ATTENTION AND PERFORMANCE IV

ATTENTION AND PERFORMANCE IV

Edited by

SYLVAN KORNBLUM

Mental Health Research Institute
The University of Michigan
Ann Arbor, Michigan

1973
ACADEMIC PRESS New York and London

ACADEMIC PRESS, INC.
111 Fifth Avenue, New York, New York 10003

United Kingdom Edition published by
ACADEMIC PRESS, INC. (LONDON) LTD.
24/28 Oval Road, London NW1

LIBRARY OF CONGRESS CATALOG CARD NUMBER: 67—20016

PRINTED IN THE UNITED STATES OF AMERICA

Contents

1 SELECTIVE ATTENTION

A Theory and the Measurement of Attention: Tutorial Review   3

Neville Moray and Mike Fitter

On the Functions of Consciousness   21

Michael I. Posner and Raymond M. Klein

v

2 PHYSIOLOGICAL CORRELATES OF ATTENTION AND PERFORMANCE

3 SEQUENTIAL EFFECTS IN REACTION TIME AND ABSOLUTE JUDGMENTS

On Expectancy and the Speed and Accuracy of Responses

Ewart A. C. Thomas

7 PERCEPTION OF TEMPORAL ORDER

The Perception of Temporal Order: Fundamental Issues and a General Model

Saul Sternberg and Ronald L. Knoll

Visual Perception of Temporal Order

Ruth Rutschmann

List of Contributors and Participants

Numbers in parenthesis indicate the pages on which the authors' contributions begin. An asterisk before a name indicates a contributor who did not participate in the conference. A dagger before a name indicates a conference participant who did not contribute to the volume.

LORRAINE G. ALLAN (737), Department of Psychology, McMaster University, Hamilton, Ontario, Canada

*TERRY R. ANDERS[1] (363), Department of Psychiatry, Massachusetts General Hospital, Boston, Massachusetts

RICHARD C. ATKINSON (583), Department of Psychology, Jordan Hall, Stanford University, Stanford, California

R. J. AUDLEY (509), Department of Psychology, University College London, London, England

DONALD BAMBER (477), Psychology Service, Veterans Administration Hospital, St. Cloud, Minnesota

JONATHAN BARON (703), Department of Psychology, McMaster University, Hamilton, Ontario, Canada

*ANNIE BESREST (209), Department of Psychophysiologie Générale, Institut de Neurophysiologie et Psychophysiologie, Centre National de la Recherche Scientifique, Marseille, France

*ALISON DAVIES (101), Department of Experimental Psychology, Oxford University, Oxford, England

STANISLAV DORNIC (119), Institute of Applied Psychology, University of Stockholm, Solna, Sweden

---

[1]Present address; Dalhousie University, Halifax, Nova Scotia.

xvii

Robert Efron (713), Neurophysiology–Biophysics Research Laboratories, Veterans Administration Hospital, Martinez, California

†Jean-Claude Falmagne, Department of Psychology, New York University, New York, New York

*Mike Fitter (3), Department of Psychology, University of Sheffield, Yorkshire, England

M. S. Gazzaniga (221), Department of Psychology, New York University, New York, New York

*David M. Green (547), Department of Psychology, University of California, San Diego, La Jolla, California

S. A. Hillyard (221), Department of Neurosciences, University of California, San Diego, La Jolla, California

I. D. John (313), Department of Psychology, University of Adelaide, Adelaide, Australia

James F. Juola (583), Department of Psychology, University of Kansas, Lawrence, Kansas

Lawrence Karlin (175), Department of Psychology, New York University, New York, New York

*Tapani Kauri (423), Department of Psychology, University of Turku, Turku, Finland

R. A. Kinchla (87), Department of Psychology, Princeton University, Princeton, New Jersey

Marcel Kinsbourne (239), Division of Pediatric Neurology, Duke University Medical Center, Durham, North Carolina

*Raymond Klein (21), Department of Psychology, University of Oregon, Eugene, Oregon

Ronald L. Knoll (629), Bell Telephone Laboratories, Murray Hill, New Jersey

Sylvan Kornblum (259), Mental Health Research Institute, The University of Michigan, Ann Arbor, Michigan

W. G. Koster (55), Instituut Voor Perceptie Onderzock Insulindelaan, Eindhoven, The Netherlands

Alfred B. Kristofferson (737), Department of Psychology, McMaster University, Hamilton, Ontario, Canada

LESTER E. KRUEGER (497), Department of Psychology, City College of the City University of New York, New York, New York

DAVID LABERGE (71), Department of Psychology, University of Minnesota, Minneapolis, Minnesota

PEKKA LEHTIÖ[2] (423), Department of Psychology, University of Turku, Turku, Finland

GREGORY R. LOCKHEAD (289), Department of Psychology, Duke University, Durham, North Carolina

R. DUNCAN LUCE[3] (547), The Institute for Advanced Study, Princeton, New Jersey

*MERRILL J. MARTZ, JR. (175), Department of Psychology, New York University, New York, New York

DAVID E. MEYER (379, 395), Bell Telephone Laboratories, Murray Hill, New Jersey

NEVILLE MORAY (3), Scarborough College, University of Toronto, Toronto, Ontario, Canada

†ROBERT E. MORIN, Department of Psychology, Kent State University, Kent, Ohio

*STANLEY M. MOSS (411), Department of Psychology, University of Massachusetts, Amherst, Massachusetts

RISTO NÄÄTÄNEN (155), Institute of Psychology, University of Helsinki, Helsinki, Finland

RAYMOND S. NICKERSON (449), Bolt, Beranek and Newman Inc., Cambridge, Massachusetts

DONALD A. NORMAN (345), Department of Psychology, University of California, San Diego, La Jolla, California

R. T. OLLMAN (571), Bell Telephone Laboratories, Holmdel, New Jersey

*STANLEY PAINE, (477), Behavior Modification Program, Rehabilitation Institute, Southern Illinois University, Carbondale, Illinois

---

[2]Present address: Department of Psychology, Division of General Experimental Psychology, University of Helsinki, Helsinki, Finland.

[3]Present address: School of Social Science, University of California at Irvine, Irvine, California.

ALLEN PARDUCCI (303), Department of Psychology, University of California, Los Angeles, California

MICHAEL I. POSNER (21), Department of Psychology, University of Oregon, Eugene, Oregon

PATRICK M. A. RABBITT (327), Department of Experimental Psychology, University of Oxford, Oxford, England

JEAN REQUIN (209), Department de Psychophysiologie Générale, Institut de Neurophysiologie et Psychophysiologie, Centre National de la Recherche Scientifique, Marseille, France

WALTER RITTER (129), Department of Neurology, and Rose F. Kennedy Center for Research in Mental Retardation and Human Development, Albert Einstein College of Medicine, Bronx, New York

RUTH RUTSCHMANN (687), Department of Psychology, Queens College, City University of New York and Biometrics Research, New York State Department of Mental Hygiene, New York, New York

ANDRIES F. SANDERS (411), Institute for Perception RVO-TNO, Soesterberg, The Netherlands

†ECKART SCHEERER, Psychologisches Institut, Ruhr Universitat, Bochum, Germany

†RICHARD SCHIFFRIN, Department of Psychology, Indiana University, Bloomington, Indiana

ROGER W. SCHVANEVELDT (395), Department of Psychology, State University of New York at Stony Brook, Stony Brook, New York

L. H. SHAFFER (435), Department of Psychology, University of Exeter, Exeter, England

†PHILIP SMITH, Department of Psychology, Stanford University, Stanford, California

†GEORGE SPERLING, Bell Telephone Laboratories, Murray Hill, New Jersey

SAUL STERNBERG[4] (629), Bell Telephone Laboratories, Murray Hill, New Jersey

*SAMUEL SUTTON (185), Biometrics Research, New York State Department of Mental Hygiene and Department of Psychiatry, Columbia University, New York, New York

---

[4]Present address: Department of Psychology, University College London, London, England.

†John A. Swets, Bolt, Beranek, and Newman, Inc., Cambridge, Massachusetts

Ewart A. C. Thomas[5] (613), Department of Psychology, University of Michigan, Ann Arbor, Michigan

Anne M. Treisman (101), Department of Experimental Psychology, University of Oxford, Oxford, England

Patricia Tueting (185), Biometrics Research, New York State Department of Mental Hygiene and Department of Psychology, Herbert H. Lehman College of the City University of New York

*R. van Schuur (55), Institut Voor Perceptie Onderzoek, Insulindelaan, 2, Eindoven, The Netherlands

Herbert G. Vaughan, Jr. (129), Department of Neurology, and Rose F. Kennedy Center for Research in Mental Retardation and Human Development, Albert Einstein College of Medicine, Bronx, New York

*Subhash Vyas (327), Department of Experimental Psychology, University of Oxford, Oxford, England

Nancy C. Waugh[6] (363), Department of Psychiatry, Massachusetts General Hospital, Boston, Massachusetts

A. T. Welford (37), Department of Psychology, University of Adelaide, Adelaide, South Australia

---

[5]Present address: Department of Psychology, Stanford University, Stanford, California.
[6]Present address: University of Oxford, Oxford, England.

Preface

When the proceedings for the first Attention and Performance conference were published, the volume was simply called *Attention and Performance*. Little did anyone, at that time, suspect that an international series had been launched. However, as I find myself taking care of the final editorial details for *Attention and Performance IV*, I am struck by the rapid developments that have taken place in the field since that first meeting. Experimental psychology has probably undergone more profound, more numerous, and more rapid changes in the last 10 years than at any other previous time. It was partly this ferment that caused the Attention and Performance symposia to emerge as an important international focus for an active group of experimental psychologists. Among the aspects of those meetings that the group cherished most was the intimacy that the small size of the meetings made possible. In order to preserve this feature in the face of mounting pressures generated by growth and success, *Attention and Performance IV* broke with its short-lived tradition and ceased trying to cover the entire field of human performance. Instead, a restricted number of topics were chosen which served as guide lines in the selection of the participants for *Attention and Performance IV*.

The seven parts of this book thus represent a small, compact subset of topics in the area of human performance. Some of the topics will be seen as contiguous and blending into one another; others may be viewed as cutting across the rest. This structure, of course, is entirely deliberate.

Each section is headed with a tutorial review, which serves to introduce a particular topic and to render it accessible to the nonexpert while at the same time making a contribution of interest to the expert as well. These tutorial papers, therefore, represent a variable mix of literature review, taxonomy, and theoretical integration. All together these reviews should make this volume of proceedings more useful to a wider audience than it would otherwise have been.

The research papers represent some of the best and most current contributions being made in these areas from laboratories all over the world. These papers also reflect a boldness, enthusiasm, rigor, and imagination which characterizes much of the current work in the field. Some of the problems being worked on today had not even been formulated 10 years ago, other problems are classics which were found intractable or sterile in the past and are now being reexamined and recast in more viable forms. Imagery, memory, attention, consciousness, and meaning, are all terms designating problem areas which are gradually making their way out of the wings onto center stage, while new technologies, new models, and new data keep changing the form and clarifying the content of these problems.

These proceedings should, therefore, be viewed as a time slice through a small segment of human performance during one of its most exciting periods.

Historical Notes and Background

The first Attention and Performance Conference was held in the summer of 1966, one week following the XVIIIth International Congress of Psychology in Moscow. Dr. Andries F. Sanders (Institute for Perception RVO–TNO, Soesterberg, The Netherlands), by capitalizing on the presence of many psychologists on the continent, was able to bring together a small group of specialists in the close to ideal surroundings of Driebergen, for an intensive 5-day exchange of research results and ideas in the area of human performance. The success of that first meeting led Dr. W. G. Koster (Institute for Perception Research, Eindhoven, The Netherlands) to plan a second meeting to celebrate the centennial of the publication of Donders' famous paper on reaction time. The second symposium on attention and performance—the Donders Centenary Symposium on Reaction Time—was held in Eindhoven in the summer of 1968. The format of that meeting followed the first rather closely. A small number of participants were invited, each expert in his own field and all working on problems of mutual interest with a strong emphasis on reaction time. Once again, the meeting was judged to be successful by the participants and the volume of proceedings included papers which have since become classics in their field. The summer of 1969 saw the XIXth International Congress of Psychology in London. Dr. Sanders, who had been responsible for the first Attention and Performance Symposium three years before, took this occasion to organize the third symposium in the series along very much the same lines that had been followed in the first two. Once again, and in spite of the fact that only one year had elapsed since the Donders Centenary, this third symposium was enormously successful and resulted in a volume of proceedings.

It was at that time that an ad hoc organizing committee was formed to review the past, discuss the present, and plan the future of the series. The committee consisted of Drs. W. G. Koster, S. Kornblum, P.M.A. Rabbitt, A. F. Sanders, S. Sternberg, and A. T. Welford. This marked the end of what, in retrospect, appears to have been the incubation period for attention and performance, and no better care could have been lavished on a budding concept than that provided by Koster and Sanders during these initial few years. In the course of the committee's discussions it became readily apparent that the series' past successes could be attributed in large part to the fact that an important need had been identified and filled by these meetings. They had provided an international forum for the vigorous exchange of research ideas and results among a small and growing group of colleagues who were working in an area which did not easily fall into the more traditional framework of learning, motivation, perception, etc. Human performance, while encompassing all of these, did not neatly fit into any one of them. Furthermore, human performance was clearly emerging as a field in its own right, and included many investigators from all over the world.

It was, therefore, with no small degree of apprehension that I accepted the ad hoc committee's charge to organize the Fourth International Symposium on Attention and Performance—the first in this new postincubation period and also the first to be held outside of the Netherlands, or even Europe. It seemed to me absolutely essential to retain the international character of the previous meetings. It was also imperative that the intimacy of the small, face to face meeting be preserved. Finally, the standards of excellence which had been set by the previous symposia pinpointed the target for Attention and Performance IV quite clearly. The meeting took place August 16–20, 1971, in Boulder, Colorado and whether or not these objectives were met will, of course, be determined by time.

Acknowledgments

Whatever the merits, successes, and assets of *Attention and Performance IV*, the bulk of the credit must unhesitatingly be given to the participants who traveled to Boulder, Colorado, from all over the world.[1] As for the proceedings, the difficult editorial task would have been utterly impossible without the dedicated help of a number of participants, and the full cooperation of all. In addition, the ad hoc organizing committee's concern, wisdom and counsel were indispensable to me in the resolution of many issues which inevitably arise in the course of organizing a symposium of this kind. Finally, the University of Michigan Mental Health Research Institute's generosity with many of its resources made my task far simpler than it would otherwise have been. These are only some of the sources to which credit must be given. There are many more that contribute to an enterprise of this kind that cannot be included in such a brief list. However, I hope that I did thank them all appropriately at the time, and am more than pleased to do so again, now.

[1]Credit must also be given to the USPHS whose grant MH 19650–01 made it possible to defray in part many of the participants' travel and living expenses, as well as some of the other costs of the conference.

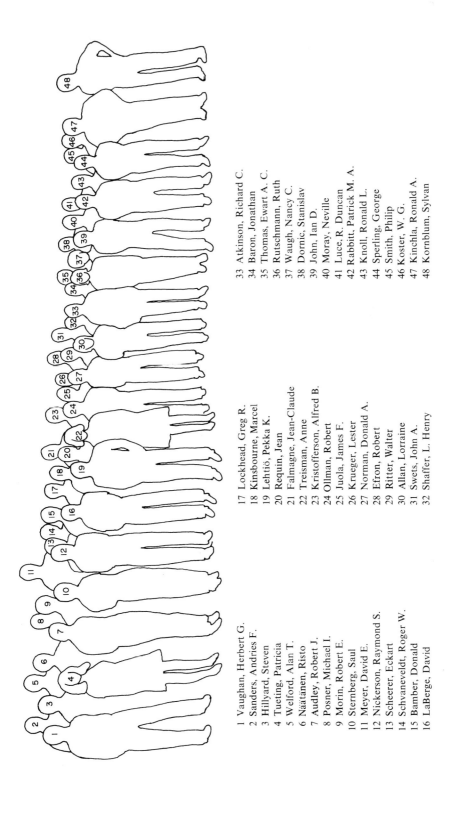

1 Vaughan, Herbert G.
2 Sanders, Andries F.
3 Hillyard, Steven
4 Tueting, Patricia
5 Welford, Alan T.
6 Näätänen, Risto
7 Audley, Robert J.
8 Posner, Michael I.
9 Morin, Robert E.
10 Sternberg, Saul
11 Meyer, David E.
12 Nickerson, Raymond S.
13 Scheerer, Eckart
14 Schvaneveldt, Roger W.
15 Bamber, Donald
16 LaBerge, David

17 Lockhead, Greg R.
18 Kinsbourne, Marcel
19 Requin, Jean
20 Lehtiö, Pekka K.
21 Falmagne, Jean-Claude
22 Treisman, Anne
23 Kristofferson, Alfred B.
24 Ollman, Robert
25 Juola, James F.
26 Krueger, Lester
27 Norman, Donald A.
28 Efron, Robert
29 Ritter, Walter
30 Allan, Lorraine
31 Swets, John A.
32 Shaffer, L. Henry

33 Atkinson, Richard C.
34 Baron, Jonathan
35 Thomas, Ewart A. C.
36 Rutschmann, Ruth
37 Waugh, Nancy C.
38 Dornic, Stanislav
39 John, Ian D.
40 Moray, Neville
41 Luce, R. Duncan
42 Rabbitt, Patrick M. A.
43 Knoll, Ronald L.
44 Sperling, George
45 Smith, Philip
46 Koster, W. G.
47 Kinchla, Ronald A.
48 Kornblum, Sylvan

1 SELECTIVE ATTENTION

A Theory and the Measurement of Attention[1]

Neville Moray　　　*Mike Fitter*

Scarborough College　　*Department of Psychology*
University of Toronto　*University of Sheffield*
Toronto, Canada　　　*Yorkshire, England*

ABSTRACT

Evidence is presented for a general theory of selective attention developed from work on vision and manual tracking, and here extended to selective listening. The model proposed is an expectancy model, in which the observer constructs an internal model of the information characteristics of the sources to be observed, and develops an aperiodic information sampling strategy from the model. A discussion follows of the problem of the measurement of attention, in particular, the relationship between the statistics of the theory of signal detection and those of information theory.

I. Introduction

Rather than add to the large number of recent reviews of selective attention (Treisman, 1969; Swets & Kristofferson, 1970; Neisser, 1967; Moray, 1969; Mostofsky, 1970; Broadbent, 1971) we propose to concentrate on drawing together work from several fields that are usually thought only to be distantly related, but which, when viewed in concert, provide a useful heuristic framework from which to develop a general theory of selective

[1]This work was partly supported by the British Science Research Council, and partly by the Canadian National Research Council.

3

attention independent of sensory modality and largely independent, at least in one sense, of the task performed by the subject.

Despite the large amount of research that has been done in the area of selective listening, theory in that area is remarkably poor. Several of the theories fit the available data equally well (or badly), and not one of them has been specified with sufficient rigor to allow detailed quantitative predictions of the outcome of experiments to be made in advance of the performance of such experiments, although some qualitative successes have occurred. Most of them are *post hoc* generalizations rather than analytic theory, and in their profusion and general lack of precision resemble an intellectual jungle in which the lush undergrowth prevents the identification of any substantial trees, and indeed may imperil the growth of the latter.

By contrast the series of models that have arisen from the work on the viewing of dynamic visual displays resembles rather the development of an 18th century formal garden, planned in advance with precision, but evolving in its development wherever unexpected details of the landscape call for rational modification; and it is from the visual work that a general theory may be developed most usefully. Although Neisser (1967) concluded that classical information theory was largely irrelevant to psychology, it has continued to be used widely in human factors engineering, and it was on classical information theory that Senders (1964) drew for the earliest analytic model of attention. The sampling theorem of information theory states that if we have a signal of bandwidth W Hz, then an ideal transmission line can transmit all the information in the signal, provided that $2W$ samples of the signal are taken per second. Senders argued that when an observer is required to transmit information from a number of sources of visual information such as the instruments in an aircraft cockpit, he is behaving as such a transmission line. It follows that there is an optimal strategy for such an observer. The instruments generate continuous functions of time, and hence the observer should sample each instrument with a sampling frequency proportional to the band width of the function it transmits, the duration of the samples being related to the discriminability of the signal. In a number of laboratory experiments, and in analyzing the eye movements of pilots flying both real and simulated aircraft, Senders found a remarkably good agreement between the data and the model (Senders, 1966; Senders, Elkind, Grignetti, & Smallwood, 1966).

This result has two important implications. First, it implies that the observer knows the value of W, the band width of the signal, with considerable precision for each instrument he observes. He therefore must have learned the statistical properties of the source, and be using such knowledge to control his sampling behavior. That is, he has constructed an internal model of the environment to which he must pay attention, and that model controls his attention. Senders therefore says that voluntary attention is, strictly speaking, a misnomer: in reality, attention is controlled by the source to which attention is being paid. To paraphrase Samuel Butler's remark that a hen is merely one egg's way of making another egg, we might say that a human being is merely a source's way of ensuring that its information is transmitted. The second implication is a methodological one—that extensive practice must be given if attention is efficiently to function, since only with such practice can the statistical properties of the source be incorporated into an internal model. From such a view point the voluntary direction of attention we usually see in laboratory experiments is merely the early, inefficient stage of acquiring a model that will eventually control behavior without the observer being aware of it.

The properties of attention therefore will be variable, not fixed, for attention will adjust itself to the requirements of the task at hand, and only rarely will fundamental limits be observable. Attention begins to take on the appearance of an acquired skill rather than the properties of a hard-wired control system of the central nervous system.

Sender's model has by now undergone considerable evolution. Elkind and Gringetti (Senders *et al.*, 1966) argued that the task was not really one in which the signal was transmitted. Rather it was to notice the moments at which the value of the signal exceeded some defined value (when, for example, the instrument reading entered a "danger zone"). They suggested that the latest observation of the instrument was used by the observer as a base line from which, using his knowledge of the statistics of the source, he could extrapolate in time, deferring his next sample from a particular source until such time as the probability of the function generated by the source exceeding the limits of safe operation would exceed some threshold probability.

Developing this approach, Carbonell (1966) was the first to make explicit the role of costs, values, and payoffs. In his model as in the others the sources queue for attention. The observer is able to use his knowledge to decide when it is probable that a source should be sampled. In addition, however, he learns the relative value of the information from the several sources, so that he can assign to each instrument a value, and can assess the cost of delaying an observation of that instrument and perhaps missing a signal, compared with the value of observing a different one. Unfortunately the solution of this sampling problem is relatively intractable mathematically unless rather restrictive simplifying assumptions are made. But it represents an attempt to introduce a kind of "meaning" into the information theory approach, and as such brings to information theory the property that many psychologists have felt it conspicuously lacked. A similar point has been made by Howard (1966) in an important paper.

Recently Sheridan (1970), has presented what is perhaps the most general model of this type, under the title, "On how often the supervisor should sample." Although the model was derived from consideration of manual control tasks, and is based on the analysis of a single source, it is readily generalizable to several sources. It incorporates Bayesian statistical decision theory, and again is concerned with the calculation of an optimal sampling interval, or distribution of intervals, if the observer knows the statistical structure of the source, and has at least a local knowledge of a recent portion of the source's history.

II. Applications to Selective Listening

Although we seem to have been getting progressively farther and farther away from attention, these models, and especially the last two, embody principles of fundamental importance to the study of attention. First, they are quantitative and precise, and, when the analytic equations can be solved, can make detailed predictions not only of the summary statistics of experiments but even to some extent of its moment to moment progress. Next, they bring out the point that in most situations, whether experimental or in real life, there will be optimal strategies available to an observer, who need not respond merely as a passive system. To employ those strategies is to minimize the time for which any given source of information need be processed, and thus to increase the time available for the monitoring of other regions of the environment, or for the performance of cognitive or response tasks. Whenever possible, organisms appear to make use of such strategies, which are of obvious biological utility. In particular, any "free time" thus gained, we suggest, will be used to monitor involuntarily any other sources of information present during an experiment.

The use of strategies requires that the observer assign values to the various sources to which he is required to attend. That assigning may be done subjectively, on the basis of past experience, or it may be defined by the experimenter. In selective listening experiments, for example, the experimenter assigns values when instructing the listener to listen only to one ear, to share his attention between the ears, and so on. The ability of the listener to make use of the value matrix will also depend on his ability to construct adequate internal models of the sources. Hence, optimal performance requires extensive practice. In the absence of such practice we may assume that the observer will bring to the experiment expectancies based upon his general experience of the world, and his particular past experience of experiments of this kind.

How may we apply these principles explicitly to the analysis of experiments on selective listening? There are a number of problems. First, few

experiments on selective listening have practiced the observers for a sufficient time to allow optimal strategies to develop. In the experiments on the
viewing of dynamic visual displays, and on manual tracking, periods of
practice of tens of hours or longer are usually employed—an order of magnitude greater than those used in most selective listening experiments. Furthermore, very few selective listening experiments have been such as allow
listeners to develop optimal strategies. There appear to have been no systematic attempts to investigate the effect of multichannel input where targets are
not equiprobable on the different channels, or where the expectancy of
target occurrence is not distributed uniformly throughout the run. (We are
currently investigating both of these problems.) However, given such defi-
ciencies in the data, how would this kind of theory account for the results
which have been accumulated to date?

Let us begin by considering a single-channel monitoring experiment in
which a listener is processing a message and trying to detect the occurrence
of some specified target, such as a letter in a stream of numerals. A model
such as Sheridan's suggests that he makes use of some kind of expectancy
about the distribution of targets. What, in an untrained subject, would be
the nature of such a distribution?

First, prose is redundant, and if the carrier message were prose, the
listener's past experience of the language would give rise to expectancies
as to the intervals between words which are significant bearers of information. These expectancies will be determined by grammar, syntax, semantics, and even prosody. Even where grammatical and semantic features are
relatively unimportant, such as carrier messages of scrambled words or
alphanumerical lists, prosody will still be present, and there will be a distribution of intervals between phoneme boundaries, syllables, word onsets, and
the like. Bearing in mind the usual rates of speech both in conversation and
in experimental materials, we may expect a range of periodicities that extends from several seconds to a few times a second. At such intervals he will
sample the incoming message. In between them he will process the information in the sample, initiate responses, and scan any other sources present.

If the observer were to shadow the message instead of merely monitoring it, his information load would be considerably greater. He now must
sample the incoming message, initiate his response, and must also monitor
his spoken output, since without such monitoring the spoken response will
not be coherent speech. Under such conditions it is likely that these tasks
will, between them, so occupy the sampling mechanism that there will be
almost no time to sample any other sources, and material in such other
sources will be missed. In a similar way the imposition of a cognitive processing task that requires control, such as translation, will tend to occupy the
processing mechanism to such an extent that his sampling rate will decrease

and his overall transmission rate fall (Treisman, 1965; Moray, 1967). It should be noted particularly that this model assumes that sampling is usually aperiodic and related to the incoming messages: only rarely will it be periodic and derived from an internal clock of fixed frequency.

The relation between monitoring and shadowing in such a model will be readily apparent. Monitoring will occupy the attention just as effectively as shadowing, provided that the overall information rate in the incoming message is high, and, perhaps more important, the variance in the intertarget interval is great, and has a low mean. Underwood (1971) presents evidence in agreement with these suggestions.

Let us now consider what will happen when attention is deliberately shared between two sources, (Moray & O'Brien, 1967; Shaffer & Hardwick, 1969). The listener now will have an expected distribution of targets for each message, and this may include expectancy as to how often targets will occur simultaneously on both channels. Initially he will bring a priori expectancies to the experiment. ("If he says there are 500 signals and that there are 10 targets, I suppose that there will be one target about every 50 signals.") But such expectancies will be modified by the observer's experience during practice runs by the way in which the targets in fact occur, and even during the experimental runs by the local statistical structure of target occurrence within a run (Baker, 1963; Michon, 1967). Since he is required to listen to both messages, it is clear that he should alternate his attention between the sources. But it is by no means clear that his best strategy is to do so as rapidly as possible. Rather, in accordance with the models we have discussed, he should use his knowledge of the recent occurrence of a target on one or both channels to dictate when he should sample that channel next. For example, since the probability of a target on a channel immediately following a target on the same channel will in general be low, he would do well, following the detection of a target on one channel, to switch immediately to the other channel and only switch back when his expectancy of the imminent arrival of a target on the original channel is so high that to delay is intolerable.

Such a system, not time locked to the periodicity of an internal clock, but stimulus locked to the statistical structure of the incoming messages, could achieve a hit rate on both channels substantially greater than the 50% that Shaffer and Hardwick (1969) seem to think must be the upper limit of a switching system. On the whole, however, there will be a loss of information from any time shared system except under certain well-defined situations, owing to the fact that the prediction of the likely moments of occurrence of targets can only be probabilistic. Targets occurring simultaneously should cause particular difficulty, as is indeed the case (Moray & O'Brien, 1967). But precise prediction of the detection of such targets will be rather difficult unless there is particular care taken during the training of observers. It would seem that simultaneous targets will be detectable only by means of very rapid switching between the channels, but this will be further dependent upon the observer *deciding that it is worth his while to make such a switch.* If he were to interpret his instructions to detect targets in both channels to mean that it is better to detect at least one of a pair of simultaneously presented targets with certainty than to respond to both with a lower chance of being right on either, then his strategy should be to spend much more time on one channel than the other, even at the cost of lowering his performance on the latter. He might choose to sample in such a way that he would detect targets on channel 1 with a probability of .9, and on channel 2 with a probability of .15, rather than to achieve an equal chance of detecting targets in the two channels, but with a probability of .65 in each case.

There are rather few time-shared listening experiments. Most of them have been performed in a selective mode, where the observer listens to one message and rejects the other. In such a case the payoff is clear—it is never correct to sample the rejected message. Even so, the listener knows that not all of the signals in the accepted message are targets, so on our model he will not be able to sample the accepted message continuously, although he will be able to bias himself strongly in that direction. His internal expectancy model will predict certain moments when the arrival of a target is highly unlikely, and during such moments the sampler will examine other sources of information, and occasionally will take samples from the wrong message. Such effects will be heightened where the instructions are at all ambiguous. Moray and O'Brien (1967), for example, asked their listeners to select one message and reject the other, but to report any targets that slipped through despite their efforts. Treisman and Geffen (1967) told their listeners to shadow one message and tap on the occurrence of a target, but only to tap when a target occurred in the other channel, which would certainly be likely to affect the bias toward the two channels differentially. All such ambiguities would tend to make the system take some samples from the rejected message, and they would tend to occur at points in the accepted message where the observer judges, consciously, that the probability of a target is low.

The model would predict further that detection of targets in the accepted message would be high, as is indeed the case. Figures for unilateral detection are usually over 90% correct (Treisman & Geffen, 1967; Moray & O'Brien, 1967; Shaffer & Hardwick, 1969). It is now well established that some, but not all, information is transmitted involuntarily from the rejected message. Little complex semantic information is transmitted, but physical characteristics such as the sex of the speaker usually can be reported. This is to be expected if only occasional short samples of the rejected message are being taken. Certain data seem to provide exceptions, such as the hearing of one's own name (Moray, 1959), switching by means of context (Treisman,

1960), and galvanic skin responses (GSR) to material in the rejected channel (Moray, 1969). But close inspection of the primary sources reveals that the upper limit of such effects is around 30% of the trials on which they could occur, and is often much lower. The only substantial exception is the very high detectability of pure tone signals embedded in or added to speech (Lawson, 1966), although even here there are very marked individual differences (Moray & Fee, 1970).

The last observation, concerning pure tones, raises the question of whether they really do have a special status, and if so, what its nature might be. Recent work in our laboratories indicates that pure tones behave rather like any other stimuli in properly controlled experiments. But there is no denying that, when presented mixed with speech, they are unusually detectable. It is possible that this results from their marked dissimilarity to the rest of the message allows them to override the sampling model and to "call" the switch. Kristofferson (1965), Stroud (1956), and Moray (1969) all have suggested that transients have a special status in determining sampling, and despite Stroud usually being thought of as a supporter of a periodic sampling system, his paper lays great stress on the importance of what he called "singularities" in the incoming signals as a means of synchronizing the clock to the properties of the message.

If the system is indeed sensitive to transients (which can be defined as marked changes in the autocorrelation of the physical parameters of the stimulus), then any sudden changes, whether pure tones, pauses, unusually loud words, or the like, when they occur in the rejected message, will increase the occasional sampling of that message, and lead to the ready identification of physical changes in the rejected message. It is interesting that at the same rate of interruption of a speech message that renders it unintelligible (Huggins, 1964) the sex of the speaker may be distinguished readily (Moray & Thorpe, 1972), which suggests that it may be possible to account for these effects on the basis of the sampling distribution alone, even without invoking transients.

III. Work in Related Fields

Before summarizing this section, it is of interest to note the increasing popularity of sampled data models in a number of related fields. Discontinuous sampling has been a possibility in skills research ever since the suggestion of Craik (1948), and a useful review is to be found in an earlier volume of the Attention and Performance Meetings (Welford, 1967). More recently, however, there has been a great increase in the support for such models by those working in the field of manual tracking and human control engineering, and frequently the adoption of sampled data models goes hand in hand with the assumption that some kind of internal model is being used by the person performing the task. We already have cited Sheridan (1970) as one example, and others are found in the work of Bekey and his group (Bekey & Neal, 1968). Excellent reviews of the internal model approach are given by Young (1969) and Kelly (1968).

Perhaps it may be worth stressing the point that in some areas the existence of internal predictive models is not a matter for doubt. It is sufficient to note that in tracking tasks a subject may not merely abolish the reaction time lag between the display and his response, but may actually introduce phase lead. Such an ability necessitates his possession of an internal model that is generating the future state of the stimulus before it occurs, and the subject must be capable of modeling the future in fast time.

IV. Summary of the Theory

We must cease to regard the properties of attention as fixed. They are largely task determined, either directly (through the interaction with transients), or indirectly (by means of the construction of an internal model of the statistical properties of the sources). There may be a few cases in which limits on performance are found, owing to the observer switching continuously at his maximum possible rate, but they are rare, and the evidence for them is distinctly thin. Attention is dynamic, with changing temporal parameters, and directed by the following:

1. the observer's model of the temporal statistics of the information source or sources he is processing, the model generating a distribution of expectancies as to the likely time of arrival of the next target;

2. the observer's model of the costs and values associated with the detection or missing of targets from the various sources;

3. (perhaps) his sensitivity to transient changes in the autocorrelation function of the physical signals.

Attention thus is seen to be rather the employment of dynamic strategies than the operation of a fixed mechanism—strategies, moreover, determined by a continually updated assessment of the informational demands of the sources being monitored. Attention thus is seen to be intimately connected with the acquisiton of skills, expectancy theory, decision theory, and probability learning. The man who successfully pays attention bears a resemblance to the virtuous man in the moral theology of Aquinas: it is not by his struggle to overcome temptation that we detect his virtue, but by the untroubled achievement of his aim.

V. Problems of Measurement

If the above model were to be successful in describing *when* we pay attention, the problem would still remain as to *how*. Just what happens at the moment when a sample is taken from one message and the others are ignored? There exists a great variety of suggestions (for example, Treisman, 1960; Treisman, 1969; Broadbent, 1958, 1971; Deutsch & Deutsch, 1963; Norman, 1969), but it is not possible to decide between them at present. On the one hand, there is the incompletely explored effect of practice, which renders present data ambiguous. For example, Moray and O'Brien (1967) found that listeners had very great difficulty in detecting two simultaneous alphanumeric targets; but recently Moray and Marks (1972) have found that after five days practice, listeners can achieve detection rates more than four times greater than those found in the earlier work. On the other hand, Moray and Fitter (unpublished) have found that after a series of experiments using three observers almost daily for three years, the three observers still cannot detect pure tone increments, when presented simultaneously, as well as in a single-channel condition.

The latter experiment is worth outlining in more detail, since some of the results raise important problems of measurement. The experiment is very similar to that already published by Moray (1970). The task for the listeners was to detect intensity or frequency increments in tone-burst trains presented in either single-channel, time-shared, or various other combinations. Targets might occur either in one channel, or the other, or simultaneously in both. The two channels were separated in frequency and sometimes in space. The tone bursts were of 100-msec duration presented every 500 msec in runs of 250 per channel. They were shaped to avoid clicks. The ratio of targets to nontargets was about 1:6.

We have analyzed performance in several ways, including statistics associated with the theory of signal detection (TSD), and the recent extension by Garner and Morton (1969) of information theory. Several authors (Broadbent & Gregory, 1963; Moray & O'Brien, 1967; Treisman & Geffen, 1967) all have found changes in d', and intuitively it would seem that ceasing to pay attention to a message must reduce the information transmitted from that message. (The use of percentage of correct detections is quite inadequate as a measure of performance, since even a casual glance at attention data shows that there are definite changes in false alarms associated with different conditions, and with individual differences.)

Let us consider for a moment what we might expect to happen to these several statistics on the various models that have been proposed. It is clear that an attenuation model such as Treisman's (1960) would predict changes in d' when a message is rejected. A response selection might lead a change in

β, although the prediction is not so clear-cut. Information transmission and d' alike would be expected to fall for a rejected message and *might* rise for an accepted one.

In the case of deliberately time-shared performance prediction is not so easy. If truly parallel processing were possible, then either channel should be as efficient as in the single-channel case, and information transmission would double. If a single channel were being shared, then the transmission per channel would fall, though whether to 50% for each input would depend on the switching rate and the type of stimulus material used. We know that in one case the relation between TSD statistics and those of information theory are well defined, since for signals such as bandwidth limited noise Taylor, Lindsay, and Forbes (1967) have shown that information is linear in $(d')^2$. More generally, we would expect that for more discriminable signals the information transmission would be greater, and hence, if we measure the information transmission in the traditional way,

$$T = H_{in} + H_{out} - H_{in, out}, \tag{1}$$

and look at the effect of attention on the proportion of available information which is transmitted,

$$T^* = 100 T / T_{max}, \tag{2}$$

where T_{max} is the maximum available information in the input, then we would expect T^* to vary with d'.

On looking at our data, we find at first that such relationships indeed appear to hold. There are marked individual differences, one subject frequently showing effects at variance with the other two, but the picture seems fairly coherent. Applying the Garner and Morton (1969) analysis, we find that for near-threshold signals there are significant changes in information transmission attributable to "state variables" (such as arousal), but as the target increments become substantially greater than threshold, the relative importance of such effects rapidly decreases, and for readily detectable targets the evidence supports the hypothesis that the two channels are being analyzed independently.

Closer inspection reveals some disturbing features. To begin with, the value of T^* fluctuates as β changes. In other words, for a given size of target the information transmission obtained is not an unambiguous measure of performance, and a little thought well reveal why this is so.

Figure 1 shows the relationship between a TSD matrix of data and an information-theory matrix. The relation between the two stimulus–response matrices is obvious. The hit and correct rejection entries in the TSD matrix form the major diagonal of the information theory matrix, which is where data must lie in order to maximize transmission. In general, any movement of data away from the diagonal will result in a fall in information transmission, and hence T^* will fall. (One can have perfect transmission with off-diagonal entries for some specified coding rule, but that does not alter the argument.) Let us consider what will happen in an experiment performed at a value of d' as shown in Fig. 1, when the observer alters his criterion. When he changes from β_1 to β_2, the entries in the FA and $f_{a/B}$ cells will increase slightly, but there will be a much greater increase in H and $f_{a/A}$. Therefore there will be a net gain for entries on the major diagonal, and information transmission (T^*) will rise as the criterion falls. On the other hand, when the criterion is lowered from β_3 to β_4, there is a small movement of data from M to H and a much larger movement from CR to FA, so that there is a net loss of entries on the major diagonal, and T^* falls. Information transmission is nonmonotonic in β for a given d'. Either too risky or too conservative a criterion will result in a less optimal value of T^*. It follows from this that to characterize experimental results adequately, we must have either d' and β, T^* and β, or all three. Either alone or together, d' and T^*, do not describe an experiment unambiguously.

The reason for this will be plain from Fig. 2, which shows the relation between d', β, and T^* for a ratio of targets to nontargets of 1:6. d' limits the maximum possible value of T^*. Thus, a d' of 2.0 means that the observer never can transmit more than about 36% of the available information, and then only if his log β has a value of .6. For a given value of d', T^* is determined by β. Hence, there can arise cases, of which there are several in our data, where in changing from one condition of attention to another d' increases while T^* decreases, since at the same time β has risen to such an extent that the data are well off to the right on the curve shown in Fig. 2.

What then is to be our measure of attention in such experiments? Measured by TSD an observer may improve: but simultaneously when measured by information transmission, his performance has declined. An attenuation model could actually increase information transmission when, according to the model, d' had decreased, provided the observer's bias changed suitably. It is obvious that we must include β or some equivalent measure of the observer's bias. But this leaves us with a very clumsy way of expressing our results. It is difficult to get a feel for what is happening if we have to describe an experiment by saying that in going from condition A to condition B the result was to change d' from 2.0 to 2.5, to change log β from 1.3 to 2.4, and T^* from 17.5 to 41.0. What we require for simplicity is a single number that represents overall performance—some standardization procedure similar to the reduction to normal temperature and pressure when doing gas-law experiments in physics. One possibility would be to scale results with respect to the value of d' at unit β, and such a transformation to "results at unit β" (RUB) is shown in Fig. 3 for the hypothetical results just mentioned.

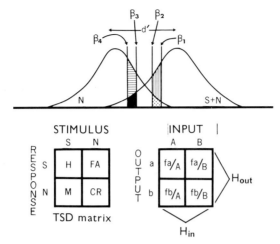

Fig. 1. The relation between TSD and information transmission.

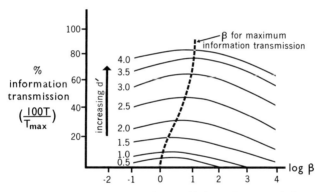

Fig. 2. The relation between d', β, and information transmission.

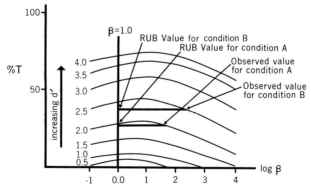

Fig. 3. RUB as a standardizing procedure.

We draw a horizontal line from the observed value of (d', β, T^*) for each condition to cut a vertical line drawn at $\beta = 1.0$ (log $\beta = .0$). Where the lines intersect, in general, will not be on the same isosensitivity curve as the original data points. Thus, condition A would have a d' of 1.9 RUB, and condition B a d' of 2.3 RUB. We then could say that the change in performance, that is, in T^*, was equivalent to a change of $0.4d'$ RUB, providing a single statistic.

The only problem now remaining is of course the greatest: what would such a change mean? We obviously are dealing with a very complex system. If we adopt the RUB convention (and if we were not to do so, we must in the future always give at least the two statistics from which the third can be derived from the curves), we must remember that our index says that performance has altered *as if* it had been caused by a change in d' of the observed amount. Moreover, the analysis in terms of T^* is very important, since, if we follow Garner and Morton, it gives us an insight into the mechanisms involved. On a RUB analysis, we should not say that attention primarily affects d'; indeed, from our data it seems more likely that the causal relationships are as follows.

Across all subjects and all conditions d' appears to increase monotonically with target intensity, as would be expected. The value of d' then is primarily determined by the physical properties of the signal. The value of d' is also affected by changes in attention conditions, but neither it nor T^* changes uniformly across conditions for different observers, or even within conditions. It seems likely that the main effect on the value of T^* is caused by the observer changing his β value from condition to condition. On the other hand, if an expectancy model of the kind outlined in the first part of this paper is indeed correct, and if information is normally taken in by means of aperiodic sampling, then we would also expect that to result in some changes in d'. Since the observer is not sampling continuously, the average duration of the signal when sampled will be reduced, since he cannot guarantee to sample at the correct instant. Thus, the effective target energy will be reduced, and the targets will be processed as if they had a lower intensity than they in fact have, and will be less easily discriminated in a time-shared mode. The size of this effect, however, will be intimately affected by the sampling strategy that the observer adopts, and hence, we may expect marked individual differences unless steps are taken to train the observers to use identical strategies, for they will make different assessments of the relative costs and values associated with different ways of processing the information. Furthermore, these costs and values also will enter into his decisions about whether there is a signal present when he does take a sample, and hence will influence β, and hence T^*, in a second way.

Overall, it would seem to be best to say that the dependent performance variable is T^*, the amount of information transmission. Its upper bound will be determined by the current value of d', itself determined in turn both by the physical parameters of the signal and indirectly by the sampling strategy of the observer. The amount by which performance falls short of the maximum possible value of T^* will be a function of the value of β at which the observer chooses to operate in a particular run of the experiment, and the value of β will be continuously modified, perhaps, as part of the model that the observer is constructing of the nature of the sources he is sampling.

VI. Conclusion

Once again we have to view attention as an intensely dynamic system, the properties of which are changing from moment to moment even within a run of an experiment. If so, attention returns to the central position in psychology to which Titchener (quoted by Swets & Kristoffersen, 1970) assigned it. Now, however, it is not so much the absolute monarch of the nervous system as a duly elected leader of the cognitive processes, and like all good leaders constantly adjusts its aims to carry out the aspirations of the people, changing its policies according to the general will. It is clear at least that Neisser's strictures about information theory are undeserved: applied with some degree of subtlety, the latter still has a great deal to contribute to psychology.

And the nature of attention? Perhaps it is neither the tangled jungle nor the 18th century garden, but rather the *Garden of Delights* of Hieronymous Bosch, full of strange and intricately contrived creatures, some more fantastical than others, but in the end, undoubtedly intelligible if only we could just find that one clue. . . .

References

Baker, C. Further towards a theory of vigilance. In D. Buckner & J. McGrath (Eds.), *Vigilance: A symposium.* New York: McGraw-Hill, 1963.

Bekey, G., & Neal, C. Identification of sampling intervals in sampled-data models of human operators. *IEEE Transactions on Man–Machine Systems,* 1968, **MMS-9,** 138–143.

Broadbent, D. E. *Perception and communication.* Oxford: Pergamon, 1958.

Broadbent, D. E. *Decision and stress.* New York: Academic Press, 1971.

Broadbent, D. E., & Gregory, M. Division of attention and the decision theory of signal detection. *Proceedings of the Royal Society (B),* 1963, **158,** 222–231.

Carbonell, J. R., A cueing model of many instrument visual sampling, *IEEE Transactions on Human Factors and Electronics,* 1966, **HFE-7,** No. 4.

Craik, K. J. W. Theory of the human operator in control systems. II. Man as an element in a control system. *British Journal of Psychology,* 1948, **38,** 142–148.

Deutsch, J. A., & Deutsch, D. Attention: Some theoretical considerations. *Psychological Review*, 1963, **70**, 80–90.

Garner, W. R., & Morton, J. Perceptual independence: Definitions, models, and experimental paradigms. *Psychological Bulletin*, 1969, **72**, 233–259.

Howard, R. Information value theory. *IEEE Transactions on Systems Science and Cybernetics*, 1966, **SSC-2**, No. 1, 22–26.

Huggins, A. W. F. Distortion of the temporal pattern of speech: Interruption and alternation. *Journal of the Acoustical Society of America*, 1964, **36**, 1055–1064.

Kristofferson, A. B. Attention in time discrimination and reaction time *NASA Report CR-194*, 1965.

Kelley, C. *Automatic and manual control*. New York: Wiley, 1968.

Lawson, E. Decisions concerning the rejected channel. *Quarterly Journal of Experimental Psychology*, 1966, **18**, 260–265.

Michon, J. A., Timing in temporal tracking. Soesterberg: Institute for Perception RVO–TNO, 1967.

Moray, N. Attention in dichotic listening: Affective cues and the influence of instructions. *Quarterly Journal of Experimental Psychology*, 1959, **9**, 56–60.

Moray, N. Where is capacity limited? A survey and a model. *Acta Psychologica*, 1967, **27**, 84–92.

Moray, N. *Attention: Selective processes in vision and hearing*. London: Hutchinson, 1969.

Moray, N. Introductory experiments in auditory time-sharing: Detection of intensity and frequency increments. *Journal of the acoustical Society of America*, 1970, **47**, 1071–1073.

Moray, N. & Fee, M. Selective attention to pure tones and speech. *Psychonomic Science*, 1970, **18(4)**, 223–224.

Moray, N., & Marks G. in preparation, 1972.

Moray, N., & O'Brien, T. Signal detection theory applied to selective listening. *Journal of the Acoustical Society of America*, 1967, **42**, 765–772.

Moray, N., & Taylor, A. The effect of redundancy on the shadowing of one of two dichotic messages. *Language and Speech*, 1958, **1**, 102–109.

Moray, N., & Thorpe, S. in preparation, 1972.

Mostofsky, D. *Attention: Contemporary theory and analysis*. New York: Appleton, 1970.

Neisser, U. *Cognitive psychology*. New York: Appleton, 1967.

Norman, D. A. *Memory and attention*. New York: Wiley 1969.

Senders, J. The human operator as a monitor and controller of multi-degree-of-freedom systems. *IEE Transactions on Human Factors in Electronics*, 1964, **HFE-5**, 2–5.

Senders, J. A re-analysis of the pilot eye-movement data. *IEEE Transactions on Human Factors in Electronics*, 1966, **HFE-7**, 103–106.

Senders, J., Elkind, J., Grignetti, M., & Smallwood, R. An investigation of the visual sampling behaviour of human observers. *NASA Report CR-434*, 1966.

Shaffer, L. H., & Hardwick, J. Monitoring simultaneous auditory messages. *Perception and Psychophysics*, 1969, **6(6B)**, 401–404.

Sheridan, T. On how often the supervisor should sample. *IEEE Transactions on Systems Science and Cybernetics*, 1970, **SSC-6**, 140–145.

Swets, J. A., & Kristofferson, A. Attention. *Annual Review of Psychology*, 1970, **21**, 339–366.

Stroud, J. M. The fine structure of psychological time. In H. Quastler (Ed.), *Information theory in psychology*. Indiana: 1956.

Taylor, M. M., Lindsay, P. H., & Forbes, S. M. Quantification of shared capacity processing in auditory and visual discrimination. *Acta Psychologica*, 1967, **27**, 223–229.

Treisman, A. M. Contextual cues in selective listening. *Quarterly Journal of Experimental Psychology*, 1960, **12**, 242–248. Treisman, A. The effects of redundancy and familiarity on translating and repeating back a foreign and a native language. *British Journal of Psychology*, 1965, **56**, 369–379.

Treisman, A. Strategies and models of selective attention. *Psychological Review*, 1969, **76**, 282–299.

Treisman, A., & Geffen, G. Selective attention: Perception or response. *Quarterly Journal of Experimental Psychology*, 1967, **19**, 1–17.

Underwood, G., & Moray, N. Shadowing and monitoring for selective attention. *Quarterly Journal of Experimental Psychology*, 1971, **23**, 284–295.

Welford, A. T. Single channel operation in the brain. *Acta Psychologica*, 1967, **27**, 5–23.

Young, L. On adaptive manual control. *IEEE Transactions on Man–Machine Systems*, 1969, **MMS-10**, 292–332.

On the Functions of Consciousness[1]

Michael I. Posner   *Raymond M. Klein*

Department of Psychology
University of Oregon
Eugene, Oregon

ABSTRACT

One aspect of attention concerns the operation of a limited-capacity mechanism sensitive to input from all modalities. Since signals which occupy this mechanism tend to interfere with one another, a probe reaction time (RT) technique is used to examine the functions which require this mechanism. It is shown that habitual encodings involving contact with long-term memory (LTM) do not require this mechanism, but rehearsal, complex transformations and response priming do. Consciousness is thought to be related intimately to the operations of the limited capacity mechanism. This usage requires an examination of the relationships of awareness, storage, verbal report, and intention to the operation of the limited capacity system.

[1]Some of these results were presented in preliminary form as an invited talk to Division 3 of the APA under the title "Time and Space as Measures of Mental Operations," August 1970. The authors thank Professor S. W. Keele for his theoretical contributions to this research. The research described here was supported by the National Science Foundation under grants GB 5960 and 21020 and by the Advanced Research Projects Agency of the Department of Defense monitored by the Air Force Office of Scientific Research under contract #F44620-67-0099.

I. Introduction

A. COMPONENTS OF ATTENTION

A recent paper (Posner & Boies, 1971) proposed a component view of attention. The overall area of attention was divided into three components: alertness, selectivity, and processing capacity. Each component was viewed as a general aspect of the field but received definition within a specific experimental task. The task involved the match of two letters presented successively. *Alertness* referred to the internal processes that took place as a consequence of providing a warning signal. *Selection* referred to the changes in dealing with the second letter as a result of the subject having been informed by the first letter what he was to look for. *Processing capacity* was defined in terms of the interference between the sequence of operations on the letters and RT to an auditory probe, which was presented at varying points in the sequence.

Probe RTs obtained during letter-matching tasks showed an improvement following the warning to prepare for the first visual letter. When the letters were separated by 1 sec, the improvement continued during the period of time following the first letter when the subject was thought to be encoding the letter. An upswing in probe RT occurred .5 sec before the presentation of the second letter. This interference effect could not be attributed to the physical occurrence of the second letter, since probe RTs were faster than .5 sec. A more marked probe interference was found following the second letter. Interference that occurs after the second letter (like that found in studies of the refractory period; see Bertelson, 1966; Smith, 1967) is confounded if the subject withholds probe responses until after completing the primary task. However, such a strategy could not account for interference effects found prior to second letter presentation, since probe responses always occur before primary task responses.

B. PROCESSING CAPACITY AND CONSCIOUSNESS

The constellation of results obtained from this study led Posner and Boies (1971) to conclude that encoding of the first letter did not require processing capacity, but that some later mental operations did. These mental operations might be related closely to the first letter (for example, rehearsal) or to preparation for the second letter (for example, generation of distinctive features, priming responses). The authors speculated that the central processor might be reserved for a subset of operations closely related to our "conscious" involvement at a given instant. Therefore, it is important to determine the exact conditions under which the interference effect is observed. The present experiments are designed to determine those conditions. The experiments seek to determine what causes the interference in probe RTs prior to the presentation of the second letter. First, we attempt to find the exact relation between first letter encoding and interference (Experiments I and II). Second, we try to see if response priming is a sufficient condition for producing interference (Experiments III and IV). Third, we try to determine if increasing the conscious processing load of the first letter affects probe RT (Experiment V).

II. Method

The general method of the studies is outlined in this section. The primary task involves the matching of two forms presented either simultaneously or successively. One major variable of the experiments in the temporal parameters. The temporal parameters for each experiment are given individually in Table 1. The first parameter is the time between the warning signal ($+$) and the occurrence of the first letter(s) (WI). The second is the time that the first letter is present (exposure duration). The third is the time between the onset of the first letter and the onset of the second letter (ISI). Finally there is the time following the feedback until the start of the next trial (ITI). Feedback was always displayed following S's response for 1 sec.

The secondary task was presented on only half of the trials. The signal was a 640-Hz tone which was presented over earphones at about 60 dB. The tone was present until the subject responded. Probe tones were presented equally often at each of eight positions, which are described individually for each experiment in Table 1. The values in Table 1 are the times following the warning signal for each probe (negative times are prior to warning). The subject never received feedback on probe RTs, nor were these times discussed with him during the experiment.

The experiments also differed in the number of subjects, total responses collected, and in the type of materials and letter match instructions. These details of the individual experiments are provided in Table 2. The first day of each experiment was practice, and data were discarded. The column marked "number of entries per cell per day" times the number of days gives the number of observations from each subject at each probe position.

All subjects were tested individually in sessions lasting about 1 hour. The materials were selected from an alphabet of 12 upper-case and 12 lower-case letters (Posner & Boies, 1971) or a set of 12 Gibson forms. The letter

Table 1. *Temporal Parameters of Experiments for Primary and Secondary Tasks*[a]

Exp.	WI	Exposure duration	ISI	ITI	Probe position							
					1	2	3	4	5	6	7	8
I	500	50, 150, 500, 1000	1000	1500–2500[b]	-500	150	550	650	800	1000	1650	1800
II	500	Until letter 2	50, 150, 500, 1000[a]	1000	-500	150	550	650	800	1000	1650	1800
II	500	Until S's response	1000	1000	-500	150	550	650	800	1000	1650	1800
III	500	2000	2000	1500–2500[b]	-500	150	600	800	1000	1500	2000	2650
IV	1000	0	0	4000	-500	100	200	500	1050	1150	1250	1400
IV	0	Until S's response	1000	4000	-500	100	200	500	1050	1150	1250	1400
V	500	1000	1000	1500–2500[b]	-500	150	550	650	800	1000	1650	1800

[a] All values are in milliseconds.
[b] Variable.

24

Table 2. *Subjects, Days, Materials, Instructions, and Number of Observations for Each Experiment*

Exp.	No. *S*s	Days	Materials	Type of match	Total trials per day	Cell *N* per *S* per day
I	7	5	Letters	Name	320	5
II	7	5	Gibson	Physical	384	24
II′	12	3	½ Letters ½ Gibson	Physical	384	12
III	6	2	Letters	½ Name ½ Physical	288	9
IV	12	3	Letters	Physical	384	12
V	7	2	Letters	½ Physical ½ Add-three	384	12

pairs used on a given trial were selected randomly from the array by a PDP-9 computer and displayed on a Tektronix 503 or 602, oscilloscope with a fast decaying P11 phosphor. The displays subtended a visual angle of less than 3°.

The subjects responded to the primary task by pressing the index finger of their right hand if the letters were "same" and their right middle finger if they were "different." The left-hand index finger was used for RTs to the secondary task. For name match instructions the first letter was always upper case and the second letter either upper or lower case, whereas physical match instructions involved either upper-case letters or Gibson forms. Equal numbers of "same" and "different" responses were used. The instructions emphasized the primary task. Feedback concerning correctness and RTs was provided after each trial but only for the letter task. The subjects were warned on the first day if they failed to respond to or anticipated the probe. All probe responses prior to a signal (anticipations) were recorded, but these almost completely disappeared after the first day. Those few subjects who deliberately waited to respond to the probe until after the primary task were excluded.

III. Results

The data from each study were summarized by a median letter match time and probe time for each subject on each experimental day. Further breakdowns by experimental condition are discussed with each experiment. The letter-matching data were of relatively little interest in the current context. Primary-task RTs varied rather little as a function of probe presentation and, in general, confirmed the results described previously (Posner & Boies, 1971).

The median-probe RTs for each probe position and subject are the basic result of the experiments. One base line for evaluating the probe RTs can be obtained from probes that occurred during the ITI. During this interval the subject is presumably relaxed and in a state of reduced alertness but is not engaged in processing any task-related information. The fastest probe times usually occur shortly following the first letter, when the subject is in a fully alerted state. Interference with the probe time can be defined either with respect to the ITI probe or with respect to the fastest fully alerted probe position.[2] We will discuss interference in relation to these two base lines.

A. Experiment I: Variable Exposure Duration

The probe RTs for Experiment I are summarized in Table 3. In this experiment the first letter remained present for a randomly varying interval of 50, 150, 500, or 1000 msec. It was then turned off and the scope remained dark until presentation of letter 2.

The results for the 1000-msec duration confirm closely those presented previously for the same condition (Posner & Boies, 1971). Probe position 6, which was .5 sec after letter 1 and .5 sec before letter 2, showed substantial interference. For each subject that probe position was longer than position 4, and for 5 of the subjects it was longer than the ITI probe. Over all exposure durations position 6 shows an RT longer than the ITI probe in 22 of 28 comparisons ($p < .01$ by sign test) and longer than position 4 in 26 of 28 comparisons ($p < .01$). As in previous work an analysis of the data excluding all RTs longer than .5 sec still shows significant interference at position 6.

The probe position at which interference begins is related to the exposure duration. When the first letter goes off after 50 msec some interference is present at 150 msec after letter 1. With 150-msec exposure duration, interference does not begin prior to 300 msec. With longer exposure durations, interference effects are delayed until 500 msec after letter 1. Once probe RTs begin to lengthen, they stay relatively long throughout the remaining interval.

---

[2]Of course, the fast RTs to probes following the first letter might be as a result of anticipations because of probe density at these positions. This view is discussed more fully in the conclusions, Section IV.

Table 3. *Probe RTs (msec) as a Function of Probe Position and First-Letter Exposure Duration*

Exposure duration	Probe position (msec following warning signal)							
	ITI[a] −500	WI[a] 150	ISI[a]				RT[a]	
			550	650	800	1000	1650	1800
50	362	338	331	371	394	394	468	412
150	354	339	331	326	346	374	482	449
500	367	338	331	317	329	406	477	417
1000	352	369	314	311	325	399	493	403

[a]Indicates primary task interval during which probe occurs.

The results of Experiment I show that the location of interference varies with the exposure duration of the first letter. Since the subject did not know when letter 1 would be removed, he presumably had to begin to process it immediately. Nonetheless, the interference effect was not present until substantially after the first letter was presented and for short durations not until it had disappeared.

If the first letter remains present during the interval, the interference appears after 500 msec. Previous work (Posner & Boies, 1971) has indicated that the subject encodes information during the first 500 msec after a letter is presented. The interference effect appears to occur at the end of this encoding process. Experiments II and II' are designed to investigate this relationship further.

B. EXPERIMENTS II AND II'

In Experiment II a Gibson form was presented for 50, 150, 500, or 1000 msec. After the specified exposure duration the first form was replaced immediately by a second form. The first form was exposed for 1000 msec on half of the trials. On these trials a probe was introduced at one of the eight positions, as shown in Table 1.

The matching RTs from the four exposure durations were used to construct an encoding function, which is shown in the upper portion of Fig. 1. The encoding function closely resembles those obtained in previous studies (Posner & Boies, 1971). Probe RTs obtained from the same subjects are shown in the lower portion of Fig. 1. The data show clearly that there is no interference with probe RTs during the encoding function. At the time encoding is largely over (.5 sec), a sharp upswing occurs. However, it is clear that the interference shown at position 6 was not as marked as obtained in

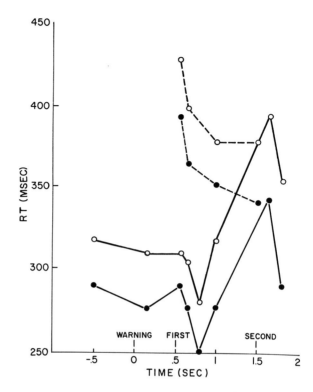

Fig. 1. Encoding functions (upper curves, dashed lines) and probe RTs (solid lines) for successive days of Experiment II: (○) days 2 and 3; (●) days 4 and 5.

the previous letter matching task. Two explanations of this seem possible. One is that the use of Gibson forms reduced the interference effect, perhaps because it did not involve naming. The second is a possible confounding, owing to the particular method of giving probes used in Experiment II. Since probes were always presented when the first form stayed present for a full second, the subject could predict the later probes easily.

To check on these possibilities Experiment II′ was run. In this experiment half of the blocks used letters and half Gibson forms. The first form remained present until the response, the second form joining it after 1 sec. Probes were presented on half the trials. Leaving the first form present until the response reduced the need for rehearsal.

The results of experiment II′ for days 2 and 3 are shown in Fig. 2. An analysis of variance of probe positions 3–6 shows that there is a significant interference effect; $F(3,33) = 26.1$ $p < .01$. Probe position 6 is longer than any of the other alerted[3] probe positions. The RT at this position is not greater than to probe position 1, however.

The results of Experiments II and II′ show conclusively that the interference effect follows the encoding of the first form. Moreover, the results of Experiment II show that interference with the probe cannot be due to a general lapse of attention since the encoding function improves throughout the delay. The most rapid drop in the encoding function is at the same time that probe RTs are showing their most rapid improvement. The results of Experiment II′ indicate that interference does not depend upon letter naming. Moreover, it does not appear that the requirement to rehearse is a necessary condition for the effect.

C. Experiment III

It is of interest to determine whether the interference effect can be delayed when the ISI is increased. Experiment III alternated blocks of physical and name matches with a fixed 2-sec interval between letters.

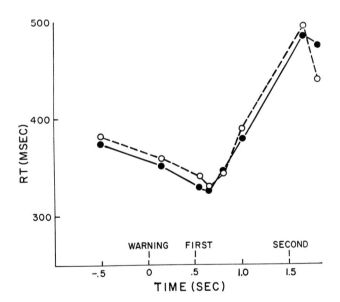

Fig. 2. Probe RTs for letter and Gibson form matching in Experiment II′: (○) Gibson; (●) letters.

---

[3]Those probes which occur during the ISI are "alerted" in this sense.

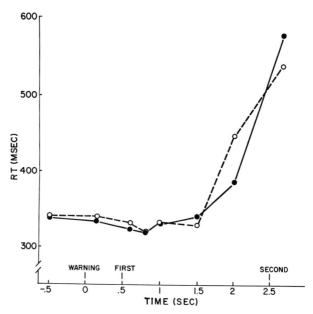

Fig. 3. Probe RTs for physical- and name-match blocks with 2-sec exposure of letter 1 (Experiment III): (○) physical match; (●) name match.

Probes were presented on half the trials at the position shown in Table 1.

The results of the experiment are presented in Fig. 3. The results show that substantial interference is present at probe position 7, which occurs 500 msec before letter 2. Of 14 comparisons, probe RTs are longer at this position than at positions 4, 5, and 6, 12 times ($p < .05$), and longer than position 1, 11 times ($p < .05$). The apparent increase in probe times at position 7 for physical over name matches shown in Fig. 3 is not reliable (only 4 of 7 comparisons are in that direction).

These results show that the interference effect is not tightly time locked to a fixed interval following first letter presentation. While it may occur at the end of encoding, it may occur sooner if the first letter is removed (Experiment I) or it may be delayed if no immediate response to letter 1 is needed.

D. EXPERIMENT IV

Experiment IV examines the role of response priming in obtaining the interference effect. In this experiment two kinds of blocks were alternated. In one type of block the subject received the first letter for 1000 msec, followed by letter 2. In the second type of block the subject received a warning signal, followed after 1000 msec by a pair of letters. The probes were presented at comparable positions when letter 1 and the warning signal are taken as time zero for their respective block types.

The results are shown in Fig. 4. It is clear both from the curve and from statistical analysis that probe position 4 shows significant interference when compared with positions 1, 2, and 3, $F(3, 33) = 6.8, p < .01$. There is a trend for the probe RTs to be longer when the first form was a letter rather than a warning signal. This is particularly true for probe position 4. However, statistical analysis shows that neither the main effect of conditions nor its interaction with probe positions reaches significance ($.05 < p < .1$).

The probe times following the *second* letter are systematically longer for the warning signal condition than for the first letter blocks. This, however, is due to the shorter letter-match RTs for sequential presentation. When the probe follows the second letter by 400 msec, which is longer than the mean successive-match RTs, the probe times approach those obtained during probe position 1.

We did not expect to find an interference effect when the first stimulus was a warning signal because there was no evidence of interference with probe times during the warning interval preceeding the first letter. Presum-

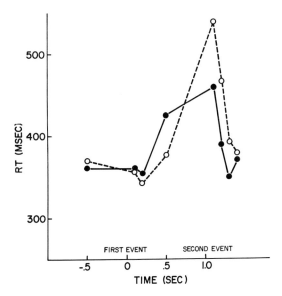

Fig. 4. Probe times for blocks of a warning signal followed after 1 sec by a letter pair (dotted line), and for letter 1 followed after 1 sec by letter 2 (solid line) (Experiment IV); (○) simultaneous; (●) successive.

ably when the subject prepares to take in information about the first letter he alerts himself in such a way as to improve not reduce RT to a probe (Posner & Boies, 1971). However, when preparation involves a motor response to the second letter, it interferes with probe RTs. This finding clearly implicates response system priming in the interference effects

E. EXPERIMENT V

Experiment V was designed to determine if stimulus-related processing can affect the degree of interference. This experiment consisted of two kinds of blocks. In the physical match blocks the subjects performed a standard matching task on the letter pairs. In the add-three blocks the subjects were required to match the input against a letter three forward in the alphabet. In order to make sure that the subjects performed the addition and could not rely upon guessing, two-thirds of the nonmatching letters were ±1 of the correct letter. Moreover, subjects who made a large number of errors were excluded from the analysis. There was a tendency of some subjects to wait until the second letter came on before attempting to count. These subjects had very long RTs in the add-three condition and were warned on the first day. A total of seven out of ten subjects were used in the analysis. The other three were eliminated because of high error rates.

The probe RTs for each condition are shown in Fig. 5. The probe data leave little doubt that the subjects received substantial interference from the add-three task. The interference clearly was established by probe position 5 (300 msec following letter 1). This study was run at a low level of practice in the primary task, but there is reason to suspect that with practice the subjects might automate the counting task and thus reduce the extent of interference shown in Fig. 5.

IV. Conclusions

To what degree is the interference effect due to processing of the primary task rather than to expectancies about or preparation for the probe? Expectancies about probes undoubtedly have an effect. However, we found anticipations or very short RTs to the probe to be negligible after the practice day. Moreover, in the studies presented in this contribution the probe position at which interference occurs has been varied from 4 through 7. In other experiments we have been able to produce maximal interference either in the center- or end-probe positions, depending upon primary task demands. Another hypothesis is that interference is due to an inability to

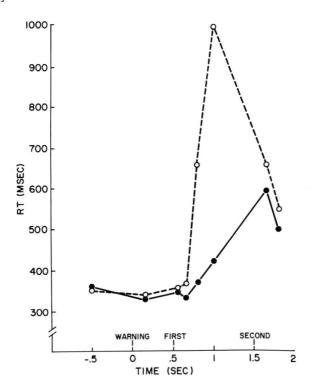

Fig. 5. Probe times for blocks of physical matches (solid line) and add-three task (dotted line) (Experiment V).

maintain optimal preparation for the probe. Studies that vary warning intervals frequently have shown an optimal period of preparation (Bertelson, 1967). However, this explanation appears inadequate to handle the effect of first-letter exposure duration and transformation difficulty on probe RTs. Thus, we conclude that the interference effect is due, at least in part, to the attention demands of operations performed upon the primary task.

Two theories about interference have dominated refractory and probe studies. The first is that all processing demands access to a single limited capacity system and the degree of interference is related to the difficulty of processing (Moray, 1967). The second is that interference is related to competition between responses (Reynolds, 1964).

Our results are difficult to reconcile with either view. Interference effects clearly occur at probe positions that are not confounded with the motor response to the primary task. Moreover, the interference effect occurs only for a subset of mental operations and not necessarily those which are most difficult. Encoding the first letter requires time and involves relating the input to past experience. However, in most experiments, it is only after encoding that interference occurs. Difficulty, as measured by the time to perform mental operations, appears to be separate from the requirement of the operation for space within the limited capacity mechanism.

The term *conscious* has been used recently in a variety of contexts (Bindra, 1970; Eccles, 1966; Gazzaniga, 1970; Sperry, 1969). The struggle for objective methods of dealing with consciousness is bound to play an important role in cognitive and physiological psychology. For several reasons the term appears to us to be closely related to the subset of operations that require access to the limited capacity system and thus produce interference. First, these operations are generally late in the processing sequence (Libet, 1966). They appear to follow habitual encodings, provided that the subject has sufficient time. Second, they are flexible. If the subject is hurried, these operations appear to take place earlier in the sequence of processing than when exposure duration is long. Third, they are not closely related to effects within any particular sensory modality. The use of auditory probes in a visual processing task was designed to avoid such within-modality effects. Finally, these operations are related to response requirements without depending upon the actual release of the motor program. This aspect fits in with the idea of consciousness as closely related to efference (Festinger, Ono, Burnham, & Bamber, 1967).

The utility of thinking of the limited capacity mechanism as related to conscious operations depends upon how this idea fits with traditional uses of the term such as awareness, intention, storage, and verbal report. Future experiments will involve relating the interference effect to other indicants of conscious operations. Perhaps then we will be able to provide a more complete account of the functions of consciousness.

References

Bertelson, P. Central intermittency twenty years later. *Quarterly Journal of Experimental Psychology*, 1966, **18**, 153–163.

Bertelson, P. The time course of preparation. *Quarterly Journal of Experimental Psychology*, 1967, **19**, 272–279.

Bindra, D. The problem of subjective experience. *Psychological Review*, 1970, **77**, 580–584.

Eccles, J. C. (Ed.) *Brain and conscious experience*. Berlin and New York: Springer-Verlag, 1966.

Festinger, L., Ono, H., Burnham, C. A., & Bamber, D. Efference and the conscious experience of perception. *Journal of Experimental Psychology Monographs*, 1967, No. 4.

Gazzaniga, M. S. *The bisected brain*. New York: Appleton, 1970.

Libet, B. Brain stimulation and the threshold of conscious experience. In J. C. Eccles (Ed.), *Brain and conscious experience*. Berlin and New York: Springer-Verlag, 1966.

Moray, N. Why is capacity limited? A survey and a model. *Acta Psychologica*, 1967, **27**, 84–92.

Posner, M. I., & Boies, S. Components of attention. *Psychological Review*, 1971, **78**, 391–408.

Posner, M. I., & Keele, S. W. Time and space as measures of mental operations, Invited address, presented at the American Psychological Association Meeting, Miami Beach, Florida, 1970.

Reynolds, D. Effects of double stimulation: Temporary inhibition of response. *Psychological Bulletin*, 1964, **62**, 333–347.

Smith, M. C. Theories of the psychological refractory period. *Psychological Bulletin*, 1967, **67**, 202–213.

Sperry, R. W. A modified concept of consciousness. *Psychological Review*, 1969, **76**, 532–536.

Attention, Strategy, and Reaction Time: A Tentative Metric

A. T. Welford

Department of Psychology
University of Adelaide,
Adelaide, South Australia

ABSTRACT

When attention is directed to a particular part of a display, reaction times to signals in that part are substantially shortened and in other parts lengthened. Experimental results are examined in terms of a serial classification model of the microbehavior underlying decisions involving choice between readily discriminable alternatives. The fit between theory and observation is remarkably close, provided some variability of the strategy used to achieve identification is assumed. The results indicate a new tentative metric for choice–reaction and identification processes. The subject is assumed to arrive at identification and choice by a series of decisions that divide the possibilities to be distinguished into dichotomies or trichotomies. Within each decision he inspects the sections of the dichotomy or trichotomy in turn until a positive observation is achieved: he does not infer presence of a signal in one section from its absence in another. The unit of measurement is taken as the *inspection time*, that is, the time taken to check the presence or absence of the signal in a section. The overall predictions of this approach approximate to an information law. At the same time they account for a number of departures from this law which have been noted in the past, especially in the case of two-choice reaction-time tasks in which one signal is more frequent than the other. A fresh experiment under these conditions was performed, and the results found to be consistent with the theory.

I. Introduction

Experiments using eight-choice reaction-time tasks in which responses were made by the different fingers of the two hands have shown that reactions by the middle and ring fingers tend to be substantially slower than those by the index and little fingers (Alegria & Bertelson, 1970; Welford, 1971). Further experiments using eight-, four-, and two-choice tasks have shown that these differences are not due to any purely motor factors but have to do with discriminability and selective attention. They are inconsistent with the serial dichotomizing and simultaneous scanning models which have usually been advanced in the past to account for the rise of reaction time with degree of choice (for example, Hick, 1952a, b; Christie & Luce, 1956) but agree remarkably well with a modified serial classification model proposed by the author some years ago (Welford, 1960, 1968).

According to this model the subject divides the total possibilities between which he has to discriminate into two, or sometimes three, classes and inspects each class in turn until he finds the one that contains the signal (or response) he seeks. He then subdivides this class into two or three, and again inspects until he finds the required subclass, and so on. Thus, with a two-choice task he sometimes achieves identification with one inspection and sometimes with two, so that if the signals are equally probable, he will on average take 1.5 inspections to make a decision. With a four-choice task, two decisions are required: one between, say, the left-hand as opposed to the right-hand pair, and a second between the members of the pair chosen. If the signals are equally probable, final choice will thus require an average of three inspections. With eight choices procedure is similar, leading to a final decision after an average of 4.5 inspections.

It is assumed that the subject can decide before the signal arrives which part of the total display he will inspect first. In a two-choice task it is therefore possible for him, by concentrating on one signal and its corresponding response, virtually always to respond after one inspection time when that signal occurs and after two inspection times when the other occurs. The difference between the reaction times to the attended and unattended signals thus provides a measure of inspection time. All inspection times are assumed to be equal, on the average, although subject to some degree of random variation.

The model accounted well for the differences between two-, four-, and eight-choice reaction times when no selective attention was given to particular signals. It also accounted well for the differences between the reaction times by different fingers in the eight-choice task if it was assumed that the lights corresponding to the index and little fingers were inspected before those corresponding to the middle and ring fingers. It also seemed to be consistent in a general way with four- and eight-choice experiments in which the subject concentrated his attention on one particular signal. No attempt was made, however, to fit the model in detail to these latter results (Welford, 1971).

The present experiments were carried out in order to obtain further evidence about the effects of selective attention upon reaction time, and to see how far the model could be used to fit results obtained under these conditions. It must be emphasized at once that the treatment at this stage is inevitably *post hoc*. It is hoped, however, to show that the type of approach implied by the model is a powerful means of accounting for several reaction-time phenomena hitherto difficult to understand.

II. Method

The apparatus, subjects and procedure were the same as those in the author's previous experiments. Eight lens-topped neon bulbs were mounted in a horizontal row so that they appeared through a 20-cm square black mask divided in half by a vertical gray line. The display was about 2.8 m in front of the subject, who sat at a table on which eight morse keys were arranged conveniently under the fingers of his two hands. The key under the left little finger corresponded to the leftmost light, the key under the left ring finger to the next light, and so on until the key under the right little finger corresponded to the rightmost light.

The lights appeared in random order except that each was presented an equal number of times in every block of 16. The lights stayed on until a key was pressed. The next light came on 3 sec after the key pressed in response to the previous light was released.

The three subjects were the author, a research student, and a graduate research assistant, both men in their 20s. The results of all three were closely similar in pattern and have therefore been pooled.

Each run consisted of 16 practice reactions which were not included in the results, followed by 200 reactions from which results were calculated. The few errors made were excluded.

III. Experiment I: Concentration upon Half the Display

Subjects performed one run under each of the following conditions:

A. eight-choice, with attention concentrated on the lights corresponding to the keys of the *right hand*;

B. eight-choice, with attention concentrated on the lights corresponding to the keys of the *left hand*;
C. four-choice, using the right hand only, with attention concentrated on the lights corresponding to the *index and middle fingers*;
D. four-choice, using the right hand only, with attention concentrated on the lights corresponding to the *ring and little fingers*.

The results of all these runs are shown in Table 1 and also, together with the results of the former eight-, four-, and two-choice tasks where there was no special concentration, in Fig. 1. It can be seen at once that the signals corresponding to the attended hand or fingers were reacted to faster, and those corresponding to the unattended slower, than when no special attention was given to particular signals. In discussing the results in detail we shall for simplicity of presentation refer to the responses, and where necessary to the lights corresponding to them, by means of the fingers concerned, thus: LL = left little, LR = left ring, LM = left middle, LI = left index, RI = right index, RM = right middle, RR = right ring, and RL = right little.

From the earlier experiments it had been found that the average difference of reaction time between attended and unattended signals in a two-choice task was about 92 msec. This figure accordingly was taken as representing one inspection time. When no special attention was given to either signal, the two-choice mean was 280 ± 5 msec. Since this should have taken, on the average, 1.5 inspection times, it was assumed that the reaction time was made up of a constant of 142 msec plus 1.5×92 msec, that is, $142 + 138 = 280$. Calculating in the same way we should expect an average of $142 + 3 \times 92 = 418$ msec for a four-choice reaction time, which is close to the figure of 415 ± 7 that was observed. For an eight-choice condition we should expect $142 + 4.5 \times 92 = 556$ msec, which is again close to the observed figure of 553 ± 8.

We shall use these quantities as yardsticks against which to measure the results of the present experiment. They apply, of course, only to the particular group of subjects concerned, although the principles behind them appear to have generality.

A. Eight-Choice Condition, Concentrating on the Right Hand

Perhaps the most likely result of concentrating on the right hand is that the initial inspection would always be of the right half of the display, so that if the signal appeared in that, it would be reached in one inspection time, whereas if it was on the left half, it would take two. It would be followed in each case by an average of three further inspections to distinguish between the four responses of the hand chosen. The results for the left hand are close

Table 1. *Mean Correct Reaction Times and 95% Confidence Limits for Experiment 1[a]*

Reacting finger	Left little	Left ring	Left middle	Left index	All left	Right index	Right middle	Right ring	Right little	All right	All fingers	Total errors
A. Eight-choice, concentrating on right hand												
	514 ±16	687 ±26	669 ±21	570 ±23	610 ±11	411 ±18	424 ±21	469 ±25	381 ±14	421 ±10	516 ±8	29
B. Eight-choice, concentrating on left hand												
	394 ±14	461 ±24	478 ±25	451 ±22	446 ±11	538 ±22	661 ±20	694 ±27	509 ±25	601 ±12	523 ±8	24
C. Four-choice, concentrating on index and middle fingers					Index and middle					Ring and little		
	—	—	—	—	336 ±9	320 ±10	352 ±10	489 ±10	446 ±13	468 ±8	402 ±6	14
D. Four-choice, concentrating on ring and little fingers												
	—	—	—	—	513 ±10	474 ±12	551 ±15	373 ±18	356 ±14	365 ±11	439 ±8	32

[a] All times are in milliseconds. Each eight-choice mean is based on 25 reactions, and each four-choice mean on 50 reactions, by each of 3 subjects, less errors.

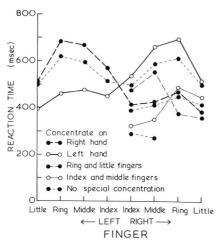

Fig. 1. Mean reaction times recorded in Experiment I, together with two-, four- and eight-choice reaction times from earlier experiments.

to expectation: $142 + 5 \times 92 = 602$ msec, which compares well with the observed figure of 610 ± 11. For the right hand the fit is not so good: we should expect $142 + 4 \times 92 = 510$ msec, whereas the observed value was 421 ± 10. It seems plausible, however, to suppose that subjects might treat the right hand reactions as a four-choice task, concentrating on two of the lights at a time, say RI + RM or RR + RL. If so, when the signal was on the right, they would reach a decision in a four-choice time, that is, 418 msec, which is indeed close to the observed value.

The time predicted for the left hand is, surprisingly, the same with either strategy, since if the right-hand reactions are treated as a four-choice task, *both* the pairs RI + RM and RR + RL would have to be inspected before the subjects turned to the left hand. The mean time thus would again include five inspection times: two to exclude the right hand and three to identify the required response among those of the left hand.

Looking at the times for individual fingers, those of the right hand correspond closely to the times for the same fingers in the four-choice condition of the earlier experiments. We should expect them all to be the same except for minor biases, such as tending to inspect RI and RL before RM and RR, and there seems to be no reason to doubt that this is so.

Times for the individual fingers of the left hand are less easy to explain. If they had been reached in the same manner as they were assumed to be in the earlier eight-choice experiments, LI and LL should have taken an average of $142 + 4.5 \times 92 = 556$ msec, which is just within the confidence limit of the observed mean of 542 ± 15. However, for LM and LR we should have expected $142 + 5.5 \times 92 = 648$ msec, which is significantly less than the observed mean of 678 ± 17. Suppose, however, that subjects adopted a slightly different strategy by initially dividing LL from the rest, and biasing their procedure so that they inspected it first on .25 of the occasions and second on .75. If they did this, LL would be reached in an average of $142 + 2 \times 92 + (.25 \times 1 \times 92 + .75 \times 2 \times 92) = 487$ msec, which is significantly although not substantially *less* than the observed mean of 514 ± 16. If LR, LM, and LI were taken as a trio in a further decision, the time for them would be $142 + 2 \times 92 + (.75 \times 1 \times 92 + .25 \times 2 \times 92) + 2 \times 92 = 625$ msec, which is again significantly but not substantially less than the observed figure of 642 ± 15.

The mean for all 8 responses was significantly less than that for the original eight-choice task with no selective attention: 516 ± 8 as opposed to 553 ± 8 msec. The saving can be attributed to the more efficient strategy of treating reaction by the attended hand as a four-choice task.

B. EIGHT-CHOICE CONDITION, CONCENTRATING ON THE LEFT HAND

The results were very similar to those for the preceding condition. The overall mean for the attended left hand, 446 ± 11 msec, fell between the means expected for the two strategies already suggested, that is, between 510 and 418 msec. It is perhaps reasonable to suppose that each strategy was followed on some occasions.

The expected values for the nonattended right hand are the same as those for the left hand in condition A. The observed means for individual fingers were all close to those expected with the second type of strategy: the expected 487 msec for RL is not significantly different from the observed 509 ± 25, and the expected 625 msec for RR, RM, and RI is close to the observed 631 ± 14. The expected mean for all 4 fingers is 591 msec, which is within the confidence limits of the observed 601 ± 12.

As in condition A, the mean for all 8 responses was significantly shorter than in the original eight-choice task: 523 ± 8 as opposed to 553 ± 8 msec. The saving again is plausibly attributed to the use of the efficient strategy of treating reaction by the attended hand as a four-choice task on a substantial number of occasions.

C. FOUR-CHOICE CONDITION, CONCENTRATING ON THE INDEX AND MIDDLE FINGERS

Two obvious strategies correspond to those considered for the eight-choice conditions. One is to bias in advance the initial decision between RI + RM versus RR + RL, so that the former is always inspected first. A further decision then distinguishes between RI and RM. This implies that the mean reaction time for RI + RM would be 142 + 92 + 1.5 × 92 = 372 msec. The other strategy is to treat RI + RM as a two-choice task so that, on average, these responses are reached in 142 + 1.5 × 92 = 280 msec. The observed mean of 336 ± 9 msec fell between these two figures and is consistent with a mixed strategy.

The expected mean for reactions by the nonattended fingers RR and RL is, as with the nonattended hand in the eight-choice case, the same for either strategy, that is, 142 + 2 × 92 + 1.5 × 92 = 464 msec, which is close to the observed value of 468 ± 8.

Differences between RI and RM and between RR and RL again can be attributed to bias in the order in which members of the pair were inspected. The mean for all four fingers, 402 ± 6, was significantly, although not substantially, less than the 415 ± 7 in the original experiments for a four-choice task in which attention was not concentrated on particular signals or responses.

D. FOUR-CHOICE CONDITION, CONCENTRATING ON THE RING AND LITTLE FINGERS

The mean reaction time by the attended fingers, 365 ± 11 msec, was only a little less than 372-msec, which was the higher of the two estimates made for condition C. However, the mean reaction time by the nonattended fingers RI and RM, 513 ± 10 msec, substantially exceeded the expected value of 464. The time for RI, 474 ± 12 msec, was close to expectation: it is the observed value of 551 ± 15 for RM that is too high. It exceeded the expected value by 87 msec, which is only a little less than one inspection time of 92 msec.

Why the time for RM was so long is not clear, but subjectively this condition seemed extremely difficult. In particular it was difficult to maintain concentration on RR as well as on RL and to distinguish RM from RR. It is possible, therefore, that some extra check was made to distinguish between these last two: for instance when the light corresponding to RM appeared, subjects might have made an extra check taking one inspection time to make sure it was not RR before deciding for RM. Whether this view is correct or not, performance was clearly slow: the overall observed mean of 439 ± 8 msec was significantly *longer* than the four-choice mean of 415 ± 7 in the former experiments.

IV. Application of the Model to Conditions with Selective Attention in Former Experiments

We shall now apply the principles used to account for the results of Experiment I to the four- and eight-choice conditions in former experiments where the subjects concentrated attention on one light and its corresponding response. The results are shown in Fig. 2 and Table 2.

Maintaining concentration on a single signal and response in four- and eight-choice conditions proved to be, subjectively at least, a difficult task: attention tended often to wander to other possible signals and responses. The effect of this can be seen in the fact that the means for the attended finger in all cases significantly exceeded the figure of 142 + 92 = 234 msec, which would be expected if it had always been reached in one inspection time.

It seems plausible to suggest that concentration had two effects: first to determine the categories into which the sources were initially divided for purposes of inspection, and second to bias the order in which inspections were made.

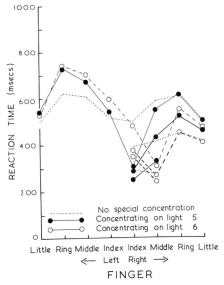

Fig. 2. Mean reaction times recorded in earlier experiments under conditions in which subjects concentrated on the light corresponding to either the right index or the right middle finger.

Table 2. *Mean Correct Reaction Times and 95% Confidence Limits for Conditions in Which Attention Was Concentrated on One Signal and Response[a,b]*

Reacting finger:	Left little	Left ring	Left middle	Left index	Right index	Right middle	Right ring	Right little	All to left of attended finger	All to right of attended finger	All fingers	Total errors
Eight-choice, concentrating on Right Index Finger												
	538 ±20	727 ±26	670 ±21	542 ±16	305 ±18	547 ±15	613 ±22	500 ±17	619 ±12	553 ±16	555 ±13	16[c]
Eight-choice, concentrating on Right Middle Finger												
	532 ±17	740 ±30	702 ±25	596 ±20	480 ±22	307 ±20	550 ±25	473 ±20	588 ±12	512 ±15	548 ±14	18
Four-choice, concentrating on Right Index Finger												
	—	—	—	—	285 ± 7	431 ±13	523 ±16	456 ±15	—	470 ± 9	424 ±10	20[c]
Four-choice, concentrating on Right Middle Finger												
	—	—	—	—	375 ±13	267 ± 8	448 ±15	410 ±11	375 ±13	429 ± 9	375 ± 9	18[c]

[a]From Welford (1971).
[b]All times are in milliseconds. Each eight-choice mean is based on 25 reactions, and each four-choice mean on 50 reactions, by each of 3 subjects, less errors.
[c]Including 1 reading missed due to a fault in the apparatus.

A. Eight-Choice Condition, Concentrating on the Right Index
   Finger

Let us assume that subjects initially divided the signals and their corresponding responses into three classes, one consisting of the whole left hand, one of RI, and one of the rest of the right hand. Let us assume also that instead of arriving first at RI once in eight times in line with the relative signal frequencies, or once in three times as they would if they gave equal weight to all three classes, they did so on half the occasions. On the remaining occasions they would arrive at RI in either 2 or 3 inspections. A method of calculating the frequencies of these is given in the Appendix. The average time taken to respond with RI works out as $142 + 153 = 295$ msec, which is reasonably close to the observed value of 305 ± 18.

As regards the left hand and the remaining fingers of the right hand, let us suppose that initial inspection is biased towards them in proportion to their relative frequencies, that is, in the ratio of 4 to 3. On this basis, the initial decision for the left hand is completed in an average of $142 + 190 = 332$ msec. If subsequent decision for the left hand proceeded according to the second strategy proposed for the unattended hand in Conditions A and B of Experiment I, the expected mean reaction time by LL would be $332 + (.25 \times 1 \times 92 + .75 \times 2 \times 92) = 493$ msec, and by LR, LM, and LI $332 + (.75 \times 1 \times 92 + .25 \times 2 \times 92) + 2 \times 92 = 631$ msec. The corresponding observed values were 538 ± 20 and 646 ± 13.

On the same basis, the initial decision for the group consisting of RM, RR, and RL would have been completed in $142 + 209 = 351$ msec. If these responses subsequently were treated as a trio, they would be reached in an average of $351 + 2 \times 92 = 535$ msec. The observed value was 553 ± 16.

The expected values for this condition are all less than those observed, but it is fair to argue that the strategies suggested are near optimal, and almost any departure from them would have lengthened reaction time.

B. Eight-Choice Condition, Concentrating on the Right Middle
   Finger

Let us assume that, in a similar manner to the foregoing condition, the subjects divided their initial inspection into 3 groups: left hand + RI, RM, and RR + RL, and managed to bias the order of inspection so as to react with RM after one inspection time on half the occasions on which the corresponding signal occurred. The expected reaction time by RM then would have been $142 + 150 = 292$ msec, which is not significantly different from the observed value of 307 ± 20.

For the left hand + RI group the initial decision would have taken $142 + 171 = 313$ msec. Let us suppose that subsequently the subjects decided between LL, RI and the rest as a trio, and that the tendency to inspect extreme positions first balanced the tendency to inspect the largest group first, so that the order of inspection was roughly equal for all three members of the trio. The decision would have taken an average of $2 \times 92 = 184$ msec giving a total mean for LL and RI of $313 + 184 = 497$ msec, which is not significantly less than the observed 506 ± 16. If LR, LM, and LI were further inspected as a trio, their expected mean would be $497 + 2 \times 92 = 681$ msec, which is close to the observed 679 ± 15.

For RR and RL the initial decision would have been completed in $142 + 229 = 371$ msec. If a subsequent decision then had been made between them, the expected reaction time would have been $371 + 1.5 \times 92 = 509$ msec, which is close to the observed value of 512 ± 15.

C. Four-Choice Condition, Concentrating on the Right Index Finger

Let us assume that the subjects made an initial decision between RI and the remaining signals and responses RM, RR, and RL, and managed to reach RI with their first inspection on half the occasions when it was presented. On this basis the expected reaction time for RI would have been $142 + 1.5 \times 92 = 280$ msec, which is close to the observed value of 285 ± 7. If they had then treated RM, RR, and RL as a trio, the expected mean reaction time for these reactions would have been $142 + 1.5 \times 92 + 2 \times 92 = 464$ msec, which is close to the observed mean of 470 ± 9.

D. Four-Choice Condition, Concentrating on the Right Middle Finger

If we assume that the subjects initially divided the possibilities into a trio RI, RM, and RR + RL, and biased their inspections so as to reach RM on the first inspection in .7, RI in .1 and RR + RL in .2 of the cases, respectively, the expected value for RM is $142 + 124 = 266$ msec, which is almost exactly equal to the observed 267 ± 8. The other expected values are, however, too high. That for RI is $142 + 252 = 394$ msec as compared with the observed 375 ± 13. That for RR and RL, assuming that a subsequent decision had to be made between them, is $142 + 176 + 1.5 \times 92 = 456$ msec as compared with the observed value of 429 ± 9.

The observed times for this condition are noteworthy in that the observed mean of 375 ± 9 msec for all 4 fingers together is very close to the basic constant time plus 2.5 inspection times, that is, $142 + 2.5 \times 92 = 372$. This is the theoretically shortest possible time for a four-choice task in terms of the present model. It can be attained only if the 4 choices are treated as two two-choice tasks, in the same manner as Condition A in Experiment I was treated as two four-choice tasks, or if subjects search serially one at a time until the correct signal and response are found. It seems possible that subjects approximated to one or other of these strategies, the search tending to be in the order RM, RI, RL, RR. Why the strategy of search should be so efficient in this condition is not clear, but it might perhaps be due to the concentration on RM tending to divide the array into 2 halves, RM + RI and RR + RL.

V. Experiment II: Effect of Unbalanced Signal Frequencies

If the model outlined in this paper is correct, or approximately so, it follows that the effects of unbalance in the frequencies of different signals will follow not the "information" each transmits, but the number of inspections needed to distinguish them. In particular, for accurate performance of a two-choice task, the maximum mean difference between the reaction times to the more and less frequent signals will be one inspection time. Hyman (1953) noted that the reaction times to more and less frequent signals were closer together than a strict information analysis would predict, but he did not give examples from his two-choice tasks. In such of the literature as the author has been able to scrutinize, there seem to have been no cases reported in which mean differences in two-choice tasks with straightforward relationships between signal and response have appreciably exceeded the 92 msec postulated as the inspection time in the present experiments. In most cases they have been much less. The same appears to be true of other cases in which different classes of response in straightforward two-choice tasks have been separated, for example in studies of repetition and alternation effects. Differences have been much greater, of course, with higher degrees of choice or with more complex relationships between signal and response.

In no case, however, has there been any way of estimating inspection time. We therefore cannot be certain that the evidence is valid support for the present model since we do not know whether the 92 msec estimated as the inspection time in our experiments is applicable more generally—it is calculated on the basis of our own subjects' results and may not be applicable to those of others. Therefore, it was decided to make a direct test, using the same subjects in a two-choice task with unbalanced signal frequencies, to see whether the reaction times to the more and less frequent signals differed by more than 92 msec.

The same apparatus was used with the lights corresponding to the right index and middle fingers only. They appeared in random order except that the former appeared 14 times and the latter twice in every 16 times. The subjects knew which would be the more frequent. Each performed one run of 200 reactions. In all other respects the arrangements were the same as in previous experiments.

Taking $1.5 \times 92 = 138$ msec as the time per bit, the mean reaction time to the more frequent signal at 0.19 bits should have been $142 + .19 \times 138 = 168$ msec, while that for the less frequent signal at 3 bits should have been $142 + 3 \times 138 = 556$ msec, a difference of 388.

In fact, the mean time for the more frequent response was 242 ± 5 msec and for the less frequent response 313 ± 13, giving a difference of only 71 msec, which is well within the figure of 92 estimated for one inspection time, and close to the difference of 69 msec expected if initial inspection had been biased to correspond with signal frequency—the difference between $142 + (.875 \times 1 \times 92 + .125 \times 2 \times 92) = 246$ and $142 + (.125 \times 1 \times 92 + .875 \times 2 \times 92) = 315$. Some slight response bias was evident in that 9 out of the 12 errors made were the result of substituting the more for the less frequent response.

VI. Discussion

From a purely factual standpoint, the results of the experiments we have outlined are indeed striking. Concentration of attention on particular signals, or groups of signals, greatly reduced the time taken to respond to them, and while it raised the times taken to respond to other signals, there was often a net gain when both were considered together. Two implications are clear. First, when considering responses to a set of signals, it is not enough to regard one response as typical of all—for example, it is not satisfactory to take the reaction times for any one finger as a reliable indication of those for other fingers. Second, there are several practical ergonomic implications, not only for the design of keyboards and consoles where certain positions which tend to capture attention are obviously indicated for those items to which reaction needs to be fastest, but also for a number of broader problems such as the design of roads, the positioning of road signs, and the control of traffic—for example, the need to divert attention to watch for traffic from side roads seems likely to impair substantially the speed of reaction time to events on the road ahead.

On the theoretical side, it must be emphasized again that the application that has been made of the proposed model is almost entirely *post hoc*, and that in fitting it to data we have made a range of assumptions. It is fair to say, however, that the assumptions have been relatively few, and that each has been made in several contexts. It therefore would be unfair to say that so many had been made that almost any data could be fitted. The author is very much aware of the many possible strategies that he postulated initially, only to find they clearly did not fit the data.

What seems to have been achieved is a tentative metric for reaction times, which in some ways approaches that of information theory, but is essentially microbehavioral rather than purely mathematical, and can explain some of the anomalies arising in the strict information theory approach. Essentially subjects are assumed to inspect in turn items or groups of items, taking them in pairs or threes, until the required degree of specificity is obtained. In this sense, the approach applies not only to choice–reaction times but to all forms of identification and selective reaction.

Many problems obviously remain. For example:

1. We have considered only cases in which both signals and responses are distinguished spatially. Can the model be extended to deal with symbolic signals and responses such as digits seen and spoken? Are these perhaps ordered in memory in such a way that they can be inspected serially?

2. The present results do not enable us to decide how far the effects of attention are due to concentration on *signals* as opposed to *responses*. Almost certainly both are involved to some extent, but how much and in exactly what ways we cannot at present say.

3. We have not attempted to account for minor biases. Why, for instance, has it been necessary to assume that some positions in the display are inspected first? Why are certain strategies pursued in some situations and other strategies in others?

We cannot at present answer these questions, but it is to be hoped that what has been said here has been challenging, or outrageous, enough to inspire the research needed to do so.

VII. Appendix: Calculating Average Numbers of Inspections When Attention Is Divided Unequally among Signals

A. Two Possible Signals or Groups of Signals

Let us suppose that two signals or groups of signals, A and B, occur with equal frequency and that attention is given to them in the proportions p_A and p_B, respectively, with $p_A + p_B = 1$.

When A occurs, it will, on p_A of the occasions, be identified in one inspection and on the remaining p_B of the occasions in two. The average number of inspections will thus be $p_A + 2p_B$. Similarly, when B occurs, it will be identified in one inspection on p_B of the occasions and on the remaining p_A of the occasions in two, so that the average number of inspections will be $p_B + 2p_A$.

B.   THREE POSSIBLE SIGNALS OR GROUPS OF SIGNALS

Similarly, let us suppose that with three signals or groups of signals, A, B, and C, each signal being equally probable, attention is given in the proportions p_A, p_B, and p_C respectively, with $p_A + p_B + p_C = 1$.

When A occurs, it will, on p_A of the occasions, be identified in one inspection and on the remaining $p_B + p_C$ occasions in two or three. On p_B of these occasions, the subject will have been inspecting B. Let us assume that having found that B has not occurred, he makes his subsequent inspections in the proportions p_A' and p_C' with $p_A'/p_C' = p_A/p_C$ and $p_A' + p_C' = 1$. Since $p_A' = p_A/(1 - p_B)$ and $p_C' = p_C/(1 - p_B)$, A will be identified in two inspections on $p_B \times p_A/(1 - p_B)$ of the occasions when the subject initially inspects B, and in three inspections on $p_B \times p_C/(1 - p_B)$ of the occasions. Similarly, if A occurs and the subject has initially inspected C, A will be identified in two inspections on $p_C \times p_A/(1 - p_C)$ occasions and in three on $p_C \times p_B/(1 - p_C)$.

Extending the same type of formulation to cases in which B and C occur, we obtain the following matrix in which each row and each column adds to unity:

		Signal or group occurring		
		A	B	C
Number of inspections required to identify	1	p_A	p_B	p_C
	2	$\dfrac{p_B \times p_A}{1 - p_B} + \dfrac{p_C \times p_A}{1 - p_C}$	$\dfrac{p_A \times p_B}{1 - p_A} + \dfrac{p_C \times p_B}{1 - p_C}$	$\dfrac{p_A \times p_C}{1 - p_A} + \dfrac{p_B \times p_C}{1 - p_B}$
	3	$\dfrac{p_B \times p_C}{1 - p_B} + \dfrac{p_C \times p_B}{1 - p_C}$	$\dfrac{p_A \times p_C}{1 - p_A} + \dfrac{p_C \times p_A}{1 - p_C}$	$\dfrac{p_A \times p_B}{1 - p_A} + \dfrac{p_B \times p_A}{1 - p_B}$

Acknowledgments

My sincere thanks are due to Mr. R. Willson who did all the programming and running of the apparatus, and also made valuable comments. The work was supported by a grant from the Australian Research Grants Committee without whose generosity it could not have been undertaken.

References

Alegria, J., & Bertelson, P. Time uncertainty, number of alternatives and particular signal-response pair as determinants of choice reaction time. *Acta Psychologica,* 1970, **33**, 36–44.

Christie, L. S., & Luce, R. D. Decision structure and time relations in simple choice behaviour. *Bulletin of Mathematical Biophysics*, 1956, **18**, 89–111.

Hick, W. E. On the rate of gain of information. *Quarterly Journal of Experimental Psychology*, 1952, **4**, 11–26. (a)

Hick, W. E. Why the human operator? *Transactions of the Society of Instrumental Technology*, **4**, 67–77. (b)

Hyman, R. Stimulus information as a determinant of reaction time. *Journal of Experimental Psychology*, 1953, **45**, 188–196.

Welford, A. T. The measurement of sensory–motor performance: survey and reappraisal of twelve years progress. *Ergonomics*, 1960, **3**, 189–230.

Welford, A. T. *Fundamentals of skill*. London: Methuen, 1968.

Welford, A. T. What is the basis of choice-reaction time? *Ergonomics*, 1971, **14**, 679–693.

The Influence of the Intensity of Tone Bursts on the Psychological Refractory Period

W. G. Koster   *R. van Schuur*

Instituut Voor Perceptie Onderzock
Insulindelaan 2
Eindhoven, The Netherlands

ABSTRACT

An experiment is described in which the subject must react to the second of two similar stimuli (1000 Hz, 15 msec). The intensity of the stimuli and the interval between them are randomly varied. The results are in contradiction with the intermittency hypothesis. They may be explained in terms of a sensitivity hypothesis. The decay in reaction time as a function of the interstimulus interval depends on the experimental conditions which suggests that other influences also play a part in such experiments.

I. Introduction

The delay (RT_2) in the reaction to a stimulus (S_2) closely preceded by another stimulus (S_1) changes when the interstimulus interval (ISI) is varied. This phenomenon is known in the literature as the psychological refractory period (Bertelson, 1966; Smith, 1967; Welford, 1967). Two groups of hypotheses have been proposed to explain the experimental results.

The *"set" hypotheses* state that before each trial the subject has an expectation about the length of ISI (Elithorn & Lawrence, 1955). Together with the conditional probability that S_2 will be presented at a particular moment, provided that it has not already been presented, an inverse relationship between RT_2 and ISI may be predicted.

The *single-channel hypotheses* state that the delay is due to a built-in restriction. All signals have to pass a single channel. In the intermittency version (Welford, 1952; Davis, 1957) a new stimulus arriving shortly after another one is not handled immediately, but must be stored until the channel is cleared. The sensitivity version (Koster & Peacock, 1969) is based on the assumption (Telford, 1931) that a new stimulus is handled upon arrival. The mechanism, not having completely recovered from handling S_1, is then less sensitive, which results in a delay in the transmission of S_2. Koster and Peacock's data obtained with visual stimuli support the assumption.

Bertelson (1966) rejects the strong version of the expectancy hypothesis stating that "delays are nothing but expectancy effects." The weaker version predicts that "delays are influenced by expectancy regarding the signals to come." The data from several experiments (Davis, 1965; Koster & Bekker, 1967) suggest that this weaker version is responsible for about only 10 msec. In these two studies the double-stimulus condition and the single-stimulus condition (in which S_1 was replaced by a trigger response by which the subject initiated each trial) were presented in separate sessions. To test the remaining two, single-channel, hypotheses an experiment was set up in which the influence of the intensity of tone bursts on RT was studied.

It is well known that RT decreases with increasing intensity. For auditory stimuli this effect has been studied extensively by Chocholle (1945). The cause of the shift in latency is less well known. A distinction may be made between a peripheral cause, the sense organ itself, and a central cause, that is, beyond the point in the brain where the information of both (or several) sense organs meet. More knowledge of the cause of the latency is crucial as the predictions of both hypotheses are cause dependent. With visual stimuli the delay in reaction with decreasing intensity is assumed to result from mainly peripheral effects (Koster & Peacock, 1969). With auditory stimuli this is less probable. Aitken and Dunlop (1968) found short latencies to clicks in the medial geniculate body that hardly changed when the intensity was increased from 55 to 105 dB SL. Studies of Gross and Thurlow (1951) showed that the latency of responses to clicks and tonal bursts in the inferior colliculus and the medial geniculate body varies inversely with intensity from 16 to 7 msec.

From studies with auditory-evoked potentials a less uniform picture is obtained. Some authors have found no effect of intensity on wave latency (Goldstein & Rodman, 1967; Davis, Mast, Yoshie, & Zerlin, 1966; Wilkinson, 1967), whereas others (Rapin, Schimmel, Tourk, Krasnegor, & Pollak, 1966) observed no effect with clicks as stimuli but a clear decrease of about 40 msec when the intensity of tone bursts (35-msec duration, 1000 Hz) was increased from 10 to 50 dB SL. In psychophysical studies using auditory stimuli (noise bursts) Sanford (1970) obtained evidence that the delay in reaction is not preperceptual.

Although the data in the literature are not uniform in this respect, there is evidence that a great proportion of the latency of auditory stimuli does not originate in the ear, but must be located in higher centers. Since there is not enough evidence to attribute the intensity effect on RT to central factors, predictions based on both hypotheses will be made for assumptions of peripheral as well as central effects.

The sensitivity model is based on the recovery of a system after the passage of a signal. For auditory stimuli there are also indications that such a mechanism exists with time parameters comparable with those found in psychophysical studies. Various authors (Abraham & Marsh, 1966; Davis *et al.*, 1966; Mast, 1965; Nelson & Lassman, 1968) found that the amplitude of an auditory-evoked potential decreased with increasing rates of stimulation, which corresponds to being inversely proportional to ISI. Tunturi (1946) reports that with auditory stimuli an absolute refractory period of 20–100 msec and a relative refractory period of 100–250 msec is found in the auditory cortex. This effect has also been observed by Erulkar (1957) in the inferior colliculus. He states: "if two stimuli are delivered in succession, one to each ear, there is an absolute unresponsive period to the second stimulus lasting from 8–150 msec according to the ear stimulated first and the strength of the second stimulus [Erulkar, 1957].

In Davis' version (1957) of the intermittency hypothesis the total RT is divided into three parts: (*a*) a sensory time ST comprising the latency in the sense organ itself and the transmission time to the brain; (*b*) a central time CT representing the time the brain is occupied with the signal; (*c*) the motor time MT consisting of the delay between a motor command in the brain and the start of the reaction. In this version an increase in the intensity of S_1, (that is, L_1), leads to a decrease in ST_1 and/or CT_1 (depending on the cause of the effect), resulting in a shorter delay. An increase in the intensity of S_2 (that is, L_2) leads to a decrease in either ST_2, thus increasing the delay, or in CT_2, and keeping the delay unchanged. With an increase in ISI, RT_2 is expected to decrease (slope -1) and to reach a particular end level. The upward deviation at the intercept of the end level and the -1 line will be .4 times the standard deviation of the data of the end level (van Schuur, 1971). The distributions are virtually normal.

In the sensitivity hypothesis an increase in L_1 may decrease ST_1; as a result the drop in sensitivity sets in earlier and so does the recovery process. A subsequent stimulus will find a more recovered system, thus resulting in shorter delay. Apart from that, a higher L_1 may produce a larger drop in sensitivity. Combination of both effects may produce shorter, constant, or longer delays as a function of L_1. An increase in L_2 may result in a decrease in ST_2; as a consequence, the signal arrives earlier in the brain centers, and the latter are not recovered as well, resulting in a longer delay. In addition, the higher intensity of S_2 may more easily overcome the reduction in sen-

Table 1. *Predictions According to the Intermittency and the Sensitivity Hypothesis for Variations in the Intensity of the Stimuli*[a]

	Increase in intensity of:	Cause of intensity effect on RT_2	
		Peripheral	Central
Intermittency	S_1	Decreased T_0	Decreased T_0
hypothesis	S_2	Increased T_0	Constant T_0
	S_1	Decreased T_0	Constant or increased T_0
Sensitivity			
hypothesis	S_2	Increased T_0	Constant or decreased T_0

[a]The calculated increase in RT_2 at ISI $= 0$ is referred to as T_0.

sitivity due to S_1. Dependent on the balance between both effects, the delay will be longer, constant, or shorter. With increasing ISI, RT will decrease exponentially until the end level is reached. For the slope at short ISI no predictions can be made.

The predictions of both hypotheses of the effect of intensity on the delay in RT_2 are summarized in Table 1. (Note the distinction made between peripheral and central causes, as stated above.) In the experiment described below the loudness (L) of the stimuli is varied from 20 to 80 dB SL to obtain reasonable differences in RT. The most simple paradigm was chosen: two identical stimuli and a reaction to the second stimulus only.

II. Experiment

A. Method

1. Apparatus

The apparatus consisted of a two-channel auditory system in which a stimulus could be produced in each channel. The stimulus consisted of a tone burst of 1000 Hz with a duration of 15 msec. No special provisions were made for switching the signal on and off at the zero crossings. The stimuli were presented dichotically through head phones to minimize extraneous peripheral effects, such as masking. The intensity of the stimuli was varied in each channel independently. The interval between the stimuli was varied. The time of reaction to a stimulus was measured to the nearest centisecond. The programming of stimulus intensity and interstimulus interval, as well as the RT measurements, was made by a specially designed device, the "Donders" (Schouten & Domburg, 1963, 1964). The subject sat in an acoustic box ("Ampliphon"). The experimenter and subject communicated through a simple intercom system.

A trial was started by depressing a trigger button. Depression of the button interrupted a light beam, which caused a light-sensitive cell to react. A piece of rubber below the button prevented unwanted acoustical signals. Another button, activating a micro switch, served as a reaction button.

2. Subjects

Four subjects took part in the experiment. All of them had been trained extensively before the experiment proper.

3. Procedure

Each subject initiated a trial by depressing the trigger button with his left hand. A stimulus was presented to his left ear 200 msec later. After a variable ISI, a second stimulus was presented to his right ear, to which he had been instructed to react with his right hand (double-stimulus condition). No immediate knowledge of result could be given.

Prior to the double-stimulus sessions, control sessions had been held in which the first stimulus was omitted in order to measure simple reaction time, RT_s (single-stimulus condition). All sessions were preceded by 10 trials to avoid warming-up effects.

B. DESIGN

In each session eight ISI values were used (25, 40, 80, 160, 250, 400, 700, and 1000 msec). Within a session ISI was varied randomly so that all values of ISI appeared equally often. Four intensity levels were used. The presentation schemes were such that all sequences of either S_2 or ISI were presented equally often, to avoid sequence effects.

In the single-stimulus condition (control) a session consisted of 128 trials, that is, four replications of each combination of ISI and L. The intensity was varied in steps of 20 dB from 10 to 70 dB SL. Altogether 14–24 sessions were held. In the double-stimulus condition a session consisted of 128 trials, that is, one replication of each combination of ISI, L_1, and L_2. A session lasted about 10 min. The intensity was varied in steps of 20 dB from 20 to 80 dB SL. The intensity levels were higher than those in the other condition because S_2 with $L_2 = 10$ dB SL was not audible when it was closely preceded by S_1, with $L_1 = 70$ dB SL. In all 36 sessions were held.

C. Results

Plotting RT for each ISI in the form of a histogram shows that most of the data approximated a normal distribution fairly well. Some reactions were made before or shortly after the presentation of S_2. Visual inspection of the histograms made it plausible to treat reaction times shorter than 80 msec as premature reactions. The same reasoning may be used for late reactions, when RT is longer than 800 msec. The data have been analyzed with and without these extreme RT. Analyses of variance were made on the data with and without the extreme values. In the latter case the number of replications in the single-stimulus condition is 51, and in the double stimulus condition it is 28.

With a large number of observations very small effects may become statistically significant in an analysis of variance. For that reason a somewhat unusual criterion was used to asses the "importance" of an effect. Given that an effect was statistically significant a ratio then was computed, consisting of the contribution to the variance of that particular effect, divided by the residual variance. If this ratio was larger than .1, then the effect was assumed to be important. The value .1 was chosen so as to get only important effects when visual inspection of the graphs led to the same conclusion.

1. Double-Stimulus Condition

In examining the relation between RT_2 and ISI, it appears that for short ISIs, there are almost no values of RT_2 less than 80 msec; excluding extreme values of RT_2 at short values of ISI would, therefore, make little difference. However, for long ISIs the effect of extreme values of RT_2 is clearly appreciable for three of the four subjects. That is, with the extreme values included, RT_2 continues to decrease with increasing ISI, whereas after the exclusion of these extreme values, the curve approaches the end level asymptotically. In contrast, exclusion does not influence the shape of the $RT_2(L_2)$ curve. In the analysis of variance the exclusion of extreme values drastically reduces the error variance. It appears that more effects reach the importance level.

The effects of subject, ISI, L_2, and the interaction of ISI and subject are found to be important in this sequence. The results are plotted in Figs. 1 and 2. The solid line through the data points is the best-fitted exponential curve representing $RT_2 = RT_n + T_o \exp(- \text{ISI}/\tau)$. The parameters differ from subject to subject. The broken line represents the predictions according to the intermittency hypothesis. The vertical solid bar represents twice the standard deviation of the individual data at ISI = 400, 700, and 1000 msec. Table 2 shows the extreme values. The percentage of $RT_2 \leq 80$ msec, increases with L_1 from .7 to 2.5%; it is independent of L_2.

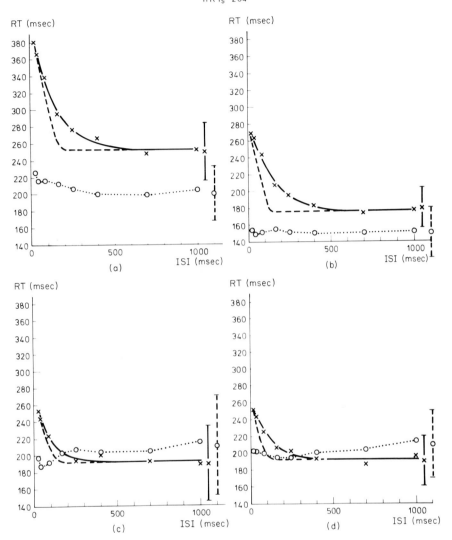

Fig. 1. Data of four subjects plotted in separate curves: (a) subject K, $RT_2 = 252 + 154$ $\exp(-ISI/135)$; (b) subject vH, $RT_2 = 176 + 116 \exp(-ISI/138)$; (c) subject vS, $RT_2 = 193 + 85 \exp(-ISI/75)$; (d) subject B, $RT_2 = 193 + 74 \exp(-ISI/101)$. The crosses refer to the delay in reaction to the second of a pair of stimuli RT_2. These values are the mean values of 448 trials, averaged over all 16 combinations of intensities. The circles indicate RT_s to a single stimulus. Each value is based on 204 trials, averaged over all four intensities. The solid line represents the predictions according to a sensitivity hypothesis, its formula being indicated above. The broken line represents the predictions according to the intermittency hypothesis.

The vertical solid bar indicates two times the standard deviation of the individual RT_2 values, the vertical dotted bar those for the individual RT_s values.

Table 2. *Percentages of Extreme RT for Each Subject for Double-Stimulus Condition*

		25	40	80	160	250	400	700	1000	Mean value
					ISI (msec)					

A. The percentages of reactions before or within 80 msec after the presentation of S_2

Subject	K	—	—	—	—	—	.2	.2	.2	.1
	B	—	—	—	.9	2.3	2.9	4.3	5.7	2.0
	vH	—	—	—	.4	.9	1.2	1.7	4.7	1.1
	vS	—	—	—	1.5	1.0	2.4	3.8	5.2	1.9
Mean value		—	—	—	.7	1.1	1.7	2.5	4.0	1.3

B. The percentages of reactions later than 800 msec after the presentation of S_2

Subject	K	1.2	.5	—	—	—	—	—	—	.2
	B	—	.2	.5	.3	—	.5	—	—	.2
	vH	.9	—	—	—	—	—	—	—	.1
	vS	.3	.2	.2	.3	—	—	—	—	.1
Mean value		.6	.2	.2	.2	—	.1	—	—	.15

Another way of analysing the data is by fitting an exponential function $RT_2 = RT_n + T_0 \exp(-ISI/\tau)$ (Koster & Peacock, 1969), in which RT_n is the end level of the RT_2(ISI) curve, T_0 is the increase in RT_2 immediately after the presentation of S_1, and τ is the time constant with which RT_2 returns to its end level. Averaged over all conditions and subjects, the value of τ is about 125 msec. It is far from being constant. As a function of L_1 it exhibits a U-shaped curve with a minimum value at $L_1 = 60$ dB SL. A low τ value is found for $L_2 = 20$ dB SL. The subjects clearly differ in their mean τ value. The mean value of T_0 is about 115 msec. For all subjects the value for the condition $L_1 = 80$ dB SL and $L_2 = 20$ dB SL is extremely high (210 msec). Elimination of the data for these values of L_1 and L_2 shows that T_0 depends only on the subjects. The increase of T_0 (10 msec) with L_1 is not significant. The value of RT_n is independent of L_1; it varies inversely with L_2.

2. Single-Stimulus Condition

For two of the four subjects rejection of extreme data has no influence on the RT_s(ISI) curve, for the other two the original data continue to decrease with increasing ISI. After rejection of extreme data, the curve is statistically horizontal. The form of the $RT_s(L)$ curve is not altered by rejection of extreme values for three of the four subjects. The analysis of variance shows the effect of stimulus intensity and subject to be of importance. No interactions reach that level. In Fig. 1 the RT_s(ISI) curves also are plotted (dotted lines) for purposes of comparison. It is worth noting that the intensities used in the single-stimulus condition differed somewhat from those used in the double-stimulus condition.

In Fig. 2 the RT_s (L) curves are plotted (broken lines) together with the RT_n(L) curves (solid lines). The RT_n values are calculated end levels of the RT_2(ISI) curves. The extreme values are given in Table 3. Both for $RT \leq 80$ msec and $RT > 800$ msec the subjects were found to differ considerably and they behaved differently with different ISIs. The overall percentage of short RT is 1.4% and that of long RT is 0.3%. More detailed results have been published elsewhere (van Schuur & Koster, 1971).

III. Discussion

The rejection of data on the grounds of arbitrary arguments is a perilous procedure (Annett, 1969). In this study we rejected less than 2% of the data, and their exclusion only occasionally influences the mean values that were

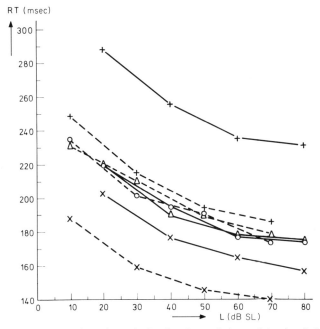

Fig. 2. For each subject the calculated values of the end levels of the RT_2(ISI) curves, RT_n, are plotted as a function of L_2 (solid lines) for subjects K (+), B (△), vS (○), and vH (×). The broken lines represent the RT_s values as a function of intensity.

Table 3. *Percentages of Extreme RT for Each Subject for the Single-Stimulus Condition*

		\multicolumn{8}{c}{ISI (msec)}	Mean value
		25	40	80	160	250	400	700	1000	

A. The percentages of reactions before or within 80 msec after the presentation of S_2

Subject	K	—	—	—	—	—	—	—	—	—
	B	—	—	—	.4	—	.8	2.5	2.1	.7
	vH	—	.5	1.7	.7	3.6	5.1	11.8	12.4	4.5
	vS	.3	.3	.8	.8	—	—	—	—	.3
Mean value		.1	.2	.6	.5	.9	1.5	3.6	3.6	1.4

B. The percentages of reactions later than 800 msec after the presentation of S_2

Subject	K	—	—	—	—	—	—	—	—	—
	B	.8	.8	—	1.3	.4	.4	—	—	.5
	vH	.8	—	—	—	—	—	—	—	.1
	vS	1.1	1.4	.6	.3	.3	1.1	—	—	.6
Mean value		.7	.5	.1	.4	.2	.4	—	—	.3

obtained, or the conclusions drawn from the analyses of variance. In the histograms of the original data, the extreme RT ≤ 80 msec and > 800 msec) clearly differ from the remaining normally distributed data. Therefore, we feel justified in basing our conclusions on the remaining data only.

We may now compare the results with the predictions according to the intermittency and to the sensitivity hypotheses. T_o is found to be only slightly dependent on L_1 and L_2. As τ varies with intensity, a correction is necessary to make estimates of RT_2 at ISI = 25 msec $[(RT_2)_{25}]$ and ISI = 40 msec $[(RT_2)_{40}]$. The increase with regard to the end level RT_n will be denoted as $T_{25} = [(RT_2)_{25} - RT_n]$ and $T_{40} = [(RT_2)_{40} - RT_n]$. The intermittency hypothesis predicts at short ISI a decrease in T of about 45 msec when L_1 increases from 20 to 80 dB SL, irrespective of the causes of the latency. In fact, T_{25} and T_{40} decrease by about 20 msec. This can be explained with the sensitivity hypothesis when the cause of the latency is either peripheral or pheripheral and central combined.

With increasing L_2 the intermittency hypothesis predicts increased or constant values of T_{25} and T_{40}; both values decrease by about 20 msec. This phenomenon is compatible with a sensitivity hypothesis that assumes a latency the cause of which is either completely central or peripheral and central combined. The intensity variations thus yield data that are compatible with a sensitivity hypothesis and not with an intermittency explanation.

Another argument against the intermittency explanation is the form of the $RT_2(ISI)$ curve (Fig. 1). Even if the fluctuations in the data are taken into account (Bertelson, 1966), there remains a clear systematic discrepancy between experimental data and predictions according to the intermittency hypothesis (Fig. 1, broken line).

An argument against both hypotheses could be the dependence of τ and hence of the slope (given the almost constant value of T_o) on the variation in intensity. As the values of τ are found to be lognormally distributed with a confidence interval of 20–450 msec, no great value can be attributed to these fluctuations.

The same is true for the change in the mean value of τ. Rubinstein's (1964) data yield a τ of 110 msec for visual as well as for auditory stimuli, whereas Koster and Peacock's data (1969) exhibit a value of 260 msec. Modality probably plays no important part. Rubinstein (1964) found the increase in RT_2 with decreasing ISI to be greater with visual than with auditory stimuli. In our studies it varied from subject to subject.

In Fig. 1 the RT_s data are plotted together with the RT_2 data. Since the intensities in the two conditions are not completely similar, the curves themselves are not simply comparable. To make them comparable, the limit values of RT_2 (that is, RT_n) are plotted in Fig. 2 as a function of L_2. The figure also shows the RT_s values as a function of intensity.

For two subjects (B and vS) the functions of $RT_n(L_2)$ and the $RT_s(L)$ are identical. From Tables 2A and 3A it is seen that the percentages of their "short-time errors" are also about the same. The RT_s values of subject K and the RT_n values of subject vH approximately coincide with that curve and the number of "short-time errors" are comparable with those of the other two subjects. Two curves, on the other hand, clearly deviate from the others. The RT_n values of subject K are much higher than expected; this is accompanied by a very low error rate (Table 2A). Subject K apparently was much more cautious in the double-stimulus condition than the other subjects. On the other hand, the RT_s values of subject vH are much lower than expected, which is associated with an extremely high error rate (Table 3A). This subject probably was somewhat too eager to obtain short RT values. As no RT-"error" tradeoff curves (Schouten & Bekker, 1967; Pew, 1969) are available, no quantitative error correction can be applied. It seems reasonable to assume that these differences between subjects and conditions can be attributed to the set of the subjects. In the present experimental setup the end level of the $RT_2(ISI)$ curve thus may be called the normal RT, RT_n, for the given stimulus characteristics. Thus, it must be concluded that the reaction time at small ISI is higher than the normal one. Consequently, contrary to what John (1964) assumed, it is unlikely to be a normal reaction time facilitated by the presentation of S_1 at longer ISI.

The RT(L) curves in this study are closely parallel to those of Chocholle (1945). Only the magnitude is different; our reaction times are 60 msec longer. This must probably be attributed to the difference between our stimulus duration (15 msec) and that of Chocholle (equal to the reaction time).

In such paradigms, in which Donders' a reactions are used, there is always the danger that some RT values are in fact reactions to S_1. The RT$_2$(ISI) curve then should exhibit a slope of -1, which is approximately the mean value found in the present experiment. This fact cannot be attributed simply to reactions to S_1, since in previous studies using visual stimuli with a comparable paradigm a slope of $-\frac{1}{2}$ to $-\frac{1}{3}$ has been found. This applies the more, since reactions to S_1 as well as anticipations would lead to many negative values of RT$_2$. In fact, the percentage of RT$_2$ values smaller than 80 msec is less than 2%. If these short RT$_2$ values are to be attributed to reactions to S_1, there should be a relation with L_1. Plotting these reaction times as histograms, the data are normally distributed for subject B (with the largest percentage of RT$_2$ ≤ 80 msec) only. In Table 4 the mean values are given together with the RT$_s$ values of the same subject.

Table 4. *Time Lapse between S_1 and R_2 for All RT$_2$ ≤ 80 msec and for Each L_1 Separately and Reaction Time to a Single Stimulus as a Function of Intensity*[a]

Double-stimulus condition		Single-stimulus condition	
L_1 (dB SL)	For RT$_2$ ≤ 80 msec ISI + RT$_2$ (msec)	L_2 (dB SL)	RT$_s$ (msec)
20	375	10	231
40	340	30	210
60	325	50	189
80	275	70	178

[a]All data taken from subject B.

From Table 4 it becomes clear that both reaction times decrease with increasing intensity, but neither the shape of the RT(L) curve nor the absolute values are identical. It seems justifiable to assume that the RT$_2$ values are based on true reactions to S_2 and that even the values of RT$_2$ ≤ 80 msec can hardly by taken to be normal reactions to S_1.

Another aspect of the results that must be discussed is the high T_0 value in the combination of $L_1 = 80$ dB SL and $L_2 = 20$ dB SL, which is found with all subjects. The most plausible explanation appears to be forward masking. Although a dichotic presentation was used, the effect may play its part with large differences in L_1 and L_2, and with short ISI. This will result in a higher threshold for S_2 and thus a smaller effective intensity and a longer RT_2.

Lüscher and Zwislocki (1949) indeed found such effects in dichotic conditions with $L_1 - L_2 = 60$ dB. From data in the literature (Elliott 1962a, b; Zwislocki, Pirodda, & Rubin, 1959) an estimate was derived for the magnitude of the effect. A 5-dB increase in threshold is estimated for ISI = 25 msec. With $L_2 = 20$ dB SL, this will result in an increase in RT_2 of 5–10 msec.

The threshold intensity of S_2 was determined in a pilot experiment, with $L_1 = 80$ dB SL and with various ISI values. With ISI = 25 msec, an increase in threshold of 10–15 dB was measured, corresponding to an increase in RT_2 of 20–30 msec, with $L_2 = 20$ dB SL. In fact, with $L_1 = 80$ dB SL and $L_2 = 20$ dB SL the increase in RT_2 at ISI = 25 msec is about 70 msec higher than normal. At ISI = 40 msec the effect is about 20 msec. Apparently the effect of forward masking is too slight to explain the total increase in T_0.

IV. Conclusion

The experimental data are in favor of a sensitivity hypothesis, both for the $RT_2(L)$ values and for the $RT_2(ISI)$ values. The cause of the intensity effect on the reaction time is assumed to be both peripherally and centrally located, in accordance with neurophysiological data. Thus far, the conclusions are similar to those based on visual data, where the intensity effect was assumed to be located peripherally. The fact that the decay time is dependent on L and is half that found with visual stimuli makes the acceptability of the hypothesis tentative.

Apparently other effects, such as "set," play a more important part than was stated previously. In another experiment more emphasis will be placed on this point.

References

Abraham, F. D., & Marsh, J. T. Amplitude of evoked potentials as a function of slow presenting rates of repetitive auditory stimulation. *Experimental Neurology* 1966, **14**, 187–198.

Aitken, L. M., & Dunlop, C. W. Interplay of excitation and inhibition in the cat medial geniculate body. *Journal of Neurophysiology*, 1968, **31**, 44–61.

Annett, J. General discussion. In W. G. Koster (Ed.), *Attention and Performance II, Acta Psychologica*, 1969, **30**, 382.

Bertelson, P. Central intermittency twenty years later. *Quarterly Journal of Experimental Psychology*, 1966, **18**, 153–163.

Chocholle, R. Variation des temps de réaction auditifs en fonction de l'intensité à diverses fréquences. *L'Année Psychologique*, 1945, **41/42**, 65–124.

Davis, H., Mast, T., Yoshie, N., & Zerlin, S. The slow response of the human cortex to auditory stimuli: Recovery process. *Electroencephalography and Clinical Neurophysiology*, 1966, **21**, 105–113.

Davis, R. The human operator as a single channel information system. *Quarterly Journal of Experimental Psychology*, 1957, **9**, 119–129.

Davis, R. Expectancy and intermittency. *Quarterly Journal of Experimental Psychology*, 1965, **17**, 75–78.

Elithorn, A., & Lawrence, C. Central inhibition—some refractory observations. *Quarterly Journal of Experimental Psychology*, 1955, **7**, 116–127.

Elliott, L. L. Backward and forward masking of probe tones of different frequencies. *Journal of the Acoustical Society of America*, 1962, **34**, 1116–1117(a).

Elliott, L. L. Backward masking: Monotic and dichotic conditions. *Journal of the Acoustical Society of America*, 1962, **34**, 1108–1115(b).

Erulkar, S. D. Single unit activity in the inferior colliculus of the cat. Cited by C. Whitfield, The physiology of hearing. *Progress in Biophysics* 1957, **8**, 30.

Goldstein, R., & Rodman, L. B. Early components of averaged evoked responses to rapidly repeated auditory stimuli. *Journal of Speech Hearing Research*, 1967, **10**, 697–705.

Gross, N. B., & Thurlow, W. R. Micro electrode studies of neural auditory activity of cat II. Medial geniculate body. *Journal of Neurophysiology*, 1951, **14**, 409–422.

John, I. D. The role of extraneous stimuli in responsiveness to signals: Refractoriness or facilitation? *Australian Journal of Psychology*, 1964, **16**, 87–96.

Koster, W. G., & Bekker, J. A. M. Some experiments on refractoriness. In A. F. Sanders (Ed.), *Attention and Performance, Acta Psychologica*, 1967, **27**, 64–70.

Koster W. G., & Peacock, J. B. The influence of intensity of visual stimuli on the psychological refractory phase. In W. G. Koster (Ed.), *Attention and Performance II, Acta Psychologica*, 1969, **30**, 232–253.

Lüscher, E., & Zwislocki, J. Adaptation of the ear to sound stimuli. *Journal of the Acoustical Society of America*, 1949, **21**, 135–139.

Mast, T. E. Short-latency human evoked responses to clicks. *Journal of Applied Physiology*, 1965, **20**, 725–730.

Nelson, D. A., & Lassman, F. M. Effects of intersignal interval on the human auditory evoked response. *Journal of the Acoustical Society of America*, 1968, **44**, 1529–1532.

Pew, R. W. The speed–accuracy operating characteristic. In W. G. Koster. (Ed.), *Attention and Performance II, Acta Psychologica*, 1969, **30**, 16–26.

Rapin, I., Schimmel, H., Tourk, L. M., Krasnegor, N. A., & Pollak, C. Evoked responses to clicks and tones of varying intensity in waking adults. *Electroencephalography and Clinical Neurophysiology*, 1966, **21**, 335–344.

Rubinstein, L. Intersensory and intrasensory effects in simple reaction time. *Perceptual and Motor Skills*, 1964, **18**, 159–172.

Sanford, A. J. Rating the speed of a simple reaction. *Psychonomic Science*, 1970, **21**, 333–334.

Schouten, J. F., & Bekker, J. A. M. Reaction time and accuracy. In A. F. Sanders (Ed.), *Attention and Performance, Acta Psychologica*, 1967, **27**, 143–153.

Schouten, J. F., & Domburg, J. The "Donders," an electronic system for measuring human reactions. *Philips Technical Review*, 1963–64, **25**, 64–74.

Smith, M. C. Theories of the psychological refractory period. *Psychological Bulletin*, 1967, **67**, 202–213.

Telford, C. W. The refractory phase of voluntary and associative responses. *Journal of Experimental Psychology*, 1931, **14**, 1–36.

Tunturi, A. R. A study on the pathway from the medial geniculate body to the acoustic cortex in the dog. *American Journal of Physiology*, 1946, **147**, 311–319.

van Schuur, R. Simulatie model van Welford. *Instituut voor Perceptie Onderzoek, Internal Report No. 203*, 1971.

van Schuur, R., & Koster, W. G. Psychologische refractaire periode I. *Instituut voor Perceptie Onderzoek, Internal Report No. 208*, 1971.

Welford, A. T. The "psychological refractory period" and the timing of high-speed performance—a review and a theory. *British Journal of Psychology*, 1952, **43**, 2–19.

Welford, A. T. Single-channel operation in the brain. In A. F. Sanders (Ed.), *Attention and Performance, Acta Psychologica*, 1967, **27**, 5–22.

Wilkinson, R. T. Evoked response and reaction time. In A. F. Sanders (Ed.), *Attention and Performance, Acta Psychologica*, 1967, **27**, 235–245.

Zwislocki, J., Pirodda, E., & Rubin, H. On some poststimulatory effects at the threshold of audibility. *Journal of the Acoustical Society of America*, 1959, **31**, 9–14.

Identification of Two Components of the Time to Switch Attention: A Test of a Serial and a Parallel Model of Attention[1]

David LaBerge

Department of Psychology
University of Minnesota
Minneapolis, Minnesota

ABSTRACT

Two tasks, detection and discrimination, were investigated in the auditory and visual modalities by means of a Donders c reaction-time method combined with a procedure which presented a cue on each trial before the stimulus appeared. The function of the cue was to control the attention of the Ss at the moment that an unexpected stimulus appeared in order to measure the amount of time involved in switching attention between the auditory and visual modalities. Comparisons of mean latencies of five Ss under eight different kinds of switching conditions led to the rejection of a serial model of attention which assumed that switching of attention and perceptual processing proceed successively. However, the data were consistent with a parallel model which assumed that perceptual processing takes place automatically, that is, while attention is located elsewhere. On the basis of the assumptions of the parallel model it was possible to isolate a component in the latency data having to do with the time it takes to switch *into* an unattended modality. The second switching component, namely, the time taken to switch *out of* an attended modality was successfully isolated assuming either a serial or a parallel attention model.

[1]This research was supported by United States Public Health Service Research Grant MH-16270-04 and The Center for Research in Human Learning through National Science Foundation Grant GS-54. The author is grateful to Laurel Reinhardt for running the experiment.

71

I. Introduction

A study by LaBerge, Van Gelder, and Yellott (1970) indicated that switching attention between visual and auditory modalities in a choice reaction time task may take more than 100 msec. The method that induced the subjects in that experiment to attend to one particular modality at the time the stimulus was presented involved presenting a cue at the beginning of each trial which indicated the stimulus most likely to occur on that trial. There were four stimuli: a red light and a high tone assigned to the left button, and a green light and a low tone assigned to the right button. On each trial, one of these stimuli served as a cue, and was followed by one of the four stimuli. Analysis of the results of this experiment showed that the cue functioned as a very effective control of what stimulus the subject expected on a trial. In fact, even when the cue predicted the stimulus on only 73% of the trials, the subject evidently treated the cue the same as when it predicted the stimulus on 100% of the trials. Thus, when the high tone was the cue, for example, and the red light followed it as a stimulus, one had considerable assurance that the subject was prepared for a high tone on that trial and then had to switch his attention to the red light before responding.

The purpose of the present study was to investigate two out of four likely components of attention switching time between the visual and auditory dimensions. The four components are

   S: time to signal the switching mechanism;
   O: time to leave the cued (origin) modality;
   D: time to enter the presented (destination) modality;
   T: time to "travel" between the origin and destination modalities.

Taken together with the time required to perceive the stimulus (P) and a residual component (R), the total reaction time L may be expressed as

$$L = (S + O + T + D) + P + R. \tag{1}$$

Equation (1) assumes that these components of latency combine additively, and this assumption will be tested in the course of the present experiment. When the stimulus presented on a trial is the same as the cue, then there is no switching involved, and

$$L = P + R. \tag{2}$$

We shall attempt to show that switching time contains at least two independent components, O and D, by varying the difficulty (or "depth") of processing of the origin and destination stimuli in a Donders c-reaction task. The situation is somewhat analogous to interrupting a person who is engrossed in reading a novel by asking him a question. We might expect that the delay in his response to the question would be longer, the more "deeply" he is attending to the novel at that particular moment. Also, we might expect that the delay in his response to the question would be longer, the more difficult the question. However, one expects longer latencies to more difficult questions even when there is no switching of attention involved. Therefore, one must consider this component when estimating the time involved in switching into a new dimension.

II. Method

The present method of manipulating levels of processing the origin and destination stimuli was to vary the type of catch trials (LaBerge, 1971a, b). The auditory cue was always a 1000-Hz tone, and the visual cue was always an orange light. The stimulus to which the subject responded by pressing a single button was also a 1000-Hz tone or an orange light. The catch stimuli for the 1000-Hz tone determined how difficult the processing of the 1000-Hz tone was. When the catch stimuli were 990-Hz tones, the task was moderately difficult. When the catch stimuli were no tones at all, the task was easy. The situation was similar for the orange light; when the catch trials were a yellow light, the task was more difficult than when the catch trials were no lights.

The tones were delivered to the subject binaurally through earphones at approximately 80 dB SPL. The orange and yellow lights each appeared as a square luminous patch of color (3×3 cm, 5-ft L) delivered by an IEE Series 10 readout approximately 40 cm from the eye of the S. There was one response button which had a vertical travel of 3 mm and required a pressure of 80 gm to register a response.

The five Ss were undergraduates at the University of Minnesota. Three of them were highly experienced in RT tasks; the other two had only a few hours of practice before they served in the present experiment. All subjects were paid by the hour.

The tasks presented to each subject can be classified into two types, switch and nonswitch. Each will be described separately.

A. Nonswitch Tasks

On each trial of these tasks a cue was presented 2 sec before the stimulus appeared. For the auditory tasks, the cue was always a 1000-Hz tone, and for the visual tasks the cue was always an orange light. The purpose of the cue was to induce the subject to focus his attention on that particular stimulus at

Table 1. *Cue–Stimulus Contingencies for Nonswitch Blocks[a]*

Cue	Stimulus	Response	Frequency	
1000 Hz	1000 Hz	Yes	20	Auditory
	Nothing	No	6	detection
1000 Hz	1000 Hz	Yes	20	Auditory
	990 Hz	No	6	discrimination
Orange	Orange	Yes	20	Visual
	Nothing	No	6	detection
Orange	Orange	Yes	20	Visual
	Yellow	No	6	discrimination

[a]Block size 26 trials.

the moment the stimulus appeared. The cue–stimulus contingencies are shown in Table 1. The type of catch trial used during a block determined whether the task was called detection or discrimination. Only one type of catch trial was used within a block of trials. Thus, there were four types of nonswitch blocks: detection and discrimination in each of two modalities.

B. SWITCH TASKS

Within a block of trials in which switching of attention was required, either an auditory or a visual stimulus could occur. Throughout a given block of trials one task was used as primary or attended task, and the other task served as the secondary or unattended task. The cue, which was the same

Table 2. *Cue–Stimulus Contingencies for Switch Blocks[a]*

Cue	Stimulus	Response	Frequency	
1000 Hz	1000 Hz	Yes	20	Primary task
	Catch[b]	No	4	(origin)
	Orange	Yes	3	Secondary task
	Catch[c]	No	1	(destination)
Orange	Orange	Yes	20	Primary task
	Catch[c]	No	4	(origin)
	1000 Hz	Yes	3	Secondary task
	Catch[b]	No	1	(destination)

[a]Block size 28 trials.
[b]990-Hz tone used for discrimination; nothing for detection.
[c]Yellow color used for discrimination; nothing for detection.

during a block, determined which task was the attended one. Table 2 shows the cue–stimulus contingencies for the switch tasks. The type of catch trial used for the attended or unattended task determined whether it was a detection or a discrimination, just as in the case of the nonswitch conditions. Therefore, it was possible to attend to an auditory discrimination and shift to a visual detection, and the like. With two modalities, two types of tasks, and two states of attention, there was a total of eight different types of switching blocks.

Each of the five subjects was tested under the eight switch conditions and the four nonswitch conditions. For a given session of eight blocks, each subject was tested for six blocks under a switch condition, and for two blocks under a related nonswitch condition. For example, within a session of eight blocks, six blocks contained a visual detection as the primary task and an auditory discrimination as the secondary task, and two blocks contained just a visual detection task. In this way visual detection performance could be compared under both switch and nonswitch conditions as an indication of how well the cue was controlling attention during switch trials. The eight blocks of a session were ordered such that nonswitch blocks occurred at positions 1 and 5, and the switch blocks occurred at positions 2, 3, 4, 6, 7, and and 8. The order in which the eight types of switch sessions was presented to a subject was varied systematically across subjects. Two eight-block sessions were given per day, with at least 1 hr of rest between sessions.

The durations of events within a trial were as follows: the cue was presented for 1000 msec, followed by 1000 msec of blank, followed by the stimulus, which terminated when the response was made unless the stimulus was a catch, in which case, it remained on for 700 msec. If the subject responded faster than his mean latency of the previous block, he has shown the digit "1" for 50 msec. If he responded to a catch trial, no feedback was given. The duration of the intertrial interval was 950 msec, and during this interval the letter "A" appeared as a trial marker. The presentation of stimuli and recording of response frequencies and latencies were controlled by a CDC 160 computer.

III. Serial and Parallel Models of Attention Switching

In order to determine whether origin and destination factors contribute to switching time, it is necessary to write out a set of equations for the mean latencies obtained under the various switching conditions. It turns out that the set of equations will differ depending upon the type of attention model that is assumed. The problem then will be to test both the models and the origin and destination factors simultaneously.

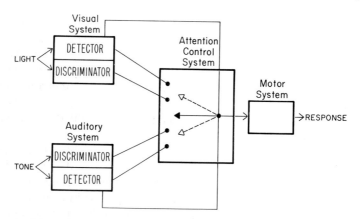

Fig. 1. Schematic representation of the relationships among the perceptual system, an attention control system, and the motor system.

To aid the descriptions of the serial and parallel models, it will be helpful to refer to Fig. 1. This diagram is similar to a scheme presented by Kristofferson (1965) and discussed by Moray (1969). Perceptual processing is assumed to be carried out by the detectors and discriminators, and the switching operations by the attention control system. It is assumed in both models that the switching mechanism is controlled by outputs from the detector analyzers. What this means is that a subject who is attending to a visual modality can be alerted to an auditory stimulus only if perception of the auditory event has direct access to the switching mechanism. Otherwise the subject would not have a way to initiate switching and to guide attention to the appropriate stimulus.

Switching of attention is represented by the movement of the pointer which reads out the contents of a perceptual analyzer into the motor system.

A. SERIAL MODEL OF ATTENTION SWITCHING

This model assumes that switching and perceiving are carried out at separate times. Perceptual processing may either precede or follow switching in this model, so that the selection process may take place prior to perceptual analyzers (Broadbent, 1957), or after the perceptual analyzers (Deutsch & Deutsch, 1963).

When an unexpected stimulus occurs, it is assumed that some initial perceptual processing of that stimulus is necessary to make contact with the switching mechanism. For both serial and parallel models it will be assumed that the detector analyzer does the perceptual processing necessary for this operation, regardless of the state of attention. Actually this assumption is not critical for purposes of this study, because the component always drops out when response latencies are subtracted from each other. However, for completeness, this component will always be included in the switching equations, and denoted as S.

B. Derivation of the Origin Indicator

To determine if "depth" of processing of the attended or primary stimulus affects switching time, one must compare latencies to a given un-attended stimulus when the origin task is a discrimination and when it is a detection. For *discrimination* of an *unattended* stimulus, the pair of equations are

$$L(\text{disc/disc}) = S + O(\text{disc}) + T + D(\text{disc}) + P(\text{disc}) + R, \qquad (3)$$

$$L(\text{disc/det}) = S + O(\text{det}) + T + D(\text{disc}) + P(\text{disc}) + R, \qquad (4)$$

where $L(\text{disc/det})$ represents the mean latency to an unexpected discrimination given that attention was focused on a detection; $O(\text{det})$ represents the time required to leave the attended detection, $D(\text{disc})$ is the time to enter the unexpected discrimination, and $P(\text{disc})$ is the time to perceive or analyze the unexpected discrimination. Subtracting Eq. (4) from Eq. (3) gives

$$L(\text{disc/disc}) - L(\text{disc/det}) = O(\text{disc}) - O(\text{det}), \qquad (5)$$

which is the indicator of the existence of the origin factor. In other words, if Eq. (5) gives a value greater than zero, then one can conclude that level of processing affects the time to switch out of an attended task, and therefore that the origin factor contributes to switching time. An additional test of the origin factor can be obtained by subtracting the pairs of equations which include *detection* as the *unattended* task, namely,

$$L(\text{det/disc}) - L(\text{det/det}) = O(\text{disc}) - O(\text{det}). \qquad (6)$$

These equations are easily written in the same form as Eqs. (3) and (4).

C. Derivation of the Destination Indicator

The procedure for determining whether the "depth" of processing of the unattended task affects switching time into the destination task involves comparing latencies to an unattended discrimination task and a detection task, given that the attended task was at a constant level. For a *discrimination* of an *attended* stimulus the pair of equations are

$$L(\text{disc/disc}) = S + O(\text{disc}) + T + D(\text{disc}) + P(\text{disc}) + R, \qquad (7)$$

$$L(\text{det/disc}) = S + O(\text{disc}) + T + D(\text{det}) + P(\text{det}) + R. \qquad (8)$$

Subtracting Eq. (8) from Eq. (7) gives

$$L(\text{disc/disc}) - L(\text{det/disc}) = D(\text{disc}) - D(\text{det}) + P(\text{disc}) - P(\text{det}). \quad (9)$$

Since $P(\text{disc}) - P(\text{det})$ is readily available from trials in which the expected stimulus occurs, this difference component can be subtracted from the obtained latency difference represented by Eq. (9), leaving the desired estimate of the destination effect, namely, $D(\text{disc}) - D(\text{det})$. An additional test of the destination factor can be obtained by comparing the pairs of switching latencies in which the *attended* stimulus is always a *detection*, namely,

$$L(\text{disc/det}) - L(\text{det/det}) = D(\text{disc}) - D(\text{det}) + P(\text{disc}) - P(\text{det}). \quad (10)$$

If it is assumed that the factor S, the time to initiate switching, is based on detection of the unexpected stimulus, then $S = P(det)$, and therefore $P(\text{det})$ occurs twice in Eq. (8). On the other hand, one might want to assume that the detection of the unattended stimulus need be carried out only once, namely, at the onset of the stimulus event, and that the contents of this perceptual process are stored and made available for readout to the motor system when switching is completed. In this case the difference between Eqs. (8) and (7) will be

$$L(\text{disc/det}) - L(\text{det/det}) = D(\text{disc}) - D(\text{det}) + P(\text{disc}). \qquad (11)$$

Unfortunately there will not be a direct estimate of $P(\text{disc})$ so that the destination factor cannot be isolated except in the event that $D(\text{disc}) - D(\text{det})$ is large relative to $P(\text{disc}) + R$. Therefore, if the serial model is confirmed, there is a possibility that the destination factor cannot be evaluated with the present data.

D.   PARALLEL MODEL OF ATTENTION SWITCHING

The parallel model assumes that perceptual processing can occur at the same time that the switching operation is going on. As in the case of the serial model, it is assumed that when an unexpected stimulus is presented, the first thing that happens is that the perceptual detector analyzes that stimulus and initiates a movement of the switching mechanism. This time component is represented as before, namely, S.

E. DERIVATION OF THE ORIGIN INDICATOR

To determine if the origin factor influences switching time, one compares the same switching latencies as in the case of the serial model, but with a slight change in the components assumed to make up these latencies. The pair of equations are

$$L(\text{disc/disc}) = S + O(\text{disc}) + T + D(\text{disc}) + R, \qquad (12)$$

$$L(\text{disc/det}) = S + O(\text{det}) + T + D(\text{disc}) + R. \qquad (13)$$

Subtracting Eq. (13) from Eq. (12) gives

$$L(\text{disc/disc}) - L(\text{disc/det}) = O(\text{disc}) - O(\text{det}), \qquad (14)$$

which is the indicator of the presence of an origin factor.

It should be noted that $P(\text{disc})$ has not appeared in Eqs. (12) and (13), even though had it been included it would have dropped out when we subtracted the equations to arrive at Eq. (14). The rationale behind this omission is based on the selection of difficulty level of the discrimination tasks used in the present study. There is evidence from a previous experiment (LaBerge *et al.*, 1970) that perceptual processing of a moderately difficult discrimination analyzer time, $P(\text{disc})$, will contribute nothing to the response latency on particular formulation of a parallel model of attention will be based on the assumption that perceptual processing of the discriminations begun at time zero will be completed *before* switching is completed, so that the discrimination analyzer time, $P(\text{disc})$, will contribute nothing to the response latency on switch trials. Since detection latencies are expected to be less than discrimination latencies, the same assumption is made for the contribution of $P(\text{det})$ to response latency on switching trials. Data from the present experiment should provide support for this assumption.

An additional indicator of the presence of the origin factor under the assumption of a parallel model can be obtained from comparing the two switching latencies based on *detection* of the *unattended* stimulus, namely,

$$L(\text{det/disc}) - L(\text{det/det}) = O(\text{disc}) - O(\text{det}). \qquad (15)$$

F. DERIVATION OF DESTINATION INDICATOR

Assuming that discrimination is completed prior to the completion of switching, the following equations represent the effect of a destination factor on switching time:

$$L(\text{disc/disc}) = S + O(\text{disc}) + T + D(\text{disc}) + R, \qquad (16)$$

$$L(\text{det/disc}) = S + O(\text{disc}) + T + D(\text{det}) + R. \qquad (17)$$

Subtracting Eq. (17) from Eq. (16) gives

$$L(\text{disc/disc}) - L(\text{det/disc}) = D(\text{disc}) - D(\text{det}) \qquad (18)$$

as the indicator of the existence of a destination factor in switching time. An additional indicator of the destination factor is the difference

$$L(\text{disc/det}) - L(\text{det/det}) = D(\text{disc}) - D(\text{det}). \qquad (19)$$

When comparing the derivations from the serial and parallel models, it may be noted that the indicator of the origin factor, namely, $O(\text{disc}) - O(\text{det})$, is estimated by the same pairs of switching latencies for both models. Therefore, it will not be necessary to know which model is correct before the origin factor can be evaluated. For the destination factor, on the other hand, the models differ in the computation of $D(\text{disc}) - D(\text{det})$ from the switching data, and so it will be necessary to evaluate the models before the destination factor can be evaluated.

IV. Results and Discussion

In Table 3 are shown the mean latencies of 5 subjects to the 1000-Hz tone and the orange color, along with the overall means. These means are based on data from all blocks, since a trend across the eight blocks of a session was not discernible by visual inspection. The means of the expected stimuli for each modality under nonswitch conditions are each based on 80 observations per subject, or a total of 400 observations. The means of the expected stimuli under the switch conditions are each based on 240 observations per subject, or a total of 1200 observations. The means of the unexpected stimuli under the switch conditions were each based on 18 observations per subject, or a total of 90 observations. The overall means are based on twice these values, or 800, 2400, and 180, respectively.

The error proportions are shown in Table 4 and the mean latency of errors are shown in Table 5. An error is defined as a response to a catch trial. Although the error proportions for the discrimination tasks are large, the mean latencies of these errors do not appear to deviate enough from the mean latencies of correct responses to warrant adjustments in these latencies for purposes of the main analyses of this study. The proportions of errors for detections are small, and the mean latency of errors for these tasks approximates the mean latency of corrects.

One of the first matters of consideration is how well the present experimental precedure controls the attention of the subjects. The relevant comparisons are between the latencies of the expected stimuli on switch blocks as compared with latencies on nonswitch blocks. These comparisons show a

Table 3. *Mean Latencies to the 1000-Hz Tone (T) and the Orange Color (O) (in milliseconds)*

Stimulus presented	Nonswitch blocks		Switch blocks					
	Expected stimulus		Expected stimulus		Unexpected stimulus/expected stimulus			
	det	disc	det	disc	det/det	det/disc	disc/det	disc/disc
1000 Hz	199	285	210	293	329	406	368	583 (467)[a]
Orange	199	278	199	281	338	417	385	442
Overall mean	199	281	204	287	333	411	376	512 (454)[a]

[a]Adjusted value based on 4 out of 5 Ss. One S gave an extremely long mean latency under this condition.

Table 4. *Proportions of Errors in Responses to Catch Trials*

Task	Nonswitch blocks Expected stimulus	Switch blocks Expected stimulus	Unexpected stimulus disc/det	disc/disc
Detection	.03	.05	—	—
Discrimination	.31	.27	.30	.15

Table 5. *Mean Latency of Errors (in milliseconds)*

Task	Nonswitch blocks	Switch blocks Expected Stimulus	Unexpected Simulus disc/det	disc/disc
Detection	218	173	—	—
Discrimination	266	265	346	428

trend toward slightly longer latencies under switch conditions, a finding which holds up when one looks at the data of individual subjects. However, the amount of difference is quite small, and therefore indicates that the subjects show the same degree of attention to the cued stimulus under both conditions. It would appear, then, that it is reasonable to assume during subsequent analyses that presentation of an unexpected stimulus always involves a switching operation out of the cued task.

Another preliminary result required before beginning the main analyses is that detection tasks and discrimination tasks show consistently different mean latencies on trials when the expected stimulus is presented. The relevant data in Table 3 indicate that $P(\text{disc}) - P(\text{det})$ equals $287 - 204$ or 83 msec for the color and tone conditions combined. That this is a very stable estimate can be seen from examining the color and tone conditions separately. This obtained difference in processing the detection and discrimination tasks should be adequate for detecting the origin and destination components of switching if they exist in any reasonable degree.

One way to test the serial and parallel models against the data obtained in this experiment is to consider the difference between the shortest switching latency $L(\text{det/det})$ and the longest switching latency $L(\text{disc/disc})$, and see if the components which make up this difference combine additively as the serial model would predict. Using the assumptions of the serial model described in Section III, the appropriate equations are

$$L(\text{disc/disc}) = S + O(\text{disc}) + T + D(\text{disc}) + P(\text{disc}) + R = 454 \text{ msec,}$$
(20)

$$L(\text{det/det}) = S + O(\text{det}) + T + D(\text{det}) + P(\text{det}) + R = 333 \text{ msec.}$$
(21)

Subtracting Eq. (21) from Eq. (20) gives

$$
\begin{aligned}
L(\text{disc/disc}) &- L(\text{det/det}) \\
&= O(\text{disc}) - O(\text{det}) + D(\text{disc}) - D(\text{det}) + P(\text{disc}) - P(\text{det}) \\
&= 121 \text{ msec.}
\end{aligned}
$$
(22)

The difference component $O(\text{disc}) - O(\text{det})$ can be estimated free of competing assumptions of the present models, since their predictions are the same with respect to this factor. Entering Table 3 with Eqs. (5) and (6) or (14) and (15) yields an estimate of $O(\text{disc}) - O(\text{det})$ of 78 msec, when the adjusted estimate of $L(\text{disc/disc}) = 454$ is used. The component $P(\text{disc}) - P(\text{det})$ is already known to be approximately 83 msec, so that the sum of two of the difference components of Eq. (22) is $78 + 83$, or 161 msec. This sum exceeds the obtained difference of 121 msec even before the third difference component $D(\text{disc}) - D(\text{det})$ is added.

The same analysis can be carried out with the unadjusted latency of 512 msec for $L(\text{disc/disc})$, and the same conclusion is reached. The sum of two of the component differences, namely $102 + 83$ msec, gives a value of 185 msec, which exceeds the obtained unadjusted sum of 179 msec, before the third component is added. Therefore, the serial model as described in this study fails.

Turning to the parallel model in which it is assumed that perceptual processing is completed by the time switching is completed, the appropriate way to rewrite Eqs. (20) and (21) is

$$L(\text{disc/disc}) = S + O(\text{disc}) + T + D(\text{disc}) + R = 454,$$
(23)

$$L(\text{det/det}) = S + O(\text{det}) + T + D(\text{det}) + R = 333.$$
(24)

Subtracting Eq. (24) from Eq. (23) gives

$$
\begin{aligned}
L(\text{disc/disc}) &- L(\text{det/det}) \\
&= O(\text{disc}) - O(\text{det}) + D(\text{disc}) + D(\text{det}) \\
&= 121.
\end{aligned}
$$
(25)

Using the parallel model's estimation equation for $D(\text{disc}) - D(\text{det})$, namely, Eqs. (18) and (19), the obtained difference is 43 msec in each case. Adding this value to the known estimate of $O(\text{disc}) - O(\text{det})$ gives $43 + 78$, or 121 msec, and the parallel model is supported. Actually, these last computations are more like a check on arithmetic than a source of independent evidence for the parallel model. The critical evidence for the parallel model emerged when the serial model failed to confirm Eq. (22).

Under the assumption of a parallel model, then, the destination factor appears to be real in the switching of attention in these tasks, since $D(\text{disc}) - D(\text{det}) > 0$, and, of course, we have independently determined that $O(\text{disc}) - O(\text{det}) > 0$, so that the origin factor appears to be real as well.

There is no way presently known to evaluate the switching factor T and the residual factor R from these data, since no experimental manipulation produced a known variation in these components. However, to bolster confidence in the indicators of origin and destination factors, an analysis of variance of the difference scores which made up the $O(\text{disc}) - O(\text{det})$ and $D(\text{disc}) - D(\text{det})$ components was carried out on the means of the five Ss. For the origin component, the overall mean difference (using unadjusted data) was significant by t test ($t = 3.65, p < .01$), using the residual mean square term of the analysis of variance to estimate the standard error term of the t test. There were no significant Fs associated with the Ss variable, nor with the four ways that the origin difference could be estimated, namely, by Eqs. (14) and (15) for both the color and the tone conditions.

For the destination component, the overall mean difference was significant ($t = 2.32, p < .05$) using the same computational procedures as in the case of the origin component. There were no significant Fs for the Ss variable, nor for the four ways that $D(\text{disc}) - D(\text{det})$ could be estimated, namely, by Eqs. (18) and (19) for both color and tone conditions.

The serial and parallel models considered here involve "stages" in the same sense as Sternberg (1969) treats them. Following his analysis, the additive and interactive effects among factors determining latencies can be summarized as follows: The factors are: (a) task (switch versus non-switch), (b) origin of switch (detection versus discrimination), and (c) destination of switch (detection versus discrimination). Factors (b) and (c) are additive in switching tasks, supporting the existence of two stages of switching. However, factors (a) and (c) interact, which provides evidence against a serial model. Since the form of the obtained interaction is negative, a parallel model is supported.

An incidental but interesting implication of these findings concerns the two functions of the perceptual detector, namely, the initiation of switching and the activation of the motor system when the task requires the subject to respond to a detection. As was assumed in both the serial and parallel models, the detector always begins to process with the onset of the stimulus and then sends its results to the switching mechanism to start its orientation to that modality. However, these data indicate that it must wait until switching is complete before it can send its contents to activate the motor system because a detection response to an unexpected stimulus was slower than to an expected stimulus. Either the contents are stored during switching and a duplicate output is produced, or another sample of stimulus input is processed when switching is complete, or, since the stimulus always remained on until the response was made, the detector is continuously reprocessing its input during switching.

Aside from the finding that level of processing apparently affects the time to switch *out of* an attention state and also the time to switch *into* an attention state, it is interesting to consider the implications of the finding that these data, taken as a whole, fit a model which assumes that processing of a discrimination and a detection proceed *while* attention is being shifted. Apparently all the perceptual analyzers begin their processing at or very near the moment the stimulus makes contact with the receptors in this particular group of tasks. It seems that perceptual processing does not need the help of a control process such as the attention system of the sort described in Fig. 1. It may well be that this is the case only for highly practiced perceptions, and that for unfamiliar patterns such as a new five-letter word, the discrimination could not go to completion until the attention system was brought to bear on the processing in some way. One would expect that perception of a pattern which required the processing of many different features might process each feature automatically, that is, without contribution of the attention system, but the combining of these features would be likely to depend upon a higher control process. Clarifying these conjectures is a likely direction of future research.

References

Broadbent, D. E. A mechanical model for human attention and immediate memory. *Psychological Review*, 1957, **64**, 205–215.

Deutsch, J. A., & Deutsch, D. Attention: Some theoretical considerations. *Psychological Review*, 1963, **70**, 80–90.

Kristofferson, A. B. Attention in time discrimination and reaction time. *NASA Report CR-194*, April, 1965.

LaBerge, D., Van Gelder, P., & Yellott, J. I., Jr. A cueing technique in choice reaction time. *Journal of Experimental Psychology*, 1971, **87**(2), 225–228. (a)

LaBerge, D. On the processing of simple visual and auditory stimuli at distant levels. *Perception and Psychophysics*, 1971, **9**(4), 331–334. (b)

LaBerge, D., Van Gelder, P., & Yellott, J. I., Jr. A cueing technique in choice reaction time. *Perception and Psychophysics*, 1970, **7**(1), 57–62.

Moray, N. *Attention: Selective processes in vision and hearing.* London: Hutchinson, 1969.

Sternberg, S. The discovery of processing stages: Extensions of Donder's method. In W. G. Koster (Ed.), *Attention and Performance II, Acta Psychologia*, 1969, **30**, 276–315.

Selective Processes in Sensory Memory:
A Probe-Comparison Procedure[1]

R. A. Kinchla

Department of Psychology
Princeton University
Princeton, New Jersey

ABSTRACT

An experiment is presented that seems to indicate our ability to remember selectively specific frequency components of a sound. In doing this, we maintain information about that component at the cost of forgetting other aspects of the sound more rapidly. A *"probe-comparison"* paradigm employed in the experiment appears to have some important advantages over other perceptual tasks employed to study "sensory memory" processes.

I. Introduction

This contribution deals with how we remember a stimulus in order to compare it with one that is perceived a few moments later. In particular, it considers the extent of our volitional control of the memory processes involved in such delayed comparisons. An experiment will be presented which seems to demonstrate our ability to remember specific frequency components of a sound selectively.

---

[1]This work was supported by National Science Foundation Grant No. GB–28435.

A number of authors (for example, Aaronson, 1967; Atkinson & Shiffrin, 1970; Kinchla & Smyzer, 1967; Massaro, 1971; Norman & Rumelhart, 1970; Sperling, 1960) have attempted to distinguish between "sensory" or "preperceptual" memory systems and higher-order or verbally mediated memory. The general idea is that a rather direct ("raw," "un-identified," "uncoded") representation of a stimulus can be held briefly in some sort of short-term memory system ("sensory register") while aspects of it are "coded" ("named," "extracted," "identified") to be used in further stages of information processing. The most familiar example of this sort is the model of visual perception proposed by Sperling (1960) in which stimulus information is extracted from a "rapidly decaying primary visual memory" through a "coding" or "naming" process; only that stimulus information successfully coded and entered into "higher" (usually verbal) memory systems can be utilized once the primary visual memory has totally "decayed." Note that the distinction between primary visual memory and subsequent forms of information retention involves the level of coding, or processing of information, as well as the duration of retention. Thus, the extent to which one would utilize the initial "sensory" memory rather than some higher level memory would depend not only on the duration of retention required, but the nature of the information to be retained as well. For example, much of the research on primary visual memory has involved stimulus displays consisting of familiar alphanumeric symbols (Estes & Taylor, 1964; Rumelhart, 1970; Sperling, 1960), and the subjects were generally required to make judgments that depended only on the "name" of each symbol. Thus, "verbal coding" of the information held in the primary visual image was both a necessary and sufficient component of the perceptual task. In contrast, suppose that a subject in such an experi-ment had been asked to compare the color of ink used to print the letters with a similar comparison color presented shortly after the letter array. It would now be of little use for him to remember the "names" of the letters, and his vocabulary of color names might provide him with less "resolution" in retaining color information than would the primary visual memory itself (at least over reasonably brief interstimulus delays). A similar argument can be made regarding one's short-term memory for spoken words. If your task were to decide whether a spoken word was in a subsequently presented list of printed words, there would be little need to "remember" the actual sound of the speaker's voice. However, if your task were to compare the pronounciation of the same word by two consecutive speakers, you might utilize an appreciably different type of memory. The point to be made here is that the period of time over which stimulus information may be *usefully* retained in some sort of primary "sensory" memory depends on both the nature of that memory process and the possibility of adequate verbal coding of the relevant stimulus features. Experiments in which the critical stimulus features can be easily coded into some verbal system may provide little insight into "sensory memory" processes.

An experimental paradigm that seems to provide a rather direct approach to "sensory memory" processes is a *delayed-comparison discrimination task*. On each of a series of trials a subject is presented with a *standard stimulus*, followed after some delay by a *comparison stimulus*. For example, the stimuli could be two brief presentations of a pure tone, and the listener could be required to decide whether the second (comparison) tone was the "same loudness" or "softer" than the first (standard) tone. It can be shown easily that his ability to accurately discriminate a small difference in loudness diminishes as the delay between the two tones is increased. Differences easily discernible when the tones occur in immediate succession may be quite difficult to discern if the tones are separated by even 1 or 2 sec. Such delayed comparison tasks have been utilized by a number of investigators, and particularly relevant work is reported in papers by Durlach and Braida (1969), Massaro (1970, 1971), and Wickelgren (1966, 1970).

In a paper entitled "A Diffusion Model of Perceptual Memory" (Kinchla & Smyzer, 1967), this author presented one approach to the analysis of perceptual memory. The basic strategy was to interpret the effect of an interstimulus delay as adding "noise" to the perceptual process in much the same fashion as external masking noise. Thus, an observer's ability to discriminate two stimuli was seen as limited by two types of noise: (*a*) *input noise*, of the sort encountered in most detection studies, either external (for example, white masking noise) or "internal" in origin; and (*b*) *memory noise*, reflecting the observer's inability to maintain a perfect representation of one stimulus until a second one was available for comparison. The basic procedure for obtaining separate measures of these two noise components can be illustrated as follows. A conventional d' discriminability measure may be calculated from a subject's performance on a particular delayed comparison task that is relatively independent of his judgmental standards (Green & Swets, 1966). Since this measure is theoretically interpreted as a kind of signal-to-noise ratio, it can be rescaled to provide a measure of the total "*perceptual noise*." Specifically, in the simplest case, d' is usually defined as follows:

$$d' = d/\sigma_N, \tag{1}$$

where d is a measure of signal strength (stimulus difference) and σ_N may be interpreted as the standard deviation of the "total perceptual noise," that is, the standard deviation of the familiar overlapping distributions of sensory states (or "likelihood ratios") in the simple "equal-variance" model of signal detection (Green & Swets, 1966). Thus, the noise variance σ_N^2 can be written as

$$\sigma_N^2 = (d/d')^2. \tag{2}$$

A measure of σ_N^2 in units of the signal strength ($d = 1$) then is given by transforming $\hat{d}'$, with the value of d' based on the subject's performance:

$$\hat{\sigma}_N^2 = (1/d')^2. \tag{3}$$

The most elementary form of the diffusion model developed by this author represents the subject's memory as a type of "random walk" or Wiener process. This leads to a simple "additive" type of memory noise and the following expression for σ_N^2:

$$\sigma_N^2 = \pi + \varphi t, \tag{4}$$

where π is the "input" component of the noise variance and φ is the rate at which the memory noise increases during the interstimulus interval t.

Having a subject make delayed comparisons at several t values (interstimulus delays) yields estimates of σ_N^2 at each value. The illustrative data shown in Fig. 1 were originally presented in the Kinchla and Smyzer paper (1967). They indicate the relation between σ_N^2 and t for three subjects in an auditory amplitude (loudness) discrimination experiment using interstimulus delays of 0, .5, 1.0, 1.5, and 2 sec. Note that the slope and intercept of the best fitting theoretical function for σ_N^2, Eq. (4), correspond to estimates of φ and π, respectively, where π is interpreted as the perceptual noise with no interstimulus delay ($t = 0$) and φ is the rate at which memory

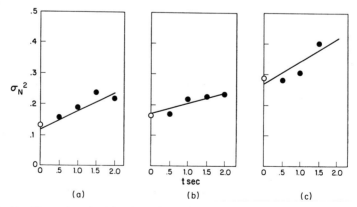

Fig. 1. Illustrative data from Kinchla and Smyzer (1967) showing delay effects in loudness comparisons: (a) Observer 1; (b) Observer 2; (c) Observer 3.

noise is accrued during the t-sec interstimulus interval. The variability of these data points about the theoretical functions does not exceed normal sampling variance, and other studies have supported the general form of these results (for example, Durlach & Braida, 1969; Tanner, 1961). In any case, the large linear components in the plots of σ_N^2 are apparent and indicate how one can separately characterize "input" and "memory" components of the total perceptual noise with measures like π and φ. It should be emphasized that the classic *"time-order error"* in amplitude comparisons is *not* represented by the measure φ, but is interpreted separately as a systematic shift in judgmental criteria (or a systematic "drift" component in the random walk process) during the interstimulus interval. This distinction is developed in both the Kinchla and Smyzer (1967) and the Kinchla and Allan (1969) papers.

A fundamental question regarding sensory memory systems is whether they are under any form of volitional or cognitive control, rather than being simply passive, fixed-parameter processes. It is clear that one has considerable volitional control over verbal memory processes, as indicated by the range of mnemonic tricks one can employ to remember verbal material. Atkinson and Shiffrin (1970) liken the variety of processing options, or "control processes," one may employ within the structural constraints of our nervous system to the variety of programs that can be run on a particular computer, given its structural constraints such as memory capacity, word size, speed, and so forth. It is clear that such "control processes" influence very early stages of perception. For example, consider the selective coding of information from primary visual memory demonstrated in the "partial report" procedure developed by Sperling (1960): an observer can selectively "scan" (process) particular elements in a brief visual array on the basis of a poststimulus auditory cue. It is not clear whether similar selective processes operate prior to any apparent coding of sensory information, such as in the simplest forms of "sensory memory." The following experiment was designed to bear on this issue.

II. An Experiment

The experiment presented here utilized what will be termed a *probe-comparison procedure* to examine a listener's ability to remember specific frequency components of an auditory stimulus. This procedure consisted of a series of test trials. On each trial the listener heard a *compound stimulus* followed by a brief silent interval and then a *probe stimulus*. The compound stimulus consisted of the simultaneous presentation of clearly audible 1000-Hz and 500-Hz tones for 100 msec. The probe stimulus was a 100-msec burst of a pure tone at one of the frequencies in the compound. The listener's task was to decide whether the probe stimulus was "equally loud" or "softer" than the corresponding frequency component in the preceding compound stimulus. Two probe amplitudes at each frequency were employed equally often and in a randomly determined sequence within each series of trials; one amplitude at each frequency was equal to that of the corresponding component of the compound, while the other was slightly lower. Thus, the listener's tendency to respond "softer" to each amplitude of a particular probe frequency can be used to calculate a d' discriminability measure, which should be relatively independent of any "response bias" effects; specifically, if $\hat{p}_0$ and $\hat{p}_1$ correspond to the proportions of "softer" responses given, respectively, the equal amplitude and lower amplitude probe at a particular frequency, then

$$\hat{d} = z(\hat{p}_0) - z(\hat{p}_1), \tag{5}$$

where $z(\hat{p}_i)$ is that value of a normal deviate exceeded with probability $\hat{p}_i$ ($i = 1$ or 0) [those readers who are unfamiliar with this type of discriminability measure are referred to Green and Swets (1966), or Kinchla and Smyzer (1967)]. The value $\hat{d}'$ then can be transformed by Eq. (4) into a measure of "perceptual noise" $\hat{\sigma}_N^2$.

The lower amplitude probe was always 2 dB lower than its component in the compound, although the absolute samplitude of that component varied slightly from trial to trial. This "roving standard" technique was employed in an attempt to increase the listener's dependence on his immediate (within-trial) memory for the particular compound used on each trial (see Durlach & Braida, 1969).

The experiment was designed to assess the effect of *three factors* on $\hat{\sigma}_N^2$. The first factor was the *interstimulus delay* (t), which was either .5, 1.0, 1.5, or 2 sec on each trial. The second factor was an *"attentional"* (*cue*) *manipulation* produced by visually cueing the listener to "attend primarily" to a particular frequency (500 or 1000 Hz) on each trial. The third factor was the *cue position* within a trial, either one second prior to the presentation of the auditory compound, or 750 msec afterwards. The object of these manipulations was simply to see whether the listener seemed to forget the "nonattended" (noncued) component more rapidly than the "attended" (cued) component, as indicated by the accuracy of his judgments at various interstimulus delays. Furthermore, would such selective effects depend critically on the availability of the attentional cue before the subject listened to the compound, or could selective processes operate exclusively on a "memory" of the compound as would be required with postcompound cueing?

A. PROCEDURE

Three paid subjects were tested during two, 320-trial, daily sessions for a total of 30 days. One session on each day involved only "prior cueing," and the other only "postcueing." A noninformative "neutral cue" came on one second before the compound on the "postcueing" trials so as to provide consistent timing information on all trials. The listeners were told to "attend primarily" to the cued frequency component, and that a bonus payment up to an amount equal to their base salary, $1.50 per hour, would be given, depending on their accuracy when tested on the cued frequency. All 16 combinations of frequency cued, interstimulus delay, and frequency tested ("probed") occurred equally often within each 320-trial session (as well as during a 32-trial "warm-up" series prior to each session). The 20 trials under each combination of conditions included 10 equal amplitude probe stimuli and 10 with an amplitude 2 dB lower than the corresponding component in the compound. The absolute amplitudes of each component of the compound were varied randomly, and independently, from trial to trial among five equally probable values: 30, 35, 40, 45, and 50 dB re the approximate "threshold" amplitude for each frequency. The subjects were isolated in separate acoustical testing chambers, listening binaurally to earphone-produced stimuli and responding on push buttons. Visual cues were small indicator lights. Each trial concluded with a 500-msec "feedback" light informing the listener as to the accuracy of his response. Each trial took from 3.7 to 5.2 sec, depending on the interstimulus delay, and there was a 500-msec intertrial period.

B. RESULTS

The results are presented in terms of the measure $\hat{\sigma}_N^2$ computed for each of the 16 conditions, for both "prior" and "post" cueing, in the manner described earlier in the paper, that is, the proportion of "softer" responses given the equal amplitude probe ($\hat{p}_0$) and the lower amplitude probe ($\hat{p}_1$) were used to calculate $\hat{d}$ by Eq. (5), and then rescaled to $\hat{\sigma}_N^2$ by Eq. (4). In order to reduce "practice" effects only the last 25 days of data from each listener were used in the analysis, providing 500 trials of data from which to calculate each value of $\hat{\sigma}_N^2$. These data are presented (data points) for individual subjects in Figs. 2, 3, and 4, and averaged over subjects in Fig. 5. The straight lines in each figure were "least-squares" fitted to each set of four data points that differed only in interstimulus delay, and indicate the interpretation leading to Eq. (4).

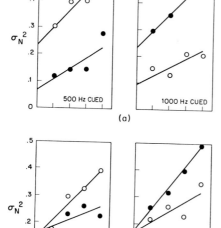

(a)

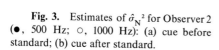

(b)

Fig. 2. Estimates of $\hat{\sigma}_N{}^2$ for Observer 1 ($\bullet$, 500 Hz; $\circ$, 1000 Hz): (a) cue before standard; (b) cue after standard.

Fig. 3. Estimates of $\hat{\sigma}_N{}^2$ for Observer 2 ($\bullet$, 500 Hz; $\circ$, 1000 Hz): (a) cue before standard; (b) cue after standard.

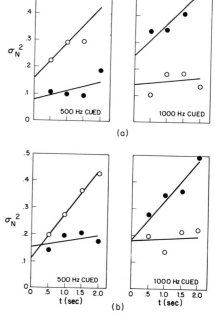

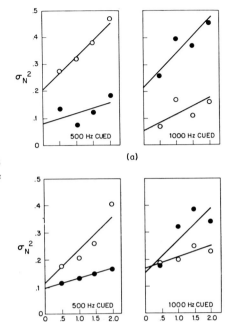

Fig. 4. Estimates of $\hat{\sigma}_N{}^3$ for Observer 3 (●, 500 Hz; ○, 1000 Hz): (a) cue before standard; (b) cue after standard.

The general pattern of results appears to be the same in each listener's data (Figs. 2, 3, and 4): *first*, $\hat{\sigma}_N{}^2$ tends to increase (accuracy diminishes) as the interstimulus delay is increased, and increases most rapidly for the "nonattended" frequency component; *second*, $\hat{\sigma}_N{}^2$ is generally larger (accuracy lower) for the "nonattended" frequency component; *third*, the straight lines fitted to the postcueing data have generally similar intercepts (π values), whereas the intercept for the nonattended frequency is higher, and for the attended frequency lower, when the cue precedes the compound. All of these features can be shown to be statistically significant ($p < .01$) and are even more obvious in Fig. 5, where the $\hat{\sigma}_N{}^2$ values in Figs. 2, 3, and 4 were averaged and fitted with straight lines (this included averaging across the particular frequency cued, since these data seemed quite comparable).

Note that a second ordinate scale, $P(C_{max})$, is indicated on the right of Fig. 5. This indicates the maximum probability of a correct response (that is, a response corresponding to the actual relation between probe and component amplitudes) for each value of $\hat{\sigma}_N{}^2$. A listener would only attain this level of accuracy if he chose an optimal "response criterion," in this case one that would lead to an equal number of "same" and "softer" responses over all conditions (see Green & Swets, 1966). Whereas the *unpracticed* observers were generally "biased" against calling the probe amplitudes

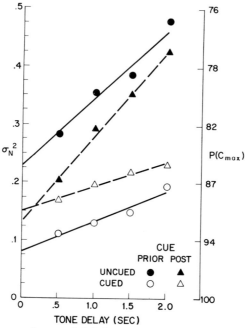

Fig. 5. Average estimates of $\hat{\sigma}_N^2$ for cued and noncued frequency at each probe position and delay.

"softer" (the so called "time-order error"), which is interpreted as a "response bias" effect by Kinchla and Smyzer (1967), this tendency virtually disappeared during the preliminary practice sessions as the listeners apparently adjusted their response criterions towards an optimal value on the basis of the "feedback" they received at the end of each trial. Thus, although some of the listeners continued to display very slight response biases, their performances were very close to the value of $P(C_{max})$ for each value of $\hat{\sigma}_N^2$. In any case, the actual proportion of correct responses is generally not a satisfactory measure of discriminability, since it is clearly influenced both by a listener's "sensitivity" and his "response criterion" (bias). While $P(C_{max})$ is a "bias-free" measure it is not linearly related to $\hat{\sigma}_N^2$, and does not have its simple "additive" property, Eq. (4).

III. Conclusions

The results seem consistent with the following interpretation. When a cue occurs after the compound, the listener must initially (at least on the average) "store" or "input" an equal amount of information about the (subsequently) cued and noncued components; thus, the σ_N^2 functions have a similar intercept. However, he can "maintain" or "rehearse" one component more effectively during the interstimulus delay as indicated by the difference in slope (φ) for the cued and noncued component. When the cue occurs prior to the compound, the listener can "store" or "input" information about the cued frequency more efficiently (π is smaller), although he does this by storing less information about the noncued frequency (π is larger). On the other hand, the rates of information loss (φ) for cued and noncued components are not appreciably influenced by cue position, since most of this loss occurs after the cue is given in either position.

Although one might argue that reduced accuracy to the cued frequency in the postcueing condition indicated an "*interference*" effect produced by the visual cue occurring immediately after the auditory compound, there is no indication of such an interference effect when the *noncued* frequency was "probed"; in fact, accuracy on this frequency was even better in the postcueing condition. Thus the results do seem to suggest selective "control processes" that operate at the level of simple sensory memory under some degree of volitional control.

IV. Some General Comments

While the type of memory process required in this probe-comparison task does not involve any *obvious* form of verbal coding, the selective memory of a specific sound component is quite similar to the selective retention of verbal material that led to the concept of "verbal rehearsal" (for example, see Atkinson & Shiffrin, 1970). Whether there are analogous "echoic rehearsal processes" that can somehow actively maintain a relatively "uncoded" or "raw" representation of sounds, or whether the selective "memory" results from selective "extraction" or "nonverbal coding" of specific stimulus features, is not clear at this point. In any case, the present results do seem especially relevant to ideas regarding "critical band" or "attentional filtering" mechanisms in hearing (see Green & Swets, 1966). Specifically, they raise the question of whether such mechanisms operate at the initial level of information storage ("input"), or at the early stages of sensory memory.

Finally, it should be emphasized that the *probe-comparison* paradigm can be employed in a variety of situations, and seems to offer a new approach to the study of selective processes in "sensory memory". The general nature of this approach is illustrated by the following *visual probe-comparison task*. Suppose the *compound-stimulus* is an array of four small colored circles (for example, red, green, blue, yellow) arranged as if in the corners of a square on a white field. A subject would fixate at a point at the center of this square just before a brief presentation of the colors. Then, following some delay, he would see at the fixation point a colored circle very similar to one of the colored circles in the preceding compound. His task would be to compare the "brightness" of the probe stimulus with its corresponding component in the compound (for example, green with green). Thus, the task would be quite similar to the auditory problem, the probe being equally bright or slightly dimmer than the corresponding component on each trial. Note that the task differs in important respects from the short-term visual memory problem used by Sperling (1960) or Estes and Taylor (1964), in that the observer is not required to code the stimuli into any (obvious) verbal system during the interstimulus period; rather, he must somehow maintain "brightness" information about each color component in order to make a delayed comparison. While this information could be "stored" as a numerical brightness estimate, it seems possible that a more primitive form of "sensory" memory might be utilized in discriminating very small brightness differences over very short delays. It seems particularly interesting to consider the influence of a "postcompound" cue directing the observer to "attend primarily" to a particular color. Would he show selective memory for that color, just as he did for the cued frequency component in the sound? This question is currently under investigation.

References

Aaronson, D. Temporal factors in perception and short-term memory. *Psychological Bulletin*, 1967, **73**, 130–144.

Atkinson, R. C., & Shiffrin, R. M. Human memory: A proposed system and its control processes. In K. W. Spence and J. T. Spence (Eds.), *The psychology of learning and motivation: Advances in research and theory*. Vol. II. New York: Academic Press, 1970.

Durlach, N. I., & Braida, L. D. Intensity perception I: Preliminary theory of intensity resolution. *Journal of the Acoustical Society of America*, 1969, **46**, 372–383.

Estes, W. K., & Taylor, H. A. A detection method and probabalistic models for assessing information processing from brief visual displays. *Proceedings of the National Academy of Sciences of the United States of America*, 1964, **52(2)**, 446–454.

Green, D. M., & Swets, J. A. *Signal detection theory and psychophysics*. New York: Wiley, 1966.

Kinchla, R. A., & Allan, L. G. A theory of visual movement perception. *Psychological Review*. 1969, **76**, 537–558.

Kinchla, R. A., & Smyzer, F. A diffusion model of perceptual memory. *Perception and Psychophysics*, 1967, **2**, 219–229.

Massaro, D. W. Preperceptual auditory images. *Journal of Experimental Psychology*, 1970, **85**, 411–417.

Massaro, D. W. The role of preperceptual images, perceptual units, and processing time in auditory perception. Studies in human information processing, Report No. 71–2. Department of Psychology, University of Wisconsin, 1971.

Norman, D. A., & Rumelhart, D. A system for perception and memory. In D. A. Norman (Ed.), *Models of human memory*. New York: Academic Press, 1970.

Rumelhart, D. A multicomponent theory of the perception of briefly exposed visual displays. *Journal of Mathematical Psychology*, 1970, **7**, 191–218.

Sperling, G. The information available in brief visual presentations. *Psychological Monographs*, 1960, **74**, 1–29.

Tanner, W. P., Jr. Physiological implications of psychophysical data. *Proceedings of the New York Academy of Sciences*, 1961, **89**, 752–765.

Wickelgren, W. A. Consolidation and retroactive interference in short-term recognition memory for pitch. *Journal of Experimental Psychology*, 1966, **18**, 250–259.

Wickelgren, W. A. Multitrace strength theory. In D. A. Norman (Ed.), *Models of human memory*. New York: Academic Press, 1970.

Divided Attention to Ear and Eye[1]

Anne M. Treisman *Alison Davies*

Department of Experimental Psychology
Oxford University
Oxford, England

ABSTRACT

Two experiments show that the limits of divided attention are reduced when stimuli are presented simultaneously to ear and eye rather than both to the ears or both to the eyes. The same improvement in a memory task is found within hearing if the stimuli differ in type—tones with words—but not in vision for spatial positions with words. The improvement is obtained in a monitoring task, whether the target items are defined as specific sounds or sights or as members of a semantic class. However, dividing attention between modalities in the monitoring task remains less efficient than focussing attention. This suggests that capacity is limited at least at two different stages—one modality specific and one shared between vision and hearing.

I. Introduction

In 1958 Broadbent put forward a theory of attention which assumed that any simultaneous sensory inputs which conveyed information to the subject would compete for a single, central, perceptual channel. The main limiting factor was the rate at which information could be transmitted by this central channel. Much of the research giving rise to this theory was done

---

[1]This research was supported by a grant from the Medical Research Council.

101

with listening tasks in which the subjects monitored, recalled, shadowed, or replied to one or both of two simultaneous speech messages, but there were some scattered experiments suggesting that the results could be generalized to tasks involving inputs from different sense modalities or different kinds of responses. [For example, Mowbray (1952) showed that monitoring a visual and an auditory message simultaneously was difficult; Broadbent (1956) found that split span experiments gave similar results in the bisensory and dichotic cases; Broadbent (1958) reports experiments in which subjects were impaired on a manual tracking task when carrying out a simultaneous speech monitoring task, the interference varying with the difficulty of the listening task.]

More recently people have extended their investigations to a wider range of tasks and stimuli and have begun to look at them in more detail, and a rather different picture is taking shape. It is clear that under some conditions we can cope with two informative inputs at least partly in parallel and that there are quite wide variations between tasks in the extent to which this is possible. Treisman (1969) suggests some general, logical distinctions which might help to structure the heterogeneous findings, and which lead to a rather different view of attention from the single channel one. It seems plausible to assume that the perceptual system consists of a number of relatively independent subsystems or "analyzers" (Sutherland, 1959), which code different aspects or dimensions of incoming stimuli, for example, their color, orientation, pitch, loudness, and spatial location. One of the main points which seems to distinguish between tasks in which some parallel processing or division of attention is possible from those in which it is not is whether the tasks involve two inputs converging onto the *same* analyzing system or the use of two *separate* analyzing systems on one or more inputs. Tasks involving the shared use of a single analyzer tend to be difficult; those which might involve different analyzers are often easier to carry out con-currently. In order to avoid circularity, one does, of course, initially need other criteria for deciding whether one or two independent analyzers are involved, but in extreme cases, such as the use of different modalities on modality-specific stimuli, there is little doubt about the independence of the early perceptual analyzers. If one finds evidence for parallel attention in these extreme cases, it would seem reasonable to extend the same explana-tion to other cases which are found to allow parallel attention. One then can use the possibility of parallel attention as a method for discovering which types or stages of analysis are shared between different kinds of stimuli and tasks. Allport, Antonis, and Reynolds (1972) recently made the same suggestion and illustrated it with two tasks involving high information rates, (shadowing speech while sight-reading music), which they found subjects could carry out in parallel with little or no interference. This contribution describes two preliminary experiments designed to explore the relations between vision and hearing within this conceptual framework. If this analysis is correct, we should both find support for it in evidence that some degree of parallel attention is possible only when it is plausible to assume that separate analyzers are involved, and also be able to use the argument in doubtful cases to discover at what level and under what conditions the two sense modalities do converge and compete for the same analyzers.

Two further alternative (though not incompatible) views of attention are as follows:

1. A modified "single-channel" theory suggests that the limits to parallel processing are set, not necessarily by the information rate in bits per second, nor by a particular central stage of analysis, but by the overall degree of either difficulty or complexity of analysis required. In other words, there is some overall limit to the capacity of the perceptual system; this can be devoted completely to one difficult task or can be divided between two or more easier ones, but only up to some limiting level (see Moray, 1967; Lindsay, 1970; Shaffer, 1971). There may well be some common pool of capacity, perhaps that involved in control processes, that would produce differences in the ease of dividing attention with differences in task complexity, but there may also be some more specific limits within the relatively independent perceptual analyzers. In these experiments we try to equate the level of difficulty of each within-modality task and then to see whether the between-modality combinations of the same tasks produce different effects on performance. This precaution often has not been taken, making the implications of results ambiguous.

2. A second possibility is that attention, at least with speech messages, is limited chiefly at the *verbal* level, that is, in tasks involving language, as seems to be the case in dichotic shadowing tasks. In these experiments we used both verbal and nonverbal tasks to test this possibility.

Evidence thus far on tasks with competing visual and auditory inputs is rather sparse and confusing. The experiments mentioned earlier suggest that in some conditions vision and hearing do compete. On the other hand, there is also evidence of some independence, even at the verbal level. For example, Mowbray (1964) and Kroll, Parks, Parkinson, Bieber, and Johnson (1970) have shown that a visual item is recalled better after interpolated auditory shadowing than an auditory item. Greenwald (1970) showed that oral reaction times (RTs) to a visual digit were faster if the same digit was simultaneously presented auditorily, while written RTs were not affected. There is also some evidence (for example, Murdock & Walker, 1969) that short-term memory parameters are different for visual and auditory stimuli and that interference in storage is at least partly modality specific. For example, Brooks (1968) showed that speaking interfered more with verbal memory and directional pointing with spatial memory. On the other hand, the results of split-span experiments (for example, Broadbent, 1956; Margrain, 1957; Dornbush, 1968; Madsen, Rollins, and Senf, 1970) are similar for dichotic and bisensory presentation, with most experiments showing marked interference between the visual and auditory items, since the span is much lower than with normal sequential presentation. Moreover, Murdock and Walker (1969) found little or no increase in memory capacity for mixed modality compared with single-modality lists, even when using sequential presentation.

II. Experiment 1: Split-Span Recall within and between Modalities

The first experiment to be reported here was done in collaboration with two students, Marilyn Harding and Viviane Nahai. We used the split-span technique to determine how far the finding of interference between simultaneous visual and auditory words is due to conversion of both sets of stimuli to a common mode of verbal representation. If this conversion could be omitted, would parallel perception and independent storage for inputs in different modalities or even for inputs of different types within each modality, become possible? Margrain (1957) in her bisensory split span experiments found considerable interaction between response mode (written or oral) and whether presentation was visual or auditory.

A. METHOD

The stimuli in the present experiment were auditory words, auditory tones, visual words and visual positions. The subjects were presented with 3 pairs of items at 3 pairs per second over 2 channels. We used all 4 combinations of the visual and auditory modalities: visual with visual V(V), visual with auditory V(A), auditory with auditory A(A), and auditory with visual A(V). A different group of 6 subjects (all undergraduates at Oxford University) was used in each of these 4 conditions. The stimuli were the words "high," "medium," "low," in different orders, either spoken or typed, or 3 tones of 250-msec duration spaced at musical intervals of a third, or 3 visual positions of a typed "o" relative to two lines

```
o    −    −
−    o    −
−,   −,   o.
```

No list contained a coincidence of items with the same description (for example, high tone with typed word "high") on both channel at once, and no channel received the same item twice within a list. The subjects were not told of these restrictions.

The previously typed visual stimuli were presented on a modified electric typewriter (used as a memory drum) that was stepped via a relay and solenoid by a synchronizing tone on the fourth track of the Uher tape recorder, which presented the auditory stimuli. A metal screen with a small window in it allowed the subjects to see only 1 or 2 stimuli at a time. If 2 visual stimuli were presented, they were in adjacent positions, both within 4° visual angle.

Each list of 3 pairs of items was preceded 1 sec earlier by a warning signal which consisted of a .5-sec burst of white noise binaurally over the headphones, together with one shift of the typewriter carriage. To equate any masking noise across conditions, all subjects wore headphones and all subjects watched and heard a sheet of paper click past on the typewriter. When only the other modality was being tested, the paper was blank or the headphones silent.

Each group of subjects received 12 lists twice over for each combination of types of stimuli, verbal or nonverbal; that is, the A(A) group had words with words, words with tones, tones with tones, and tones with words. The first complete run through the 4 sets of 12 lists was for practice, and only the second run through was used in analyzing the data. The order of lists was different in each condition and the order of conditions was counterbalanced across the subjects. The subjects were all asked to fixate a central marker line, whether 1 or 2 items were presented. They were instructed to give chan-nel-by-channel recall, always starting with the left-hand channel, their responses taking the form of mimicking the input [repeating aloud the audi-tory words, writing the initial letter of the visual ones (L, M, or H), singing back the tones and marking in the visual positions on a prepared response sheet]. Notice that the stimuli all could be coded as the words "high, medium, low," but the mimicking responses did not *require* this in the case of the tones and visual positions.

B. Results

The mean results are shown in Fig. 1. Analysis of variance showed that the lists in different modalities were significantly better recalled than lists in the same modality [($F(1, 20) = 27.3$ and 50.0 for first and second channels, respectively, $p < .001$], and also that lists comprising both verbal and non-verbal items were better recalled than lists of either type singly [$F(1, 20) =$

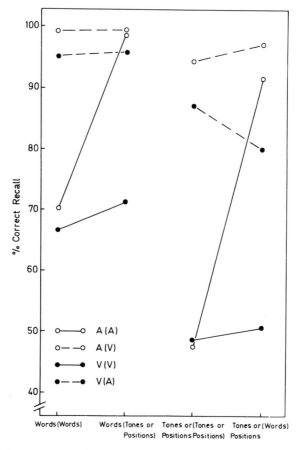

Fig. 1. Mean percentage of correct items recalled in correct positions in each condition of Experiment 1. "Words (tones)," for example, shows the mean percent words correct when these were presented with tones.

23.7 and 15.8, $p < .001$]. However, in separate analyses for each modality combination [V(V), A(A), V(A), and A(V)], only the A(A) condition showed a significant effect of whether the stimuli in the two channels were of the same or different types (both words or both tones, compared to half of each).

C. DISCUSSION

It is interesting that visual items, although recalled significantly less well than auditory items [$F(1, 20) = 8.7$ and $14.1, p < .01$], still averaged nearly 90% correct when paired with auditory stimuli and showed almost no loss when recalled second. The decrement between first and second channel recall for these items was only 4%. This contrasts markedly with Margrain's (1967) and Dornbush's (1968) findings of almost complete loss of visual items when recalled second in a bisensory split span experiment. In their experiments all responses to one list were made in the *same* way (either spoken or written). We also found rapid loss of the visual items recalled second in our experiment, but only for those visual items that had been presented with other visual items, that is, visual words with positions, visual words with visual words, and visual positions with visual positions. Thus, the rapid decay in the visual store appears to depend on interference from other competing visual items, rather than occurring automatically within the first 1 or 2 sec of time. (The interference might come from the other visual stimuli or from monitoring the written responses. Further experiments are needed to determine which.) With the auditory items, the decrement on the second channel was also greater when the first channel had the same type of stimuli: 21% for auditory words with auditory words and tones with tones, and a mean of only 2% for all other conditions.

Clearly the conditions showing interference between stimuli are those in which the same stimuli are presented in the same modality, and also the condition in which words and spatial positions are both presented visually. It appears then that, when no common response code is involved, partly or wholly independent perceptual and memory systems are available for auditory tones, auditory words, and visual stimuli, but that visual words and spatial patterns, like pairs of auditory words or pairs of visual words, converge and interfere at some stage between input and recall. Moray and Jordan's results (1966) suggest that at least part of the difficulty with pairs of auditory words arises at the response stage since subjects who were required to type responses to right-ear items with the right hand and to left-ear items with the left hand did better than those required to recall all items orally in alternating order. However, their subjects were still getting only 72% of lists correct in the bimanual response task, even after extensive practice, which is considerably less than our subjects' scores on auditory words with tones or visual items. The independence of auditory words and tones may be related to the apparent hemispheric specialization shown to occur with these auditory stimuli, for example, by Milner (1962) and by Kimura (1967).

However, from these and other heterogeneous results, it is still far from clear just what distinguishes tasks in which parallel analysis is possible, either within or between modalities, from those between which it is impossible to divide one's attention. The whole effect here might depend on differential interference with specific stored traces caused by recall responses which matched them or differed in modality or type [see Margrain's (1967) account of her results]. Alternatively, it might be primarily a perceptual effect, since the type of recall response required might determine how the item is processed perceptually during the presentation. The second experiment to be described concentrates on the perceptual limits by using a task which minimizes memory and response load.

III. Experiment 2: Monitoring in One or Two Modalities

In this experiment we again attempted to vary whether 1 or 2 sets of analyzing mechanisms were involved by presenting simultaneous lists either both in the same modality or each in a different modality, and we also varied the level of analysis required by defining the target items in terms of either a modality-specific, physical property or a semantic property. We tried approximately to equate the complexity of analysis required by using the same lists of words for the subjects to monitor in all conditions and by choosing physical forms of presentation that, in pilot experiments, had proved equally difficult within each modality. Two lists of words were presented simultaneously and the subjects were asked to monitor both lists for the occurrence of a target word. Physically defined targets were all words containing either the letters "END" or the sound "end" (for example "lender," "pretend," "endear"); semantically defined targets were all animals' names (for example, "baboon," "bee," "mussel").

It seemed likely that the physically defined targets would be identified by the separate auditory and visual systems, while the semantic targets would be identified within a common semantic system, which we assume to be shared between modalities. Figure 2 then shows the simple, preliminary schema we were testing. If the limits to attention arise in the shared use of a single analyzing system, the only easy condition should be that in which the subjects monitor for physical targets in different modalities. If, on the other hand, the difficulty in dividing attention lies in the parallel use of separate analyzers, the physical targets in different modalities should produce the most difficult monitoring tasks. If the limits arise mainly at the linguistic level, monitoring for semantic targets should be equally difficult, whether within or between modalities. The diagram is, of course, incomplete in many ways. For example, it is possible that higher levels can influence the tests carried out at lower levels. Moreover, some demand on capacity is likely to be imposed by the central control mechanisms which determine the sequence and nature of the perceptual operations carried out on each input. Memory stores have been omitted since they were irrelevant to the task we used. This simple flow diagram was set up simply as a first approximation to guide the initial experiments.

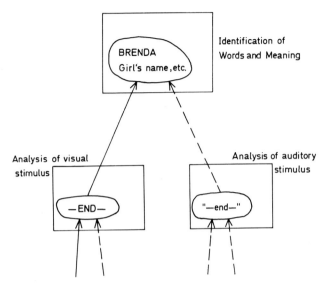

Fig. 2. Schema illustrating possible levels of convergence and competition within perceptual analyzing systems.

A. METHOD

We found in preliminary experiments that the methods which appeared to give approximately equal difficulty of monitoring within each modality were as follows: the auditory words were spoken by the same female speaker at a rate of 2 pairs per second and were presented dichotically at equal subjective loudness. The visual lists were presented on the modified electric typewriter described earlier, approximately synchronized with the auditory words by tones on the fourth track of the tape. One word was typed immediately below the other in each pair, and the pair occupied approximately 1.5 by .5° visual angle. To make the visual condition as difficult as the auditory, the words had to be further degraded by the addition of the letter "x" at either end of each word, and the superimposition of a mask consisting of black dots on a transparent screen placed over the viewing window.

The lists consisted of 16 pairs of words up to 7 letters long, chosen randomly from the dictionary.[2] Each list contained just one target word and its position varied randomly with the constraint that it appeared once in each

---

[2] We are grateful to Professor U. Neisser for making his pool of background and semantic target words available to us.

list position between 3 and 14 inclusive in every set of 12 lists; positions 1, 2, 15, and 16 were never used. Whichever 2 channels were not used for experimental lists in each condition presented the words "zero" and "nought," respectively, repeated in synchrony with the experimental words. This was to equate any peripheral masking effects across conditions.

The same example of a target word was never used twice. Six out of 12 targets were presented in each modality in the mixed modality condition, in each ear in the auditory condition, and in each position in the visual condition. Four sets of 12 lists were prepared for each type of target word, and the same sets of lists were monitored by 2 subjects in each of the 4 conditions, V(V), A(A), V(A), and A(V), making 8 subjects tested in each condition. The order in which the subjects were tested on the 4 conditions and 2 types of target word was counterbalanced using a Latin square design. The subjects were given 2 practice lists in each condition immediately before the 12 experimental lists. The targets used in the practice lists were the sound or letters "—ING—" in the physical target conditions and any Christian name in the semantic target conditions.

The subjects were told to look at or listen to each member of each pair, and to press a key if they saw or heard a target word. They were told that there would be one target word per list of 16 pairs, and they were encouraged to avoid errors. Their RTs were measured from the onset of the first synchronizing tone in each list, which triggered an Advance electronic timer. These times were corrected later by measuring on an ultraviolet recorder and subtracting the interval between the onset of the first tone and the onset of the target word. Eight further subjects were tested under the same conditions, with the modification that they were told in advance which channel would receive the target in each list. They therefore were free to focus their attention exclusively on 1 of the 2 lists, as far as this was possible.

The subjects were volunteer research students or undergraduates at Oxford University or Oxford Technical College, and were paid 30 p per hour. The experiment took one session of about $1\frac{1}{2}$ hr.

B. RESULTS

The mean percent targets detected and the mean false positive rates per list in each condition are given in Fig. 3, and the mean correct RTs in Fig. 4. The occurrence of an anticipation error (a false positive response to an incorrect word which preceded the correct target word in the list) precluded a correct detection for that list, so the percentage of correct detections was calculated as a proportion of the lists without anticipation errors. The mean number of anticipation errors never exceeded 1 out of the 12 lists in any of the conditions tested, and averaged .55. The false positives include any anticipation error and any response with a latency of more than 3 sec, unless the subject commented (as he was asked to) that he had just made an unusually slow response. Approximately half these false positives were recognized spontaneously as such by the subjects. To convert these false positives to probabilities, they were divided by the number of "words at risk," these being defined as any word in either list up to the pair which contained a detected target, plus all words in lists in which no target was detected, plus all words presented up to 1 sec before a false positive error. This gave the following percentages of false positives in the divided attention condition: .30, .48, and .47 for A(A), V(V), and mixed lists with "—end—" targets, respectively, and .39, .48, and .44 for corresponding lists with "animal" targets, respectively. If one uses these mean percentages of detections and false positives to estimate d' values for the different conditions with divided attention, essentially the same pattern of results is obtained, the increases in d' for between versus within modality monitoring being .51 and .86 for visual and auditory "end" targets, and .62 and .54 for visual and auditory "animal" targets.

The correct detections and RTs were subjected to analyses of variance; for the percentage of detections the arcsine of each mean was used. In the divided attention group, the effect on correct detections of changing from within- to between-modality monitoring was highly significant; $F(1, 7) = 40.04, p < .001$. The only other significant effect was the interaction between target type ("end" or "animal") and modality of target word; $F(1, 7) = 6.72, p < .05$. This reflects the fact that with visual presentation the subjects found it easier to monitor for words containing "end," while with auditory presentation they did better with the semantic targets. The RTs were slightly faster with between- than within-modality monitoring (except for visual "end" targets), but the effect here did not reach significance.

The subjects monitoring with focused attention did significantly better than those dividing their attention; $F(1, 14) = 69.6, p < .001$. In this group auditory monitoring was slightly better than visual $[F(1, 7) = 5.8, p < .05]$, both auditory and visual monitoring were better on average when the competing list was visual rather than auditory $[F(1, 7) = 9.2, p < .025]$, and this difference was more marked for the "end" than for the "animal" targets $[F(1, 7) = 6.9, p < .05]$.

The RTs were all appreciably faster for the subjects monitoring with focused rather than divided attention. However, as Ninio and Kahneman (1971) also found in a similar monitoring task with dichotic presentation, the RT distributions were not consistent with the assumption that performance with divided attention results from two separate states, one in which the subject happens to have focused his attention on the correct list and one in which he has not. If the subjects had to switch their attention on 50% of the trials, one would expect half the RTs in divided attention to approximate the

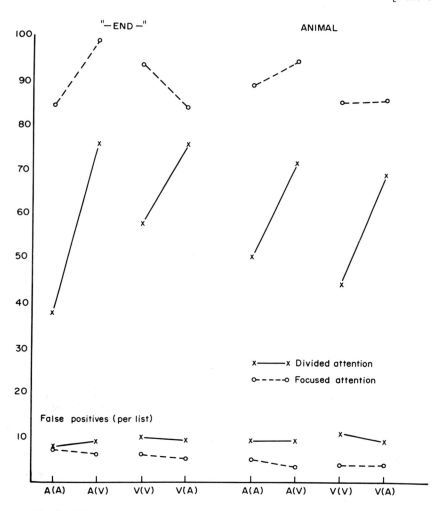

Fig. 3. Mean percent targets detected (out of total lists without anticipation errors) and percent false positives per list in Experiment 2.

mean of those with focused attention and the other half to be appreciably slower. But in fact the difference between the means of the two *fastest* RTs with focused and with divided attention was almost as great as the difference between the means of *all* RTs with focused and with divided attention (.20 compared with .23 sec).

IV. Discussion

What can we conclude from these results? When both inputs are in the same modality, the subjects attempting to monitor both detect appreciably

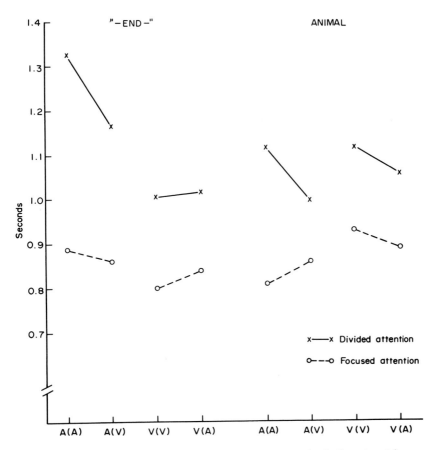

Fig. 4.   Mean correct RTs with focused and divided attention in Experiment 2.

less targets than are detected by the subjects monitoring only one of the two. This confirms again that marked perceptual limits are present when two inputs converge on the same analyzing mechanisms at either of the two levels involved in our talks. However, the main finding, as in the first experiment, is the considerable increase in the subjects' ability to divide their attention between two inputs when these are in different modalities rather than the same modality. This suggests that the effect in the first experiment was not due only to memory or response factors. There is clearly some modality-specific perceptual capacity that cannot be redeployed to inputs in another modality when required. This means that there is effectively more capacity available when two modalities are monitored than one. These results then conflict with the suggestion that all processing capacity is interchangeable between different types of analysis, storage and control. One possible arti-factual explanation could be that the effective synchronization in time of arrival at central perceptual mechanisms is better for stimuli in the same than in different modalities. If central "synchrony" causes difficulty, this could explain the inferior performance within modalities. To check on this possibility we ran a control experiment in which we deliberately introduced an average asynchrony of $\frac{1}{6}$ sec between paired auditory words in the dichotic condition. When 8 subjects monitored 12 desynchronized and 12 synchronized lists for "animal" targets, they detected a mean of 48% with desynchronized presentation and 47% with synchronized presentation. There is therefore no indication that this degree of asynchrony makes the monitoring task any easier at all.

Another question considered earlier was whether the limits to attention might arise only at higher levels of language processing. In our tasks it does not seem that the main bottleneck occurs at the semantic level. The particular examples of physical and semantic targets that we chose are, of course, arbitrary ones, and so it is difficult to draw general conclusions from their relative difficulty. However, the semantic task, involving higher-level linguistic analysis, is certainly not the only one to reveal perceptual limits. In fact, if we maintain the plausible assumption of a single semantic system shared by vision and hearing, our results suggest that the limit to capacity in monitoring within modalities for semantic targets did not arise at the semantic level. This is because, if the ceiling to detections in the A(A) and V(V) semantic conditions had been set by the subjects' ability to classify each word as an animal or not, there would have been no room for improvement in the between-modality semantic condition. However, with the present choice of targets, there clearly was some spare capacity within the semantic system, which could not be used in the within-modality condition because the limits to capacity at the earlier modality-specific stages prevented sufficient inputs (identified words) reaching the semantic level. Whether the true limit to capacity at the semantic level is reached in the between-modality conditions cannot be decided from the present results. If the hint, shown with the auditory lists, of a smaller improvement for semantic than for physical targets is reliable, it would suggest that semantic limits are beginning to be reached in the between modality condition.

Can we draw any further conclusions about the stages of analysis at which processing is parallel and those at which convergence and competition occur? There are two further aspects of the results with divided attention to account for: (1) the absence of any interaction between target type (physical versus semantic) and between- versus within-modality monitoring; (2) the fact that, even with inputs in different modalities, performance is still worse with divided than with focused attention.

1. We had suggested that with the physically defined targets monitor-

ing two modalities might involve entirely separate analyzers, whereas with semantic monitoring the visual and auditory inputs would converge on a common semantic system and so might still show limits which would be removed with the physical targets. One reason for our failure to find this may be simply that the particular semantic classification task we chose was too easy at the presentation rate we used. It would be interesting to test a more difficult semantic monitoring task, to see whether the relative improvement with between- versus within-modality monitoring would then be shown no longer. Another possibility, of course, is that each modality actually has its own separate semantic system.

2. However there is a third, more plausible possibility, which would also account for the fact that divided attention is worse than focused attention, even with the inputs in different modalities. This is that the so-called "physical" monitoring task we used in fact involved some higher-level verbal limits as well. For example, the subjects might have identified the auditory words as such and then converted them to spellings, or identified the visual words and converted these to sounds. The fact that the target would be the same in both lists after conversion (always the syllable "end") might have encouraged Ss to do this. Alternatively the fact that "END" is itself a word as well as a syllable might have allowed the subjects to monitor for this particular target as a word, albeit embedded in other words. So the failure to find a greater increase in detection of the "end" targets between modalities might be due to the subjects' strategy of monitoring the visual and auditory inputs at the *verbal* level, with both inputs again converging on the same analyzer. One might need some totally nonverbal target (such as a change of voice and of typeface) to preclude convergence on common analyzers and so allow an adequate test of our initial hypothesis.

If this account is correct, then the present experiment has shown limits to perceptual capacity at *two* different levels at least, one which is relatively peripheral and modality specific, and one which is shared between modalities, but probably located earlier in verbal processing than the semantic level. The between-modality improvement over within-modality monitoring with both types of targets shows the increased capacity at the early modality-specific levels of verbal processing; the remaining limits to monitoring different modalities with both types of targets reflect the competition at later verbal stages which are shared between modalities. In the focused attention condition, only half the words need be monitored, so that neither the modality-specific nor the verbal limits any longer impair performance to any extent. One reason why the detection rates in some conditions are lower than 100%, even with focused attention, may be that the focused-attention condition involves the additional task of excluding the irrelevant channel. (This varied randomly from list to list and the subjects reported sometimes having trouble remembering which list they were supposed to monitor.) Thus, differences in the ease of excluding the irrelevant words may account for the differences between conditions shown by these subjects. For example, a competing auditory message appeared most difficult to exclude when the subjects were monitoring for the syllable "—END—," whether in another auditory or in a visual list, while the most difficult target to search for was a visually presented animal name.

References

Allport, D. A., Antonis, B, & Reynolds, P., On the division of attention: A disproof of the single channel hypothesis. *Quarterly Journal of Experimental Psychology*, 1972, **24**, 225–235.

Broadbent, D. E. Successive responses to simultaneous stimuli. *Quarterly Journal of Experimental Psychology*, 1956, **8**, 145–152.

Broadbent, D. E. *Perception and communication.* Oxford: Pergamon, 1958.

Brooks, L. R. Spatial and verbal components of the act of recall. *Canadian Journal of Psychology*, 1968, **22**, 349–368.

Dornbush, R. L. Input variables in bisensory memory. *Perception and Psychophysics*, 1968, **4**, 41–44.

Greenwald, A. G. A double stimulation test of ideomotor theory with implications for selective attention. *Journal of Experimental Psychology*, 1970, **84**, 392–398.

Kimura, D. Functional asymmetry of the brain in dichotic listening. *Cortex*, 1967, **3**, 163–178.

Kroll, N. E. A., Parks, T. E., Parkinson, S. R., Bieber, S. L. & Johnson, A. L. Short term memory while shadowing: Recall of visually and of aurally presented letters. *Journal of Experimental Psychology*, 1970, **85**, 220–224.

Lindsay, P. H. Multichannel processing in perception. In D. I. Mostovsky (Ed.), *Attention: Contemporary theory and analysis.* New York: Appleton, 1970.

Madsen, M. C., Rollins, H. A., & Senf, G. M. Variables affecting immediate memory for bisensory stimuli: Eye–ear analogue studies of dichotic listening. *Journal of Experimental Psychology Monograph Supplement*, 1970, **83**, No. 3, 16.

Margrain, S. A. Short term memory as a function of input modality. *Quarterly Journal of Experimental Psychology*, 1967, **19**, 109–114.

Milner, B. Laterality effects in audition. In V. B. Mountcastle (Ed.), *Interhemispheric relations and cerebral dominance.* 1962, Baltimore; Maryland: Johns Hopkins Press. Pp. 177–195.

Moray, N. Where is capacity limited? A survey and a model. In A. Sanders (Ed.), *Attention and performance. III. Acta psychologica*, 1967, **27**, 84–93.

Moray, N., & Jordan, A. Practice and compatibility in 2-channel short-term memory. *Psychonomic Science,* 1966, **4**, 427–8.

Mowbray, G. H. Simultaneous vision and audition: The detection of elements missing from overlearned sequences. *Journal of Experimental Psychology*, 1952, **44**, 292–300.

Mowbray, G. H. Perception and retention of verbal information presented during auditory shadowing. *Journal of the Acoustical Society of America*, 1964, **36**, 1459–1465.

Murdock, B. B., Jr., & Walker, K. D. Modality effects in free recall. *Journal of Verbal Learning and Verbal Behavior*, 1969, **8**, 665–676.

Ninio, A., & Kahneman, D. Reaction time in focused and in divided attention (in preparation).

Shaffer, L. H. Attention in transcription skill. *Quarterly Journal of Experimental Psychology*, 1971, **23**, 107–112.

Sutherland, N. S. Stimulus analysing mechanisms. In *Mechanisation of thought processes*, Vol. 2. London: Her Majesty's Stationery Office, 1959. Pp. 575–609.

Treisman, A. M. Strategies and models of selective attention. *Psychological Review*, 1969, **76**, 282–299.

Order Error in Attended and Nonattended Tasks

Stanislav Dornic

Institute of Applied Psychology
University of Stockholm
Solna, Sweden

ABSTRACT

Order errors were studied in the recall of a memory task (auditory messages) presented under different conditions, in which the subjects (*a*) attended to a tracking task during the presentation of the messages, or (*b*) attended to the messages themselves. No significant difference was found between these conditions in the percentage of correct messages with the correct order of items. The percentage of correct messages with a wrong order was, however, significantly lower when the subjects did not attend to the presentation of the memory task. The results are interpreted as being due to the fact that the retention of item information in the recall of nonattended tasks is probably bound to the retention of order information.

I. Problem

Experiments on the retention of nonattended stimuli represent laboratory models of many everyday situations. Several different approaches to these problems have been employed during the past few years. One of the most effective methods used in this area is a so-called shadowing, introduced by Cherry (1953): the subject is required to "shadow," that is, to repeat messages presented to him, at the same time being presented with another message. Using this method, retention of stimuli from the rejected channel can practically be reduced to zero (Moray, 1959).

However, to get a more differentiated insight into what is happening to the nonattended stimuli, we need at least some partly successful retention of the nonattended messages. For this purpose, a method might be useful in which both the tasks (the one to be attended to and the subsidiary one) are basically different, the task to be attended to being simple enough to allow the subjects to retain some of the material from the rejected channel. A divided attention technique, recently used for a different purpose (for studying the effect of a memory task on tracking performance; see Johnston, Greenberg, Fisher, & Martin, 1970) was employed in the present experiment; this method seems to meet the above requirement.

Special attention in the analysis of the data obtained in the present experiment was paid to the occurrence of order error in the recall of the attended and nonattended tasks. Many studies have been devoted to this problem in short-term memory research, particularly since Crossman (1960) and Brown (1959) suggested that order information and item information might be stored separately. Studies by Aaronson and Sternberg (1964) and by Conrad (1965) have brought new and interesting facts and shed more light on the problems under study. It is nevertheless obvious that the problem deserves further investigation.

II. Method

The task to be attended to was represented by a typical tracking task not involving or requiring any verbalization and not preventing the subject from recall.

The tracking device was situated in front of the subject. A 3-mm thick black line drawn on a white background and visible in a 5 × 5 cm square opening, moved toward the subject at a speed of 12 mm/sec. The line was bending irregularly in the left–right direction. The subject's task was to follow the line by means of a pen attached to a simple mechanism that made it possible to move the pen in the left–right direction, thus enabling the subject to draw a continuous line inside the moving stimulus line. Any failure to follow the task was clearly visible on the white background. This task was defined as the one to be attended to. The relation between the speed and the number of deviations from the line was determined empirically and made it possible for the subject to cope successfully with the task, providing that he was fully concentrating on it.

The memory task consisted of auditory messages of digits and letters presented by a tape recorder at a rate of 1 item per .75 sec. Each message consisted of 7 items: 4 digits and 3 consonants. The vocabulary involved all decimal digits except for 0, and 17 consonants. None of the items was repeated within one message. With regard to well-known findings (Conrad, 1959, 1965), acoustic similarity of the individual items within messages was avoided or reduced to minimum.

Four experimental conditions were used. In the first condition, the subjects attended to the tracking task during the presentation of the memory task, but not during recall. Ten sec after the tracking task had been started, the first message was presented. Two sec after the message had been finished, the tracking task was stopped (the apparatus was switched off), and a red light came on, indicating that the subject should start the recall. About 2 sec after the recall, the tracking task began again. Following an interval of 10 sec, another message was presented, and so on. This condition will be referred to as condition TM (T standing for tracking and M for messages).

In condition MM, which served as control condition, only the memory tasks were presented, the subjects being instructed to attend to them. The intervals between the individual messages and recalls were the same as in condition TM, the subjects being cued to recall by means of the red light.

In condition TT, the messages were both presented and recalled simultaneously with the tracking task, the other conditions being equal.

Finally, in condition MT, the messages were always presented alone, without the tracking task. Immediately after the end of each message, the tracking task was started, 2 sec later, the red signal for recall was presented, and so on.

As mentioned above, the tracking task was defined as the primary, "more important" one, and the subjects were instructed fully to concentrate on it, the number of errors in this task being defined for them as the main criterion of their performance.

Thirty messages were presented within each experimental condition. All four conditions were repeated twice, under two different instructions concerning recall strategies. Instruction 1 required serial recall, while in instruction 2, the subjects were told to recall the messages in the way and order they preferred. The order of conditions was randomized.

Since the two instructions might have interfered with each other, two groups of subjects were used, one for each instruction. Altogether 42 female university students between the ages of 20 and 22 years participated in the experiment, 20 in one group and 22 in the other.

Since the experimental procedure, particularly that in condition MT, required a certain amount of practice, all subjects were adequately trained.

III. Results and Discussion

A preliminary analysis showed that the instruction concerning the recall strategies did not have any clear-cut influence on the results. Data obtained from all 42 subjects therefore were treated together.

Three scores were employed to analyze the successfulness of recall in the individual conditions: (A) percentage of messages in which all the items were recalled, regardless of whether or not they recalled in the correct order; (B) percentage of correctly recalled messages, with correct order; (C) percentage of messages in which all the items were recalled but in a wrong order. (See Table 1.)

First, let us compare conditions TM and MM. Performance according to score A (percentage of correctly recalled messages with as well as without the correct order) was considerably better when memory task was attended to (condition MM, 86%) than when it was not attended to (condition TM, 74%). The difference is statistically significant at the .05 level. This result should, of course, be expected.

However, this difference is due to the considerably higher occurrence of recalls with all the items correct but with a wrong order (score C, 25% in condition MM versus 15% in condition TM; the difference is highly significant: $p < .01$). Score B reveals almost no difference.

A comparison of conditions TT and MT shows similar relationships as stated above with the difference that attending to the tracking task during recall resulted in a generally lower performance. Statistical significance was found in score A as well as in score C (in both cases, $p < .05$), but not in score B.

It follows from the present data that the subjects' concentration on the

Table 1. *Recall of Messages in the Four Experimental Conditions*[a]

Condition	Message presentation	Recall	Score (%)		
			A	B	C
TM	Tracking	No tracking	74	59	15
MM	No tracking	No tracking	86	61	25
TT	Tracking	Tracking	66	48	18
MT	No tracking	Tracking	79	54	25

[a]Score A: percentage of messages in which all the items were recalled, regardless of the order. Score B: percentage of correctly recalled messages, with correct order. Score C: percentage of messages with all the items correct but in a wrong order.

tracking task during the presentation of messages did not have any clear-cut effect on the more mechanical way of recall, that is, on "parroting back" the items in their original order. The lower overall performance in conditions TM and TT appears to be caused by the fact that the retention of item information was bound to the retention of order information; having forgotten the order, the subjects lost at the same time a great deal of item information.

The above findings remind us of the results of an earlier experiment on the effect of alcohol on short-term memory (Dornic, Myrsten, & Frankenhaeuser, 1971). The results were rather similar. In the more difficult condition, that is, under the influence of a large dose of alcohol, there was almost no decrease in the number of correctly recalled messages with the correct order, but a significant decrease was found in item information alone. It was as if alcohol had not affected the more "primitive" or "mechanical" way of coding, and the items could be recalled easily only as long as they were "pasted together," according to the order of their presentation, in the subjects' "echo boxes," as the often-cited Waugh's (1961) subject called his experience. In another experiment (Hockey & Hamilton, 1970), noise was shown to impair recall of item information rather than that of order information.

The present results seem to support the idea of two different mechanisms or levels of storage in immediate memory. In order to avoid confusion (the labels "sensory," "perceptual," "primary," "secondary" are used by different authors in a different sense), they will be referred to only as "lower" and "higher" storage mechanisms, respectively. The main difference between these two mechanisms lies in the fact that a trace formed by the lower storage mechanism carries order information and does not require attention, while the higher mechanism requires attention and does not necessarily carry order information.

The lower storage mechanism can be characterized as echoic in nature. It stores the arriving information in the order presented in the form of connected chain traces, primarily according to their physical features rather than according to their meaning. This system does not necessarily involve activation of the stimulus names in long-term memory. The higher mechanism involves identification of the arriving stimuli according to their meaning or to their names already stored in long-term memory, rather than according to their physical features. The traces of the individual items within messages thus may become more "independent" or "loose" and less connected together in the order of presentation.

The existence of the lower storage mechanism might seem to be inconsistent with the well-known findings, indicating the existence of an automatic initial analysis of the signals even on nonattended channels (for example, Norman, 1968). However, a selective mechanism working on the principle of a "lowered threshold" for important information may account for the fact that the lower storage mechanism does not necessarily involve activation of the stimulus names in long-term memory.

The present data, however, do not allow any generalization, and the above differentiation of the two storage mechanisms represents only a tentative attempt to account for the data obtained.

Finally, the problem of the origin of order errors should be mentioned briefly. There is disagreement in the literature as to the question of whether order errors in recall are mainly a consequence of misperceiving the item order during stimulus presentation or are a consequence of forgetting the order during retention. Some authors emphasize the role of perceptual factors (for example, Ladefoged & Broadbent, 1960; Aaronson, 1967), whereas other authors feel that order errors are due in large part to memory (for example, Conrad, 1965; Moray & Barnett, 1965; Wickelgren, 1965). The present findings do not appear clearly to support either the perceptual or the memory hypothesis: both factors might have been equally involved. It is true that, when attending to the tracking task, the subjects had poorer conditions for the perception of messages. It must be taken into account, however, that retention starts from the beginning of the message presentation. Thus, concentration on the tracking task impaired conditions for retention as well.

References

Aaronson, D. Temporal factors in perception and short-term memory. *Psychological Bulletin*, 1967, **67**, 130–144.

Aaronson, D., & Sternberg, S. effects of presentation rate and signal-to-noise ratio on immediate recall. Paper presented at Eastern Psychological Association, Philadelphia, 1964.

Brown, J. Information, Redundancy and decay of the memory trace. In N.P.L. Symposium No. 10, London: H.M. *Mechanisation of thought processes*. Stationery Office, 1959.

Cherry, E. C. Some experiments on the recognition of speech, with one and with two ears. *Journal of the Acoustical Society of America*, 1953, **24**, 975–979.

Conrad, R. Errors of immediate memory. *British Journal of Psychology*, 1959, **50**, 349–359.

Conrad, R. Order Error in Immediate Recall of Sequences. *Journal of Verbal Learning and Verbal Behavior*, 1965, **4**, 161–169.

Crossman, E. R. W. F. Information and serial order in human immediate memory. In C. Cherry (Ed.), *Information theory*. London: Butterworth, 1960.

Dornic, S., Myrsten, A. L., & Frankenhaeuser, M. Effect of alcohol on short-term memory. *Reports from the Psychological Laboratories*, the University of Stockholm, 1971, No. 336.

Hockey, G. R. J., & Hamilton, P. Arousal and information selection in short-term memory. *Nature*, 1970, **226**, 866–867.

Johnston, W. A., Greenberg, S. N., Fisher, R. P., & Martin, D. R. Divided attention: A vehicle for monitoring memory processes. *Journal of Experimental Psychology*, 1970, **83**, 164–171.

Ladefoged, P., & Broadbent, D. E. Perception of sequences in auditory events. *Quarterly Journal of Experimental Psychology*, 1960, **12**, 162–170.

Moray, N. Attention in dichotic listening: Affective cues and the influence of instructions. *Quarterly Journal of Experimental Psychology*, 1959, **11**, 59–60.

Moray, N., & Barnett, T. Stimulus presentation and methods of scoring in short-term memory Experiments. *Acta Psychologica*, 1965, **24**, 253–263.

Norman, D. A. Toward a theory of memory and attention. *Psychological Review*, 1968, **75**, 522–536.

Waugh, N. C. Free versus serial recall. *Journal of Experimental Psychology*, 1961, **62**, 496–502.

Wickelgren, W. A. Short-term memory for repeated and non-repeated items. *Quarterly Journal of Experimental Psychology*, 1965, **17**, 14–25.

2 PHYSIOLOGICAL CORRELATES OF ATTENTION AND PERFORMANCE

Physiologic Approaches to the Analysis of Attention and Performance

Herbert G. Vaughan, Jr.   Walter Ritter

*Department of Neurology and
Rose F. Kennedy
Center for Research
in Mental Retardation
and Human Development,
Albert Einstein College of Medicine,
Bronx, New York*

ABSTRACT

By averaging the brain potentials related in time to stimuli and to motor responses, the timing and localization of neural processes underlying simple and complex sensorimotor sequences can be studied in man and in experimental animals. These "event-related potentials" (ERP) have been classified as sensory-evoked potentials (EP), motor potentials (MP), association-cortex potentials (ACP), and steady potential shifts (SPS), each with a characteristic temporal course and intracranial origin. The present limitation of definitive information on the quantitative relationship of ERP with underlying neuronal processes and with psychological variables must dictate great caution in relating them to complex psychological constructs such as attention. Physiological attempts to demonstrate modulation of sensory input associated with selective attention have been largely unsuccessful. This failure reflects an unduly constricted conceptual formulation of attention as well as inadequacies of earlier experimental approaches. Effective physiological approaches to the analysis of attention will require knowledge of the higher order cerebral mechanisms which underlie cognitive processes.

¹Psychophysiological Studies of Sensorimotor Processes, NIMH Grant No. MH-06723, 1962. H. G. Vaughan, Jr., L. D. Costa, and W. Ritter, investigators.

129

I. Introduction

Behavioral scientists must rely primarily upon patterns of stimulus and response contingencies to infer the nature of information processing mechanisms within the organism. The lack of data on the timing and location of relevant neural activity leads to uncertainty concerning both the existence and the temporal characteristics of physiologically distinct processing stages (Sternberg, 1969a, b).

Statistical methods for the analysis of brain potentials recorded from human scalp electrodes and from chronically implanted micro- or macroelectrodes in experimental animals have made it possible to study the spatiotemporal patterning of neural activity during the course of behavioral sequences.

The potentialities of the new methods for studying brain function have attracted many investigators with widely varying backgrounds and interests. It is perhaps not surprising that one of their main concerns has been with the possible value of human brain potentials as indices or correlates of "higher" psychic processes. Among these psychological entities, none has excited greater interest than attention. Unfortunately, attempts to study the physiology of processes, which are not only complex but often conceptually elusive, in the absence of a sound technical, behavioral, and physiologic foundation, can be expected to produce a confused and sometimes actively misleading body of experimental data, despite occasional provocative and suggestive findings. It is no secret that this is the present status of physiologic studies of attention, both in man and in experimental animals. The situation may be summarized briefly by the assertion that while the reticular system, especially in·its thalamic extension, is generally implicated in the physiologic mechanisms of attention, no conclusive electrophysiologic manifestations of attention have been demonstrated in the behaving organism. We shall consider subsequently some of the experiments in this area, which make it abundantly clear that past efforts to define physiologic correlates of attention have run afoul of serious experimental and conceptual snags.

During the past decade, we have developed a program of research with the objective of defining the timing and location of cerebral activity involved in sensorimotor processes. Our approach followed the conceptual tradition initiated by Donders (1868), which was formulated in neurological terms by von Monakov (1911) as the "chronological localization of cerebral function," and more recently elaborated by Wiener (1948) and von Neumann (1958). Although the pace of our quest has often seemed discouragingly slow, frustrated by the many uncertainties inherent in the analysis of human brain potentials, we can now assert with some confidence that tools for a physiologic approach to the analysis of human experience and behavior are at hand. We believe that the productive physiologic analysis of psychological processes requires the integration of studies in man and experimental animals. This strategy involves an initial exploration of human brain potentials to establish the timing and localization of brain activity associated with well defined sensory and motor events. Some of this information is now available, and will be briefly described below. In order to more fully define the sequence of cerebral processes involved in simple sensorimotor sequences, especially the role of subcortical structures and cortical areas not readily accessible to scalp recordings, concurrent studies must be made in chronically implanted primates trained to carry out tasks identical to those performed by the human subjects. Furthermore, studies in the behaving animal are required to define the relationship between the slow (EEG) potentials and the firing patterns of individual neurones. The latter data will provide a bridge between behavioral physiology and cellular neurobiology, which is concerned with the intimate mechanisms of neural activity. Although both of these approaches to the analysis of neuroelectric activity must proceed at their own pace, it is essential for investigators who concentrate on one level of analysis to articulate their findings with data at other levels. To date there has been disappointingly little effort in the neurobehavioral sciences to achieve this experimental coordination. Psychologically elegant studies of human brain potentials may be physiologically meaningless due to a failure to evalute their intracranial sources. Conversely, neurophysiologists are willing to relate psychological processes to electrophysiological data obtained in anesthetized animals without due concern for the speciousness of such formulations.

During the early development of any scientific area, experimental techniques must be devised and perfected. This usually proceeds most rapidly in relative independence of other disciplines and extraneous procedural concerns. Once the stage is technically set, however, all of the relevant variables in a particular domain of inquiry must be considered in the design and execution of fruitful experiments. In behavioral physiology, the scope of investigation is both extensive and resistant to the experimental isolation of subsystems. Despite the undoubted value of techniques such as ablation and electrical stimulation for defining relationships of brain to behavior, electrophysiologic study of the behaving organism represents the primary tool for dissecting the role of the brain in generating experience and behavior. We shall consider in outline the strategy with which such investigations may proceed.

II. An Empirical Strategy for Linking Psychological and Physiological Variables

The founders of experimental psychology recognized that an understanding of information processing mechanisms required the determination of their temporal characteristics. Reaction time (RT) experiments formed the crucial paradigm for such an analysis. Unfortunately, these early studies could not lead to a definition of central mechanisms, since they postulated serial mechanisms in which complicating stages were both additive and exclusive. In the absence of confirmatory physiologic data, such an assumption could not be sustained, and RT methods fell from favor until the recent resurgence of interest in information flow models of behavioral mechanisms.

Despite the early emphasis (Sherrington, 1906) on reflex mechanisms, physiologic studies of sensorimotor sequences in the behaving organism have been rare (Cruikshank, 1937; Bernhard, 1940; Monnier, 1949). However, with the advent of computer averaging of brain potentials and methods for chronic implantation of animals with both macro- and microelectrodes, there has been an increasing use of the RT paradigm in physiological studies (Vaughan, Costa, Gilden, & Schimmel, 1965; Evarts, 1966; Vaughan, Costa, & Gilden, 1966; Miller & Glickstein, 1967). The logical attractiveness of the RT method derives from the opportunity it provides for the analysis of concomitant variations of psychological and physiological variables. In man, there is the additional possibility of detecting and subjecting to quantitative analysis the physiological processes that underlie conscious experience, since the temporal course of various sensory experiences can be defined experimentally (for example, Haber & Standing, 1970; Efron, 1970a, b). The basic behavioral strategy is an elaboration of the original method of Donders. This approach recently has been imaginatively extended by psychologists (for example, Sternberg, 1969a, b) so as to provide behavioral paradigms for probing such physiologically obscure processes as memory retrieval.

From a physiologic standpoint, however, the analysis of even simple sensorimotor sequences is procedurally and analytically complicated. For the behavioral scientists, stimulus and response are events whose physical parameters are discrete and unambiguous. However, the physiologic response of the sensory receptors and the physiologic measures of motor response (that is, action potentials in motor nerve or the electromyogram) are relatively prolonged and rather variable, even though the external stimulus and response remain physically constant. Thus, a brief (< 1-msec) light flash elicits activity in the optic nerve lasting up to 100 msec. And though the instantaneous break of a key contact comprises the usual behavioral measure of RT, physiologic measurements of the response depict an EMG burst that begins between 30 and 80 msec before the contact break and persists for around 250 msec, even with intentionally brief contractions. Furthermore, in simple RT tasks, the motor response begins long before the termination of central neural activity generated by the stimulus. Due to this extensive temporal overlap of physiologic activity, notions of information processing involving additive, exclusive serial processes must be oversimple. We must also admit the operation of parallel processes and feedback mechanisms, which are well-known features of neural systems, even of reflex organization. Finally, the physiologic state existing at the time of stimulation interacts with the stimulus generated activity, as well as conditioning the probability and characteristics of motor response. Thus, we encounter a set of variables, even when conceptualized in the simplest possible fashion, that seems virtually inaccessible to empirical dissection. It is this undoubted complexity of brain mechanisms that leads many physiologists to despair of a meaningful physiologic analysis of the intact, functioning mammalian nervous system, and to turn either to approaches that utilize "simple" nervous systems such as that of the mollusk *Aplysia* or focus upon artificially circumscribed microphysiologic aspects of mammalian brain physiology. Both of these approaches are valuable in the elucidation of neural mechanisms, but they must not be imbued with greater significance than they possess for understanding the neural mechanisms of behavior. Studies of this sort, no matter how successful, cannot provide us with information at the level of analysis required to define the neural mechanisms involved, for instance, in perception, memory, and other cognitive processes. If we recognize that presently feasible studies in behaving man and primates will provide us with gross but crucial data on the identity of the structures and the sequencing of neural processes involved in a given behavior, we need not deprecate the value of these relatively crude methods. However, it is essential for the meaningful use of these data that every effort be directed toward the isolation and identification of specific processes, both by appropriate behavioral manipulations and a skillful application of available techniques for statistical and biophysical analysis of the neuroelectric data.

III. The Analysis of Event-Related Cerebral Potentials

In the behaving organism, the electrical potentials recorded from the brain, whether EEG obtained from scalp electrodes in man or action potentials of individual neurones sensed by extracellular microelectrodes in experimental animals, possess only statistically reliable relationships with stimulus or response variables. In the case of single unit activity, this reflects the probabilistic aspect of neural mechanisms. But in the case of the EEG, variability is introduced by contribution of innumerable neuronal generators, which differ in location and orientation as well as in their physiological relationship with the psychological variable under consideration. Thus, both a statistical and a biophysical analysis are required to extract from a given set of EEG recordings data on the timing, strength, and origin of the neural signals related to a reference stimulus or motor response.

Since these event-related potentials (ERP) are obscured by the concurrent spontaneous EEG activity, reliable ERP measurements require the computation of averaged potentials. The amplitude ratio between the ERP and random background activity present in the average is proportional to the square root of the number (N) of samples, so that the relative contribution of residual background activity to average ERP variance can be estimated for a given N, given knowledge of the EEG and ERP amplitudes. If the number of samples constituting an average is appropriately chosen for a given ratio of ERP to background activity and meticulous attention is paid to maintain stable experimental conditions, highly reliable recordings can be obtained. In computing averaged ERP, it is usually assumed that the potentials are time locked to the reference event. While this is true, to a reasonable approximation, for the initial portions of stimulus elicited cortical activity, neural processes further along in the processing of information show an increasingly variable temporal relation to the stimulus. A similar situation exists when averaging with respect to a motor act. Whenever significant temporal variability in neural activity relative to the averaging reference is present, errors in estimation of both the timing and amplitude of the potentials on individual trials will occur. An equally serious problem is presented by the volume conduction of brain potentials from their intracranial sources. Workers have tended to make assumptions about the sources of sensory-evoked potentials, based more upon tradition than thorough analysis. Most, when recording sensory evoked potentials, have placed their electrodes in the general vicinity of the primary projection area when interested in modality-specific responses, and at the vertex when concerned with the so-called "nonspecific" response. These practices have precluded the definition of relations between ERP and their intracranial generators. The localization of the sources of the ERP recorded in a given situation requires a detailed spatial mapping of the potential distribution and an analysis based upon volume conduction theory (for example, Vaughan & Ritter, 1970).

It is useful to classify the presently known averaged ERP into four groups (Vaughan, 1969), taking both the temporal relation to the reference event and the location of intracranial sources into consideration.

A. STIMULUS-EVOKED POTENTIALS (EP)

The transient cortical responses elicited by brief stimuli arise after a brief latency (15–50 msec or more, depending upon sensory modality and stimulus parameters) and last for 200–250 msec in the waking state (Fig. 1). These EP are composed of several sequential positive and negative deflections that vary with stimulus parameters and recording techniques so as to preclude a standardized nomenclature. The least ambiguous designation indicates the polarity and peak latency (in milliseconds) of each component

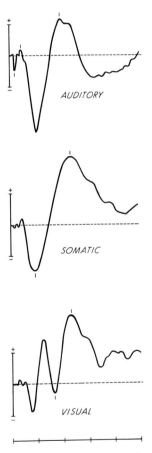

Fig. 1.   Composite averaged EP obtained from 8 adult subjects: Each trace represents the computer average of 4800 individual responses. The EP have been recorded from electrodes placed at the point of maximum amplitude for each modality referred to an inactive electrode on the nose. Calibration: 10 μV, 100 msec per division. (Reprinted from Vaughan, 1969.)

(for example, P100, N150, P200). Variations in EP across subjects tend to be more prominent in component amplitude rather than latency, so that a "standard" sequence of components may generally be identified across subjects for given experimental conditions, despite rather striking variations in the configuration of the overall waveforms. The sensory EP reflect changes in stimulus parameters with considerable sensitivity, but the effects are neither simple nor necessarily quantitatively similar across subjects. This has led to a generally confused picture of the relationships between EP parameters and stimulus variables. The lack of straightforward relationships between stimulus and EP measures derives in large part from the composite physiological nature of the EP, which reflects a variety of physiological activities in a very large and heterogeneous neuronal population. Due to the uncertainties concerning the contribution of activity of single neurons to any specific EP, interpretations of changes in amplitude of a given EP component in terms of underlying neural activity are exceedingly dangerous. Inasmuch as the EP are believed to represent a summation of postsynaptic potentials from a large number of cellular elements oriented in various directions, neither the polarity nor the amplitude of EP can indicate unambiguously increases or decreases of neural activity as measured by their output of action potentials. This fact constitutes an important general limitation of EP amplitude measures as indexes of underlying neural activity. While in some cases relationships between EP and firing patterns do exist, these relationships have to be validated directly over a wide range of conditions in experimental animals before inferences can be drawn. Such data are not yet available in behaving animals and, until they are, EP amplitude data must be interpreted with great circumspection.

The scalp distributions of EP to auditory, visual, or somatosensory stimulation are widespread. Furthermore, as can be seen in Fig. 2, the amplitudes of their later components are maximal at or near the vertex. These observations gave rise to a long and strongly held belief that these so-called "vertex potentials" reflect activity in a diffusely projecting thalamocortical system. As we shall see, this presumption has had implications for evoked potential investigations of attention. However, careful mapping of the EP, combined with an analysis based upon a quantitative volume conduction model, shows that the scalp EP distributions are, in fact, consistent with intracranial sources in and near the respective primary cortical projection areas. Thus, the localization of maximum auditory EP amplitude near the vertex reflects the orientation of auditory cortex within the Sylvian fissure, perpendicular to the overlying scalp, rather than the proximity of active cortex to the recording electrode. In fact, electrodes placed directly over the primary auditory cortex show no EP at all (Vaughan & Ritter, 1970). In addition to their occipital generators, the visual EP show a secondary source

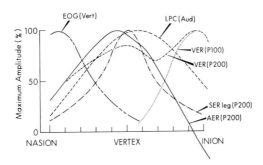

Fig. 2. Amplitude distributions for various ERP components recorded along the mid-sagittal line. Each distribution has been scaled with reference to the point of maximum amplitude. Abbreviations: AER, auditory-evoked response; SER, somatosensory-evoked response; VER, visual-evoked response; LPC, late positive component of the ACP; EOG, electrooculogram. P_{100} and P_{200} refer to the positive components which peak at 100 and 200 msec, respectively.

in the precentral region, which presumably reflects the polysensory projections to motor cortex described by Albe-Fessard and Liebeskind (1966). The somatosensory responses also arise from precentral as well as postcentral areas (Vaughan, Costa, & Ritter, 1968; Stohr & Goldring, 1969; Goldring, Aras, & Weber, 1970). A similar motor cortex projection for auditory EP has not as yet been observed.

Changes in EP amplitude recorded from a single scalp electrode may reflect alterations in either the magnitude or the spatial distribution of the cortical response. Due to volume conduction considerations, a less extensive source equal in strength to a larger one will produce a smaller EP. Thus, in order to make inferences concerning the significance in changes of EP amplitude, it is necessary to determine the response distribution. Despite the critical importance of data on the intracranial sources of EP, this factor rarely has entered into the design and interpretation of experiments involving EP measures.

The complex relationships that have been demonstrated between stimulus parameters and EP measures make it impossible to presume a simple relationship between the EP and sensation. Relatively few studies have directly sought such relationships, but some encouraging results have been obtained. For example, Vaughan and Silverstein (1968) found a close quantitative relationship between the amount of brightness suppression in a metacontrast experiment and the reduction in area of the P_{200} component of the visual EP. It is likely, however, now that methods for more precisely defining intracranial sources are available, that attempts to directly relate perceptual and EP variables may be rewarding. We recently have begun to analyze the spatial extent of cortical response to various kinds of visual stimuli, including pictorial and verbal material. These studies suggest that changes in luminance of unpatterned stimuli elicit responses predominantly in striate cortex, whereas patterned stimuli produce relatively sizable prestriate EP. Thus, future studies of EP and visual function will have to take into account changes in source geometry due to stimulus parameters.

The duration of the EP might conceivably reflect the duration of physiological processes underlying perception of a brief stimulus. Thus, Efron (1970b) has concluded that visual perceptions have a minimum duration in the range 120–240 msec, and that the auditory minimum duration lies between 120 and 170 msec. These times are similar to the period of the large EP deflections, which begin 50 msec or so after the stimulus. It should be profitable to directly explore this relationship, and to extend the analysis to a consideration of possible EP correlates of short term visual storage (Averbach & Sperling, 1961).

B. The Motor Potentials (MP)

The ERP related to motor acts have been designated "motor potentials" (Gilden, Vaughan, & Costa, 1966). These potentials, derived from scalp recordings by averaging with respect to onset of a repeated muscle contraction, comprise three components (Fig. 3).

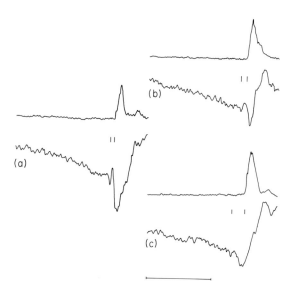

Fig. 3. Rectified and averaged EMG (upper trace) and average MP (lower traces) associated with (a) unilateral facial contraction, (b) clenching fist, and (c) foot dorsiflexion. Upward deflections are positive in polarity. Time line: 1 sec. (Reprinted from Vaughan *et al.*, 1968.)

1. A slow negative shift called the "readiness potential" by Kornhuber and Deecke (1965) precedes the onset of contraction by as much as one second.

2. A sharp negative or positive–negative deflection shortly precedes the contraction by an interval that depends both on the nature of the motor task and the specific muscle utilized. For the same task, differences in delay between this component of the MP and the onset of EMG activity (the corticomuscular delay, CMD) reflects the length of the conduction path from brain to muscle. In various tasks (for example, self-paced contractions as compared with RT), differences in the CMD seem to reflect changes in the time required for organization of the motor act.

3. A large, slow positive potential accompanies and follows the contraction to complete the MP.

The three components of the MP possess a similar scalp distribution, their maximum overlying the precentral region in a position corresponding to the somatotopic organization of motor cortex (Vaughan et al., 1968). For hand movements, an ipsilateral as well as a contralateral focus of activity is present, which varies considerably in relative prominence from individual to individual.

The functional significance of the three MP components can only be surmised. It seems reasonable to suppose that the slow shift generated within motor cortex reflects preparatory mechanisms, but whether these represent primarily an excitatory or inhibitory cortical state or, what is more likely, a complex organizational process representing establishment of a specific motor set is entirely unknown. Interpretation of the phasic antecedent potential is on somewhat firmer ground, since its timing is comparable to the surge of pyramidal tract neuron activity which has been recorded before hand movements in the monkey (Evarts, 1966). The functional significance of the large, positive component is obscure. Although it first was thought to reflect kinesthetic feedback, limb deafferentation fails to alter it (Vaughan, Bossom, & Gross, 1970).

Although the MP can be recorded in isolation only when self-paced movements are performed, they can be uncovered in recordings containing concurrent EP, as in RT experiments, by subtracting the data recorded during a no-response condition from that obtained during the sensorimotor task. This technique permits an estimate of CMD in RT tasks (Vaughan et al., 1965; Vaughan & Costa, 1968).

However, due to the variable RT on the trials entering into each average, it is necessary to segregate trials with similar RT so as to synchronize both the stimulus and the response. Data obtained by this procedure are depicted in Fig. 4. It can be seen that the ERP averages recorded from occipital and motor regions in a simple visual RT task vary primarily in ampli-

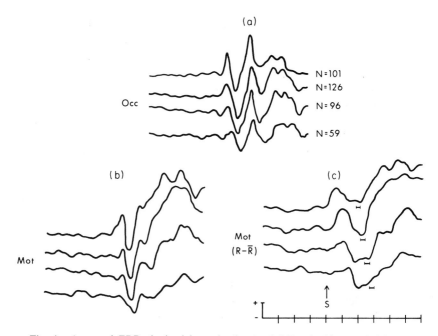

Fig. 4. Averaged ERP obtained in a simple visual RT task: (a) recorded from mid-occipital electrode referred to linked ears; (b,c) taken from an electrode placed overlying the estimated position of the left-hand area also referred to linked ears. ERP data has been segregated into four sets according to RT: 180–210 msec; 210–240 msec; 240–270 msec; 270–300 msec. The number of individual trials in each average is indicated to the right of the upper traces. Sets (a) and (b) depict ERP recorded during performance of the RT task. The data in set (c) are obtained by subtracting a comparable number of trials on which no response was made to the visual stimulus. By this method the cerebral potentials (MP) related to the motor response are uncovered and approximately synchronized (± 15 msec). Note that the EP recorded from occipital and motor leads show primarily a decrease in amplitude with increasing RT with only minor shifts in latency, whereas the timing of the motor potentials follows the RT more closely. Calibration: 2.5 μV, 100 msec/division.

tude when divided into four ERP sets corresponding to increasing RT. When the visual EP recorded in response to the same stimuli under a no-response condition are subtracted from the RT data, the MP associated with the motor responses are disclosed. These MP progressively increase in latency approximately in parallel with the RT increase of each set.

C. Association Cortex Potentials (ACP)

When a stimulus becomes potentially significant for the organism, either by its unexpected presentation or incorporation into a task requiring its identification, a new potential appears. This was originally described as a long-latency positive component of the EP by Sutton, Braren, and Zubin (1965), who found it when *S*s were required to guess the identity of a subsequent signal selected from a small set of possible stimuli. Later, it was discovered that a similar component appeared whenever a stimulus was presented unexpectedly (Ritter, Vaughan, & Costa, 1968) or when a sensory discrimination was required (Ritter & Vaughan, 1969). By mapping the distribution of cortical responses obtained under conditions eliciting this late component, we found (Vaughan, 1969; Vaughan & Ritter, 1970) that these potentials could be readily differentiated from the sensory EP on the basis of their topography, which was consistent with an origin in the parietotemporal cortex. Accordingly, we designate these responses "association cortex potentials." Although overlapping the sensory EP in time, the earlier components of the ACP can be observed for auditory stimulation by placing the active recording electrode on the null-potential line for the specific auditory EP overlying the Sylvian fissure. Then it is seen that the ACP begins only a short time later than the specific EP and comprises predominantly a negative-positive waveform, of which only the latter peak ("P_3") is ordinarily visible in the averaged scalp record (Fig. 5).

The ACP differ importantly from the EP in respect to the factors determining their latency and amplitude: EP parameters being primarily defined by stimulus variables, and the ACP by task variables or stimulus

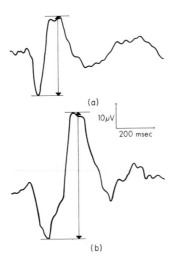

(a)

10μV

200 msec

(b)

Fig. 5. Average auditory EP (a) to 100 tones presented at 2-sec intervals, (b) ACP to 20 tones presented at irregular, infrequent intervals. Arrows indicate the P_{200} component of the auditory EP and the late positive component of the ACP, sometimes called P_3 or P_{300}. (Reprinted from Vaughan & Ritter, 1970.)

significance. In contrast to the EP, which are stable in latency for given stimulus parameters, the ACP show remarkable fluctuations in latency. Both the nature and difficulty of the task (as objectively defined by RT) are associated with shifts in peak latency of the positive component of the ACP, which varies from about 300 msec to at least 550 msec in the vigilance and discrimination tasks we have studied. More difficult tasks are associated with longer latency and generally smaller ACP. Furthermore, within a block of trials, the latency of individual ACP can be seen to vary widely. Reaction time and ACP latency have a product moment correlation of about .7 in vigilance tasks so that an average ACP, whether computed with reference to stimulus or response, does not depict accurately either the average amplitude of individual ACP or changes in amplitude across conditions in which the variability in latency of the ACP differ. Any situation in which the dispersion of ACP latency (and RT) is increased will yield average ACP of diminished amplitude, even though the individual ACP amplitudes were to remain constant. As yet, all of the factors influencing averaged ACP amplitude have not been elucidated, but, among them, latency variability must always be considered. Since most experiments to date have not assessed such variance, P_3 amplitude measurements must be viewed with caution for this reason, as well as for the previously stated limitations on the validity of ERP amplitude measures.

D. THE STEADY POTENTIAL SHIFTS (SPS)

Potential shifts of greater duration than the transients heretofore described (that is, > 500 msec) are commonly called steady potential shifts. These were initially described by Köhler, Held, and O'Donnell (1952) in response to auditory and visual stimulation in cats and human subjects. Steady potential shifts were later described as correlates of changes in arousal level (Caspers, 1963), and in motivational state (Rowland, 1968). However, the most celebrated SPS was proposed by Walter and colleagues (Walter, Cooper, Aldridge, McCallum, & Winter, 1964) as a cortical sign of conditioning. This negative SPS, designated the "contingent negative variation" or CNV, appeared following the warning signal in a fixed fore-period simple RT task.

Although the CNV was described initially as a cortical sign of expectancy, attention or development of a conditioned response to the pairing of the "conditional" and the "imperative" stimuli, and was alleged to originate from widespread sources in frontal cortex, subsequent investigations by Walter and others have led to a number of modifications and qualifications of the early descriptions. Low, Borda, Frost, and Kellaway (1966) suggested that the "CNV" reflected, primarily, conative processes. As already mentioned, averaging of EEG traces with respect to a self-paced motor contraction in the absence of external stimulation yields a slow negative shift morphologically similar to the CNV. This "readiness potential" is largest over the central region contralateral to the responding hand (Vaughan et al., 1968; McAdam & Seales, 1969). It seems likely therefore, that, in experiments which require preparation for a motor response, the CNV does reflect, at least in part, processes related to motor set. However, a number of experiments have substantiated the assertion by Walter and colleagues that an overt motor response is not required for the prior appearance of a negative SPS. These shifts have been reported prior to regular repetitive stimulation to which subjects' attention was directed (Faidherbe, 1967), but in most instances the anticipated stimulus either provides information or signals the onset of a perceptual or cognitive task (Walter, 1967; Donald, 1970; Donchin, Gerbrandt, & Leifer, 1971). These experiments seem to rule out the necessity of a motor response for development of the CNV and provide support for a functional interpretation involving a more general state of expectancy. An analysis of the spatial distribution of the SPS recorded in these experiments has not been carried out so that it is not known whether the sources are similar to those found in the SRT paradigm. We (Vaughan, 1969) as well as others (Garcia-Austt & Bûno, 1969) have observed negative SPS overlying the occipital region in tasks requiring a visual discrimination, but these potential shifts have not been reliably reproducible in repeated experiments on the same subject, and are not found at all in some subjects. Others also have experienced difficulty in obtaining reliable SPS data, despite careful attention to the technical requirements for recording them. Several investigators (for example, Hillyard & Galambos, 1970; Straumanis, Shagass, & Overton, 1969) have noted that the CNV is frequently contaminated by negative shifts due to vertical eye movements, so that the localization of the CNV to the anterior frontal region has been called into question. A CNV map obtained under conditions in which eye movements were controlled (Cohen, 1969) indicates a maximum amplitude overlying central and anterior parietal cortex. In view of the possibility that a number of intracranial sources may be contributing to the scalp-recorded SPS, suggested by the earlier animal data, as well as the existence of extracranial sources of potential shifts (skin and corneoretinal potentials) a good deal of work remains to distinguish fact from artifact in human scalp SPS recordings.

IV. Some Approaches to the Analysis of Attention and Performance

The problem of attention, despite a recent vigorous resurgence of interest in the psychological and physiological aspects of this venerable topic, still embodies most of the nebulous empirical and conceptual difficulties which disposed the behaviorists to expunge the term from the psychological vocabulary. At a recent conference on Attention in Neurophysiology, Berlyne (1969) commented: "Hitherto, there has been a tendency for neurophysiologists to assume that the psychologists know what attention is and for psychologists in turn to assume that the neurophysiologists know." Physiologists, as might be gathered from this remark, have generally taken a fairly casual view toward the need for a precise behavioral definition of attention. Their conception of attention seems to be rather simple. Attention has to do with whether or not *stimulus* information reaches some unspecified level within the nervous system. It is assumed that the afferent activity generated by unattended stimuli gets suppressed somewhere along the way, and, conversely, that activity generated by attended stimuli is likely to be enhanced relative to neutral stimuli. Thus, physiological contributions have been limited to speculation on the neural structures involved in the enhancement or suppression of sensory input, and attempts to demonstrate the existence of the postulated afferent modulation.

Thinking on the physiological basis of attention has been dominated during the past two decades by the important insights which have been gained into the role of the reticular formation in the modulation of arousal. Penfield (1938), arguing from clinical experience with the effects of epilepsy and electrical stimulation of the cortex on the conscious state, proposed that consciousness is mediated by mechanisms located within the central core of the brain, near the midbrain and hypothalamus. This prescient suggestion was provided experimental support by Magoun and his colleagues (Moruzzi & Magoun, 1949; Lindsley, Schreiner, Knowles, & Magoun, 1950), who demonstrated the critical role of the midbrain reticular formation in the EEG and behavioral manifestations of arousal. Subsequently, the notion that the "nonspecific" thalamic nuclei, which are the cerebral extensions of the brain-stem reticular formation, control focal and phasic shifts in cortical activation related to selective attention has gained wide currency (Jasper, 1960). As yet, however, direct physiologic evidence for or against this hypothesis has not been presented. Furthermore, it is not known what sort of modulation has to be accounted for by the mechanisms of attention attributed to the thalamic reticular system.

For a number of years, experimental studies in this field were dominated by Hernandez-Peon (1961) and his co-workers. He employed two basic experimental procedures:

1. Sensory-evoked potentials were recorded to monotonously repeated stimuli. It was presumed that the animal would attend initially to the stimuli and then, when the stimuli were found to be insignificant, ignore them. The EP amplitudes were assumed to covary with these fluctuations in attention. The experimental approach was comparable to studies of habituation of the orienting reflex (Sokolov, 1963).

2. Repetitive stimuli whose evoked responses were monitored were delivered before, during, and after presentation of a highly significant stimulus in another sensory modality. It was assumed that the repeated stimuli were not attended during presentation of the distracting stimulus.

In both experimental situations, it was reported that potentials recorded at the first nucleus of the respective sensory pathways were attenuated when the stimuli were presumed to be unattended. These findings led to the hypothesis of afferent neuronal inhibition, which postulated a centrifugal inhibitory action of the reticular formation on the specific sensory nucleus when a perceptual or behavioral response in that modality was suppressed. The experimental findings of Hernandez-Peon have been criticized extensively and effectively (Horn, 1965; Worden, 1966) so that the role of centrifugal modulation of afferent activity in sensory and attentive processes remains undefined.

A major flaw in the hypothesis of afferent neuronal inhibition is its inconsistency with the evidence from psychological studies (Moray, 1959) that unattended sensory data reach far enough along in processing so that stimuli carrying significant semantic information can elicit responses. Since these responses are dependent not upon the physical parameters, but rather on the cognitive significance of the stimulus, peripheral input attenuation would seem at most to represent but a limited feature of attentional mechanisms.

Other efforts to detect evidence of attentional effects on input have observed EP at the cortical level. Many of these studies have employed human averaged EP as the physiologic index. The experimental approaches again have employed habituation of EP as a criterion of loss of attention, or have sought EP changes when attention is paid to one class of stimuli while another set is being ignored concurrently. The several studies of EP habituation in man and experimental animals have utilized averages of sequential blocks of stimuli, often presented over long periods of time. Gradual decrements in EP amplitude across stimulus blocks have been identified with waning of attention (for example, Garcia-Austt, 1963). Three criticisms can be directed toward these studies. First, there is no behavioral evidence to link decrement in EP amplitude to decrease in sensory response. Thus, a direct relation between EP amplitude and attention must be viewed merely as an assumption. Second, arousal level has not been controlled in these studies, so that gradual response decrements might well be related to waning of alertness rather than to changes specific to attention. Finally, habituation of orienting responses to nonsignificant stimuli requires but a few unreinforced stimulus presentations, rather than the hundreds or thousands of stimuli utilized in the average response studies. It was to deal with the latter objection that we devised a method for stimulus by stimulus assessment of changes in the human averaged auditory EP (Ritter *et al.*, 1968). We presented short blocks of stimuli, each block separated by several minutes of distracting activity. The EP to each of the individual stimuli within a block then was averaged across blocks to evaluate the stimulus by stimulus change in EP. With this technique, we found a striking attenuation in amplitude of EP over the first few stimuli, but only when an interstimulus interval (ISI) of 2 sec was employed. When the stimuli were separated by 10 sec, no amplitude decrement occurred. This sort of result has been employed in the literature as evidence for habituation, since a characteristic of habituation is its acceleration with shortening of the ISI. Nevertheless, the relevance of such findings for attention seems doubtful. The stimuli employed in these experiments were tone bursts. When the procedure was repeated using brief light flashes with a 2-sec ISI, no decrement in EP amplitude was observed. There is no reason to suppose that, when stimuli are presented at the rate of 1 every 2 sec, attention rapidly wanes if the stimuli are tones but is maintained if the stimuli are flashes. A more reasonable explanation is based on the fact that the maximum amplitude of auditory EP is obtained with an ISI of about 10 sec (Davis, Mast, Yoshie, & Zerlin, 1966), whereas it is under 2 sec for visual EP recorded under the conditions employed in our study. Thus, EP were maximal in amplitude for the first stimulus of a run and decreased rapidly to the appropriate steady-state amplitude if subsequent stimuli were delivered at intervals less than that required for full recovery (as with the 2-sec. ISI for tones), and maintained their amplitude when subsequent stimuli permitted full recovery (as with the 10-sec ISI for tones and the 2-sec ISI for flashes).

Of greater significance for physiologic correlates of attention was our discovery that stimuli unexpected by virtue of their timing or physical parameters elicited a large, long latency (300-msec) potential, which we subsequently identified as an ACP. These stimuli were associated with subjective orienting (when the tones were presented during reading). Association cortex potentials were seen only with unpredictable stimulus changes and, in contrast to the amplitude changes in the earlier components, were not dependent upon the ISI.

Directly concerned with selective attention are the experiments which direct the attention of the subject to one class of stimuli to the exclusion of another, either by requiring a response to one and not the other, or merely by instruction to attend (Tecce, 1970). The results of these experiments have been discouragingly inconsistent. Most of the human studies have been concerned with amplitude changes in the P_{200} EP components. This wave has been viewed as a nonspecific response reflecting activity in the "diffuse" projections from midbrain and thalamus, without, however, any direct evidence for this presumption. Although some studies have found increments in amplitude to attended or cue stimuli as compared with unattended or neutral stimuli, as a whole the changes were rather small, inconsistent across subjects, and sometimes opposite in direction. Similarly discordant results have been obtained in animal experiments on selective attention.

The main criticism addressed to both the animal and human experiments on selective attention is that the amplitude of sensory-evoked potentials is affected by the S's state of arousal, and that, when state of arousal for attended versus unattended stimuli is controlled, as in Näätänen's vigilance experiments (1967), no differences in amplitude of the P_{200} component may be found between relevant and irrelevant classes of stimuli.

Perhaps the most serious reservation concerning attempts to relate attention to enhanced EP has to do with the contribution that such a finding might make toward elucidating the mechanism underlying attention. If EP were indeed blocked early in the afferent pathways, this could reflect an important part of the mechanisms subserving attention. But no investigator has suggested how small changes in cortical EP amplitude could clarify the physiology of attention. One possibility involves a threshold mechanism, such that only neural activity reflected by an EP exceeding a certain amplitude would be interconnected with later processing stages. The difficulty with this or any other attempt to relate the amplitude of sensory EP to the mechanisms of attention is that the amplitude of EP is affected by a number of factors, including state of arousal, stimulus intensity, and interstimulus interval. Thus, the amplitude of the P_{200} auditory EP component is five times bigger with a 6-sec ISI than with a .5-sec ISI (Davis *et al.*, 1966). Since the effect of interstimulus interval on the amplitude of EP is independent of whether the S attends the stimuli and has no apparent correlation with sensory magnitude, it is difficult to believe that much smaller changes in EP amplitude reflect the means by which the nervous system accomplishes selective attention.

On the other hand, if it could be shown that attended stimuli elicit a physiological response not elicited at all by unattended stimuli, a case could be made for this response as a correlate of the postulated attentional mechanism. It would be attractive to consider the ACP as a candidate. However, stimuli do not elicit ACP merely by instructional direction of attention to them. Our experience indicates that ACP are generated only when:

1. stimuli not requiring an overt response are presented infrequently (> 30-sec ISI) either alone or imbedded within sequences of dissimilar stimuli (Ritter *et al.*, 1968);

2. repeated stimuli to which a motor response is required are presented at somewhat shorter intervals (Ritter & Vaughan, unpublished data; Bostock & Jarvis, 1970);

3. tasks requiring a discrimination between stimuli, as in choice RT, vigilance, and in sequential paired comparison (Ritter & Vaughan, 1969);

4. the stimulus informs the subject as to the correctness of a prior guess (Sutton *et al.*, 1965).

The first condition can be considered as *eliciting* an attentional (orienting) response in contrast to the others wherein attention is directed in *anticipation* of the cue stimulus.

Common to all of the situations in which an ACP is elicited is the element of stimulus uncertainty, whether in timing or physical parameters. Thus, we might suppose that ACP are generated when the occurrence of a specific stimulus is not predicted in advance of its appearance. This hypothesis could account for some odd aspects of ACP behavior. We observed that ACP were present only in response to the signal stimuli in a vigilance task where the signals occurred in 10% of the trials (Ritter & Vaughan, 1969). This result is consistent with the tendency for ACP to be larger with decreasing probabilities of stimulus occurrence, whether in the guessing situation of Sutton and colleagues (Tueting, Sutton, & Zubin, 1971) or when no overt task or significance is associated with the stimuli, as in our early experiments. Yet, when the difficulty of the discrimination between infrequent signals and frequent nonsignals was increased, ACP were observed to *all* stimuli. This result led us to conclude that the ACP could not merely reflect stimulus uncertainty or the occurrence of a mismatch in the comparison between a template for predicted stimulus and the (infrequent) signal stimulus, but must be related to a less clearly specifiable operation which we vaguely designated "cognitive stimulus evaluation." One possibility is that this mechanism involves selection and retrieval from the set of relevant templates, only one of which can be held in readiness at a given time. Present data do not permit further speculation on the functional significance of the ACP, but it is clear from the nature of the conditions under which it is elicited that it must represent some stage of information processing between stimulus and response related processes.

Further progress in elucidating the physiology of attentive processes will require a more satisfactory definition of the behavioral features of the construct. In risking a definition of attention that might provide a suitable focus for future physiologic investigations, we are inclined to consider the properties that seem on purely experiential grounds to comprise the salient features of attention. While it may not be possible to formulate an operational definition suitable for experimental analysis on this basis, the essential features of attention are identified most readily from phenomenological data. Attempts to reduce attention to a strictly behavioral concept seem to be no more sensible or productive than the pretension that sensation is a form of behavior. A clear distinction must be made between the demands for experimental objectivity and the characterization of the phenomena that are being subjected to analysis. Thus, perception, cognition, emotion, and volition are attributes of experience, and their behavioral manifestations are both functionally derivative and temporally subsequent. We know that sensations, thoughts, and emotions can be elicited by electrical stimulation of the appropriate brain regions. The electrical stimulus elicits physiological responses underlying the experiences which in principle, can be recorded and analyzed. So the sequencing of ordinary subjective experience must be associated with concurrent physiologic processes that we can detect and study. Thus, from a physiologic standpoint, a comprehensive definition of attention comprising the full range of its experiential and behavioral attributes may be preferable to a fragmentary and incomplete definition based only on experimentally observable parameters. Accordingly, we mention the following properties that seem characteristic of attention:

1. Attention may be directed selectively toward sensations, thoughts, emotions, or actions, singly or in combination. This multiplicity of object seems to us a key feature of attention, entirely neglected in experimental approaches that focus exclusively upon the role of attention in input modulation. The various objects of attention interact in an apparently restrictive manner. Thus, involvement in a difficult motor task tends to reduce the capacity to engage concurrently in unrelated cognitive or perceptual activity. Similarly, deep thought seems to be accompanied by a screening out of interfering sensations and to preclude all but automatic motor activity.

2. As a corollary of the first point, the capacity of attention is limited. But this limitation seems to be flexible and dependent upon the nature of the task under consideration as well as the content of the material. Thus, when attentively contemplating an esthetic experience, the amount of sensory information being actively incorporated into the experience is enormously greater than that processed during a difficult sensory discrimination task. Yet in both instances, objects outside the "focus of attention" are largely excluded from consciousness, despite the apparent disparity in the quantity of information being processed.

3. Attention may be generated by external or internal events, either involuntarily or apparently under volitional (that is, cognitive) control.

These are the "passive" and "active" modes of attention described by James (1890).

4. Attention seems to be involved primarily in situations wherein shifts in mode of information processing are required. From a teleological viewpoint, attention may be regarded as a process which permits or facilitates adaptive modifications of information processing.

The most difficult aspects of attention to deal with experimentally are those in which the processing of stimuli are not the primary consideration; thus, we may attend to internal events, cognitive, affective or conative, that may or may not become manifest as overt behavior. Such manifestations of attention are only experienced by the individual and may, of course, be subsequently reported by him, despite the absence of immediate overt behavioral expression. It is these aspects of attention that provide the strongest evidence for relating attention to the physiologic processes underlying conscious experience, since the unifying factor in all aspects of attention, whether or not it is associated with external stimulation, is the selective awareness of a limited set of brain operations. From a physiologic standpoint, such a process would necessarily involve the interaction of a number of brain mechanisms, subserving sensation, motor functions, drives, and language, that possess some identified structural substrates. Other components, such as the neural systems implicated in short- and long-term memory, remain largely unknown, even as to location. A useful physiologic formulation of attention will nevertheless require knowledge of when and where these processes occur within the brain.

Experimental approaches of necessity will converge from the two directly observable events: stimulus and response. Analysis of the neurophysiological substrate of perceptual selectivity will increasingly involve studies of the cortical and thalamic regions that receive projections from the primary projection areas. Study of the human association cortex potentials can be expected to articulate with complementary work in animals, such as the ongoing analysis of the role of inferotemporal cortex and pulvinar in vision (Gross, in press). Working in the opposite direction, we are currently (Arezzo & Vaughan, unpublished) recording the potentials that accompany hand movements in monkeys from a large number of cortical and subcortical locations, in an attempt to trace the spatiotemporal sequence of neural activity leading to voluntary movements.

In our view, meaningful direct experimental approaches to the physiological mechanisms underlying selective attention remain to be formulated. The burden of our argument rests upon the belief that the processes collectively labeled "attention" represent the highest order of cerebral organization, and that their elucidation will involve the analysis of dynamic connections among many brain systems. Once it is acknowledged that attention must be viewed as a manifestation of extraordinarily complex and varied neural transactions, the fruitless search for simple "neurophysiological correlates of attention" finally will be abandoned.

References

Albe-Fessard, D., & Liebeskind, J. Origine des messages somatosensitifs activant les cellules du cortex moteur chez le singe. *Experimental Brain Research*, 1966, **1**, 127–146.

Averbach, E., & Sperling, G. Short term storage of information in vision. In C. Cherry (Ed.), *Information theory*. London: Butterworth, 1961. Pp. 196–211.

Berlyne, D. E. The development of the concept of attention in psychology. In C. R. Evans and T. B. Mulholland (Eds.), *Attention in neurophysiology*. New York: Appleton, 1969. Pp. 1–26.

Bernhard, C. G. Contributions to the neurophysiology of the optic pathway. *Acta Physiologica Scandinavica*, 1940, **1**, Suppl. 1.

Bostock, H., & Jarvis, M. J. Changes in the form of the cerebral evoked response related to the speed of simple reaction time. *Electroencephalography and Clinical Neurophysiology*, 1970, **29**, 137–145.

Caspers, H. Relations of steady potential shifts in the cortex to the wakefulness-sleep spectrum. In M. A. B. Brazier (Ed.), *Brain function*, UCLA Forum in Medical Sciences, No. 1. Berkeley: University of California Press, 1963. Pp. 177–214.

Cohen, J. Very slow brain potentials relating to expectancy: the CNV. In E. Donchin and D. B. Lindsley (Eds.), *Averaged evoked potentials: methods, results, evaluations*, NASA SP-191. Washington, D.C.: National Aeronautics and Space Administration, 1969. Pp. 143–198.

Cruikshank, R. M. Human occipital brain potentials as effected by intensity-duration variables of visual stimulation. *Journal of Experimental Psychology*, 1937, **21**, 625–641.

Davis, H., Mast, T., Yoshie, N., & Zerlin, S. The slow response of the human cortex to auditory stimuli: Recovery process. *Electroencephalography and Clinical Neurophysiology*, 1966, **21**, 105–113.

Donald, M. W. Direct-current potentials in the human brain evoked during timed cognitive performance. *Nature*, 1970, **227**, 1057–1058.

Donchin, E., Gerbrandt, L. K. & Leifer, L. Is the contingent negative variation contingent on a motor response? *Electroencephalography and clinical Neurophysiology*, 1971, **31**, 299.

Donders, F. C. Die Schnelligkeit Psychischer Prozesse. *Archiv für Anatomie und Physiologie und wissenschaftliche Medizin*, 1868, 657–681.

Efron, R. The minimum duration of a perception. *Neuropsychologia*, 1970, **8**, 57–63. (a)

Efron, R. The relationship between the duration of a stimulus and the duration of a perception. *Neuropsychologia*, 1970, **8**, 37–55. (b)

Evarts, E. V. Pyramidal tract activity associated with a conditioned hand movement in the monkey. *Journal of Neurophysiology*, 1966, **29**, 1011–1027.

Faidherbe, J. Étude de la signification psychophysiologique de certaines composantes lentes des potentiels évoqués électroencéphalographiques. *Archives Internationales de Physiologie et de Biochimie*, 1967, **75**, 861–864.

Garcia-Austt, E. Influence of the states of awareness upon sensory evoked potentials. *Electroencephalography and Clinical Neurophysiology Suppl. 24*, 1963, 76–89.

Garcia-Austt, E., & Bûno, W., Jr. Relationships between visual evoked responses and some psychological processes. In C. R. Evans & T. B. Mulholland (Eds.), *Attention in neurophsiology*. New York: Appleton; 1969. Pp. 258–280.

Gilden, L., Vaughan, H. G., Jr., & Costa, L. D. Summated human EEG potentials associated with voluntary movement. *Electroencephalography and Clinical Neurophysiology*, 1966, **20**, 433–438.

Goldring, S., Aras, E., & Weber, P. C. Comparative study of sensory input to motor cortex in animals and man. *Electroencephalography and Clinical Neurophysiology*, 1970, **29**, 537–550.

Gross, C. G. Visual functions of inferotemporal cortex. In R. Jung (Ed.), *Handbook of sensory physiology*. Vol. 7, Part 3. New York: Springer Publ. In press.

Haber, R. N., & Standing, L. G. Direct estimates of the apparent duration of a flash. *Canadian Journal of Psychology*, 1970, **24**, 216–229.

Hernandez-Peon, R. Reticular mechanisms of sensory control. In W. A. Rosenblith (Ed.), *Sensory communication*. New York: MIT Press and Wiley, 1961. Pp. 497–520.

Hillyard, S. A., & Galambos, R. Eye movement artifact in the CNV. *Electroencephalography and Clinical Neurophysiology*, 1970, **28**, 173–182.

Horn, G. Physiological and psychological aspects of selective perception. In D. S. Lehrman, R. A. Hinde, and E. Shaw (Eds.), *Advances in the study of behavior*. Vol. I. New York: Academic Press, 1965. Pp. 155–215.

James, W. Attention. In *Principles of psychology*. Vol. 1. New York: Holt, 1890. Pp. 402–458.

Jasper, H. H. Unspecific thalamocortical relations. In J. Field (Ed.), *Handbook of physiology*. Section I: *Neurophysiology*. Vol. II. Washington: American Physiological Society, 1960. Pp. 1307–1321.

Köhler, W., Held, R., & O'Donnell, D. N. An investigation of cortical currents. *Proceedings of the American Philosophical Society*, 1952, **96**, 290–330.

Kornhuber, H. H., & Deecke, L. Hirnpotentialänderungen bei Willkürbewegungen und Passiven Bewegungen des Menschen: Bereitschaftspotential und Reafferente Pontentiale. *Pflügers Archiv*, 1965, **284**, 1–17.

Lindsley, D. B., Schreiner, L. H., Knowles, W. B., & Magoun, H. W. Behavioral and EEG changes following chronic brain stem lesions in the cat. *Electroencephalography and Clinical Neurophysiology*, 1950, **2**, 483–498.

Low, M. D., Borda, R. P., Frost, J. D., & Kellaway, P. Surface-negative, slow-potential shift associated with conditioning in man. *Neurology*, 1966, **16**, 771–782.

McAdam, D. W., & Seales, D. M. *Bereitschaftspotential* enhancement with increased level of motivation. *Electroencephalography and clinical Neurophysiology*, 1969, **27**, 73–75.

Miller, J. M., & Glickstein, M. Neural circuits involved in visuomotor reaction time in monkeys. *Journal of Neurophysiology*, 1967, **30**, 399–414.

Monnier, M. Retinal time, retinocortical time, alpha blocking time and motor reaction time. *Electroencephalography and Clinical Neurophysiology*, 1949, **1**, 516–517.

Moray, N. Attention in dichotic listening; affective cues and the influence of instructions. *Quarterly Journal of Experimental Psychology*, 1959, **11**, 56–60.

Moruzzi, G., & Magoun, H. W. Brain stem reticular formation and activation of EEG. *Electroencephalography and Clinical Neurophysiology*, 1949, **1**, 455–473.

Näätänen, R. Selective attention and evoked potentials. *Annales Academiae Scientiarium Fennicae B151*, 1967, **1**, 1–226.

Penfield, W. The cerebral cortex in man. I: The cerebral cortex and consciousness. *Archives of Neurology and Psychiatry*, 1938, **40**, 417–442.

Ritter, W., & Vaughan, H. G., Jr. Averaged evoked responses in vigilance and discrimination: a reassessment. *Science*, 1969, **164**, 326–328.

Ritter, W., Vaughan, H. G., Jr., & Costa, L. D. Orienting and habituation to auditory stimuli: A study of short term changes in average evoked responses. *Electroencephalography and Clinical Neurophysiology*, 1968, **25**, 550–556.

Rowland, V. Cortical steady potential (direct current potential) in reinforcement and learning. In E. Stellar and J. M. Sprague (Eds.), *Progress in physiological psychology*. New York: Academic Press, 1968 Pp. 1–77.

Sherrington, C. S. *The integrative action of the nervous system.* New York: Scribner, 1906.

Sokolov, Y. N. *Perception and the conditioned reflex.* New York: Macmillan, 1963.

Sternberg, S. Memory scanning: Mental processes revealed by reaction-time experiments. *American Scientist*, 1969, **57**, 421–457. (a)

Sternberg, S. The discovery of processing stages: extensions of Donders' method. In W. G. Koster (Ed.), *Attention and performance II.* Amsterdam: North-Holland Publ. 1969. Pp. 276–315. (Reprinted from *Acta Psychologica*, 1969, **30**.) (b)

Stohr, P. E., & Goldring, S. Origin of somatosensory evoked scalp responses in man. *Journal of Neurosurgery*, 1969, **31**, 117–127.

Straumanis, H., Shagass, C., & Overton, D. A. Problems associated with the application of the contingent negative variation to psychiatric research. *Journal of Nervous and Mental Disease*, 1969, **148**, 170–179.

Sutton, S., Braren, M., & Zubin, J. Evoked potential correlates of stimulus uncertainty. *Science*, 1965, **150**, 1187–1188.

Tecce, J. J. Attention and evoked potentials in man. In D. I. Mostofsky (Ed.), *Attention: contemporary theory and analysis.* New York: Appleton, 1970. Pp. 331–366.

Tueting, P., Sutton, S., & Zubin, J. Quantitative evoked potential correlates of the probability of events. *Psychophysiology*, 1971, **7**, 385–394.

Vaughan, H. G., Jr. The relationship of brain activity to scalp recordings of event-related potentials. In E. Donchin and D. B. Lindsley (Eds.), *Averaged evoked potentials. methods, results, evaluations.* NASA SP-191. Washington, D.C.: National Aeronautics and Space Administration 1969. Pp. 45–94.

Vaughan, H. G., Jr., & Costa, L. D. Analysis of electroencephalographic correlates of human sensorimotor processes. *Electroencephalography and Clinical Neurophysiology*, 1968, **24**, 288.

Vaughan, H. G., Jr., & Ritter, W., The sources of auditory evoked responses recorded from the human scalp. *Electroencephalography and Clinical Neurophysiology*, 1970, **28**, 360–367.

Vaughan, H. G., Jr., & Silverstein, L. Metacontrast and evoked potentials: a reappraisal. *Science*, 1968, **160**, 207–208.

Vaughan, H. G., Jr., Costa, L. D., Gilden, L., & Schimmel, H. Identification of sensory and motor components of cerebral activity in simple reaction-time tasks. *Proceedings of the 73rd Convention of American Psychological Association*, 1965, **1**, 179–180.

Vaughan, H. G., Jr., Costa, L. D., & Gilden, L. The functional relation of visual evoked response and reaction time to stimulus intensity. *Vision Research*, 1966, **6**, 645–656.

Vaughan, H. G., Jr., Costa, L. D., & Ritter, W. Topography of the human motor potential. *Electroencephalography and Clinical Neurophysiology*, 1968, **25**, 1–10.

Vaughan, H. G., Jr., Bossom, J., & Gross, E. G. Cortical motor potential in monkeys before and after upper limb deafferentation. *Experimental Neurology*, 1970, **26**, 253–262.

Von Monakov, C. Lokalisation der Hirnfunktionen. *Journal für Psychologie und Neurologie*, 1911, **17**, 185–200.

von Neumann, J. *The computer and the brain.* New Haven: Yale Univ. Press, 1958.

Walter, W. G. Slow potential changes in the human brain associated with expectancy, decision and intention. In W. Cobb and C. Morocutti (Eds.), *The evoked potentials.* Amsterdam: Elsevier, 1967. Pp. 123–130. (Electroencephalography and Clinical Neurophysiology, Supplement 26.)

Walter, W. G., Cooper, R., Aldridge, V. J., McCallum, W. C., & Winter, A. L. Contingent negative variation: an electrical sign of sensorimotor association and expectancy in the human brain. *Nature*, 1964, **203**, 380–384.
Wiener, N. *Cybernetics*. New York: MIT Press, 1948.
Worden, F. G. Attention and auditory electrophysiology. In E. Stellar and J. M. Sprague (Eds.), *Progress in physiological psychology*. New York: Academic Press, 1966. Pp. 45–116.

The Inverted-U Relationship between Activation and Performance: A Critical Review[1,2]

Risto Näätänen

Institute of Psychology
University of Helsinki
Helsinki, Finland

ABSTRACT

Behavioral efficiency of an organism is discussed in relation to the intensity aspect of its physiological responses. It frequently has been claimed, especially by proponents of activation-level theories, that the relationship between "activation" and performance follows the form of an inverted U. According to these theories, there exists for each kind of performance an "optimal level of activation," usually of a moderate degree, at which the highest behavioral efficiency is reached. Data claimed to support the inverted-U curve is reviewed and it is concluded that the down turn of this curve after the "optimal level of activation" is an artifact of relatively uncontrolled behavioral direction, as well as of the ecological unrepresentativeness of such experiments. It is proposed that behavioral efficiency increases as a negatively accelerating function of the intensity of physiological response, as long as the patterning of the response remains appropriate with regard to the kind of performance involved.

[1]Supported by Suomen Kulttuurirahasto (The Finnish Cultural Foundation) and Valtion Urheilulautakunta (National Sports Council of Finland).

[2]This paper has gained much by the constructive comments of Drs. J. I. Lacey and B. C. Lacey. It reached its final form during my visit to Dr. D. B. Lindsley, whose suggestions and advice greatly contributed to it.

155

I. Introduction

Behavior is generally regarded as varying in two basic dimensions, direction and intensity. The former concerns the qualitative, the latter the quantitative aspect of behavior. In the earlier phases of psychology, the directional aspect of behavior held the dominating position. This tendency was related apparently to methodological developments, which did not permit profound and many-sided measurements of the intensity of different organismic functions. The development of electrophysiological measuring techniques however, has made itself felt in the sphere of psychology and has made it possible to study the graded intensity of such organismic functions in relation to behavior. One of the main, and extreme, developments along these lines has been the activation-level theory propounded by, among others, Duffy (1962) and Malmo (1959). Probably the most important promise of this approach lies in its possibility to provide, as claimed, the different degrees of excellence of various kinds of actions and performances of the organism with a physiological correlate, which, according to the proponents of this theory, is measurable with the technical means available. This correlate would be the general intensity level of the physiological processes of the organism. According to Duffy (1962, p. 158), there is an "optimal level of activation" for many kinds of performances at which performance reaches its highest excellence, and that the individual's "level of activation" may be either too low or too high for producing the best quality of work of which he is capable.

> When activation is too low, as for example in drowsiness or extreme relaxation, it might be expected that the individual would lack alertness. He might fail to respond to cues, or his response might lack force and speed. When, on the other hand, his level of activation is too high, there might be excessive impulsion to action and reduction of what Easterbrook (1959) has called "the range of cue utilization" [Duffy, 1962, pp. 158–159].

Before entering into a further investigation of this claim for the existence of the inverted-U shaped relationship between the "level of activation" (or "activation") and performance and reviewing experimental evidence held to lend support to such a conception, it is emphasized that many investigators in the field have opposed the view according to which the human organism can be regarded as a functional unity to a considerable and behaviorally significant degree in its activation processes. Lacey's (1967) criticism has been especially penetrating in an article in which he challenges the activation-level concept and causal connections between certain physiological and behavioral states that usually are considered to be very intimately interlinked.

II. Basic Claims of the Activation-Level Theory

I extract the essentials, as I can see them, of the claims of the activation-level theory in the following two points:

1. The organism can be regarded as more or less a functional unity in its activating processes, in the sense that *intraindividual* correlations exist between changes in various measures of the CNS, the ANS and behavioral activation, justifying the idea of speaking about a certain level of activation varying from the physiological state of deep sleep to that related to intensive emotions, excitement and motivation, prevailing in the organism at any moment (see, however, Lacey, 1967).

2. The activation-level concept is very useful for psychology as well as for any other discipline pursuing research on human performance, for the various points of the activation continuum are intimately related to certain kinds of behavioral phenomena and states as well as to certain characteristics of performances in tasks virtually of any sort.

Let us consider the latter of the aforestated basic proposals involving the usefulness of the activation-level concept to human-performance research, which specifically is raised in the frequent claims for the existence of the inverted-U shaped relationship between "activation level" and performance (for example, Duffy, 1962; Hokanson, 1969, pp. 26–28; Malmo, 1959; Sternbach, 1966, p. 72). These authors seem to understand the "level of activation" of the organism in a performance situation as an intervening variable of critical significance to performance. I try to illustrate what I see as a common nucleus of their thinking by the following schema (Fig. 1). It does not attempt to incorporate the permanent and semipermanent characteristics of the organism that also affect the intervening variables concerned, as well as performance.

In this schema, $S_1, S_2, \ldots, S_n$ represent, of course, the task and the external conditions for its performance, and R the output of the organism in the dimensions of the experimental task. Arrows 1 and 2 together depict the total influence of the immediate environmental factors (S factors) on the performing organism. In Fig. 1 arrow 1 represents the effect of the physical energy of the sensory stimuli on the organism. It is a well-established neurophysiological fact that nonspecific activating effects of sensory stimuli on both ascending and descending reticular activating systems of the lower

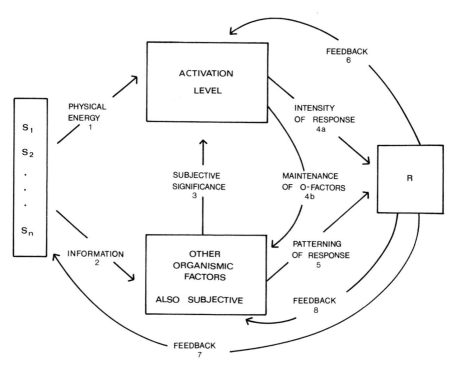

Fig. 1. An activation-level schema for behavioral performance.

brain stem, as well as on the diffuse thalamic projection system, result in increased activation in many other parts of the organism (Lindsley, 1951, 1960, 1961, 1970).

Arrow 2 represents other effects of stimulation on the organism than that described by 1. More specifically, the affecting element here is the information-containing characteristics of the sensory stimuli. These effects are related to the *directional aspect* of the behavior. They represent the cognitive aspects of the influence of the stimulus situation on the organism, in other words, the perception and interpretation of the stimulus situation by the organism.

Arrow 3 describes the generally activating effects of this perceiving and interpreting process in the organism under conditions in which the situation is experienced as containing demands in some way. [Duffy (1962) speaks about the incentive and threat values of the situation.] Activation theorists apparently also would like to include under 3 another activating effect in addition to those originating from the incentive and threat values of the situation, namely, that connected with anticipatory reactions with regard to the expected stimuli and preparatory to the intended response (Näätänen, 1970a).

Arrows 4a and 4b are of special importance to the present schema. They represent the effect of the "level of activation" on performance, both directly (4a), and indirectly (4b), via "other organismic factors" and arrow 5. These concern the second main claim of the activation-level theory as interpreted by the present author, and relate to the main topic of this paper. The usefulness of the activation-level concept on human-performance research is understood here to be mainly determined by the strength of arrows 4a and 4b.

Arrow 5 represents the effect of the directional aspect of behavior on performance, which is reflected in the organism by the patterning of its activation. In an ideal case, it is concentrated on, or located in, most appropriate mechanisms and functions of the organism with respect to the task in question (Arnold, 1942; Daniel, 1939; Davis, 1942, 1948; Freeman, 1938; Henderson, 1952).

Finally, there are in the schema representations of feedback processes (arrows 6, 7, and 8) of the performance situation. Again, the "purely" physiological side is separated from the perceptual and "interpretational." Arrow 6 represents the direct response feedback upon "activation level." Muscular responses are known, among others, to activate the reticular formation (Caspers, 1961). The perceptual and "interpretational" effect, on the other hand, is mediated by the changes in the stimulus situation (including experimenter's reactions) that are interpreted by the organism, mainly in terms of the goals of the experimental task as conceived by it (arrow 7). There also exists a more direct feedback route, that based on the subject's estimations concerning his performance, neither mediated by the external changes of the situation as a result of the response nor by the experimenter (arrow 8).

III. Direction versus Intensity of Behavior as a Determinant of Performance

In the author's view, the "level of activation" or "activation" (or what has been tried to measure preferably by a combination of different physiological measures) *as such* is of a lesser importance to success in performance than generally is thought. "Level of activation" is not so much a determinant of performance as it is an indicator of the state of those processes that really are of great significance for performance: patterning of activation, or more exactly, the appropriateness of the activation pattern of the organism with respect to the type of task in question. Even this is understood to be reflected by the "level of activation" in a rather indirect and uncertain way (Näätänen, 1964). Let us consider, for example, an organism functioning very well at a moderate "level of activation," usually referred to as the "optimal level of activation." It is proposed herein (experimental evidence pertinent to the point made will be presented later in this paper) that the high quality of performance under such conditions does not result from that certain "level of activation," but rather it is the appropriateness of the activation pattern that is connected with both the high level of performance and the moderate "level of activation." Under these conditions, the behavior of the organism has only one direction, that dictated by the experimental task. The phase of the inverted-U shaped curve involving the progressively deteriorating performance with increasing "level of activation," *after* the "optimal" level has been reached,[3] is suggested to be an artifact of the change of direction in behavior farther and farther away from that of the task at hand as "activation" increases under conditions in which this deteriorating effect has been observed (Näätänen, 1964, 1970b). In the earlier of these investigations, I have discussed the phenomena of divergent demands of the performance situation upon the organism extensively. The following main types of divergence are proposed:

A. Other Tasks
    1. A second task
    2. Preparation for another task
    3. Residuals of another task
B. Other Stimuli
C. Other Reactions
    1. Anxiety reactions
    2. "Trying harder" reactions

---

[3]The initial rise of performance level comprising the first part of the inverted-U curve is not dealt with although what is said certainly has implications also in respect to this phase of the curve. Generally, the increase in behavioral efficiency with increases in the changes of physiological responses is considered a valid phenomenon; it is proposed that behavioral efficiency continuously increases with increasing physiological changes as long as the appropriateness of their pattern to the performance in question prevails. This increase of behavioral efficiency is assumed to be a negatively accelerating function of the intensity of the physiological changes, asymptotically approaching a straight horizontal line, following many other input–output functions. Note that according to the author, even when of extreme intensity these patterned physiological responses never break their own pattern because of the intensity, contrary to the conceptions of activation-level theorists (see, for example, Duffy, 1962). They can be diffused only by central events, by those which induce and control them.

3. Task-specific fatigue reactions
4. Reactions connected with becoming too conscious of one's own performance
5. Loose associations and other irrelevant reactions
D. Other Organismic States than the "Basic" State
1. Continuous contact with the environment
2. General exhaustion
3. Other ongoing processes
4. Artificial states

A. OTHER TASKS

This refers to those experimental situations in which two or more tasks are presented to the subject simultaneously or in close succession. In this group, point (1) is by far the most important to the present discussion and will be considered extensively.

1. A Second Task

It is a common usage in studies dealing with the relationship between "activation" and performance to employ a second task in order to vary "activation". This is done most frequently by asking the subject to pull on a dynamometer (or to push a lever, and similarly,) with a force in a certain proportion to the subject's maximal strength. Under such conditions, the inverted-U curve has been a common finding (Courts, 1939, 1942; Freeman, 1938; Meyer, 1953; Shaw, 1956; Shore, 1958), although there are also experiments in which no sign of the inverted-U curve could be observed (Murphy, 1966; Pinneo, 1961; Duffy, 1962, pp. 158–163 and 185–186; Hokanson, 1969, pp. 27–28). The majority of these studies seems to favor the U curve, however. As the decrement of performance level in these investigations generally has occurred only when heavy physical efforts have been performed simultaneously (the force applied on the dynamometer equaling from one-half to three-fourths of the subject's maximal strength), it might be the increasing demands of this additional task, rather than the increase in the "level of activation" induced by it, that caused performance to deteriorate. The greater the force applied by the subject to the pulling on the dynamometer or to an equivalent task introduced to increase muscle tension, the more his attention probably was directed also to that task and the more divergence prevailed in the patterning of his muscular tension as related to the patterning required by the mere test performance. In an organism in such a state, not only the *intensity* of the physiological changes but presumably also the *direction* of behavior is varied. The inverted-U relationship obtained under such experimental conditions is understood to be an artifact of the change of the direction of behavior farther and farther away from that of the test performance as the demands of the second task increase.

Studies trying to relate the intensity aspect of physiological changes to performance should be conducted by keeping the directional aspect of behavior constant while the former is manipulated. For this reason a second task, such as pulling on the dynamometer, cannot be employed *simultaneously* with the experimental task. The measurement of the test performance should take place under organismic states differing from each other only with respect to the intensity of physiological changes. This kind of experimental approach was attempted in the Institute of Psychology of the University of Helsinki, by scheduling the second task during a period immediately preceding the experimental task (Näätänen, 1970b).

"Activation" was varied by having the subject ride a bicycle-ergometer set at different power levels for a couple of minutes. During a short period after the induction of the desired "level of activation" (evaluated by the heart rate[4]), the subject could concentrate on the experimental task without interference from the task performed for the manipulation of the heart rate. The period during which the experimental task could be performed was, of course, rather short (30 sec), for the differing degrees of induced heart rate begin to decrease and converge soon after the physical effort is halted. Figure 2 represents the mean course of the heart rate of the subjects during the experimental task, ensuring that there was only a negligible amount of overlapping of different heart-rate levels induced by cycling at different power levels, and that the activation measure employed demonstrated sufficient experimental variation.

The experimental tasks performed involved simple reaction time (finger press) and the speed of arm movement (maximal speed of extension of the right arm, flexed at the elbow). Figure 3 shows the effect of the induced heart-rate increase on the simple reaction time, randomized interstimulus intervals varying from 1.5 to 2.5 sec as measured during the 30-sec period immediately after cycling (Näätänen, 1970b). Although the heart rate was varied almost as extensively as possible in a waking human subject, statistical tests conducted did not show any connection between the heart rate and the

---

[4] I do not mean to accept heart rate and induced muscle tension as equal or even valid estimators of the construct of the "activation level," but many forms of these theories would accept such a statement. Hence, these experiments can be considered to be central to the kind of theorizing they do.

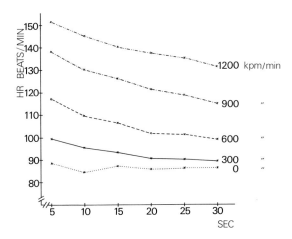

Fig. 2. The mean course of heart rate (HR) for different power levels [kpm (kilopond meters)/min] during the 30-sec period immediately after cycling. (From Näätänen, 1970b. Reproduced by permission of the Institute of Psychology, The University of Helsinki.)

reaction time.[5] To ascertain that a relationship between these two variables would have been obtained by scheduling the reaction-time task and cycling to be performed simultaneously, a control study (Näätänen, unpublished) was arranged in which the same subjects (except one) performed the same reaction-time task while still cycling (after cycling for a couple of minutes without any reaction-time measurements) under conditions as similar to those of the main experiment as possible (Fig. 4). This time the same statistical procedures, which did not yield any hint toward even the slightest level of statistical significance in the main study, now clearly demonstrated a relationship between these two variables. The deterioration of the reaction speed with increase of the heart rate was very clear-cut. The linear component of this deterioration was shown by an analysis of regression; it was statistically highly significant for the data of all three subjects, whereas the curvilinear component reached the .05 level only for one subject.

[5]There were two complicating factors involved in the experimental design applied. First, a 30-sec period for a performance is unusually short, and second, the performance level, of course, was measured only during rapidly *decreasing* values of the heart rate. These facts may bear consequences for the subject's performance but not for the utility of the results obtained in testing the activation-level theory, which yields differential predictions for activation-performance relationships neither for decelerating, accelerating, or steady heart rate nor for short or longer tasks.

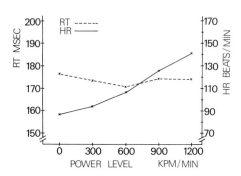

Fig. 3. Heart rate (HR) and simple reaction time (RT) for different power levels [kpm (kilopond meters)/min] during the 30-sec period immediately after cycling. (From Näätänen, 1970b. Reproduced by permission of the Institute of Psychology, The University of Helsinki.)

Fig. 4. Simple reaction time (RT) for different power levels [kpm (kilopond meters)/min] during cycling, separately for each subject. (From Näätänen, unpublished data.)

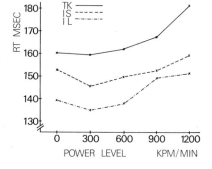

The similar study involving the relationship between the heart rate and the speed of arm movement provided results that were in agreement with those of the simple reaction-time experiment: the heart rate did not bear any relationship to the speed of movement under such experimental conditions (Fig. 5). Again, variance and regression analyses performed were very consistent in showing that these results were not statistically significant.

These Helsinki studies constitute a beginning in a series of experiments in progress in our laboratory to clarify human performance under different degrees of induced heart rate. In this series of experiments we are moving from simple types of motor and sensorimotor performance to more complicated ones also involving cognitive aspects.

Another kind of demonstration to show that it is not the increased "activation" that affects performance, but rather the exposure of the subject to a dual task, can perhaps be found in Murphy's investigation (1966) in which the simultaneous pull on a dynamometer contaminated the reaction speed in proportion to the amount of the force applied on the first experimental days but later did not exert any influence on it. On the basis of the reported results, it cannot be decided with full certainty, however, that it

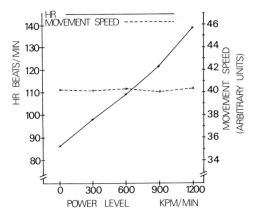

Fig. 5. Heart rate (HR) and speed of arm movement (in arbitrary units) for different power levels [kpm (kilopond meters)/min] during the 30-sec period immediately after cycling. (From Näätänen, unpublished data.)

really was the divergent demands, introduced by the induction of the second task, rather than the increased muscle tension, that subjects learned to tolerate, as the experiment progressed.

2. Preparation for Another Task

It is proposed that when anticipatory reactions of an approaching situation are set going in a performance situation, an increased number of perhaps divergent functions of the organism is involved (Lacey & Lacey, 1970). In such circumstances the criterion performance level can be lowered when there is interaction of simultaneous responses (Freeman & Kendall, 1940; Malmo, 1966; Meyer, 1953).

3. Residuals of Another Task

The time needed for the complete dissipation of a reaction is longer than generally believed. Bourne (1955) cites R. C. Davis as stating, in a personal communication to him, that 4 min is the length of time needed for the dissipation of induced dynamometric tension (see also Bartoshuk, 1959; Duffy, 1962, pp. 266–268; Peake & Leonard, 1971). If the tension residual is a patterned one, the possibility exists that it interferes with the task performance, especially if the response mechanisms involved in both tasks overlap, which may lead to data favoring the U-curve function (see Bourne, 1955).

B. OTHER STIMULI

If a stimulus not belonging to the experimental task, such as noise, is used to vary "activation," it is possible that the *specific* effects of such a stimulation when intense, rather than the nonspecific effects, are responsible for the performance deterioration. During loud auditory stimulation we often feel ourselves irritated and annoyed, which is by no means a necessary experience in connection with high "activation." Rather, it is something specific to this kind of stimulus situation, and it probably is this specific aspect that is to blame for difficulties in concentrating on a task under such conditions rather than increased "activation" as such. However simple and unpatterned the noise stimulation might be physically (for example, "white noise"), the organismic response pattern to it may be very complicated (Davis, 1950; J. I. Lacey, Kagan, B. C. Lacey, & Moss, 1963).

Another problem under this category consists of inadequately controlled background stimuli not intended by the experimenter to be present in the experimental situation. Such stimuli may evoke response patterns in the organism that vary with respect to their intensity and pattern (Davis, 1950). These response patterns presumably interfere with the task performance, depending on the intensity and degree to which they overlap the response patterns of the task proper, as previously explained. Here again we may have a factor contributing to the inverted U.

C. OTHER REACTIONS

1. Anxiety Reactions

The subject in an experimental situation is seldom engaged only with the experimental task. He often spends a considerable amount of "energy" in worrying about the outcome of the experiment, for example, failure stress (Lazarus & Eriksen, 1952), or the strange-looking and threatening experimental device, etc. He is anxious, "nervous," and emotional. These additional reactions as a rule raise "activation" (Beam, 1955; Peake & Leonard, 1971; see, however, Lacey et al., 1963) and cause performance to deteriorate (Beam, 1955; Birch, 1945; Cowen, 1952; Taylor & Spence, 1952). If there is variation in the strength of these anxiety reactions across different trials and experimental sessions, conditions may exist appropriate for the production of data that some would like to interpret as supporting the inverted-U curve.

For example, let us consider a sprinter immediately before the firing of the starter's gun. If, while concentrating on making a good start, he is also anxious as to whether he is going to be dropped out from the team, or what nasty things his coach is going to say if he loses the race, there presumably are two patterns in his skeletal–muscular system: one involving the muscles needed in the start, shadowed by a more diffusely spread static tension induced by anxiety and fear of failure. Apparently these patterns also have a central equivalent in the firing patterns of cortical cells related to motor control. A performance probably can reach its highest excellence only when the relevant systems are activated and the irrelevant are not, especially the antagonist muscles. That is, the pattern prevailing in the organism must be very sharp or differentiated, in addition to being appropriate with regard to the requirements of the task (Arnold, 1942; Daniel, 1939; Davis, 1948; Henderson, 1952; Meyer, 1953).

A separate important category under this heading consists of *reactions to experienced failure and difficulties*. This would result in some patterns of physiological change (the increased threat value of the situation is likely to evoke fear reactions with diffuse physiological responses). It would probably not be good for the performance and might contribute to the inverted-U curve.

2. "Trying Harder" Reactions

In a performance task, the subject often aims at increasing his level of performancy by "trying harder" *intentionally*. There is the risk, however, that this surplus excitation forced into the performing motor systems would not be suited to the prevailing pattern, and instead would be reflected by a general increase in the tension of the performing limbs, including the antagonist muscles, and would perhaps affect the whole organism. During such trials, performance may deteriorate while measures of "activation" show increased values, that is, the inverted-U shaped curve appears.

3. Task-Specific Fatigue Reactions

Surwillo (1956) refers to data indicating that, under conditions where the (objective) muscular effort is held constant, the action-potential amplitude is greater at fatigue than at the time of initial contraction. During these fatigue trials muscular activation seems to increase whereas performance deteriorates. If experimental conditions, as well as the treatment of the data, are not balanced completely within an experimental day and between days, these and similar phenomena might be able to yield a spurious relationship between "activation" and performance of the form involved in the inverted U.

4. Reactions Connected with Becoming (too) Conscious of One's Own Performance

This means a kind of diversion of behavioral direction of the subject in an experimental situation in which he simultaneously performs the task and observes himself performing the task. Thus, the latter perceptual and cognitive processes may extend well beyond those belonging to the task performance and its feedback loop. The anxiety reactions (Section C,1) are not necessarily involved.

Consider, for example, a person trying to fall asleep and his inability to do so because of his intention and of attempted acts to promote sleep. Or, have you ever tried to think of nothing? Generally it does not succeed; we soon think that "we don't think." If we cannot concentrate solely on the experimental task at hand, but also concentrate on watching ourselves performing the task, our attention is divided between the task itself and the whole situation, including the performer of the task. Under these conditions there is apt to be deterioration of performance and probable increases in physiological responses, that is, the data suggest an inverted-U curve. This problem has been discussed extensively elsewhere (Näätänen, 1964). It should be emphasized that the aspect of "unnaturalness" of experimental situations, when compared with performance situations of everyday life, promotes perceptual and cognitive processes of this kind.

5. Loose Associations and Other Irrelevant Reactions

These are the subject's reactions to other stimuli of the experimental situation or to past stimuli that do not belong to the task. Nor do these reactions seem to bear any connection to its consequences. During such coincidences of stimuli or reactions during task periods physiological measures probably yield changes indicating increased "activation," whereas performance does not necessarily improve. Such a condition might have existed in a reaction-time study by Lansing, Schwartz, and Lindsley (1959) in which the reaction time was not correlated with the spontaneous, unstimulated, blocking of α waves, but was (negatively) correlated with blocking under alerted conditions (a warning signal delivered). It is proposed here that the α blockade was produced differentially in the two conditions, in the alerted condition by the expectancy or anticipation of the stimulus and in the nonalerted condition by more diverse and extraneous causes, for example, free associations. This, in turn, is understood to be related to the reaction-time differences obtained. Studies showing the decreasing effect of expectancy on the reaction time are numerous (for example, Näätänen, 1970c).

D. OTHER ORGANISMIC STATES THAN THE "BASIC" STATE

1. Continuous Contact with the Environment

This has been discussed extensively elsewhere (Näätänen, 1964). It is understood to be a biological process which prevents us from concentrating on any task so wholeheartedly that perceptual contact with the rest of environment breaks down. If there had been in some stages of the evolutionary-chain organisms capable of doing this, they would have been caught by their enemies under these highly concentrated states. It is another sign of "Nature's wisdom" (in addition to creating us) that at all times we continue to scan our environment and maintain a state of readiness of varying intensities to meet the unexpected. This assumption gains support from the studies indicating drastically increased levels of performance in various tasks under hypnotic states. It seems to be justified to think that the continuous perceptual contact with the environment and diffuse readiness state are stopped by hypnotic instructions, and, therefore, all the resources of the organism are available for performance. Also the directional aspect of behavior (patterning of activation) can be assumed to be more appropriate than without hypnosis, owing to the effective specific instructions of the hypnotist. The increased level of performance under hypnosis thus is explained via increased "energy" and the more appropriate patterning of the energy release with regard to the task during this state. It seems to me that those attempting to clarify the persistent problems of attention and performance have ignored far too long the investigation of human performance under hypnosis, which provides us with a potentially powerful means to vary attention (Leuba, 1946).

What was said in this section relates to the inverted-U question via assumed variation in the intensity of these continuous processes. When they are intense, "activation" probably is increased but the level of performance may be decreased as there already is an activation pattern interfering with the response pattern of the experimental task.

2. General Exhaustion

Malmo (1959; see also Malmo, 1958) writes:

> when a man is deprived of sleep for some 60 hr his activation level appears to be higher than it was before he had suffered sleep loss. Physiological indicants reveal an upward shift in activation level that is gradual and progressive throughout the vigil [p. 373].

Also food and water deprivations increase "activation" (Malmo, 1959). It is well known that, after a certain point, deprivations cause deterioration of performance. Therefore, higher values of physiological activation may become associated with decreasing performance level.

3. Other Ongoing Processes

These refer to all other kinds of processes of the organism that follow it to the experimental situation (for example, chronic worrying about another person). If their degrees vary from moment to moment during an experimental session or between different sessions, increased "activation" values again are in danger of being coupled with decreased levels of performance.

4. Artificial States

Induced by agents such as electrical stimulation, drugs, and lesions, these states usually are of such a kind that continuous application or increase of the agent inducing such a state necessarily results in performance deterioration. Fuster's (1958) well-known experiment with electrical stimulation applied to the reticular formation of a monkey frequently is referred to as a demonstration of the inverted-U curve. The moderate intensity of such a stimulation improved accuracy and speed of visual discrimination reaction, whereas higher intensities had the opposite effect. Simultaneously with stimulation at high intensities, there were also observable motor effects such as generalized muscular jerks. At least most of these "artificial" states involve side effects that may invalidate reliable conclusions concerning the connection between "activation" and performance (see Lacey, 1967). Human electric-chair experiments at Sing-Sing and San Quentin with even stronger electrical stimuli have provided even more dramatic demonstrations of the inverted-U function.

IV. General Discussion and Conclusions

The views presented here as well as in 1964 (Näätänen, 1964), represent my feeling that there is an urgent need for synthesis between general and specific aspects of "activation," after the long-lasting dominance of the nonspecific aspect, in order to progress in our continuous attempts to discover the physiological bases of behavioral phenomena. Similar reemphasis on specific factors can be observed in Lacey's influential writings (Lacey, 1967) when he, for example, refers to striking "directional fractionation" phenomena of some ANS and CNS changes and emphasizes specific situational determinants of physiological response patterns. Similar tendencies also can be detected in Lazarus' (1967a, b) conceptions concerning the importance of cognitive determinants of stress and emotions.

The evidence produced to support the inverted-U shaped relationship between "activation" and performance is considered to a great extent a product of the particular era of psychophysiology and physiological psychology during which, as far as human-performance research is concerned, the qualitative aspect of behavior was subordinated to the quantitative to the extent that even the necessity to control strictly the qualitative aspect was often ignored. This contribution has aimed at classifying the different forms this oversight has adopted and at demonstrating that the claims for the existence of the inverted-U curve between values of different activation measures or their combinations and performance mainly rest on inadequate experimental evidence.

Critical consideration of the available evidence makes it necessary to say a word of caution with regard to the manner in which we interpret and apply such important theoretical elaborations as Lindsley's (1952, 1970) famous activation continuum, especially the relations proposed between certain points along such a continuum and certain degrees of behavioral efficiency. The deterministic or causal manner in which the observations and proposals, such as those of Lindsley (1952, 1960, 1961, 1970), are frequently misunderstood is challenged here.

Present evidence lends support only to the idea of correlative or probabilistic relationships between certain stages of the activation continuum and their respective behavioral correlates (see Lacey, 1967). For example, the probability may be that during a very high degree of cortical activation behavioral efficiency really is "poor (lack of control, freezing up, disorganized)" (Lindsley, 1952), but obviously he did not intend or say, that this should necessarily be the case every time when the EEG demonstrates a very high degree of activation. The high probability that behavioral efficiency really is poor, when this kind of EEG prevails, may result from the common situational characteristics underlying such an EEG, which often include elements releasing strong emotional reactions in the subject. This is a kind of ecological unrepresentativeness of experimental situations (see Brunswik, 1956). It might be possible under certain experimental conditions to induce an EEG showing an extreme degree of activation even in a subject whose behavior could be characterized as especially efficient, having only one direction, that of the experimental task. It might be that large physiological changes are not necessarily harmful for performance (Näätänen, 1970b), whereas the specific elements connected with these and affecting their patterning might be.

References

Arnold, M. B. A study of tension in relation to breakdown. *Journal of General Psychology*, 1942, **26**, 315–346.

Bartoshuk, A. K. Electromyographic reactions to strong auditory stimulation as a function of alpha amplitude. *Journal of Comparative and Physiological Psychology*, 1959, **52**, 540–545.

Beam, J. C. Serial learning and conditioning under real-life stress. *Journal of Abnormal and Social Psychology*, 1955, **51**, 543–551.

Birch, H. G. The role of motivational factors in insightful problem-solving. *Journal of Comparative Psychology*, 1945, **38**, 295–317.

172 NÄÄTÄNEN [Part 2

Bourne, L. E., Jr. An evaluation of the effect of induced tension on performance. *Journal of Experimental Psychology*, 1955, **49**, 418–422.

Brunswik, E. *Perception and the Representative Design of Psychological Experiments.* (2nd ed.). Berkeley: Univ. of California Press, 1956.

Caspers, H. Changes of cortical D. C. potentials in the sleep–wakefulness cycle. In G. E. W. Wolstenholme and M. O'Connor (Eds.), *The nature of sleep.* London: Churchill, 1961. Pp. 237–253.

Courts, F. A. Relation between experimentally induced tension, muscular tension and memorization. *Journal of Experimental Psychology*, 1939, **25**, 235–256.

Courts, F. A. The influence of practice on the dynamogenic effect of muscular tension. *Journal of Experimental Psychology*, 1942, **30**, 504–511.

Cowen, E. L. The influence of varying degrees of psychological stress on problem-solving rigidity. *Journal of Abnormal and Social Psychology*, 1952, **47**, 512–519.

Daniel, R. S. The distribution of muscle action potentials during maze learning. *Journal of Experimental Psychology*, 1939, **24**, 621–629.

Davis, R. C. The pattern of muscular action in simple voluntary movement. *Journal of Experimental Psychology*, 1942, **31**, 347–366.

Davis, R. C. Motor effects of strong auditory stimuli. *Journal of Experimental Psychology*, 1948, **38**, 257–275.

Davis, R. C. Motor responses to auditory stimuli above and below threshold. *Journal of Experimental Psychology*, 1950, **40**, 107–120.

Duffy, E. *Activation and behavior.* New York: Wiley, 1962.

Easterbrook, J. A. The effect of emotion on cue utilization and the organization of behavior. *Psychological Review*, 1959, **66**, 183–201.

Freeman, G. L. The optimal muscular tensions for various performances. *American Journal of Psychology*, 1938, **51**, 146–150.

Freeman, G. L., & Kendall, W. E. The effect upon reaction time of muscular tension induced at various preparatory intervals. *Journal of Experimental Psychology*, 1940, **27**, 136–148.

Fuster, J. M. Effects of stimulation of brain stem on tachistoscopic perception. *Science*, 1958, **127**, 150.

Henderson, R. L. Remote action potentials at the moment of response in a simple reaction-time situation. *Journal of Experimental Psychology*, 1952, **44**, 238–241.

Hokanson, J. E. *The physiological bases of motivation.* New York: Wiley, 1969.

Lacey, J. I. Somatic response patterning and stress: Some revisions of activation theory. In M. H. Appley and R. Trumbull (Eds.), *Psychological stress: Issues in research.* New York: Appleton, 1967. Pp. 14–44.

Lacey, J. I., & Lacey, B. C. Some autonomic-central nervous system interrelationships. In P. Black (Ed.), *Physiological correlates of emotion.* New York: Academic Press, 1970. Pp. 205–227.

Lacey, J. I., Kagan, J., Lacey, B. C., & Moss, H. A. The visceral level: Situational determinants and behavioral correlates of autonomic response patterns. In P. H. Knapp (Ed.), *Expression of the emotions in man.* International Universities Press, 1963. Pp. 161–196.

Lansing, R. W., Schwartz, E., & Lindsley, D. B. Reaction time and EEG activation under alerted and nonalerted conditions. *Journal of Experimental Psychology*, 1959, **58**, 1–7.

Lazarus, R. S. Cognitive and personality factors underlying threat and coping. In M. H. Appley and R. Trumbull (Eds.), *Psychological stress: Issues in research.* New York: Appleton, 1967. Pp. 151–181. (a)

Lazarus, R. S. Stress theory and psychophysiological research. *Försvarsmedicin*, 1967, **3**, 152–177. (b)

Lazarus, R. S., and Eriksen, C. W. Effects of failure stress upon skilled performance. *Journal of Experimental Psychology*, 1952, **43**, 100–105.

Leuba, C. Hypnosis as a method of controlling variables in psychological experiments. *American Journal of Psychology*, 1946, **59**, 686–690.

Lindsley, D. B. Emotion. In S. S. Stevens (Ed.), *Handbook of Experimental Psychology*. New York: Wiley, 1951. Pp. 473–516.

Lindsley, D. B. Psychological phenomena and the electroencephalogram. *Electroencephalography and Clinical Neurophysiology*, 1952, **4**, 443–456.

Lindsley, D. B. Attention, consciousness, sleep and wakefulness. In J. Field, H. W. Magoun, & V. E. Hall (Eds.), *Handbook of physiology. Section I: Neurophysiology*. Volume III, Washington, D.C.: American Physiological Society, 1960. Pp. 1553–1593.

Lindsley, D. B. The reticular activating system and perceptual integration. In D. E. Sheer (Ed.), *Electrical stimulation of the brain*. Austin, Texas: Univ. of Texas Press, 1961. Pp. 331–349.

Lindsley, D. B. The role of nonspecific reticulo-thalamo-cortical systems in emotion. In P. Black (Ed.), *Physiological correlates of emotion*. New York: Academic Press, 1970. Pp. 147–188.

Malmo, R. B. Measurement of drive: An unsolved problem in psychology. In M. R. Jones (Ed.), *Nebraska symposium on motivation 1958*. Lincoln: Univ. of Nebraska Press, 1958. Pp. 229–265.

Malmo, R. B. Activation: A neuropsychological dimension. *Psychological Review*, 1959, **66**, 367–386.

Malmo, R. B. Cognitive factors in impairment: A neuropsychological study of divided set. *Journal of Experimental Psychology*, 1966, **71**, 184–189.

Meyer, D. R. On the interaction of simultaneous responses. *Psychological Bulletin*, 1953, **50**, 204–220.

Murphy, L. E. Muscular effort, activation level, and reaction time. *Proceedings of the 74th Annual Convention of American Psychological Association*, 1966, 1–2.

Näätänen, R. Reaktioaikakokeissa esiintyvän suoritusvalmiuden aktivaatiotasoteoreettista tarkastelua. (Readiness and activation in reaction-time experiments.) Unpublished Phil. Lic. thesis, University of Helsinki, 1964.

Näätänen, R. Evoked potential, EEG, and slow potential correlates of selective attention. In A. F. Sanders (Ed.), *Attention and Performance III, Acta Psychologica*, 1970, **33**, 178–192. (a)

Näätänen, R. Activation and performance I: Heart rate and the simple reaction time. *Institute of Psychology*. The University of Helsinki, 1970, No. 4. (b)

Näätänen, R. The diminishing time-uncertainty with the lapse of time after the warning signal in reaction-time experiments with varying fore-periods. *Acta Psychologica*, 1970, **34**, 399–419. (c)

Näätänen, R. Heart rate and the simple reaction time during physical exercise. Unpublished data.

Näätänen, R. Heart rate and the speed of arm movement. Unpublished data.

Peake, P., and Leonard, J. A. The use of heart rate as an index of stress in blind pedestrians. *Ergonomics*, 1971, **14**, 189–204.

Pinneo, L. R. The effects of induced muscle tension during tracking on level of activation and on performance. *Journal of Experimental Psychology*, 1961, **62**, 523–531.

Shaw, W. A. Facilitating effects of induced tension upon the perception span for digits. *Journal of Experimental Psychology*, 1956, **51**, 113–117.

Shore, M. F. Perceptual efficiency as related to induced muscular effort and manifest anxiety. *Journal of Experimental Psychology*, 1958, **55**, 179–183.

Sternbach, R. A. *Principles of Psychophysiology*. New York: Academic Press, 1966.

Surwillo, W. W. Psychological factors in muscle-action potentials: EMG gradients. *Journal of Experimental Psychology*, 1956, **52**, 263–272.

Taylor, J. A., and Spence, K. W. The relationship of anxiety level to performance in serial learning. *Journal of Experimental Psychology*, 1952, **44**, 61–64.

Response Probability and Sensory-Evoked Potentials[1]

Lawrence Karlin   Merrill J. Martz, Jr.

Department of Psychology
New York University
New York, New York

ABSTRACT

Evoked potentials to stimuli conveying various amounts of response information as measured by *a priori* response uncertainty were studied in an
experiment in which information was delivered either 1 sec before (condition
W) or at the time when (condition N) a fast choice response was required.
Increase in response information produced enhancement of P_3 beyond that of a
rare-stimulus control in both conditions, but the effect was greater in condition N.
The overall size of P_3 was also greater in this condition. It was concluded
that P_3 enhancement was indirectly related to the cognitive aspects of stimulation
through the mediation of momentary or "phasic" arousal factors.

I. Introduction

A number of recent studies have found that human averaged evoked
potentials (EP) to infrequent, unpredictable stimuli yield enhanced late
positive deflections. Results of this kind observed in different types of task
have been interpreted to mean that these deflections (variously called P_3,

---

[1] This research was performed through support from the NIH Biomedical Services Support
Grant to New York University and by a Grant-in-aid from the New York University Arts and
Science Research Fund.

P_{300}, and LPC, with latencies ranging from about 300 to 500 msec) are related to orienting behavior (Ritter, Vaughan, & Costa, 1968), evaluation of cognitive significance (Ritter & Vaughan, 1969), stimulus uncertainty (Sutton, Braren, Zubin, & John, 1965) and stimulus probability (Teuting, Sutton, & Zubin, 1971).

The present study is a further examination of the possible role of informational variables in producing P_3 enhancement when stimulus frequency is held constant. Our purpose in controlling stimulus frequency was to minimize the differential effects of any factors such as the orienting response (Sokolov, 1963) that might be associated with the immediate sensory impact of stimulation. In this way we hoped to determine the effect of stimulus meaning at a somewhat higher level of abstraction than would be provided by manipulation of stimulus frequency alone. The present experiment thus compared EP to two equally rare, unpredictable stimuli that instructed the subject to make responses that occurred with unequal frequency. We therefore varied the degree of *a priori* response uncertainty, which was reduced by occurrence of a given stimulus while holding stimulus uncertainty constant.

In an effort to manipulate any arousal factors that might be involved in P_3 enhancement, we also varied the urgency or speed with which the response information was needed.

II. Method

The subject's task was to respond to a given stimulus as fast as he could by pressing one of two thumb switches which he held in his hands. There were two conditions of this experiment, the "wait" (W) and "now" (N) conditions.

In each trial of condition W a signal stimulus presented by a loud speaker 5 ft in front of the subject was selected from one of three 20-msec tones of differing pitch (3600, 2040, and 950 Hz). To increase discriminability among the tones, the middle tone actually consisted of two sequential frequencies (1880 and 2100 Hz) so it sounded like a "chirp." The signal tones told the subject which response to make 1 sec later to the reaction stimulus, which was always a click. In half the runs the subject was instructed to respond with his left thumb to the click after hearing the middle tone and in the other half with his right thumb. The high and low tones always instructed the subject to respond with right and left thumbs, respectively.

There were four such runs counterbalanced with respect to which response followed the middle tone and given in ABBA order. Each run consisted of 128 trials in which high and low tones occurred on 16 trials each, the middle tone occurring on the remaining 96 trials. There was a 5 sec interval between trials. In a given run the frequent response was made to one of the rare tones as well as to the middle tone so it occurred on 112 (87.5%) trials. The rare response was made to the other rare tone on the remaining 16 (12.5%) trials. The three signal stimuli thus may be classified as (a) rare tone followed by rare response (RR), (b) rare tone followed by frequent response (RF), and (c) frequent tone (always the middle tone) followed by frequent response (FF). These stimuli were presented in quasi-random order, with the constraints that the same rare stimulus was never immediately repeated, and both rare stimuli were approximately equally spaced throughout the run. Prior to the first run a practice run of 24 trials was administered.

In addition to the experimental stimuli, a small light located above the loudspeaker was turned on for 3 sec, beginning 1 sec prior to the signal stimulus and ending 1 sec after the reaction stimulus. The subject was instructed to fixate the light when it appeared and to refrain from blinking while it was on.

Condition N was the same as condition W except that the subject was instructed to respond immediately to the signal stimuli and to ignore the subsequent click.

Three of the ten subjects had served as subjects in earlier pilot experiments. All were young adults of whom seven were female. Each condition was given on a separate day with order counterbalanced over subjects.

The experiment was conducted in a sound-proof room and lasted about 2 hr. There were breaks of a few minutes between runs. Within runs there were shorter breaks of 30 sec every couple of minutes in order to forestall fatigue and eye irritations. We recorded the electroencephalograms (EEG) from the vertex referred to linked ears and the electrooculograms (EOG) from above and below the right eye, using Beckman miniature biomedical electrodes leading to a Beckman dynograph and a Honeywell 7600 recorder. The time constants were set for 10 sec for the EEG channel and 1 sec for the EOG channel. The various trial types were selectively averaged with a CAT-1000, using a 4-sec epoch that began .5 sec before the onset of the fixation stimulus. For evoked potentials to both the signal and reaction stimuli we measured five peaks (N_1, P_2, N_2, P_3, and N_3) with respect to the voltage levels at the onset of these stimuli, and these onset levels in turn were measured with reference to the level at the onset of the fixation stimulus in order to reflect contingent negative variation (CNV) amplitudes (Walter, Cooper, Aldridge, McCallum, & Winter, 1964).

III. Results

Illustrative tracings of EP to RR, RF, and FF stimuli for one subject are shown in Fig. 1. The EOG tracings at the bottom of the figure show little correlation with the EP tracings. Similar results were obtained for the remaining subjects. Note that in Condition W the CNV occurs in two segments, the first initiated by the warning light and the second by the signal stimuli, with recovery following the reaction stimulus. As expected in condition N, recovery from CNV followed the tones which in this condition served as both signal and reaction stimuli. Similar results in this respect were obtained for the remaining subjects.

The peak amplitudes of EP to the signal tones illustrated by Fig. 1 were measured for each subject with respect to voltage at stimulus onset and then averaged over all subjects. These averages are plotted in Fig. 2.

Of major interest are the differences in P_3 to the signal stimuli in Condition W. A two-way analysis of variance using the subject-by-stimulus interaction as the error term yielded a significant F of 4.07 ($F_{.05} = 3.55$). This result was examined in greater detail by making separate tests of the three possible stimulus comparisons (Winer, 1962). We found that stimulus frequency effects (RF versus FF), while in the expected direction, were not

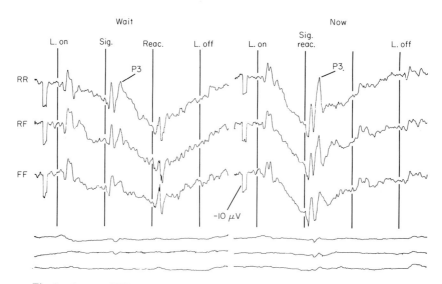

Fig. 1. Averaged EP to RR, RF and FF stimuli in "wait" and "now" conditions for one subject. Lower tracings are EOG. Averages are based on 64 trials over a 4-sec epoch. Gain of the EOG channel was one-fifth that of the EEG channel.

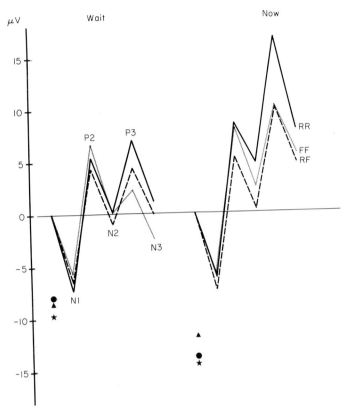

Fig. 2. Schematic EP to signal stimuli in both conditions showing peak deflections averaged over 10 subjects. The different types of signal stimuli are indicated as follows: solid line, RR; dashed line, RF; dotted line, FF. Note that the response was made immediately to the signal tone in the "now" condition but one sec later in the "wait" condition. All peaks were measured as deviations from the averaged voltage level at stimulus onset. Therefore, all stimulus onsets were adjusted to zero in the figure. The actual averaged voltages at the various signal stimulus onsets are indicated by the first set of points in each condition as follows: star, RR; triangle, RF; circle, FF.

significant ($F = 1.44$, $F_{.05} = 5.12$). The effect of differences in response frequency (RR versus RF) was also not significant ($F = 3.52$) although the effect was greater. Finally the comparison involving both effects (RR versus FF) was significant ($F = 6.8$).

Using the same kind of two-way analysis of variance, a highly significant effect ($P < .01$) of stimulus type was obtained in condition N, but it is obvious from Fig. 2 that this effect was due only to response frequency (RR versus both RF and FF) since no difference attributable to the effects of stimulus frequency (RF versus FF) was obtained.

The tones and clicks in conditions W and N differed with regard to whether or not a reaction was made in response to them. Thus, the task was effectively terminated immediately after the tone of condition N and the click of Condition W. This difference in turn affected the roles these stimuli played in generating and terminating preparatory states as inferred from baseline changes, which were identified in Fig. 1 as stages of the CNV. Further relevant data are shown in Table 1, where the voltages at the onsets of the three types of signal tone and of the clicks following each type of tone are given. The first set of values in both conditions giving the voltages at tone onset (shown also in Fig. 2) indicate the development of CNV initiated by the preceding fixation stimulus, since all these points are markedly negative. The greater negativity shown at the onsets of the tones in condition N indicates, as might be expected, a more rapid development of CNV. Condition N also shows recovery from CNV following the tones, since the voltages at click onsets are nearly zero. On the other hand, condition W shows a further development of CNV following the tones, since the voltages at the subsequent click onsets have increased in negativity. Note that this increase is least at the onset of the clicks that follow the FF stimuli, perhaps indicating that the subject finds the response to the clicks in this case least difficult (Low & McSherry, 1968; Waszak & Obrist, 1969).

From Fig. 1 and Table 1, therefore, it can be seen that EP to the signal stimuli in both conditions may have been riding on opposed base-line trends, that is, further development of CNV in Condition W and recovery from CNV in Condition N. But since the differences in P_3 to the three types of signal stimuli were within-condition comparisons and since the major comparison of interest (RR versus RF) was in the same direction in both conditions, it is not likely that the opposed CNV trends are importantly involved

Table 1. *Voltage (CNV) (in microvolts) at Tone and Click Stimulus Onset Relative to Voltage at Fixation Stimulus Onset*

Signal stimulus type	Condition			
	W		N	
	Signal tone	Reaction click	Signal and reaction tone	click
RR	−9.80	−17.40	−14.45	−1.25
RF	−8.45	−16.50	−11.85	−0.00
FF	−8.15	−11.45	−13.75	−1.75

in this aspect of the results. However, the differences in overall P_3 obtained in Conditions W and N might have reflected the effects of the opposed CNV trends. To check this possibility for each subject we remeasured P_3 relative to the average of N_2 and N_3. Thus, the new P_3 was measured with respect to a point in Condition N that should minimize CNV recovery effects and in Condition W with respect to a point that should minimize the effects of further development of CNV. Table 2 shows the values of P_3 to each type of signal stimulus determined in this way for conditions W and N.

The results given in this table are consistent with the plotted results for the "uncorrected" P_3 amplitudes shown in Fig. 2, and are somewhat more internally consistent. First, the differences due to stimulus type in conditions N and W are in the same direction as in Fig. 2 with a difference $(p < .10)$ now appearing between P_3 to the RF and FF stimuli of condition N. Second, not only is the overall effect of stimulus type significant, but the difference between P_3 to the RR and RF stimuli in Condition W is now significant $(p < .05)$.

Of additional interest are the reaction times (RT) to the various stimuli in conditions N and W shown in Table 3. On the average RT were about 200 msec shorter in Condition W. Although differences in the sensory attributes of the reaction stimuli were not controlled across conditions (that is, clicks in Condition W versus tones in condition N), it is likely that most or all of the difference in RT can be attributed to the advance information supplied by the signal stimuli of condition W. This information converted the choice reaction of Condition N into essentially a simple reaction in condition W.

IV. Discussion

The results of the present study showed that with frequency of stimulus occurrence controlled, the amplitude of P_3 to a given rare stimulus increased when the stimulus reduced a greater amount of uncertainty about which response was to be made. Thus, these results lend further support to a number of earlier studies, which have suggested that P_3 is related in some way to the cognitive or meaningful aspects of stimulation.

We also found that the speed with which the information was needed affected P_3. This conclusion is based on a comparison of P_3 across conditions W and N. The amplitudes of P_3 were greater in Condition N than in Condition W even when allowance was made for differential base-line shifts (see Table 2). In evaluating this result the possible confounding effects of overt motor response (Vaughan, Costa, & Ritter, 1968) also need to be considered because they occurred in closer temporal proximity to the signal stimuli of

Table 2. *Corrected P_3 (in microvolts) by Signal Stimulus Type and Condition*

Signal stimulus type	Condition	
	W	N
RR	6.45	10.50
RF	4.92	7.65
FF	3.44	5.70

Table 3. *Reaction Time (in milliseconds) by Condition and Signal Stimulus Type[a]*

Signal stimulus Type	Condition			
	W		N	
	Mean	SD	Mean	SD
RR	200	51.6	453	81.5
RF	194	50.5	401	74.9
FF	183	56.8	345	75.9
Mean:	192		400	

[a] Note that the reaction stimulus in Condition W was a click and in Condition N, a tone.

Condition N. While we cannot rule out this possibility conclusively, the RT data of Table 3 do not indicate a motor response factor because differences in P_3 amplitude are not related systematically to differences in RT. Furthermore, the high variability of RT, especially in condition N, should reduce appreciably the size of any effects time locked to the response. Finally, a previous study (Karlin, Martz, Brauth, & Mordkoff, 1971), which examined the question of EP modulation by motor potentials, also did not find supporting evidence.

The fact that response urgency increased both the overall level of P_3 as well as P_3 to the RR stimuli, when compared to the other two stimulus types, suggests another interpretation that might combine cognitive and arousal factors. If the effect of increased urgency is to increase general cortical arousal, which in turn is reflected in an enhanced P_3, it may be that the enhancement produced by the RR stimuli does not directly reflect the specific processing of the greater response uncertainty but rather the consequences of such processing. Specifically, we suggest that as a result of rapid (cognitive) analysis of stimulus significance during the first 200 msec following stimulus onset, the subject develops a level of cortical arousal determined by task difficulty. This arousal level we assume would be reflected by P_3 amplitude, and since it occurs as a momentary response to the stimulus, we call it "phasic arousal." Thus, it could be argued that the subject develops a set to make a given response to the FF stimuli that does not have to be changed in response to the RF stimuli. It is the need for changing this set in response to the RR stimuli, which we assume to be associated with momentary development of greater arousal, that produces a large P_3 to these stimuli. When the set can be changed more leisurely, as in condition W, the corresponding values of P_3 are smaller.

Finally, we should note that related suggestions have been made in earlier discussions to account for EP modification by the cognitive aspects of stimulation such as "general mental activity" (Uttal, 1967), "selective arousal" (Chapman, 1969) and "self-mobilization" (Karlin et al., 1971).

References

Chapman, R. M. Discussion. In E. Donchin & D. B. Lindsley (Eds.), *Averaged evoked potentials*, NASA SP-191, Washington, D.C.: National Aeronautics and Space Administration, 1969. Pp. 262–275.

Karlin, L., Martz, M. J., Jr., Brauth, S., & Mordkoff, A. M. Auditory evoked potentials, motor potentials and reaction time. *Electroencephalography and Clinical Neurophysiology*, 1971, **31**, 129–136.

Low, M. D., & McSherry, J. W. Further observations of psychological factors involved in CNV genesis. *Electroencephalography and Clinical Neurophysiology*, 1968, **25**, 203–207.

Ritter, W., & Vaughan, H. G., Jr. Average evoked responses in vigilance and discrimination: A reassessment. *Science*, 1969, **164**, 326–328.

Ritter, W., Vaughan, H. G., Jr., & Costa, L. D. Orienting and habituation to auditory stimuli: A study of short term changes in average evoked responses. *Electroencephalography and Clinical Neurophysiology*, 1968, **25**, 550–556.

Sokolov, E. N. *Perception and the conditioned reflex*. Oxford: Pergamon, 1963.

Sutton, S., Braren, M., Zubin, J., & John, E. R. Evoked potential correlates of stimulus uncertainty. *Science*, 1965, **150**, 1187–1188.

Tueting, P., Sutton, S., & Zubin, J. Quantitative evoked potential correlates of the probability of events. *Psychophysiology*, 1971, 7, 385–394.

Uttal, W. R. Evoked brain potentials: Signs or codes? *Perspectives in Biological Medicine*, 1967, **10**, 627–639.

Vaughan, H. G., Jr., Costa, L. D., & Ritter, W. Topography of the human motor potential. *Electroencephalography and Clinical Neurophysiology*, 1968, **25**, 1–10.

Walter, W. G., Cooper, R., Aldridge, V. J., McCallum, W. C., & Winter, A. L. Contingent negative variation: An electrical sign of sensorimotor association and expectancy in the human brain. *Nature*, 1964, **203**, 380–384.

Waszak, M., & Obrist, W. D. Relationship of slow potential changes to response speed and motivation in man. *Electroencephalography and Clinical Neurophysiology*, 1969, **27**, 113–120.

Winer, B. J. *Statistical principles in experimental design.* New York: McGraw-Hill, 1962.

The Relationship between Prestimulus Negative Shifts and Poststimulus Components of the Averaged Evoked Potential[1]

Patricia Tueting

*Biometrics Research,
New York State Depart-
ment of Mental Hygiene
and Department of
Psychology Herbert H.
Lehman College of the
City University of New
York*

Samuel Sutton

*Biometrics Research,
New York State Depart-
ment of Mental Hygiene
and Department of
Psychiatry, Columbia
University, New York, New York*

ABSTRACT

Four formulations were considered concerning the possible relationship between averaged pre- and poststimulus waveforms. An adequate formulation must account for data showing that although a prestimulus negative shift tends to be associated with changes in the vertex averaged evoked potential, especially a positive enhancement of P_3 (and possibly of the P_2 and N_2 components), pre- and poststimulus activity can also be dissociated. For example, it is possible to find functional relationships between evoked potential amplitude and certain experimental variables while controlling for differential contribution of prestimulus activity by presenting stimulus conditions in an unpredictable trial sequence. Further research is required in order to determine the exact nature of association and dissociation between pre- and poststimulus activity with particular attention to the possibility of an overlapping of components from different neurological sources in some experimental designs.

[1]This work was supported by Grants MH 14580 and MH 19812 from the National Institute of Mental Health, United States Public Health Service.

185

Electrical activity has been recorded prior to and after the occurrence of the stimulus of interest in certain classes of experiments. A prestimulus slow negative shift, often referred to as the contingent negative variation or CNV (Walter, Cooper, Aldridge, McCallum, & Winter, 1964), appears to be a correlate of both sensory and motor processing. The CNV develops when the subject is supposedly expecting (Walter *et al.*, 1964) the arrival of a salient stimulus within a defined time period. Increases in the magnitude of the negative shift have been reported with manipulations of attention and correspondingly decreases have been reported with manipulations which induce distraction in the subject (McCallum, 1969; Tecce & Scheff, 1969). In addition, the CNV has been related to concepts of readiness (Karlin, 1970), motivation (Irwin, Knott, McAdam, & Rebert, 1966; Rebert, McAdam, Knott, & Irwin, 1967), conation (Low, Borda, Frost, & Kellaway, 1966), and arousal (Tecce, 1971).

A poststimulus increase in amplitude of the N_1 and P_2 components of the vertex-evoked potential, which have approximate peak latencies of 100 msec and 200 msec, respectively, has been linked with vigilance and decision (Eason & Harter, 1969; Picton, Hillyard, Galambos, & Schiff, 1971; Satterfield, 1965; Spong, Haider, & Lindsley, 1965), uncertainty (Tueting, 1968; Tueting, Sutton, & Zubin, 1970), discrimination (Davis, 1964), key pressing (Spong *et al.*, 1965), and counting (Gross, Begleiter, Tobin, & Kissin, 1965). Further, an increase in a later positive component (with a latency of about 300 msec) of the vertex-evoked potential (P_3) has been reported when the stimulus is task relevant (Donchin & Cohen, 1967), delivers information resolving uncertainty (Sutton, Tueting, Zubin, & John, 1967; Weinberg, Walter, & Crow, 1970), occurs unpredictably (Ritter, Vaughan, & Costa, 1968), occurs with low probability (Tueting *et al.*, 1970), or requires a difficult discrimination (Ritter & Vaughan, 1969).

Because of the emphasis on poststimulus activity in many studies and because of the lower-frequency cutoff required for the slow prestimulus activity, measurement of both pre- and poststimulus activity has been undertaken in only a few studies. However, the possibility of a relationship between the prestimulus[2] negative shift and the amplitude of certain evoked potential[3] components, particularly P_3, has been suggested (Donchin &

---

[2]Our use of the term prestimulus is only for purposes of clarity and simplicity. Actually, the typical CNV design has two stimuli, S_1 and S_2, with the CNV appearing between the two stimuli. In relation to this design, our use of the term prestimulus means prior to the second stimulus, S_2.

[3]Following the usage in the literature, the term evoked potential in this paper is limited to poststimulus activity—in the CNV design we are referring to the response to S_2. This is not meant to imply that other potentials such as the CNV may not in many experimental designs be "evoked."

Smith, 1970; Karlin, 1970; Näätänen, 1967, 1970; Weinberg *et al.*, 1970). The view is based on data that indicate that conditions that are associated with the appearance of the negative shift are similar to the conditions that are sometimes associated with dramatic increases in the amplitude of P_3. For example, Donchin and Smith (1970) found larger CNV and P_3 for relevant stimuli as compared with irrelevant stimuli when relevant and irrelevant stimuli were presented in a predictable sequence. Such data appear to seriously question whether certain late components reflect processing of stimulus information which is independent of, or at least in addition to, processing prior to stimulus presentation. There is frequently the implication that differences in evoked potential amplitude related to such constructs as selective attention and cognition are completely or partially accounted for by prestimulus processing and are in this sense trivial (Karlin, 1970; Näätänen, 1967, 1970).

Although the controversy has revolved mainly around the relationship between the prestimulus negative shift and the amplitude of the P_3 component of the evoked potential, other evoked-potential components have been implicated, Järvilehto and Fruhstorfer (1970) have suggested that a central dominant prestimulus slow negative potential and N_1 of the auditory-evoked potential might both be "signs of the same functional system, one representing a more tonic, the other a more phasic activity [p. 315]." Näätänen (1967, 1970) argued that the P_2 component reflected prestimulus arousal rather than poststimulus selective attention. He found that subjects showing enhancement of P_2 for relevant stimuli also tended to have large prestimulus negative shifts (Näätänen, 1970). Although prestimulus activity was not recorded, Sheatz and Chapman (1969) reported that both P_2 (Peak 1) and P_3 (Peak 2) were enhanced for relevant stimuli when relevant and irrelevant stimulus conditions were alternated. The N_2 component of the evoked potential, when measured separately, has been reported to decrease in amplitude with increased uncertainty (Tueting, 1968) and with increased vigilance (Wilkinson, Morlock, & Williams, 1966), both of which are conditions likely to elicit a CNV (Friedman, 1971; Wilkinson & Haines, 1970). Picton and his colleagues (1971) found a larger CNV and larger N_1-P_2 and P_2-N_2 when subjects were listening to clicks in order to detect infrequent fainter clicks than when subjects were reading a book and ignoring the clicks. In a considerable number of studies, only peak-to-peak measures, N_1-P_2, N_1-P_3, P_2-N_2, are reported. The absence of corresponding base line-to-peak measurements complicates the issue of differential effects on particular components.

Because several evoked-potential components have been reported to change in amplitude with nonsensory changes in information processing requirements, the following discussion sometimes refers to the "late" components (N_1, P_2, N_2, P_3, N_3, P_4) of the vertex-evoked potential. However, it cannot be disregarded that certain of these components have different sources (W. R. Goff, Matsumiya, Allison, & G. D. Goff, 1969; Vaughan & Ritter, 1970) and are known to vary systematically with sensory parameters of the stimulus. Moreover, Ritter and his associates (1968) have reported that P_3 amplitude is increased when an auditory stimulus is unpredictable while P_2 amplitude is not.

The issue of the relationship between prestimulus negativity and post-stimulus activity can be summarized in terms of four overlapping, but nevertheless different, hypotheses. These four formulations will serve as a framework for the following discussion and will indicate the complexity and problems involved in relating pre- and poststimulus activity.

Formulation 1: There is a direct relationship between the prestimulus negative shift and certain poststimulus components, particularly P_3.

This hypothesis was suggested originally by the fact that the return to base line of the prestimulus negative shift often appears to correspond in time with the peak of the P_3 component. Karlin (1970) suggested that P_3 represents "reactive change" due to the termination of "readiness" processes, which are ongoing and are probably represented by the prestimulus negative shift. Although researchers are rightly hesitant at this stage to directly state that the mechanism involved in the prestimulus negative shift is the same mechanism involved in the poststimulus activity, the implication is often there. Karlin (1970), in a review criticizing evoked-potential studies that reported a correlation between cognitive processing (for example, selective attention) and poststimulus activity, states in his abstract that: "The possibility is examined that certain low voltage changes, such as contingent negative variation and other so called 'readiness' potentials, are associated with reactive change and *produce* [italics ours] the positive enhancement in evoked potentials as reported in many of the experiments [p. 122]."

The fact that the CNV and P_3 are often evoked by the same kinds of experimental manipulations (Donchin, Gerbrandt, Leifer, & Tucker, 1972; Donchin & Smith, 1970; Friedman, 1971; Karlin, 1970; Weinberg et al., 1970) would tend, of course, to support this formulation. Unfortunately, there is a lack of clear quantitative data relating pre- and poststimulus activity that might further support Formulation 1, and reports of dissociation between the prestimulus negative shift and evoked-potential amplitude are particularly damaging to this hypothesis. Evidence for dissociation will be discussed later.

Formulation 2: Both the prestimulus negative shift and certain components (particularly P_2 and possibly P_3) of the averaged evoked potential *increase in amplitude as a function of an underlying process of nonspecific arousal.*

The second formulation has been made most explicitly by Näätänen (1967, 1970) in the context of his critique of selective attention experiments that compare evoked potentials to task-relevant and task-irrelevant stimulus conditions. He pointed out that experimental designs involving regular alternation of relevant and irrelevant stimuli (Satterfield, 1965; Spong *et al.*, 1965), and larger N_1-P_2 for relevant stimuli, do not control for the possibility of a greater level of nonspecific arousal prior to the presentation of task-relevant stimuli as compared with task-irrelevant stimuli. In support of the prestimulus activation hypothesis he found that when relevant and irrelevant stimuli were alternated, a larger prestimulus negative shift and greater α desynchronization preceded relevant stimuli. Most important to his hypothesis, he reported a failure to find selective attention effects for the P_2 component of the evoked potential when he controlled for differential prestimulus factors by random presentation of relevant and irrelevant stimulus conditions.

Hartley (1970), who also used random presentation of relevant and irrelevant stimulus conditions, found data in support of Näätänen for the P_2 component, although he defined relevance in terms of a duration discrimination task rather than in terms of a vigilance task. Hartley did not present measurements of the P_3 component, although a component at that latency can be seen in some of the examples he reported.

Contrary to Näätänen and Hartley, several studies have shown that the averaged evoked potential does reflect selective attention even when controlling for prestimulus effects by randomizing the presentation of relevant and irrelevant stimulus conditions. Donchin and Cohen (1967) found a difference in P_3 amplitude using a quasi-random presentation order. Näätänen discounted the finding that P_3 was larger for the relevant visual stimulus than for the irrelevant visual stimulus when stimuli were presented in random order because of the greater likelihood of peripheral confounding for visual stimuli as compared with auditory stimuli. The respective views of Donchin and Cohen and Näätänen on "anticipation of relevant stimuli and evoked potentials" are well documented (Donchin & Cohen, 1969a, b; Näätänen, 1969a, b). Eason and Harter (1969), who randomized relevant and irrelevant stimulus conditions, also found a difference in evoked-potential amplitude as a function of the relevance of the stimulus. From the examples given, it appears that N_1, P_2, and P_3 were all enhanced substantially for relevant stimuli. Further evidence for poststimulus enhancement of positive components for relevant stimuli that could not be predicted in advance has been reported by Chapman (1969). Clearly, the issue of whether the averaged evoked potential reflects selective attention requires further investigation because of the contradictory findings.

The hypothesis that the prestimulus negative shift reflects nonspecific arousal has been studied by using a design in which evoked-potential amplitude to an irrelevant tracer stimulus presented during the negative shift is compared to the evoked-potential amplitude obtained to the same stimulus presented during the intertrial interval. Increased amplitude (Näätänen, 1967) and decreased latency (McAdam, 1969) of the evoked potentials to stimuli presented during the CNV as compared with stimuli presented during the intertrial interval have been used to support the arousal hypothesis. However, it is possible that a stimulus presented during the CNV has a time-marking function that a stimulus presented during the intertrial interval does not have (Karlin, 1970) and therefore inferences with regard to the arousal hypothesis from these experiments are tenuous. Moreover, Donald and Goff (1971) in a variation of this design found dissociation between the amplitude of the CNV and the amplitude of the P_3 component of the evoked potential. In their experiment, P_3 varied as a function of the relevance of the stimulus to the subject's task independently of the CNV level.

Näätänen (1967) suggested that arousal reflected in the CNV and in the evoked potential might be of extralemniscal reticular origin. While it is generally agreed that components within the first 100 msec carry modality-specific information (Goff et al., 1969), it has been suggested recently that N_1-P_2 of the vertex auditory-evoked potential (Vaughan & Ritter, 1970) originates in temporal auditory cortex, although conflicting data have been reported by Kooi, Tipton, and Marshall (1971). It has also been reported that P_2 of the somatosensory-evoked potential is dependent upon the integrity of the primary somatosensory areas (Williamson, Goff, & Allison, 1970). These data, if upheld, would seem to rule out a simple notion of extralemniscal reticular arousal involvement in these components, but rather would implicate these components in reflecting further cortical processing of stimulus information.

Formulation 3: Both the prestimulus negative shift and the late components of the evoked potential reflect independent psychological experimental variables that may occur together in some experimental designs, and the correlations obtained between these measures is a function of this overlap.

Formulation 4: The pre- and poststimulus processes are related, but additional processing of stimulus information is also reflected independently in certain evoked-potential components.

Since there is no evidence which at the present time would separate Formulations 3 and 4, they are discussed together. Essentially, Formulation 3 proposes complete independence except that our present experimental designs do not always adequately disentangle the relevant psychological variables. In Formulation 3, the pre- and poststimulus processes covary by "coincidence," that is, the psychological variables independently controlling these processes vary together. On the other hand, Formulation 4 posits both dependence and independence. A dependent relationship between the pre- and poststimulus processes is proposed, but this is not one of complete determinism. Formulation 4 further suggests that at least the poststimulus process may be involved in further processing that is independent of the prestimulus state of electrical activity.

Both Formulations 3 and 4, as opposed to Formulations 1 and 2, would be supported by evidence of dissociation between the prestimulus negative shift and the poststimulus components of the evoked potential. The "ideal" experiment would be to create conditions that would elicit a component such as P_3 and no prestimulus negative shift, or the inverse, a prestimulus negative shift and no P_3. A late positive component without a CNV can be seen in the data of Friedman (1971) and Jenness (1972), and indicates that for these subjects the presence of the CNV is not a sufficient or a necessary condition for the elicitation of P_3. Friedman (1971) found that while six out of eight subjects showed larger CNV[4] and P_3 for the uncertain condition as compared with the certain condition this association was not true for the remaining two subjects. In these subjects, a positive shift was found, although the P_3 data for these two subjects were not different from the other six subjects. These data could indicate the possibility of an uncontrolled factor in the experiment related to the CNV but not necessarily to P_3. Jenness (1972) showed that a large late component (which could not be identified with certainty as being P_2 or P_3) in the response to the feedback click in a discrimination situation was preceded by a prolonged positive shift.

Some recent experiments, while inconclusive for the issue of the relationship between pre- and poststimulus activity, indicate a direction for further research. Bevan (1971) reported that N_1–P_2 amplitude of the auditory-evoked response to S_1 (prior to the CNV) in an S_1–S_2 paradigm was reduced by 65% in hyperbaric air, while the CNV showed no change. Unfortunately, he did not report whether or not there was any change in the response to S_2. It would also be informative to determine the effect of sleep loss on

---

[4]In Friedman's design, the prestimulus negative shift was measured between a subject-initiated button press and a subsequent stimulus. Therefore, this is not the classical CNV which uses the S_1–S_2 paradigm.

the evoked response to S_2, since sleep loss has been reported to eliminate or greatly reduce the CNV (Naitoh, Johnson, & Lubin, 1971).

While it is true that dissociation between the CNV and amplitude of certain late components is often found, it is also true that association is found in many experiments (Donchin & Smith, 1970; Donchin *et al.*, 1971a; Näätänen, 1967, 1970). Moreover, both association and dissociation have been reported in the same studies. Small and Small (1970) failed to find a significant correlation between the amplitude of a prestimulus slow wave and the amplitude of the averaged evoked potential in a simple CNV design. Although the CNV and a late positive component both may be present, the late positive component has been reported to vary in amplitude as a function of the experimental variable, while amplitude of the CNV does not. Donchin and his associates (1972) have reported that a late positive component varies as a function of the type of task required of the subject (motor, selective motor, predictive or computational). The CNV, although present for all tasks, did not. Lombroso (1969) found that a late positive component reflected response selection in a choice reaction time design, whereas a prestimulus negative shift failed to do so.

We would like to present some evidence from our laboratory relevant to the issue of the relationship between pre- and poststimulus processing. On the whole, this evidence supports Formulation 4 in that there is neither complete independence nor complete dependence between pre- and poststimulus activity. Evidence for dissociation apparently does not preclude weak positive correlations between the CNV and poststimulus components, particularly P_3. In all of these studies, however, it was possible to obtain systematic functions relating the amplitude of some components of the evoked potential to the experimental variable, whereas no such systematic function was obtained for the CNV, even if present. Two major factors in the ability to obtain this kind of dissociation were that all experimental conditions were presented in an unpredictable sequence and the experiments yielded quantitative functions.

I. Pitch Discrimination Study

Jenness (1972) conducted an experiment involving slow improvement in accuracy of performance in a very difficult pitch discrimination. In his design, the two responses that the subject made did not have equal salience, since one of the two discriminative responses was rewarded with a high monetary payoff if correct (and a corresponding loss if incorrect), whereas the other discriminative response had no monetary consequences, whether correct or incorrect. The motor response of the subject indicating his discrimination was delayed to avoid, as much as possible, overlap of the motor potentials with the evoked response to the stimulus to be discriminated.

Over the ten days of the experiment, late components in the response to the stimuli being discriminated became increasingly differentiated with respect to the relative amplitude of $N_2 - P_3$, $P_3 - N_3$, and $N_3 - P_4$. This differentiation paralleled the behavioral accuracy of discrimination. However, no systematic relation to the behavioral level of accuracy emerged in the CNV preceding the stimuli to be discriminated, nor was the CNV preceding correct discriminations in any way different from the CNV preceding incorrect discriminations.

In addition, as shown in Fig. 1, the slow base-line shift, while present, seemed to be independent of the amplitude of the evoked potential. The largest evoked potential was obtained for a click giving feedback to the subject concerning his accuracy, and it was preceded by a prolonged positive (rather than negative) shift in all subjects; however, the same click when it served as the click to be discriminated was preceded by a negative shift in most subjects. In addition, there was considerable between-subject variability in slow base-line shifts.

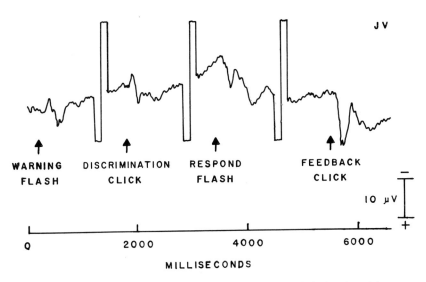

Fig. 1. Vertex electrical activity (earlobe reference) recorded during the trial sequence when the discrimination click was the hot stimulus. The waveform is interrupted by three calibrating pulses. The feedback click-evoked response amplitude was actually larger than is shown because of the fact that the feedback click was only presented for correct discriminations while the average has been divided by the total number of trials in which the discrimination click was the hot stimulus.

II. Threshold Study

Hillyard and his colleagues (Hillyard, Squires, Bauer, & Lindsay, 1971) reported that P_3 is systematically related to d', which is a behavioral measure of the sensitivity of the subject in the threshold situation—P_3 increases as the accuracy of detection increases (due to increased intensity). He also reported that the CNV was slightly larger prior to correct detections where P_3 was present, than prior to incorrect detections where P_3 was absent. The latter finding could be interpreted as suggesting that the subject was in a state of greater readiness or alertness preceding correct identifications than preceding incorrect identifications.

Paul (1971) of our laboratory has replicated this experiment and also found that P_3 was linearly related to d'. An example of one of these experi-

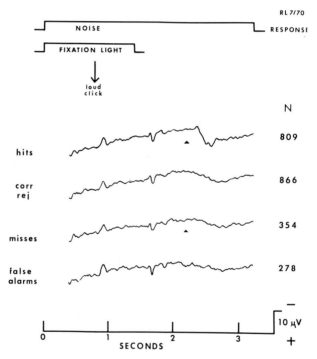

Fig. 2. Averaged evoked responses for one subject recorded from vertex to earlobe. Data for the early portion of the trial, the evoked response to noise and fixation light onset are not shown. The subject's key press response, which indicated his discrimination, was made at the offset of the noise. The occurrence of the threshold click is shown as a triangle below the waveforms for hits and misses. The number of trials in the average is shown at the right of the waveform.

ments is shown in Fig. 2. Four stimulus–responses categories are possible in this type of threshold experiment: (*a*) hits, the threshold stimulus is present and the subject detects it; (*b*) correct rejections, the threshold stimulus is absent and the subject says it is absent; (*c*) misses, the threshold stimulus is present and the subject fails to detect it; and (*d*) false alarms, the threshold stimulus is absent and the subject thinks he detects a stimulus. Note that the evoked potential to the threshold click is present for the hit category only. It is not present for misses even though the stimulus was actually presented. Nor is it present for absent clicks, regardless of whether the subject thought he heard a click or not, as indicated by his behavioral response.

Figure 3 shows that the CNV was not consistently larger preceding correct identifications than preceding incorrect identifications as Hillyard

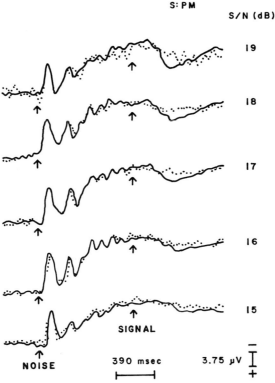

Fig. 3. Averaged vertex data (earlobe reference) for one subject. The first arrow indicates the onset of a ready signal and the second arrow indicates the presence or absence of the threshold click. Waveforms for correct (solid line) and incorrect (dotted line) detections are superimposed at various intensity levels of the threshold click. Numbers at the right of the waveforms give the relative intensity of the clicks.

and his colleagues (1971) reported. Note also that P_3[5] is large for correct detections and absent for incorrect detections despite essentially identical CNVs. On the other hand, Paul found small but consistently positive correlations between the CNV and P_3 as a function of d'. The P_3 component was larger at intensities at which the subject was more accurate and the CNV also tended to be larger.

Paul also systematically manipulated the criterion of the subject in two different ways, by varying monetary payoff or by varying signal probability. The P_3 component for hits was found to be related monotonically to the degree of cautiousness of the subject, while the prestimulus negative shift failed to vary as a function of criterion.

In summary, both association and dissociation between the CNV and P_3 were demonstrated in the threshold data. There was a low positive correlation between the CNV and P_3 as a function of sensitivity but not as a function of criterion. Also in Paul's data, large differences in P_3 for correct and incorrect detections were preceded by identical CNVs, which is in conflict with Hillyard's findings. However, even when there are CNV differences for correct versus incorrect detections, these differences are small compared with the large P_3 differences for the same conditions (Hillyard et al., 1971).

III. The Guessing Paradigm

The guessing design may aid in the separation of perceptual and response contributions to pre- and poststimulus waveforms. When the subject guesses what stimulus will occur on the next trial, response selection occurs prior to stimulus presentation. The subject makes no response following stimulus presentation, and therefore the evoked potential cannot be confounded by response contingent neurological processing as it may be in reaction time or discrimination designs.

In these experiments, the alternative stimuli (high or low band-pass clicks) were presented unpredictably, except that their relative probability of occurrence was varied. The subject was told the relative probabilities with which the two stimuli would be presented, and the subject's guessing probabilities were also recorded.

---

[5]The identification of this component as P_3 follows Hillyard et al. (1971) and is based both on latency considerations as well as on the more complete shape of the evoked potential at higher intensities of the stimulus in the same subjects. Further study is required in order to identify conclusively the late positive component reported in guessing experiments, in choice reaction time experiments and in discrimination and threshold experiments as the same component (P_3).

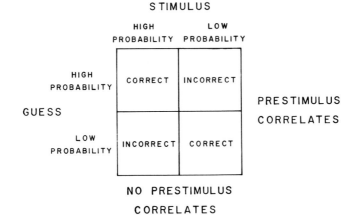

Fig. 4. Four-cell table describing the experimental design. Low versus high probability stimuli were presented randomly, and therefore averaged evoked potentials associated with column differences should not reflect differential prestimulus processes. However, row-averaged evoked responses could possibly reflect the subject's guessing response, which was a prestimulus event.

Figure 4 summarizes the design. If evoked responses are averaged separately by columns (as a function of the stimulus) prestimulus differences would be surprising since stimulus conditions were randomized by trial. On the other hand, it would not be surprising to find differences when averaging separately by rows—as a function of whether the subject guessed the low-probability stimulus, which might be considered to be a "risky" bet, or whether he guessed the high-probability stimulus, which might be considered to be less "risky." Since the guess occurs prior to the stimulus, it might conceivably be reflected in prestimulus activity.

The results are shown in Fig. 5. The response to the warning flash (S_1) shows a clear N_1-P_2 response, followed by a slow negative rise in amplitude of approximately 8 μV during the S_1-S_2 interval. The negative shifts were relatively small compared with the CNV amplitudes found in other studies but small amplitude is not surprising, considering that the subject was not required to make an overt response to the second stimulus (Irwin *et al.*, 1966).

The evoked response to the click (S_2) shows a large N_1-P_3 of about 20 μV. Note that in the upper pair of waveforms, averaged by stimulus, P_3 is larger for the low-probability click than for the high-probability click, but the two CNVs are essentially identical. However, in the lower pair of waveforms, which are averaged according to the guess, both the CNV and P_3 are larger when the subject guesses the low-probability event.

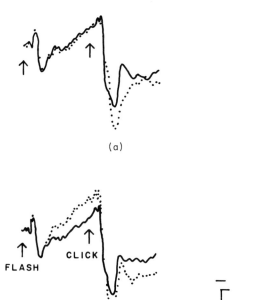

(a)

(b)

Fig. 5. Averaged evoked potentials from vertex to earlobe for one subject: (a) (. . . .) low-probability stimulus, (———) high-probability stimulus; (b) (. . . .) guess low probability, (———) guess high probability. The first arrow indicates the time of occurrence of a ready flash, and the second arrow marks the occurrence of the high or low band-pass click that informed the subject of the correctness of his guess. The upper two waveforms show differences as a function of stimulus probability and the lower two waveforms show differences as a function of the subject's guessing behavior.

Considerable variability was noted in seven replications of this experiment. Not all subjects showed larger amplitude CNV and P_3 for averaged potentials associated with guessing the low-probability event. There was no monetary payoff for correct guesses, and lack of incentive could have accounted for the variability in the results, since motivation has been reported to increase the CNV amplitude (Irwin *et al.*, 1966).

In another set of five experiments of similar design, a payoff schedule was instituted. The alternative stimuli, instead of being single high versus single low band-pass clicks, were either same pairs of clicks (high followed by high or low followed by low) or different pairs of clicks (high followed by low or low followed by high). The interclick interval was 2 sec, the intertrial interval was 11–12 sec, and the intensities of the low click and of the high click were equated subjectively. The experimenter varied the probability that same or different pairs of clicks would be presented according to a preset program. The subject was instructed to guess "same" or "different," and on alternate blocks of trials he was informed that same click pairs had a high probability of occurring (different click pairs, a low probability) or that different click pairs had a high probability of occurring (same click pairs, a low probability).

In this design, findings were consistent across five experiments in three subjects. When the averages were separated according to whether the subject guessed the low- or high-probability event, P_3 amplitude was larger when the subject guessed the low-probability event in four out of five cases.[6] The negative shift was also larger when the subject guessed the low-probability event, but the CNV differences were consistently smaller than the P_3 differences. In the one case where P_3 was smaller for the low-probability event, the prestimulus negative shift preceding the low-probability event was also smaller. The guessing experiments, then, like the threshold experiments, demonstrate both association and dissociation—association when averaging as a function of the guess, dissociation when averaging as a function of the stimulus.

IV. Probability Study

Friedman (1971) of our laboratory recently replicated probability experiments (Tueting *et al.*, 1970) in which the subject guessed prior to the event whether one of two auditory stimuli would be presented. In different blocks of trials the two stimuli had different relative probabilities, and the subject could not predict whether the frequent or the infrequent stimulus would be presented on the next trial. He confirmed the fact that the late components of the evoked response were larger when stimulus probability was low and smaller when stimulus probability was high. But the CNV showed no relationship to these probability manipulations, as shown in Fig. 6, which compares the effects of stimulus probability on the CNV and N_1–P_3.

In another experimental condition, the subject was told the identity of each stimulus prior to its occurrence, instead of being required to guess. Here in the certain condition, both the CNV and the late components of the

---

[6]The finding of no difference in P_3 amplitude for same versus different pairs of clicks indicates that sensory sameness versus differentness is not reflected in P_3 amplitude in this situation. It also would indicate that the probability effect cannot be explained in terms of inadequate recovery. These results are also contrary to a simple interpretation in terms of habituation for the probability effect since in the present study what must be habituated is the sameness or differentness of the click pairs.

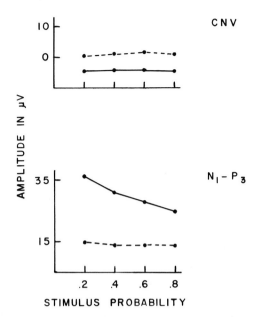

Fig. 6. Base line-to-peak amplitude of the CNV (top) and peak-to-peak amplitude of N_1–P_3 (bottom) averaged across eight subjects: The figure shows the effects of stimulus probability on the CNV and N_1–P_3 amplitude for both certain (dashed line) and uncertain (solid line) conditions.

evoked potential were reliably smaller than in the uncertain (or guessing) condition. In addition, there were individual differences among subjects in the CNV. Two of the eight subjects showed a prestimulus positive shift instead of a negative shift, but both the positive shift subjects and the negative shift subjects showed larger N_1–P_3 for the uncertain than for the certain condition.

In summary, in Friedman's experiments the late components but not the CNV followed the selective effects of stimulus probability. On the other hand, the two measures varied together across two experimental conditions which might be thought of as involving a difference in interest, or motivation, or uncertainty.

V. Discussion

A number of experiments have shown that when the negative shift preceding a stimulus is large, one or more components of the evoked potential to the subsequent stimulus are also large (see for example, Donchin *et al.*,

1972). In addition, if the conditions of the experiment are arranged so that the subject can predict which stimulus requires more information processing, a larger CNV may precede relevant stimuli and one or more late components may be increased in amplitude (Donchin & Smith, 1970; Näätänen, 1970).

Evidence presented in this paper shows that both the prestimulus negative shift and late components are larger in an uncertain condition than in a certain condition (Friedman, 1971). It was also reported that making a high-risk guess is associated with larger CNV and P_3 than making a low-risk guess. The CNV preceding an accurate discrimination (which yields a large P_3) was reported by Hillyard and his associates (1971) to be larger than the CNV preceding an inaccurate discrimination (which yields a smaller or absent P_3). McAdam and Rubin (1971) also reported larger negative shifts to be associated with greater accuracy of perception, while a late positive component (P_{302}) was not associated with accuracy. However, neither Paul (1971) nor Jenness (1972) were able to support a relationship between the CNV and whether the subject makes an accurate or an inaccurate discrimination. Finally, Paul also found that both the CNV and P_3 increase in amplitude as sensory sensitivity increases.

When the subject cannot predict which stimulus is relevant, systematic changes may be obtained in late components (Donchin & Cohen, 1967; Eason & Harter, 1969). Both P_2 and P_3, but not the CNV, change in amplitude systematically with stimulus probability when the subject is guessing which of two stimuli will be presented (Friedman, 1971). The P_3, N_3, and P_4 components, but not the CNV, change systematically with behavioral accuracy as a difficult discrimination is learned (Jenness, 1972). Jenness (1972) also found that the entire evoked-potential waveform changes as a function of whether the stimulus is the stimulus to be discriminated or whether the same stimulus has a feedback function. The response to the feedback click is much larger in amplitude and is preceded by a positive rather than by a negative shift in base line. Finally, Donchin and his associates (1972) have reported that a poststimulus positive component, but not the CNV, varies as a function of the task required of the subject.

In view of the findings of dissociation between the CNV and P_3, Formulations 1 and 2, although parsimonious, are by themselves inadequate. The hypothesis that the CNV reflects prestimulus readiness and that P_3 reflects poststimulus reactivity (Formulation 1) is not supported. Even in those situations where dependence between pre- and poststimulus processes is found, the relationship is weak and no systematic quantitative relationships have been demonstrated. In none of the experiments in which both the CNV and P_3 are found to vary together is the magnitude of the change of the same order. Changes in P_3 are often three or four times larger than changes in the

CNV (Friedman, 1971; Hillyard *et al.*, 1971; Paul, 1971). In some subjects, no CNV or even a small positive, instead of a negative, shift is found, but the changes in P_3 are just as systematic in these subjects as in subjects that do show a negative shift (Friedman, 1971; Jenness, 1972; Paul, 1971).

The hypothesis that both the prestimulus negative shift and the late components of the evoked potential reflect nonspecific arousal (Formulation 2) is similarly inadequate in light of the many reports of dissociation. It is also in conflict with the data of Donald and Goff (1971) and McAdam (1969), who did not find differences in evoked potential amplitude for stimuli presented during a CNV. Moreover, the notion that P_2 primarily reflects arousal presents some difficulties in view of the reported relatively localized cortical representation of this component. There is as yet no anatomical or physiological evidence relating P_2 or P_3 to extralemniscal arousal (Williamson *et al.*, 1970), nor any evidence in human subjects relating negative shifts to stimulation of the reticular formation. The hypothesis that extralemniscal arousal modulates the amplitude of certain late components requires further study.

At this writing, there is no evidence that can be used to distinguish between Formulation 3 and Formulation 4. Since both hypotheses provide for both association and dissociation, the evidence available on association and dissociation cannot be used to support one against the other. Formulation 3 would suggest that we concentrate on attempting to make the separation between pre- and poststimulus processes on the psychological level—by finding the experimental manipulations that affect one but not the other potential. Formulation 4 would suggest that more research is needed to determine to what extent the two potentials share a common mechanism and to what extent the poststimulus activity reflects additional independent processing of stimulus information.

It is highly probable that Formulation 4 must be true to some extent as the poststimulus evoked potential often can be seen riding on a positive process, which may be assumed to be the return of the prestimulus negative shift to base line. Actually, even the "return to base line" appears to be too simple a statement, as the poststimulus positive process often overshoots the base line, and has sometimes been referred to as a positive rebound. In any case, the overlap of the evoked potential with the positive shift would tend to summate with and perhaps distort all evoked-potential components. In fact, it may even be the positive-shift portion of the compound or overlapped poststimulus potentials that may be responsible for the degree of association found between pre- and poststimulus processes.

The positive shift and the overlap may be seen directly in Paul's data (1971). In the categories of correct rejections, misses, and false alarms, the negative shift resolves into a positive shift with the change in direction beginning somewhere in the vicinity of the time of presentation of the stimulus to be detected (S_2). These categories yield no evoked potential, and the positive shift may be seen with clarity, particularly in the correct rejections waveform. In the hits waveform, an evoked potential may be seen to the detected stimulus, and it is clear that it is overlapped with the positive return since by the time the evoked potential is over, the tracing is back to base line.

Other instances of overlap of potentials have been reported. Järvilehto and Fruhstorfer (1970) have identified at least two components of the CNV, a central dominant potential that seems to be related to readiness and a frontal dominant potential which seems to be related to uncertainty. They reported that it is the frontal dominant potential that is related to the P_3 component of the evoked potential reported to be correlated with the resolution of uncertainty described by Sutton (Sutton et al., 1967). Vaughan (1969) has differentiated motor potentials that can be localized over motor cortex from other steady potential shifts. According to Vaughan, a steady potential shift preceding a visual discrimination can be localized over the occipital cortex. In addition, experiments with monkeys also suggest the possibility of multiple sources of the prestimulus base-line shift (Borda, 1970; Donchin, Otto, Gerbrandt, & Pribram, 1971; Symmes, Healy, & Chase, 1971).

An overlap of poststimulus components is also possible. McAdam and Rubin (1971) have considered the possibility of an overlap between P_{300} of the stimulus-evoked potential and P_2 of the motor potential. Vaughan, Costa, Gilden, and Schimmel (1965) also have identified overlapped poststimulus sensory and motor components when a motor response is required upon stimulus presentation. An overlap of the somatosensory-evoked potentials with the vertex potential has been recently reported by Donald (1971).

At the present time, however, it is not possible to argue conclusively for Formulation 4. More work is required on this problem, keeping in mind certain technical considerations. It is essential to record prestimulus activity as well as poststimulus activity, using amplifiers that are sufficiently open on the low-frequency end, and simultaneously to monitor extracerebral potentials that could contaminate cortical activity. It is also desirable to use multiple electrode locations in order to obtain an adequate topographical distribution of the components involved in a particular study, and to report both peak-to-peak and base line-to-peak measurements of all components. Both measurements are required because peak-to-peak measurements may be less contaminated by base-line shifts, whereas peak-to-peak measurements alone are not sufficient because components like P_2 and N_2 may react differently to the same conditions.

When a behavioral task is required in response to the stimulus, an attempt should be made to separate the relative contribution of sensory and motor components (Vaughan *et al.*, 1965). Separation can be attempted by looking at different tasks in an otherwise similar situation, for example, requiring versus not requiring a reaction time in a guessing task, or by holding motor requirements constant across experimental conditions to be compared. More data is required on the difference between immediate and delayed responding, since delayed responding is used frequently as a control for overlap. Studies that utilize response time locking as well as stimulus time locking in the same experiment would also be informative. The advantage of using the uncertainty situation where the subject predicts what the next stimulus will be is that an overt response is not required to the relevant stimulus, thus avoiding the generation of brain activity related to the response.[7]

Randomization by trial of the experimental conditions is a procedure for controlling for differential prestimulus effects and for obtaining a dissociation between pre- and poststimulus processes. Unfortunately, the implementation of randomization is difficult, and therefore many laboratories are still using easier block designs. When complete unrestricted randomization is used and conditions are equally likely, there is no opportunity for the subject to expect the next trial presentation to be one condition over another. Thus, there should be no differences in prestimulus processes as a function of the experimental conditions even though CNVs may be present prior to all stimuli depending upon the other conditions of the experiment. Any "unpredictable" presentation order that uses a restricted random presentation order is not an adequate control because subjects learn the restriction quickly with repeated trials and the presentation order becomes to some degree predictable.

There is a great need for parametric research designs in order to obtain functional relationships and quantitative data in relation to pre- and poststimulus processes. By using appropriate control techniques and parametric experimental designs the relative contribution to specific late component amplitude from pre- and poststimulus processes can be assessed systematically. It then can be determined more conclusively whether Formulation 3, or Formulation 4, or a new hypothesis is the best way to describe the relationship between the prestimulus processes and particular late components of the evoked potential.

---

[7]The assumption that the response component is eliminated would not be entirely true if there are covert startle reflexes in response to the informative stimulus.

Acknowledgments

We thank David Friedman, Marion Hartung, David Jenness, Robert Laupheimer, Robert Levit, Dina Paul, Raymond Simon, and Joseph Zubin for assistance with various aspects of this work, and Dr. M. Wallach, Director of Brooklyn State Hospital, for providing the facilities for carrying out this research.

References

Bevan, J. The human auditory evoked response and contingent negative variation in hyperbaric air. *Electroencephalography and Clinical Neurophysiology*, 1971, **30**, 198–204.

Borda, R. P. The effect of altered drive states on the contingent negative variation (CNV) in rhesus monkeys. *Electroencephalography and Clinical Neurophysiology*, 1970, **29**, 173–180.

Chapman, R. M. Conference discussant. In E. Donchin & D. B. Lindsley (Eds.), *Average evoked potentials*, NASA SP-191. Washington, D.C.: NASA, 1969. Pp. 262–275.

Davis, H. Enhancement of evoked cortical potentials in humans related to a task requiring a decision. *Science*, 1964, **145**, 182–183.

Donald, M. W. Topography of long-latency somatosensory responses in the human brain: a re-examination. Paper presented at the Society for Neuroscience, Washington, D.C., October 1971.

Donald, M. W., & Goff, W. R. Attention-related increases in cortical responsivity dissociated from the contingent negative variation. *Science*, 1971, **172**, 1163–1166.

Donchin, E., & Cohen, L. Averaged evoked potentials and intramodality selective attention. *Electroencephalography and Clinical Neurophysiology*, 1967, **22**, 537–546.

Donchin, E., & Cohen, L. Anticipation of relevant stimuli and evoked potentials: A reply to Näätänen. *Perceptual and Motor Skills*, 1969, **29**, 115–117. (a)

Donchin, E., & Cohen, L. Further reply to Näätänen. *Perceptual and Motor Skills*, 1969, **29**, 270. (b)

Donchin, E., Gerbrandt, L. K., Leifer, L., & Tucker, L. Is the contingent negative variation contingent on a motor response? *Psychophysiology*, 1972, **9**, 178–188.

Donchin, E., Otto, D., Gerbrandt, L. K., & Pribram, K. The dependence of the distribution of slow cortical potentials recorded in the rhesus on the task imposed on the monkey. Paper presented at the Society for Neuroscience, Washington, D.C., October 1971.

Donchin, E., & Smith, D. B. D. The contingent negative variation and the late positive wave of the average evoked potential. *Electroencephalography and Clinical Neurophysiology*, 1970, **29**, 201–203.

Eason, R. G., & Harter, M. R. Effects of attention and arousal on visually evoked cortical potentials and reaction time in man. *Physiology and Behavior*, 1969, **4**, 283–289.

Friedman, D. The effects of stimulus uncertainty on pupillary dilation response and the vertex evoked potential in man. Unpublished doctoral dissertation, The City University of New York, 1971.

Goff, W. R., Matsumiya, Y., Allison, T., & Goff, G. D. Cross-modality comparisons of average evoked potentials. In E. Donchin & D. B. Lindsley (Eds.), *Average evoked potentials*, NASA SP-191. Washington, D.C.: NASA, 1969. Pp. 95–142.

Gross, M. M., Begleiter, H., Tobin, M., & Kissin, B. Auditory evoked response comparison during counting clicks and reading. *Electroencephalography and Clinical Neurophysiology*, 1965, **18**, 451–454.

Hartley, L. R. The effect of stimulus relevance on the cortical evoked potentials. *Quarterly Journal of Experimental Psychology*, 1970, **22**, 531–546.

Hillyard, S. A., Squires, K. C., Bauer, J. W., & Lindsay, P. H. Evoked potential correlates of auditory signal detection. *Science*, 1971, **172**, 1357–1360.

Irwin, D. A., Knott, J. R., McAdam, D. W., & Rebert, C. S. Motivational determinants of the "contingent negative variation." *Electroencephalography and Clinical Neurophysiology*, 1966, **21**, 538–543.

Järvilehto, T., & Fruhstorfer, H. Differentiation between slow cortical potentials associated with motor and mental acts in man. *Experimental Brian Research*, 1970, **11**, 309–317.

Jenness, D. Auditory evoked response differentiation with discrimination learning in humans. *Journal of Comparative and Physiological Psychology*, 1972, **80**, 75–90.

Karlin, L. Cognition, preparation, and sensory-evoked potentials. *Psychological Bulletin*, 1970, **73**, 122–136.

Kooi, K. A., Tipton, A. C., & Marshall, R. E. Polarities and field configurations of the vertex components of the human auditory evoked response: a reinterpretation. *Electroencephalography and Clinical Neurophysiology*, 1971, **31**, 166–169.

Lombroso, C. T. The CNV during tasks requiring choice. In C. R. Evans & T. B. Mulholland (Eds.), *Attention in neurophysiology*. New York: Appleton, 1969, Pp. 64–69.

Low, M. D., Borda, R. P., Frost, J. D., & Kellaway, P. Surface-negative, slow-potential shift associated with conditioning in man. *Neurology*, 1966, **16**, 771–782.

McAdam, D. W. Increases in CNS excitability during negative cortical slow potentials in man. *Electroencephalography and Clinical Neurophysiology*, 1969, **26**, 216–219.

McAdam, D. W., & Rubin, E. H. Readiness potential, vertex positive wave, contingent negative variation and accuracy of perception. *Electroencephalography and Clinical Neurophysiology*, 1971, **30**, 511–517.

McCallum, C. The contingent negative variation as a cortical sign of attention in man. In C. R. Evans & T. B. Mulholland (Eds.), *Attention in neurophysiology*. New York: Appleton, 1969. Pp. 40–63.

Näätänen, R. Selective attention and evoked potentials. *Annals of the Finnish Academy of Science* (Helsinki: Suomalaisen Tiedeakatemian Toimituksia), 1967, **151**, 1–226 (Separate).

Näätänen, R. Anticipation of relevant stimuli and evoked potentials: A comment on Donchin's and Cohen's "Averaged evoked potentials and intramodality selective attention." *Perceptual and Motor Skills*, 1969, **28**, 639–646. (a)

Näätänen, R. Anticipation of relevant stimuli and evoked potentials: A reply to Donchin and Cohen. *Perceptual and Motor Skills*, 1969, **29**, 233–234. (b)

Näätänen, R. Evoked potential, EEG, and slow potential correlates of selective attention. In A. F. Sanders (Ed.), *Attention and performance III*. Amsterdam: North-Holland Publ., 1970. Pp. 178–192.

Naitoh, P., Johnson, L. C., & Lubin, A. Modification of surface negative slow potential (CNV) in the human brain after total sleep loss. *Electroencephalography and Clinical Neurophysiology*, 1971, **30**, 17–22.

Paul, D. Late components of the auditory average evoked potential and binary decisions in signal detection tasks. Unpublished doctoral dissertation, Columbia University, 1971.

Picton, T. W., Hillyard, S. A., Galambos, R., & Schiff, M. Human auditory attention: A central or peripheral process? *Science*, 1971, **173**, 351–353.

Rebert, C. S., McAdam, D. W., Knott, J. R., & Irwin, D. A. Slow potential change in human brain related to level of motivation. *Journal of Comparative and Physiological Psychology*, 1967, **63**, 20–23.

Ritter, W., & Vaughan, H. G. Averaged evoked responses in vigilance and discrimination: a reassessment. *Science*, 1969, **164**, 326–328.

Ritter, W., Vaughan, H. G., Jr., & Costa, L. D. Orienting and habituation to auditory stimuli: a study of short term changes in average evoked responses. *Electroencephalography and Clinical Neurophysiology*, 1968, **25**, 550–556.

Satterfield, J. H. Evoked cortical response enhancement and attention in man: A study of responses to auditory and shock stimuli. *Electroencephalography and Clinical Neurophysiology*, 1965, **19**, 470–475.

Sheatz, G. C., & Chapman, R. M. Task relevance and auditory evoked responses. *Electroencephalography and Clinical Neurophysiology*, 1969, **26**, 468–475.

Small, J. G., & Small, I. F. Interrelationships of evoked and slow potential responses. *Diseases of the Nervous System*, 1970, **31**, 459–464.

Spong, P., Haider, M., & Lindsley, D. B. Selective attentiveness and cortical evoked responses to visual and auditory stimuli. *Science*, 1965, **148**, 395–397.

Sutton, S., Tueting, P., Zubin, J., & John, E. R. Information delivery and the sensory evoked potential. *Science*, 1967, **155**, 1436–1439.

Symmes, D., Healy, M., & Chase, K. Slow potential correlates of reaction time performance in monkeys. Paper presented at the Society for Neuroscience, Washington, D.C., October 1971.

Tecce, J. J. Contingent negative variation and individual differences. *Archives of General Psychiatry*, 1971, **24**, 1–16.

Tecce, J. J., & Scheff, N. M. Attention reduction and suppressed direct-current potentials in the human brain. *Science*, 1969, **164**, 331–333.

Tueting, P. Uncertainty and averaged evoked response in a guessing situation. Unpublished doctoral dissertation, Columbia University, 1968.

Tueting, P., Sutton, S., & Zubin, J. Quantitative evoked potential correlates of the probability of events. *Psychophysiology*, 1970, **7**, 385–394.

Vaughan, H. G., Jr. The relationship of brain activity to scalp recordings of event related potentials. In E. Donchin & D. B. Lindsley (Eds.), *Average evoked potentials*, NASA SP-191. Washington, D.C.: NASA, 1969. Pp. 45–94.

Vaughan, H. G., Jr., Costa, L. D., Gilden, L., & Schimmel, H. Identification of sensory and motor components of cerebral activity in simple reaction-time tasks. *Proceedings of the 73rd Convention of the American Psychological Association*, 1965, **73**, 179–180.

Vaughan, H. G., Jr., & Ritter, W. The sources of auditory evoked responses recorded from the human scalp. *Electroencephalography and Clinical Neurophysiology*, 1970, **28**, 360–367.

Walter, W. G., Cooper, R., Aldridge, V. J., McCallum, W. C., & Winter, A. L. Contingent negative variation: an electric sign of sensorimotor association and expectancy in the human brain. *Nature*, 1964, **203**, 380–384.

Weinberg, H., Walter, W. G., & Crow, H. J. Intracerebral events in humans related to real and imaginary stimuli. *Electroencephalography and Clinical Neurophysiology*, 1970, **29**, 1–9.

Wilkinson, R. T., & Haines, E. Evoked response correlates of expectancy during vigilance. In A. F. Sanders (Ed.), *Attention and performance III*. Amsterdam: North-Holland Publ., 1970. Pp. 402–413.

Wilkinson, R. T., Morlock, H. C., & Williams, H. L. Evoked cortical response during vigilance. *Psychonomic Science*, 1966, **4**, 221–222.

Williamson, P.D., Goff, W. R., & Allison, T. Somato-sensory evoked responses in patients with unilateral cerebral lesions. *Electroencephalography and Clinical Neurophysiology*, 1970, **28**, 566–575.

Development of Expectancy Wave and Time Course of Preparatory Set in a Simple Reaction-Time Task: Preliminary Results

Annie Besrest   Jean Requin

Département de Psychophysiologie Genérale
Institut de Neurophysiologie et Psychophysiologie
Centre National de la Recherche Scientifique
Marseille, France

ABSTRACT

The cortical expectancy wave (EW) of 12 human subjects was analyzed in a variable interstimulus-interval (ISI), simple reaction-time (RT) task. The experimental design involved four conditions that differed in the subjective conditional probability (CP) distributions of the executive signal, considered as the major determinant of preparation time course. Changes in subjective CP were obtained either by varying the frequency distribution of ISIs or by introducing a time mark in the RT context. While the RT–ISI length relationship differs only slightly between experimental conditions, EW development appears strictly related to the hypothesized preparatory process timing.

I. Introduction

Since its discovery by Walter (1964), the slow surface-negative cortical potential, which is elicited by the warning signal (WS) and develops during the interstimulus interval (ISI) of an experimental paradigm such as a reaction time (RT) experiment, has been considered to be dependent on a number of psychological factors. By varying the significance or the probability of the executive signal (ES), this so-called expectancy-wave (EW) phenomenon has been shown to be related to attention, motivation, expectancy, conation, preparatory set, and decision making. However, the experimental situation always involves the same subject cognitive set, which can be defined as making some response to a significant future event. Moreover, the predictive value of EW amplitude for response efficiency has been demonstrated (Hillyard & Galambos, 1967; Waszak & Obrist, 1969; Besrest & Requin, 1969). Thus, the broadest interpretation of EW is probably to consider this phenomenon as a special index of preparatory processes.

Founded on this general hypothesis, the present experiment was an attempt to investigate the relationship between the development of EW and the time course of preparation in a simple-RT situation with variable ISI. It was based upon a theoretical model previously described and tested (Requin & Granjon, 1969a, b; Durup & Requin, 1970). In a manner analogous to the ideas developed by Nickerson (1967), Thomas (1970), and Näätänen (1970), that model related the time course of preparation in RT experiments to the subjective distribution of conditional probabilities (CP) of the ES. The relationship between preparation level and ISI length can be predicted from the complex effects of time elapsed since the WS. That is, with a rectangular frequency distribution of ISI, the CP of the ES increases with time; however, the uncertainty as to its precise occurrence in time also increases. Two experimental paradigms can be used to analyze these opposing effects. The first is to introduce a recurring time marker between the WS and the ES during a RT trial. The role of the marker is to render the time-estimation error constant for all the ISI durations. The second procedure involves a modification of the frequency distribution of ISI so as to obtain "nonaging" ISI or foreperiods; in this way one also obtains a rectangular distribution of CPs.

The precise purpose of the present study was to examine the time course of the EW amplitudes in a RT experiment where the subjective CP distribution of the ES was tentatively modified by varying ISI distribution and information about elapsed time.

II. Method

A. REACTION TIME DEVICE

The experiment was conducted in a sound-shielded air-conditioned box. The WS was a brief tone of 1000 Hz; the ES was the weak illumination of a lamp. The time marker was a click delivered every .5 sec between the WS and the ES. The response was made by depressing a lever with the right foot, which stopped the clock that had begun with the onset of the ES.

B. Experimental Design

The combination of two ISI distributions with and without the time marking click defined four experimental conditions.

In conditions A and B, four different values of ISI were used in a series: .5, 1.0, 1.5, and 2.0 sec; these were presented equiprobably, that is, in a rectangular frequency distribution. A series consisted of 48 trials. No click was presented in condition A; in condition B, the clicks were presented so as to appear at the four possible times of ES occurrence.

In conditions C and D, six different values of ISI were used, ranging from .5 to 3.0 seconds, in half-second steps. The ISI frequency distribution was so chosen as to obtain the same value of CP (.33) of ES occurrence at the end of the four shortest ISIs. A series consisted of 81 trials. In condition D, the click intervened in the same way as in condition B; there was no click in condition C.

The sequential effects were exhaustively counterbalanced in all series. Six subjects were given conditions A and B in the same session and in the order ABAB; six different subjects were given conditions C and D in the order CDCD.

C. Physiological Recordings

The electroencephalogram (EEG) was recorded with a vertex electrode referred to the earlobe, and the electroculogram (EOG) was recorded between the upper and lower eyelids. Silver–silver chloride electrodes were connected to dc amplifiers through a special device permitting adjustments of the dc level input during intertrial interval. The output of the amplifiers was connected to a tape recorder.

D. Analysis of the Data

After selecting the correct samples of the EEG recordings, the analog data were converted to digital form. For each trial the data analyzed began 500 msec before the WS, and extended 500 msec after the ES; a 20-msec integrating interval was used. In conditions C and D this conversion was limited to the four shortest ISIs. These data then were analyzed on a computer. For each trial, the program first computed the base line for that trial; the base line was defined as the average level value observed during the 500-msec period preceding the WS. This value then was used as a reference level for estimating the data collected during the ISI.

For each of the two experimental conditions that had been presented to a subject the mean EEG level per 20-msec period was computed for successive periods, and averaged across all values of ISI; confidence limits were also calculated. The averaging method thus involved a decreasing number of observations from the WS to ES of the 2-sec ISI duration t-tests between conditions A and B or C and D then were calculated.

In order to compare the time course of EW between all the experimental conditions, a mean expression for the data within groups was estimated, based on the commonly held assumption that the EW amplitude would be the same for all the subjects during the 500-msec period after the WS, at the end of which the ES conditional probability was approximately identical in all the experimental conditions.

The RT means, with their confidence limits, were calculated for each experimental condition and ISI duration, for each subject separately, and for all subjects grouped together.

III. Results

A. REACTION TIME DATA

Figure 1 shows the mean RTs at each ISI value for the four experimental conditions. In condition A, RT appears to decrease slightly with increasing ISI duration; there also seems to be a tendency for the median ISI to be optimal. Introducing the markers in condition B results in an increase in the mean RT level. All the results obtained in conditions C and D can only be described in terms of trends. There is a slight decrease of RT with ISI length in condition C, and a slight decreasing relationship in condition D, without any difference between mean performance levels.

The RT variance is correlated with the RT mean. It decreases with ISI length in condition D and tends to decrease or to be stable in conditions A, B, and C.

B. ELECTROENCEPHALOGRAM DATA

Figure 2 shows a complete analysis of the data obtained with two subjects, each of them performing in two experimental conditions. Successive events appear on the EEG recordings: the evoked potential (EP) to

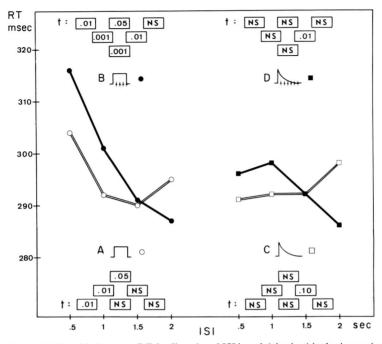

Fig. 1. Relationship between RT (ordinate) and ISI length (abscissa) in the 4 experimental conditions, defined with conventional symbols schematizing the shape of the ISI distribution and the presence (arrows) or absence of the time-marking click, all the subjects grouped together. The statistical significance of *t*-tests calculated between RTs observed for all the ISI durations are indicated in each experimental condition.

the WS, the development of the EW during the entire ISI, with EPs to clicks in conditions B and D, the EP to the ES, and, finally the sharp decrease of the EW with the response. The absence of ocular artifacts during the ISI can be seen readily. Within each experimental condition, a correlation appears between the slope of the RT–ISI length relationship and the time course of EW amplitude. The latter variable tends to increase or to remain up, while the RT tends to decrease with ISI length, and vice versa.

Figure 3 contains all the averaged EEG data for the 12 subjects in the four experimental conditions. It can be noted that introducing the time-marking click had a systematic effect. Except for one subject (5, in conditions C and D), the EW amplitude decreases during the ISI in conditions A and C and increases or keeps up in conditions B and D.

The differences in the EW amplitudes between experimental conditions with and without the time-marking click can be analyzed in Fig. 4, where all the statistically significant *t*-tests comparing conditions A versus B or C versus D are summarized. This analysis confirms that introducing

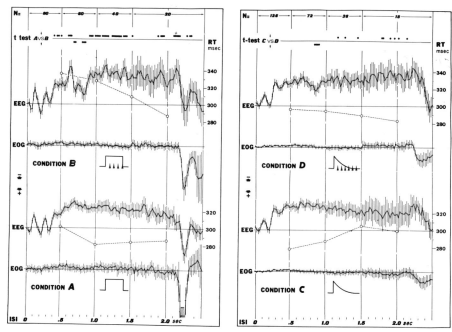

Fig. 2. Reaction times and averaged physiological recordings data for two subjects. One of them performed in conditions A and B (left), the other in conditions C and D (right). In each experimental condition, evolutions during the ISI (abscissa) of the mean RTs (ordinate on right) and of the mean levels of EEG and EOG recordings (expressed by arbitrary but comparable units within one session) are shown for each 20-msec period. Their confidence limits at the $p = .05$ probability threshold are indicated. The averaging method involved a decreasing number of observations from the WS to the ES of the 2-sec ISI duration. This is indicated at the top of the figure. The statistically significant t-tests ($p = .05$) between the mean levels of the EEGs recorded in conditions A and B or C and D are indicated by circles, above an horizontal line when B > A or D > C, below this line in the opposite cases.

the markers resulted in an increase in the EW amplitude, and that EPs to successive clicks also disturbed the time course of the slow-EEG wave.

A comparison of the time course of the EW between all the experimental conditions is shown in Fig. 5. It appears that differences in EW amplitude not only result from the introduction of the time-marking click (conditions A versus B and C versus D) but also depend on the shape of the objective CP distributions of the ES (conditions A versus C and B versus D). The clearest differences in the development of the EW appear when these effects intervene in opposite directions (conditions B versus C); note that there is no difference between conditions A and D, where these effects are compensated. All these comparisons are congruent with RT results, according to the slope of the RT–ISI length relationship.

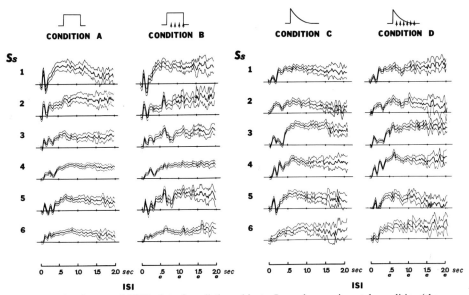

Fig. 3. Averaged EEG data for all the subjects. In each experimental condition (the characteristics of which are recalled by the conventional symbol) and for each subject (numbered from 1 to 6 in each group), the mean EW-amplitude time course during the ISI (abscissa) is indicated, with its confidence limits, at the $p = .05$ probability level. Within each subject, a direct comparison of EW amplitude between conditions A and B or C and D is valid.

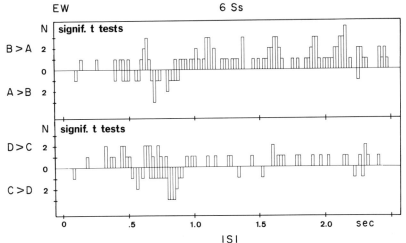

Fig. 4. Distributions during all the successive 20-msec periods of the ISI of statistically significant t-tests ($p = .05$) between conditions A and B or C and D, all the subjects collected. Each histogram shows the number of t-tests, which statistically confirm that EW amplitude in individual data is greater (above 0 on ordinate) or smaller (below 0) in conditions B and D than in A and C.

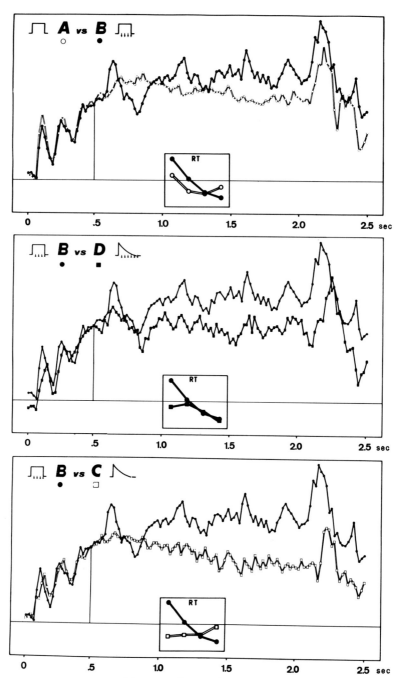

Fig. 5. Comparison of all the experimental conditions of averaged EEG data for the 12 subjects. The averaging method is based upon the commonly held assumption that the EW amplitude is the same for each subject during .5 sec after the WS (vertical line). Comparisons between experimental conditions with and without the clock are presented

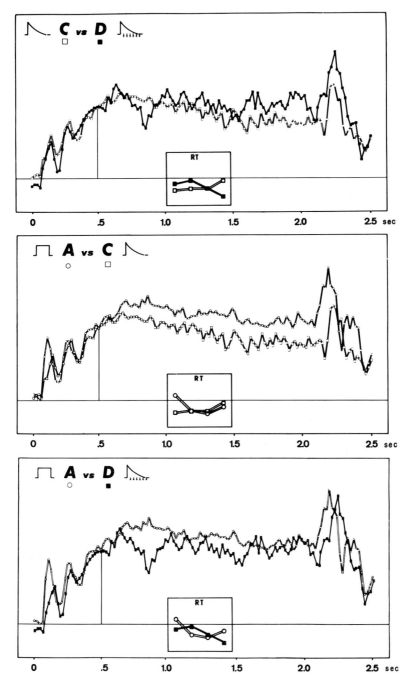

at the top of the figure. Comparisons between experimental conditions that differ on the shape of the ISI distribution are shown in the center of the figure. Comparisons between experimental conditions with these two combined factors are indicated in the inferior part of the figure. For each comparison, the corresponding RT–ISI length relationship is inserted.

IV. Discussion

Referring to the shape of the RT–ISI length relationships, which was predicted from the model introduced at the beginning of this paper, the observed latencies cannot be considered to be very convincing results. Nevertheless, it should be noted that all these relationships are in accord with the expected direction of the slope. However, the magnitude of the changes of gradient that result either from modifying the ISI distribution or from reducing time uncertainty is quite small. Discrepancies from previous results (Requin & Granjon, 1969a) most probably could be explained by the disturbing effects on RT that results from the restraining conditions imposed by the physiological recordings, rather than by the differences between the ranges of the ISIs used. These data otherwise confirm that the introduction of the time-marking click involves some interacting effect with the ES, which can explain the increase in mean RT level.

The EEG data lend themselves to a sounder interpretation. In spite of the unsolved methodological problem regarding the validity of comparing different EW amplitude levels from different subjects, and hence different groups, the EW development appears to be congruent with the expected time course of preparatory processes, within each experimental condition and within each group. However, the role of EPs to clicks in conditions where time uncertainty was reduced must be discussed. One possible suggestion is that the increase in EW amplitude with time in such conditions is the result of the cumulative effects of later components of successive EPs. In such a case, the problem of the interaction between EW and EP amplitudes, which was investigated by Näätänen (1967), would be very complex. However, merely modifying the shape of the frequency distribution of the ISIs, that is, from a rectangular to a Poisson distribution, involves similar changes in the EW development. The single CP variable, which was hypothesized, thus appears to be a sufficient explanation of the EEG data observed. Nevertheless, the idea that time marking is related to some cumulative physiological effects during the ISI suggests that EPs to clicks, modulating a slow-wave phenomenon, could provide the physiological substrate of CP-integration mechanisms.

V. Conclusion

The development of the EW during the ISI appears to be a sensible index of the changes in time of the subjective CP of an expected event. Thus, in spite of slight differences between the RT–ISI length relationships in the four experimental conditions, physiological concomitants of preparatory processes are found to be more predictable than response latencies calculated according to the theoretical model that was proposed. Perhaps this is not a methodological paradox if one remembers that that model only described the time course of the intervening preparation variable, but not the corresponding RTs. The RTs themselves depend on a complex unknown transfer function. Moreover, the unidimensional EW amplitude parameter is probably related to the energy mobilized by the whole situational context. Therefore, one could not predict specific cue efficiency when the preparatory process is divided, as, for example, in the possible "go–no go" situation prompted by the time-marking clicks, which in some conditions precede the ES.

Acknowledgments

We thank M. Granjon, M. Marinopoulos, and G. Reynard for assistance with various aspects of this work.

References

Besrest, A., & Requin, J. Onde d'expectative et niveau de performance dans une situation de temps de réaction. *Comptes Rendus des Séances de la Société de Biologie*, 1969, **163**, 1875.

Durup, H., & Requin, J. Hypothèses sur le rôle des probabilités conditionnelles du signal d'exécution dans le temps de réaction simple. *Psychologie Française*, 1970, **15**, 37–46.

Hillyard, S. A., & Galambos, R. Effects of stimulus and response contingencies on a surface negative slow potential shift in man. *Electroencephalography and Clinical Neurophysiology*, 1967, **22**, 297–304.

Näätänen, R. *Selective attention and evoked potentials.* Helsinki: Finnish Academy of Science, 1967.

Näätänen, R. The diminishing time-uncertainty with the lapse of time after the warning signal in reaction-time experiments with varying fore-periods. *Acta Psychologica*, 1970, **34**, 399–419.

Nickerson, R. S. Expectancy, waiting time and the psychological refractory period. *Acta Psychologica*, 1967, **27**, 23–34.

Requin, J., & Granjon, M. The effect of conditional probability of the response signal on the simple reaction time. *Acta Psychologica*, 1969, **31**, 129–144.   (a)

Requin, J., & Granjon, M. Relation entre le niveau d'excitabilité médullaire et la probabilité conditionnelle d'apparition du signal d'exécution pendant la période préparatoire à une réponse motrice. *Canadian Journal of Psychology*, 1969, **23**, 347–365.   (b)

Thomas, E. A. C. On expectancy and average reaction time. *British Journal of Psychology*, 1970, **61**, 33–38.

Walter, W. G. The contingent negative variation: An electrocortical sign of significant association in human brain. *Science*, 1964, **146**, 434.

Waszak, M., & Obrist, W. D. Relationship of slow potential changes to response speed and motivation in man. *Electroencephalography and Clinical Neurophysiology*, 1969, **27**, 113–120.

Attention Mechanisms following Brain Bisection[1]

M. S. Gazzaniga　　*S. A. Hillyard*

Department of Psychology　*Department of Neurosciences*
New York University　　*University of California, San Diego*
New York, New York　　*La Jolla, California*

ABSTRACT

Brain bisection that disconnects the cortical–cortical connections between the cerebral hemispheres was found to have a profound effect upon the attentional processes that are active during learned sensory–motor performance tasks. In most cases in the split-brain primate, the quantity of information that can be processed by the two hemispheres working in concert on separate tasks is substantially greater that when only one task is being solved. It is as if the split-brain operation adds an extra data-processing channel with selective attentional capabilities for the parallel processing of dual tasks. This suggests that the neuroanatomical basis of interference between concurrent tasks in normal primates is due in large part to the intact cortical–cortical connections.

At the same time, when a lateralized motor response set was induced by a particular task, substantial interhemispheric interaction was evident in the split-brain primate. Present evidence, including bilateral recordings of the cortical electroencephalogram (EEG), suggests that this disruption of one hemisphere's activities by the other occurs at the motor response end of processing rather than by disrupting the sensory or perceptual analysis of inputs.

[1]Aided by USPHS Grant MH 17883-02 and NASA Grant NGR-05-009-83. The human split-brain surgery was performed by P. J. Vogel and J. E. Bogen.

221

I. Introduction

This contribution examines the question of whether the bilateral symmetry of the telencephalic structures in the primate brain permits the operation of two independent attentional systems when the interhemispheric connections are transected. The extent to which this "split-brain" operation enables the "parallel processing" of sensory information and motor coordinations in the separated hemispheres indicates the relative roles of cortical and brainstem structures in mediating different types of selective processes.

The concept of attention has been used to describe selective processes at any of several points in a sensory–motor performance sequence. Some theorists define attention in purely perceptual terms as a process that enhances the detection of selected stimuli to the exclusion of others (Berlyne, 1970). Another view emphasizes the selective retrieval from memory of learned associations and expectations that govern behavioral sequences (Hochberg, 1970). Finally, there is the older idea of attention as the holding of a specific response in readiness (that is, response set).

Most of the studies reported here were not designed to differentiate between these and the numerous other varieties of attention. Hence, we use the term *attentional processes* in a general sense to indicate those brain mechanisms that enable either the selection of specific stimuli, the retrieval of conditioned associations, or the execution of specific conditioned responses. Thus, our measure of attention is the overall quantity of selective information transmitted through the nervous system from receptor to effector as revealed in the pattern of stimulus–response correlations, or simply stated, the overall information processing capacity.

The experiments described in Section II demonstrate that mechanisms of selective attention can operate simultaneously and independently (that is, in parallel in the two disconnected half-brains, such that the net information transmitted is greater than when either hemisphere works alone). In a few instances, the two hemispheres working simultaneously and independently can process exactly twice as much information as either working alone. In contrast, the studies described in Section III reveal departures from parallel processing in the form of a blocking of one hemisphere's performance brought about by problem solving in the other. Such evidence is interpreted as showing that bilateral coordination mechanisms in the brainstem can influence the expression of selective sensory and motor processes in the cortex, in certain tasks where one hemisphere predominates.

II. Parallel Processing in the Separated Hemispheres

The studies reported here have been carried out in either split-brain monkeys or human patients, the latter having undergone brain-bisection surgery in an effort to control the interhemispheric spread of epileptic seizures. In both instances surgical disconnection of the hemispheres included the corpus callosum and anterior commissure. In the monkeys the optic chiasm was sectioned as well. This surgery disconnects only the cortical–cortical interhemispheric exchange system and produces the well-known split-brain effects. These effects include the creation of separate and distinct cognitive systems within each hemisphere that are capable of learning, emoting, and processing at least some language, as well as certain other abilities (Gazzaniga, 1970).

Some studies in man that demonstrate parallel processing in terms of duplicate, simultaneous perceptions in the two sides are represented in Fig. 1. These tests showed that each hemisphere could register information briefly presented (100 msec) to it and could subsequently respond correctly, even after a prior and contradictory response from the other. For example, in Fig. 1d when the word "HE*ART" is flashed with the fixation point occurring between the "HE" and the "ART," thus making "ART" projected exclusively to the left hemisphere and "HE" to the right, the subject responds verbally that he saw only the word "ART." When the left hand subsequently is allowed to choose a card from a series, however, it passes over a card with "ART" or "HEART" printed on it and chooses one with "HE" (Gazzaniga, Bogen, & Sperry, 1965).

This same kind of phenomenon is seen in Fig. 1a, where the subjects say they saw a "triangle"; yet the left hand will subsequently pick up a "square." Here again the "angle" is flashed exclusively to the left hemisphere while the half-square goes to the right half-brain. In addition to the separation of percepts, the subjects tend towards figure completion and say they saw a "triangle" instead of the actual stimulus of an "angle."

In Fig. 1b an immediate spoken response "IKE" is made by the patient, even though the right hemisphere is reportedly superior in facial-recognition tasks (Milner & Teuber, 1968). Even when there is such a tendency for one hemisphere to predominate in the processing of particular kinds of information, the other nonetheless can register similar stimuli.

Each hemisphere also can process letter information separately and concurrently. In Fig. 1c each half-brain has to remember as many letters exclusively flashed to it as possible. In normal man, as good a score is obtained when 8 letters (4 in each half-field) are flashed to both hemispheres

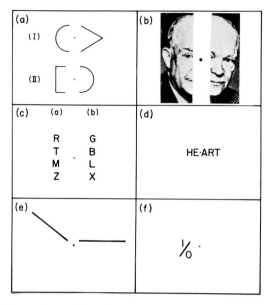

Fig. 1. (a) Figure closure: (I) patient says, "I saw a "triangle" in (II) a "circle." Yet in subsequent free choice test using left hand patient will pick a card with the figure C for (I) and I for (II). (b) Face recognition: right hemisphere dominance for this kind of task does not cause left hemisphere block. There may be specialization, but it is more one of degree. (c) ST memory: the patient remembers more information when both visual fields are presented with four letter stimuli than when either field is stimulated alone. Normal subjects do not improve, however, upon dual presentations. (d) Triple word test: splits immediately say upon presentation of the word "HEART," "ART" when fixation falls between "HE" and "ART." When the left hand is allowed to choose from a series of cards, it retrieves the card "HE" even though "ART" and "HEART" are among the choices. (e) Visual orientation: two lines are flashed simultaneously. The right-field stimulus is immediately reported accurately. If a nonverbal manual response is allowed, there is a strong tendency to make a hand movement in the form of the flashed lines. (f) Choice reaction time: each hemisphere is found to be equally fast at responding to "1" versus "0" pattern discriminations when using the contralateral hand (Gazzaniga & Hillyard, 1971); this is not a test of parallel processing, since two hemispheres acted successively rather than simultaneously.

as when only 4 are flashed to one. In split-brain subjects, the double-field presentation increases the half-brain score (Gazzaniga, 1968). Although the total score achieved by the patients fails to exceed that for normal subjects, the important point is that when one hemisphere has reached its limit of information storage; the other has an additional independent processing capacity.

As in the normal subject, spatial information in the split-brain patient is also registered appropriately. In Fig. 1e both half-brains can note the orientations of lines projected to them simultaneously and subsequently can gesture appropriately (Gazzaniga et al., 1965).

Perhaps the clearest example of parallel processing in the separated hemispheres comes in our double-discrimination and reaction-time (RT) experiment (Gazzaniga & Sperry, 1966). In this study both pre- and postoperative scores were collected in two of the split-brain patients tested.

First, a single red–green discrimination task was presented in the right visual field. While the subjects fixated on a central dot, reaction times were recorded from the onset of each 100-msec stimulus to the subjects response. The correct response was to hit a translucent response button directly in front of the "correct" light, which was either red or green on a given run.

In the subsequent double-discrimination task each subject was required to respond to the brighter of two stimuli, which simultaneously appeared in the opposite, left visual field and along with the red–green discrimination. Now, with the right hand responding to the right visual-field red–green discrimination and the left hand responding to the left visual-field light–dark discrimination, the reaction time score was found to increase in normal subjects and in the patients tested before their operation (Table 1). Following callosal section, the double task of performing the red–green and the light–dark discriminations was performed at the same speed as the single task. Thus, sectioning cortical–cortical connections seems to eliminate the interhemispheric response interference exhibited by normal subjects when solving simultaneously presented two-choice tasks.

In animal studies there are several reports that give additional support to the notion of double-attentional mechanisms. These are summarized in Fig. 2. In Fig. 2a split-brain monkeys proved able to handle a great deal more visual information presented bilaterally in a brief flash than normal subjects. In the final phase of testing, each half-brain was presented exclusively with a spatial pattern of lights, which in fact were 4 two-choice light–dark discriminations presented to each hemisphere. First, 2 two-choice problems are presented; one to each hemisphere. When the animal succeeds, 2 more are added, now making 4 problems; 2 to each hemisphere. When proficiency is reached, 2 more are added, making 3 problems for each hemisphere, and so on. As a result, the task starts out being simple and becomes more complex only if the animal succeeds at each step along the way. Normal monkeys stop performing accurately when 6 lights appearing in any of 12 possible buttons are illuminated and left on for 800 msec. After the monkeys' brains are split, they can solve in a 200-msec flash which of 8 lights randomly occurring on 16 possible buttons are presented. Here, each half-brain sees only 4 lights and, when working in alternation, each

Table 1. *Reaction Times to Visual Stimuli (in msec)*[a]

Subject	Right hand (Trials 1–10)		Right hand–Left hand (Trials 11–20)				Right hand (Trials 21–30)		$p(M_2-M_1)$	$p(M_2-M_4)$
	M_1	SD	M_2	SD	M_3	SD	M_4	SD		
Normal and preoperative										
GRN	438	57	695	97	694	96	391	56	< .005	< .005
TRB	465	120	770	140	800	120	496	83	< .005	< .005
HML	380	55	470	88	464	95	374	73	< .05	< .025
SRP	439	228	574	70	678	88	376	64	< .005	< .005
Case III (AA)	704	176	1272	213	1110	254	629	117	< .005	< .005
Case IV (LB)	727	158	1667	750	1227	580	682	149	< .005	< .005
Operated										
Case I (WJ)	1150	138	869	92	798	104	848	110	n.s.	n.s.
Case II (NG)	766	156	777	153	869	224	706	280	n.s.	n.s.
Case III (AA)	705	175	724	170	741	199	582	237	n.s.	n.s.
Case IV (LB)	700	152	594	92	566	114	600	161	n.s.	n.s.

[a]Right hand responds to red–green discrimination in right half visual field.
Left hand responds to bright–dark discrimination in left half visual field.
Probability calculated from paired observations by one-tailed t test. n.s. > .05

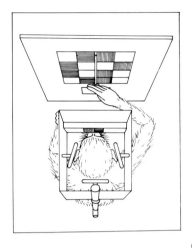 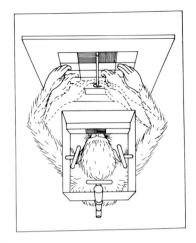

(a)

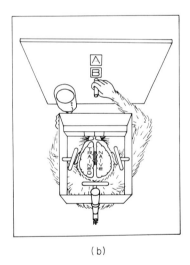

Fig. 2. The split-brain monkey is activating a start switch which initiates a spatial discrimination. Here, four lights pseudo-randomly appearing on any of eight possible response panels are projected to one hemisphere while four others are simultaneously projected to the other. The lights are left on for only 200 msec following split-brain surgery, and each level of lights, starting at the bottom, must be responded to before advancement is allowed to the next row. (b) The trained hemisphere works while the naive half-brain watches.

(b)

hand starts at the bottom of the panel and proceeds upward, hitting the correct buttons along the way (Gazzaniga & Young, 1967).

In Fig. 2b a naive half-brain, one which has not been trained on a visual discrimination observes the errorless performance of a knowledgeable half-brain. After 40 "observation" trials, the naive half-brain is tested separately, and it is discovered it too has learned the problem. Here with one half-brain clearly taking the lead and initially directing responses, the other half nonetheless is capable of attending to the relevent cues. Here again it would seem clear the responses of the "one" brain do not necessarily interfere with the attentional process of the other (Johnson & Gazzaniga, 1970).

DISCUSSION

These studies indicate that independent, parallel processing channels exist in the two separated hemispheres. The human patients are capable of perceiving and interpreting verbal, pattern, and spatial stimuli correctly and simultaneously in each half-brain. The clearest evidence of dual information-processing channels comes from the multiple-choice light experiment in the monkey; each hemisphere can process 4 bits of information (4 two-choice problems) when disconnected from the other, while only an average of 3 bits per hemisphere are transmitted in the normal animal. In other words, the severing of the cortical–cortical connections actually increases the net channel capacity of the nervous system.

The simultaneous double-discrimination RT experiment also provides strong evidence of dual-attentional mechanisms, which are freed to operate in parallel following callosal section. This suggests that the corpus callosum normally mediates an integration of the selective processes of the two hemispheres, which has the effect of restricting the total number of stimulus–response transactions permissable in the normal condition. From this, it would seem fair to propose that cortical–cortical interactions in general precipitate interference in multiple sensory–motor tasks (see Treisman and Davies's contribution to this volume).

Since two separate stimulus–response sequences may be executed concurrently in the commisurotomized primate, for the kinds of tasks described we can reject the notion of a stimulus–response selection mechanism residing in the brain stem that can only "energize" one behavioral sequence at a time. Indeed, the double-discrimination RT experiment suggests that the corpus callosum integrates the sensory fields such that attention only can be linked to one portion of it at a time.

III. Interhemispheric Interaction and Lateralization Response Systems

In the previous section, the selective attentional processes functioned bilaterally to an extent that permitted simultaneous and comparable performance from the two hemispheres. In the types of tasks now considered, the active response systems are strongly lateralized, and there is a concomitant disruption of learning and performance in the contralateral half-brain.

It has been reported, for example, that if a chiasm–callosum-sectioned monkey is restricted to the use of only one hand when learning a visual pattern discrimination, it is generally found upon subsequent testing that only the contralateral eye–brain has learned the problem, despite equivalent exposure to the visual stimulus–respond–reward contingency (Trevarthen, 1962). The mechanism by which such a strongly lateralized "response set" interferes with processing of the disconnected hemisphere is unresolved. In most cases it is difficult to ascertain whether the "supressed" hemisphere is subjected to an inhibition of its sensory–perceptual apparatus, a disruption of its selective, learned stimulus–response chains, or simply a decoupling of its processing from motor output.

Trevarthen (1970) has reported one of the few cases where perceptual suppression *per se* seems to have occurred in a split-brain patient. A "unilateral neglect" of one visual half-field occurred when a visually guided pointing task to a spatial target was lateralized to either the right or the left hand. For example, when the left hand (largely under control of the right cerebrum) aimed at a visual form, the portions of the target in the right visual field (projecting to the contralateral hemisphere) at times were blocked out of perception, according to the subject's verbal report. The implication is that the normal pathways from the geniculostriate system to the speech apparatus in the left hemisphere are somehow inhibited via brainstem connections, while the right hemisphere is actively directing the motor outflow. A similar process of interhemispheric suppression of visual perception as a function of lateralized response set (in this case, speech set in normal subjects) was proposed by Kinsbourne (1970) to explain the relative increase in detection thresholds in the left visual field during verbalization. Similarly, a blocking of somesthetic sensations from one-half of the body has been reported as a function of attentional and response sets in the split-brain patients (Gazzaniga, Bogen, & Sperry, 1963).

Not all types of lateralized response sets, however, result in a profound suppression of perceptual sensitivity in the ipsilateral sensory fields of the split-brain patient. During a strong right-hemisphere response set created by demanding a prompt thumb press from the left hand in a choice reaction-time (RT) task (see Fig. 1), visual pattern cues flashed to either hemisphere were discriminated and responded to with equal speed (Gazzaniga & Hillyard, 1971).[2] Moreover, a strong left-hemisphere verbal response set to name a small flashed numeral as fast as possible did not prevent the accurate

[2]This patient could control the left hand from either hemisphere with equal facility, etc.

discrimination and storage of an unpredictable series of numbers by the right hemisphere (Gazzaniga & Hillyard, 1971). While some degree of perceptual suppression may have existed in the right hemisphere in the latter study, it was not sufficient to prohibit discrimination of the 1° stimulus patterns flashed for 100 msec. The quality of the response set that determines the degree of contralateral perceptual suppression is not clear, but the available data suggests that the sensory-guided motor acts in which feedback or reafference must be monitored and utilized maximize suppression, whereas balistic, triggered movements tend not to interfere with contralateral perception.

The initiation of motor activity by one hand also can block the execution of well-learned responses controlled from the opposite hemisphere of split-brain primates. A demonstration of this is given in experiments by Trevarthen (1970), where the two hemisphere–hand combinations of a split-brain baboon had learned separate, complementary motor components of a manipulative latch-box problem; often when one hand spontaneously began to perform its own manipulations, there was total inhibition and neglect of the other, which assumed a reflex grasping posture. Less severe apraxia of the limb of the nonperforming hemisphere has been observed in other contexts as well, indicating that a lateralized response set can restrict the contralateral motor outflow via brainstem connections. The experiment described below in commissurotimized man illustrates that preparation to respond lateralized to the minor hemisphere at times may retard normal sensory–motor performance by the dominant left-hemisphere–right-hand ensemble.

LATERALIZATION OF WARNING STIMULUS AND RESPONSE IN A FOREPERIOD RT TASK

This experiment was designed to create expectancy of an impending tone and motor response in only one of the surgically separated hemispheres of a human patient, in order to study the extent to which the contingent negative variation (CNV) or expectancy wave (Walter, Cooper, Aldridge, McCallum, & Winter, 1964; Besrest and Requin's contribution to this volume) might be lateralized to the "expectant" half-brain (Hillyard, 1971). Besides yielding evidence of the mechanism of this electrophysiological sign of expectancy and preparatory set, some unexpected behavioral interactions were observed between the two hemispheres when one of them was warned and alerted and the other governed the motor response.

In this task, a button was pressed with one hand to a loud tone burst, which followed a visual warning signal presented exclusively to one or the other hemisphere on a given trial. The warning was a 1° numerical pattern flashed for 100 msec to either the right or left of a fixation point. When this flash was the number "1," it signified that, after a 1.3-sec foreperiod, a tone that demanded a prompt press would occur. On the other half of the trials, the warning flash was the number "0," followed by no tone and hence no response. Each subject was given 4 blocks of 25 RT trials each, the right hand responding on blocks 1 and 4 and the left hand on blocks 2 and 3. Within each block the warning signal was randomized from trial to trial among the 4 possibilities of "1" and "0" flashed to the right and left sides. Intertrial intervals were randomized between 10 and 30 sec.

In Table 2 the mean RTs of button presses following tone onset are compared for the different hand–hemisphere combinations in the three subjects. The RTs for the dominant right hand following the alerting of the minor (right) hemisphere were prolonged significantly in relation to those of the other combinations, which did not differ significantly from each other. Subject NW was not able to bring the left hand under sufficient voluntary control to perform the button press; this was an extreme case of the left-sided apraxia sometimes observed in adult commissurotomy patients (Gazzaniga, 1970). While neurological patients often have great variability in their RTs from one run to the next due to effects of practice, motivation, and the like, we believe the significant effect shown in Table 2 to be reliable since comparisons were made within a hand-use condition (right versus left

Table 2. *Reaction Times (in msec, ± standard error) for Button Press to Tone following Selective Warning of Right and Left Hemispheres, Respectively*

Response made by	Warning signal flashed to	
	Right hemisphere	Left hemisphere
Subject NG		
Right hand	$1050 \pm 82 (p < .01)$[a]	390 ± 43
Left hand	430 ± 57	370 ± 48
Subject LB		
Right hand	$345 \pm 42 (p < .025)$[a]	257 ± 12
Left hand	260 ± 12	255 ± 12
Subject NW		
Right hand	$447 \pm 30 (p < .025)$[a]	360 ± 17

[a]The p values are two-tailed significance levels of the comparison of mean RT in right-hand-right-hemisphere condition against the other means, using analysis of variance.

visual field), and the sequence of hand-use conditions was balanced for order effects.

Our initial hypothesis for these delayed RTs—that the motor-response set induced in the left hemisphere during right-hand usage had suppressed the attentional and perceptual capacity of the right hemisphere to detect the warning cue—was inconsistent with other results. First, in subject NG the RTs for this condition (averaging 1050 msec) scarcely overlapped with the other RTs and were much longer than even the simple, unwarned RT, which ranged between 300 and 500 msec for NG.[3] Thus, there appeared to be an active inhibition of the normal control of the right hand by the left hemisphere, brought about by the selective warning of the right hemisphere. One possible mechanism for this might be that the alerted right hemisphere attempted to take control of the right hand via ipsilateral pathways, resulting in competitive interference between the response on the two sides in attempting to control the same hand. The absence of such interference for the left-hemisphere–left-hand combination is probably a consequence of the capacity of both hemispheres for controlling the left hand in simple acts, whereas the right hand is controlled predominantly from the left hemisphere (Gazzaniga & Hillyard, 1971).

A second reason to doubt the occurrences of perceptual suppression in the right hemisphere when the right hand was in use is the CNV evidence from all subjects, indicating that the warning flashes were being discriminated accurately. Figure 3, for example, shows CNVs recorded simultaneously over the right and left hemisphere, with scalp electrodes placed 5 cm lateral to the midline-referred-to linked electrodes behind the ears. Each tracing is the CNV computer averaged over 12 trials under the indicated stimulus and hand-usage conditions. The CNVs following the "1" are larger that those after the "0" since this wave constitutes an index of a preparatory process variously characterized as expectancy, preparatory set, or motor priming (Cohen, 1969). This difference in CNVs during right-hand usage (Fig. 3, left column, compare top and bottom tracings) indicates that the right hemisphere in fact did discriminate the "prepare to act" signal ("1") from the "no-go" cue ("0"). This suggests that the CNV can serve as a measure of perception of the light-tone contingency in a hemisphere that has its motor output suppressed, presumably on account of the response set lateralized in the other hemisphere. Use of the CNV as an indicator of perception and comprehension of "sign-significate" relationships may prove to be a useful

_____

[3]Simple RTs in subject LB were also faster (range 260–405 msec; mean 312) than in the right-hand–left-hemisphere combination but the difference is not as striking. Simple RTs were not measured for subject NW.

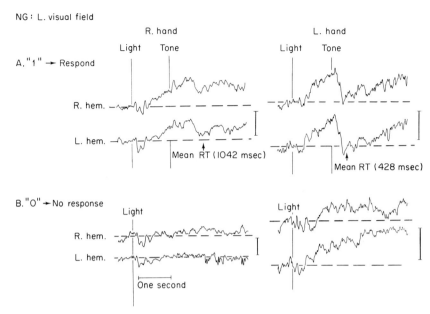

Fig. 3. Computer-averaged CNV, ($N = 12$) recorded simultaneously from the scalp over the right and left hemispheres under conditions of right- and left-hand usage with the right hemisphere warned. Nonpolarizing electrodes were placed 5 cm to the right and left of the vertex, along the interaural line. Records are shown only for those trials (one-half of total) when the warning flash was given to the left visual field. Trials containing eye-movement artifacts were excluded from these averages; DC amplification was used. Calibrations: $20\mu V$.

clinical tool as a test of mental functioning in pathological states of motor paralysis.

The CNV was bilaterally symmetrical in two of the patients (NG, LB) under all visual-field–hand combinations (Figs. 3 and 4; Table 3). The small right–left discrepancies in CNV amplitude can be attributed to spontaneous EEG variations, measurement error, and scalp-placement asymmetries. More importantly, the right–left differences in these patients did not correlate with either hand usage or which hemisphere was warned. In subject NW, however, a larger asymmetry was found in both CNV amplitude and waveform, with larger CNVs localized above the warned hemisphere during the S_1–S_2 interval. In addition, it appears (Fig. 5) that the CNV is incremented *after* the tone onset above the hemisphere that controls the response.

Caution must be exercised when inferring a bilaterality of brain processes from these findings of CNV symmetry in two patients and a small departure from this in a third (average asymmetry in NW was 6 out of $27\mu V$). First, the possibility must be considered that electric fields generated in one

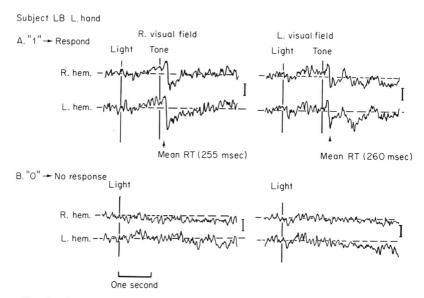

Fig. 4. Computer-averaged CNVs ($N = 12$) from subject LB in the same experiment as in Fig. 4, but here only records taken with the left hand in use are presented. The four pairs of CNVs (from right and left scalp) were from trials when the warning cue was a "1" and a "0," presented to right and left visual fields, respectively. Calibration: 20 μV.

hemisphere may spread to the other side by volume conduction. Available evidence, however, indicates that field spread would not contribute more than a small fraction of the observed contralateral negativity. The CNVs are greatly attenuated over even small, localized cortical lesions (McCallum, Walter, Winter, Scotton, & Cummings, 1970), and those EEG and evoked-potential fields that are slow and diffuse like the CNV spread to the lateral portions of contralateral scalp by less than 20% after hemispherectomy (Hazemann, Olivier, & Fischgold, 1969) and unilateral amytal injections (Barlow, Rovit, & Gloor, 1964). Second, it is possible that on some trials the "unwarned" hemisphere received stimulus information by extracranial crosscueing (Gazzaniga, 1970), since control tests showing that the cue was lateralized were done only on a few trials within an experiment. Third, a bilaterally symmetrical component conceivably might have arisen from an artifactual source such as the skin or tongue [but not from eye movements that were controlled (Hillyard, 1973)].

Despite these reservations, our results do suggest that a substantial portion (somewhere between 50 and 100%) of the CNV in the foreperiod RT task is bilaterally symmetrical and therefore is governed from bilaterally activated structures in the brainstem or thalamus. Whether there is an

Table 3. *Bilateral Symmetry of CNVs from Right and Left Hemispheres, Quantified as the Mean Amplitude (in μV) over the .30 Sec Prior to Tone Onset*

	Warning signal ("1") flashed to	
Response made by	Right hemisphere	Left hemisphere
Subject NG		
Right hand		
Right Hemisphere	13.4	15.7
Left Hemisphere	10.7	15.1
Left hand		
Right Hemisphere	19.2	17.0
Left Hemisphere	18.5	16.3
Subject LB		
Right hand		
Right Hemisphere	7.1	3.5
Left Hemisphere	4.2	6.1
Left hand		
Right Hemisphere	7.2	11.2
Left Hemisphere	4.3	8.7
Subject NW		
Right hand		
Right Hemisphere	30.4	28.2
Left Hemisphere	20.2	30.5

asymmetrical CNV component in addition, as NW's data suggest, is more speculative. It has not been established whether the CNV in this RT task can be decomposed into two or more distinctive portions, each with a different behavioral correlate and physiological generator, or whether the CNV is a unitary phenomenon. While anatomically different types of CNV have been distinguished in purely sensory versus purely motor tasks (Järvilehto & Fruhstorfer, 1970; Hillyard, 1973), there is no evidence that the CNV during foreperiod RT tasks is a composite of these components. In fact, if the asymmetrical, purely motor "readiness potential" (Kornhuber & Deecke, 1965) were such a component, the foreperiod RT CNVs should also be asymmetrical in normal subjects, which has yet to be demonstrated (Cohen, 1969; Otto, 1972). Therefore, while it is attractive to propose a lateralized, task-specific CNV additive with a bilateral "generalized" CNV [as McAdam and Whitaker's (1971) experiments suggest], the present evidence is inconclusive.

Serious questions may be raised concerning the psychological correlates

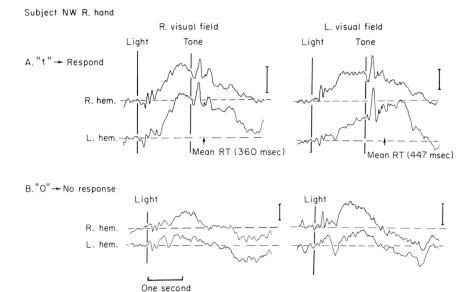

Fig. 5. Computer-averaged CNV (N = 12–15) from subject NW, who was able to respond only with the right hand (same notation as in Figs. 4 and 5). Calibration: 20 μV.

of "the CNV." Our evidence, though clearly preliminary, weighs against the entire CNV being a direct physiological index of the patterned neuronal activity underlying expectancy or motor preparation, since these processes were activated only in the warned hemisphere. While the bilateral portion of the CNV may yet prove to be generated in conjunction with specific psychological states such as attention, motivation, or response set, and may in fact be necessary for high levels of performance, its functional seems to be relatively nonspecific, since it is present in the nonperforming hemisphere.

IV. General Discussion

It emerges from these experiments that there is frequently more "channel capacity" in a split-brain primate than in a callosum-intact normal primate. Exceptions to this principle were found only in certain tasks eliciting a response set that was strongly lateralized to one hemisphere. In such cases a disruption of contralateral processing was observed. At present, however, the evidence is insufficient to decide whether the lateralized response set interferes with the contralateral performance sequence at the perceptual, retrieval from memory, or motor output stages. Only Trevarthen's (1970) report suggests that perceptual interference may occur. In all other demonstrations of interhemispheric interactions, interference between the response outputs of the two sides can explain the results.

Assuming that such interference occurs at the output end, it may be proposed that the responsible brainstem mechanisms function normally to coordinate response outputs from the two sides when they operate in compatible or cooperative tasks. It seems, however, that at times the output of one hemisphere can preempt this brainstem coordinator and deny output to the other. A fundamental question then is to specify the property of a given task that determines whether subcortically mediated interhemispheric interference will occur. We can speculate that such interaction occurs when one hemisphere is generating those sorts of responses that require preparation. Perhaps putting a response in readiness and holding it requires extensive physiological management, which produces a general inhibition of competing response systems.

In addition to the above, the role of the forebrain commissures in integrating the attentional processes of the two cerebral hemispheres is revealed by the increases of total processing capacity upon the removal of the corpus callosum. It is as if in the normally interconnected brain the callosum is involved in inhibiting the transmission of information undergoing processing extraneous to the dominant cognitive activity under consideration. The brain cannot consider all things at all times, and perhaps order only is brought about by what amounts to a cognitive counterpart of a reciprocal inhibition kind of mechanism.

In summary, the foregoing studies are consistent with the proposal that commissural mechanisms act more to integrate the sensory sphere of activity, while the brainstem is involved in coordination and selection of response outputs.

References

Barlow, J. S., Rovit, R. L., & Gloor, P. Correlation analysis of EEG changes induced by unilateral intracarotid injections of amobarbital. *Electroencephalography and Clinical Neurophysiology*, 1964, **16**, 213–220.

Berlyne, D. Attention as a problem in behavior theory. In D. Mostofsky (Ed.), *Attention: Contemporary theory and analysis*. New York: Appleton, 1970.

Cohen, J. Very slow brain potentials relating to expectancy: The CNV. In E. Donchin & D. B. Lindsley (Eds.), *Average evoked potentials: Methods, results, evaluations*, NASA SP-191. Washington D.C.: NASA, 1969. Pp. 143–163.

Gazzaniga, M. S. Short-term memory and brain-bisected man. *Psychonomic Science*, 1968, **12**(5), 161–162.

Gazzaniga, M. S. *The bisected brain*. New York: Appleton, 1970.

Gazzaniga, M. S., & Hillyard, S. A. Language and speech capacity of the right hemisphere. *Neuropsychologia*, 1971, **9**, No. 3, 273.

Gazzaniga, M. S., & Sperry, R. W. Simultaneous double discrimination response following brain bisection. *Psychonomic Science*, 1966, **4**(7), 261–262.

Gazzaniga, M. S., & Young, E. D. Effects of commissurotomy on the processing of increasing visual information. *Experimental Brain Research*, 1967, **3**, 368–371.

Gazzaniga, M. S., Bogen, J. E., & Sperry, R. W. Laterality effects in somesthesis following Cerebral commisurotomy in man. *Neuropsychologia*, 1963, **1**, 209–215.

Gazzaniga, M. S., Bogen, J. E., & Sperry, R. W. Observations on visual perception after disconnection of the cerebral hemispheres in man. *Brain*, 1965, **88**, 221–236.

Hazemann, P., Olivier, L., & Fischgold, H. Isilateral somesthetic evoked potentials recorded from the scalp of a hemispheretomized man. *Compt Rendue Academie Science (D) Paris D*, 1969, **268**, 195–198.

Hillyard, S. A. The psychological specificity of the contingent negative variation and late evoked potential (P300). *Electroencephalography and Clinical Neurophysiology*, 1971, **31**, 302–303. ○(a)

Hillyard, S. A. The contingent negative variation. In R. F. Thompson & M. M. Patterson (Eds.), *Methods in physiological psychology*. Vol. I. *Bioelectric recording techniques*. New York: Academic Press, In press 1973.

Hochberg, J. Attention, organization, and consciousness. In D. Mostofsky (Ed.), *Attention: Contemporary theory and analysis*. New York: Appleton, 1970.

Järvilehto, R., & Fruhstorfer, H. Differentiation between slow cortical potentials associated with motor and mental acts in man. *Experimental Brain Research* 1970, **11**, 309–317.

Johnson, J. D., & Gazzaniga, M. S. Interhemisphere imitation in split-brain monkeys. *Experimental Neurology*, 1970, **27**, 206–212.

Kinsbourne, M. The cerebral basis of lateral asymmetries in attention. In *Attention and Performance III*. A. F. Sanders (Ed.), Amsterdam: North Holland Publ. 1970.

Kornhuber, H. H., & Deecke, L. Hirnpotential-anderungen bei Willkurbewegungen und passiven Bewegungen des Menschen: Bereitschaftspotential und reafferente Potential. *Pflugers Archiv*, 1965, **284**, 1–17.

McAdam, D. W., & Whitaker, H. A. Language production: Electroencephalographic localization in the normal human brain. *Science*, 1971, **172**, 499–502.

McCallum, W. C., Walter, W. G., Winter, A., Scotton, L., & Cummings, B. The contingent negative variation in cases of known brain lesion. *Electroencephalography and Clinical Neurophysiology*, 1970, **28**, 210.

Milner, B., & Teuber, H. Alteration of perception and memory in man: Reflection on methods. In L. Weiskrantz, (Ed.), *Analysis of behavioral change*. New York: Harper, 1968. Pp. 268–375.

Otto, D. A. The effect of modifying response and performance feedback parameters on the CNV in humans. *Electroencephalography and Clinical Neurophysiology, Supplement*. In press 1972.

Trevarthen, C. B. Double visual learning in split-brain monkeys. *Science*, 1962, **136**, 258–259.

Trevarthen, C. B. Experimental evidence for a brain-stem contribution to visual perception in man. *Brain Behavior and Evolution*, 1970, **3**, 338–352.

Walter, W. G., Cooper, R., Aldridge, V., McCallum, W. C., & Winter, A. L. Contingent negative variation: An electric sign of sensorimotor association and expectancy in the human brain. *Nature*, 1964, **203**, 380–384.

The Control of Attention by Interaction between the Cerebral Hemispheres

Marcel Kinsbourne

Division of Pediatric Neurology
Duke University Medical Center
Durham, North Carolina

ABSTRACT

Each cerebral hemisphere guides attention towards contralateral space, and the two hemispheres are in mutually inhibitory balance. In right-handed subjects, the left hemisphere chiefly subserves linguistic processes, and the right hemisphere subserves spatial processes. It is proposed that cognitive activity lateralized to one hemisphere overflows so as to cause contralateral orientational shifts. This model, which can account for laterality effects in perception, is experimentally validated by showing that:

1. Gaze and head turning occur contralateral to the preponderantly active hemisphere when subjects engage in verbal or spatial thought.
2. Concurrent subvocalization (that is, left-hemisphere activity) introduces right-sided advantage into right-handed subjects' ability to detect a gap in a briefly exposed square.
3. Concurrent subvocalization induces right half-field superiority for recognition of briefly presented nonsense shapes by right-handed subjects.

In left-handed subjects, both verbal and spatial processes appear to be programmed from one hemisphere at a given time.

I. Introduction

Throughout the evolutionary ascent from worm to man, behavior is controlled by a basically mirror symmetrical central nervous system. Each of its two laterally adjacent but separate divisions can control the full range

239

of behavior characteristic of the species (Trevarthen, 1969). Each exerts this control within contralateral space. Whereas bisymmetrical lesions reduce the animal's behavioral repertoire, unilateral lesions leave the repertoire intact but reduce the arena within which it may be deployed.

The two divisions are linked at various levels by transverse commissures. When corresponding decisions are formulated within each half-central nervous system, information flow along transverse commissures coordinates these decisions, so that the output mechanism may receive unequivocal instruction. Where conflicting decisions are formulated on the two sides, inhibitory interaction across commissures (Horridge, 1965) establishes decisive priorities for the organism as a whole by amplifying a small initial imbalance into a decisive one.

The bisymmetrically represented capabilities of subhuman species have in common a precise reference to external space (pursuit of prey, grooming) or are very simple and stereotypic (mating calls); comparable processes in man retain this archaic bisymmetry. Major departures from structural and functional complementarity occur in flatfishes in relation to their gross somatic asymmetry (Hubbs & Hubbs, 1945) and in birds in relation to the development of bird song (Nottebohm, 1971). The most strikingly asymmetrical lateralization is that of the highest mental functions in man. Man has command over novel processes underlying linguistic, numerical, and other abstract forms of thought, which in their fully developed form need not be programmed with reference to specific points in space. Phylogenetically, verbalization originates in animal vocalization which is often directed towards a specified point. Ontogenetically, this spatial reference may be observed when babies vocalize as they point in a given direction. But when speech has become fully internalized, spatial reference is missing. The types of behavior that thus far have been shown to derive from cerebrally lateralized neural substrates, including bird song, seem to share this characteristic of freedom from spatial reference.

The cerebrum is a highly linked system, with but few synapses separating any neuron from any other. Within the cerebrum, asymmetrically lateralized facilities without spatial reference develop in addition to the bisymmetrically represented facilities that guide behavior precisely in space. Given such cerebral organization, we can predict how distribution of attention might be distorted by concurrent lateralized higher mental activity. This contribution presents some behavioral experimental tests of those predictions as applied to the visual system of intact man, and inferences about brain organization are drawn from the outcomes.

When animals endowed with cerebral cortex look in various directions [the localized or investigating orienting reaction of Sokolov (1960)], their synergic head and eye movements are under cerebral control; each hemisphere programs the motions of looking in the opposite direction (Crosby, 1953), whereas the hemispheres in equal balance direct head and gaze in the vertical plane. The areas primarily involved are the left and right frontal eye fields, which are mutually inhibitory (Leyton & Sherrington, 1917). Thus, looking in any given direction is programmed as the vector resultant of the opposing activities of the two frontal eye fields.

Prior to gross eye and head movements, shifts of visual attention may occur (Lipp, 1910). There is some neuropsychological evidence that these premotor shifts also are programmed by the cerebral hemispheres, much as are the overt eye movement that they represent in latent form (Kinsbourne, 1970a).

II. A Model

The following model is equally applicable to head movement, eye movement, and premotor attention shift in the lateral plane. Each hemisphere is in a reciprocally inhibitory relationship with the other, and the paired midbrain output facilities have a similar reciprocal relationship (Sprague & Meikle, 1965). When hemispheric activity is in exact balance, attention is centered upon the median plane (Fig. 1). When one hemisphere

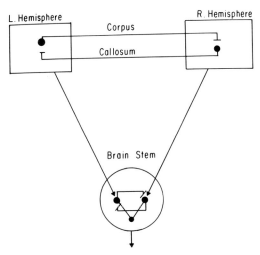

Interaction of equal opposing orientational
tendencies

Fig. 1.   Interaction of equal opposing orientational tendencies.

is more active than the other, either because it is stimulated or because the other is depressed (for instance by a lesion), attention deviates in a direction contralateral to the more active hemisphere (Fig. 2). Kinsbourne (1970b) elaborated this system to accommodate the addition, in man, of asymmetrically lateralized cerebral functions. The highly linked organization of each hemisphere permits significant cross talk between lateralized higher mental function and the orienting control mechanism on the same side so that visual attention becomes biased toward contralateral space, not for purposes of information retrieval but secondary to the asymmetrical cortical activity (Fig. 3).

To test this model of hemispheric control of attention selection for location we first determine whether lateralized cerebral activity elicits contralateral orientation. We shall present experimental evidence that subjects *spontaneously* turn their gaze and head in the direction congruent with the putatively more active hemisphere. The second step–to show that these spontaneous, unconsciously chosen directional tendencies actually allow subjects to process information more *effectively*—remains to be taken.

III. Orientational Shifts While Thinking

When two persons engaged in dialogue face one another, it is an every-day observation that when one asks a question that cannot be answered immediately, the respondent averts his eyes from the questioner's face while thinking and looks back when ready to respond. In its naturalistic setting, this behavior could be interpreted variously though inconclusively as a purposive looking away or a motor rearrangement secondary to the central cognitive process or both.

It could be argued that in order to think effectively, subjects need to minimize distraction from input and therefore look away from highly informational areas such as the human face, towards relatively featureless expanses of space. Or, one might even adopt an interactional view. Pending the response, the questioner has ascendancy over the questioned, who therefore averts his gaze. Again, in line with the mechanisms proposed here the gaze deviation might be secondary to the intellectual effort being directed sideways where it involves one hemisphere more than the other, vertically where it involves both to a comparable extent.

Support for the notion that direction of gaze deviation is not random but subject to individual differences is afforded by reports that subjects look sideways rather than up or down and show internal consistency in their preferred direction of "lateral gaze behavior" (Day, 1964; Duke, 1968). Bakan (1969) speculated that left deviators and right deviators differ as

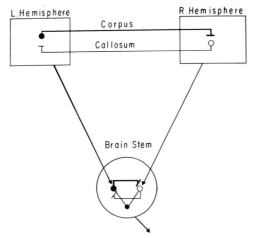

Orientational bias due to left hemisphere
activation

Fig. 2.

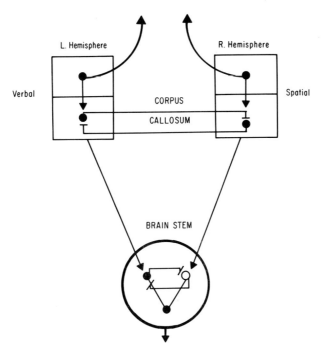

EFFECT OF LATERALIZED CEREBRAL ACTIVITY
ON DIRECTION OF
ORIENTATION

Fig. 3.

243

regards their cerebral organization. Whereas right deviators use verbal (left hemisphere) modes of thinking, left deviators are more apt to think in preverbal or representational modes more characteristic of the right hemisphere (Bogen, 1969). However, it is hard to sort out endogenous factors from cues possibly afforded by the experimenter as he confronts the subject, including the experimenter's own subconscious lateral gaze behavior. Lack of control of the appearance of the background injects further uncertainty into the paradigm. It is necessary first to make sure that the lateral gaze tendency is not due to the need to look away from a highly structured visual field straight ahead. Kinsbourne (1972) eliminated this source of error and tested three predictions derived from the attentional model: (a) mode of questioning will determine direction of gaze deviation within an individual; (b) head deviation, which is equally integral to the orienting mechanism, will give substantially similar results; (c) by virtue of differences in their lateralization of hemispheric function, left-handers as a group will predictably differ from right-handers as regards their head and eye deviations.

Twenty left-handed and 20 right-handed undergraduates participated. Each subject faced a homogeneous surface while questioned by the experimenter sitting behind him. Three sets of 20 questions were asked: verbal, numerical, and spatial. Audio–visual recordings were made, and the data were analyzed for the first gaze deviation and the first change in head position [in excess of 5° (Edwards, Antes, Adams, & Truman, 1971)] after each question had been spoken by the experimenter. Oblique movements were recorded in terms of the closest cardinal direction: up, down, left, or right. The findings showed that lateral gaze behavior survived the substitution of a homogeneous surface for the previously used naturalistic setting. This supported the view that lateral gaze resulted from an endogenously triggered mechanism. Further, the findings for eye and for head movements were largely congruent, supporting the notion that both represent an orienting synergism such as can be elicited by the stimulating electrode at the cortical level (Penfield & Rasmussen, 1957). We therefore shall speak of direction of orienting to subsume both gaze and head deviations.

The right-handers overwhelmingly oriented to the right after verbal questioning. They tended to look up after numerical questions and up and to the left after spatial questions. Left-handers showed far less communality in that some looked right and some left after verbal questions. Unexpectedly, the left-handers who looked right with verbal questioning almost always also did so with spatial questioning, whereas those who looked left in the verbal condition usually also looked left in the spatial condition. Numerical questioning gave results less closely correlated with either of the other conditions. In all three conditions vertical gaze deviations were far less common with left-handers than with right-handers.

A further experiment contrasted verbal and spatial responses holding the form and contents of questioning completely constant. Having listened to a spoken sentence, subjects either repeated it verbatim or transformed it into a set of spatial relationships drawn on paper after a 5-sec delay. The results were much as before. Right-handers looked right for verbal responses and up and left for spatial responses. Left-handers looked either right or left for both. The findings of the second experiment extend those of the first as they show that direction or orientation is determined not by the mode of input but by the mode of thought that the task elicits. In general, these results confirm the effect of mode of cognitive set on orienting behavior while thinking. They show that individuals do not look in one characteristic direction only when thinking. Rather, one can relate direction of orientation to laterality of cerebral representation (where known) within a given individual. Thus, the hypothesis of cross talk due to hemispheric sharing between a lateralized higher mental process and the cortical mechanism for looking in a given direction is supported. In addition, the findings suggest new hypotheses about the cerebral organization of left-handers.

Right-handers behaved as expected from the fact that, overwhelmingly, verbal processes are represented in their left hemisphere whereas spatial processes are somewhat more represented in their right hemisphere. No such predictions could be made for left-handers, whose lateralization of function is known to be more variable but is not thoroughly understood (Hecaen & Sauget, 1971). Clinical data suggest that left-handers more frequently than right-handers sustain language deficits with unilateral cerebral disease; these deficits are less severe and more transient than those of right-handers (Conrad, 1949; Humphrey & Zangwill, 1952; Milner, Branch, & Rasmussen, 1964), and these facts may be related to the observation that individual left-handers orient in the same direction while engaged in both verbal and in spatial thought, in either of two ways: (a) left-handers concentrate their laterality of verbal and of spatial thought in one hemisphere (the right in some cases, the left in others), leaving the other hemisphere relatively empty of those functions; (b) both verbal and spatial functions are represented in both hemispheres of many left-handers (Conrad, 1949; Hecaen & Sauget, 1971), but at any one period of time, only one hemisphere is used in programming the appropriate behavior. The latter interpretation would fit with the relatively sparse incidence of vertical orienting movements in this group. If vertical orientation indicates concurrent function of the two hemispheres, this perhaps is what left-handers are less well able to achieve.

Such differences in cerebral organization would be expected to have some psychometric correlates. They also might account for some of the higher incidence of a variety of developmental retardation syndromes among left-handers.

Having shown that cognitive functioning elicits overt orientational shifts that depend in direction on the cerebral distribution of that activity, we may now inquire whether covert shifts of attention at speeds faster than those possible for voluntary eye movements can also be generated in this way. Our goal is both to test the model further and to contribute toward a comprehensive explanation of laterality effects in perception.

The attentional model has two parts: prestimulus and poststimulus effects. Prestimulus effects consist of attention directed in advance to one side of a display because the contralateral hemisphere is already active prior to presentation of the stimulus. Poststimulus effects are those involved in the processing of the perceptual trace that remains after the very brief stimulus has been shown. Poststimulus effects depend on whether the direction in which attention is focused is congruent with the hemispheric location of the processes called into play by the nature of the task. Thus, for example, even if the subject is told ahead of time that the stimulus (a word) will appear on the left side of the display, he will have more difficulty in processing it because his attention has been drawn to the left (which necessarily involves activating the right, nonverbal hemisphere) than if he were warned of and shown a word on the right, in which case his attention shift to the right would activate the left, verbal hemisphere. In the latter case, the two activities–orienting to the right and verbal processing—are compatible because programmed by the same hemisphere.

In summary, the attentional model predicts both prestimulus and poststimulus effects that interact with the direction from which the stimulus comes. The prestimulus effect can be demonstrated by manipulating the distribution of preparatory cerebral activity, holding the task constant. The poststimulus effect should be similarly demonstrable by manipulating the nature of the task, holding preparatory state constant.

We shall discuss experiments which bear upon the prestimulus effects. The poststimulus effects have not yet been fully validated, but relevant observations will be discussed later.

IV. Prestimulus Effects

A. GAP DETECTION DURING SUBVOCALIZATION

Twenty right-handed undergraduates viewed black-on-white outline squares (Fig. 4) presented singly and subtending 2° of visual angle in the test field of a Scientific Prototype two-channel tachistoscope. Half the squares were complete, and half were interrupted by a single gap (subtending 6' of visual angle) in the center of either the right or the left vertical. Half the squares of each type were presented in such a way that their right-side vertical was precisely in the median plane and centered upon the fixation point; for the other half, the left-side vertical was centered on the fixation point. We arrive at four types of square with gap: the square left of fixation, the gap in the left half-field (Fig. 4a); the square right of fixation, the gap in the right half-field (Fig. 4b); the square left of fixation, the gap in the median plane (Fig. 4c); the square right of fixation, the gap in the median plane (Fig. 4d). For each subject, initial trials established an exposure duration at which he detected gaps with better than chance success but not perfectly. These durations were below 10 msec and thus far too short to permit changes in eye position in response to the appearance of the stimulus (Bartz, 1962). Then each subject was run under two conditions (counterbalanced between subjects):

1. Standard: in which gap detection was the only requirement.

2. Verbal: in which 6 words were read to the subject before each trial and he was required to retain them in memory until he had made the gap judgment, and then to recall them.

This experiment partially replicates Kinsbourne (1970b), and further experimental details are as in the earlier report.

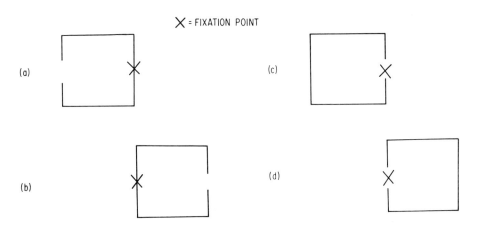

Fig. 4.   Stimuli for gap detection.

As in the previous experiment, the findings showed that false, positive gap detections were rare. Accuracy of gap detection was related to gap location and condition by the χ^2 test of significance. Two comparisons were made.

1. Peripheral Gaps.

There was a nonsignificant trend for mean recognition of gaps in left half-field to be greater than in right half-field in the standard condition ($t = 1.20, p > .05$). This is reminiscent of Knehr's observation in 1941 that Landolt C acuity is better to the left of fixation. With concurrent subvocalization, right-sided gaps were significantly more frequently recognized than left-sided gaps ($t = 3.23, p < .01$) (Fig. 5).

According to the attentional model, subvocalization (the covert rehearsal of word lists while watching for the stimulus) activates the left hemisphere of right-handed subjects and should bias attention to the right. The

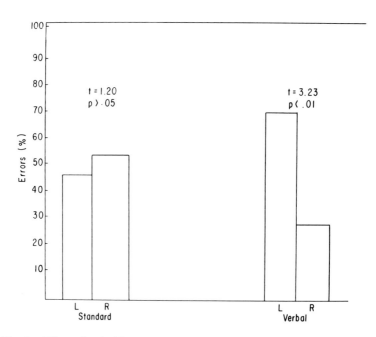

Fig. 5. Effect of coincident verbal activity on visual sensitivity ($N = 20$ peripheral errors).

shift of recognition efficiency to the right with subvocalization was thus as predicted. The result replicates that obtained by Kinsbourne (1970).

2. Central Gaps.

The second comparison extends the generality of this finding and further validates the model. Kimura's (1966) switchboard model for perceptual asymmetries makes differential predictions for stimuli located in the left and in the right visual half-fields. Verbal stimuli are best processed when presented in the right half-field, because this gives them more direct access to the left hemisphere. Some spatial stimuli are processed best when presented on the left, which gives them direct access to the right hemisphere. The attentional model makes predictions not in terms of absolute location but rather in relation to the lateral extremities of the stimulus display, left side versus right side, irrespective of location. When orientation is controlled by the right hemisphere, the left end of the display first attracts attention; under left-hemisphere control, the right end is searched first. In the case of the square, the critical feature—the gap—is located half of the time to its left and half of the time to its right. Thus, irrespective of the absolute location of the square, the left-hemisphere type of orientation confers advantage when the gap is on the right of the display and vice versa. When the two central-gap conditions are compared, we have a rigorously controlled situation, as the two gaps are identically located at the fixation point. The difference resides in the (irrelevant) rest of the square. Kimura's theory predicts no difference in detection scores for these two displays. The attentional model predicts the actual result, which was as follows.

In standard circumstances, there is a nonsignificant trend toward better detection of the central gap in the left side of the square that is located to the right of center (Fig. 4d; $t = 1.83, p > .05$). During subvocalization, there is a nonsignificant trend toward better detection of the central gap to the right of the square that is located to the left of center. (Fig. 4c; $t = 1.09, p > .05$). The change from standard to verbal condition is significant (Fig. 6; $\chi^2 = 4.12, p < .05$). The results are as predicted by the attentional model, according to which there would be a shift from right-hemisphere to left-hemisphere preponderance as subvocalization is introduced.

In a sense, this paradigm takes its place within the by now formidable inventory of laterality effects in perception (White, 1969; Harcum, 1973), in that the stimuli were centered left and right of fixation, respectively. Viewed in this way, it is apparent that subvocalization not only biases detection but also can reverse laterality effects, since for central gap detection the left square was actually the better stimulus under left hemisphere set (though this paradox is resolved by the attentional model). However, a more

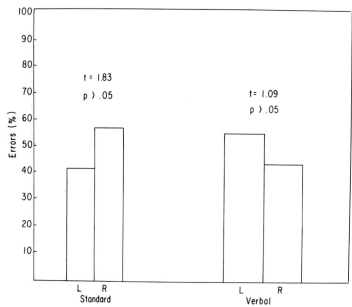

Fig. 6. Effect of coincident verbal activity on visual sensitivity ($N = 20$ central errors, $X^2 = 7.12, p < .05$).

direct demonstration that subvocalization can modify the lateral distribution of visual recognition ability was reported by Bruce and Kinsbourne (1971) as follows.

B. FORM RECOGNITION DURING SUBVOCALIZATION

Whereas explicitly verbal stimuli (words, letters) successively exposed to one or the other side of fixation yield a reliable right half-field superiority, visual forms have given inconsistent results. Geometric forms and drawings of familiar objects generally yield no laterality effect (Bryden, 1960; Bryden & Rainey, 1963). Meaningless forms (hard to verbalize) should give left-sided advantage, but they have not been found to do so (Terrace, 1959; Bisiach, 1966). Bruce and Kinsbourne (1971) did not find lateral asymmetry when subjects were shown an individual nonsense shape (Attneave, 1954; Vander-plas & Garvin, 1959) to the left or right of fixation and subsequently picked it out of a five-shape recognition ensemble by forced choice. When the paradigm was supplemented by adding the requirement to remember six words while performing the perceptual task, a firm right half-field superiority was established. This result further supports the attentional model and in addition suggests why left half-field superiorities in vision are so hard to obtain. Even if the stimulus material itself is not easily amenable to verbalization, concurrent subvocalization by the subjects might counteract a left-sided bias. The subjects' subvocalization during these rather slow-moving, monotonous tasks are hard to control; stray verbal thoughts as attention wandered might account for Bruce and Kinsbourne's (1971) unexpected but replicated finding that, within a block of trials under standard conditions, an initial left-field advantage is counteracted by a terminal right-field advantage.

If subvocalization induces left-hemisphere preponderance, then a comparable concurrent nonverbal activity should induce right-hemisphere preponderance in right-handers. Music (Darwin, 1969; Spellacy, 1970) for dichotic musical chords suggested itself for this purpose (Kimura, 1964; Gordon, 1970). Subjects listened to a dichotic pair of chords, held them in memory while performing the perceptual task, then chose the two chords they had heard from a recognition ensemble of four successive chords. This method was applied both to gap detection and to shape recognition but in neither case was effective in biasing performance to the left. However, in a preliminary report, Goodglass, Shai, Rosen, and Berman (1971) applied the attentional model to music by having subjects hum in concordance with a series of musical notes, the last of which occurred just before the presentation of a nonsense shape either to the right or to the left of fixation. A significant left lateral advantage for recognition resulted. Recently, we have been able to demonstrate a left visual half field advantage for recognition of nonsense shapes viewed while subjects were silently rehearsing previously heard melodies.

It is clear that concurrent, lateralized hemispheric activity can bias attention so as to yield perceptual asymmetries comparable to those that have frequently been found empirically. If concurrent, lateralized activity can have this effect, it becomes conceivable that the stimuli and task themselves are capable of eliciting lateralized cognitive activity sufficient to generate the range of laterality effects (White, 1969); this mechanism obviates the need to resort to transcallosal degradation of information as an explanatory principle (Kimura, 1966). This is convenient insofar as one does not know how much threshold decrement would be expected on the basis of information spillage at one synapse. Nor can one comfortably equate transcallosal conduction time with latency differentials ranging from 4 to 40 msec (Efron, 1963; Kerr, Mingay, & Elithorn, 1963; Filbey & Gazzaniga, 1969; Jeeves & Dixon, 1970). The attentional model has the further advantage that it accommodates the effectiveness of contralateral concurrent auditory messages (Kimura, 1961; Treisman & Geffen, 1968) or noise (Corsi, 1967; Murphy & Venables, 1970) in amplifying dichotic asymmetries without need for further assumptions. These latency differentials may well be related to differential activation of the hemispheres, due either to the nature of the task or to intercurrent subvocalization. Nevertheless, Kimura's switchboard model cannot be dismissed unless and until it is shown experimentally that the attentional model can account for the bulk of the variance in typical laterality paradigms. In advance of such experimentation we now further analyze the mechanisms involved in this model.

Perception is influenced by preparation for action (Mach, 1959). Lateralized cerebral activity prior to the stimulus could induce an anticipatory sideways shift of visual attention or even of eye position [as observed empirically by Terrace (1959) for verbal material except when it was randomized with nonverbal material]. Quite apart from that, the lateralized preparatory state may make the system more amenable to a lateral shift in one than in the other direction when the stimulus appears, so that the speed of orientation to an eccentric stimulus may vary with lateralized preparatory set. In this connection, it is noteworthy that gaze reaction time and head-turning reaction time are shorter for glances to the right than to the left (Van der Meer, 1959; Bartz, 1962; Gabersek, 1963).

The relative contribution of pre- and poststimulus factors to perceptual asymmetry can be assessed by determining the residual asymmetry after differential expectancy is eliminated. If verbal and nonverbal materials are randomized, will each still give rise to its appropriate laterality effects?

On Kimura's model, each will do so as before; on the attentional model the difference in effectiveness of processing material in one as compared to the other half-field will be reduced to the extent that it is a result of biased expectancy.

V. Poststimulus Effects

Once a stimulus has appeared, attention has to be shifted to one or the other side to engage it. It may be that the left hemisphere is more efficient in processing verbal material while orienting somewhat to the right, whereas the right hemisphere processes nonverbal material better while orienting to the left. Poststimulus factors are particularly important in paradigms in which a laterality effect is demonstrated for a complex display such as letter sequence. The serial identification involved can be quite time consuming, and initial orienting advantage (prestimulus effect) is unlikely to account for the magnitude of asymmetries in such situations, which are substantially greater than when only single stimuli are used (Mishkin & Forgays, 1952;

Bryden, 1966; Harcum, 1973). Heron (1957) accounted for the asymmetry by invoking biases in preferred direction of scan brought about by directional habits acquired in the process of learning to read. Without necessarily disputing this interpretation, we would suggest that, when orientation is directed to the right, the left hemisphere may be more efficient in the rate at which it encodes verbal material. This effect would be concordant with the Western left-to-right reading habit, but not with the Hebrew and Arabic right-to-left direction of scan.

We have argued that activation of a hemispherically lateralized process results in an orientational bias towards contralateral space. Conversely, a lateral orienting response might facilitate processes programmed by the hemisphere which elicited the orientational bias. Thus, process and orientation would be mutually supportive. A quite different case is that in which the same hemisphere is called upon to program two independent processes at the same time. There mutual interference would be expected and seems to occur (Kinsbourne & Cook, 1971; Kreuter, Kinsbourne, & Trevarthen, 1972).

VI. Conclusion

In this paper, we have demonstrated by observing normal human behavior that the two cerebral hemispheres are in reciprocal balance in their control of lateral attention manifested in lateral gaze, head turning, or merely premotor shifts of visual attention. Measurable shifts of attention give us a behavioral criterion for lateralizing any chosen higher mental function in intact man (as, for instance, we investigated the laterality of numerical thought). We thereby make a begining toward the definition of a behavioral space, in topological rather than Euclidean correspondence to the cerebral cortical neuronal system. Within this space can be plotted the relative proximity of diverse cerebral processes as indicated by the extent to which they are mutually supportive in situations in which they are congruent and mutually interfering when they are directed towards unrelated goals.

References

Attneave, F. Some informational aspects of visual perception. *Psychological Review*, 1954, **61**, 183–193.

Bakan, P. Hypnotizability, laterality of eye movements and functional brain asymmetry. *Perceptual and Motor Skills*, 1969, **28**, 927–932.

Bartz, A. E. Eye movement latency, duration and response time as a function of angular displacement. *Journal of Experimental Psychology*, 1962, **64**, 318–324.

Bisiach, E. Differenze destra-sinistra nel vicoscimento di stimoli visivi complessi. *Rivista di Patologia Nervosa e Mentale*, 1966, **87**, 393–396.

Bogen, J. E. The other side of the brain: II: An appositional mind. *Bulletin of Los Angeles Neurological Society*, 1969, **34**, 135–162.

Bruce, R., and Kinsbourne, M. The effects of attention on lateral asymmetries in visual perception, 1971. Unpublished.

Bryden, M. P. Tachistoscopic recognition of non-alphabetical material. *Canadian Journal of Psychology*, 1960, **14**, 78–86.

Bryden, M. P. Left–right differences in tachistoscopic recognition: Directional scanning or cerebral dominance? *Perceptual and Motor Skills*, 1966, **23**, 1127–1134.

Bryden, M. P. & Rainey, C. A. Left-right differences in tachistoscopic recognition. *Journal of Experimental Psychology*, 1963, **66**, 568–571.

Conrad, K. Über áphasische Sprachstorungen bei hirnverletzten Linkshandern. *Nervenarzt*, 1949, **20**, 148–154.

Corsi, P. M. The effect of contralateral noise upon the perception and immediate recall of monaurally presented verbal material. Unpublished master's dissertation, McGill University, 1967, Montreal.

Crosby, E. C. Relations of brain centers to normal and abnormal eye movements in the horizontal plane. *Journal of Comparative Neurology*, 1953, **99**, 437–479.

Darwin, C. J. Auditory perception and cerebral dominance. Unpublished *doctoral dissertation*, Cambridge University, 1969, Cambridge, England.

Day, M. E. An Eye-movement phenomenon relating to attention, thought and anxiety. *Perceptual and Motor Skills*, 1964, **19**, 443–446.

Duke, J. D. Lateral eye movement behavior. *Journal of General Psychology*, 1968, **78**, 189–195.

Edwards, D. C., Antes, J. R., Adams, R. W., & Truman, G. A. Comparison of "first-eye-movement" detection methods. *Perceptual and Motor Skills*, 1971, **32**, 435–441.

Efron, R. The effect of handedness on the perception of simultaneity and temporal order. *Brain*, 1962, **86**, 261–284.

Filbey, R. A., & Gazzaniga, M. S. Splitting the normal brain with reaction time. *Psychonomic Science*, 1969, **17**, 335–336.

Gabersek, V. Étude électro-oculographique des temps de réaction oculomoteurs chez les sujets normaux. *Le Travail Humain*, 1963, **26**, 255–272.

Goodglass, H., Shai, A., Rosen, W., & Berman, M. New observations on right–left differences in tachistoscopic recognition of verbal and non-verbal stimuli. Paper presented at the International Neuropsychological Society, Washington, D.C., August 1971.

Gordon, H. W. Hemispheric asymmetries in the perception of musical chords. *Cortex*, 1970, **6**, 387–398.

Harcum, E. R. Lateral dominance as a determinant of temporal order of responding. In M. Kinsbourne (Ed.), *Asymmetry of hemispheric function*. London: Tavistock Press, 1973. In press.

Hecaen, H., & Sauget, J. Cerebral dominance in left handed subjects. *Cortex*, 1971, **7**, 19–48.

Heron, W. Perception as a function of retinal locus and attention. *American Journal of Psychology*, 1957, **70**, 38–48.

Horridge, G. A. *Interneurons*. London: Freeman, 1965.

Hubbs, C. L., & Hubbs, L. C. Bilateral asymmetry and bilateral variation in fishes. *Papers of the Michigan Academy of Science, Arts and Letters*, 1945, **30**, 229–310.

Humphrey, M. E., & Zangwill, O. L. Dysphasia in left-handed patients with unilateral brain lesions. *Journal of Neurology, Neurosurgery and Psychiatry*, 1952, **15**, 184.

Jeeves, M. A., & Dixon, N. F. Hemisphere differences in response rates to visual stimuli. *Psychonomic Science*, 1970, **20**, 249–251.

Kerr, M., Mingay, R., & Elithorn, A. Cerebral dominance in reaction time responses. *British Journal of Psychology*, 1963, **54**, 325–336.

Kimura, D. Cerebral dominance and the perception of verbal stimuli. *Canadian Journal of Psychology*, 1961, **15**, 166–171.

Kimura, D. Left–right differences in the perception of melodies. *Quarterly Journal of Experimental Psychology*, 1964, **16**, 355–358.

Kimura, D. Dual functional asymmetry of the brain in visual perception. *Neuropsychologia*, 1966, **4**, 275–285.

Kinsbourne, M. A model for the mechanism for unilateral neglect of space. *Transactions of the American Neurological Association* 1970, **95**, 143–145. (a)

Kinsbourne, M. The cerebral basis of lateral asymmetries in attention. *Acta Psychologica*, 1970, **33**, 193–201. (b)

Kinsbourne, M. Eye and head turning indicates cerebral lateralization. *Science*, 1972, **176**, 539–541.

Kinsbourne, M., & Cook, J. Generalized and lateralized effects of concurrent verbalization on a unimanual skill. *Quarterly Journal of Experimental Psychology*, 1971, **3**, 341–345.

Knehr, C. A. The effect of monocular vision on measures of reading efficiency and perceptual span. *Journal of Experimental Psychology*, 1941, **29**, 133–154.

Kreuter, C., Kinsbourne, M., & Trevarthen, C. Are disconnected cerebral hemisphere independent channels? Effects of unilateral loading on bilateral finger tapping. Unpublished, 1972.

Leyton, A. S. F., & Sherrington, C. S. Observations on the excitable cortex of the chimpanzee, orangutan and gorilla. *Quarterly Journal of Experimental Physiology*, 1971, **11**, 135.

Lipp, O. Über die Unterschiedsempfindlichkeit im Sehfeld unter dem Einflusse der Aufmerksamkeit. *Archiv der Gesamten Psychologie*, 1910, **19**, 313–394.

Mach, E. *The Analysis of sensations*. Republication of the 1914 edition, translated by C. M. Williams, New York: Dover, 1959.

Milner, B., Branch, C., & Rasmussen, T. Observations on cerebral dominance. In A. V. S. de Reuck & M. O'Connor (Eds.), *Disorders of language*, CIBA Foundation Symposium, Churchill: London, 1964.

Mishkin, M., & Forgays, D. G. Word recognition as a function of retinal locus. *Journal of Experimental Psychology*, 1952, **43**, 42–48.

Murphy, F. H., and Venables, T. H. Ear asymmetry in the threshold of fusion of two clicks: A signal detection analysis. *Quarterly Journal of Experimental Psychology*, 1970, **22**, 288–300.

Nottebohm, S. The ontogeny of bird song. *Science*, 1970, **167**, 950–956.

Penfield, W., & Rasmussen, T. *The cerebral cortex of man*. New York: McMillan, 1957.

Sokolov, E. N. Neuronal models and orienting reflex. In M. A. B. Brazier (Ed.), *The central nervous system and behavior*. New York: Josiah Macy Foundation, 1960.

Spellacy, F. J. Lateral preferences in the identification of patterned stimuli. *Journal of the Acoustical Society of America*, 1970, **47**, 574–578.

Sprague, J. M., & Meikle, T. H. The role of the superior colliculus in visually guided behavior. *Experimental Neurology*, 1965, **11**, 115–146.

Terrace, H. S. The effect of retinal locus and attention on the perception of words. *Journal of Experimental Psychology*, 1959, **58**, 382–385.

Treisman, A., & Geffen, G. Selective attention and cerebral dominance in perceiving and responding to speech messages. *Quarterly Journal of Experimental Psychology*, 1968, **20**, 139–150.

Trevarthen, C. Brain bisymmetry and the role of the corpus callosum in behavior and conscious experience. Paper presented at the International Colloquium on Interhemispheric Relations, Smolenice, Czechoslovakia, 1969.

van der Meer, H. C. *Die Links—rechts Polarisation des Phenomenalen Raumes*. Gröningen: Wolters, 1959.

Vanderplas, J. M., & Garvin, E. A. The association value of random shapes. *Journal of Experimental Psychology*, 1959, **57**, 147–162.

White, M. J. Laterality differences in perception: A review. *Psychological Bulletin*, 1969, **72**, 387–405.

3 SEQUENTIAL EFFECTS
IN REACTION TIME AND ABSOLUTE JUDGMENTS

Sequential Effects in Choice Reaction Time:
A Tutorial Review[1]

Sylvan Kornblum

Mental Health Research Institute
The University of Michigan
Ann Arbor, Michigan

ABSTRACT

This paper reviews the experimental data on sequential effects in one-to-one and many-to-one choice reaction-time (RT) tasks. The results of many studies make it clear that some variables, such as stimulus probability, transition probability, number of alternatives, and stimulus–response (S–R) compatibility all have systematic, and sometime differential, effects on the RT for repetitions and nonrepetitions; other variables, such as time lag, appear to have more equivocal effects. By viewing the mean RT of a set of trials as a weighted sum of the RT for proper subsets of those trials, certain methodological issues arise which are also briefly discussed.

I. Introduction

The purpose of this review is to summarize some of the experimental findings on sequential effects in choice reaction-time (RT) tasks. With that end in mind, the data and relevant methodological questions have been emphasized, whereas explanatory conjectures and theoretical treatments

[1]Preparation of this manuscript was helped in part by grant NSF GB 30644.

259

have been excluded from consideration (however, see the review for the two-choice case by Audley in this volume). This approach to the area has revealed some remarkable consistencies as well as inconsistencies among the results. The former leave little doubt that sequential effects are a robust aspect of performance in choice RT tasks and cannot be regarded as ancillary aberrations, or epiphenoma; the latter cast serious doubts on some of the simplistic conjectures that have been put forth to account for these results.

For purposes of convenience and coherence this paper begins with some procedural and definitional statements. These are followed by a historical note where some of the principal issues are stated. The body of the paper is then presented in two major sections, the first dealing with one-to-one tasks and the second with many-to-one tasks. Data that could not be accommodated within this rubric then are considered briefly before the exposition is brought to a close.

II. Definitions, Procedures, and Methodological Considerations

The term *sequential effect* may be defined as follows: If a subset of trials can be selected from a series of consecutive trials on the basis of a particular relationship that each of these selected trials bear to their predecessor(s) in the series, and the data for that subset differ significantly from the rest of the trials, then the data may be said to exhibit sequential effects.[2]

If sequential effects are known to be present in a set of experimental results, then analytical procedures that assume independence between trials are no longer appropriate for that set of data. One must, therefore, seek either to exclude or isolate these nonindependent trials for separate analyses, or design one's experiments so as to eliminate, or minimize them (see LaBerge, Van Gelder, & Yellott, 1970). Alternatively, one could design one's experiments so as to exploit these sequential dependencies and take advantage of their presence in order to investigate some of the underlying psychological processes in such tasks. In either case, some procedures must be used to determine the presence or absence of sequential effects. Procedures that partition the data with that end in mind are briefly listed below.

---

[2]Repetitions and nonrepetitions of various kinds will be our principal concern in this paper. Clearly, many other kinds of sequential effects exist (for example in psychophysical experiments, in absolute judgments, etc.), however, these will not be considered in this paper.

A. First-Order Sequential Effects

This procedure assigns trials to mutually exclusive and exhaustive subsets on the basis of the relationship that exists between trial n and its immediate predecessor, trial $n - 1$.

1. One-to-One Mapping (1:1).
If the stimulus and response on trial n are the same as on trial $n - 1$, then trial n is classified as a *repetition* (Rep); if they are not the same, then it is a *non-repetition* (N-Rep).
Since Rep and N-Rep partition the data, it follows that the overall mean reaction time $(\overline{\text{RT}})$ is the sum of the mean RT for Rep$(\overline{\text{RT}}_r)$ and N-Rep$(\overline{\text{RT}}_{nr})$ each weighted by its own probability of occurrence, that is,

$$\overline{\text{RT}} = p_r(\overline{\text{RT}}_r) + p_{nr}(\overline{\text{RT}}_{nr}). \tag{1}$$

2. Many-to-One Mapping (n:1).

In tasks where different stimuli are mapped onto the same response, it is entirely possible to repeat the response on two consecutive trials for which the stimuli themselves differ. The 1:1 classification scheme is, therefore, ambiguous in the $n{:}1$ case. However, Bertelson (1965) has proposed an unequivocal procedure for partitioning such $n{:}1$ data. Consider a task in which the stimuli S_A and S_B are mapped onto response $R_1 (n{:}1)$, and stimulus S_C is uniquely mapped onto response R_2, that is,

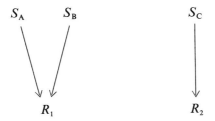

One possible sequence of trials in such a task could be the following:

  trial 1 (S_A, R_1);   trial 2 (S_C, R_2);   trial 3 (S_C, R_2);
  trial 4 (S_B, R_1);   trial 5 (S_B, R_1);   trial 6 (S_A, R_1).

Whenever the response is not repeated, neither is the stimulus; the class of N-Rep is, therefore, clear-cut and unambiguous (see trials 2 and 4 above).

However, on trials where response R_1 is repeated (n:1), the stimulus may (trial 5) or may not (trial 6) have been repeated. Bertelson distinguishes between these two cases of response repetitions in the n:1 case by calling the former an *identical* trial (Id), and the latter an *Equivalent* trial (Eq); N-Rep in n:1 tasks have come to be called *Different* trials (Diff).

Since Id, Eq, and Diff partition the data, Eq. (1) is equally applicable to the n:1 case, except, of course, for the obvious fact that the probability of response repetition [p_r in Eq. (1)] is the sum of the probability of Id (p_{Id}) and Eq (p_{Eq}), that is,

$$\overline{RT} = p_{Id}(\overline{RT}_{Id}) + p_{Eq}(\overline{RT}_{Eq}) + p_{Diff}(\overline{RT}_{Diff}).$$

It is worth noting that the overall mean RT for a particular stimulus is simply the weighted sum of the mean RT of these three partitions for that stimulus. Some of the implications of this point will be considered in the discussion of the experimental results of n:1 tasks.

B. kth-ORDER SEQUENTIAL EFFECTS.

In contrast to first-order procedures in which a particular trial is compared to its immediate predecessor, kth-order procedures assign the trials to k mutually exclusive and exhaustive subsets on the basis of the relationship that trial n may have to its k predecessors. This procedure yields a much finer-grained data base than does the first-order classification.

1. Repetitions.

If the stimuli and responses on trial n and on the k trials that precede it are the same, then trial n is classified as the kth-*consecutive repetition* (see, for example, Falmagne, 1965). Consecutive Id or Eq trials may also be distinguished in this manner by using the criteria appropriate for those partitions.

2. Nonrepetitions.

At least two types of kth-order N-Reps have been considered in the literature.

a. kth Consecutive Nonrepetitions. If the stimulus and response on trial n differ from the stimulus and response on trial $n - 1$, and those in turn differ from the stimulus and response on trial $n - 2$, and so on for k preceding consecutive trials, then trial n is classified as the kth consecutive N-Rep. This procedure is used rarely and is presently of doubtful value, except possibly in the two-choice, 1:1 case (see, for example, Hale, 1969).

b. Number of Intervening Trials.   In this procedure, given the S–R pair on trial n, the sequence of preceding trials $n - 1, n - 2, \ldots, n - k$ is searched until a match with the original S – R pair is found. These two successive occurrences of the same S – R pair thus would be separated by k intervening trials ($k \geqslant 1$), and trial n would be classified as a N-Rep, k trials removed from its previous occurrence in the series (see, for example, Hyman, 1953); clearly if $k = 0$, then trial n is a repetition.

This basic procedure also has been elaborated to make more detailed discriminations in the data. Smith (1970) was able to demonstrate that significant differences in RT on trial n were obtained depending on whether the intervening trials themselves were Reps or N-Reps, the former being faster than the latter.

C. Exhaustive k-Tuples

This procedure yields the most detailed classification of all, in that all the possible different sequences of length k are considered separately (see, for example, Remington, 1969, 1971). The larger the number of alternatives, the more difficult this becomes, for the number of different sequences of length k that are possible with N different alternatives is N^k.

Since practically all the RT data in the past two decades have been reported in the form of average measures for series, conditions, individual stimuli, Reps, or N-Reps, it may be useful to keep the "weighted sum" nature of these average measures in mind if only to retain the continuity between these gross measures and the more detailed aspects of the data that we are now considering. Thus, Eqs. (1) and (2) may be expressed in a more general form to include kth-order sequential effects, or any other partition of the data, that is,

$$\overline{RT}_s = \sum_k p\,(S_k)\overline{RT}_{sk}, \tag{3}$$

where $\overline{RT}_s$ is the average RT for a particular sequential effect, for example, Rep, or N-Rep; $\overline{RT}_{sk}$ is the average RT for the kth order sequential effect being investigated, that is, the kth consecutive Rep, or N-Rep with k intervening trials; $p(S_k)$ is the probability of the kth order sequential effect (where $\sum_k p\,(S_k) = 1.00$).

The probability $p(S_k)$ will, of course, vary with k differences in the number of alternatives, stimulus probability, transition probability, etc. That is, the weighting of these partitions in the overall average will vary with different conditions.

III. Setting the Stage and Formulating the Problem

Aside from a study by Hansen (1922, pp. 365–366), who noted the occurrence of sequential effects in his choice RT error data, Hyman (1953) was the first to report sequential effects in a systematic fashion. His stimuli consisted of 8 lights located at the corners of two concentric squares. The responses were verbal, and the intertrial interval was approximately 10 sec. His observations deal with both repetitions, and nonrepetitions. First he noted that ". . . whenever a stimulus was immediately followed by itself in the series, S seemed to respond unusually fast to it . . . [Hyman, 1953, p. 195]"; second, he observed that the RT to a particular stimulus increased with the first two stimuli that intervened between two successive occurrences of the same stimulus, and after that, the RT decreased (except in the two-choice condition). These observations were tangential to Hyman's principal thesis, and remained of peripheral interest to the area until Bertelson's series of studies in the early 1960s. It was Bertelson's first study (1961) that set the stage for subsequent work in this field.

Bertelson's experiment consisted of a two-choice task in which neon lights were used as stimuli, and key presses as responses; the mapping was 1:1. The stimuli themselves were equiprobable but differed in their transition probabilities, that is, for condition REP, $p(i|i) = .75$, for condition ALT, $p(i|j) = .75$ ($i \neq j$), and for condition RAND, $p(i|i) = p(i|j) = .5$. The experiment was conducted as a serial task with two different time intervals between a response and the onset of the next stimulus (R–S interval). In one condition the R–S interval was 50 msec; in the other it was 500 msec. The first analysis considered only the first-order effects in the data; the second analysis went into kth order effects. Some of the results of the first analysis are plotted on Fig. 1.

The abscissa of Fig. 1 represents the conditional probability of a stimulus. The data points for the repetitions and nonrepetitions plotted at $p(i|j) = .5$ are all from the same experimental series, since $p(i|j) = p(i|i)$. However, the Rep and N-Rep data plotted at the other values of $p(i|j)$ are each from different experimental series. That is, at $p(i|j) = .25$ the Rep data are taken from the ALT conditions, the N-Rep data are taken from the REP condition, and so on. Since stimulus transition probability has an effect on RT, the data must be normalized with respect to transition probability in order to be comparable.

From Fig. 1, it can be seen that the RT for Reps and N-Reps are both inverse functions of their respective conditional probabilities. This effect was noted briefly by Bertelson (1961): ". . . in both redundant conditions the mean RT to the preponderant event (i.e. the event with the higher conditional probability) is shorter . . . [p. 98]."

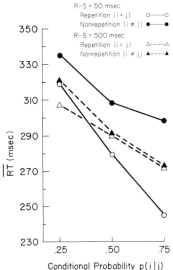

Fig. 1. Two-choice RT for Rep and N-Rep from Bertelson's study (1961) plotted as a function of the conditional probability of the stimuli. The stimuli themselves, were equiprobable.

The second major result concerns the effect of the R–S interval. At the short, 50-msec interval the RT for Reps is considerably faster than that for N-Reps. When that interval is increased to 500 msec, two different effects are in evidence: the RT for Reps goes up, and the RT for N-Reps goes down. The net effect, of course, is to reduce the difference between Reps and N-Reps in all but the low $p(i|j)$ condition; however, it is important to note the two components contributing to this reduction. It is, therefore, not sufficiently informative merely to report the changes in this difference, as has occasionally been done (that is, changes in the magnitude of the "repetition effect"), but the manner in which this change occurs must be reported as well.

In his last analysis, Bertelson calculated the mean RT for each of the k ($k = 1, \ldots, 6$), consecutive repetitions and nonrepetitions and found that, with the exception of the RAND condition, the RT for Rep and N-Rep both decreased with increasing values of k.

The findings from that study were instrumental in calling attention to the importance of sequential effects in choice RT.

IV. One-to-One Choice Reaction Time Tasks

A. The Effect of Absolute Probability

The inverse relationship between the overall mean RT and the probability of a stimulus is one of the best documented propositions in the area of choice RT. In comparison to that vast body of evidence, data dealing with the effects of stimulus probability on Reps and N-Reps are relatively meager. However, some direct evidence does exist that can be brought to bear on the question.

In a study the principal objective of which was the development of a stochastic model that would account for choice RT data in terms of sequential preparatory processes, Falmagne (1965) reports the results of a six-choice RT experiment. The stimuli consisted of the digits 1 through 6, the responses were key presses, and the R–S interval was 760 ± 20 msec. Each of the 6 stimuli was presented with a different probability ranging from .01 to .56. The overall mean RTs for the stimuli follow the customary inverse relationship with stimulus probability. The separate mean RT for Reps and N-Reps follow the same pattern, in that they both decrease inversely with stimulus probability, the Rep being faster than the N-Rep. However, for the low-probability stimuli (.01, .03, and .06) the data are far too few and variable to be included in this generalization.

It is interesting to note that the decrease in RT attributable to stimulus probability appears to be about the same for Rep and N-Rep. This should be borne in mind in connection with the effects of the number of alternatives (discussed in detail later). There, it will be seen that an increase in the number of equiprobable alternatives increases the RT for N-Rep more than for Rep. Since changes in the number of alternatives are accompanied by changes in stimulus probability, these findings suggest that stimulus probability and number of alternatives are separate factors.

Similar results were found by Krinchik (1969) in a study where the probability of some of the stimuli was kept fixed at either .92, .5, or .067 as the number of alternatives was varied from two, to four, to eight. The stimuli were geometrical figures, the responses were key presses, and the inter-stimulus interval was 7 sec (including a warning signal and foreperiod). The RT for Rep and N-Rep both decreased with increasing stimulus probability. There also appears to be an interaction between stimulus probability and number of alternatives, which lends further support to the proposition that stimulus probability and number of alternatives are separate factors.

Additional evidence on the effects of stimulus probability is present in the results of a five-choice study by Leonard, Newman, and Carpenter (1966). Using the digits 1–5 as stimuli, key presses as responses, and a 100-msec R–S interval, Leonard constructed two sets of random stimulus sequences. In one set the critical stimulus, the digit "3," occurred with a probability of .68; in the other that probability was .44; the remaining stimuli were equiprobable. As the probability of the critical stimulus increased, the RT for Reps and N-Reps both decreased (Reps being faster than N-Reps). Leonard's data (Leonard et al., 1966, Figs. 3 and 4) also suggest that the N-Reps decreased at a slightly faster rate than the Reps.

B. The Effects of Transition Probability

1. Two-Choice Conditions

The effects of transition probability that Bertelson (1961) first reported were verified subsequently in two separate experiments by Kornblum (1967, Figs. 1 and 2). In both experiments neon lights were used as stimuli, and key presses as the responses. The stimuli themselves were equiprobable, with transition probabilities that varied in the range between .1 and .9. In one experiment the R–S interval was 270 msec; in the other, it was 137 msec. The mean RTs for Reps and N-Reps were inversely related to their respective transition probabilities in both experiments. However, the difference between Reps and N-Reps was affected by the R–S interval. At the longer interval of 270 msec, the RT for Reps and N-Reps appears to be identical for all values of transition probability; at the shorter R–S interval of 137 msec, the RT for Reps was slightly faster than that for N-Reps.

Further analysis of the two-choice data at the shorter, 137-msec R–S interval, indicated that the decrease in RT with transition probability could be described by a linear equation in $p(i|j)$, that is, $\overline{RT}_r = 321 - 105p(i|i)$ and $\overline{RT}_{nr} = 323 - 65p(i|j)$. Whereas the intercepts are almost identical, the slope of the Reps was more than half again as steep as the slope of the N-Reps. Such a large difference in slope appears to occur in the two-choice case only.

2. More-Than-Two-Choice Conditions

The effects of transition probability were investigated next in a four- and eight-choice task (Kornblum, 1967). The stimuli, again, were neon lights, the responses were key presses, and the R–S interval was 137 msec. The stimuli were equiprobable and the conditional probabilities $p(i|j)$ ranged from .05 to .8. The results replicated the patterns that had been found in the two-choice case. Both the Reps and N-Reps were inverse linear functions of their respective conditional probability: (a) four-choice, $\overline{RT}_r = 328 - 85p(i|i)$, $\overline{RT}_{nr} = 373 - 79p(i|j)$; (b) eight-choice $\overline{RT}_r = 368 - 111p(i|i)$, $\overline{RT}_{nr} = 451 - 104p(i|j)$. [Note that the slopes for Reps and N-Reps are much more nearly the same within the four- and the eight-choice conditions than they were in the two-choice conditions.]

The linear decrease in the mean RT for Reps and N-Reps received further confirmation from the results of two four-choice experiments (Kornblum, 1969) in which the stimuli were equiprobable and the conditional probabilities were varied from .05 to .6. One experiment was run serially with an R–S interval of 140 msec and neon lights as stimuli. The other experiment was run discretely with approximately 3 sec between successive stimulus presentation; the digits 1–4 were used as stimuli. Key presses were used as the responses in both experiments.

At this point let us pause briefly and recall that the overall mean RT for Rep and N-Rep can be expressed as a weighted sum of kth-order Rep and N-Rep, respectively [see Eq. (3)]. In a number of experiments, it has also been shown that the mean RT for the kth Rep or N-Rep [that is, $\overline{RT}_{sk}$ in Eq. (3)] varied with k. In particular, the mean RT for Rep decreases with each successive value of k (see, for example, Bertelson, 1961; Falmagne, 1965; Hale, 1969) and the mean RT for N-Rep appears to increase as the number of intervening items gets larger (see, for example, Hyman, 1953; Falmagne, 1965). Furthermore, the probability of the kth-order Rep or N-Rep (p_{sk}) changes with k as well as with stimulus transition probability. Thus, the linear decrease of $\overline{RT}$ with conditional probability which has been reported above, or other similar changes in the overall mean RT for Rep and N-Rep could, in principle, be an artifactual consequence of the sheer differences in weights, or p_{sk}, for different conditions. To guard against such a possibility, the data of the last two experiments (Kornblum, 1969) were analyzed in greater detail.

Figure 2 illustrates the results of a kth-order analysis of the Rep and N-Rep for the serial and discrete experiments. The abscissa for the Rep indicates the first six successive repetitions; the abscissa for the N-Rep indicates the number of intervening trials up to seven. Except for the upward displacement of the data for the discrete experiment (note the change in values on the ordinate), the results from the two experiments are quite similar. The greater the probability of a repetition, the faster is the RT for the first Rep; the greater the probability of nonrepetition, the faster is the RT for the first N-Rep (that is, with one intervening trial). Whereas successive Rep continue to decrease in the discrete case, this effect is greatly attenuated by the probability of Rep in the serial case. However, in both the serial and in the discrete experiments the RT for N-Rep increases as the number of intervening trials increases.

The result that we wished to verify is clear from these data, that is, the inverse relationship reported between transition probabilities and the overall mean RT of Rep and N-Rep is evident at the level of the first Rep and N-Rep as well.

C. The Effects of the Number of Alternatives

The discussion in the previous section focused on evidence related to the effects of transition probability on Rep and N-Rep, where it will be recalled, some of the data were drawn from experiments in which the number of alternatives had also been a variable (Kornblum, 1967). The transition probability effect was expressed by the negative slope of RT with

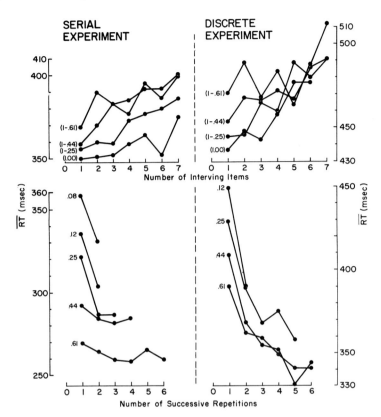

Fig. 2. Mean RT for kth successive Rep, and N-Rep with k intervening items from Kornblum's (1969) serial and discrete four-choice experiments. The probability values that label each curve, refer to the probability of Rep and N-Rep (as complementary values) for each series. The stimuli themselves were equiprobable. Note that different ordinates are used for each set of data.

respect to $p(i|j)$; the effect of the number of alternatives, on the other hand, appears to be reflected in the differences in the intercepts of the lines. Referring back to the linear equations, note that as the number of alternatives increases from two to four to eight, the intercept for the Rep increases from 321 to 328 to 368 msec and the intercept for the N-Rep increases from 323 to 373 to 451 msec. That is, an increase in the number of alternatives (which in this experiment is confounded with a decrease in stimulus probability) has a dual effect. First, the RT for both Reps and N-Reps increases with the number of alternatives, and second, the increase is greater for the N-Reps than for the Reps. The latter, of course, would result in a greater "repetition effect" (that is, greater difference between Reps and N-Reps) as the number of alternatives increased. This dual effect is confirmed by

Krinchik's experiment (referred to above) in which stimulus probability and number of alternatives were not confounded by virtue of the probability for some stimuli having been kept fixed as the number of alternatives was varied (Krinchik, 1969). Several additional studies provide either partial or total confirmation for these findings.

Hale (1969) used the digits 1–8 as the stimuli, key presses as the responses, and an R–S interval of 100 msec in constructing a two-, four-, and eight-choice task. His results indicate that the RT for Reps and N-Reps both increase with the number of alternatives, the increase for N-Rep being greater than for Rep in going from four to eight alternatives. Similar findings are also evident in the two- and four-choice data from a study by Schvaneveldt and Chase (1969); however, in that study, the increase for Rep and N-Rep appears to be the same.

A comparison of the results of two separate experiments by Remington does confirm the overall, as well as the differential, increase of N-Reps with the number of alternatives. Using horizontally arranged neon lights as the stimuli, key presses as the responses, and a 4-sec interstimulus interval (which includes a warning signal and a foreperiod), Remington conducted a two-choice (1969) and a four-choice (1971) experiment for which the data in the equiprobable conditions are comparable for our purposes. In comparing the two-choice with the four-choice data, the Rep increased from 284 to 366 msec, whereas the N-Rep increased from 295 to 400 msec.

Indirect evidence on this question is provided from a study by Bertelson (1963), whose central concern was the effect of S–R compatibility on sequential effects. Using two horizontally arranged neon lights as the stimuli, key presses as the responses, a crossed-over stimulus response assignment, and a 50-msec R–S interval, Bertelson obtained a mean RT of 333 msec for Reps and 443 msec for N-Reps in this, the most incompatible of his two-choice conditions. In his most compatible four-choice task he used the numerals 1–4 as stimuli, key presses as the responses, and a 150-msec R–S interval; the mean RTs in that experiment were 422 and 565 msec for Reps and N-Reps, respectively. By comparing the results of his slowest two-choice task with his fastest four-choice task, the data are compatible with the finding of a differential increase in the RT for Reps and N-Reps as the number of alternatives is increased.

D. STIMULUS AND RESPONSE EFFECTS

1. Partial Response Repetitions.

Some of the more successful recent studies addressing themselves to the question of identifying stimulus and response factors in choice RT tasks have relied on many-to-one (n:1) paradigms in the design of their experiments. However, many-to-one mapping is not a necessary requirement for such inquiries, although the uncritical use of the terms "stimulus" and "response" may make it appear so. Ordinarily, these terms are used to refer to the two opposite extremes of a long chain of events that begins at one end with a sensory event and terminates at the other end with a motor act. It would be naive to assume that the complex sequence that intervenes between these two end points is amenable to a simplistic dichotomy; some of the events may be closer to one end than to the other, but few are a pure case of either. Thus, "response factor" may encompass more than the actual overt motor act, and may include some of the processes that lead up to that final act. When viewed in this manner, motor acts on two consecutive trials need not necessarily be identical and coincide in every respect (and they probably do not) in order to speak of response repetitions; it may be sufficient for some of the response-associated processes to overlap on two consecutive trials, and one could then speak of a partial response repetition.

This approach was pursued by Rabbitt (1965) in a ten-choice task in which the stimuli were ten horizontally arranged lights, and the responses consisted of pressing the appropriate one of ten switches with the index finger of the left (for lights 1–5) or right hand (for lights 6–10); the R–S interval was 20 msec. The stimuli were presented randomly, with the proviso that no stimulus followed itself in the series. The omission of stimulus repetitions precluded the repetition of two identical responses; however, it did not eliminate two consecutive responses being made with the same hand. These constituted partial response repetitions for which Rabbitt reported a mean RT of 534 msec; the mean RT for trials calling for a switch in hands was 581 msec.

A similar finding emerges from a more detailed analysis of the data from Kornblum's four-choice serial experiment (1969), which was described in Section IV,B,2; the four stimulus lights were mapped onto the middle and index fingers of the left and the right hands in their most natural order. Repetitions, of course, occur when the response on trial n is the same as on trial $n - 1$. However, several classes of partial response repetitions may be distinguished among the nonrepetitions. For instance, when a response with the left middle finger is followed by a response with the left index finger, the left-hand response is a response component common to two consecutive trials and constitutes a partial response repetition. Similarly, if we consider the two index fingers to be anatomically symmetrical, as are the two middle fingers, then two response equivalence classes may be constructed so that when a response with the left index finger is followed by a response with the right index finger, the index response is the common response component for those two trials and constitutes another partial response repetition. Four different types of transitions are, therefore, possible with the particular S–R mapping used in this experiment: pure repetitions (HF), where both the hand and the finger were the same; pure non-repetitions ($\overline{HF}$), where neither the hand nor the finger were the same; and partial response repetitions ($H\overline{F}$) and ($\overline{H}F$), where respectively either the hand, or the finger were the same. The data for these four transitions are presented in Fig. 3. Clearly, the pure repetition data (HF) are fastest. However, the most striking feature of these results is the distinction that emerges among the N-Rep. Without exception, the RT on trials with partial response repetitions, when the hand is the same but the finger is not ($H\overline{F}$), is faster than when neither the hand nor the finger are repeated. Even though the finger repetitions ($\overline{H}F$) do not have an effect on the RT data, they do have marked effects in the error analysis (see Kornblum, 1969). These data,

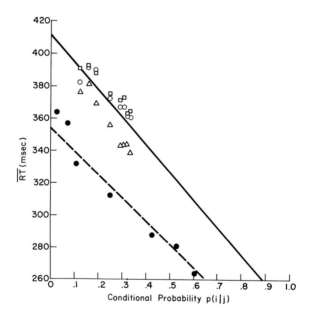

Fig. 3. Mean RT for Rep and N-Rep as a function of the conditional probability of Rep and N-Rep; the data are from Kornblum's (1969) four-choice serial experiment (●, HF repetitions). Three types of N-Rep are distinguished: (Δ) $H\overline{F}$, Rep of hand, with N-Rep of finger; (□) $\overline{H}F$ N-Rep of hand with Rep of finger; (○) $\overline{HF}$ N-Rep of either hand or finger. The lines are the best fitting straight lines for the overall means of the Rep and N-Rep data.

together with Rabbitt's results are evidence in support of a response factor in sequential effects.

2. *S–R Compatibility.*

The effects of S–R compatibility are subsumed under the heading of stimulus and response effects because they deal with a critical stage in the processing sequence that extends between the sensory event and the motor act. Indeed, that stage is the very juncture between the two, and cannot be considered separately from either. (See also Rabbitt's contribution to this volume.) The question that we shall address ourselves to, however, is an empirical one: do changes in S–R compatibility have a differential effect on Reps and N-Reps? All the available evidence appears to point to an affirmative reply.

Bertelson (1963) used a two-choice task in which a pair of horizontally and another pair of vertically arranged lights served as stimuli, key presses were used as responses, and the R–S interval was 50 msec. An ordering of the four possible mappings from the most to the least compatible, or fastest to slowest, yields the following data: direct correspondence was fastest, the two vertical conditions were next, and the crossed condition was slowest. If that ordering is maintained, and the RT for Rep and N-Rep are now examined, the RT for Reps increased by 13 msec for each successive condition, whereas the RT for N-Reps increased by 33 msec per condition. The net effect, of course, is to increase the difference between Rep and N-Rep by 20 msec for each successive condition. Similar results with a four-choice task are reported in the same study. In that experiment, the digits 1–4 were mapped in either an ascending or descending left-to-right order onto four keys, and an R–S interval of approximately 150 msec was used. The increase in incompatibility increased the RT for Reps by 96 msec, and the RT for N-Reps by 269 msec. It is interesting to note that even though the tasks in the two-choice and the four-choice conditions are not the same, the differential effects of compatibility on Rep and N-Rep appear to be amplified by an increase in the number of alternatives.

Shaffer conducted a series of two- and three-choice experiments (Shaffer, 1965, 1966, 1967) in which the stimuli were either two horizontally arranged lights, or three lights at the vertices of an equilateral triangle; the responses were key presses and the R–S interval was varied among the experiments. An unusual feature of Shaffer's studies was the presentation, on each trial of a signal that specified the particular S–R mapping to be used on that trial. Consecutive trials, therefore, could differ either in the mapping, or in the physical stimulus, or in the response that was called for.

The fastest RT was obtained on Rep trials, when neither of these three aspects had changed. The largest increase in RT occurred on trials on which the mapping rule had changed; when the mapping rule had been repeated but the stimulus had not, the RT was intermediate. However, the difference between this and the latter conditions was of questionable statistical significance.

Keele (1969) reports the results of a six-choice experiment in which horizontally arranged lights were used as stimuli, key presses as the responses, and an intertrial interval (otherwise left unspecified) of either 2, 4, or 8 sec was incorporated in the experimental design. Two levels of compatibility were obtained by mapping the lights onto the keys in the most direct natural order for one condition, and in a purely arbitrary fashion for the other condition; the latter was the less compatible mapping. In the compatible condition the RT for Rep and N-Rep did not differ from each other. The effect of the incompatible mapping was twofold: first, it increased the RT for Rep and N-Rep, and second, it increased the N-Rep far more than the Rep.

Several experiments were run by Schvaneveldt and Chase (1969) in a study where the effects of S–R compatibility and the number of alternatives were among the variables under investigation. In one experiment (Experiment II), the stimuli consisted of illuminated knobs, the subsequent depression of which constituted the response. In two other experiments (Experiments III and IV) the stimuli were the digits 1–4 and the responses were key presses. In Experiment III, the digits were assigned to the keys in a left-to-right ascending order; in Experiment IV, that assignment was random. The conditions in Experiment IV were run as a four-choice task only, whereas the conditions in Experiments II and III were run as a two- and a four-choice task. The intertrial interval was systematically varied from .1 to .5, and to 1.00 sec in all the experiments. The results presented in Table 1 are the mean RTs for Rep and N-Rep as calculated from Figs. 2 and 3 of their paper (Schvaneveldt & Chase, 1969).

The effects of compatibility are readily apparent from a comparison

Table 1. *RT Data from Schvaneveldt and Chase (1969)*

	Two-choice		Four-choice	
	Rep	N-Rep	Rep	N-Rep
Experiment II (Knobs, most compatible)	378	367	419	415
Experiment III (Digits, less compatible)	431	460	570	609
Experiment IV (Digits, least compatible)	—	—	540	625

of the results of Experiments II and III within the two- and four-choice conditions. It will be recalled that Experiment III has a less compatible task than Experiment II. This decrease in compatibility increases the RT for Rep and N-Rep by 53 msec and 93 msec respectively, in the two-choice condition, and by 151 and 194 msec respectively, in the four-choice condition. The differential susceptibility of Rep and N-Rep to the effects of S–R compatibility is thus clearly demonstrated.

It is of interest to note that unlike the interaction that was reported in most other studies, the Schvaneveldt and Chase data indicate that an increase in the number of alternatives appears to increase the RT for Rep and N-Rep about equally; that is, sequential effects and number of alternatives seem to be additive. However, the effects of both of these factors interact with S–R compatibility, which confirms our previous conjecture in that regard (Kornblum, 1969).

V. Many-to-One Choice Reaction Time Tasks

The use of 1:1 tasks makes it difficult, although not impossible, to distinguish between stimulus and response effects. Among the advantage of using n:1 tasks is the multiple mapping, which makes it possible to vary stimulus and response probabilities, transitions, or alternatives, separately. Thus, for example, with n:1 mapping, response repetitions may be generated by both stimulus repetitions and nonrepetitions, as we have already noted. In the same paper where Bertelson (1965) first distinguishes between these two types of response repetitions he also reports the results for these different types of transitions.

The stimuli were the digits 2, 4, 5, and 7, and the responses were two key presses. The digits 2 and 4 were mapped onto the left response and the digits 5 and 7 were mapped onto the right response; the stimuli and responses were equiprobable, and the transitions were random; the R–S interval was 50 msec. The RTs averaged across the four subjects who participated in the experiments were 500 msec for Diff, 404 msec for Eq, and 393 msec for Id.

Rabbitt (1968) investigated the effects of mapping eight stimuli onto either two, four, or eight (1:1) responses; in one additional condition he used four stimuli mapped onto two responses. The stimuli were the digits 1 through 8, the responses were key presses, and the mapping was straightforward; the R – S interval was 20 msec. Within conditions, the results of the last 300 out of a total of 3000 trials confirmed the order of RT that Bertelson had found for his three types of transitions: Id < Eq < Diff. However, the difference in the RT between Eq and Diff emerged only after extensive training; furthermore, the difference between Id and Eq was much larger than that found by Bertelson. Similar results are reported by Eichelman (1970) in a letter-naming task. Rabbitt finds that the RT for Id does not differ between conditions, although the RT for Rep is longest in the 1:1 task. In contrast, the RT for Diff and Eq transitions does differ among all conditions.

Smith (1968) reports the results of a 2:1 task in which the stimuli consisted of the digits 1 and 2 presented on either a red or a green background; the responses were two key presses. The red–1 and green–2 were mapped onto the left key, and the green–1 and red–2 were mapped onto the right key. The stimuli and responses were equiprobable, and the transitions were random. The R–S interval was 6 sec, including a 1 sec warning signal and a 1-sec foreperiod. The RT for Id was 807 msec, for Eq, 937 msec, and for Diff, 875 msec. This is the only experiment in which the RT for Eq is reported to be longer than for Diff in a 2:1 equiprobable situation. However, the conjunctive combination of attributes (digits and colors) that define the stimuli in this task also present an extraordinarily difficult coding problem for the subject, particularly in the case of Eq trials, where both stimulus attributes change, but the response does not.

A. THE EFFECTS OF TRANSITION PROBABILITY

The many-to-one paradigms that have been discussed up to now have been used to try to disentangle the effects of stimulus and response probability. Some of these will be examined below. However, let us first review the results of an experiment from our own laboratory in which the effects of changing the probability of the transitions themselves was investigated.

The stimuli, the responses, and the mapping were the same as were used by Bertelson (1965). The digits 2 and 4 were mapped onto the left key, and the digits 5 and 7 were mapped onto the right key. The stimuli and response were equiprobable, and the R–S interval was 100 msec. The three principal conditions of the experiment were determined by three probabilities-of-response repetitions. In one condition the probability-of-response repetition was .3, in another it was .5, and in the last, it was 7. Six different subjects were assigned to each of these three conditions. Within each condition there were five experimental series, which differed in their probability of Id and Eq trials. In two of these five series, either the probability of Id or the probability of Eq was made equal to the probability-of-response repetition; in these series, therefore, a response repetition always was obtained either as a result of an Id or of an Eq transition. In another series, the probability of Id and Eq were made equal; thus, given that a response repetition had occurred, it was equally likely that

Table 2. *Experimental Conditions and Results (Means of Medians) of n:1 Study*

p(R)[a]	Series	Identical (Id)				Equivalent (Eq)				Different (Diff)			
				SEM[c]				SEM[c]				SEM[c]	
		p_{Id}[b]	$\overline{RT}$	Within	Between	p_{Eq}[b]	$\overline{RT}$	Within	Between	p_{Diff}[b]	$\overline{RT}$	Within	Between
.3	1	—	—	—	—	.30	438	11.99	16.10	.70	420	3.63	8.64
	2	.08	405	13.55	14.57	.22	442	16.23	14.72	.70	423	6.51	9.58
	3	.15	377	15.43	10.73	.15	454	23.86	15.01	.70	413	8.50	5.33
	4	.22	381	10.24	8.30	.08	469	26.00	25.35	.70	421	8.33	6.62
	5	.30	389	7.35	9.77	—	—	—	—	.70	415	9.17	8.03
.5	1	—	—	—	—	.50	427	8.08	11.20	.50	479	5.87	9.14
	2	.15	380	7.21	10.36	.35	425	6.54	10.72	.50	475	6.22	5.75
	3	.25	382	7.47	7.25	.25	440	10.98	13.31	.50	475	5.34	7.71
	4	.35	376	7.77	10.50	.15	443	9.82	7.25	.50	476	6.89	5.59
	5	.50	380	7.04	16.46	—	—	—	—	.50	465	8.05	7.35
.7	1	—	—	—	—	.70	371	8.26	7.51	.30	497	12.00	8.09
	2	.18	343	7.39	5.74	.52	374	7.38	3.49	.30	484	8.18	9.93
	3	.35	354	10.73	8.45	.35	405	10.16	7.45	.30	481	10.69	8.18
	4	.52	343	9.09	7.57	.18	411	12.14	6.62	.30	478	9.38	6.39
	5	.70	314	9.45	6.24	—	—	—	—	.30	474	10.82	8.57

[a] Probability of response repetition.
[b] Probability of Id, Eq, or Diff.
[c] Standard error of the mean within and between subjects.

277

it had been brought about by a stimulus repetition or nonrepetition. In the remaining two series, the probability of identical and equivalent were widely separated (see Table). Subjects were run for 500 trials on each of the five series within a condition. The results for the last three replications are shown in Table 2.

The RT for Id is faster than that for either Eq or Diff, in all three conditions. In the two conditions where the probabilities of response Rep are .5 and .7, the RT for Eq is faster than for Diff. However, where the probability of response Rep is .3, the RT for Eq is longer than that for Diff. This result will be examined shortly. Within each of the three conditions, there is an overall trend in the RT for Id and Eq to decrease as these particular transition probabilities increase. However, the magnitude of that trend is relatively minor when compared with the magnitude and consistency of the effects that changes in the probability of response repetitions and nonrepetitions have on RT. Figure 4 illustrates this effect for those series in which response repetitions were brought about by identical or equivalent transitions exclusively (series 1 and 5). The abscissa represents

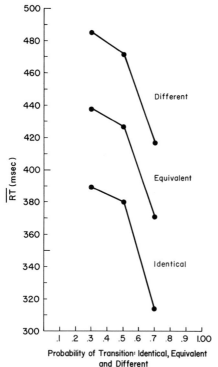

Fig. 4. Mean RT for Id, Eq, and Diff transitions as a function of the probability of these transitions. The stimuli and responses themselves were equiprobable.

the probability of the particular transition. The data points plotted for Diff are the means for Diff for series 1 and 5. For example, the RT for Diff, which is plotted at .3, is the mean of Diff for series 1 and 5 in the condition where the probability of response Rep was .7. The .3 and .7 data for Diff, therefore, are taken from different conditions than the data for Id and Eq. This manner of plotting the data (that is, normalizing it with respect to probability) resolves what at first sight might have appeared to be an incongruous result in the .3 condition, where the RT for Diff fell halfway between Id and Eq. Figure 4 also suggests that varying the probability of response repetitions and nonrepetitions has the same effect on the RT for repetitions, irrespective of the kind of transition, and on the RT for nonrepetitions. The three curves appear to be parallel, even though the decrease in RT is certainly not linear with transition probability.

These results suggest the presence of both stimulus and response transition factors in $n{:}1$ RT tasks. Support for a stimulus transition factor comes from the difference between Id and Eq, which is maintained across different values of the probability of response repetitions. That is, given that a response has been repeated, whether the stimulus itself is repeated (Id) or not (Eq) appears to make a substantial difference in the RT obtained. The presence of a response transition factor is indicated by the inverse relationship between the RT for all three transitions and the probability of those transitions. Finally, the stimulus and response transition factors appear to be additive.

B. The Effects of Stimulus and Response Probability

These results, which indicate that substantial RT differences are obtained for the three types of transitions in $n{:}1$ tasks, cast a slightly different light on studies that have used the $n{:}1$ paradigm to distinguish between stimulus and response effects.

In particular, let us consider the paradigm that was first introduced in Section III, where the stimuli S_A and S_B were mapped onto response R_1, and stimulus S_C was uniquely mapped onto response R_2. Consider the case where $p(S_A) > p(S_B) = p(S_C)$, and where all the transitions are randomly determined by those stimulus probability, to generate probabilistically independent sequences.

The probability of a response Rep occurring on stimulus S_C is, of course, given by $p^2(S_C)$, while the probability of a response N-Rep is given by $p(S_C) - p^2(S_C)$. Let us now consider stimulus S_B, whose probability is equal to that of stimulus S_C. The probability of a response Rep occurring with S_B has two components; one of them is given by $p^2(S_B)$, which is the probability of Id transitions and is also equal to $p^2(S_C)$, and the other is given by the product $p(S_B) \times p(S_A)$, which is the probability of Eq transitions for stimulus S_B. Thus, even though the stimulus probabilities themselves are equal, that is, $p(S_C) = p(S_B)$, the probability of a response Rep for S_B is greater than for S_C, that is, $p^2(S_B) + p(S_B)p(S_A) > p^2(S_C)$. With this mapping, the magnitude of the difference in the probability of response repetitions for S_C and S_B increases with any increase in the probability of S_A. Thus, as $p(S_A)$ increases, not only does the probability of Id transition for S_C decrease, but the probability of Diff for S_B decreases simultaneously with an increase in its probability of Eq transitions. Given these differences in the probability of response repetitions for S_B and S_C, and the fact that Eq RTs are faster than Diff RTs, it follows that the mean RT to S_B would be faster than to S_C [see Eq. (2)], even though the stimulus probabilities are equal.

This conclusion is in accord with some of the results obtained by LaBerge and Tweedy (1964), LaBerge, LeGrand, and Hobbie (1969), Dillon, (1966), Biederman and Zachary (1970), and others. These authors interpreted their results as supporting either a stimulus-factor or a response-factor hypothesis. For example, LaBerge and Tweedy (1964) report that when a high- and a low-probability stimulus both were mapped onto the same response, the RT was faster for the high-probability stimulus than for the low-probability stimulus; a similar result also was reported by Bertelson and Tisseyre (1966). Those results are clearly consistent with the above analysis. However, the near equality in RT that LaBerge and Tweedy report for the low-probability ($p = .1n:1$), stimulus and the stimulus uniquely mapped onto the other response ($p = .4$) is as puzzling to us as it was to them. In contrast, all the results of LaBerge et al. (1969) are in complete accord with our analysis. Dillon (1966) reports the results of four different experiments in which the stimuli consisted of four pairs of auditorily presented letters, and the responses were two key presses. The letters in each pair were matched in probability. One letter was uniquely mapped onto one response and constituted the "critical" stimulus; its match and all the remaining six letters were mapped onto the other response. The subjects were instructed that when a stimulus was presented, they were not to make a response unless that stimulus was accompanied by an additional signal, the probability of which was varied—this was the response–demand signal. Two important features of this experiment make it particularly interesting from our viewpoint. First, stimulus repetitions were not allowed to occur; second, the stimulus matched in probability with the critical stimulus was never presented on a trial following the critical stimulus. These two constraints generated experimental sequences that not only eliminated response repetitions to the critical stimulus, but also forced every presentation of its matched member in the pair to occur as the result of an Eq transition. In principle, therefore, most of Dillon's results could be accounted for in terms of the sequential effects in his data. Finally, Biederman and Zachary (1970), in trying to distinguish between stimulus and response probability effects in choice RT, report that they found no differences in the RT between Id, Eq, and Diff transitions. However, in their examination for sequential effects they averaged the RT for these various transitions across all their experimental conditions, thus washing out whatever differences there might have been between transitions as a result of differences in transition probabilities.

The fact that the results of these various experiments, in addition to those of many binary classification tasks (see Nickerson's contribution to this volume), can be accounted for, in principle, by the "weighted sum" type of argument does not necessarily imply that sequential effects do, in fact, account for these data. For instance, even though the results of Hawkins and Hosking (1969) and Hawkins, Thomas, and Drury (1970) are consistent with a sequential analysis, they report that they did not find sequential effects in their data, which therefore, excludes a sequential "weighted sum" argument explanation for their results. However, we have shown that the appropriate sequential analyses must be performed if the "weighted sum" argument is to be ruled out as an explanation for the results of many experiments that are intended to address themselves to other questions.

C. ADDITIONAL STUDIES

The most carefully developed theoretical treatments of sequential effects are to be found in Falmagne (1965), Falmagne and Theios (1969), Theios and Smith (1970), and Laming (1968). In addition to these explicitly stated models, which fall outside the scope of this review, two conjectures have been entertained by a number of investigators, which have given rise to a series of studies dealing with the effects of time lag and guessing behavior on sequential effects. These will now be considered briefly.

1. The Effects of Time Lag.

The term "time lag" is being used in its generic sense to denote two types of intervals: It either refers to the R−S interval, or to the intertrial interval (iti), which may or may not include a warning signal or foreperiod. The experimental investigations of the effects of time lag rest on two premises. First, sequential effects are hypothesized as being attributable, in part, to the operation of memory dependent, residual (Hyman, 1953), or inertial processes (Bertelson, 1961) that favor repetitions; second, it is assumed that whatever these processes may be, their effects will be at-

Table 3. *Studies, Conditions, and Data* on Time Lag*

Study	No. of choices	Stimuli	Responses	S–R correspondence	Shift in R–S or iti (sec)	Shift in RT for N-Rep ($\overline{RT}_{nr}$)	ΔRT_{nr}	Shift in RT for Rep ($\overline{RT}_r$)	ΔRT_r	Shift in difference ($\overline{RT}_{nr} - \overline{RT}_r$)
Bertelson (1961)	2	Lights	Key press	Direct	.05 → .50	308 → 291	−17	279 → 290	+11	29 → 1(−)
Bertelson and Renkin (1966)[a]	2	Symbolic	Key press	Not applicable	Regular					
					.05 → .20	437 → 421	−16	353 → 350	− 3	84 → 71(−)
					.20 → 1.00	421 → 421	0	350 → 375	+ 25	71 → 46(−)
					Random					
					.05 → .20	457 → 450	− 7	370 → 378	+ 8	87 → 72(−)
					.20 → 1.00	450 → 424	−26	378 → 400	+ 22	72 → 24(−)
Entus and Bindra (1970)	2	"Circle size"	Key press	Not applicable	2 → 10.00	687 → 645	−42	679 → 684	+ 5	8 → −39(−)
Hale (1967a)	2	Digits	Key press	Direct	.10 → .60	459 → 393	−66	420 → 376	− 44	39 → 17(−)
					60 → 2.00	393 → 399	+ 6	376 → 405	+ 29	17 → 6(−)
Hale (1967b)	2	Digits	Key press	Direct	4.00 + FP of:					
					.60 → 2.00	362 → 379	+17	375 → 383	+ 8	13 → 4(−)
					2.00 → 4.00	379 → 386	+ 7	383 → 404	+ 21	4 → 18(+)

Schvaneveldt and Chase (1969)[a,b]	2	Lit buttons	Button press	Direct	.10 → .50	376 → 359	−17	400 → 373	− 27	−24 → −14(+)
					.50 → 1.00	359 → 360	+ 1	373 → 365	− 8	−14 → − 5(+)
					1.00 → 2.50	326 → 310	−16	330 → 325	− 5	−6 → −15(−)
					2.50 → 8.50	310 → 310	0	325 → 314	− 11	−15 → 4(+)
	4	Lit buttons	Button press	Direct	.10 → .50	427 → 410	−17	430 → 421	− 9	−3 → −11(−)
					.50 → 1.00	410 → 417	+ 7	421 → 410	− 11	−11 → 7(+)
					1.00 → 2.50	372 → 362	−10	363 → 355	− 8	9 → 7(−)
					2.50 → 8.50	362 → 371	+ 9	355 → 361	+ 6	7 → 10(+)
Keele (1969)[c]	6	Lights	Key press	Indirect	2.00 → 4.00	740 → 760	+20	620 → 615	− 5	120 → 145(+)
					4.00 → 8.00	760 → 710	−50	615 → 650	+ 35	145 → 60(−)
Smith (1968)	4	2 digits on 2 backgrounds	Key press	Arbitrary	2.00 → 4.00	845 → 930	+85	725 → 837	+112	120 → 93(−)
					4.00 → 8.00	930 → 945	+15	837 → 880	+ 43	93 → 65(−)

*Note: all data are in milliseconds.

[a]Data taken from the figures.

[b]The first two and the last two comparisons are from two different experiments involving two different groups of subjects, which account for the differences between the two 1.00-sec conditions.

[c]The data for the direct, compatible situation are difficult to extract from the figure; the data in the table are approximate.

tenuated, or will decay in time. Given the present state of theoretical developments, and the inconsistent effects of time lag among these experiments, both assumptions appear to be gratuitous, at best. For instance, Williams (1966) reports a faster RT for N-Rep in her two-choice experiments, with iti values ranging from $\frac{1}{2}$ to 1 full sec, and from 12 to 15 sec. Hyman (1953), on the other hand, while reporting similar results for his own two-choice condition, finds much faster RTs for Reps than N-Reps with three or more alternatives, using an iti of approximately 10 sec.

The results from studies that deliberately set out to investigate the effects of time lag are summarized in Table 3. The data in that table illustrate the effects of time lag on the magnitude of the *difference* between N-Rep and Rep (that is, the repetition effect) as well as on the RT for N-rep and Rep themselves. Given the latter, which is much more informative, the former is redundant; however, the data on the "repetition effect" is included merely for the sake of convenience. Thus, for instance, both Smith (1968) and Keele (1969) find that increasing time lag reduces the magnitude of the difference between N-Rep and Rep. However, in Smith's case, this reduction is the result of a differential increase in the RT for both Rep and N-Rep, whereas in Keele's case, it is brought about by an increase in the RT for Reps and a decrease in the RT for N-Reps. An analysis merely in terms of the "repetition effect" is, therefore, insufficient. A cursory examination of Table 3 fails to reveal the presence of large systematic effects of time lag except for its possible interaction with S–R compatibility (see Keele, 1969; Smith, 1968; Bertelson & Renkin, 1966). The data with respect to the effects of time lag are, therefore, equivocal at this time. The further study of this variable would appear to require a far clearer, and more precise theoretical statement than we now have, of the questions being posed.

2. Guessing Habits. [3]

When Hyman (1953) first reported the presence of sequential effects in his data, he suggested that in addition to a residual effect which facilitated reaction to a stimulus that had just been seen and reacted to, the subjects' "verbal expectancies" might be another factor underlying some of his results. This suggestion recently has been subjected to several attempts at experimental verification.

---

[3]Several studies that have used subjects' guesses as a measure of "expectancy" are not included in this review because the guessing data were related to overall mean RTs irrespective of the transitions between trials (for example, Bernstein & Reese, 1965; Bernstein, Schurman, & Forester, 1967; Hinrichs & Krainz, 1970).

Williams (1966), whose results of a series of two-choice experiments indicated a generally faster RT for N-Rep than for Rep, had one condition in her study in which subjects stated which stimulus, or response, they expected on the next trial. Irrespective of whether they had been asked to guess the next stimulus or the next response, the two-choice RT for the correctly guessed event was considerably faster than that for the incorrectly guessed event; however, the RT for N-Rep remained faster than for Rep.

In one of the conditions of his two-choice study, Hale (1967a) required subjects to make a verbal prediction about the next stimulus. The predictions were made only on trials that followed the occurrence of one of the two stimuli, and had to be made within the 2-sec R–S interval of the experiment. The overall results indicated that the prediction task itself increased the RT for Rep and N-Rep by about 60 msec, and the RT for correctly predicted stimuli was about 80 msec faster than that for incorrectly predicted stimuli. For incorrect predictions the RT for Rep was longer than for N-Rep; however, there was no difference between Rep and N-Rep for the correctly predicted stimuli.

Keele (1969) had subjects predict the next stimulus within the 5- sec iti of a four-choice experiment, which included a compatible and an incompatible mapping. Even though there are no sequential effects in his data, the RT for correctly predicted stimuli was faster than that for incorrectly predicted stimuli. This advantage of correct predictions was greater for the incompatible (~ 200 msec) than for the compatible mapping (~ 80 msec).

Schvaneveldt and Chase (1969) recorded subjects' guesses independently of an RT task for random sequences of two and four events and then computed the conditional probabilities of the guesses, given the preceding three trials. The data of several two- and four-choice RT experiments then were related to these guessing probabilities with the following results. In their two-choice compatible conditions, they found a high negative correlation [$r < (-.9)$] between RT and the guessing probability for a particular stimulus. In the less compatible two-choice condition the magnitude of this correlation was reduced, and the RT for Rep was faster than for N-Rep. The data for their most compatible four-choice condition appear to show a weak relationship with guessing probability. However, as was true of their incompatible two-choice data, their incompatible four-choice data are unrelated to guessing probabilities, and also show marked effects of Rep and N-Rep.

The results of these experiments indicate that whereas the RT for correctly predicted events is generally faster than for incorrect predictions, the differences between Rep and N-Rep are maintained, regardless of the outcome of such guesses. As was true of the experiments on time lag, the experimental attempts to assess the relative contributions of "expectancy" (as measured by verbal guessing habits) to the sequential effects of choice RT are inconclusive.[4]

VI. Concluding Remarks

This brief review of sequential effects in one-to-one and many-to-one choice RT tasks has restricted itself to a consideration of experimental results and methodological issues. The results indicate that some variables, such as stimulus probability, transition probability, number of alternatives, and S–R compatibility all have systematic, and sometime differential, effects on the RT for repetitions and nonrepetitions. It is equally clear that other variables, such as time lag, have more equivocal effects that require further investigation. However, the pervasiveness and the orderliness of sequential effects that has been demonstrated by these studies should guide the design of future experiments whether such experiments address themselves directly to a more detailed study of sequential effects, or whether they seek to exclude such effects from their results.

References

Bernstein, I. H., & Reese, C. Behavioral hypotheses and choice reaction time. *Psychonomic Science*, 1965, **3**, 259–260.

Bernstein, I. H., Schurman, D. L., & Forester, G. Choice reaction time as a function of stimulus uncertainty, response uncertainty and behavioral hypotheses. *Journal of Experimental Psychology*, 1967, **74**(4), 517–524.

Bertelson, P. Sequential redundancy and speed in a serial two-choice responding task. *Quarterly Journal of Experimental Psychology*, 1961, **12**, 90–102.

Bertelson, P. S–R relationships and reaction times to new versus repeated signals in a serial task. *Journal of Experimental Psychology*, 1963, **65**, 478–484.

Bertelson, P. Serial choice reaction time as a function of response versus signal-and-response repetition. *Nature*, 1965, **206**(4980), 217–218.

Bertelson, P., & Renkin, A. Reaction times to new versus repeated signals in a serial task as a function of response-signal time interval. *Acta Psychologica*, 1966, **25**, 132–136.

Bertelson, P., & Tisseyre, F. Choice reaction time as a function of stimulus versus response relative frequency of occurrence. *Nature*, 1966, **212**(5066), 1069–1070.

Biederman, I., & Zachary, R. A. Stimulus versus response probability effects in choice reaction time. *Perception and Psychophysics*, 1970, **7**(3), 189–192.

---

[4]The liberal borrowing of such terms as "positive" and "negative recency" from the area of probability learning, where their meaning is quite precise (see Jarvik, 1951), also appears to be unwarranted at this time.

Dillon, P. J. Stimulus versus response decisions as determinants of the relative frequency effect in disjunctive reaction-time performance. *Journal of Experimental Psychology*, 1966, **71**(3), 321–330.

Eichelman, W. H. Stimulus and response repetition effects for naming letters at two response-stimulus intervals. *Perception and Psychophysics*, 1970, **7**(2), 94–96.

Entus, A., & Bindra, D. Common features of the "repetition" and "same–different" effects in reaction time experiments. *Perception and Psychophysics*, 1970, **7**(3), 143–148.

Falmagne, J. C. Stochastic models for choice reaction time with applications to experimental results. *Journal of Mathematical Psychology*, 1965, **2**(1), 77–127.

Falmagne, J.-C., & Theios, J. On attention and memory in reaction time experiments. *Acta Psychologica*, 1969, **30**, 316–323.

Hale, D. J. Sequential effects in a two-choice serial reaction task. *Quarterly Journal of Experimental Psychology*, 1967, **19**(2), 133–141.   (a)

Hale, D. J. Sequential analysis of effects of time uncertainty on choice reaction time. *Perceptual and Motor Skills*, 1967, **25**, 285–288.   (b)

Hale, D. J. Repetition and probability effects in a serial choice reaction task. *Acta Psychologica*, 1969, **29**, 163–171.

Hansen, F. C. Serial action as a basic measure of motor capacity. *Psychological Monographs*, 1922, **31**, 320–382.

Hawkins, H. L., & Hosking, K. Stimulus probability as a determinant of discrete choice reaction time. *Journal of Experimental Psychology*, 1969, **82**, 435–440.

Hawkins, H., Thomas, G. B., & Drury, K. B. Perceptual versus response bias in discrete choice reaction time. *Journal of Experimental Psychology*, 1970, **84**, 514–517.

Hinrichs, J. V., & Krainz, P. L. Expectancy in choice reaction time: Anticipation of stimulus or response? *Journal of Experimental Psychology*, 1970, **85**, 330–334.

Hyman, R. Stimulus information as a determinant of reaction time. *Journal of Experimental Psychology*, 1953, **45**(3), 188–196.

Jarvik, M. E. Probability learning and a negative recency effect in the serial anticipation of alternative symbols. *Journal of Experimental Psychology*, 1951, **41**, 291–297.

Keele, S. W. Repetition effect: A memory-dependent process. *Journal of Experimental Psychology*, 1969, **80**(2), 243–248.

Kornblum, S. Choice reaction time for repetitions and non-repetitions: A re-examination of the information hypothesis, *Acta Psychologica*, 1967, **27**, 178–187.

Kornblum, S. Sequential determinants of information processing in serial and discrete choice reaction time. *Psychological Review*, 1969, **76**(2), 113–131.

Krinchik, E. P. The probability of a signal as a determinant of reaction time. *Acta Psychologica*, 1969, **30**, 27–36.

LaBerge, D., & Tweedy, J. R. Presentation probability and choice time. *Journal of Experimental Psychology*, 1964, **68**(5), 477–481.

LaBerge, D., LeGrand, R., & Hobbie, R. K. Functional identification of perceptual and response biases in choice reaction time. *Journal of Experimental Psychology*, 1969, **79**(2), 295–299.

LaBerge D., Van Gelder, P., & Yellott, J., Jr. A cueing technique in choice reaction time. *Perception and Psychophysics*, 1970, **7**(1), 57–62.

Laming, D. R. J. *Information theory of choice reaction*. London: Academic Press, 1968.

Leonard, J. A., Newman, R. C., & Carpenter, A. On the handling of heavy bias in a self-paced task. *Quarterly Journal of Experimental Psychology*, 1966, **18**(2), 130–141.

Rabbitt, P. M. A. Response-facilitation on repetition of a limb movement, *British Journal of Psychology*, 1965, **56**(2, 3), 303–304.

Rabbitt, P. M. A. Repetition effects and signal classification strategies in serial choice-response tasks. *Quarterly Journal of Experimental Psychology*, 1968, **20**(3), 232–240.

Remington, R. J. Analysis of sequential effects in choice reaction times. *Journal of Experimental Psychology*, 1969, **82**, 250–257.

Remington, R. J. Analysis of sequential effects for a four-choice reaction time experiment. *Journal of Psychology*, 1971, **77**, 17–27.

Schvaneveldt, R. W., & Chase, W. G. Sequential effects in choice reaction time. *Journal of Experimental Psychology*, 1969, **80**(1), 1–8.

Shaffer, L. H. Choice reaction with variable S–R mapping. *Journal of Experimental Psychology*, 1965, **70**(3), 284–288.

Shaffer, L. H. Some effects of partial advance information on choice reaction with fixed or variable S–R mapping. *Journal of Experimental Psychology*, 1966, **72**(4), 541–545.

Shaffer, L. H. Transition effects in three-choice reaction with variable S–R mapping. *Journal of Experimental Psychology*, 1967, **73**(1), 101–108.

Smith, M. C. Repetition effect and short-term memory. *Journal of Experimental Psychology*, 1968, **77**(3), 435–439.

Smith, P. G. Choice reaction time as a function of stimulus sequence: Implications for the order of memory search. Report 70–7, Wisconsin Mathematical Psychology Program, September 1970.

Theios, J., & Smith, P. G. Sequential dependencies in choice reaction times. Report 70–8, Wisconsin Mathematical Psychology Program, October 1970.

Williams, J. A. Sequential effects in disjunctive RT; Implications for decision models. *Journal of Experimental Psychology*, 1966, **71**, 665–672.

Choosing a Response[1]

Gregory R. Lockhead

Department of Psychology
Duke University
Durham, North Carolina

ABSTRACT

This contribution reviews and presents some results which show that the name subjects choose for a stimulus is based on their judgment of the value of that stimulus and is then modified by consistent response processes. These response processes show up in the form of consistent effects of the sequences of previous values on the subjects' choice of a name for the current stimulus. The effects occur in different types of studies: in absolute judgments (of several different variables), in magnitude estimations, and in guessing random sequences.

Some experimental manipulations affect performance but do not change these sequential effects. This is taken as evidence that the factors studied, long-term memory and criteria variances in the studies conducted, are independent of response system processes.

I. Introduction

The typical psychophysical experiment involves a large number of trials of presenting a stimulus to a subject and obtaining a judgment. Each judgment may be of the relation between that stimulus and some standard

[1]This research was supported by Research Grant No. MH-18617 from the National Institute of Mental Health.

289

(method of constants); a judgment of the name of an attribute of the stimulus as previously learned (method of absolute judgments or single stimuli); a judgment of the relative category or location to which that stimulus belongs in the set of stimuli (methods of single stimuli and category judgments); a judgment of the presence or absence of an attribute (most threshold studies and detection tasks); a judgment of the relation between that stimulus and the just previous one (methods of limits, adjustments, and fractionation); or a judgment of an amount for the stimulus in relation to some previously learned modulus (method of magnitude estimation). Although this list is not intended to be exhaustive, and although there have been several modifications to many if not to all of the standard techniques, there is a common attribute to all of them. A presented stimulus is judged and responded to with some type of name.

The name may be relative, such as larger or quieter. It may be absolute, such as "3" or "Philip." The name may be supposed to refer to a relation to a previously learned scale (as in indirect scaling methods such as category judgments) or to an absolute scale (as in direct scaling methods such as magnitude estimation). In any case, the stimulus must be named. To accomplish this, the subject must employ a memory of the scale or the modulus, and in most cases he must employ his memory of at least the previous stimulus in the sequence.

As an example, consider a standard magnitude estimation task. The subject must judge the magnitude of the presented stimulus, compare his short-term memory of this magnitude with his memory of the just previous stimulus, and then calculate the relation between them. In some studies, he then must multiply this result by his memory of the name or magnitude he assigned to the previous stimulus. The resulting name or number is the subject's estimation of the magnitude of the stimulus presented. Although the magnitude of the stimulus might have been judged directly, the selection of a name for the response requires considerable activity and judgment. This paper reports some of the effects of judgment and response processes on the subject's selection of a name for the stimulus presented to him.

Although psychophysical tasks are tedious for the subject, consider the plight of the experimenter. For several subject hours per day, and for several days in a row, his task consists of selecting the next stimulus according to a proscribed procedure, presenting it (generally automatically) and then, usually, giving feedback (hopefully automatically). The sane experimenter must discover some activity that will keep him at the task since only the most unusual individuals are intrinsically motivated by this aspect of their investigations. One activity that he is likely to engage in involves an attempt to predict, before the response, what the subject will call the stimulus. Since the tasks are always structured so that the subjects perform better than chance but still make many errors, it is easy to indulge in this game. It is also easy for the experimenter to get the idea that he can predict the subject's response with greater accuracy than can the statistician, who knows only the stimulus value and the mean and variance of the subject's responses to each stimulus in the set. We generally consider the subject's errors to result largely from random perturbations in both the subject and in the stimulus apparatus (see the general methods of describing the Gaussian response distributions). But if the experimenter's introspections are correct, there must be something else, something like sequential dependencies, that provides this predictability.

II. Some Observed Sequential Dependencies

With this possibility of being able to predict the subjects' responses in mind, Morris Holland looked at some data from an absolute judgment study in several different ways. The result was the discovery of very regular relations between the judgment of the current stimulus and the sequence of previous stimuli in the experiment. The results have been presented in detail elsewhere (Holland & Lockhead, 1968) and the typical result is shown here (Fig. 1).

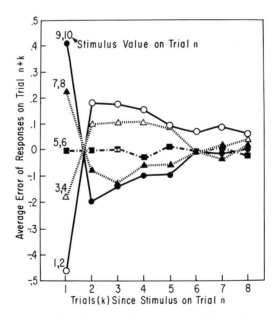

Fig. 1. The average effect of the stimulus on a given trial on the responses on the next eight trials.

The experiment reported in Figure 1 was one of absolute judgments of loudnesses. There were 10 1000-Hz tones, which varied in loudness in subjectively equal steps. The .5-sec duration tones were randomly presented to subjects for identification. Responses were the numerals 1–10, ordered with the loudnesses, such that 1 was the quietest tone and 10 was the loudest tone. Feedback followed each response. Each of the three subjects gave 150 responses in each of 18 sessions for an average of 810 responses per stimulus. The average performance was 41% correct. The results presented are collapsed over subjects and over pairs of stimuli for ease of presentation. All subjects showed the same effects.

Figure 1 shows a marked tendency for subjects to underestimate the value of a stimulus when it follows a low-intensity tone and to overestimate the stimulus when it follows a high-intensity tone. That is, responses to the current stimulus are assimilated toward the value of the immediately previous stimulus. For example, when the stimulus on the immediately previous trial ($k = 1$) was a 1 or a 2 (low intensity), the average response to the randomly selected subsequent stimulus was smaller than would be predicted from the overall average of the subject's responses to that stimulus. When the stimulus on the previous trial was a 9 or a 10 (loud), the average error was positive.

Further, for this particular condition, there is the opposite relation (contrast) between the subject's choice of a response to the current stimulus and the value of the stimulus which occurred two trials earlier ($k = 2$). If a low stimulus occurred two trials ago, there is a marked tendency for the subject to overestimate the magnitude of the current stimulus. If a high-valued stimulus occurred two trials ago, the current stimulus tends to be underestimated. This contrast between the response to the current stimulus and the value of earlier stimuli is enduring and continues for at least 5 trials, and perhaps for as many as 8 trials, back in the sequence.

This general result has been observed now in a number of different studies, but with modifications that depend on the conditions of the experiment. These various effects, reported earlier (Ward & Lockhead, 1971), are summarized here in Fig. 2. In general, it is seen that we have always obtained some assimilation followed by some contrast and that the magnitude of these effects, and whether they are primarily associated with previous stimuli or previous responses, depends on the experimental situation. It appears to generally be the case that, when the subject's task is to judge which particular stimulus has been selected out of a set of previously learned stimuli that vary on a single psychological dimension, his response is assimilated towards the value of the previous stimulus and contrasted with earlier stimuli in the sequence. (It may be necessary to have several members in the stimulus set for the generalization to hold.)

When the task is relatively easy, so that the subject is performing well above chance, the sequential effects between the previous stimuli and the current response are very similar to those between the previous response and the current response (compare Fig. 2a and b). This result is expected since stimuli and responses are highly correlated when the task is easy. It is not possible to tell from these results whether the sequential effects are related to stimuli or to responses, or to both.

If the task is made more difficult, such that the subjects are performing only slightly better than chance, stimuli and responses are not so highly correlated. In this case, the contingencies between previous stimuli and the current response appear much as they do with the easy task (Fig. 2c), but the first-order contingencies between previous and current responses largely disappear (Fig. 2d). Thus, the effects appear to be associated with the stimuli or with the feedback. The data reported are from a study of absolute judgments of line lengths with feedback given.

If we now withhold feedback from the subject, the results change again. As shown in Fig. 2e and f, when subjects are not given the correct name for the stimulus they just judged, the assimilative effects are large, last for several trials before there is a suggestion of contrast, and are much more associated with the previous responses than with the previous stimuli. The last is the reverse of the effect of increasing task difficulty while giving feedback.

The next set of data helps to clarify the nature of these effects. As the task was made difficult, we observed that contingencies between the current response and the previous response disappear, whereas those between current responses and the previous stimulus or feedback increase. This result is seen in the extreme when the task is made impossible, when the stimulus apparatus is turned off, and the subject has to guess which stimulus was selected although it was not presented to him. In this case (Fig. 2g and h) there are again marked contingencies between the response and the previous stimulus (the feedback) but there is no regular relation between the current response and the previous response. This assimilation of the current response to the previous stimulus (which was never presented) turns to contrast 2 to perhaps 6 trials back. It is not possible that these results are due to relations between memory processes and stimulus values, as suggested earlier by Holland and Lockhead (1968), because no stimuli were presented.

III. Choice of a Response

These various results taken together allowed Ward and Lockhead (1971, p. 77) to propose that the sequential effects are entirely due to response-system processes. The suggestion is summarized here. When stimuli vary over a large physical range, or when there is a large number of stimuli to be identified even though the physical range may not be large, the subject is uncertain as to exactly which is the "correct" name. He may

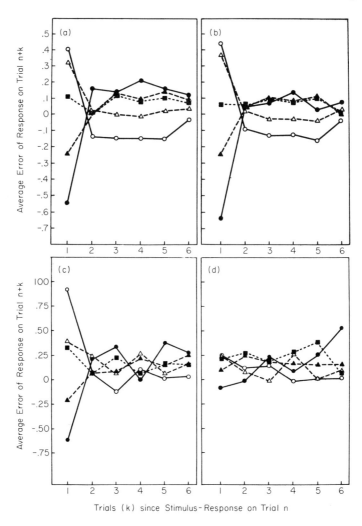

Fig. 2. The average effect of the stimulus (left columns) and of the response (right columns) on a given trial on the responses on the next six trials where the "stimulus"–response value on trial n are (●) 1, 2; (▲) 3, 4; (■) 5, 6; (△) 7, 8; (○) 9, 10. The stimuli

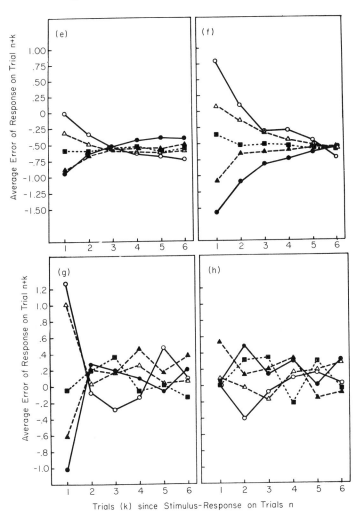

were loudnesses for (a) feedback, stimulus analysis; (b) feedback, response analysis; (e) no feedback, stimulus analysis; (f) no feedback response analysis; line lengths for (c) difficult, stimulus analysis; and (d) difficult, response analysis; and they were nothing for (g) guessing, "stimulus" analysis and (h) guessing, response analysis.

know that the stimulus was fairly loud, or relatively light, or near the mid-point of the scale. But with many stimuli possible, any of several responses or names are acceptable to him. Thus, a particular stimulus near the middle of a 10-category stimulus scale is mapped by the subject onto the middle of his internalized stimulus scale. Since this scale is not precise, and data on channel capacity show that it is not, this stimulus may be mapped as about a 4 or a 5 or a 6. Any of these names might be equally acceptable to the subject as his response. Since there are these several alternative acceptable responses, something other than sensory or judgment processes is employed to decide which one to select.

Assuming that subjects have a criterion of minimum average error, and assuming that they attend to the distribution of differences between successive stimuli as well as to the probability of occurrence of stimuli, we proposed that they select as their response that acceptable one which best matches the probability distribution of successive stimulus differences. With 10 stimuli it is more likely that randomly chosen successive stimuli differ by 1 or 2 category steps than by, to be extreme, 8 or 9 steps. Only 2% of all differences are as large as 9 steps, the 10 following the 1 and the 1 following the 10, whereas 10% of the differences are of 0 step (stimulus repetition) and 18% are of 1 step. Thus, small differences between successive stimuli are more likely than are large differences when the particular stimuli are ignored. If the subjects select responses based partly on this strategy of maximizing with respect to the distribution of successive differences between stimuli, assimilation is the necessary result. When the middle stimulus chosen as an example follows a low stimulus, it is likely to be called a 4. If it follows a high stimulus it is likely to be called a 6.

Although simplistic, this notion does account for all of the first-order contingencies determined thus far. As the task becomes more difficult, the magnitude of the assimilation increases because there are now more acceptable responses to a particular stimulus, and thus the tendency to maximize according to successive differences between stimuli can have a greater effect. When no feedback is provided, the subject's previous response is his best information concerning the value of that stimulus. Thus, his current response is assimilated to that response. The previous response was itself assimilated to the response prior to it; thus, the cumulative assimilation effect without feedback (Fig. 2e and f).

It is further suggested that the contrast of responses to stimuli further back in the sequence results from the subject's tendency not only to use the available responses equally often (Parducci, 1965) but also to attempt to do this over a small number of trials (Ward & Lockhead, 1971). Assume that, when one response area predominates over a few trials, the subject's response scale is adjusted to increase the probability of use of another part of it. If this occurs, contrast several trials back is the necessary result.

All of the sequential effects observed thus far are accountable for by a combination of these two response system processes: a tendency to maximize according to the distribution of successive stimulus differences and a tendency to use response alternatives equally often over the past several trials.

IV. Memory and Response Processes

Long-term memory has been reported to affect absolute judgment performance when feedback is not provided (Tresselt, 1947; Wever & Zener, 1928). We asked if memory also affects judgments in such a task when feedback is given after every trial (Ward & Lockhead, 1970). A major interest of the study was to determine the relation between sequential effects (which are a response-produced process) and memory effects, which are not a result of response processes.

Subjects were asked to judge loudness levels in a study very similar to that reported in Fig. 1. After making 2500 judgments (500 judgments on each of 5 days) the subjects were asked to judge a new set of tones on the sixth day. These new tones were generated by simply adding or subtracting 5 dB to each of the original stimuli. That is, the scale was shifted either up or down by 5 dB, but the subjects were not told that any change had taken place. Three subjects received feedback after each trial and three had no feedback. In either case, there was a marked effect on performance. The constant error shifted towards the mean of the previous stimulus distribution, and the effect of the previous day's scale was surprisingly tenacious. Even when the scale was moved up first, and then down and then back up on successive days the constant errors tracked the previous day's scale, whether or not feedback was provided. Thus, long-term memory has a marked effect on the judgment of the current set of stimuli.

The sequential effects were also marked and took the same form as those already reported. When no feedback was given, assimilation was found for at least two trials back, followed by contrast through 6 trials back (Fig. 3a and b). When feedback was provided there was assimilation one trial back followed by contrast 2–6 trials back (Fig. 3c and d). These sequential effects were superimposed on the constant error shift such that the figures are displaced by the magnitude of the long-term memory effect. Since the sequential effects (response effects) are superimposed on the scale shift (memory effects) but are not affected in form by the change in constant error, it may be reasonable to infer that the memory effects are response process independent. If so, and if this methodology is useful in isolating the locus of effects, perhaps the deter-

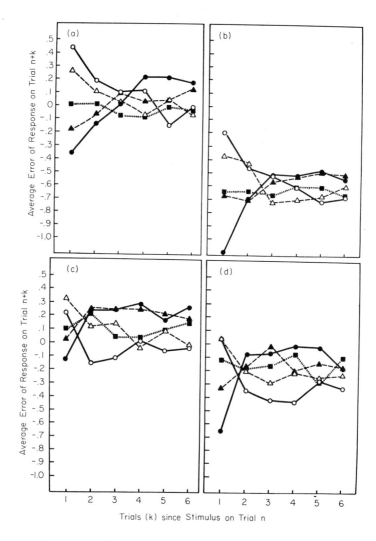

Fig. 3. The average effect of the stimulus on a given trial on the responses on the next six trials, where the stimulus value on trial *n* is as given in Fig. 2 for 1–10.(a) No feedback, up :CE = +.04; (b) no feedback, down :CE = −.61; (c) feedback, up :CE = +.12; (d) feedback, down :CE = −.20. The stimulus series was increased 5 dB from the previous day (left column) or decreased 5 dB (right column); feedback was not given (a and b) or followed each trial (c and d).

mination of response process effects in different studies can teach us something about the judgment process. Two studies conducted with this in mind, the investigation of sequential effects in magnitude estimations and when the stimulus range is varied in absolute judgments, are reported below.

V. Magnitude Estimations and Response Processes

If direct scaling methods, such as magnitude estimation, fractionation and cross-modality matching, provide a measure of sensory transduction free of judgment-based factors, then they ought not to provide sequential effects. If the results of such studies depend on more than the stimulus domain chosen, then they may reflect response processes. Poulton's review (1968) shows that the exponent of the power function for a particular stimulus domain depends on several variables. At least some of these, for example, the position of the stimulus in the stimulus ensemble and the size of the modulus, may be response-dependent factors. If so there should be sequential effects with magnitude estimations just as there are with absolute judgments.

Ward (1970) showed that there are sequential effects in a magnitude estimations of loudnesses task. The average error of responses to the current stimulus was assimilated to the value of the stimulus on the previous trial, and this assimilative effect extended for four trials back in the sequence. The first-order effects looked much like those obtained from the category judgment task performed by the same subjects. If these sequential effects are due to response processes, subjects must use a judgment process which is common in both magnitude estimation and category judgment tasks. If so, "It would seem that simply giving subjects different sets of instructions may not assure that they are doing anything fundamentally different when judging the stimuli [Ward, 1970, p. 54]."

VI. The Stimulus Range and Response Processes

The stimulus ensemble in an absolute judgment task is usually structured so that adjacent stimuli are separated by equal discriminability steps. When the physical size of these steps is increased, performance improves up to some point. Beyond that limiting point, or channel capacity, increases in the size of the steps do not affect performance. That the stimuli are not identified more accurately, when the physical distance between successive stimuli is increased, means that judgmental accuracy measured in physical units actually gets worse. That is, the subject's average error necessarily increases in proportion to the increased stimulus spacing. Since an increase in stimulus spacing produces a corresponding increase in stimulus range, the subject's average error is proportional to the stimulus range. Gravetter and Lockhead (1970) have demonstrated that this relation between range and performance is general and not limited to judgments at channel capacity. Accuracy in identifying a particular physical stimulus in an absolute judgment task is determined by the range over which the stimuli are being judged.

This is a general property of measuring devices. Consider a voltmeter as an example. If a 1% accurate meter is set at the 10-V range, an 8-V input will be recorded as 8 ± 0.1 V. If the meter is set to the 100-V range, the same input will be recorded as 8 ± 1.0 V. Thus, the meter appears to become less reliable as the physical range it is set to cover increases. Just as with people, the accuracy of the measuring device is proportional to the range over which it "expects" to vary.

We know that increases in the variance of the responses to a particular stimulus in an absolute judgment task are accompanied by increases in the magnitudes of the sequential effects (Holland, 1968). Thus increases in response variability might be due to response system processes. Alternatively, they may reflect increased variability in the subjective scale which would in turn be reflected by increases in the magnitudes of the sequential effects. This would be because there are now more acceptable alternative responses, just as when the judgment task is made difficult, and thus more opportunity for response system processes to affect the responses.

To separate these possible effects, we obtained absolute judgments, with feedback, of 10 line lengths under two conditions. In the normal condition the separations between successive stimuli were equal. In the spread condition, the shortest line was made much shorter and the longest line much longer; the other 8 stimuli were kept at their original values. Thus, the stimulus range was increased while the number of stimuli was kept constant and most of the interstimulus distances were unchanged. As with loudnesses (Gravetter & Lockhead, 1970), performance on the middle stimuli becomes more variable when the scale is spread. Also as before, there is assimilation followed by contrast to all stimuli in the normal condition. However, the first-order effects in the spread condition are different. There is little if any assimilation to stimuli 1 and 10, the extreme stimuli, and perhaps there is contrast to them, whereas responses are assimilated to stimuli 2–9, just as is found in the normal condition. All of the higher-order effects again look much as they do in the normal condition, contrast to all of the stimuli. Thus, when the range of the stimulus scale is increased either uniformly or nonuniformly, responses (or criterial boundaries) become more variable. But the sequential effects remain the same only when the interstimulus distances are equal.

Because increases in the scale consistently produce increased response variability but do not consistently produce response process effects, the results are interpreted as evidence that the range effect is attributable to the judgmental, or other such, system and not to response processes.

References

Gravetter, F. J., & Lockhead, G. R. Criterial dispersions and the stimulus range. *Proceedings of the 78th Annual Convention of the American Psychological Association*, 1970, **5**, 41–42.

Holland, M. K. Channel capacity and sequential effects: The influence of the immediate stimulus history on recognition performance. Unpublished doctoral dissertation, Duke University, 1968.

Holland, M. K., & Lockhead, G. R. Sequential effects in absolute judgments of loudness. *Perception and Psychophysics*, 1968, **3**, 409–414.

Parducci, A. Category judgment: A range-frequency model. *Psychological Review*, 1965, **72**, 407–418.

Poulton, E. C. The new psychophysics: Six models for magnitude estimation. *Psychological Bulletin*, 1968, **69**, 1–19.

Tresselt, M. E. The influence of amount of practice upon the formation of a scale of judgment. *Journal of Experimental Psychology*, 1947, **37**, 251–260.

Ward, L. M. Some psychophysical properties of category judgments and magnitude estimations. Unpublished doctoral dissertation, Duke University, 1970.

Ward, L. M., & Lockhead, G. R. Sequential effects and memory in category judgments. *Journal of Experimental Psychology*, 1970, **84**, 27–34.

Ward, L. M., & Lockhead, G. R. Response system processes in absolute judgment. *Perception and Psychophysics*, 1971, **9**, 73–78.

Wever, E. G., & Zener, K. E. The method of absolute judgment in psychophysics. *Psychological Review*, 1928, **35**, 466–493.

A Range-Frequency Approach to Sequential Effects in Category Ratings

Allen Parducci

Department of Psychology
University of California
Los Angeles, California

ABSTRACT

Sequential effects implied by the range-frequency approach are illustrated using a game played with a computer. The player makes a succession of choices, analogous to the sequence of stimuli chosen by the experimenter in psychophysical research. The successive payoffs to the player represent the category ratings his choices would elicit as stimuli. Calculation of the payoffs is based only on the most recent choices, the value of each successive payoff depending on how the player's current choice compares with the frequency distribution of his recent prior choices. As in psychophysical research, trial-by-trial sequential effects are usually small. However, the average payoff is much greater for choices ordered in a periodically ascending series than when the same choices are made in reversed order.

Practical concern with sequential effects can be illustrated by a somewhat farfetched example. Suppose that somewhere, bathed in nutrient fluid, there lived a disembodied human brain, a brain whose sole stimulation came through electrodes implanted in one of its "pleasure centers." Suppose also that this brain's hedonic life were determined by the amount of juice, higher voltage at any given moment yielding greater pleasure. Suppose finally that an altruistic psychologist could control the juice by means of a switch with nine levels, switching from level to level in whatever sequence he chose. *What sequence of levels would give the greatest pleasure?*

I. The Computer Game as a Sequential Range-Frequency Model

One answer to this question is incorporated into a game played with a computer. On each of a succession of trials, the player (an altruistic psychologist) punches one of nine keys, indicating his choice of levels for that trial. In return, a teletype prints out the payoff (amount of pleasure) associated with that particular choice on that particular trial.

Payoffs in the game depend on the relationships among the different levels chosen by the player. The specific nature of this dependency, which is the concern of this contribution, is suggested by analogy with psychophysical research where category ratings depend on the physical relationships among the different stimuli presented for judgment. For example, the same weight may be rated "very heavy" when it is the heaviest of the stimuli in the experimental series, "very light" when it is the lightest. In the computer game, the payoff represents the rating the disembodied brain would make if it could rate different levels of stimulation in the same way that experimental subjects rate different psychophysical stimuli.

The task for the altruistic psychologist is to select and order the different levels of brain stimulation so as to make these hypothetical ratings as high as possible. The computer game is thus a model of how such ratings are made. The model is relativistic in character, and it is based on the range-frequency theory of judgment (Parducci & Perrett, 1971).

A. RANGE-FREQUENCY THEORY

This theory assumes that exposure to a stimulus sequence establishes a frequency distribution of subjective values. The relative position of each stimulus in this frequency distribution is described by two principles of judgment, and each of the actual ratings reflects a compromise between these two principles. According to the *range* principle, which gives special importance to the two extreme values defining the range of this subjective distribution, the rating of a particular stimulus depends on what proportion of the range is below its own subjective value. According to the *frequency* principle, on the other hand, the rating depends on the proportion of all stimulus presentations that have values below the value of the one being rated. When stimuli are evenly distributed over the subjective range, the two principles work together to produce the same rating. When the stimuli are unevenly distributed, the category rating is a compromise between the values predicted from the range and frequency principles.

Systematic manipulation of the physical values presented for judgment provides the evidence for range-frequency theory (see, for example, Birnbaum, 1971; Parducci, 1963; 1965). In the most extensive tests (Parducci &

Perrett, 1971), subjects rated the sizes of squares presented in different sets, each with a different probability distribution of sizes. The squares composing a particular set were presented successively in a long, random series. A specific range-frequency model, the one from which the computer game was developed, was used to predict the mean rating of each square, averaged over its many presentations. With the assumption that the subjective range was the same for all sets with the same physical end points (largest and smallest squares), it was possible to predict the radically different curvilinear forms of the plots of mean ratings against stimuli. These predictions seem a clear improvement upon those from alternative approaches. Since functions cross and recross when plotted for the same stimuli in different sets, the linearity entailed by either a simple range model (see, for example, Johnson & Mullally, 1969) or by the theory of adaptation level (Helson, 1964) could not be obtained by monotonic transformation of the stimulus or response scales (see Birnbaum, 1971).

B. THE SEQUENTIAL MODEL

Sequential considerations are incorporated into the computer game by basing the calculation of each successive payoff exclusively on the player's nine most recent choices. Earlier choices are dropped from the computer's memory and thus do not enter into the calculation of the payoff for the current choice. To simplify the game, the alternative choices (1–9) are interpreted as equally spaced on a psychological scale of range values.

Following each successive choice by the player, the computer determines the range of the nine most recent choices. It then calculates the proportion of this range that is cut off by the player's current choice. This is the range value corresponding to the level of choice on that trial, that is, the rating this choice would elicit as a stimulus if ratings conformed only to the range principle. Consider, as an example, the following sequence of choices: 1–5–4–5–5–4–5–1–3. The current choice 3 is halfway between the two extreme values, 1 and 5, and therefore has a range value of .5. More generally, the range value for the current choice R_c is calculated using the following equation:

$$R_c = (S_c - S_{min})/(S_{max} - S_{min}), \qquad (1)$$

where S_c is the current choice, and S_{max} and S_{min} are the greatest and smallest of the nine most recent choices.[1] Substitution in Eq. (1) gives the range value

---

[1] When all nine have the same value, both numerator and denominator of Eq. (1) are 0 so that the ratio is undefined. In this special case, R_c is assigned the value .5.

of the ninth or final choice in this sample sequence: $R_c = (3 - 1)/(5 - 1) = .5$. If 7 had been chosen in place of one of the 5's in this sequence, S_{max} would have been 7 and substitution in Eq. (1) would give $R_c = (3 - 1)/(7 - 1) = .33$.

The frequency value for the current choice is the proportion of the last nine choices that it exceeds. This is the rating the current choice would elicit as a stimulus if ratings conformed only to the frequency principle. Reordered with respect to rank, the nine values of the sample sequence become 1–1–3–4–4–5–5–5–5, with the most recent choice (3) exceeding two of the values still held in memory. Its frequency value F_c is given by

$$F_c = (r_c - 1)/(9 - 1), \tag{2}$$

where r_c is the rank of the current choice, and the constants 9 and 1 are the greatest and smallest of the possible ranks.[2] Substitution in Eq. (2) gives $F_c = (3 - 1)/(9 - 1) = .25$ as the frequency value for the ninth or final choice. In calculating r_c, ties are assigned their mean rank. For example, if the last choice had been a 1 instead of a 3 (placing three rather than two 1's in memory), r_c would have been 2.0 (the mean of ranks 1, 2, and 3), and F_c would have been $(2 - 1)/(9 - 1) = .125$.

The payoff P_c for the current choice, that is, the rating this choice would elicit as a stimulus if ratings followed a range-frequency compromise, is simply the mean of the associated range and frequency values:

$$P_c = (R_c + F_c)/2. \tag{3}$$

Thus, for the original sample sequence, $P_c = (.5 + .25)/2 = .375$. Since the range and frequency values can vary from 0 to 1.0, the possible payoffs must also vary between 0 and 1.0. Application of this model to psychophysical data requires a linear transformation to take account of the arbitrary unit and zero point of the rating scale. For example, if ratings were made on a scale from 1 to 6, the current rating would be $5(P_c) + 1$.

II. Implications for Sequential Effects

Successive repetitions of the same choice, whatever its value, yield a payoff of .5 as soon as the computer's memory is filled with the repeated choice. Subsequent choice of a higher level brings the top payoff, 1.0; but an immediate return to the repeated level produces a drop to .22. This is a sequential effect in the sense that the payoff for a given choice depends

---

[2]Unlike S_{max}, which varies with the value of the highest choice in memory, the highest possible rank is always equal to the total number of choices in memory.

upon the particular order or sequence of prior choices. Had the run of repetitions been broken by a lower choice (with a payoff of 0), the return to the repeated level would have elicited a rating of .78. These sequential effects depend only upon changes in the frequency distribution of the nine choices in memory, and thus they occur even when the overall distribution of choices (which includes those from earlier trials) is the same for the sequences being compared.

Although changes in range and frequency values are often correlated, the choice on a given trial may affect one without affecting the other. Consider the sequences 3–3–3–3–3–1–9–6–5 and 3–3–3–3–3–1–9–4–5, which differ only in the second to last choice (6 versus 4). The range value of the final choice is .5 for both sequences, but the frequency values are .75 and .87, respectively, so that the difference in payoff is .06. The first-order sequential effect would have been .17 if the memory were restricted to the last four choices but only .005 if it included the last 100 choices.

A. ASSIMILATION VERSUS CONTRAST

The sequential effects in the computer game are always in the direction of *contrast*: the payoff for the choice on Trial n varies inversely with the value of the choice on some preceding trial, such as Trial $n - 1$—if it is affected at all by the earlier choice. The payoff *is* affected whenever the prior choice establishes one of the endpoints of the range of choices in memory. Equation (1) implies that the greater the value of this end point, regardless of whether it is S_{max} or S_{min}, the lower is the value of R_c. The rank of the current choice, and hence F_c, will also be lower if the earlier. choice is above rather than below the current choice.

This predicted contrast is the direction of the *overall* distribution effects actually obtained in experiments with category ratings. Indeed, it was these effects that the nonsequential range-frequency models were designed to explain (see, for example, Parducci & Perrett, 1971). The predicted contrast is also consistent with the popular notion that the perceptual or judgmental magnitude of a stimulus varies inversely with the magnitude of the preceding stimulus. Furthermore, it is consistent with the strongest of the first-order sequential effects obtained in psychophysical experiments, those recognition experiments in which the task is to discriminate which of two stimuli is presented on each of a long succession of trials (see, for example, Parducci & Sandusky, 1965; Tanner, Haller, & Atkinson, 1967). However, it is not consistent with the trial-by-trial sequential effects obtained when there are many different stimulus values. Garner (1953), Lockhead and his associates (see, for example, Ward & Lockhead,

1971), and our own unpublished analyses provide evidence for first-order *assimilation* rather than contrast.

This presents a worrisome problem: how can first-order sequential effects be in the opposite direction from the overall distribution effects? One answer to this apparent contradiction lies in the reversed direction of *higher-order* sequential effects. Ward and Lockhead (1971) report contrast, rather than assimilation, to the values of stimuli presented three, four, or five trials back in the sequence; and we find it in similar analyses of our own data. This contrast appears to be exactly large enough to balance out the first- and second-order assimilation.

Another consideration with respect to the opposed directions of the distribution and the first-order effects is that the latter are very small. The absolute magnitude of the greatest assimilation appears to be on the order of only 10% of the range of permissible category ratings. Systematic shifts in the judgment of a given stimulus may span up to one-third of the range of category ratings for different distributions with the same end points, and the earlier example with lifted weights illustrates how variation of the stimulus range can produce shifts from the highest to the lowest values of the rating scale. That first-order effects should be relatively small is an implication of the computer game, at least when ratings are averaged over the many occurrences of the same short subsequence of stimuli in the random series used in such research. Unless the capacity of memory were even smaller than the nine values assumed for the present version of the game, the value of the preceding choice in a random series would make, on the average, only small changes in the range and frequency values for the current choice.

The deduction of the effects of variation in the overall distribution from the first-order sequential effects in the two-choice recognition experiments (Parducci & Sandusky, 1965; Tanner *et al.*, 1967) may raise false hopes that a similar analysis would work for the usual category-rating scales which involve many more stimuli and responses. The two-choice experiments appear to be special cases in which the immediately preceding stimulus can serve as a standard so that any clear change, in either direction, identifies both stimuli. Guessing habits also may loom larger in the two-choice experiments and in the work with informational feedback after each response. When the subject is in doubt, his optimal strategy may be either to repeat or to shift his previous response, depending upon what he has learned about the stimulus sequence (Sandusky, 1971; Ward & Lockhead, 1971). In experiments using more than two stimuli, however, the subject can never be sure about his identification of any particular value. As a consequence, the immediately preceding stimulus does not afford a reliable anchor for the scale of judgment.

B. EFFECTS OF LONGER SEQUENCES

The computer game illustrates the practical potential of systematic manipulation of sequence. With the nine-unit memory, a periodically ascending series of five successive 1's, five 2's, and so on, up to five 9's, and then five 1's again, five 2's, and so on, yields an expected or mean payoff of .82 per choice. This is clearly a sequential effect because the same choices made in a periodically descending series (that is, the reversed order) would yield an average payoff of only .18 per choice.

The ascending series pays so well because, except for the first eight trials at the beginning of each ascent, the successive choices all have high frequency values and are all at the top of the range of values in memory. This strategy produces about the same average payoff for repetition runs of up to length eight, that is, eight 1's, eight 2's, and so on. The number of repetitions at each level that would produce the highest mean payoff for the entire sequence varies directly with the number of choices in memory. The devastating effect of the periodic drop from 9's down to 1's lasts just until the higher choices drop from memory.

The superiority of the ascending series is hardly surprising when only the first ascent is considered. Who would not want to arrange things so that they got better and better and better? But problems arise when things cannot get any better, when the end of the line has been reached. In the computer game, the solution is a sudden drop to the lowest level. It is a good solution in the sense that the payoffs for the second and subsequent ascents will also be high, much higher than those for the complementary sequences of a periodically descending series. It is interesting that this implication of the computer game is contrary to a simple adaptation-level model in which the adaptation level for the current choice is equal to the mean of the last nine choices and the payoff for the current choice is proportional to its algebraic difference from adaptation level. This adaptation-level model yields identical values of the mean payoffs for the two series.

Although there appears to be no published evidence on periodically ascending or descending series, a pilot study by Jennie Shamey in our laboratory found striking differences in the predicted direction. The stimuli, varying concentrations of 2-butanol, were rated with respect to the strength of their odors. This task was picked because discrimination of the intensity of odors is very poor, suggesting that effects of prior presentations are unusually transitory, that is, memory might hold fewer values than would be the case for other dimensions. All six experimental subjects made higher ratings for the periodically ascending than for the periodically descending series.

III. Concluding Comments

Given the paucity of research on the effects of longer sequences, one can speculate freely about alternative designs of the computer game as a model of sequential effects in judgment. A probabilistic rule for the disappearance of particular choices from memory seems more attractive than restriction to a fixed number of the most recent choices. For example, there could be a fixed probability that any particular choice would disappear on any particular trial,[3] or some choices might have lower probabilities for disappearance. The two choices that define the end points of the range, particularly if quite separated from the values of the less extreme choices, might be granted a more secure position in memory.

There could also be allowance for systematic drift in the values of prior choices while they remained in memory. This could model the *central-tendency effect* (Hollingworth, 1910) in which the point of subjective equality shifts toward the values of other stimuli. Thus, the effective value of a prior choice could shift toward the mean of the other values in memory. There is some evidence that an analogous phenomenon occurs in category-rating experiments (Parducci & Marshall, 1962), and it may provide a partial explanation of the small first-order assimilation found in such experiments.

The presence of earlier choices in computer memory need not be interpreted as memory in a traditional sense. It seems possible that judgments may be affected by earlier presentations that would not necessarily be remembered on a test for recognition. The computer memory can be thought of as simply the subjective representation of those values affecting the payoff. In the computer game, the overt values of the choices are placed directly in memory. In psychophysical applications, the physical values of the stimuli first must be transformed into subjective values. The model itself provides the basis for this subjective scaling of the stimuli (Parducci & Perrett, 1971).

The practical concern with finding sequences that maximize the payoffs is more easily illustrated by the example of the disembodied brain than by examples from everyday life. The special feature of the brain example is that stimulation consists solely of the sequence of levels chosen by the psychologist. And yet, judgments on any of the value dimensions of everyday life must also be affected by particular sequences of events. Insofar as one could identify and estimate values for these events, the computer game could serve as a source of hypotheses about the effects of different sequences.

---

[3] Using Monte Carlo simulation, Chris Thomas in our laboratory demonstrated that probabilistic memory reduces but does not eliminate the advantages of periodically ascending series.

Several points might bear reiteration. First, although experimental studies of the effects of sequence have concentrated on trial-by-trial analysis of random sequences of presentation, the effects of even the immediately preceding stimulus on the present judgment are usually small. Furthermore, these first-order effects can be in the opposite direction from the effects of the overall frequency distribution of stimuli. Consequently, trial-by-trial analysis does not seem to provide a promising basis for understanding the more influential processes of judgment. The computer game, as a tentative model of sequential effects, emphasizes the practical effects of controlling longer sequences of stimuli. The game suggests that for a given set of stimuli, high mean ratings can be obtained by presenting the individual values in a periodically ascending sequence.

References

Birnbaum, M. H. Psychophysical judgment: An integral model. Paper presented at Western Psychology Association Meetings, San Francisco, April, 1971.

Garner, W. R. An informational analysis of absolute judgments of loudness. *Journal of Experimental Psychology*, 1953, **46**, 373–380.

Helson, H. *Adaptation-level theory*. New York: Harper, 1964.

Hollingworth, H. L. The central tendency of judgment. *Journal of Philosophy, Psychology, and Scientific Method*, 1910, **7**, 461–468.

Johnson, D. M., & Mullally, C. R. Correlation-and-regression model for category judgments. *Psychological Review*, 1969, **76**, 205–215.

Parducci, A. Range-frequency compromise in judgment. *Psychological Monographs*, 1963, **77**(2, Whole No. 565).

Parducci, A. Category judgment: A range-frequency model. *Psychological Review*, 1965, **72**, 407–418.

Parducci, A., & Marshall, L. M. Assimilation vs. contrast in the anchoring of perceptual judgments of weight. *Journal of Experimental Psychology*, 1962, **63**, 426–437.

Parducci, A., & Perrett, L. F. Category rating scales: Effects of relative spacing and frequency of stimulus values. *Journal of Experimental Psychology Monograph*, 1971, **89**, 427–452.

Parducci, A., & Sandusky, A. Distribution and sequence effects in judgment. *Journal of Experimental Psychology*, 1965, **69**, 450–459.

Sandusky, A. Signal recognition models compared for random and Markov presentation sequences. *Perception & Psychophysics*, 1971, **10**, 339–347.

Tanner, T. A., Haller, R. W., & Atkinson, R. C. Signal recognition as influenced by presentation schedules. *Perception & Psychophysics*, 1967, **2**, 349–358.

Ward, L. M., & Lockhead, G. R. Response system processes in absolute judgment. *Perception & Psychophysics*, 1971, **9**, 73–78.

Sequential Effects in Absolute Judgments
of Loudness without Feedback

I. D. John

Department of Psychology
University of Adelaide
Adelaide, Australia

ABSTRACT

An analysis of sequential effects in two-, three-, and ten-stimulus absolute judgments of loudness without feedback is presented. It is suggested that judgments are mediated by a self-regulating structure that is partially isomorphic with the properties of the task. This results in two tendencies which give rise to the observed sequential effects: (*a*) a tendency to repeat the error of the previous trial and (*b*) a tendency to underestimate the difference in magnitude between stimuli on successive trials.

I. Introduction

A model of the judgment process to account for sequential effects in ten-stimulus absolute-judgment tasks, both with and without feedback, has been put forward by Ward and Lockhead (1971). The model, which is based on the evidence presented in a series of papers (Holland & Lockhead, 1968; Ward & Lockhead, 1970, 1971), attempts to account for sequential effects in terms of two-response system processes, one of which, it is suggested, also accounts for the central tendency effect in judgment.

Although Ward and Lockhead (1971) have not been explicit on this point, it may be inferred from their comments in a previous paper (1970) that the model is not meant to apply to two-stimulus absolute-judgment tasks, since they have suggested that performance in these tasks requires a qualitatively different kind of judgment. In two-stimulus tasks without feedback, the responses tend to be contrasted with the previous stimulus rather than assimilated to it (Kinchla, 1966; Parducci & Sandusky, 1965; Tanner, Haller, & Atkinson, 1967).

In ten-stimulus tasks without feedback, Ward and Lockhead (1971) have suggested that the subject first determines a range of acceptable responses for the stimulus presented on the current trial (trial n). The final choice within this range then is made by taking into account the response on the previous trial (trial $n - 1$) and selecting an acceptable response that tends to minimize the response–response difference. An implication of this hypothesis is that for any given response on trial $n - 1$, performance on trial n should be independent of the stimulus on trial $n - 1$. This implication has been examined and confirmed for ten-stimulus tasks with feedback (Holland & Lockhead, 1968), but does not seem to have been examined for a task without feedback.

One aim of this contribution is to examine an alternative conceptualization of the microbehavior of absolute judgments without feedback. There is a body of evidence (see for example, Eriksen & Hake, 1957; John, 1969, 1972) which suggests that, in judgment tasks using the method of single stimuli, the extreme stimulus values are more adequately internalized and have a functional significance that is not shared by the intermediate stimuli. Evidence of this kind provides the basis of Eriksen and Hake's (1957) subjective standard hypothesis, which states that the internalized representations of the extreme stimuli serve as the basis for an implicit comparison of the stimulus presented. As it stands, this hypothesis raises more questions about the judgment process than it satisfactorily answers, and at best provides an inadequate account, since the existence of sequential effects is evidence of determinants of behavior other than those envisaged by the hypothesis.

If judgments are mediated by a structure representing the properties of the stimulus array, in which the extreme stimuli are better defined than the intermediate stimuli, the stimulus presented on any trial could be located within the structure by extrapolation from the end points. The stimulus also could be located by extrapolation from the point in the structure defined by the recollection of the previous stimulus and response. If the properties of the mediating structure are completely isomorphic with the properties of the task, an errorless performance would result but inadequacies of the structure would produce response errors. Extrapolation from the point defined by the recollection of the previous stimulus and response would tend to produce response errors of the kind associated with the previous trial. However, a tendency of this kind cannot be continued indefinitely because, as the response scale is truncated at both ends, it would give rise to impermissible responses. Situations in which there is a contradiction between the response indicated by extrapolation from the extreme stimuli and extrapolation from the characteristics of the previous trial would signal the necessity for some change in the mediating structure. Such situations are likely to arise when a high stimulus follows a previous overestimation, or a low stimulus follows a previous underestimation. These situations should also be characterized by a reduction in the range of acceptable responses, and in that sense could be regarded as potentially more informative than other trials. They also should result in greater response accuracy and less uncertainty, as indicated by independent performance measures such as confidence and latency. This means that even in the absence of explicit feedback, potential sources of information might be available for exploitation by the subjects, and these would be associated most frequently with the extreme stimulus values.

This conceptualization therefore envisages performance as mediated by what is essentially a self-regulating cognitive structure in which the extreme stimulus values are more adequately represented because there is potentially more information available to the subject about these values.

This conceptualization by itself cannot entirely account for sequential effects since low stimuli tend to result in positive errors of judgment, and in ten-stimulus tasks such trials tend to be followed by trials on which there is a negative error. On the other hand, low responses tend to be associated with negative errors of judgment, and such trials tend to be followed by trials on which there are negative errors that are larger in magnitude than those which follow low stimuli. This suggests that there must be at least two processes operating whose summation is revealed in an analysis of sequential effects in terms of previous responses, and whose opposition is revealed in an analysis in terms of previous stimuli.

II. Method

Three groups of two Ss each completed one practice and a number of experimental sessions in an absolute-loudness judgment task. For each group the task involved two, three, or ten stimuli; Ss in the first group completed five, and those in the other groups completed ten experimental sessions.

The stimulus consisted of a 1000-Hz tone of approximately 90 dB s.p.l., which could be attenuated in 1-dB steps. It was presented through muffed earphones and was available to S by pressing a morse key at any time after the appearance of a warning light, which signaled the commencement of the trial. The signal continued as long as the key was pressed.

The S was seated in an experimental room with constant masking noise provided by an exhaust fan, and could communicate with E in an adjoining room by intercom. Instructions required S to identify the stimulus on each trial by means of the appropriate number from "one" to "two," "three," or "ten," as was appropriate for the particular experimental condition, and subsequently to report the confidence of his judgment on a scale from "A" to "D." Each session, lasting about 45 min, consisted of 201 trials in which the stimuli were presented in a random order derived from random-number tables.

For purposes of analysis confidence judgments were transformed to scores by allocating values of 1–4 to each of the categories in ascending order of confidence. Stimulus sampling times (times for which the stimulus key was depressed) were standardized for each S for each session, using the convention $\overline{X} = 50$ and $SD = 10$, to produce sampling time scores. In summarizing the data the various performance measures were determined for each individual S, and are reported as the means of the measures for the two Ss for each condition. For the ten-stimulus condition the data were collapsed over adjacent pairs of stimuli and responses to reduce the variability.

III. Results

A. SEQUENTIAL DEPENDENCIES

Figure 1 shows the effects of previous stimuli and previous responses on the average error of response on the current trial. The results for the ten-stimulus condition are comparable to Ward and Lockhead's results (1970, Fig. 2) although the variability is greater. They show that the assimilation of the response on trial $n + 1$ to the response on trial n is greater than to the stimulus on trial n. It may also be seen that assimilation tends to decrease in magnitude as a function of the remoteness of previous trials in the sequence, and that this process is more rapid for previous stimuli than that for previous responses.

There is an indication that the initial assimilation of the response on trial $n + 1$ to the stimulus on trial n changes to contrast as successively more remote trials are considered. The initial assimilation of the response on trial $n + 1$ to the response on trial n is reduced as successively more

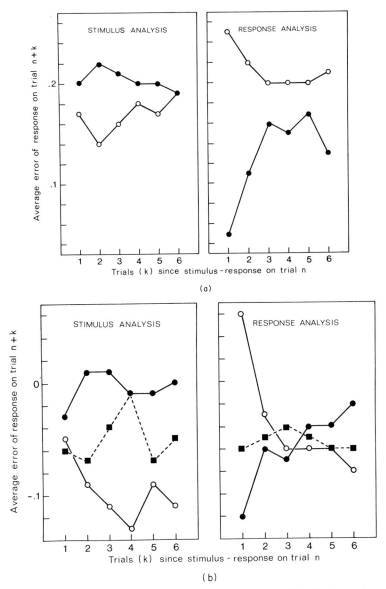

Fig. 1.   Average error of response on trial $n + k$ as a function of the stimulus and response on trial n. (a) Two-stimulus condition (there are in excess of 600 observations per point): stimulus–response value on trial n, (●) 1: (○) 2, (b) Three-stimulus condition (there are in excess of 1000 observations per point): stimulus–response value on trial n, (●) 1; (■) 2; (○) 3. (c) Ten-stimulus condition (there are in excess of 500 observations per point): stimulus–response value on trial n, (●) 1, 2; (▲) 3, 4; (■) 5, 6; (△) 7, 8; (○) 9, 10.

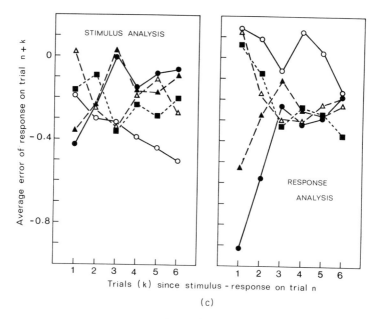

Fig. 1. (**continued**)

remote trials are considered, but it cannot be confirmed from these data that contrast effects eventually result.

For the two- and three-stimulus conditions, although the response on Trial $n + 1$ is assimilated to the response on trial n, it is contrasted with the stimulus on trial n. That is, the two-stimulus condition is not unique in producing contrast to the stimulus on the preceding trial.

B. Effects of the Previous Response

A detailed picture of the effects of the previous response on the judgment of stimuli on the current trial is provided in Fig. 2. In this figure the average error of response on trial n as a function of the response on trial $n - 1$ has been plotted with the stimulus on trial n as the parameter. For the two- and three-stimulus conditions the results indicate a tendency for the type of error on trial $n - 1$ to be repeated on trial n for all stimuli. Low responses will represent on the average negative errors whereas high responses will represent positive errors, and since the trend of the functions for the two and three stimulus conditions increases positively, they may be said to reflect a tendency to repeat such errors on the subsequent trial.

For the ten-stimulus condition, although the general trend of the function is positively increasing, the individual functions for extreme

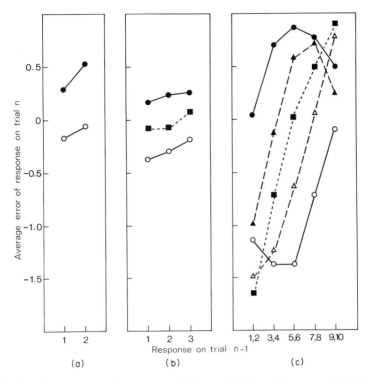

Fig. 2. Average error of response on trial n as a function of the response on trial $n - 1$ (there are in excess of 80 observations per point). (a) Stimulus on trial n for two-stimulus condition, (●) 1; (○) 2. (b) Stimulus on trial n, for three-stimulus condition, (●) 1, (■) 2; (○) 3. (c) Stimulus on trial n, for ten-stimulus condition, (●) 1, 2; (▲) 3, 4; (■) 5, 6; (△) 7, 8; (○) 9, 10.

stimuli on Trial n are curvilinear. That is, the tendency to repeat the error of trial $n - 1$ is reduced for extreme stimuli on trial n. It must be noted that this does not arise because of the truncation of the response scale, since high responses on trial $n - 1$ will represent on the average positive errors and will only restrict the range of acceptable responses on trial n to stimuli of greater magnitude. This finding that judgments of extreme stimuli are less subject to contextual influences is consistent with the view that they are comparatively more effectively internalized than stimuli in the middle range.

C. Effects of Type of Error on Subsequent Responses

The tendency to repeat the error of the previous trial is illustrated further in Fig. 3. The average error of response on Trial n as a function of the response on trial $n - 1$ has been determined for each kind of response

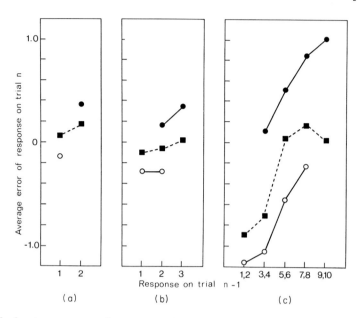

Fig. 3. Average error of response on trial n as a function of the response on trial $n - 1$ for overestimates, correct estimates, and underestimates on trial $n - 1$ (there are in excess of 20 observations per point): response on trial $n - 1$, (●) overestimate; (■) correct; (○) underestimate. (a) Two-stimulus condition. (b) Three-stimulus condition. (c) Ten-stimulus condition.

(overestimation, correct, and underestimation) for each condition. The data are presented with response on trial $n - 1$ as the abscissa, and kind of response on trial $n - 1$ as the parameter. The pattern of results is similar for each condition, and the clear separation of the functions indicates that for a given response on trial $n - 1$ the error on trial n will be determined by the type of performance on trial $n - 1$. This finding is inconsistent with the prediction derived from Ward and Lockhead's (1971) model.

D. PERFORMANCE ON POTENTIALLY INFORMATIVE TRIALS

It has been predicted that on trials preceded by a positive error of judgment, accuracy and confidence should be relatively greater and sampling speed relatively lower for high stimuli than for low stimuli. The opposite result should be observed on trials preceded by a negative error of judgment. These predictions may be seen to have been confirmed by an inspection of Figs. 4, 5, and 6. In Fig. 4 the average error of response on trial n has been plotted as a function of the stimulus on Trial n with performance on trial $n - 1$ as the parameter. For each of the three experimental con-

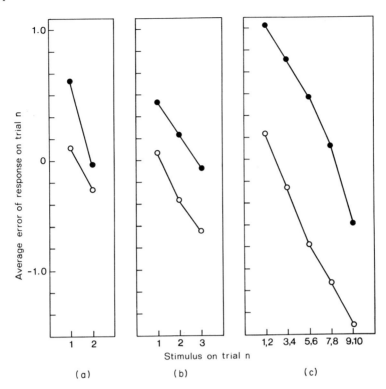

Fig. 4. Average error of response on trial n as a function of the stimulus on trial n following overestimates and underestimates on trial $n - 1$ (there are in excess of 200 observations per point): (●) overestimate on trial $n - 1$; (○) underestimate on trial $n - 1$. (a) Two-stimulus condition. (b) Three-stimulus condition. (c) Ten-stimulus condition.

ditions, the average error of response for high stimuli is smaller following an overestimate on trial n-1, and for low stimuli it is smaller following an underestimate on trial $n - 1$.

In Fig. 5 average confidence on Trial n has been plotted as a function of the stimulus on Trial n, with performance on trial $n - 1$ as the parameter. Confidence is greater for judgments of high stimuli following an over-estimate on trial $n - 1$ and for low stimuli following an underestimate on trial $n - 1$. The crossing over of the functions in the predicted manner is a distinctive feature of the data for each of the three conditions.

The average sampling time score on trial n is shown in Fig. 6 as a function of the stimulus on trial n, with type of performance on Trial $n - 1$ as the parameter. In this figure the crossing over of the functions in the predicted manner is once more apparent.

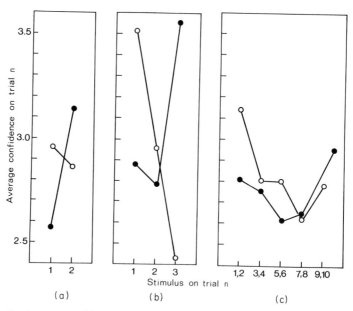

Fig. 5. Average confidence on trial n as a function of the stimulus on trial n following over-estimates and underestimates on trial $n - 1$ (there are in excess of 200 observations per point): (●) overestimate on trial $n - 1$; (○) underestimate on trial $n - 1$. (a) Two-stimulus condition. (b) Three-stimulus condition. (c) Ten-stimulus condition.

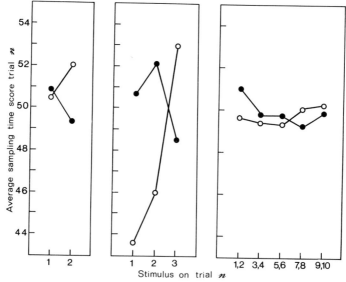

Fig. 6. Average sampling time score on trial n as a function of the stimulus on trial n following overestimates and underestimates on trial $n - 1$ (there are in excess of 200 observations per point): (●) overestimate on trial $n - 1$; (○) underestimate on trial $n - 1$. (a) Two-stimulus condition. (b) Three-stimulus condition. (c) Ten-stimulus condition.

E. Underestimation of Stimulus–Stimulus Differences

In Fig. 7 the average response on trial n as a function of the stimulus on trial n has been plotted with, stimulus on trial $n - 1$ as the parameter. The analysis is confined to extreme stimuli on trial $n - 1$, and only trials following a correct response on trial $n - 1$ have been considered in order to eliminate the effects of any tendency to continue the error on the previous trial. The two functions are clearly separated for each experimental condition and in relative terms, this separation is more marked for the ten-stimulus condition than for the two- and three-stimulus conditions.

At first sight this might appear to provide evidence for a type of response bias such as Ward and Lockhead (1971) have postulated, but which has already been questioned in this paper. Comparison of this result with findings in other areas suggests an alternative interpretation.

Stevens (1957) has drawn attention to a phenomenon that he has termed "psychophysical hysteresis," and which is observed when subjects are required to make bisections of sensory magnitudes. If the two stimuli are presented in ascending order of magnitude, then the stimulus value chosen as bisecting the interval between them is consistently greater than if the two stimuli are presented in descending order. Such an effect could be interpreted as a bias toward underestimation of the difference between the first

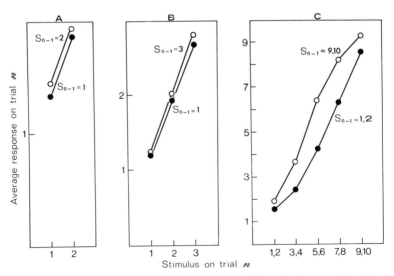

Fig. 7. Average response on trial n as a function of the stimulus on trial n following a correct response on trial $n - 1$ (there are in excess of 30 observations per point). (a) Two-stimulus condition. (b) Three-stimulus condition. (c) Ten-stimulus condition.

standard presented and the variable stimulus. It is difficult to see this effect
as representing the operation of a bias of the kind suggested by Ward and
Lockhead (1971) since it is observed when nonnumerical responses are
required, such as adjustment of a variable stimulus (Stevens, 1961), or
moving a cursor along a line to represent the value of the variable stimulus
(John, unpublished data, 1967).

The data presented in Fig. 7 therefore are more parsimoniously interpreted as representing the operation of a bias or tendency toward underestimation of the difference in magnitude between stimuli on successive trials
rather than a bias toward production of adjacent responses on successive
trials. Therefore, the question may be posed as to how such a tendency could
be established in tasks of this kind.

It has already been noted that even in the absence of explicit feedback
certain types of trials are more informative to subjects than others, and these
seem to constitute a source of implicit feedback capable of influencing or
reinforcing behavior. A similar point can be made about the estimation of
differences between successive stimuli. Low stimuli in general will be over-
estimated, and when followed by overestimation or correct estimation of the
difference between that stimulus and a subsequent high stimulus, this will
produce an unacceptable response alternative (that is, one which goes
beyond the allowable range) on a proportion of occasions. The same situation will also obtain in the case of low stimuli following high stimuli.

It can be seen, therefore, that underestimates of stimulus–stimulus
differences will tend to be positively reinforced, whereas correct estimates
and overestimates will tend to be negatively reinforced. Such differential
reinforcement should result in the establishment of a tendency to consistently underestimate stimulus–stimulus differences. A corollary of such a
tendency will be a relatively greater frequency of usage of the middle-
response categories than the end-response categories, which is, of course, an
alternative way of describing the central tendency of judgment.

IV. Discussion

It has been argued that in absolute judgment tasks without feedback
the subject exhibits two tendencies: (a) error continuation, a tendency to
continue any error of judgment on successive trials; and (b) stimulus difference underestimation, a tendency to underestimate the difference between stimuli on successive trials. In this experiment the tendency to
difference underestimation is relatively stronger for the ten-stimulus condition than for the two- and three-stimulus conditions.

When the analysis of sequential effects is made in terms of previous stimuli, the results for trial $n + 1$ express the opposition of these two processes. In ten-stimulus tasks the tendency to underestimate stimulus difference is sufficiently strong to overcome the error continuation tendency, and the net result is assimilation of the response on trial $n + 1$ to the stimulus on trial n. In two- and three-stimulus tasks, when the tendency to underestimate stimulus difference is relatively weaker, the error continuation tendency predominates, and responses on trial $n + 1$ are contrasted with the stimulus on trial n. When the analysis is made in terms of the effects of the previous response, the results express the summation of the two tendencies, and in all conditions assimilation of the response on trial $n + 1$ to the response on trial n is observed.

The data presented do not permit firm conclusions to be drawn about the precise factors underlying sequential effects on trials succeeding trial $n - 1$. A tendency to use available responses equally often over a larger number of trials, as has been suggested by Ward and Lockhead (1971), may well operate, but the following considerations would also seem to be involved.

On trials succeeding trial $n + 1$, the tendency to underestimate stimulus differences should have no net effect because, as the stimuli are presented in random order, the mean difference between stimuli on successive trials will be constant. On the other hand, the error continuation tendency will continue until restrictions on the response scale are encountered. Following such an encounter there will be a tendency for the direction of error to be reversed on the subsequent trial. Thus, following an error on trial n the probability of repeating the direction of that error diminishes and the probability of reversing the direction of that error increases on subsequent trials. It is this process that seems to account, at least in part, for the attenuation of assimilation effects on subsequent trials and the eventual appearance of contrast effects.

Acknowledgment

The assistance of D. Colquhoun in analyzing the data is gratefully acknowledged.

References

Eriksen, C. W., & Hake, H. W. Anchor effects in absolute judgments. *Journal of Experimental Psychology*, 1957, **53**, 132–138.
Holland, M. K., & Lockhead, G. R. Sequential effects in absolute judgments of loudness. *Perception and Psychophysics*, 1968, **3**, 409–414.

John, I. D. Stimulus discriminability in the magnitude estimation and category rating of loudness. *Perception and Psychophysics*, 1969, **6**, 78–80.

John, I. D. The role of subjective standards in the category judgment of lifted weights. *Australian Journal of Psychology*, 1972, **24**, 93–102.

Kinchla, R. A. A comparison of sequential effects in detection and recognition. *Experimental Psychology Series*, Psychology Department, New York University, Technical Reports, **1**, 1966.

Parducci, A., & Sandusky, A. Distribution and sequence effects in judgment. *Journal of Experimental Psychology*, 1965, **69**, 450–459.

Stevens, S. S. On the psychophysical law. *Psychological Review*, 1957, **64**, 153–181.

Stevens, S. S. To honor Fechner and repeal his law. *Science*, 1961, **133**, 80–86.

Tanner, T. A., Haller, R. W., & Atkinson, R. C. Signal recognition as influenced by presentation schedules. *Perception and Psychophysics*, 1967, **2**, 349–358.

Ward, L. M., & Lockhead, G. R. Sequential effects and memory in category judgments. *Journal of Experimental Psychology*, 1970, **84**, 27–34.

Ward, L. M., & Lockhead, G. R. Response system processes in absolute judgment. *Perception and Psychophysics*, 1971, **9**, 73–78.

What Is Repeated in the "Repetition Effect"?

Patrick M. A. Rabbitt   *Subash Vyas*

Department of Experimental Psychology
University of Oxford
Oxford, England

ABSTRACT

Previous experiments on the "repetition effect" have considered only repetitions of individual signals or repetitions of individual responses. The present series of experiments demonstrates that, as well as these factors, facilitation is achieved of coding "rules" relating signals to responses. Early in practice errors are related to the possibilities of confusions between these rules. Later in practice the importance of rules in mediating repetition–facilitation appears to diminish.

Together with earlier work demonstrating facilitation by partial repetition of motor movements, or facilitation by the sequencing of some motor movements rather than others, these facts appear to require a new taxonomy, and consequent new interpretations of phenomena loosely subsumed as "repetition effects" in the literature to date.

I. Introduction

In serial, self-placed, choice reaction-time tasks human subjects respond faster when successive signals, and so responses, are identical than when one signal follows another to which a different response must be made. This "repetition effect" is now extremely well documented, and many of the factors affecting its magnitude have been investigated (see, for example, Bertelson, 1961, 1963, 1965; Bertelson & Renkin, 1966; Kornblum, 1969; Rabbitt, 1965, 1967, 1968, 1969; Remington, 1969; Williams, 1966). Certain

327

logical obscurities arise, however, if models for the repetition effect are based solely upon considerations of transitions between signals, on the one hand, on transitions between responses on the other, or upon some combination of both. A consideration of three different lines of experiments makes this clear.

An obvious first question is whether reaction time (RT) to repeated signals is reduced because the subject repeats a particular act of identification or because he makes the same motor movement twice in succession. Bertelson (1965) required his subjects to make one response to the onset of either of two signals (for example, A_1 or A_2) and a different response to the onset of either of a different pair (for example, B_1 or B_2). Therefore, three kinds of transition between successive events could occur:

1. "identical transitions" when both signal and response were repeated (A_1 follows A_1 or B_2 follows B_2, and so forth);
2. "equivalent transitions" in which the signal was not repeated although the response was (A_1 follows A_2 or B_2 follows B_1, and so forth);
3. "new transitions" when neither the signal nor the response were repeated (A_1 follows B_1 or B_2 follows A_2, and so forth).

Four highly practiced subjects (1500 trials) showed no differences in RT for identical and for equivalent transitions. New RT, however, remained substantially slower than either. Bertelson (1965) therefore concluded that the "repetition effect" in this type of simple, self-paced, choice RT task was entirely due to facilitation of processes concerned with the programming and execution of motor acts, and that facilitation of perceptual recognition by stimulus repetition contributed little or nothing to the effect.

An extended replication of this experiment suggested a slightly different interpretation; (Rabbitt 1968). Early in practice the subjects gave equivalent RTs equal to new RTs, with identical RTs much faster than either (responses 300–600). Late in practice the difference between new RTs and identical RTs remained, and although the difference between equivalent RTs and identical RTs diminished to 10–40 msec. Even after 3000 trials the equivalent RTs remained significantly slower than the identical RTs. The rate at which practice reduced equivalent RTs to approach identical RTs was inversely proportional to the size of the total signal ensemble and to the number of response classes (2 or 4) into which the signal ensemble had to be partitioned.

In very loose terminology we might suggest that the repetition effect for equivalent signals depends upon the learning of a rule associating signals to responses. When this rule is unfamiliar, or is made more difficult, learning is slower. Potentially, therefore, we may think of three rather than two stages of processing at which repetition effects may occur: (a) repetition of a signal (perceptual processing), (b) repetition of a response (motor programming and response execution), and (c) repetition of a rule relating members of a common signal set to the same response.

A similar suggestion occurs from a second series of experiments investigating the motor side of repetition effects. Rabbitt (1965) found that successive, though dissimilar, movements with the same hand were made faster than successive equivalent movements with alternate hands. In another study Rabbitt (1967) found that subjects make successive responses with alternate hands, or with alternate feet, faster than equivalent responses involving a hand movement following a foot movement, or vice versa. Further, when hand and foot movements followed each other, successive movements with contralateral limbs were made faster than successive movements with ipsilateral limbs. Since none of these transition effects depended upon repetitions of identical signals or responses it seems that they occur because some transitions between motor acts are easier than others. Again, loosely, we may say that sequential effects appear to be mediated not merely by repetition of individual signal or response events but also by the repetition, or partial repetition, of motor programming rules intervening between the encoding of a signal and the execution of a motor response to it.

Finally, some very recent experiments have shown that repetition effects are not mediated simply (and in some cases not at all) by immediate (1-back) transitions but rather by patterns of sequential dependencies that may involve strings of as many as five successive signals and responses (Remington, 1969). Systematic variations in the conditional probability structure of signal sequences are reflected in changes in rank order for string segments of at least this length (Remington, 1969) and are, surprisingly, affected little by activity interpolated between responses and successive signals (Keele, 1969). Again it is clear that the repetition of a single signal or of a single response is not completely decisive in determining the observed repetition effect. On the assumption that the subject is extracting a set of hierarchical "rules," reflecting stochastic properties of a signal sequence, "rule-mediated" repetition effects appear to be the norm rather than the exception even in very simple, serial choice RT tasks.

While all these data reveal a loose common logical link in their reference to coding "rules" of various kinds, and in the effects of their repetition or alternation, an ostensive demonstration of such a "rule," or "rule repetition effect" is not made directly by any of them. A derived hypothesis would imply that we may design tasks to show "repetition effects" of at least three kinds: signal repetition effects, response repetition effects, and repetition effects mediated by the repeated application of a common rule mapping signals on to responses—even when neither particular signals nor particular responses are repeated.

In view of the fact that the balance of the effects of signal and response repetitions appears to alter radically with practice (Rabbitt, 1968), it is naive to suppose that these processes will be separate and independent. It seems much more likely that they will be found to interact in complex ways.

The most stringent test for a rule-repetition effect would be a demonstration that repetition of an S–R "mapping" or "coding" rule, without entailed repetition of a particular signal or of a particular response, affects RT on immediately successive trials. Experiment I was an attempt to show this.

II. Experiment I

A. METHOD

The Subjects were 12 experimentally naive students at Oxford College of Technology, between 17 and 22 years of age.

Procedure.

A signal presenting and reaction timing apparaturs (MRC APRU "Sparta" Mk. 2) allowed various kinds of signals to be presented to Ss in pre-programmed random order. The onset of any one of 8 possible signals required a press response on any one of 8 keys, inset into a desk at which S sat. A response on any key caused the display to change to the next state in the sequence in less than 50 msec. Preprogrammed random sequences of 301 signals allowed Ss to continue responding in this way in a self-paced mode. The Sparta recorded on punched tape each successive signal presented to the S, as well as the key pressed in answer to it ("errors" could be identified precisely), and measured and recorded the elapsed time between the onset of each signal and the moment of key press (RT) to within 0.01 sec.

Two separate groups of Ss responded to different kinds of signals. Group 1 (Neon/Number) faced a vertical 3 ft square, matt black display screen across the center of which four neon bulbs $\frac{1}{2}$ in. wide were set 3 in. apart in a horizontal line. A "Digitron GS 10-in. display tube was also inset in the screen 3 in. below the center of an imaginary line joining the second and third bulbs. In this group Ss received different instructions as to which were the "correct" allocations of signals to response keys. If the S's fingers from left to right are imagined to be numbered from 1 to 8, two patterns of signal–finger allocations were used. Half the Ss responded with fingers 1, 3, 5, and 7 to the onset of "Digitron" numerals 1, 2, 3, and 4, respectively. They responded with the alternate fingers (2, 4, 6, and 8) to the onset of any one of the neon bulbs in corresponding left-to-right order across the display. The remaining Ss reversed neon and number allocations. For both types of signal the interval between response and successive display onset was 20 msec.

Group 2 (Letter/Number) Ss faced a 3 × 2-in. "Bina-Vue" display screen. They might receive as signals, in random order, any of the four letters A, B, C, or D or any of the four digits 1, 2, 3, or 4. Signal–response allocations were made on a similar principle to those described for Group 1. That is, half the Ss responded to letters A, B, C, and D with fingers 1, 3, 5, and 7, respectively, and to digits 1, 2, 3, and 4 with fingers 2, 4, 6, and 8, whereas the remainder reversed this mapping.

Four different sequences of 301 successive signals were programmed using a Linc 8 computer to generate random octal sequences in which all signals, and transitions between signals, were approximately equiprobable. The Ss were told to "respond as fast as you can and make as few errors as possible." Each S was tested on the 4 different sequences in random order during a single experimental session. Errors were monitored during the experiment during the first two runs. Only data from the last two unmonitored runs were combined for analysis by a Linc 8 data-sort program.

B. RESULTS

The sort program detected errors and listed them for inspection, but eliminated errors and the three responses following each error from the computation of mean correct RTs (these responses are atypical in various ways; see Rabbitt, 1969). No S made more than 7.8% errors; the mean error score was 5.2%.

An error analysis was performed for each group classifying errors as confusions within and between responses appropriate to the signal classes "Neon" and "Number" (Group 1) or "Letter" and "Number" (Group 2). The resulting matrices are presented in Table 1.

A χ^2 test was applied to the error-confusion matrix obtained for each group, and was significant in both cases ($p < .01$). It is evident from inspection of the matrices that this asymmetry arose because the subjects in Group 1 made "Neon" responses mainly to the wrong "Neon" signals and "Number" responses mainly to the wrong numbers, while confusions between these classes were rare. The same was true of "Letter" and "Number" confusions made by the subjects in Group 2. We may conclude that confusions within classes were more frequent than confusions between classes. This impression was statistically validated by Wilcoxon matched-pairs signed-ranks tests carried out across the subjects' data for each group ($p < .01$ in both cases).

The RT data provide a consistent picture. The sort program separated sequences of correct responses into all possible 64 transition states. The out-

Table 1. *Percentages of Confusions within and between Stimulus Classes in Conditions 1 and 2 of Experiment 1.*

A. Condition 1: neon lamps and digitron display

		Class of stimulus for correct response	
		Neon	Digit
Class of stimulus to which wrong response was made	Neon	36%	15%
	Digit	18%	41%

B. Condition 2: letter and digit stimuli

		Class of stimulus for correct response	
		Letter	Digit
Class of stimulus to which wrong response was made	Letter	34%	20%
	Digit	17%	29%

put included the number of observations (N), the summed RT, the mean RT ($\bar{X}$), and the standard deviation (σ) for each cell of the transition matrix. Of these 64 transitions eight represent cases where the same signal, and implicity the same response, were repeated immediately. The data were collapsed to obtain overall means and standard deviations for these "Identical" transitions. The remaining 56 can be classified into transitions within signal classes (Neon following Neon or Number following Number) and transitions between signal classes (Number following Neon or vice versa). This "category

Table 2. *Mean Reaction Times and Standard Deviations (σ) for Transitions between Signals in the Two Conditions of Experiment I*

Transitions	Mean RT (msec)	σ	Transitions	Mean RT (msec)	σ
A. Experiment I, Condition 1: neon lamps and digit displays			B. Experiment I, Condition 2: letter and digit displays		
Identical stimulus	364	32	Identical stimulus	394	47
"Same stimulus class"	483	56	"Same stimulus class"	652	74
"New stimulus class"	547	69	"New stimulus class"	698	68

transition" analysis was made for each group and mean RTs are given in Table 2.

A separate analysis of variance was applied to data across subjects for these three transition classes within each group. For Group 1 terms for differences between subjects and between transition classes were significant ($p < .01$ in each case) but there was no significant interaction. The same was true of Group 2. Accordingly S^2 was applied to rank-order RTs between transition classes. In both groups identical transition RT was significantly faster than within-class transition RT ($p < .01$). In Group 1 within-transition class RT was significantly faster than between-transition class RT ($p < .01$), and Group 2 the same was true ($p < .05$).

In serial-choice RT tasks in which heterogenous signal populations are used it seems that, early in practice, successive presentations of signals from the same arbitrary subset facilitates RT. This classification of signals into arbitrary subsets of "Neons and Numbers" or "Letters and Numbers" seems an idiosyncratic quirk on the part of the subjects unless the S–R mapping allocations used in this experiment are carefully considered. If fingers are considered as being numbered from 1 to 8 from left to right across the keyboard, the signal sets implicitly defined "odd" or "even" fingers. It follows that if a subject remembered whether Neons, Numbers, Letters, or Digits represented "odd" or "even" sets of fingers, he could derive from this rule the correct response to any displayed signal. Had Group 1 conditions alone been used, the transition-class RT data might have been partially explained in terms of persistence of fixation of a signal source (neon lamps or "Digitron" display) after each response. This objection cannot apply to Group 2 data.

It seems that in addition to "stimulus repetition effects" and "response repetition effects" we must consider further repetition effects resulting from the use of a common S–R mapping rule for a subset of signals on the display. Two previous studies (Bertelson, 1965; Rabbitt, 1968) found that with arbitrary categorizations of a signal set repetitions of "same-class" (that is, "equivalent") signals facilitated RT. The present data show that this effect, at least early in practice, cannot be attributed to repetition of a common response, since class repetition facilitation occurs even when different responses are made.

Traditional demonstrations of S–R coding effects (Fitts & Biederman, 1965) have been concerned with the relative spatial allocations of signals to which the subject responds and the switches he uses to answer them. In the present context investigation of such situations has the advantage that they involve learning of allocations which are arbitrary, rather than conceptually related to the subjects' previous experience. Experiment II was made to extend the data in this way.

III. Experiment II

A. METHOD

The Subjects were 8 experimentally naive students from the Oxford College of Technology, between 17 and 19 years of age.

Procedure

The Sparta timing apparatus was used to present random sequences of 301 successive signals on 8 neon lamps mounted 3 in. apart in an horizontal line across the center of a 3 ft square vertical matte-black display panel. Responses were made on the keyboard used in Experiment I. Each S was instructed in a different system of allocation of fingers (keys) to lamps. Four of the lamps required "directly correspondent" (DC) responses; that is, each of these was answered by the corresponding key in left-to-right order across the keyboard. The DC lamps were different for each S and were selected by reference to an octal random number table. The other 4 lamps were answered by randomly chosen "noncorrespondent" (NC) keys. These NC allocations again were different for each S, and were chosen by reference to adjacent numbers in an octal random number table, with obvious necessary constraints.

Eight different, random signal sequences were generated by Linc 8 program. Each of the 8 Ss ran through these sequences in a different order.

The first two runs were necessarily training runs during which the S was interrupted to point out errors, and could refer to a chart of his S–R allocations mounted above the lamps on the display. Subsequent runs were carried out without intervention by E or reference to the chart, except at the end of each run when any persistent confusions were pointed out.

Each individual test sequence lasted for 4–6 min, with intervening rest pauses of 10-min during which the performance was analyzed and discussed. The experiment was completed over two sessions of approximately 1 hr each, given on different days. Data were analyzed using the same sort programs described for Experiment I. The results of runs 3 and 4 (day 1) and runs 7 and 8 (day 2) were pooled to give data for early and relatively late practice sessions.

B. RESULTS

Confusion matrices for errors within and between DC and NC classes were generated as for Experiment I both for early practice sessions (9.2–28.4% errors) and for late practice sessions (6.8–12.6% errors). These data

Table 3. *Percentages of Confusions between Responses in Classes of Directly Correspondent (DC) and Noncorrespondent S–R Pairings, Early and Late in Practice in Experiment II*

A. Early practice sessions

		Class of S–R mapping rule for correct response	
		DC	NC
Class of S–R mapping rule of error response	DC	17%	4%
	NC	29%	50%

B. Late practice sessions

		Class of S–R mapping rule for correct response	
		DC	NC
Class of S–R mapping rule of error response	DC	4%	0%
	NC	44%	52%

are given in Table 3. χ^2 tests were applied to both matrices, and were significant in each case ($p < .01$). Again it seems that the asymmetry of the error matrices was due to a tendency to confuse DC responses with other DC responses and NC responses with other NC responses. This was checked by Wilcoxon's tests applied as in Experiment I. The trend was significant both early ($p < .01$) and late ($p < .05$) in practice.

Table 4. *Mean Reaction Times and Standard Deviations (σ) for Transitions between Signals Either Directly Correspondent (DC) or Not Correspondent (NC) to the Required Response Keys (Data for Early and Late Practice Sessions in Experiment II)*

Transitions	Mean RT (msec)	σ	Transitions	Mean RT (msec)	σ
A. Experiment II, early practice sessions: DC and NC S–R pairings			B. Experiment II, late practice sessions: DC and NC S–R pairings		
Identical stimulus	404	41	Identical stimulus	392	32
"Same class"	818	97	"Same class"	743	57
"New class"	945	151	"New class"	801	91

The RTs for correct responses were also sorted and collapsed precisely as described for Experiment I. The data for both practice conditions are given in Table 4.

A separate analysis of variance was carried out for each condition of practice. At both levels of practice significant terms were obtained for differences between transition conditions and S subjects ($p < .01$), with no interaction between them. Accordingly S^2 tests were made to rank-order means for transition classes. Early in practice the RTs for identical transitions were faster than those for other transition classes ($p < .01$), and the RTs for transitions within DC and NC classes were significantly faster than those for transitions between these classes ($p < .01$). Late in practice the difference between identical transitions and within-class transitions appeared to be maintained ($p < .01$), but the difference between within-class and between-class transitions, while still significant ($p < .05$), was reduced. To investigate this further an overall analysis of variance was made for the combined data from the two practice levels. Significant terms appeared for differences between subjects ($p < .01$), between levels of practice ($p < .01$), and between transition classes ($p < .01$). There were also significant interactions between practice and subjects ($p < .05$) and between practice and transition-class differences ($p < .05$). It seems that we may assume that the "repetition effect" for transition classes is diminished by practice.

Once again it seems that repetition of the use of an arbitrary S–R coding rule facilitates RT in self-paced sequential tasks, even when neither a particular response nor a particular signal is repeated immediately. This effect, however, seems to diminish with practice.

The literature on transition effects contains a great deal of information about cases where both a signal and the response to it are immediately repeated (see, for example, Bertelson, 1961, 1963; Bertelson & Renkin, 1966; Leonard, Newman, & Carpenter, 1967) and some data on cases in which a response may be repeated although a particular signal is not (Bertelson, 1965; Rabbitt, 1968). As we have seen, the latter data must now be considered to confound repetition or alternation of the S–R mapping rules with repetition or alternation of responses. No situation has been reported in which subjects may receive successive, identical, or different signals but in which responses are *never* repeated. The investigation of such a task seemed to have the advantages of a methodological innovation, and to usefully allow extension of our present very loose concepts as to what an "S–R coding rule" might be. Experiment III was accordingly made as a preliminary investigation.

IV. Experiment III

A. METHOD

The Subjects were 16 miscellaneous persons (5 research students in psychology, 3 technicians, 2 secretaries, and 6 psychologically and experimentally naive students from Oxford College of Technology, five of whom were women.) Their ages ranged from 17 to 32 years.

Procedure

The aim of the experiment was to discover whether Ss who spontaneously generated words from superordinate noun classes responded faster when successive, different nouns had to be generated from the same superordinate class than when successive nouns were generated from different classes.

The superordinate classes "Animals," "Christian Names," "Oxford Colleges," and "English Counties" were chosen on the basis of pilot experiments as providing classes that were easily comprehensible to Ss and from which they could quickly generate many subordinate instances (for example, "Cat," "George," "Mary," "Oriel," or "Rutland") without repeating themselves.

Each of the Ss was randomly assigned a different pair of these four superordinate class names. For each such class pair a Linc 8 system was programmed to present a random list of 50 superordinate class names one at a time on a CRT display. The names (signals) used were the words "ANIMAL," "NAME," "COUNTRY," or "COLLEGE," as appropriate, in block capitals.

The words were displayed simultaneously on two CRT's, one being monitored by the E and the other being placed in the S's cubicle. The Ss' display was located in a dark, sound-attenuating booth and was viewed through an optical system incorporating a head and chin rest to stabilize the mouth position. An experimental run began with E's verbal command "Ready," after which a fixation spot appeared on the center of the display for precisely 2 sec. The first of the random list of class names then appeared. The S responded as quickly as possible by saying aloud a subordinate noun from that class (for example, (Animal → Dog; Name → John). All Ss were told that speed of response was essential and that the experiment was a memory test in which they must never use the same subordinate noun twice during the entire series of 50 presentations.

The S's verbal response triggered a voice key, operated (within < .001

sec) through a microphone fixed by his mouth. The voice key immediately caused the computer to switch off the display presented, and after a 200-msec dead time the next display in the series appeared. The interval between the onset of each display and S's verbal response was timed by the computer to within 0.001 sec. At the end of the run the computer printed out the list of class names (signals), in order of presentation, with the RT associated with each. All S's responses were tape-recorded so that this list could subsequently be checked for errors (i.e. wrong subordinate class nouns and repeats).

B. RESULTS

Errors (repeated subordinate class items, as no other errors occurred) constituted 1.8% of the responses. All errors, and the response following each error were eliminated from subsequent analysis (3.6% of responses were lost in this way). The remaining "correct" responses were classified in terms of two transition classes: "superordinate class repeat" and "new superordinate class." The means and standard deviations of RTs summed over Ss are, respectively, 1304 msec (σ 302) for the repeated superordinate category and 1978 msec (σ 502) for the alternated superordinate category.

A Wilcoxon matched-pairs signed-ranks test was made across the subjects to compare RTs for repeated superordinate-class responses with RTs for new superordinate-class items. As the above suggests, "repeats" were faster than "new responses" ($p < .01$).

V. Discussion

The implications of Experiment III for semantic theories are not profound. Successive production of words from the same superordinate semantic class—however loosely the latter is defined—will imply the successive production of words likely to be strongly associated with each other. Disjunction of semantic classes will lower the probability of such associations. Further, most contemporary semantic theories that do not invoke mechanisms of relative association strength as a sole parameter (see Morton, 1970) would also predict facilitation under these conditions.

However, in the context of experiments analyzing choice RT transition effects, Experiment III is unique in that it shows a completely response-independent repetition effect. That is, while signals (class names) might be identical on successive presentations, responses never were. These data therefore show a repetition effect that may be attributed to the facilitation of perceptual analysis of successive signals by repetition, but which may be attributed much more probably to the repeated use of what may be loosely described as a "coding rule" or "memory search rule." Facilitation by repetition of identical or similar motor acts cannot possibly be a factor.

Considered together, Experiments I, II and III have implications for the design, analysis, methodology, and purpose of future studies of the "repetition effect." All previous literature has been based on the assumption that the process of identifying a signal and the process of selecting and making a response to it are two sequential and separate operations. Recent theoretical reviews have made strong claims that the complexity, and so implicitly the duration, of these processes are independent of each other so that observed RT represents some simple sum of their durations (Sternberg, 1969). The possibility that further "translation" or "retrieval" processes intervening between signal identification and response execution are similarly independent, sequential, and so simply additive in their contributions to observed RT has also been suggested (see Briggs & Blaha, 1969).

The present experiments show that facilitation of RT can occur when any one of a variety of "S–R mapping rules" (Experiments I and II), or "memory retrieval rules" (Experiment III) is applied in immediate succession. However, when all the present data are considered together, the independence of such "mapping," "coding," or "retrieval" rules on the one hand, from processes of signal identification and response selection on the other seems rather dubious. It is indifferent to the general implications of this point what precisely the rules determining commonality of sets of signals (Experiments I and II) or of sets of responses (Experiment III) may be. For example, one possible explanation of Bertelson's (1965) and Rabbitt's (1968) results might be that practice adaptively changes the nature of the perceptual "tests" that subjects apply to signals. Eventually, late in practice, a point is reached when all "perceptual tests" for signals in a common response class are made in parallel (see Neisser, 1963, 1967; Neisser, Novick, & Lazar, 1963). Repetition of an "equivalent" signal thus may become as facilitating as repetition of an "identical" signal, since the same tests will be made in each case. Further, there is no reason to suppose that such "composite" or "class" tests are adequate to discriminate any signal *within* a given response class from any other signal *in the same class*, since they would be most efficient if designed to discriminate *between* rather than *within* signal classes (Rabbitt, 1967). Similarly, for Experiment III, we might postulate that associations between nouns in the same superordinate class are "stronger" than associations between nouns in different superordinate classes. The adequacy of these hypotheses, or of any of an endless rival list limited by the ingenuity of theoreticians rather than by the data available, is not necessary to establish the general point: neither the complexity and the consequent duration of processes of signal identification and classification, nor the complexity and duration of processes of response selection and execution are independent of learned coding rules intervening between these processes. The application of these rules is facilitated by repetition, and their nature possibly is modified by practice (Experiment II).

These experiments add to the diversity of the phenomena that have been subsumed in the literature under the blanket term of "repetition effects." It now seems possible, and necessary, to apply a simple preliminary taxonomy to possible sources of sequential facilitation between signals and responses in serial self-paced tasks.

1. *Perceptual identification.* When successive signals are physically identical and require the same response, repetition effects are very marked. Even after considerable practice, RTs for repetitions of identical signals may be significantly faster than RTs for transitions between physically different signals to which the same response is appropriate (Rabbitt, 1968).

2. *Signal coding.* When successive signals are physically distinct, but require the same response, practiced subjects show marked repetition effects (Bertelson, 1965; Rabbitt, 1968). This is also the case when successive signals belong to the same, arbitrary, conceptual "class" (for example, Experiment I) or when unpractised subjects must learn unfamiliar S–R assignments (Experiment II). In Experiment I response repetition was not involved. Thus, facilitation in this experiment, and possibly also in the Bertelson (1965) and Rabbitt (1968) studies, must refer to repetition of an S–R coding rule and not simply to the repetition of a motor act.

3. *Signal–response mapping.* The repetition of arbitrary spatial rules by which Ss are instructed to "map" signals on to responses shows facilitation where neither signal nor response repetition occurs (Experiment II). The extent of this facilitation is modified by practice.

4. *Response "retrieval" or "selection."* Even when responses are always physically distinct, RT is faster when successive responses are made from a common semantic category than when they are made from disjunctive categories (Experiment III).

5. *Response programming.* Certain sequences of physically different motor responses are easier to make than others. This may refer to successive responses with the same type of limb (for example, hands and feet) (Rabbitt, 1967) or to laterality of limbs (Rabbitt, 1965). Also, certain sequences of finger movements are made faster and more accurately than others (Rabbitt & Vyas, 1970). None of these effects is signal dependent in any way.

6. *Response execution.* While there is no literature to support the hypothesis directly, it must at least be left open whether the successive employment of identical contractions or relaxations of particular muscle groups facilitates RT.

With the possible exception of effects completely dependent on muscular physiology (6 above) there is no *prima facie* reason to suppose that (*a*) these processes are all functionally successive in time, without overlap, or (*b*) the complexity and duration of any one of these processes does not affect the complexity and duration of others. On the contrary, a listing of these processes seems simply to offer a temporary taxonomy of convenience in terms of which any particular experiment in the literature may be evaluated. For the moment it seems wise to commit ourselves only to the generalization that "repetition effects" also may be mediated by the repetition of coding "rules" developed by, or previously familiar to the subject in classifying a particular set of S–R transformations that the experimenter wishes him to learn and use. Such repetition effects need not entail the repetition of particular signals or of particular responses, but evidently may affect the relative times taken for signal coding for response selection and organization, and for the patterns of errors made.

This generalization appears unpromisingly weak. Nevertheless, it offers a useful methodology for the future investigation of cognitive processes carried on by subjects in learning to improve their performance, even at what are apparently very simple, serial choice RT tasks. It is the nature, and the limitations, of such cognitive rule systems that now seems a more interesting and challenging topic for further investigation rather than the testing of relatively simple inflexible nonadaptive algebraic "models" for serial-choice RT.

References

Bertelson, P. Sequential redundancy and speed in a serial two-choice responding task. *Quarterly Journal of Experimental Psychology*, 1961, **13**, 90–102.

Bertelson, P. S–R relationships and reaction times for new versus repeated signals in a serial task. *Journal of Experimental Psychology*, 1963, **65**, 478–484.

Bertelson, P. Serial choice reaction-time as a function of response versus signal-and-response repetition. *Nature*, 1965, **206**, 217–218.

Bertelson, P., & Renkin, A. Reaction times to new versus repeated signals in a serial task as a function of response-signal time interval. *Acta Psychologica*, 1966, **25**, 132–136.

Briggs, G. E., & Blaha, J. Memory retrieval and central comparison times in information processing. *Journal of Experimental Psychology*, 1969, **79**, 395–402.

Crossman, E. R. F. W. The information capacity of the human operator in symbolic and non-symbolic control processes. In *Information theory and the human operator*. WR/D2/56. London Ministry of Supply, 1956. Pp. 231–249.

Fitts, P. M., & Biederman, I. S–R compatibility and information reduction. *Journal of Experimental Psychology*, 1965, **69**, 408–412.

Griew, S. Information gain in tasks involving different stimulus-response relationships. *Nature*, 1958, **182**, 1819.

Keele, S. W. Repetition effect: A memory-dependent process. *Journal of Experimental Psychology*, 1969, **80**, 243–248.

Kornblum, S. Sequential Determinants of information processing in serial and discrete choice Reaction Time. *Psychological Review*, 1969, **76**, 113–131.

Leonard, J. A., Newman, R. C., & Carpenter, A. On the handling of heavy bias in a shelf-paced task. *Quarterly Journal of Experimental Psychology*, 1967, **18**, 130–141.

Morton, J. A functional model for memory. In Norman, D. (Ed.), *Models of human memory.* New York: Academic Press, 1970. Pp. 203–254.

Neisser, U. Decision-time without reaction-time. Experiments in visual scanning. *American Journal of Psychology*, 1963, **76**, 376–385.

Neisser, U. *Cognitive psychology.* New York: Appleton, 1967.

Neisser, U., Novick, R., & Lazar, R. Searching for ten targets simultaneously. *Perceptual and Motov Skills*, 1963, **17**, 955–961.

Rabbitt, P. M. A. Response facilitation on repetition of a limb-movement. *British Journal of Psychology*, 1965, **56**, 303–304.

Rabbitt, P. M. A. Times for transitions between hand and foot responses in a self-paced task. *Quarterly Journal of Experimental Psychology*, 1966, **18**, 334–339.

Rabbitt, P. M. A. Learning to ignore irrelevant information. *American Journal of Psychology*, 1967, **80**, 1–13.

Rabbitt, P. M. A. Repetition effects and signal classification strategies in serial choice-response tasks. *Quarterly Journal of Experimental Psychology*, 1968, **20**, 232–240.

Rabbitt, P. M. A. Psychological refractory delay and response-stimulus interval duration in serial, choice-response tasks. *Acta Psychologica*, 1969, **30**, 195–219.

Rabbitt, P. M. A., & Vyas, S. M. An elementary preliminary taxonomy for some errors in laboratory choice RT tasks, *Acta Psychologica*, 1970, **33**, 56–76.

Remington, R. J. Analysis of Sequential effects in choice reaction times. *Journal of Experimental Psychology*, 1969, **82**, 250–257.

Sternberg, S. The discovery of processing stages: Extensions of Donder's method. *Acta Psychologica*, 1969, **30**, 276–315.

Williams, J. A. Sequential effects in disgunctive reaction time: Implications for decision models. *Journal of Experimental Psychology*, 1966, **71**, 665–672.

4 ORGANIZATION AND CODING IN MEMORY

Learning and Remembering: A Tutorial Preview[1]

Donald A. Norman

Department of Psychology
University of California, San Diego
La Jolla, California

ABSTRACT

When one examines the structure of long-term memory, it becomes clear that there is more to it than a simple set of pigeon holes in which facts are kept. To represent the meaningful component of memory properly requires a richly interconnected network structure, although this structure can be described as labeled, directed graphs or as lists or even as formulas in predicate calculus, depending upon the bias of the theorist. When the emphasis is on problem solving, on thought, and on the understanding of language, then it is seen that the properties required both of the memory and of the processes that use it are somewhat different from those normally studied in the psychological literature. Hence, we will need both new classes of theories and new types of experiments to determine the ways by which the human memory system represents data, operates upon those data, and uses language. This paper summarizes and previews some experimental and theoretical studies on the nature of language, memory, learning, and thought.

[1]This tutorial article contains a review of work that has been done by a variety of people and a hint of the direction in which I expect the field to continue developing: hence the word "preview" in the title. There is very little (if any) new thought presented in this paper that has not been presented by me or by others elsewhere; e.g., the research on the memory model was done by Peter Lindsay, Donald Norman, and David Rumelhart and can be found in Rumelhart, Lindsay, and Norman (1972). This paper does not contain an exhaustive literature review, but such selectivity is consistent with the nature of a tutorial paper. The work on the memory model was supported by a grant from the National Institute of Neurological Disease and Stroke, United States Public Health Service NS–07454.

What is memory about? It is not just a repository of past experiences, for a sheer compilation of facts is not an adequate basis for human cognitive processes. Rather, there must be method to the memory. Memory must be used, and its organizational structure and coding must reflect that use. We use memory to answer questions about the world, about ourselves, and even about itself. Whatever the organizational structure, it must be one that is flexible enough to allow access to it in a variety of ways, precise enough to be capable of logical deduction when that is required, and powerful enough to contain not only records of past events, but also programs for actions. We humans can perform actions both in reality (such as reading a paper) or mentally (such as thinking of reading a paper). Mental actions bear many resemblances to physical ones, but they serve different purposes, in part allowing a sequence of real operations to be planned previous to their execution. The memory system must permit actions to be thought, as well as to be performed. Moreover, if mental planning is to be useful, it must be remembered, just as a real action must be remembered. And the memory structure must be flexible enough to distinguish among things done, things experienced, things thought, and things remembered.

I. Memory Representation

If concepts are stored within the memory system, and if these concepts are to be related to others, then the natural formal representation is by either a list structure or by a directed, labeled graph. The two representations are, in fact, one and the same—the differences simply being one of notational convenience. Moreover, once a graph or list structure is devised, then it is possible to represent them by means of a set of ordered triples of the form (**aRb**), where **a** and **b** are concepts (nodes in the graph space) and **R** is the relation obtaining between **a** and **b** (the labeled, directed link or arc between the nodes). By a labeled, directed graph I mean simply that (**aRb**) $\neq$ (**bRa**). That is, the meaning of the relation depends upon the direction in which it is applied. These notational schemes are the basis of numerous memory structures now being tested by several groups of psychologists (for example, Anderson, 1972; Kintsch, 1972; Quillian, 1969; Rumelhart, Lindsay, & Norman, 1972) and by numerous computer science groups as well. Nico Frijda's excellent review of research on the simulation of human memory introduces this topic well (Frijda, 1972), so his discussion will not be repeated here. The paper by Hunt (1971) also serves as a good review and introduction to this area, as does the collection of Collins and Quillian (1972), Kintsch (1972), and Rumelhart *et al.* (1972) in the book edited by Tulving and Donaldson (1972). In the discussion that follows, I will use the representation scheme developed by my collaborators at La Jolla (Peter Lindsay and David Rumelhart) primarily because it is most convenient and natural for me, but also because the common, important features of this form of representation are independent of the exact scheme that I follow. (For more details, see Rumelhart *et al.*, 1972; or Lindsay & Norman, 1972, Chapters 10–13.)

A. CONCEPTS, EVENTS, AND EPISODES[2]

When examining the kinds of things that must be represented in a model of human long-term memory, it is convenient to distinguish among three classes of information: *concepts, events*, and *episodes. Concepts* refer primarily to particular ideas. An *event* is action based, denoting a scenario with its associated actors and objects. An *episode* is a series of events or actions. Although these different classes of information can be logically distinguished, they are all represented in the same memory format. To introduce the main ideas, I will only briefly illustrate the types of relations that are useful for representing concept, event, and episode information.

1. Encoding Concepts

When it comes to defining concepts in the memory system, three types of functional relations are of primary importance: the classes to which a concept belongs, the characteristics which define it, and the examples of that concept. Three relations can specify an important class of functional relations: *isa*, as in *John isa person* and *dog isa animal*; *is* and *has*, as in the definition of property relations: *has* (in the sense of has-as-parts) for objects, as in *animal has feet*; *is* for qualities, as in *John is fat*. To specify an *example* relation, the inverse of *isa* is used; *animal isa-inverse dog*, meaning an example of animal is dog.

Although these three relations are neither necessary nor sufficient to define concepts, they provide crucial information needed during the manipulation of the conceptual information in the memory system.

2. Encoding Events

An event is a scenario with actions, actors, and objects. In general, a verb describes the action that is taking place, so the representation centers around the verb. We treat an action as a relation that can take various arguments. The exact interpretation of the event depends on the arguments of the relation.

---

[2]This section is modified from Rumelhart, Lindsay, and Norman (1972).

For example, consider the observation:

$$\text{The rock rolled down the mountain.} \quad (1)$$

This represents an event centered around the critical action *roll*. The "rock" is the *object* rolling down the mountain (set in motion by some anonymous actor); "down the mountain" specifies the *path* of the action; the *time* is in the past. The encoding of this information into the memory structure is shown in Fig. 1A.

Now consider the further information:

$$\text{The hut is tiny.} \quad (2)$$

$$\text{The hut is at the river.} \quad (3)$$

The action here centers around the relation *is*: in this case, "tiny" is a *quality*, "river" a *location*, and "hut" is the *object* of the relation *is*. This produces Fig. 1B. Now consider:

$$\text{The rock crushed the hut.} \quad (4)$$

The "rock" is the *instrument* which acts on the *object* "hut." Hence the structure of Fig. 1C.

The last structure, Fig. 1D, shows the complete representation of the event:

$$\text{The rock that rolled down the mountain}$$
$$\text{crushed the tiny hut at the river.} \quad (5)$$

Note that this is the first testable aspect of the model: that different related sentences form a single unified conceptual structure. Indeed, when Bransford and Franks (1971) asked subjects to learn the individual sentences (1)–(4) above and later tested for recognition, they found that it was the full concept, sentence (5), that was recognized even though it had never been shown to the subjects.

Primary and Secondary Nodes.   There are problems when a single concept or event must be referred to many times, but in different circumstances. Suppose that we are using the act *hit* in the two sentences:

$$\text{John hits the ball.} \quad (6)$$

$$\text{Peter hits the cat.} \quad (7)$$

The difficulty is shown in Fig. 2A. We need to separate the two uses of the act *hit*. We do this by distinguishing between the definitional node for *hit*, the *primary* (or type) node, and the particular use of that node, the *secondary* (or token) node. We represent secondary event nodes by encircling them. The secondary node for an *event* is connected to the primary node by the relation

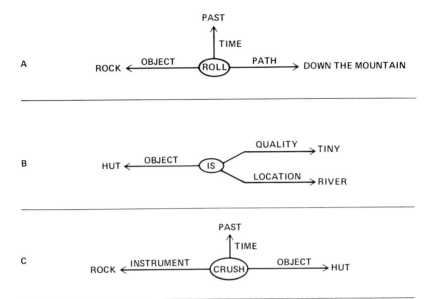

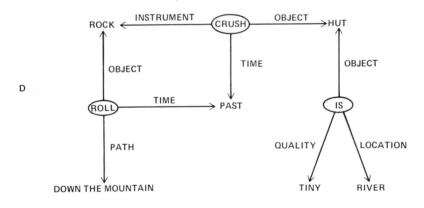

Fig. 1.

act. When a secondary node is shown in diagram form by a circle, the *act* relation is assumed to exist: hence, the encoding diagrammed in Fig. 2B.

Similar problems and solutions arise with concept nodes. Secondary concepts are enclosed in angular brackets: <animal>. This can be read as

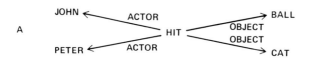

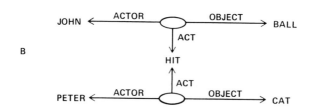

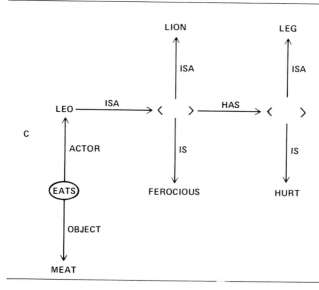

Fig. 2.

"this animal" or "token animal." Secondary concepts are connected to their primary nodes by the relation *isa*. Thus, the illustration in Fig. 2C depicts the concept:

$$\text{Leo, a ferocious lion with a hurt leg, eats meat.} \qquad (8)$$

3. Encoding Episodes

The representation of an event is centered around a single action. An *episode* is a cluster of events or actions. The interrelations within the event clusters are encoded by special arrows called *propositional conjunctions*. Two of these conjunctions are the *then* relation, which leads to the next event in an action sequence, and the *while* relation, which interconnects events with unspecified temporal order. The *then* and *while* arrows are illustrated in the episode of Fig. 3:

$$\text{John murders Mary at Luigi's.} \qquad (9)$$

This mechanism for clustering events into episodes has considerable flexibility for representing temporal information in the memory system.

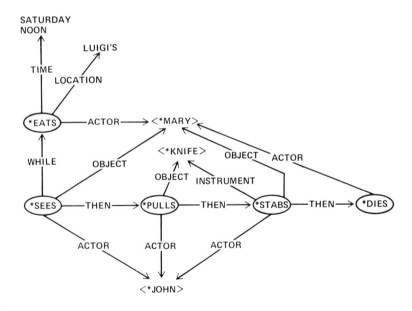

Fig. 3.

Time is defined locally within the context of a specific event sequence. Since any level of embedding is allowed, any level of time scale can be defined.

In general, conjunctions like *then* and *while* provide an organizing principle for events similar to that provided by *isa* in clustering concepts. Events can be grouped into hierarchical structures when several may have general properties in common. The *while* and *then* links specify the temporal relations within each instance.

This conceptualization of event clusters is crucial to the memory model, for it allows us to encode the procedures for retrieving, manipulating, and evaluating stored information—the *processes* of the model—in the same way we encode the conceptual and event information. An event is simply an action or relation among several arguments. An episode is a sequence of events—the equivalent of a subroutine. The *act* relation can be interpreted as the enactment of that subroutine. Thus, the actions involved in internal processing can be represented in exactly the same format as external action sequences that have been observed by the system. The flow of action in an episode is a process of the memory system. The only difference between external event sequences and internal processes is whether the system (person) actually performs operations or simply does them mentally as it follows through the specification of an episode.

It is interesting to note that a number of functions used by the interpretive system during processing can also be used during the actual execution of that same event. When following the events shown in Fig. 3, the *act* relation means to examine the definition of *stab* to find the arguments required. *Stab* may specify that a *person*, an *object*, and a *pointed instrument* are needed. This provides the plan for searching for specific arguments in the observational sequence or for making inferences about arguments that may be missing in the memory of an event. If one is only "thinking" about the event sequence, then missing arguments do not matter. But if one is trying to execute the sequence (that is, if one wishes to stab someone), then the missing arguments must actually be filled before proceeding with the action.

The ability to encode processes and episodes directly into the data base has important theoretical implications, for it allows the procedures that operate on concept and event information to operate on themselves. Conceptual, event, and episode information is completely intermixed in the memory system, and all are represented in this same format. The *then* links are used interchangeably to lead to the next event in an observed action sequence or the next process to be executed by the interpreter. If the action called for can be executed, it will be; if not, the system simply continues evaluating the processing network.

4. General Features of the Representational Format

To summarize, there are several fundamental aspects of this process model. The basic element of information in the memory network is the event, consisting of a set of nodes interconnected by a relation. A node is a functional cluster of information that can represent a concept, event, or episode in the system and may have any number of relations attached to it. Secondary nodes may be derived from primary nodes; higher-order nodes may be defined by the concatenation of lower-order ones.

Relations among nodes are directed and labelled. Relational labels are the basic means of encoding logical or semantic functions which interconnect nodes. Though a distinction has been made between the representation of concrete concepts, events, and episodes, these three types of information are in fact encoded in identical formats, and completely intermixed in the memory structure. Together they form the total body of knowledge that the system has at any given time.

B. LEARNING AND LOCAL HIERARCHIES

One thing that results from any network consideration is a hierarchical organization when small local areas are examined. Consider how a network develops. Suppose a child is learning about birds. He sees his first instance and forms a concept that I will describe in words as that of a living creature that flies. With more experience, more attributes of birds come to be known, perhaps that they have wings and eat worms. The next important step comes in the realization that one instance might differ from earlier ones. Now a new node must be created in the memory system, one that is the same as the earlier node with some distinguishing characteristic: suppose it is the relation–concept pair *has red-breast*. If a third bird is added, one that is the same as the first except that it *is black*, then we are starting to develop a simple hierarchical structure: consider the question, Does the third bird fly? To find out, we examine the information stored about it and discover no answer to the question. But because the third bird is described as a special instance of the first, and because the first does fly, we can deduce that the third does also. Thus, by the simple process of creating the network by relating new concepts to old ones as much as possible, with discriminating information where necessary, we have built the form of hierarchical network described and tested in the several experiments of Collins and Quillian (1969, 1972).

The network I have just described grew from the top down as new concepts were *discriminated* from the old. It is also possible to grow a network from the bottom up by *generalizing* among the concepts. Suppose that all instances known of birds *have wings*. Then it should be possible to generalize this information and add it to the higher level concept. As a result, it need no longer be added to any new nodes that get formed when new instances of birds arrive.

If three basic principles are used in learning the memory structure, then many of the simple hierarchical structures studied in recent years by psychologists interested in the organization of memory emerge. The three principles would seem to be:

1. *No forgetting or erasure*: once information is entered within the network, it stays.
2. *Generalization*: the process by which information common to a number of nodes can be added to higher level nodes.
3. *Discrimination*: the process by which one node is subdivided into two, each with a set of features that discriminate them from one another and with common features remaining on a higher level node.

II. The Analysis of Language

Few of our experiences happen without a surrounding contextual framework. Presumably the memory structure has evolved to understand a present experience within the total context in which it appears. So must it be with language. Just as the preceding sentence was perfectly intelligible even though it was linguistically ungrammatical, so must many grammatical utterances be uninterpretable (at least without ambiguity) unless the contextual information is considered.

Most linguistic analyses have been concerned with the structure of single sentences. Linguists make their livelihood looking for subtleties in meanings and structures, putting stars on those sentences that are ungrammatical for the analysis under consideration. But to the psychologist, much of the game of linguistics simply is not relevant. People talk in order to communicate. They rely upon hints and phrases to reference the relevant concepts and events. It matters not whether the utterances of speech are grammatical or potentially ambiguous. What does matter is that the listener be able to reconstruct the proper memory structure from the sequence of utterances. It may well be that an analysis of how language is used in discourse might give us clues to the nature of memory structures.

An important consideration in the analysis of language is the identification of the proper referent. A conversation might discuss sets of objects or events. Later on, one of the speakers wishes to refer to a particular instance: what linguistic cues must be used to get the listener to the proper referent?

Some starts in such experimental studies have been made. Olson (1970) has used a communication strategy to study the use of pronouns and modifiers in the use of language for communicating instructions. Similar strategies might be insightful for studying the memory structures involved in the use of language as a medium for understanding.

There are numerous ways to do the grammatical analysis of a sentence. Some are more formal than others: some yield more psychological insight into the processes involved than others. One procedure for analysis rapidly growing in favor among psychologists is the case grammar of Fillmore (1968, 1969) [see Kintsch's (1972) discussion]. Case grammar provides a very compelling description of sentence structure, for it emphasizes the roles played by each component. Thus, in the sentence

$$\text{John wrote on the wall.} \qquad (10)$$

the action of writing requires certain roles to be fulfilled. For one, it requires an actor to initiate the event. For this sentence, the actor must be either human or pseudohuman (it could be a computer). An instrument of the writing is also required, an inanimate object that is capable of making marks. And a location is also required, the place where the writing is performed. Hence, for sentence (10) we have

event:	write
time:	past
actor:	John
location:	on the wall.

With the sentence

$$\text{The pencil wrote on the wall.} \qquad (11)$$

pencil is the instrument of the action, for the semantics of the sentence tell us that pencil, being inanimate, cannot be an actor and, because it is capable of making marks, it is a logical candidate for instrument. Thus, although John and pencil are both subjects of their respective sentences, the semantics unambiguously tell us their roles in the episode.

The difference between the roles of John and the pencil is consistent with the linguistic fact that they can be combined into a single sentence like

$$\text{John wrote on the wall with a pencil.} \qquad (12)$$

but not into a sentence like

$$\text{A pencil wrote on the wall with John.} \qquad (13)$$

Case grammar is an important analytical tool for psychologists, but beware, it is far from being the whole story. Case grammar is rich enough to accept sentence (12) and reject sentence (13), but what does it do with sentence (14):

$$\text{The typewriter wrote on the wall.} \qquad (14)$$

To analyze that sentence and to realize the anomaly we need a deeper understanding of the underlying concepts than is provided by the case usage.

Consider this sentence:

$$\text{Hubert grew flowers in the yard.} \qquad (15)$$

Formally, Hubert is the actor who initiates the act of growing flowers (the object being grown) in the yard (the location). Or is Hubert the actor? Actually, it is the plant that does the growing; how can a person cause a plant to grow? Consider

$$\text{Hubert grew flowers in the yard with fertilizer.} \qquad (16)$$

Fertilizer is the instrument of the growing, right? No, not really. The instrument is really a whole conceptual act, that is, of Hubert spreading fertilizer on the ground, causing the plant to grow. That is, the reason that Hubert is not the actor of sentence (15) nor the fertilizer the instrument of sentence (16) is that there is a whole conceptual action involved in growing plants, and that action is causally related to the growth. The instrument of "grew" is that whole conceptual activity. To analyze even simple sounding phrases often requires consideration of a good deal of other things: a set of actions are implied; causality gets invoked.[3]

This last analysis of the sentence has been taken from the work of Roger Schank (Schank, 1972: also described briefly in Hunt, 1971). In my opinion, this conceptual analysis is of great potential importance to psychologists, for it lays bare a good deal of the processing that we know intuitively does go on in the understanding of a sentence, but which is not captured by the work of most linguistic theorists.

Schank's analysis brings us back to the problem of memory representation, for now it starts to become clear how memory structure must interact with linguistic processing. Thus, the memory system must know not only simple word definitions and simple lexical constraints, such as those that rule out sentence (13), but rather a deeper understanding of how the concepts being discussed actually operate in realistic contexts.

Perhaps the most important implications of this memory structure for

---

[3]In fact, now we see that Fig. 1C and D are wrong: the *instrument* of the act of crushing is the entire event of the *rock rolling down the mountain*. Hence, the *instrument* relation should point directly at the event *roll*, not at *rock*.

research in psycholinguistics is the realization that the psychological unit is much larger than that of a single sentence. Schank's work emphasizes how the analysis of a single sentence carries with it a conceptual structure far richer than that of the surface structure of the sentence itself. Moreover, the memory structure that corresponds to the meaning of linguistic strings would seem to be based around the total episodic structure that is being experienced. It would be hoped that experimentation aimed at bringing out the interrelationships of the psychological structures would bring more insight into our understanding of psycholinguistic processes.

Even if we wish to understand how single sentences are encoded, the most illuminating research seems to come from a consideration of the memory for groups of sentences. Thus, I have already discussed how Bransford and Franks have demonstrated how separate sentences can be integrated together into whole conceptual paradigms. Anderson (1972) and Anderson and Bower (1971) have been especially clever at teasing out the possible memory structures by means of tests based on interrelated groups of sentences. For example, consider the two sentences

$$\text{The man photographed the bicycle.} \qquad (17)$$

$$\text{The girl rode the bicycle.} \qquad (18)$$

Both have a common object: the bicycle. Suppose we do a probed recall experiment: which probe do you think would act as a better cue for the object of the sentence

$$\text{The man photographed ————.} \qquad (19)$$

or

$$\text{The girl photographed ————.} \qquad (20)$$

Common sense says that sentence (19) should be best, for the clue is part of sentence (17), whereas sentence (20) involves a crossover with the subject combined with the inappropriate verb. Nonetheless, Anderson and Bower showed that structural models of the class being discussed here (in particular, they examined the Rumelhart, Lindsay, and Norman model) all predict that the two should be almost equal in their power. And, indeed, the experimental results support that counter-intuitive prediction.[4]

---

[4]Anderson and Bower went on to show that when they did the experiment "properly," they got the intuitive result. However, it took 20 min just to explain the procedure to their subjects, so I will not try to duplicate that task here. More important to us, their papers illustrate some exciting new directions to take in the exploration of memory structures.

III. Learning

Given the form of memory representation, the psychology of learning takes on a new look. From the point of view of the memory structure, the process of learning is the process of adding new nodes and relations to the existing memory structure. This means that the learner has two things to do: first he must identify his present experience with previous ones. Then, he must note the similarities and differences, and either create new structures or add to previously acquired ones. The generalization and discrimination processes discussed earlier should play a major role in these processes.

It is useful to discuss three different areas of learning: the learning of concepts, the learning of actions, and the learning of rules.

A. LEARNING CONCEPTS

Here, the learner has to add new structures into the memory system. Presumably, he does this by noting the similarities and differences among the present experience and previously acquired ones and then uses the principles of generalization and discrimination either to build new structures or to add to the existing ones.

B. LEARNING ACTIONS

Actions differ from concepts primarily in that they are not complete in themselves: a concept like *house* may need to be specified to get it from the general term to a specific instance, but nonetheless, it is a unitary concept by itself. An action such as *get*, however, requires some more information: *get* can be treated as a function which has missing arguments.

The action *get* implies a transfer of information from one location to the location of the actor. Probably a basic *transfer* concept underlies actions such as get, take, give, move, run, walk, stroll, and fetch. These words all differ in their implicit and explicit specification of the arguments of the *transfer* function. Hence, *get* requires explicit specification of an object and an actor, with the implicit assumption that the location of the object be changed from its previous location (which may have to be specified) to the location of the actor, as in

John got the newspaper from the hall.   (21)

Thus, in learning of actions, not only must the physical acts to be performed be acquired, but also the prerequisites that accompany the actions must be established. It turns out, conveniently enough, that many of the classical examples of problem solving can be expressed as problems of "filling in" the missing arguments of an action. For the monkey-and-the-stick problem—the monkey who must learn to use a stick in order to get a banana hung out of the reach of his arms—the whole solution of the task relies upon the identification of the fact that the instrument of the action *get* cannot be satisfied by hands alone, but rather must be extended artificially.

Actions have the property that they both exist within the memory structure as information, and also that they constitute an executable set of instructions for performing the action. Thus, not only can one learn the actions of *get* so that experiences which involve the perception of the act of getting can be understood, but also one can then do it if necessary either mentally or physically. In the latter case, the action must have all its proper arguments filled by concrete examples in order for the act to be successful.

C. LEARNING RULES

Rules differ from concepts and acts in that they denote a set of actions to be performed conditionally upon the satisfaction of prior conditions. Thus, to learn rules, one needs to learn both the proper conditions for their execution and the proper act to be taken. By the specification of rules in this conditional format, they become analogous to more simple concepts and events in the memory structure (see Lindsay & Norman, 1972, Chapter 13) so that the same operations that apply to the learning of concepts and actions may also apply to rules. Rumelhart (personal communication) is studying the rules for rule acquisition. It now appears that reasonably straightforward processes can account for the learning of rather complex behavior: the parsing of English sentences. A good deal of the grammar—both syntactical and semantic—may be acquired through the experiences of the language user. If his study proves successful, then it will demonstrate how rather complex rules can be developed by reasonably simple principles. In fact, although he has had to devise a learning theory specific to rules, the important breakthrough here was the development of an adequate representational scheme—the addition of the concepts of causality and conditionality to the memory structure.

IV. Testing the Memory Structure

There are major unsolved problems involved in the testing of memory structure. For one thing, if I am correct about the nature of the network and about the close correspondence between memory for concepts, actions, and rules, then it may be impossible ever to measure directly some of the features. If a memory representation can both be stored but also activated to perform some action, then it is difficult to see how one devises critical tests of its structure.

One immediate test, of course, simply is one of adequacy: do the concepts discussed here work; are they capable of performing the complex behavior found in human thinking? The answer to this question comes about through simulation of such structures: the papers collected by Minsky (1968) and the theses of Becker (1970) and Winograd (1972) indicate the direction that such simulation efforts might take.

Some features of the network representation are subject to test. As we have seen, Anderson (1972) and Anderson and Bower (1971) have examined some of the linguistic implications of these graph structures. Bransford and Franks (1971) have shown how ideas may be represented as single complexes, so that upon later test a subject may be aware of the total ideas but be unable to recreate how he had acquired them. The reaction time studies of Collins and Quillian (1969), Landauer and Freedman (1968), and Meyer (1970) get at related but differing aspects of the network. Kiss (1968) has developed large network structures.

There are numerous ways of going about the business of examining memory hierarchies. At the moment, the best procedures would seem to be those that involve reaction time measures, or sorting tasks, or free associations. Unfortunately, most of the effort so far seems to have been expended to prove or disprove specific notions about the existence of or the details of memory hierarchies. I would expect these studies to be of minimal value. It is difficult to imagine a memory structure that did not have the basic principles of hierarchical organization. If material stored in memory also contains information about its relationships to other stored information, then the properties of a hierarchy must result of necessity. It does not seem to matter whether the memory system is organized into lists or graph structures or even if it is essentially disorganized, but with an efficient parallel access scheme (such as a content-addressable access): the end result is that the necessity to recognize the generalities and the differences among different memory concepts produces the hierarchical result.

Experimental studies which average the results across different subjects may have minimal value. For if one starts to postulate learning mechanisms, perhaps ones akin to the three rules stated previously, then it is readily seen that although each individual person may use the same basic rules to develop his memory structure, and although the same principles are involved for each separate individual, we can expect large individual variation in the exact structures that are derived. It will be the accidental sequence of encounters with the world that determine the way the structure develops, and it would seem that little can be gained by studies that attempt to characterize the memory structure from data averaged across individuals.

The trick is to determine the representation of information within long-term memory. Clearly, this is a difficult task, but one worthy of our attention, for once you start to consider the basic problem, then suddenly a number of the properties of the long-term memory become apparent, a number of important issues raise themselves as candidates for further investigation, and a number of issues heretofore thought to be important are seen to be irrelevant.

References

Anderson, J. R. FRAN: A simulation model of free recall. In G. H. Bower (Ed.), *The psychology of learning and motivation*. Vol. 5. New York: Academic Press, 1972.

Anderson, J. R., & Bower, G. H. Associationism vs. Gestalt theory: The nature of the memory trace for sentences—Part II. Unpublished manuscript, 1971.

Becker, J. D. An information-processing model of intermediate-level cognition. *Stanford Artificial Intelligence Project Memo AI–119*, 1970.

Bransford, J. D., & Franks, J. J. The abstraction of linguistic ideas. *Cognitive Psychology*, 1971, **2**, 331–350.

Collins, A. M., & Quillian, M. R. Retrieval time from semantic memory. *Journal of Verbal Learning and Verbal Behavior*, 1969, **8**, 240–247.

Collins, A. M., & Quillian, M. R. How to make a language user. In E. Tulving & W. Donaldson (Eds.), *Organization and memory*. New York: Academic Press, 1972.

Fillmore, C. J. The case for case. In E. Bach & R. T. Harms (Eds.), *Universals in linguistic theory*. New York: Holt, 1968.

Fillmore, C. J. Toward a modern theory of case. In D. A. Reibel & S. A. Schane (Eds.), *Modern studies in English*. Englewood Cliffs, New Jersey: Prentice-Hall, 1969.

Frijda, N. H. The simulation of human memory. *Psychological Bulletin*, 1972, **77**, 1–31.

Hunt, E. What kind of computer is man? *Cognitive Psychology*, 1971, **2**, 57–98.

Kintsch, W. Notes on the semantic structure of memory. In E. Tulving & W. Donaldson (Eds.), *Organization and memory*. New York: Academic Press, 1972.

Kiss, G. R. Words, associations, and networks. *Journal of Verbal Learning and Verbal Behavior*, 1968, **7**, 703–713.

Landauer, T. K., & Freedman, J. L. Information retrieval from long-term memory: Category size and recognition time. *Journal of Verbal Learning and Verbal Behavior*, 1968, **7**, 291–295.

Lindsay, P. H., & Norman, D. A. *Human information processing*. New York: Academic Press, 1972.

Meyer, D. E. On the representation and retrieval of stored semantic information. *Cognitive Psychology*, 1970, **1**, 243–300.

Minsky, M. (Ed.) *Semantic information processing*. Cambridge, Massachusetts; MIT Press, 1968.

Olson, D. Language and thought: Aspects of a cognitive theory of semantics. *Psychological Review*, 1970, **77**, 257–273.

Quillian, M. R. The teachable language comprehender: A simulation program and theory of language. *Communications of the ACM*, 1969, **12**, 459–476.

Rumelhart, D. E., Lindsay, P. H., & Norman, D. A. A process model for long-term memory. In E. Tulving & W. Donaldson (Eds.), *Organization and memory*. New York: Academic Press, 1972.

Schank, R. C. Conceptual dependency: A theory of natural language understanding. *Cognitive Psychology*, 1972, in press.

Tulving, E., & Donaldson, W. (Eds.) *Organization and Memory*. New York: Academic Press, 1972.

Winograd, T. Procedures as a representation for data in a computer program for understanding natural language. *Cognitive Psychology*, 1972, **3**, 1–191.

Searching through Long-Term Verbal Memory[1]

Nancy C. Waugh   *Terry R. Anders*[2]

Department of Psychiatry
Massachusetts General Hospital
Boston, Massachusetts

ABSTRACT

Subjects were required to decide whether a given letter occurred within a particular subsequence of the alphabet in its natural order. They were also required to name letters drawn from known subsequences on seeing them. In both cases the independent variable was the length of the subsequence from which the letter was selected, while the dependent variable was the subject's reaction time. The results are consistent with the hypothesis that information in very long-term memory may be subject to parallel rather than serial search.

I. Introduction

In what can surely be called a series of classical experiments, Sternberg (1966, 1967a, b) has demonstrated the operation of serial, exhaustive scanning in human memory. The process seems to typify retrieval and recogni-

---

[1]This work was supported by Research Grant No. MH-08119 from the National Institute of Mental Health, United States Public Health Service. Deborah Baker, Karen Graf, Timothy Lillyquist, and Roseanna Means collected the data and helped analyze them; their assistance is gratefully acknowledged.
[2]Present addresses: University of Oxford, Oxford England; and Dalhousie University, Halifax, Nova Scotia, respectively.

tion in a situation of the following sort: Initially the subject sees a short list of familiar symbols (called the positive, or target, set) arranged in an unfamiliar order. Immediately thereafter, he is presented with a test item—either a symbol that appeared in the list he just saw, or one that did not. His task is to make one response if he believes that the test item is also a target item and another if he thinks it is not. It is assumed that in order to perform the task, the subject must in some sense scan the set of target items in memory so as to discover whether any one of them matches the test item. The time that it takes him to respond is assumed to reflect the nature of his search through the memorized list.

Two significant results have emerged from studies that follow the prototype just described. First, response time has been found to increase as a rectilinear function of list length. It accordingly has been inferred that the scanning of verbal memory for a given item's presence is a serial process; that is, the search proceeds item by item, only one target (or, strictly speaking, only one target item's representation in memory) being examined and compared with the test item at any given time. Second, the latencies of positive and negative responses have been found to increase at the same rate as a function of list length. This result has suggested that the search is exhaustive, such that every individual item in the positive set must be sampled exactly once before a decision is made. The process is a rapid one (each comparison between target and test items taking only about 30–40 msec), and is apparently not specific to the recognition of novel liguistic information. There is evidence (gathered by Sternberg and A. Treisman and reported by Sternberg, 1969) that sets of faces and geometric forms are similarly subjected to high-speed scanning in short-term memory; there also is evidence (Sternberg, 1969) that relatively familiar lists in longer-term, secondary (Waugh & Norman, 1965), or "inactive" memory can also undergo the same sort of sequential retrieval as lists that have been very recently learned (and are therefore still available in primary or "active" memory). The serial scanning of memorized information (even though it is sometimes self-terminating rather than exhaustive: see Anders, 1971; Theios, Smith, Haviland, & Traupmann, 1971) therefore seems to be a phenomenon of some generality, at least in the binary classification tasks by means of which psychologists commonly study recognition.

The question arises as to whether the process is in fact universal. Common sense and everyday experience suggest that it is not. For instance, if anyone were to be asked whether November is among the first three months of the year, it is difficult to imagine that he would retrive the list *January, February, March, . . . , December* (or even the list *January, February, March*) before making the appropriate reply. It would seem quite likely, on the other hand, that he would have to first generate and then sequentially scan the list *April, August, December* (or possibly the list *April, August, December, . . . , September*) when asked whether November was among the first three months of the year, all twelve of them now arranged alphabetically. What is the difference between the two tasks? Mainly that the months of the year in their natural order form a short yet very familiar series of words; but arranged in any other order, they probably do not.

These examples are not meant to suggest in any way that introspection and common sense are infallible guides in the domain of scientific psychology. Everyone will certainly agree that they are not, especially when it comes to mental processes that last for only a few milliseconds. But it is usually a sound heuristic principle to try to discover the limits of one's generalizations—and that is basically why the present study was undertaken. There must exist some limit to the generalization that, in order to decide whether a certain stimulus is a member of a certain memorized set, one has to conduct a sequential and exhaustive search of the set. There is intuitive reason to suppose that highly overlearned sets may furnish exceptions to that rule.

The effects of overlearning on the time that it takes to retrieve verbal information from memory may in fact be analogous to the effects of overlearning on response latencies in the conventional disjunctive-reaction task, wherein responses are mapped onto stimuli in one-to-one correspondence (see Brainard, Irby, Fitts, & Alluisi, 1962; Burrows & Murdock, 1969; Davis, Moray, & Treisman, 1961; Morin & Forrin, 1962; Morin, Konick, Troxell, & McPherson, 1965; Mowbray & Rhoades, 1959). In the latter case, the effect of extended practice is to eliminate—or, in any event, greatly to attenuate—the usual dependence of choice reaction time on the number of alternative stimuli. The general purpose of the present study was to determine whether the time required to classify a verbal item as a member of an extremely familiar list is similarly independent of the number of other items in the list.

We therefore selected as well-known a series of symbols as we could think of—the letters of the alphabet in their natural order—and asked our subjects to decide whether or not a given letter fell within a given portion of the alphabet. The length of this positive subseries ranged from 1 to 12 letters. All of them occurred in the first half of the alphabet. Since Wingfield and Branca (1970) have shown that subjects will sometimes scan whichever of two complementary sets is the smaller, the positive and negative sets that were selected for the present study always contained the same number of letters; whenever they included two or more, the letters were drawn from consecutive positions in the alphbet. It should be emphasized that the subject always knew exactly which letters were included in both sets. The specific aim of the experiment was to discover whether his reaction time—the time he took to decide whether a given letter belonged to the positive set—could be better described by a hypothesis of serial scanning or by one of parallel search.

II. Method

A. APPARATUS AND GENERAL PROCEDURE

The stimuli, lower-case letters (Letra-Set Schoolhouse type), were mounted onto 2-in. slides and were displayed on a Keystone rear-projection screen by means of a Kodak Carousel 650 slide projector. Each appeared 1.5 in. high on the screen and was viewed by the subject from a distance of approximately 2 ft.

Reaction times were measured by a Hunter Model 120A Klockounter and were recorded manually. A timing cycle began whenever a photo-relay was activated by a newly projected slide, and it terminated whenever a noise-operated relay (Hunter Model 325S) was activated by the subject's vocal response. Each trial was initiated by the experimenter and was preceded by a verbal warning. The click of a slide's dropping into place in the projector (some 250 msec before the onset of the visual stimulus) served as an additional signal. The stimulus subsequently remained in view until the subject had made his response. The interval between trials was approximately 2 sec.

B. EXPERIMENTAL CONDITIONS

Each of 8 subjects served in 10 experimental sessions on 10 consecutive weekdays. A given session lasted for approximately 45 min and included a block of trials that represented one of five experimental conditions. The conditions were distinguished by the number of letters included in the positive set—either 1, 3, 6, 9, or 12—and will henceforth be designated as *conditions*, *1*, *3*, . . . , and *12*. For one group of four subjects, the positive set included the letters *a, abc, abc · · · f, abc · · · i,* or *abc · · · l*; while the negative set included the letters *z, xyz, uvw · · · z, rst · · · z,* or *opq · · · z*, respectively. For the other four subjects, the positive sets were *l, jkl, ghi · · · l, def · · · l,* and *abc · · · l*; and the corresponding negative sets were *o, opq, opq · · · t, opq · · · w,* and *opq · · · z*. Two of the four individuals in each group underwent the conditions, labeled according to set size, in the order 1 through 12 and then 12 through 1; the other two underwent them in the order 12 through 1 and then 1 through 12.

Each such block of *classification trials* included 144 stimuli. They were presented one at a time, and the subject was to decide whether each was a member of the positive set. He was to say "Yes" if he though that it was; otherwise he was to say "No." Positive and negative stimuli were equally likely to occur within each block, as were the specific exemplars of each. The order in which they were presented was unsystematic, subject to the restriction that the sequence of positive and negative responses be exactly the same under each condition.

C. CONTROL CONDITIONS

1. Both before and after each block of 144 experimental trials, the subject also underwent a similar series of 36 trials (to give a total of 72 per session) in which he did not classify the stimuli but simply called out their names. The original purpose of these *naming trials* was to determine whether the time taken to classify a letter depended in any way on the time taken to identify it. (The assumption that an item must be fully identified before it is classified proved to be suspect. The latencies recorded on the naming trials proved to be of interest in and of themselves, however, and will be described independently of the experimental data.)

2. In another set of control trials, administered at the end of the fifth experimental session, the subject, on preinstructions from the experimenter, simply called out the name of each letter of the alphabet (with the exception of *m* and *n*) or the word "yes" or "no" at the onset of a red light. (The slide projector was not employed in this phase of the study.) The time elapsing between the onset of the light and the subject's response was measured in the same way as before. The reason for including this task was to determine whether there were any large or systematic differences in the amount of time taken to activate the noise-operated relay by the various vocal responses that were required of the subject.

3. Under a third and final control condition (*condition* 0), the subject saw either a given letter (always an *a* or an *l*) or no letter at all projected on the screen (in which case he saw a protracted flash of light). His task was to say "Yes" if he saw a letter (which he did 50% of the time) and to say nothing if he did not. Otherwise the procedure was the same as under the various experimental conditions. Each subject underwent a total of 144 such trials after he had completed the last experimental session. In effect, therefore, this block of trials actually comprised an eleventh experimental session. The purpose of the task was to arrive at some estimate of the subject's vocal reaction time when he saw a letter just as he had in the experiment proper but did not have to identify it or classify it. (This latency, of course, should be somewhat longer than a simple reaction

time, since the subject did have to make a discrimination, even though it was a very crude one. The reason for including the blank trials was to prevent the subjects from anticipating the verbal stimulus.)

At the beginning of the first experimental session, the subject was given detailed instructions with respect to both the naming and classification tasks. He was admonished always to respond both as rapidly and as accurately as possible. These instructions were followed by 36 practice trials in which each member of a mixed series of red and blue slides projected on the Keystone screen was responded to with the name of its color. The subject then was asked to classify each member of a similar series of stimuli as either red or not red. The proper responses were "yes" to a red stimulus and "no" to a blue one. Finally, the subject was told which letters he was to name or classify throughout the remainder of the session. He received similar instructions (but did not view the colored slides) at the beginning of each subsequent session.

The subjects, paid volunteers, were students or laboratory assistants of both sexes. All were in their late teens or early twenties. None had ever served in an experiment of this sort.

III. Results

A. Errors and Practice Effects

No latency associated with an incorrect response was included in the analysis of the results. The overall incidence of erroneous classifications was low (less than 5%) and did not vary systematically across the five experimental conditions. Neither did the incidence of naming errors, which amounted to approximately 1%. Preliminary analysis of the classification data revealed the existence of practice effects for both groups of subjects, such that reaction times were slightly but consistently lower during the second half of the experiment than during the first. No systematic trends were evident across sessions 6–10, however.

The reader will recall that one of the control tasks, condition 0, wherein letters were not to be named or classified but simply responded to on being seen, was not administered until the end of the experiment. The latencies recorded under that condition conceivably can provide an empirical estimate of a value that seems frequently to have been discussed but seldom measured—namely, the zero intercept of the function relating reaction time to the number of different stimuli to be responded to. In order to make that value as comparable as possible to those observed under Conditions 1–12, and in view of the practice effects just described, the data for the first five sessions were discarded.

B. CLASSIFICATION LATENCIES

The first question to be asked with respect to the classification times is whether the latencies of positive and negative responses were in any way different. As may be seen in Table 1, they were in fact effectively identical under each of the five experimental conditions (negative responses taking about 3 msec less, on the average, than positive ones), and they were pooled accordingly wherever possible. What this result means is that, everyday intuition and common sense notwithstanding, the subject probably conducted an exhaustive rather than a self-terminating search of the positive set before making his response. Otherwise the latencies associated with negative responses should have exceeded those associated with responses to positive stimuli, or should in any event have increased at a different rate with set size. (This result would also be consistent with an exhaustive search of either the negative set only, or of both sets; or with a self-terminating search, originating at some random point, of both sets. In postexperimental interviews, however, the subjects consistently declared that they had dealt with the positive set. It will accordingly be assumed that they did. This assumption, of course, it subject to future empirical verification. One means of verifying it would be to vary the size of the negative set while holding constant the size of the positive set.)

The next question to be asked is whether some letters where more difficult to classify than others. Inspection of the mean classification times measured under condition 12 (the only condition under which every subject saw all of the 24 letters presented in the experiment) suggested that it did take somewhat longer to say "yes" or "no" to letters in the middle of the alphabet than to letters at either extreme. An analysis of variance performed on the times taken by each individual to classify each letter under condition 12 indicated that this tendency was not statistically reliable, however; $F(8, 24) < 1.00$.

Table 1.   *Mean Classification Time (in milliseconds) for Positive and Negative Stimuli as a Function of the Size of the Positive Set.*

	Stimulus	
Condition	Positive	Negative
1	347.1	340.2
3	385.4	383.7
6	427.0	419.1
9	455.0	453.0
12	482.0	483.5

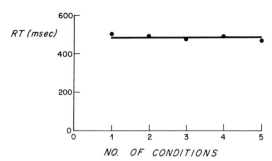

Fig. 1. Mean time to classify a letter under condition 12 as a function of the total number of conditions under which it was presented.

In Fig. 1 the classification latencies measured under condition 12 have been averaged across letters that were presented under an equal number of conditions. Thus, the leftmost point in this figure represents the mean time taken to classify those letters that appeared only under condition 12 (*j, k, l, o, p, q* for one group of subjects and *a, b, c, x, y, z* for the other), whereas the rightmost point represents the average time taken to classify those that appeared under all five of conditions 1–12 (*a* and *z* or *l* and *o*, respectively). Here it is quite evident that the time taken to classify a given letter did not depend on how frequently it was seen throughout the course of the experiment. That this time did vary with the number of letters to be classified under a given condition—that is, with the size of the positive set—is quite evident in the results shown in the next two figures.

Figure 2 shows mean classification time as a function of the size of the positive set. Each point is based on approximately 1100 observations.

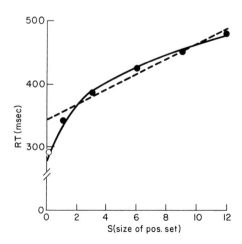

Fig. 2. Mean classification time as a function of the number of letters in the positive set. The dashed [RT = 341.95 + 12.23S] and the solid [RT = 273.24 + 64.47$f(S)$] lines are the theoretical functions which best describe the filled circles according to the serial and the parallel hypotheses, respectively.

The rectilinear function has been fitted by a method of least squares to the data gathered under conditions 1–12 and represented by the five filled circles. If it is assumed that a serial and exhaustive search of the positive set's representation in memory precedes each response, then it can be said that each target letter requires approximately 12 msec to be inspected. The open circle plotted at the zero intercept represents the average latency (283 msec) measured under condition 0 (wherein the subject responded "Yes" to a given letter without having to identify or categorize it); it lies considerably below the value of 343 msec predicted by the rectilinear function. The standard error of estimate (calculated for the five rightmost points in Fig. 2) is 7.09 msec. If one ignores the empirical estimate of the zero intercept, then a rectilinear function appears to describe the classification data very adequately.

The question now to be considered is whether a hypothesis of parallel search can fit them equally well. The simplest such model assumes that the inspection times associated with the various items share a common exponential distribution, such that the probability of observing a reaction time of $t + k$ msec when the positive set contains only one item is

$$f_{a,1}(t) = ae^{-at} + k. \tag{1}$$

Here the constant k is the time taken to preprocess (Smith, 1968) a stimulus and initiate a response (or, alternatively, to perform all of those acts that do not include classifying the stimulus), and a is a constant that characterizes the rate at which stimuli are classified. The expected value of the time taken to perform an exhaustive parallel search of S items in memory (Christie & Luce, 1956; Feller, 1966; Rapoport, 1959) is $1/a(1 + \frac{1}{2} + \cdots + 1/S) + k$. (For large values of S, interestingly enough, it can be shown that this formula is approximately equivalent to $b \log_2 S + c$. Thus, an information-theory and a parallel-search model could at times be very difficult to distinguish one from the other.)

The hypothesis just described has been applied to the results of the present experiment and is represented by the solid curve in Fig. 2. In accordance with the model, the independent variable $f(S)$ was defined as $(1 + \frac{1}{2} + \frac{1}{3} + \cdots + 1/S)$; the curved line was fitted by a method of least squares to reaction times as a function of $f(S)$. The data gathered under condition 0 and represented by the open circle were not included in the calculations. According to the model, the average amount of time required to inspect one item is approximately 64 msec, while the residual component of the reaction times is approximately 273 msec. The standard error of estimate—again excluding the point representing Condition 0—was 6.92 msec (as opposed to 7.09 for the rectilinear function). A parallel-search hypothesis therefore provides a somewhat more accurate description of the data than does a serial model, even when the empirical estimate of the zero intercept is not taken into consideration.[3]

C. NAMING LATENCIES

We originally had intended to perform a stage analysis of the data, whereby the time taken to see and name a given letter would be subtracted from the time taken to see it and denote to which subset of the alphabet it belonged. We had hoped thereby to estimate the time required simply to classify an item as a member of a particular subseries, independently of the time taken to identify it and then generate an appropriate response. Our initial hypothesis was that, in the classification task, the subject initially perceived, or preprocessed, a stimulus; he then identified it; he then classified it; and he then finally responded "yes" or "no." We presumed that in the naming task, on the other hand, he had only to perceive it, identify it, and initiate the appropriate response. (Fortunately enough, the times taken either to say "yes" or "no" or to pronounce a given letter name, as measured under the second control condition, were all effectively equivalent. Therefore, the time taken to *initiate* a preselected response was effectively the same under all conditions, and need not be taken into consideration in any comparison of naming and classification latencies.)

The data that we obtained, however, were difficult to reconcile with our hypothesis. Some subjects occasionally took longer to name certain letters than they did to classify them, so that the results of the stage analysis were untidy and not very enlightening and therefore probably not worth describing to the reader in any detail. It would appear that two basic processes—the complete identification of a letter, including the retrieval of its name, and its classification as a member of a familiar subset (such as *abc* or *xyz*)—occur in parallel (at least to some extent) rather than in series. This conclusion is consistent with the suggestions made by Davis, *et al.* (1961) and by Neisser (1967) to the effect that very familiar decisions can become preattentive; it is also consistent with data of a rather different nature reported by Posner (1970), which indicate that the name of an item need not necessarily be retrieved before the item is classified as a digit or

---

[3]When this value (283 msec) is in fact included in the least-squares calculations, the parallel-search hypothesis provides a much more accurate description of the data. According to the serial-search model, inspection time per item is now approximately 15 msec (as opposed to 12), and the residual reaction time is approximately 321 msec (as opposed to 342). The parallel-search model, on the other hand, now predicts an average inspection time of 60 msec per item (as opposed to 64) and an intercept of 286 msec (as opposed to 273). The standard error of estimate is now considerably larger for the rectilinear than for the curvilinear function (17.18 versus 7.64 msec, respectively).

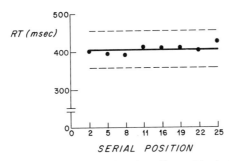

Fig. 3.   Mean time to name a letter as a function of its position in the alphabet (estimated across successive, nonoverlapping groups of three, and excluding *m* and *n*).

a letter. What the result seems to mean in the present context is that the subject need not become fully aware that a given symbol is, for instance, the letter *e* before he begins to decide that it belongs in the first half of the alphabet.

In accordance with data reported by other investigators, the results of the present study indicate that naming latencies do depend to some degree on the size of the ensemble of items to be named. Figure 3 indicates that the time taken to name a given letter as such did not vary systematically nor to any great extent with its serial position in the alphabet. Figure 4 is analogous to Fig. 2. The rectilinear function was fitted by a method of least squares to the reaction-times measured when the subject was required to discriminate between 2 or among 6, 12, 18, or 24 letters. The data obtained under condition 0 were here again ignored in the calculations. Note that the theoretical intercepts of the functions shown in Figs. 2 and 4 are almost the same (approximately 342 and 339 msec, respectively); but the slopes of the lines are quite different (12.23 msec to classify an item but only 2.94 msec to retrieve its name).

The curvilinear function shown in Fig. 4 was fitted to the naming latencies by the same procedure that was followed with the classification times (see Fig. 2). According to our calculations, the parallel-search model predicts the naming latencies much better than does the hypothesis of serial search even when condition 0 is excluded from consideration: the standard errors of estimate are 11.96 and 7.05 msec, for the rectilinear and curvilinear functions, respectively.[4]

---

[4]If the mean reaction time measured under condition 0 *is* included in the least-squares estimates, the parallel-search model fits the data even more closely, the standard error of estimate dropping from 7.05 to 6.51 msec, whereas the serial-search model proves conversely to be less accurate, with the standard error of estimate increasing from 11.96 to 18.60 msec. According to the parallel-search model, the time taken to retrieve a letter's name is 29.91 msec, whereas according to the serial model, it is 4.20 msec. Residual reaction times are 290.26 and 319.34 msec, respectively. The former value is of course much closer to the 283 msec actually measured under condition 0.

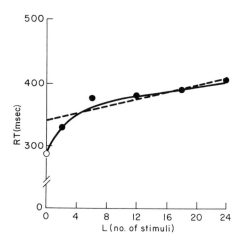

Fig. 4. Mean naming latency as a function of the number of letters to be named. The dashed [$RT = 339.26 + 2.94L$] and the solid [$RT = 287.54 + 30.79f(L)$] lines are the theoretical functions which best describe the filled circles according to the serial and the parallel hypotheses, respectively.

Since the greatest increment in reaction times occurred when the number of letters to be named or classified increased from 2 to 6, we wondered whether the latencies measured under the former condition could have been contaminated by a "repetition effect" (Bertelson, 1961), such that a given stimulus would be responded to relatively rapidly when it was the same as its immediate predecessor and relatively slowly otherwise. Runs of two or more identical stimuli occurred frequently under condition 1 and seldom under conditions 3–12. The existence of a repetition effect under condition 1 would thereby tend to reduce the mean reaction times measured under that condition relative to those measured under condition 3. It accordingly might lend a spurious curvilinearity to the function relating reaction time to the number of alternative stimuli: what would otherwise be a straight line with zero slope for the classification times would instead appear to be a monotonically increasing, negatively accelerated function. This hypothesis was not supported by the data, however; some subjects responded relatively rapidly to stimulus alternations and others, to stimulus repetitions. The net effect was that alternated and repeated stimuli were responded to with equal speed, on the average.

We also analyzed the data exactly as described above but including only the letters *a* and *z* or *l* and *o*, each of those pairs being the only two stimuli that were responded to under every condition by a given individual. The results of this analysis were almost exactly the same as those illustrated in Figs. 2 and 4. In the interest of reliability, therefore, we have chosen to describe the mean latencies estimated across all of the letters responded to under a given condition.

IV. Discussion

The results of the present study may be summarized as follows:

1. When a subject must decide whether a given letter occurs in a given portion of the alphabet, the time that it takes him to do so can be described quite accurately by a hypothesis that assumes a serial and exhaustive search of the subseries of letters in question. His reaction time can be predicted somewhat more accurately, however, by a hypothesis that assumes an exhaustive but parallel scanning of that set, wherein the individual letters share a common and exponentially distributed inspection time.

2. If an empirically estimated zero intercept of the function relating reaction time to number of stimuli is taken into consideration, the parallel-search hypothesis fits the data much more closely than its serial-search counterpart. (In order to draw this conclusion, of course, one must be willing to assume that the latencies measured under condition 0 provide a valid measure of that point—that is, of the time that it takes an individual to make exactly the same reaction to exactly the same stimulus as under conditions 1–12, but without his having to classify the stimulus before initiating his response.)

3. A parallel-search hypothesis predicts the time taken to identify and name the letters in a well-defined ensemble more precisely than does a hypothesis of serial search, both when the empirical zero intercept (as defined above) is considered and when it is not. The parallel model, more-over, predicts zero intercepts for both the naming and classification functions that are very similar to each other and to the value actually observed. The serial model does not. The repeated coincidence between the zero intercept as predicted by the parallel-search hypothesis and the condition-10 data, as observed in both the naming and the classification tasks, is striking and suggestive.

4. The data evidently fail to support the hypothesis that the com-plete identification of a letter and its classification are independent pro-cesses that do not overlap in time. Evidently the two processes do overlap in time, so that binary classification seems to proceed on the basis of in-complete identification.

The absolute values measured for the classification times of stimuli in extremely familiar lists are considerably lower than any reported previously; the average value of approximately 13 msec per item observed in the present study is considerably less than the 40 or so msec reported for the retrieval of digits from unfamiliar lists in "active" memory, and it is even less than the 100 or so msec reported for their retrieval from "inactive" memory (Sternberg, 1969). The average increment in naming latency per item with increasing ensemble size was much smaller. The value of approximately 3.5 msec measured in the present study is consistent with values reported by Davis *et al.* (1961), by Brainard *et al.* (1962), and by Morin *et al.* (1965).

One is almost forced to conclude, on the basis of the data described above, that information which is presumably stored in secondary or "inactive" memory, such as an initially unfamiliar list of letters memorized at the beginning of one experimental session (Sternberg, 1969), is retrieved in a very different way from information which has been very highly overlearned and which may thereby be said to reside in tertiary (Waugh, 1970a), as opposed to secondary, memory. Information that is stored in secondary memory is recalled relatively slowly, while information in primary memory (Waugh, 1970b) is recalled relatively rapidly; information in tertiary memory is recalled even more rapidly (Waugh & Holstein, 1968). It is as though verbal information were transferred, in the process of being overlearned, from a slow-access store from which it had to be retrieved via a series of steps to a rapid-access store from which it could be retrieved directly.

In summary, then, the results of this study are by and large more consistent with a hypothesis of parallel search of very long-term verbal memory than with one of serial search. Just why this hypothetical parallel search should be exhaustive, rather than self-terminating, is not intuitively obvious. But neither is it intuitively obvious why serial scanning for presence— when it does take place—should be exhaustive and not self-terminating. It is worth bearing in mind, therefore, that some hypothesis other than the two tested here may fit the data with a greater degree of intuitive plausibility, and perhaps even more closely.

References

Anders, T. R. Retrospective reports of retrieval from short-term memory. *Journal of Experimental Psychology*, 1971, **90**, 251–257.

Bertelson, P. Sequential redundancy and speed in a serial two-choice responding task. *Quarterly Journal of Experimental Psychology*, 1961, **12**, 90–102.

Brainard, R. W., Irby, T. S., Fitts, P. M., & Alluisi, E. A. Some variables influencing the rate of gain of information. *Journal of Experimental Psychology*, 1962, **63**, 105–110.

Burrows, D., & Murdock, B. B., Jr. Effects of extended practice on high-speed scanning. *Journal of Experimental Psychology*, 1969, **82**, 231–237.

Christie, L. S., and Luce, R. D. Decision structure and time relations in simple choice behavior. *Bulletin of Mathematical Biophysics*, 1956, **18**, 89–112.

Davis, R., Moray, N., & Treisman, A. Imitative responses and the rate of gain of information. *Quarterly Journal of Experimental Psychology*, 1961, **13**, 78–89.

Feller, W. *An introduction to probability theory and its applications.* Vol. II. New York: Wiley, 1966.

Morin, R. E., & Forrin, B. Mixing of two types of S–R associations in a choice reaction time task. *Journal of Experimental Psychology*, 1962, **64**, 137–141.

Morin, R. E., Konick, A., Troxell, N., & McPherson, S. Information and reaction time for "naming" responses. *Journal of Experimental Psychology*, 1965, **70**, 309–314.

Mowbray, G. H., & Rhoades, M. V. On the reduction of choice reaction times with practice. *Quarterly Journal of Experimental Psychology*, 1959, **11**, 16–23.

Neisser, U. *Cognitive psychology.* New York: Appleton, 1967.

Posner, M. I. On the relationship between letter names and superordinate categories. *Quarterly Journal of Experimental Psychology*, 1970, **22**, 279–287.

Rapoport, A. A study of disjunctive reaction times. *Behavioral Science*, 1959, **4**, 229–315.

Smith, E. E. Choice reaction time: an analysis of the major theoretical positions. *Psychological Bulletin*, 1968, **69**, 77–110.

Sternberg, S. High-speed scanning in human memory. *Science*, 1966, **153**, 652–654.

Sternberg, S. Retrieval of contextual information from memory. *Psychonomic Science*, 1967, **8**, 55–56. (a)

Sternberg, S. Two operations in character recognition: some evidence from reaction-time measurements. *Perception and Psychophysics*, 1967, **2**, 45–53. (b)

Sternberg, S. Memory-scanning: mental processes revealed by reaction-time experiments. *American Scientist*, 1969, **57**, 421–457.

Theios, J., Smith, P. G., Haviland, S. E., & Traupmann, J. Memory scanning is a serial, self-terminating process. Report 71–1, Wisconsin Mathematical Psychology Program, 1971.

Waugh, N. C. Primary and secondary memory in short-term retention. In K. Pribram & D. E. Broadbent (Eds.), *Biology of memory.* New York: Academic Press, 1970. (a)

Waugh, N. C. Retrieval time in short-term memory. *British Journal of Psychology*, 1970, **61**, 1–12. (b)

Waugh, N. C., & Holstein, E. C. Recall latencies of highly overlearned items. *Psychonomic Science*, 1968, **11**, 143.

Waugh, N. C., & Norman, D. A. Primary memory. *Psychological Review*, 1965, **72**, 89–104.

Wingfield, A., & Branca, A. A. Strategy in high-speed memory search. *Journal of Experimental Psychology*, 1970, **83**, 63–67.

Verifying Affirmative and Negative Propositions: Effects of Negation on Memory Retrieval

David E. Meyer

Bell Telephone Laboratories
Murray Hill, New Jersey

ABSTRACT

Some current theories of sentence processing assume that negation does not influence the duration of memory retrieval during sentence verification. This assumption was tested by measuring reaction time of true-false judgments of affirmative and negative propositions about semantic categories, for example, SOME DOCTORS ARE MALES and NO ELMS ARE METALS. Effects of the set relation between categories and of category size were larger for negatives than for affirmatives. The results support the view that sentence negation requires extra processing capacity, and thereby reduces the rate of searching long-term memory.

I. Introduction: The Problem of Sentence Negation

In psycholinguistic research, the problem of sentence negation has received considerable attention (Clark, in press; Gough, 1965; Greene, 1970; McMahon, 1963; Miller, 1962; Slobin, 1966; Wales & Grieve, 1969; Wason, 1959, 1961, 1965). One major finding from this work is that negative sentences are usually harder to understand than affirmatives. There are several possible explanations for the greater difficulty of negatives. Following the work of Chomsky (1957), one prominent view has been that negation influences the forming of a sentence representation, or "deep structure." For example, Miller and McKean (1964) suggested that negative sentences may require an extra operation, which transforms them into a positive format.

A. The Encoding and Comparison Model

A more elaborate, but related view has been expressed independently by Chase and Clark (in press), and by Trabasso (1970). Their theory explains how a person makes true–false judgments about whether sentences correctly describe specified referents, such as pictures and other classes of objects. According to the theory, there are four separate stages in sentence verification. During stages 1 and 2, respectively, representations are formed of the sentence and the objects that it describes. Then in stage 3, these representations are compared. Depending on whether they match in prescribed ways, a response of either "true" or "false" is executed in stage 4.

This *encoding and comparison* (EC) *model* can be applied to situations where either the referents of a sentence are within immediate view, or information about them is stored in memory (Clark, in press; Trabasso, Rollins, & Shaughnessy, 1971).[1] The following example illustrates one possible application. Suppose that a person must judge the truth of the statement FIVE IS SMALLER THAN THIRTEEN (see McMahon, 1963). Here the referents are the integers 5 and 13. The model holds that in stage 1, a representation is formed of the order relation asserted by the sentence, for example, "5 < 13." In stage 2, a representation of the true order relation between the referents is formed from memory, for example, "5 < 13." Then in stage 3 the two representations are compared, and because they match, a "true" response is produced in stage 4. On the other hand, events are somewhat different in judging the statement FIVE IS NOT SMALLER THAN THIRTEEN. For this case, stage 1 results in a sentence representation like "5 ≮ 13",[2] whereas the output of stage 2 is again "5 < 13." When the two representations are compared during stage 3, a mismatch occurs, so that a "false" response is produced in stage 4.

The model is testable with reaction time (RT) data from true-false judgments of sentences (Chase & Clark, in press; Trabasso, 1970). Under certain circumstances (for example, McMahon, 1963, Experiment IIIa; Slobin, 1966), it has been found that RTs are longer for negative sentences and also for false ones. Here the model would presume that negation increases sentence-encoding time (stage 1) and that falsehood increases comparison time (stage 3). When such effects of negation and truth value occur, the model implies that they should be additive, because sentence encoding and

---

[1] It should be noted that the present discussion by necessity oversimplifies the original model, which incorporates a number of special cases (Chase & Clark, in press; Clark, in press; Trabasso, 1970). For example, the full model permits reversing the order of stages 1 and 2, and includes several different forms of representation for the sentence and its referents.

[2] Here the symbol ≮ denotes "not less than."

comparison are separate stages (see Sternberg, 1969). Despite variability in the data, at least some evidence has been interpreted as supporting this additivity prediction.

Other properties of the model have not been tested fully. In particular, the model makes two important assumptions: (*a*) representations of the sentence and its referents are formed successively, and (*b*) negation does not affect the time to create a representation of the referents. Thus, for sentences that describe pictures in immediate view, the model assumes that negation does not affect the duration of picture encoding during stage 2. Similarly, for sentences such that stage 2 relies on stored information about the referents, it is assumed that negation does not affect the duration of memory retrieval. This last point is illustrated by the above example concerning numerical sentences, for which the model would presume that negation does not affect the time to retrieve a representation of the true order relation between integers.

B. A Reaction-Time Method for Studying Negation and Memory Retrieval

This contribution outlines and uses a method for discovering possible effects of negation on memory retrieval, thereby testing the EC model and other theories of sentence processing. The method involves measuring RT of true–false judgments about logical propositions concerning semantic categories (Meyer, 1970). Like other approaches (Chase & Clark, in press; Trabasso, 1970), it examines predictions of additive effects on RT, but of a different sort than studied previously.

Results are reported here for two types of proposition: *particular affirmatives* (PA) having the form SOME S ARE P, and *universal negatives* (UN) having the form NO S ARE P. In each proposition, the symbols "S" and "P" denote the *subject category* and *predicate category*, respectively. From the two types of proposition, actual test stimuli are constructed with semantic categories (for example, DOCTORS and MALES) as subject and predicate categories, yielding propositions like SOME DOCTORS ARE MALES and NO DOCTORS ARE MALES.

There are several reasons for studying PAs and UNs together. First, one proposition is affirmative and the other negative, yet both include the same number of words. Second, the propositions express fundamental information about semantic categories. Third, differences in judging PAs and UNs cannot be attributed to differences in the knowledge they require, since both types of proposition concern whether S and P *intersect*, that is, have common exemplars. For example, if a person says SOME DOCTORS ARE

MALES, then he is asserting that there is at least one DOCTOR who is a MALE.[3] On the other hand, this assertion is denied if he says NO DOCTORS ARE MALES. Thus, the same information about DOCTORS and MALES must be retrieved to evaluate either proposition.

Certain variables are already known to affect judgments about whether two categories interesect (Meyer, 1970). One variable is the *set relation* of S to P. There are four possible set relations between nonidentical subject and predicate categories:

1. S is a *subset* of P, for example, HOTELS are a subset of BUILDINGS.
2. S is a *superset* of P, for example, FLUIDS are a superset of WINES.
3. S and P partially *overlap*, for example, DOCTORS and MALES overlap.
4. S and P are *disjoint*, for example, ELMS and METALS are disjoint.

In each of the first three relations, S intersects P. The set relation between S and P determines the truth value of PAs and UNs. Particular affirmatives are true for the subset, superset, and overlap relations, whereas universal negatives are true for the disjoint relation.

Another critical variable is *category size*, which refers to the number of exemplars that S and P contain. While there are several ways to vary category size, the present experiment employs a method introduced by Landauer and Freedman (1968). It involves sampling pairs of nested categories, for example, DOCTORS and PERSONS, where one category is by definition a subset of the other. When used as subject or predicate categories, such nested pairs provide a natural variation in category size. A "small" category like DOCTORS or a "large" category like PERSONS can be substituted in the sentence frame SOME———ARE MALES, varying the size of S while maintaining an overlap relation between S and P.

C. Application of the Model to Judging PAs and UNs

If the EC model is correct, then as depicted by Fig. 1, the following sequence of operations ought to occur in judging PAs and UNs. First, the proposition is encoded during stage 1. The output of this process presumably

---

[3]In typical usage, PAs are sometimes interpreted to mean SOME BUT NOT ALL S ARE P, which differs from their formal meaning as used in the present experiment. However, people quickly learn the correct logical meaning if they do not already know it. For example, propositions like SOME HOTELS ARE BUILDINGS soon lead to the most rapid and accurate "true" responses (Meyer, 1970), even though such propositions are false under the common "misinterpretation" of PAs mentioned above.

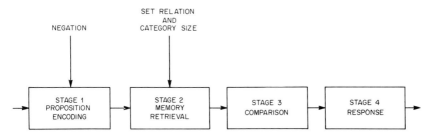

Fig. 1. Application of the EC model to judging particular affirmatives and universal negatives. Horizontal arrows indicate the sequence of operations during a judgment. Vertical arrows show the influence of negation, set relation, and category size on these stages.

represents what the proposition asserts. When the proposition is SOME S ARE P, then stage 1 has an output like "S ∩ P,"[4] since PAs assert that the subject category intersects the predicate category. Conversely, UNs would be represented as "S ⋒ P." In stage 2, stored information about the referents is retrieved to form a representation of whether S and P actually intersect; for example, when memory reveals that the two categories are disjoint, stage 2 has a result like "S ⋒ P." Then during stage 3, the outputs of the first two stages are compared. Depending on whether a match is found, a true–false response occurs in Stage 4. For example, these four operations should be executed in judging the proposition NO DOCTORS ARE MALES. Because this proposition asserts that DOCTORS and MALES are disjoint categories, encoding it (stage 1) would represent S and P as categories that do not intersect. However, retrieving information from memory (stage 2) should reveal that DOCTORS and MALES have members in common; the output of the second operation would thus represent S and P as intersecting categories. When the results of the first two stages are then compared, a mismatch ought to occur (stage 3), leading to a "false" response (stage 4).

D. PREDICTIONS OF THE EC MODEL

Based on previous research (Meyer, 1970), one may suppose that set relation and category size affect the duration of memory retrieval (stage 2). Now suppose further that negation does not affect retrieval, but has an effect on sentence encoding (stage 1), as proposed by Chase and Clark (in press), and by Trabasso (1970). Then the assumed influence of these factors is indicated by the vertical arrows in Fig. 1. Since the model involves a series of stages, the

---

[4]Here the symbol ∩ denotes the relation of set intersection.

effect of negation is expressible as an additive component of RT, which is a sum of stage durations (Sternberg, 1969). The model therefore predicts that the effect of negation should not interact with effects of set relation and category size. This is also a property of related models (see Miller & McKean, 1964) that assume negation adds an extra stage to sentence processing. The property can be tested by searching for significant effects of negation, set relation, and category size. Wherever these occur, the set-relation and category-size effects should be quantitatively the same for UNs as for PAs (Sternberg, 1969). In contrast, if negation influences memory retrieval, one might expect to find a systematic pattern of interactions.

At the same time, one must note an inherent limitation of the method. The factors of negation and set relation are confounded with truth value. PAs are false only for the disjoint relation, and in this case, UNs are true. Certain interactions of negation with set relation thus fail to provide a firm test of the EC model. In particular, it is known that RT for judging PAs is shorter when S and P intersect than when they are disjoint (Meyer, 1970). If the magnitude of this set-relation effect is less for UNs, one may conclude nothing from it about the influence of negation on memory retrieval. Such an interaction could result from an effect of truth value. If there is a bias favoring "true" responses, as has been found in some experiments (Clark, in press; Trabasso et al., 1971), then RT would ordinarily tend to be shorter for UNs when S and P are disjoint than when they intersect. Because of this, the discussion below gives more emphasis to the three set relations in which S intersects P.

II. Procedure

Twelve employees at Bell Laboratories were divided randomly into two groups of six subjects each. The subjects were run individually for two 1-hr sessions. During the first session, subjects in group 1 judged the truth of UNs, while subjects in group 2 judged PAs. During the second session, the tasks of the two groups were interchanged.[5]

A session included three practice blocks and six test blocks of 24 trials. On each trial, the subject was presented with a visual ready signal, which consisted of a sentence frame for the proposition to be judged, for example,

---

[5]The design thus had the property that during a session, subjects were never uncertain about whether a UN or PA would be presented next. This means that the effects of negation reported later cannot be attributed to a lesser expectancy for negative propositions.

SOME ——————— ARE ——————— . The display was similar to that described by Meyer (1970, Experiment II). When the subject was ready, he pressed a foot-switch that started a 1-sec foreperiod. At the end of the foreperiod, the blanks of the frame were filled with the names of two categories. The subject read the proposition and decided whether it was true or false. He pressed a key with the right index finger to respond "true" or another key with the left index finger to respond "false." Reaction time was measured in milliseconds from the onset of the complete proposition until the response. The subject was instructed to respond as quickly and accurately as possible. Immediately after each trial, he was informed about the speed and accuracy of the re-sponse, after which there was a 2-sec intertrial interval. The stimuli were presented in a random order on each trial block, and half of the propositions were true.

A total of 864 propositions served as test stimuli, of which 144 PAs and 144 UNs were used for any one subject. The presentation of the test stimuli was balanced across subjects. In half the propositions presented to a subject, S and P were disjoint; the other three set relations were represented with equal frequencies in the remaining half. Stimuli were chosen on the basis of dictionary definition (*Webster's Third New International Dictionary*, 1964). The manipulation of set relation and category size was similar to that de-scribed by Meyer (1970, Experiment II). The propositions were grouped

Table 1. *Examples of Particular Affirmatives in Which Set Relation and Category Size Vary*

Set relation	Truth value	S size	P size	Particular affirmatives
Subset	True	Small Large	Constant	SOME THRONES ARE FURNITURE SOME CHAIRS ARE FURNITURE
Superset	True	Small Large	Constant	SOME ROCKS ARE GRANITE SOME SOLIDS ARE GRANITE
Overlap	True	Small Large	Constant	SOME DOCTORS ARE MALES SOME PERSONS ARE MALES
Disjoint	False	Small Large	Constant	SOME TROUSERS ARE BRIDGES SOME GARMENTS ARE BRIDGES
Subset	True	Constant	Small Large	SOME HOTELS ARE BUILDINGS SOME HOTELS ARE STRUCTURES
Superset	True	Constant	Small Large	SOME FLUIDS ARE WINES SOME FLUIDS ARE DRINKS
Overlap	True	Constant	Small Large	SOME PETS ARE DUCKS SOME PETS ARE BIRDS
Disjoint	False	Constant	Small Large	SOME ELMS ARE STEELS SOME ELMS ARE METALS

into pairs for each set relation of S to P. In half of these pairs, the size of S varied, whereas P was constant; in the other half, the size of P varied, whereas S was constant. Words used for the different set relations and levels of category size were approximately matched in frequency (Thorndike & Lorge, 1944) and length. The same categories appeared in both PAs and UNs. Examples of the types of PAs used as test stimuli are shown in Table 1. The upper half contains pairs of propositions in which the size of S varies for each set relation, while P is constant. In the lower half, the size of P varies and S is constant. Corresponding UNs were obtained by replacing the quantifier SOME with the quantifier NO, which reverses the truth value for each set relation.

III. Results

A treatments-by-subjects analysis of variance (Winer, 1962) was performed on mean RTs of correct responses. The relative frequency of errors was approximately .09 averaged over subjects. Mean error rates were similar for PAs and UNs, and otherwise tended to correlate positively with mean RTs.

A. Main Effects of Negation and Set Relation

Mean RTs of correct responses, averaged over category size and subjects, are shown in Fig. 2 as a function of proposition type and the three set relations where S intersected P. For reasons discussed at the end of Section I, data from the disjoint relation shall be considered later. In Fig. 2, mean RTs for UNs are over 200 msec longer than for PAs. The main effect of negation was significant at the .05 level; $F(1,10) = 9.9$.[6] The main effect of set relation was significant at the .01 level; $F(2,20) = 10.6$. The mean RT was approximately 86 msec longer for the overlap relation than for the subset relation. Interactions between the effects of set relation and negation are discussed below.

B. Main Effects of Category Size

Table 2 presents mean RTs as a function of category size, with the data averaged separately for the subset, superset, and disjoint relations. Results in the upper half of the table show the effects of varying the size of S, while

---

[6]Here and elsewhere, error terms for the reported F ratios were derived from the interactions of treatments by subjects within groups.

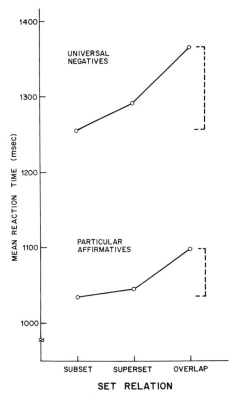

Fig. 2. Mean RT for particular affirmatives and universal negatives as a function of set relation. Dashed braces indicate the comparative magnitudes of the set-relation effect for the two types of proposition.

those in the lower half give the effects of varying P. The design requires this kind of comparison for two reasons: either S or P was constant while the size of the other varied; different categories were used in changing the sizes of S and P for a given set relation. F ratios in the right column indicate the statistical significance of the category-size effects for each relation. These effects ranged from approximately 50 to 150 msec in magnitude. Data for the overlap relation have been omitted because neither the main effect of category size nor its interaction with negation was statistically significant in this case; $F(1,10) < 1.0$.[7]

_____

[7] The failure to find a category-size effect for the overlap relation is consistent with results of previous research involving PAs (Meyer, 1970, Experiment II). Because of this failure, manipulating category size in the overlap relation does not provide a firm test of the EC model. In order to test a theory of stages by looking for additivity between two factors like negation and category size, both factors must have significant main effects or they must interact significantly (Sternberg, 1969).

Table 2. *Mean RT as a Function of Category Size and Proposition Type*

Set relation	S size	P size	Mean RT (msec) PA	UN	F(1, 10)
Subset	Small Large	Constant	1088 1012	1326 1194	23.2***
Superset	Small Large	Constant	973 1109	1173 1350	58.6***
Disjoint	Small Large	Constant	1160 1177	1302 1380	8.4*
Subset	Constant	Small Large	953 1084	1170 1332	13.8**
Superset	Constant	Small Large	1097 998	1389 1254	12.7**
Disjoint	Constant	Small Large	1150 1205	1314 1386	36.4***

*p < .05.   **p < .01.   ***p < .001.

C. INTERACTIONS OF NEGATION WITH SET RELATION AND CATEGORY SIZE

The most reliable interaction of negation with category size occurred for the disjoint relation, where increasing the size of S produced a 60-msec larger effect for UNs than PAs; $F(1,10) = 3.3$. Neither this nor any other single interaction of negation with category size (Table 2) or set relation (Fig. 2) reached the .05 significance level. Acceptance of the additivity hypothesis on the basis of these data would be consistent with the EC model (Section I). However, the overall pattern of interactions leads one to question the model.[8]

First consider the interaction between negation and set relation, as shown in Fig. 2. Here the magnitude of the set-relation effect depicted by the dashed braces is over 70% larger for negatives than affirmatives (109 msec compared with 63 msec). This difference can be broken into two orthogonal contrasts that both reveal the same pattern: (a) the difference between mean RTs for the superset and subset relations is greater in the case of UNs than

---

[8] In this respect, it is important to remember that a prediction of additivity is a type of null hypothesis. Such a hypothesis may be accepted wrongly if the error terms for testing separate interactions are relatively large. More powerful tests can be obtained by considering whether the pattern of interactions is systematic.

Table 3. *Observed Magnitudes of Category-Size Effects for UNs versus PAs*

Set Relation	Effect of S size (msec)		Effect of P size (msec)	
	PA	UN	PA	UN
Subset	76	132	131	162
Superset	136	177	99	135
Disjoint	17	78	55	72

PAs; (*b*) the difference between the overlap relation and the average from the preceding two relations is also greater for UNs than PAs.

Next consider the results for category size presented in Table 2. In each of the six rows, which involve orthogonal contrasts, the magnitude of the category-size effect is also larger for UNs than PAs; that is, there is a "positive interaction" between the effects of negation and category size. This is seen more clearly in Table 3, which shows absolute values of the differences between mean RTs for small and large categories. Here magnitudes of the category-size effects, viewed as a function of set relation, range from about 20% to over 300% greater for UNs than PAs.

The preceding results include a total of eight orthogonal contrasts that provide tests of the EC model, two for set relation and six for category size. In each case, the effects of these variables were larger in magnitude for UNs than PAs. If the model is correct, this pattern of positive interactions would have to occur by chance, since the model implies that the effects of negation should be additive with those of set relation and category size; that is, the effects of set relation and category size should be the same for UNs and PAs (Section I). As evidence against the model, a simple sign test shows the probability is less than .01 that all the interactions would be in the same direction by chance.

D. EFFECT OF TRUTH VALUE

Table 4 presents mean RT for the disjoint relation, compared to the mean from those relations where S intersected P. Notice that the disjoint relation required more time than the average from the others [$F(1, 10) = 25.0, p < .001$], but that the difference was less in the case of UNs than PAs [$F(1, 10) = 4.0, p < .10$]. This "negative interaction" contrasts with the above positive interactions. However, it is not inconsistent with them, because the results are subject to an effect of truth value arising from a bias in favor of "true" responses (see Section I, D). Such a bias could produce the

Table 4. *Mean RT for the Disjoint
Relation*

Set relation	Mean RT (msec)	
	PA	UN
Disjoint	1173	1346
Intersect	1058	1304

negative interaction, since UNs are true for the disjoint relation, whereas PAs are false. When S and P are disjoint, the bias would tend to decrease RT for UNs and increase it for PAs.

Is the positive interaction between negation and the other set relations (Fig. 2) also due to response bias? Probably not. Here the results for PAs would suggest that the bias to respond "true" was strongest when S was a P subset, since RT of correct ("true") responses to PAs was shortest for the subset relation. This would mean that the bias to respond "false" must have been weakest when S was a P subset. Thus, if response bias was the only contributing factor, RT of correct ("false") responses to UNs should have been longest for the subset relation. But as the results indicate, this did not happen.

Similarly, the positive interactions between negation and category size (Table 3) cannot be explained by an effect of truth value. If the latter factor mediated these interactions, then the effects of category size should have been always larger for false propositions, or always larger for true propositions. But this failed to happen. When S was a subset or superset of P, a larger category-size effect occurred for false propositions (that is, UNs); on the other hand, when S and P were disjoint, the effect of category size was larger for true propositions (that is, UNs again).

IV. Discussion

In some respects, the EC model seems to fit the data reasonably well. It can explain the main effect of negation, which might be attributed to greater difficulty of encoding UNs than PAs (stage 1). The observed effect of truth value also falls within the model's framework (Clark, in press; Trabasso, 1970). However, the pattern of positive interactions of negation with set relation and category size indicates a possible need to revise the model.[9] It appears that in addition to increasing sentence-encoding time, negation may increase the duration of memory retrieval (stage 2), contrary to original assumptions.[10] This would explain why the magnitudes of set-relation and category-size effects were larger for UNs than PAs. The remainder of the chapter outlines one revision of the model that provides for such an influence of negation on retrieval.

Let us start by considering what happens to a sentence representation formed in stage 1, before it enters the comparison process of stage 3. Under the original EC model, nothing was said about how the sentence representation is maintained temporarily during stage 2 (Chase & Clark, in press; Trabasso, 1970). Now make the following further assumptions. Suppose that prior to stage 3, the representation is kept in a short-term store, and that maintaining the store takes processing capacity whose total amount is limited (Broadbent, 1971). Suppose further that the representation of a negative sentence is more complex than an affirmative (Chase & Clark, in press), so that holding a negative representation in short-term storage requires more processing capacity (see Krueger, in press).

Next consider stage 2 of the model. Suppose that for PAs and UNs, this operation entails a retrieval process in which memory is searched to determine whether the subject category actually intersects the predicate category. For example, it has been proposed elsewhere that retrieval may involve searching for the name "S" among stored names of categories that intersect P (Meyer, 1970). On this assumption, the set relation and sizes of S and P influence the number of items searched before the retrieval process terminates; for example, when S and P are disjoint, increasing the size of P in-

---

[9]The data also provide evidence against some related models of sentence processing (Miller & McKean, 1964), which predict no interaction of negation with set relation and category size (Section I).

[10]Alternatively, it is conceivable that the interactions were not caused by negation, but by a difference in *logical mood* such that the negatives were "universal" propositions, whereas the affirmatives were "particular." However, at least two points suggest that negation and not logical mood was the critical variable. First, the RT data for UNs had a pattern different from results obtained earlier for the proposition ALL S ARE P, which is a *universal affirmative* (UA; see Meyer, 1970, Experiment I). If logical mood was an important factor in the present experiment, then results from UNs should have been more similar to those from UAs. Second, if logical mood rather than negation was crucial, then the results in Section III would indicate that *particular negatives* (PN; that is, SOME S AREN'T P) should be more easily judged than UAs. This follows because the experiment reported here produced shorter RTs for "particular" propositions than for "universal" ones. But contrary to the second implication, results of unpublished studies by the author at Bell Laboratories show that RT is actually longer for PNs than for UAs. In addition, other data from these experiments support the conclusion that negation influences memory retrieval.

creases the items searched to determine that S does not intersect P (Meyer, 1970). Finally, suppose that the rate of search depends directly on the amount of available processing capacity, so that decreasing capacity reduces search rate.

Given these added assumptions in the model, it necessarily follows that negation would increase retrieval time, and thereby increase the magnitudes of set-relation and category-size effects. For example, consider judging a proposition in which PENCILS form the subject category and DOGS the predicate category, so that S and P are disjoint. When the proposition is an affirmative like SOME PENCILS ARE DOGS, stage 2 involves searching for the word PENCILS at a rate of r items per millisecond among a total of n words like COLLIES, PETS, MAMMALS, etc., which denote categories that intersect DOGS. Now if the size of P is increased by replacing DOGS with a larger category like ANIMALS, then a total of $n + \Delta n$ items (that is, COLLIES, PETS, MAMMALS, ..., plus words like ELEPHANTS and HORSES) would have to be searched instead. Increasing category size would therefore produce an increase of $\Delta n/r$ msec in total search time for affirmatives. On the other hand, for negative propositions like NO PENCILS ARE DOGS, the search would occur at a reduced rate of $r - \Delta r$ items per millisecond. Hence, the effect of increasing category size on total search time would be $\Delta n/(r - \Delta r)$ msec, which is greater than the effect for affirmatives. Such an interaction is qualitatively consistent with the data observed in the present experiment, and thus the revised model appears to warrent further testing.[11]

In conclusion, there are a number of open questions. It remains uncertain whether the preceding arguments would apply to other types of sentence. Do negative sentences describing pictures within a person's immediate view reduce capacity for picture encoding? Krueger (in press) has collected data that suggest this may be the case. An important problem is to determine the range of situations where one can apply the EC model as originally formulated (Chase & Clark, in press; Trabasso, 1970), and to discover which situations require revising the theory. Of course, the notions suggested here provide only one alternative. Other possibilities are that sentence encoding and memory retrieval may be dependent parallel processes, and factors like set relation and category size may influence sentence

---

[11]One possible test involves examining the observed interactions in more detail. If negation reduces the rate of memory search, one might predict that the interactions are "linear" in form; that is, negation should produce relatively constant percentage increases in the magnitudes of set-relation and category-size effects. With one exception for the disjoint relation, where the effect of S size was over 300% larger for UNs than PAs, the data satisfy this prediction fairly well.

encoding as well as memory retrieval. Although no attempt has been made to distinguish among these alternatives, there are ways to test them. One method is to vary factors that influence processing capacity, for example, discriminability, and memory load (see Krueger, in press). If the present hypothesis is correct, then such factors should interact with the effects of sentence negation. The procedure outlined here is one step toward applying this approach.

Acknowledgment

I thank A. S. Coriell, K. H. Smith, and S. Sternberg for helpful suggestions.

References

Broadbent, D. E. *Decision and stress*. New York: Academic Press, 1971.

Chase, W. G., & Clark, H. H. Mental operations in the comparison of sentences and pictures. In L. Gregg (Ed.), *Cognition in learning and memory*. New York: Wiley, in press.

Chomsky, N. *Syntactic structures*. The Hague: Mouton, 1957.

Clark, H. H. Semantics and comprehension. In T. A. Sebeok (Ed.), *Current trends in linguistics*, Vol. 12. The Hague: Mouton, in press.

Gough, P. B. Grammatical transformations and speed of understanding. *Journal of Verbal Learning and Verbal Behavior*, 1965, **4**, 107–111.

Greene, J. M. The semantic function of negatives and passives. *British Journal of Psychology*, 1970, **1**, 17–22.

Krueger, L. E. Sentence–picture comparison: A test of additivity of processing time for feature-matching and negation-coding. *Journal of Experimental Psychology*, in press.

Landauer, T. K., & Freedman, J. L. Information retrieval from long-term memory: Category size and recognition time. *Journal of Verbal Learning and Verbal Behavior*, 1968, **7**, 291–295.

McMahon, L. E. Grammatical analysis as part of understanding a sentence. Unpublished doctoral dissertation, Harvard University, 1963.

Meyer, D. E. On the representation and retrieval of stored semantic information. *Cognitive Psychology*, 1970, **1**, 242–299.

Miller, G. A. Some psychological studies of grammar. *American Psychologist*, 1962, **17**, 748–762.

Miller, G. A., & McKean, K. A chronometric study of some relations between sentences. *Quarterly Journal of Experimental Psychology*, 1964, **16**, 297–308.

Slobin, D. I. Grammatical transformations and sentence comprehension in childhood and adulthood. *Journal of Verbal Learning and Verbal Behavior*, 1966, **5**, 219–227.

Sternberg, S. The discovery of processing stages: Extensions of Donders' method. In W. G. Koster (Ed.), *Attention and performance II, Acta Psychologica*, 1969, **30**, 276–315.

Thorndike, E. L., & Lorge, I. *The teacher's wordbook of 30,000 words*. New York: Columbia Univ. Press, 1944.

Trabasso, T. Reasoning and the processing of negative information. Invited address presented at the meeting of the American Psychological Association, Miami Beach, 1970.

Trabasso, T., Rollins, H., & Shaughnessy, E. Storage and verification stages in processing concepts. *Cognitive Psychology*, 1971, **2**, 239–289.

Wales, R. G., & Grieve, R. What is so difficult about negation? *Perception and Psychophysics*, 1969, **6**, 327–332.

Wason, P. C. The processing of positive and negative information. *Quarterly Journal of Experimental Psychology*, 1959, **11**, 92–107.

Wason, P. C. Response to affirmative and negative binary statements. *British Journal of Psychology*, 1961, **52**, 133–142.

Wason, P. C. The contexts of plausible denial. *Journal of Verbal Learning and Verbal Behavior*, 1965, **4**, 7–11.

Webster's Third New International Dictionary. Springfield, Massachusetts: Merriam, 1964.

Winer, B. J. *Statistical principles in experimental design.* New York: McGraw-Hill, 1962.

Retrieval and Comparison Processes
in Semantic Memory

Roger W. Schvaneveldt   *David E. Meyer*

Department of Psychology   *Bell Telephone Laboratories*
State University of New York   *Murray Hill, New Jersey*
at Stony Brook
Stony Brook, New York

ABSTRACT

One useful procedure for studying semantic memory involves judging whether two strings of letters are both words. Decisions in the task are faster if the two strings are commonly associated words. Two classes of models could explain this effect. One class attributes the effect to processes that occur in accessing stored information about the words. A second class attributes the effect to comparing the words semantically. Such models were tested in an experiment where three horizontal strings of letters appeared simultaneously in an array from top to bottom. Subjects responded "yes" if the three strings were all words, and "no" otherwise. Both positive and negative responses were faster if two of the strings were commonly associated words. Reaction time also depended on the number and position of nonwords in the display. The results suggest that stimulus items were processed serially, that facilitation occurred in accessing stored information about associated words, and that excitation spreading between memory locations may be responsible for the association effect. Implications for a theory of semantic memory are considered.

I. Introduction: The Lexical-Decision Task

As a result of growing interest in human semantic memory, psychologists have devised a number of reaction-time (RT) tasks. One useful procedure involves judging whether a string of letters is an English word (Landauer

& Freedman, 1968; Meyer & Ellis, 1970; Rubenstein, Garfield, & Millikan, 1970). Reaction time in this *lexical-decision task* is a function of several factors, such as the frequency and number of different meanings a word has. Although the task is relatively simple, it presumably involves fundamental memory processes that occur in more complicated activities such as reading prose.

In a recent series of experiments, we used the lexical-decision task to study a dependence between retrieval operations (Meyer & Schvaneveldt, 1971). Two strings of letters were presented simultaneously on each trial. The stimuli were arranged horizontally in a visual display, with one string of letters centered above the other. Each stimulus was either a pair of non-words (for example, PABLE–REAB), a word and a nonword (for example, KNIFE–SMUKE), or a pair of words. Half of the word pairs involved commonly associated words (for example, BREAD–BUTTER and NURSE–DOCTOR), while the remaining half consisted of unassociated words (for example, BREAD–DOCTOR and NURSE–BUTTER). In one experiment, subjects responded "yes" if both strings of letters were words, and "no" otherwise. In a second experiment, subjects responded "same" if the strings were either both words or both nonwords, and "different" otherwise.

The results of the two experiments revealed a substantial effect of association within pairs of words. In the yes–no experiment, pairs of associated words were judged an average of 85 msec faster than pairs of unassociated words. The same–different experiment produced a 117 msec association effect, which was not significantly different from the effect obtained in the yes–no experiment. The position of nonwords in the display also affected RT. In the yes–no experiment, negative responses were faster when the top item in the stimulus was a nonword than when it was a word. Given that the top item was a nonword, the lexical status of the bottom item did not affect RT significantly.

To account for these results, we proposed a two-stage retrieval model (Meyer & Schvaneveldt, 1971). According to the model, stimulus processing begins with the top string of letters in the display. The first stage involves a decision about whether the top string is a word, whereas the second stage involves a decision about the bottom string. The model presumes that if the first decision is negative in the yes–no experiment, then retrieval terminates and the subject responds "no." Otherwise, both stages are executed and the response depends on the outcome of the second decision. In the same–different task, both stages of retrieval normally are completed. The outcomes of the two decisions are then compared, and the subject responds "same" if the decisions match; otherwise, he responds "different." An outline of this model is shown in Fig. 1.

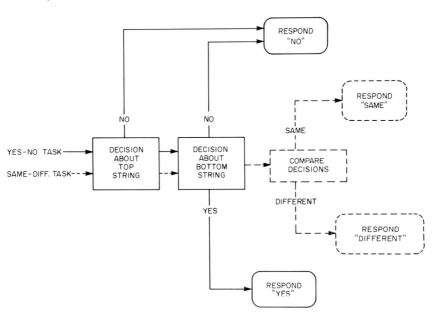

Fig. 1. A two-stage model for lexical decisions.

Our motivation for proposing the model was quite simple. The model explains two major findings in the yes–no experiment: (*a*) negative responses were faster when the top string was a nonword; (*b*) the lexical status of the bottom string had relatively little effect when the top string was a nonword. Since the association effects were similar in the yes–no and same–different experiments, there is reason to believe that the same basic retrieval operations occurred in the two experiments. The additional operation of comparing decisions for a match would then explain why "same" responses took more time than "yes" responses, and why "different" responses took more time than "no" responses.

Further elaborating the model, we suggested that the association effect occurs in accessing information for the second lexical decision. We assume that memory is organized by meaning, and that associated words are located "nearer" to each other in memory. As a result of this organization, the duration of the second retrieval stage presumably depends upon the first stage. We considered two possible mechanisms that might produce such a dependence between retrieval operations. The first is based on the concept of neural excitation. According to this view, retrieving information from a particular memory location produces a spread of excitation to nearby locations. The increase in activity at these locations facilitates retrieval, making it easier to access information stored there (see Collins & Quillian, 1970;

Warren, 1970). In addition to this *spreading-excitation model*, we suggested another alternative, which we call a *location-shifting model*. This second model assumes that stored information can be "read out" of only one memory location at any given instant, that time is required to "shift" read-out from one location to another, and that shifting time increases with the distance between locations. Thus, the association effect occurs because shifting to nearby locations is faster than shifting to more distant locations. Unfortunately, our first two experiments could not distinguish between the spreading-excitation and location-shifting models.

While our model attributes the association effect to a dependence between retrieval operations, other types of model also could explain our findings. Most semantic memory tasks include several conceptually distinct operations in addition to retrieval. For example, tasks involving two or more words often require comparing semantic information about each of the items. Effects of association (or semantic relatedness) have been observed in a number of these tasks (Collins & Quillian, 1969; Kintsch, Crothers, & Berman, 1970; Meyer, 1970; Schaeffer & Wallace, 1969). Such results have led to a view that semantic comparisons between words are responsible for association effects. One version of this *semantic-comparison model* attributes the association effect to changes in response criterion as a function of semantic similarity encountered during the comparison process (Schaeffer & Wallace, 1970). The semantic-comparison model holds that semantic similarity between words may be encountered before the stimuli have been evaluated along all critical dimensions. This semantic similarity produces a bias toward the positive response (for example, "yes," "same," "true"). Thus, positive responses are initiated more rapidly when semantic similarity is present. In contrast, negative responses (for example, "no," "different," "false") are slowed by semantic similarity. Further support for the semantic-comparison model, as well as other models attributing the association effect to response bias, comes from experiments demonstrating an inhibitory effect of association on negative responses (Collins & Quillian, in press; Schaeffer & Wallace, 1970); for example, semantic similarity slows the judgment that two words belong to different superordinate categories. Thus, it is possible that semantic comparisons produced the association effect we observed in the lexical-decision task. This possibility must be considered, even though one might argue for various reasons that the semantic-comparison model does not apply to lexical decisions (see Meyer & Schvaneveldt, 1971).

The present study has three purposes. First, it provides a test between the spreading-excitation and location-shifting models. Second, it provides evidence about the applicability of the semantic-comparison model to lexical-decision tasks. Third, it provides additional data about the serial nature of retrieval operations in lexical decisions. The experiment uses a

procedure where three horizontal strings of letters are presented simultaneously in an array from top to bottom. Stimuli consist of either three words,
or a combination of words and nonwords. The subjects respond "yes" if all
three strings of letters are words, and "no" otherwise. Reaction time is
measured as a function of two factors: (a) degree of association between
words in the stimulus; and (b) position of the words and nonwords in the
stimulus display. An important feature of the procedure is that degree of
association varies orthogonally with the required response.

Each of the models makes firm predictions about RT of positive responses. We should emphasize that the predictions assume that the strings of
letters are processed serially from top to bottom. This assumption can be
tested directly from variations of RT with the position of nonwords in the
display. When a single nonword is present in the stimulus display, the RT of
negative responses should increase linearly as the position of the nonword
changes from top to bottom.

If the strings of letters are processed serially beginning with the top item
in the array, then the location-shifting model implies that degree of association should affect RT, and that this effect will depend upon the position of
the associated words in the display. For example, suppose that the stimulus
includes two associated words like BREAD and BUTTER, together with an
unassociated word like STAR. Then the unassociated word can appear in
one of three stimulus positions: top, middle, or bottom. When the unassociated word is in the top or bottom position, the associated words will be processed in immediate succession. In this case, the location-shifting model
predicts that the associated words will facilitate retrieval, thereby making
RT faster. However, when the unassociated word is in the middle position,
there should be no association effect. The reason for this is quite simple.
Between accessing information from the memory locations of the two associated words, retrieval must be shifted elsewhere in memory to the location
of the unassociated word. Thus, the shorter distance separating the associated
words in memory becomes irrelevant to retrieval time.

On the other hand, the spreading-excitation model ordinarily would
predict that the associated words should facilitate retrieval, regardless of
the position of an unassociated word. Because excitation may decay, facilitation could be less when the unassociated word is in the middle position. However, unless the decay is very rapid, the effect should not disappear completely. Similarly, the semantic-comparison model would predict that facilitation
should occur for positive responses whenever associated words are present
in the stimulus.

Each of the models also makes predictions about negative responses.
For example, suppose that the stimulus includes two associated words and a
nonword, and that the nonword is in the bottom stimulus position. Then the

spreading-excitation and location-shifting models predict that association should facilitate retrieval and shorten RT. If the nonword is in the middle or top position, both models predict that there should be no association effect. This happens because the assumed serial retrieval-process would terminate before information is accessed about the associate in the bottom stimulus position. In contrast, the semantic-comparison model predicts that association slows negative responses (Collins & Quillian, in press; Schaeffer & Wallace, 1970). Association effects on negative responses therefore provide a test of the retrieval versus comparison models in this experiment.

As a convenient shorthand for referring to the different stimulus types, we shall adopt the following notation. Let A represent a word that is associated with at least one other word in the stimulus, let U represent a word that is unassociated with all other words in the stimulus, and let N represent a nonword. Then three letters such as AUA will refer to a stimulus like BREAD–STAR–BUTTER, where the words are arrayed from top to bottom and the top word is associated with the bottom word.

To summarize, Table 1 outlines the predictions of the various models. The predictions are for positive and negative stimuli involving associated words, as compared with corresponding stimuli in which none of the words are associated. For example, the semantic-comparison model predicts that RT of "no" responses should be slower for stimuli of type AAN than for those of type UUN.[1]

II.   Method

The subjects were ten technical assistants at Bell Laboratories and ten high school students. Each subject was tested individually in a single session lasting approximately 1 hr. The subject was seated in a darkened room throughout the experiment, which was controlled by a General Automation 18/30 computer.

A session was divided into ten blocks of 21 trials each. During the first two blocks, the subject practiced the task. The remaining eight blocks consisted of test trials. A small fixation point was presented on the screen of a cathode ray tube at the start of each trial. The fixation point served as a

---

[1]The model's predictions for stimuli of types ANA and NAA depend on temporal properties of the semantic-comparison process. With various assumptions about these properties, one would predict that association either inhibits or does not affect negative responses to stimuli ANA and NAA.

Table 1. *Predicted Effects of Association on Reaction Time: Retrieval versus Comparison Models*

			Predicted reaction time		
Stimulus[a]	Example	Correct response	Location shifting	Spreading excitation	Semantic comparison
AAU	BREAD BUTTER STAR	"Yes"	Faster	Faster	Faster
AUA	BREAD STAR BUTTER	"Yes"	No effect	Faster	Faster
UAA	STAR BREAD BUTTER	"Yes"	Faster	Faster	Faster
AAN	BREAD BUTTER SATH	"No"	Faster	Faster	Slower
ANA	BREAD SATH BUTTER	"No"	No effect	No effect	Slower or no effect
NAA	SATH BREAD BUTTER	"No"	No effect	No effect	Slower or no effect

[a] A = associated word; U = unassociated word; N = nonword.

warning signal and remained visible throughout a 1 sec foreperiod. At the end of the foreperiod, the fixation point was removed and a stimulus was presented that subtended approximate visual angles of 2.2° horizontally and 2.0° vertically. The stimulus consisted of three horizontal strings of letters displayed visually in an array from top to bottom, with the top word centered at the same position as the fixation point. The subject pressed a key labeled "yes" with his right index finger if the three strings were all words, otherwise pressing a "no" key with the left index finger. The subjects were instructed to examine the stimulus from top to bottom, and to respond as quickly and accurately as possible. The RT was measured in milliseconds from the onset of the stimulus to the response. The response terminated the display, and the screen remained blank for 2 sec before the next trial. If the subject made an error, this interval was extended to 4 sec, during which a display appeared to indicate the occurrence of an incorrect response. After the trial block, the subject was informed of his mean RT, total number of correct responses, and total number of errors for the block.

Each subject was paid an initial sum of $1.25 for participating in the experiment. In addition, subjects were paid a bonus for responding quickly and accurately. This bonus was computed from a system whereby 1 point was awarded for each correct answer, n points were deducted for the nth error that occurred on each trial block, and 1 point was deducted for each .1 sec in mean RT on a block. The subject was paid 1.5¢ for each point in the net total he scored under the system, and the average bonus was approximately $1.25.

Separate sets of stimuli, which consisted of various combinations of words and nonwords, were presented during the practice and test blocks. Words in the test stimuli were chosen from standard association norms and included the stimulus and response members from 80 pairs of frequently associated words (Bousfield, Cohen, Whitmarsh, & Kincaid, 1961; Palermo & Jenkins, 1964). Nonwords in the test stimuli were constructed from the 160 words of the paired associates. This procedure involved two steps. First, the initial letter of each word was altered by replacing vowels with other vowels and consonants with other consonants. Second, for those strings that involved two or more syllables, the modified initial syllable of each string was interchanged randomly with the initial syllable from one of the other multisyllable strings. The resulting nonwords were matched with the words in length and general orthography.

This collection of words and nonwords then was used to form 13 different types of test stimuli. The test stimuli varied in three respects: (a) level of association between the words in the stimulus, (b) the number of nonwords contained in the stimulus, and (c) the display positions of the words and nonwords in the stimulus. Two levels of association were possible between any two words in a stimulus. Either the two words were *associated* in that they occurred together in the association norms, or the words were *unassociated*. The unassociated words did not occur together in the norms, and were obtained by randomly permuting the words belonging to the paired associates.

The left half of Table 2 uses the notation of Section I to summarize the 13 stimulus types, together with their frequencies of occurrence in the experiment. To represent the various types, a different set of 144 test stimuli was assigned to each subject. The peculiar characteristics of individual words were controlled by balancing the presence of each word in all possible stimulus types and in all possible display positions. A similar balancing procedure was used for the nonwords. During the test blocks, each subject was also presented an additional eight stimuli of type *AAA*, eight stimuli of type *UUU*, and eight stimuli of type *NUU*. These "filler stimuli" were constructed from a separate set of words (Bilodeau & Howell, 1965) and non-

Table 2. *Stimuli and Data from the Three-String Experiment*

Stimulus type[a]	Correct response	Relative frequency	Mean RT (msec)	Mean errors (%)
AAU		.095	1093	3.4
AUA	"Yes"	.095	1090	4.4
UAA		.095	1073	3.1
UUU		.048	1175	3.8
AAN		.048	1151	13.1
ANA	"No"	.048	1029	6.3
NAA		.048	827	5.0
UUN		.095	1222	12.5
UNU	"No"	.095	1010	4.4
NUU		.048	864	3.1
UNN		.048	992	1.3
NUN	"No"	.048	814	2.5
NNU		.048	769	1.3

[a]*A* = associated word;   *U* − unassociated word;   *N* = nonword.

words, and served to balance a number of conditional stimulus probabilities. For example, the level of association between any two words in a stimulus was eliminated as a cue about the correct response. The various types of stimuli were presented on each test block in proportion to their frequency over the entire stimulus set. Stimuli of type *NNN* were not included in the experiment. Approximately 43% of the stimuli required a "yes" response. Given these constraints, the order of stimulus presentation was randomized for each subject.

III. Results and Discussion

The right half of Table 2 summarizes mean RTs of correct responses and mean error rates for the various types of test stimuli. The data from the filler stimuli are excluded because they involved a different set of words and nonwords than used in the test stimuli.

A. EVIDENCE OF SERIAL PROCESSING

Let us first consider the mean RTs for stimuli that included two unassociated words and a single nonword (*UUN*, *UNU*, and *NUU*). These data reveal that the position of the nonword in the display had a significant effect;

$F(2, 38) = 69.7, p < .001$. When the nonword was the top item in the display, negative responses were relatively fast, and there was an approximate linear increase in RT as the position of the nonword varied from top to bottom. This linear increase accounts for approximately 99% of the variation in mean RT with position of the nonword, and the residual variation was not significant. The slope of a least-squares line fit to the data was 179 msec per unit change in position of the nonword. This estimate is quite similar to the value of 183 msec per unit change that we obtained earlier for stimuli involving two strings of letters (Meyer & Schvaneveldt, 1971).

The data for stimuli involving two unassociated words and a nonword suggest that processing included a substantial serial component. In particular, the data appear as if the subject processed the stimulus items sequentially from top to bottom, stopping as soon as a nonword was discovered. We therefore shall assume that the processing order was consistent enough for testing the retrieval models discussed in Section I.

B.   EFFECTS OF ASSOCIATION ON POSITIVE RESPONSES

The mean RTs for positive responses revealed a significant effect of association; $F(1, 19) = 27.1, p < .01$. Reaction time averaged 90 ± 17 msec faster for stimuli that included two associated words and one unassociated word (AAU, AUA, and UAA) than for stimuli with three unassociated words (UUU).[2] The magnitude of the association effect did not depend significantly on the position of the unassociated word in the stimulus. In particular, the effect was not attenuated significantly when an unassociated word was displayed in the middle position, separating associated words in the top and bottom display positions. These results are summarized in Fig. 2.

As we argued previously, each of the models predicts that association should speed positive responses. The spreading-excitation and semantic-comparison models imply that some effect should occur regardless of the position of the words in the display. Our data are therefore consistent with these models. However, the location-shifting model predicts that the association effect should be eliminated when an unassociated word is displayed between two associated words. Since the effect was not even attenuated significantly in this case, we have substantial evidence against location shifting.

---

[2]Here and elsewhere we are reporting RT differences plus or minus one standard error. Error terms were derived from treatments-by-subjects interactions computed in an analysis of variance.

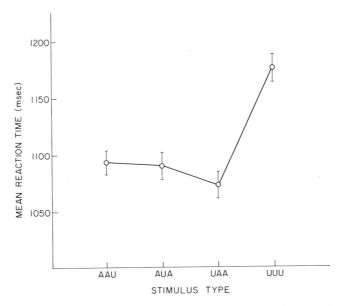

Fig. 2.   Mean RT (±1 standard error) for positive responses to stimuli involving associated and unassociated words.

C.   EFFECTS OF ASSOCIATION ON NEGATIVE RESPONSES

In contrast to positive responses, the negative responses revealed association effects that depended upon the position of items in the display. When two words were displayed above a nonword, RT was 71 ± 23 msec faster if the two words were associated (AAN versus UUN); $F(1, 19) = 9.86$, $p < .01$. Thus, the effect was comparable to the association effect for positive responses (AAN-UUN versus AAU-UUU); $F(1, 19) < 1.0$. However, when the nonword appeared in the middle display position, the association effect was -19 ± 20 msec (ANA versus UNU), which was not significant; $F(1, 19) < 1.0$. Finally, when the nonword was in the top position, the effect was 37 ± 25 msec (NAA versus NUU), which also was not significant; $F(1, 19) = 2.05$, $p > .10$. Thus, the association effect with a nonword in the bottom position was significantly larger than the average effect with a nonword in the middle or top position; $F(1, 19) = 4.6, p < .05$. Furthermore, the association effect with a middle nonword was not significantly different from the effect with a top nonword (ANA–UNU versus NAA–NUU); $F(1, 19) = 2.6, p > .10$. A summary of these results is shown in Fig. 3.

The effects of association on negative responses give evidence against the semantic-comparison model. As discussed earlier, this model predicts

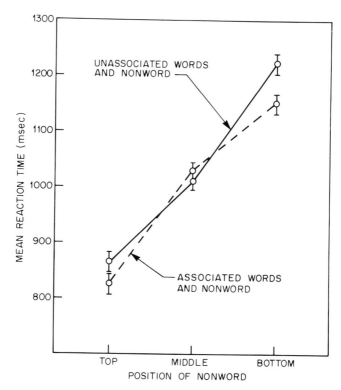

Fig. 3. Mean RT (±1 standard error) for negative responses to stimuli involving one nonword.

that association should inhibit negative responses (Schaeffer & Wallace, 1970), whereas our data show a net facilitation for the negatives. In addition, the results rule out several response-bias explanations of the association effect (see Trabasso, Rollins, & Shaughnessy, 1971). The effect is consistent with predictions of both the location-shifting and spreading-excitation models, assuming that the stimulus items were processed serially. The serial-processing assumption is further supported by the fact that a significant association effect occurred only when the nonword was in the bottom display position.

D. Reaction Time for Stimuli Including Two Nonwords

Although we have argued for serial processing, some of the data leave open questions about the exact nature of processing. There is little doubt that a substantial serial component was present in the processing of the three strings of letters. However, inconsistencies appear in the RTs to stimuli with two nonwords. When two nonwords were presented in the top and middle display positions, the mean RT was 95 ± 35 msec faster than when a single nonword appeared in the top position (*NNU* versus *NUU*); $F(1, 19) = 7.5$, $p < .025$. If processing was strictly serial from top to bottom, then there should have been no difference between these two stimulus types. The occurrence of a difference suggests that a nonword in the middle position was processed at least occasionally when a nonword was also present in the top position, contrary to the serial processing assumption.

A comparison between stimulus types *NUN* and *NUU* yields a smaller difference of 50 ± 33 msec; $F(1, 19) = 2.3$. While this difference is not significant, it might be interpreted as further evidence that stimulus processing was not strictly serial from top to bottom. The data suggest that if there was a nonword in the top position, then a nonword in the bottom position was processed less often than a nonword in the middle position. It is interesting that an even smaller difference (18 ± 14 msec) occurred for stimuli of type *UNN* versus *UNU*.

E. ERRORS

Error rates in the experiment averaged approximately 5% over the various stimulus types, and tended to correlate positively with RT. Error rates were significantly higher ($p < .01$) for stimuli of types *UUN* and *AAN*. This suggests that processing of the stimuli occasionally terminated before the bottom display position had been examined. Such a strategy is not surprising, since "yes" was the correct response for approximately 75% of the stimuli with words in the top and middle positions (see Meyer & Schvaneveldt, 1971). In general, the other stimulus types did not differ significantly in error rates.

IV. Conclusions

Taken as a whole, the data for negative responses support a belief that stimulus processing was not strictly serial from top to bottom. This suggests at least two possible conclusions. First, processing may have been strictly serial, but may have varied in the stimulus position at which it started. For example, the subject sometimes could have begun processing with the middle string and only later processed the top string. Second, processing may have occurred from top to bottom, but with some overlap in the execution of operations for each string of letters.

Despite these conclusions, there is little doubt that stimulus processing was substantially serial from top to bottom, as indicated by the data for stimuli that included two unassociated words and a single nonword. The uniform effects of association on positive responses therefore suggest a rejection of the location-shifting model. At the same time, the effects of association on negative responses rule out the semantic-comparison model as discussed here. Thus, of the theories proposed in Section I, only the spreading-excitation model is completely consistent with our findings. Because association affected positive responses without regard to the position of the associated words, it appears that excitation may not decay significantly over a period of 200–400 msec. This inference follows from three considerations: (a) the estimated time to process a word is approximately 200 msec; (b) substantial facilitation occurred for stimuli where an unassociated word was displayed between two associated words; (c) for stimuli of this type, the middle unassociated word was usually processed before the bottom associate.

Assuming our conclusions are correct, one might speculate about the way in which spreading excitation facilitates retrieval. For example, suppose that serial retrieval-operations occurred in processing the stimulus from top to bottom, but that these operations overlapped temporally to some extent. Then one could argue that excitation affected the starting times of these operations, as well as perhaps influencing their durations. In particular, excitation may have permitted the operations to begin sooner and also may have lessened the times they took. It is conceivable that initiation of the operations is "linked" to some extent, so that the starting time of one operation determines how soon thereafter another operation begins.

Our results, of course, do not permit dismissing contributions of comparison processes or response bias in other semantic memory tasks. A comprehensive model of semantic memory may have to incorporate more than one type of processing operation to explain the entire spectrum of association effects. However, the present findings suggest that retrieval processes must play a central role in such a theory.

Acknowledgments

This work was accomplished while the first author was visiting assistant professor at the University of Colorado. Appreciation is expressed to the University and to the Institute for the Study of Intellectual Behavior for their support. We thank M. Grondin for preparing the stimuli at the University, A. S. Coriell for helping with the apparatus at Bell Laboratories, and B. Kunz for testing subjects. The paper has also benefited from the comments of E. Crothers, W. Kintsch, T. Landauer, R. Olson, P. Polson, S. Sternberg, T. Trabasso, and S. Young.

References

Bilodeau, T. A., & Howell, D. C. Free association norms by discrete and continuous methods. ONR Technical Report No. 1, Contract Nonr-475(10), 1965.

Bousfield, W. A., Cohen, B. H., Whitmarsh, G. A., & Kincaid, W. D. *The Connecticut Free Associational Norms*, Report No. 35. Department of Psychology, University of Connecticut, Storrs, 1961.

Collins, A. M., & Quillian, M. R. Retrieval time from semantic memory. *Journal of Verbal Learning and Verbal Behavior*, 1969, **8**, 240–247.

Collins, A. M., & Quillian, M. R. Facilitating retrieval from semantic memory: The effect of repeating part of an inference. In A. F. Sanders (Ed.), *Attention and Performance III.* Amsterdam: North-Holland Publ., 1970.

Collins, A. M., & Quillian, M. R. Experiments on semantic memory and language comprehension. In L. W. Gregg (Ed.), *Cognition in Learning and Memory.* New York: Wiley, in press.

Kintsch, W., Crothers, E. J., & Berman, L. N. The effects of some semantic and syntactic properties of simple sentences upon the latency of judgments of semantic acceptability. Technical Report, Quantitative Psychology Program, University of Colorado, 1970.

Landauer, T. K., & Freedman, J. L. Information retrieval from long-term memory: Category size and recognition time. *Journal of Verbal Learning and Verbal Behavior*, 1968, 7, 291–295.

Meyer, D. E. On the representation and retrieval of stored semantic information. *Cognitive Psychology*, 1970, **1**, 242–300.

Meyer, D. E., & Ellis, G. B. Parallel processes in word-recognition. Paper presented at the meeting of the Psychonomic Society, San Antonio, Texas, November 5–7, 1970.

Meyer, D. E., & Schvaneveldt, R. W. Facilitation in recognizing pairs of words: Evidence of a dependence between retrieval operations. *Journal of Experimental Psychology*, 1971, **90**, 227–234.

Palermo, D. S., & Jenkins, J. J. *Word association norms: Grade school through college.* Minneapolis: Univ. of Minnesota Press, 1964.

Rubenstein, H., Garfield, L., & Millikan, J. A. Homographic entries in the internal lexicon. *Journal of Verbal Learning and Verbal Behavior*, 1970, **9**, 487–494.

Schaeffer, B., & Wallace, R. J. Semantic similarity and the comparison of word meanings. *Journal of Experimental Psychology*, 1969, **82**, 343–346.

Schaeffer, B., & Wallace, R. J. The comparison of word meanings. *Journal of Experimental Psychology*, 1970, **86**, 144–152.

Trabasso, T., Rollins, H., & Shaughnessy, E. Storage and verification stages in processing concepts. *Cognitive Psychology*, 1971, **2**, 239–289.

Warren, R. E. Stimulus encoding and memory. Unpublished doctoral dissertation, University of Oregon, 1970.

The Effects of Input Modality and Vocalization at Presentation on Intratrial Rehearsal

Andries F. Sanders

Institute for Perception RVO–TNO
Soesterberg, The Netherlands

Stanley M. Moss[1]

Department of Psychology
University of Massachusetts
Amherst, Massachusetts

ABSTRACT

It has been repeatedly suggested that the amount of intratrial rehearsal in memory span tasks depends on input modality (auditory, visual) and treatment at presentation of the items (vocalization, silent reading). This hypothesis is further investigated in the present paper. In one experiment, the subjects received near-span lists of successively presented visual items. The items of each list were partly vocalized at presentation and partly nonvocalized. Recall accuracy improves when vocalization is followed by nonvocalization, whereas a decline is found when nonvocalization is followed by vocalization. These results are consistent with the hypothesis that cumulative rehearsal occurs with silently read lists while vocalization preempts this rehearsal process.

A similar experiment on the mutual effects of successive auditory and visual sublists showed an improvement when auditory items were followed by visual items, but no systematic effects were found in the reverse condition. The question whether auditory presentation provides less opportunity for intratrial rehearsal than visual perception remains dubious, therefore.

In the discussion, alternative explanations of the results are considered and some possible implications are suggested.

---

[1]On sabbatical leave at the Institute for Perception, Soesterberg, The Netherlands. Now returned to the University of Massachusetts.

411

I. Introduction

It has been found repeatedly that the recall accuracy of nonrecent items in serial recall of near-span lists is hardly affected by sensory factors. This finding lends support to the notion of a central processing and storage mechanism that is independent of factors as input modality (auditory, visual) or treatment at presentation of visual items (vocalization, silent reading) (Murray, 1966; Conrad & Hull, 1968; Crowder & Morton, 1969). On the other hand, separate visual and auditory storage mechanisms are assumed at the precategorical level. This assumption is partly based upon pronounced differences in recency when either auditory or visual inputs are involved. The precategorical acoustical store (PAS) is likely to have a greater persistence than its visual counterpart (Fig. 1).

While it is parsimonious to accept the notion that upon categorization the central processing is the same, regardless of input modality or treatment at presentation, there is some evidence that this is not the case. The main objection concerns some evidence that the two factors—input modality and vocalization at presentation—differ with respect to opportunities for intratrial rehearsal. Most rehearsal seems to occur with silently read visual material, while minimal rehearsal takes place with vocalized visual items. If, in spite of different opportunities for rehearsal, the primacy parts of the serial-position (SP) curves are about the same, then this would mean that the vocalized and, possibly, the auditory items gain their strength from a different source than the nonvocalized visual items, that is, not from rehearsal. In turn, this could mean different central processes due to sensory factors, which would have consequences with respect to the distinction between PAS and the central postcategorical store.

The evidence concerning differential opportunities for intratrial rehearsal stems mainly from Routh (1970), who found that an additional task, writing down each item at presentation (monitoring), had a seriously negative effect on nonvocalized visual lists, whereas the recall of vocalized visual items was hardly affected. The adverse effect on monitoring in the

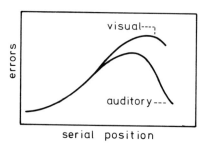

Fig. 1.   A schematic representation of the modality effect. The auditory curve includes both auditory presentation and vocalization at presentation of visual items.

former case is ascribed by Routh to interruption of ongoing cumulative rehearsal (see also Corballis & Loveless, 1967). The absence of an effect of monitoring when added to vocalization would imply that vocalization itself preempts rehearsal. With respect to input modality, Routh (1971) found that nonvocalized visual and auditory lists were equally affected by the monitoring task. This would suggest that both input conditions provide equally good opportunities for intratrial rehearsal. Several other studies suggest, however, that rehearsal is preempted at least to some degree in the case of auditory presentation. Thus, the recall accuracy of visually presented items is found to increase at slower rates of presentation, whereas no comparable gains are found with auditory presentation (Sherman & Turvey, 1969; Moss & Sharac, 1970). Sherman and Turvey have suggested that rehearsal of earlier auditory items would interfere with the assimilation of later items. A similar effect would not occur with visual items because of the dissimilarity between the presented items and their silently rehearsed articulations.

The aim of the present study is to present further evidence on the effects of input modality and vocalization at presentation on intratrial rehearsal. One possible approach is to study the effect of subsequent vocalization or auditory presentation on earlier nonvocalized visual items and vice versa. Reduction of rehearsal in the former conditions would adversely affect the recall of the early visual items, as compared with a completely nonvocalized visual list. In addition, if rehearsal is a cumulative process, then the recall accuracy of the visual items should be inversely related to the *number* of subsequent vocalized or auditory items. The converse is also predicted, that is, an increase of recall accuracy of auditory or vocalized visual items when followed by more and more nonvocalized items.

II. Experiment 1

A. METHOD AND PROCEDURE

Seven consonants were successively presented on a Nixie tube display at a rate of 1 item per second. The consonants were taken from the subset F, H, J, K, S, T, X, Z, and occurred only once in a trial. The start of a list was preceded by a neutral warning signal that was separated from the first item by a 1-sec interval. After presentation of a list the subjects had 8 sec for verbal recall before arrival of the next warning signal. The sequence of events and their timing was controlled by the PSARP apparatus (Van Doorne & Sanders, 1968). The shift from vocalization (V) to nonvocalization ($\overline{V}$)

or vice versa was indicated by a marker, which always appeared below the same consonant in a block of trials. In the V → V̄ condition the subjects were instructed to read aloud all consonants up to but not including the marked consonant and to read silently the remaining consonants. The instructions for the V̄ → V condition were the reverse. Since the eight consonants were randomly distributed across the seven SPs, the marker appeared with approximately equal frequency at all positions, including the case where the marker did not occur at all (position C). Instructions for recall of the lists stressed recall in strict temporal order. In case of partial forgetting, guessing was encouraged. The responses were scored according to the principle of a correct item in a correct position. Eight paid students from the University of Utrecht participated as subjects under both experimental conditions, V → V̄ and V̄ → V, in a counterbalanced order. In each condition they received 10 practice trials followed by 120 experimental trials divided over four blocks of 30 trials each, two trial blocks on each of two daily sessions over two consecutive days.

B. Results

Proportions of correct recall (P_i) were calculated for each subject at each SP under both conditions. To exclude possible ceiling effects all proportions were given a $\log[(1 - P_i)/P_i]$ transformation prior to being subjected to statistical analyses.

The mean proportion of recall errors are summarized in Fig. 2. Each panel represents a different SP, showing mean recall accuracy of earlier V or V̄ as a function of marker position. The data on postmarker items were omitted in view of the absence of any systematic differences either between later V and V̄ or between any of these and comparable items in completely vocalized and nonvocalized lists, where the marker appeared at position 1. Marker position C represents the trials were no marker was presented at all, which means also complete V or V̄. These data seem to be the most suitable controls with respect to the effects under discussion. Separate analyses of variance were applied to each SP for the premarker data. The difference between conditions V̄ → V and V → V̄ was significant beyond the 5% level at SPs 1, 2, 4, and 6, indicating a generally higher degree of recall accuracy for V → V̄, as compared to V̄ → V. The marker position was significant only at SP 3 ($p < 0.05$), but the interactions between marker position and V → V̄, V̄ → V were significant beyond the 5% level at all SPs. This indicates that the recall accuracy of V → V̄ increased as compared with a completely vocalized list, while it decreased at V̄ → V as compared with a completely nonvocalized list. These conclusions were substantiated by the results on *post hoc* Newman–Keuls analyses.

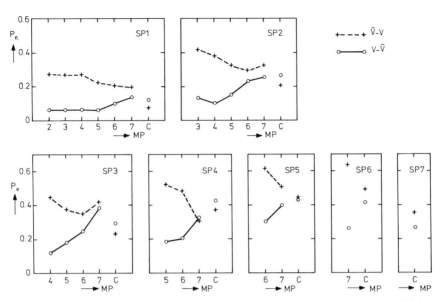

Fig. 2. Mean proportion of recall errors at each SP of V, when followed by $\bar{V}$ ($\circ$) and of $\bar{V}$, when followed by V ($+$) as a function of marker position.

It should be noted that the negative effect on $\bar{V}$ is already maximal in the case of merely one vocalization, whereas the positive effect on the recall of V in the V → $\bar{V}$ condition grows gradually as a function of the number of later $\bar{V}$.

C. Discussion

The results of Experiment 1 are roughly in line with the predictions from the hypothesis that V preempts rehearsal. Recall accuracy of early V is enhanced by later $\bar{V}$, suggesting that early vocalizations can be rehearsed better during later $\bar{V}$. Later V acts negatively on early $\bar{V}$, which is also suggestive of rehearsal preemption. However the two effects are far from symmetrical: one V is sufficient to produce the complete decrement of the silently rehearsed portion of the SP curve (Fig. 2, $\bar{V}$ → V, SP 1–3). It follows from the notions of cumulative rehearsal that the later in the sequence vocalization starts, the more opportunities are available for rehearsing the early items—within the limits of the memory span.

Thus, in the case of mere rehearsal preemption, recall accuracy should be inversely related to the number of subsequent V, in the same way as the recall accuracy of vocalized items increased monotonically with more opportunity to rehearse, that is, more nonvocalized items. The one V at

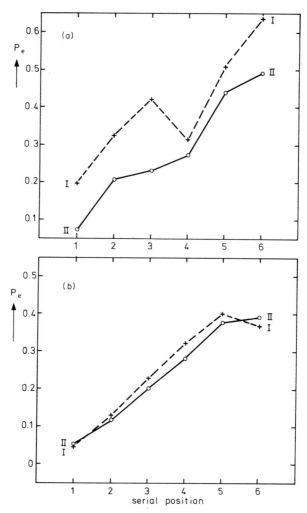

Fig. 3. The effect of (a) one vocalization (I) or (b) one auditorily presented item (I) at SP 7 on recall accuracy of earlier silently read visual items. The solid lines (II) represent the control curves where no marker or transition occurred.

SP 7 removes almost the whole primacy effect (Fig. 3a), which is generally ascribed to intrapresentation rehearsal (for example, Murdock 1968). Thus, vocalization may do more than preempt rehearsal; it may interfere directly with the traces established by the earlier rehearsal of nonvocalized items, which clearly occurs at a postcategorical level. Before a discussion of the possible consequences of these findings, the second experiment, dealing with auditory and visual presentation, will be reported.

III. Experiment 2

A. METHOD AND PROCEDURE

The consonant sequences and the procedures were similar to those employed in the previous experiment. What differed was the mode of presentation: the consonant sequences were presented over a closed-circuit TV and audio system. The stimuli were taped from the original Nixie tube display, with an audio portion replacing the pictoral representations at critical points in each consonant sequence. The auditory items were spoken by the experimenter at the same rate as the visual items. Within each trial block the transition from auditory to visual (pictoral), and vice versa, began with the same consonant, as was the case in Experiment 1. The transitions occurred with approximately equal frequency at all SPs, including the case, where no transition took place (position C). As in the previous experiment, two experimental conditions were employed: (a) auditory–pictoral (A → P) and pictoral–auditory (P → A). Under both conditions Ss were instructed neither to whisper nor mouth the consonants during their presentation.

Eight new paid students from the University of Utrecht participated as subjects under both of the experimental conditions in a counterbalanced order.

In each condition they received 10 practice trials followed by 120 experimental trials divided over four blocks of 30 trials each. Two trial blocks in each of four experimental sessions were conducted over a 7-hr period.

B. RESULTS

The mean proportion of recall errors are summarized in Fig. 4, which is similar to Fig. 2. Each panel represents a different SP as a function of the position of modality transition under the A → P and P → A conditions. As in the previous experiment the data were transformed and separate analyses of variance were applied to each SP for the data points representing the effects of the number of subsequent auditory or pictoral items on recall of early items. The data on recall at post marker positions were omitted for similar reasons as in Experiment 1. The main effect of modality was significant at the 5% level for SPs 5 and 6, indicating an overall higher degree of recall accuracy for A → P as compared with the recall accuracy of P → A. Transition position was significant at the 5% level or less at SPs 3–6. This effect reflects a general increase in recall errors as the shift in

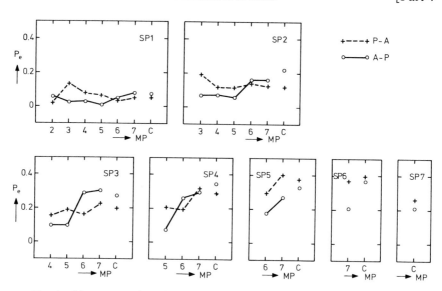

Fig. 4. Mean proportion of recall errors at each SP of A, when followed by P (O) and of P, when followed by A (+) as a function of transition point.

modality occurs later in the sequence. The interaction between modality and transition position was significant at 5% or less for SPs 1–4 and 6. The means of these interactions present different configurations at different SPs. Under the A → P condition, there is, in general, a decrease in the recall accuracy of auditory items when followed by fewer pictoral items that resembles the results of Experiment 1, where recall accuracy of vocalized items was found to decrease when followed by fewer nonvocalized items. On the other hand, the recall accuracies of early pictoral items did not differ systematically if followed by either auditory items or pictoral items. The only exceptions were a poor recall accuracy at SPs 1 and 2 when the transition to auditory items occurred at position 3 and a significant increase in recall accuracy at SP 1 when the transition occurred at SP 2. All foregoing conclusions were substantiated by *post hoc* Newman–Keuls analyses.

C. DISCUSSION

The results are similar to those of Experiment 1 in that auditorily presented items were recalled better when followed by pictoral items as compared with more auditory items. This is in line with the assumption that visual presentation provides more opportunity to rehearse than auditory presentation. However, this is not confirmed by the complementary evidence—the effect of P → A. The finding that, in general, recall of early P was not affected by later A suggests equal opportunity to rehearse under both presentation modes.

What seems clear from these results is that auditory presentation does not have the strong negative effect on traces, established by previous rehearsal, as was found with vocalization. The difference between the effect of a single vocalization and a single auditory item is clearly shown in Fig. 3. The question as to whether auditory presentation preempts rehearsal to some degree remains dubious, since the results point into opposite directions. Any attempt to reconcile the results remains speculative, but at least two opposite views might be outlined.

1. In the P → A condition, the subjects continue to rehearse P after the transition, at the cost of postcategorical processing of the auditory items. This may be an efficient strategy only if a limited number of auditory items is presented. The poor recall of P items when transition occurs at SP 3 may support this view, but the good recall of the one pictoral item, when transition occurs at SP 2, would require additional speculation, for example, the notion of distinctiveness. In general, the explanation holds that rehearsal is preempted when processing auditory material, but it allows for some selective control on the processes involved.

2. An alternative view could be that rehearsal opportunities are equal for visual and auditory material. The facilitation in the A → P condition would result from precategorical retrieval of the auditory items. This would be less possible when more auditory items are presented, so that the gain should diminish when transitions occur later in the list.

A similar explanation could be offered for the results on V → $\overline{V}$ in Experiment 1. In fact, this view is quite in line with the interpretation of earlier work on recall of lists made up from different inputs (see, for example, Broadbent & Gregory, 1961).

A main objection against application of the second view to the results on V → $\overline{V}$ comes from a subsequent experiment by the authors (Sanders & Moss, in preparation). It was found that in the V → $\overline{V}$ condition, the recall accuracy of V did not depend on the number of $\overline{V}$ when the latter items required an overt nonvocal classification response at presentation. A PAS theory would not predict this result since no extra vocal element was introduced and since the time intervals remained unchanged. A rehearsal preemption theory, on the other hand, is at least consistent with the result. Whether the same conclusion can be drawn with respect to A → P remains to be shown.

IV. General Discussion

The results of the present studies confirm the hypothesis that treatment at presentation—and perhaps input modality to a lesser degree—affects the opportunity for intratrial rehearsal. Hence, the major problem concerns the question posed earlier: how do vocalized—and perhaps auditory—items acquire their strength to produce similar recall accuracy at the primary portion of the SP curve? Although the results of the present experiments provide no direct information on this issue it seems reasonable to suppose that visual presentation involves a process that may incorporate successive elements into organized rehearsal groups. Vocalization, on the other hand, may produce stronger individual traces of the items. The observation that the response latencies for vocalized items were larger than for nonvocalized items in a probe experiment (Moss, in preparation) lends some support to the notion that there is a less structured organization of the items with vocalization. Vocalized—and possibly auditorily presented—items may develop associations largely on the basis of proximity only. If there is some truth in these speculations, the laws of interference theory would be of more relevance to the latter cases than to silently read material.

The strength of the individual items could result from either the overt character of the articulatory responses or the acoustic feedback of the vocalized items or from both of these factors. Articulatory responses are considered to be of crucial importance in the activation and maintenance of postcategorical STM traces (Crowder & Morton, 1969; Crowder, 1970), and they may be more effective if overt as compared to covert. Further reinforcement of the postcategorical traces might be due to the subsequent acoustic feedback. If auditory presentation preempts rehearsal to some degree, a certain contribution of acoustic elements toward stronger articulatory traces seems to be a necessary assumption. The fact that the evidence on rehearsal preemption appears to be more stringent with respect to vocalization suggests at least a strong contribution of the act of vocalization (see also Crowder, 1970). The latter factor is also likely to produce the negative effect on the traces, established by earlier rehearsal of nonvocalized visual items (see Experiment 1). Much more research is required to evaluate the relative contributions of these factors. As stated earlier, the distinction between PAS and the postcategorical storage mechanism would become less relevant if acoustic factors contributed greatly to the strength of the individual traces at the postcategorical level.

There is one final point worth noting. The control conditions in the two experiments reported above are similar to the visual and auditory conditions used by other investigations (Murray, 1966; Conrad & Hull,

1968; Crowder & Morton, 1969; Crowder, 1970), who found a pronounced recency effect when acoustic traces were involved.

A closer look at these data points in Figs. 1 and 3 indicates that very little, if any, recency effect was obtained in the vocalized and auditory conditions, which obviously poses a serious discrepancy. The only distinguishable difference between the present control conditions and the other studies is that of mixed versus separate blocks of visual and vocalized (or auditory) items. The mixed blocks might effect the subjects' strategies of organization and emphasis (see, for example, Murdock, 1968). However, if retrieval of recent acoustic items is due to PAS, then the subjects' strategy would have no predominant effect. Thus, the present findings, if found to be general, would cast some doubt upon the explanation of the modality effect in terms of PAS.

Acknowledgments

The authorship is equally shared. The authors are indebted to Drs. Wagenaar and Trumbo for valuable criticisms on earlier draft.

References

Broadbent, D. E., & Gregory, M. On the recall of stimuli presented alternately to two sense organs. *Quarterly Journal of Experimental Psychology*, 1961, **13**, 103–110.

Conrad, R., & Hull, A. J. Input modality and the serial position curve in short term memory. *Psychonomic Science*, 1968, **10**, 135–136.

Corballis, M. C., & Loveless, T. The effect of input modality on short term serial recall. *Psychonomic Science*, 1967, **7**, 275–276.

Crowder, R. G. The role of one's own voice in immediate memory. *Cognitive Psychology*, 1970, **1**, 157–178.

Crowder, R. G., & Morton, J. Precategorical acoustic storage (PAS). *Perception and Psychophysics*, 1969, **5**, 365–373.

Moss, S. M., & Sharac, J. Accuracy and latency in short term memory: Evidence for a dual retrieval process. *Journal of Experimental Psychology*, 1970, **84**, 40–46.

Murdock, B. B., Jr. Serial order effects in short term memory. *Journal of Experimental Psychology Monograph Supplement*, 1968, **76**, 2.

Murray, D. J. Vocalization-at-presentation and immediate recall with varying recall methods. *Quarterly Journal of Experimental Psychology*, 1966, **18**, 9–18.

Routh, D. A. "Trace strength," modality and the serial position curve in immediate memory. *Psychonomic Science*, 1970, **18**, 355–357.

Routh, D. A. Independence of the modality effect and amount of silent rehearsal in immediate serial recall. *Journal of Verbal learning and Verbal Behavior*, 1971, **10**, 213–218.

Sherman, M. F., & Turvey, M. T. Modality differences in short term serial memory as a function of presentation rate. *Journal of Experimental Psychology*, 1969, **80**, 335–338.

Van Doorne, H., & Sanders, A. F. PSARP: A programmable stimulus and response processor. *Behavior Research Methods and Instrumentation*, 1968, **1**, 29–32.

An Experiment in Memory Scanning

Pekka Lehtiö   *Tapani Kauri*

Department of Psychology
University of Turku
Turku, Finland

ABSTRACT

In this contribution the role of the spatial coordinates in retrieval in visual memory is investigated. An experimental situation is used in which the subject has to recall successively parts of a memorized picture in order to perform a recognition task. The results show that recognition latencies in this task are dependent on the physical distances between the successive parts of the original picture.

I. Introduction

One of the central problems of memory research is that of the logical structure of information within memory. For recent statements of this problem, the reader is referred to books and papers by Neisser (1967), Norman (1970), and Reitman (1970). This problem is independent of the theoretical bias of the psychologist. Even if we adopt some kind of extreme reconstruction or problem-solving approach to memory retrieval, we still have to assume that information about past events is somehow controlling these constructive activities (Neisser, 1967).

Most of the recent efforts to develop a detailed theory of information structure in memory deal with semantic memory (for example, Collins &

Quillian, 1969; Kintsch, 1970; Meyer, 1970). In these models of memory the organization of long-term storage is described by a network, which arises when items of information are interconnected by pointers or markers describing different kinds of relationships among these items. These models lead to testable predictions about retrieval latencies when subjects using this information have to decide whether sentences are true or false (Collins & Quillian, 1969), and about clustering in free recall (Kintsch, 1970).

Models relying on verbal representation of information only are unable to explain results obtained in the area of visual memory (Haber, 1970). Haber puts forward a suggestion that there is one kind of memory system for pictorial material and another for linguistic material. The results obtained by Shephard and Chipman (1970) on similarity judgements of internal representations of the shapes of states are also indicative of a nonverbal form of memory trace. Kintsch, in his marker theory of memory, makes a provision for nonverbal memory by proposing a set of sensory markers.

One way to test hypothesis about the organization of visual memory is to examine the act of perception in vision. The study of the mechanics of perceiving a complex visual object has shown that the perception of an object is derived from a succession of separate fixations (Yarbus, 1967). Eye movement recordings show that the observers attention is usually held only by certain key regions of the picture (Mackworth & Morandi, 1967). The important implications of such a process have been pointed out by many writers (see Hebb, 1967; Neisser, 1967): the perception of unified things must result from an integrative or organizing process operating in time. Hebb (1967) suggests that motor process connected to eye movements have this organizing function both in perception and in imagery. This idea may be in line with Yarbus' finding that the perception of a picture is usually composed of a series of "cycles" of eye movements, all of which have much in common.

It is obvious that we are not ordinarily aware of the successive nature of visual perception. Our perceptual experience of seeing a landscape, for instance, has an apparently continuous quality, though our central vision is focused only on a part of the visual field. A memory image has introspectively a sharply different quality. We experience that we are able to have a clear image of only a limited part of the scene. It is interesting to speculate that this phenomenon might have its explanation in the fact that we are able to recall only those chunks of information that corresponded to our original fixations and that this information is available for central processing sequentially.

The present experiment is designed to investigate the role of the spatial coordinates in retrieval in visual memory. An experimental situation is used in which the subject has to recall successively parts of a larger picture in order to perform a recognition task. This situation may be described as the scanning of a memory image. The question is whether the recognition latencies in this task are dependent on the physical distances between the successive parts of the original picture.

II. Method

A. APPARATUS

The stimuli were projected on a screen by a Kodak Carousel projector equipped with a solenoid-operated shutter for exposure control. The viewing distance was 180 cm.

Two response keys, labeled YES and NO, were mounted on the table so that the subject could conveniently depress them while resting his palms on a flat surface.

The experimenter initiated the exposure by depressing the start button. This operation also started a printing electronic interval timer. When the subject pressed the response key, it stopped the timer and closed the shutter. The timer recorded the reaction times (RTs) in units of 1 msec.

B. STIMULUS MATERIAL

Three sets of stimulus slides were prepared, one for each part of the experiment.

1. Practice Set

The stimulus set for the practice trials consisted of an inspection slide and 12 test slides. The inspection slide was a 5×3 rectangular matrix consisting of five different meaningless geometrical patterns, each pattern was repeated three times. The cells occupied by these patterns were chosen randomly. When projected on the screen, the overall size of the image was 50×30 cm. In the test slides just one of the 15 cells was occupied by a pattern. In 6 of the test slides the pattern was the same as the pattern in the corresponding location of the inspection slide. For these 6 slides a positive response was required. In the other 6 slides, requiring a negative response, the inspection and test slides had different patterns in the occupied cell.

2. Test Set

The stimulus set for the experimental trials consisted of an inspection slide and 12 test slides. The inspection slide was a black and white picture of a landscape photographed from a children's book by Richard Scarry. A line drawing of this picture is presented in Fig. 1a. (Parts of Fig. 1a are shaded to make the description of the test slides easier; the original picture was unitary.) In the original picture the name of each object was printed near the object. On the screen, the size of the picture was 40 × 70 cm.

Six of 12 test slides were produced by photographing parts of the original landscape. Five of the shaded areas were used for each slide (Fig. 1b). They were arranged side by side in a row. Details used in each of the six slides are shown in Table 1. The size of each part on the screen was 12 × 12 cm. The distances shown in Table 1 were computed by summing the

Fig. 1. (a) Line drawing of the picture memorized in Part II of the experiment. (b) An example of test pictures used in Part II of the experiment. [From RICHARD SCARRY'S BEST WORD BOOK EVER, Copyright © 1963 by Western Publishing Company.]

Table 1. *Summary of the Properties of*
the Six Positive Test Slides of the Test Set

Test slide	Parts used[a]	Distance (cm)
1	3, 6, 7, 4, 10	72.5
2	6, 3, 5, 7, 4	72.5
3	4, 2, 1, 10, 8	133.5
4	5, 8, 4, 9, 3	121.0
5	9, 1, 3, 2, 6	215.0
6	10, 5, 2, 6, 1	234.5

[a]Numbers refer to Fig. 1a.

distances measured between the middle points of the adjacent part pictures from the projected 40 × 70 cm image of the inspection slide.

The other 6 test slides of this set were produced by photographing four of the parts of Fig. 1a and one part from another landscape. The latter landscape was from the same book and drawn by the same artist, which secured a very similar overall appearance between it and the inspection slide. The position of the extraneous detail was randomized. A positive response was required for the first six test slides and a negative response for the other 6 slides.

3. Recognition Set

This set consisted of 18 slides, each one showing either one of the ten details (of Fig. 1a) used in construction of test slides of the test set, or one of eight details from the other landscape, which was used as a distractor.

C. INSTRUCTIONS AND TRIAL PROCEDURES

The experiment consisted of three parts. In this section the parts are described in the order in which they were performed.

1. Part I

The practice slides were used. The subject was seated in front of the screen, and the inspection slide of the practice set was projected on the screen. The subject was instructed to look at the stimulus matrix so that he could afterwards remember the patterns in their correct positions. The subject saw the matrix on the first occasion for 1 min. He then was asked to describe verbally what he had seen—what kind of patterns there were and where they were located. This was followed by another 1-min presentation of the inspection slide.

The subject then was given the following instruction: "I will now show you parts of the previous figure. Each picture will show one square of it. It is your task to state as soon as possible if the pattern is in its correct position. If you think it is in the right position, push the YES key as soon as possible. Otherwise push the NO key as soon as possible. It is important to work quickly. Do you have any questions?"

After the instructions, the subject was shown the test slides of the practice set. RTs were not recorded in the practice trials.

2. Part II

The test set slides were used. This part formed the experiment proper. The inspection slide of the test set was projected first on the screen. The experimenter then read the following instructions: "I will now show you another slide. It presents a landscape. Watch it carefully and try to form a memory image of it. The picture will be shown for one and a half minutes. Describe the picture while you are watching it." Immediately after presentation, the subject was asked to recall as many details of the picture as possible. This was followed by a second presentation of the inspection slide for one and a half minutes.

Before the test slides the subject was given the following instructions: "I will now show you parts of the landscape just seen. In each slide there are five pictures in a row. It is your task to look at all the pictures as rapidly as possible to see if they all are from the landscape shown you before. If you think all the pictures are parts of that landscape, push the YES key. If the row pictures contains a picture which was not in the original landscape, push the NO key as soon as possible. Any "wrong" pictures are clearly different and they are easily recognizable. It is again important that you work as quickly as possible. Do you have any questions?"

After the instructions were given, the subject was shown the test slides of the test set. All RTs and errors were recorded. Additional instructions encouraging the subject to work as fast as possible were given prior to the second, fifth, eighth, and eleventh slide.

The 12 test slides were presented in accordance with a 12×12 Latin square design. The same Latin square was replicated three times, three subjects being assigned randomly to each row of the square. Each slide then appeared once in each column. This design was chosen to counterbalance the learning effects when the subject learned the part pictures themselves. It also concealed from the experimenter the identity of positive and negative instances during the experiment.

3. Part III

The slides of the recognition set were used. The subject was told that part pictures used to construct the slides of the previous phase would be shown, one by one, and that he had to push the YES key as soon as possible if the picture was part of the original landscape, and the NO key if it was not. Eighteen slides were presented in accordance with a 18 × 18 Latin square. Two subjects were assigned to each row of the square.

No knowledge of results was given to the subject during any part of the experiment.

D. SUBJECTS

The subjects were children ranging in age between 13 and 16 years. The 36 subjects, 15 girls and 21 boys, whose results are reported below were all pupils of Lieto comprehensive school. One subject was excluded because of an exceptionally high error rate.

III. Results

1. Part I of the experiment was used for training only and the results were not recorded.

2. The subjects made errors on 6.9% of their responses in Part II of the experiment. Of these 24 errors, 15 were false positives and 9 false negatives.

An analysis of variance was performed on the data of Part II. We were interested in the positive responses only, because in these data we can assume that all part pictures were recognized before the response occurred. Prior to the analysis of variance, all response latencies for negative responses were deleted from the original 12 × 12 Latin square. In addition, the response latencies for identical positive slides occupying two adjacent columns in the original Latin square were grouped to form a 6 × 6 Latin square. The logarithmic transformation was performed on the RTs before the analysis in order to stabilize the cell variances.

The analysis of variance showed a significant interaction between the distance of adjacent part pictures and the order of presentation ($p < .05$). The mean latencies of correct positive responses for each test stimulus therefore were used to establish the relationship between the distance of the adjacent part pictures and RT. This function is presented in Table 2. The product moment correlation coefficient between distance and mean RT is .88, which is significant ($p < .025$).

Table 2. *Sum of Distances between Adjacent Part Pictures and Mean Response Latencies for Positive Test Slides in Part II of the Experiment*

		Mean RT (msec)						
Test slide distance (cm)		Position in the order of presentation						Overall mean RT (msec)
		1	2	3	4	5	6	
1	72.5	2958	2196	2364	2252	2644	1732	2358
2	72.5	3052	2652	2464	2460	2383	1956	2495
3	133.5	2905	2480	2437	2140	2172	3076	2780
4	121.0	2691	2910	2514	2629	2612	3322	2780
5	215.0	5802	3755	2214	2422	2330	3474	3334
6	234.5	4184	3677	2655	3149	2259	2050	2996

All 6 test slides were permutations of the same 10 part pictures. The significant interaction between distance of adjacent part pictures and the order of presentation appears to indicate that the subjects gradually learn to recognize the separate part pictures without reference to the original memory image. The mean RT for each positive test slide in different positions of the order of presentation also are given in Table 2. In this way the interpretation of the significant interaction effect between distance and order is facilitated. In this table we can see that the distance effect decreases with the serial position of the test slide.

The results of Part II thus establish a distinct relationship between the total distance between the successive part pictures (in the original memorized picture) and the RT for the recognition of all of them.

Table 3. *Mean Response Latencies of Part Pictures*

Part picture[a]	Mean RT (msec)
1	1182
2	1184
3	1249
4	1223
5	1327
6	1160
7	1108
8	1099
9	1264
10	1270

[a]Numbers refer to Fig. 1a.

3. An alternative explanation of the significant differences between the RTs to the 6 test slides in Part II of the experiment is that the recognition latencies for individual part pictures differ. When these part pictures are combined to form a test slide, the differences in recognition latencies then reflect differences between part-picture RTs.

To test this hypothesis the recognition latencies for each part picture were measured in Part III of the experiment. The analysis of variance for the 10×10 Latin square containing the 10 part pictures used in Part II revealed a significant difference between the RTs for these pictures. The mean response latency for each picture is shown in Table 3. The product moment correlation between the sum of response latencies for the part pictures of each test slide and the RTs to the corresponding slides is $+.05$. This explanation is rejected as the coefficient is not statistically significant.

IV. Discussion

The results of this experiment suggest that when the subject is performing a recognition task in which he has successively to recognize parts of a memorized picture, the recognition time for a series of part pictures is dependent upon the distance between adjacent part pictures in the original display. This result holds only when subjects have to refer to the memory representation of the original picture in order to recognize the part pictures. When part pictures are presented as test stimuli, subjects remember them individually and recognition time is no longer dependent on the spatial properties of the original picture.

It is obvious that the variation in recognition time for test slides may not be explained by reference to the variation of recognition times of different part pictures of a test slide. There are significant differencies in recognition latencies of separate part pictures as shown in Part III of the experiment, but the effects of these latencies are balanced in a series of part pictures. The same part pictures also occurred in many different test slides. The best way to exclude this possibility of course, would be to construct test slides so that the distance effect could be estimated with the same part pictures.

The generality of the findings reported here may be limited by the fact that in Part I subjects were instructed to deal in terms of spatial coordinates. In some other situations spatial properties might have no effect on recognition latencies. It is true that Part I of the experiment gave the subject a powerful set to localize the information presented and that the data do not provide any clue for assessment of the generality of the findings. In any event it is difficult to believe that any single stimulus dimension could be important in organizing all material stored in human memory.

It is tempting to try to find a suitable explanation for the results reported in this paper. At least two possible alternatives may be outlined. First, it may be assumed that the subject stores in memory the informational units of the original picture in a form that may be represented by a multicomponent ordered feature vector and that the spatial coordinates are elements of such a vector. In order to recognize a part picture, the subject has to localize the memory trace of that part picture. When he has to localize successively different memory traces corresponding to different part pictures, the subject may make efficient use of the spatial information of the memory traces located initially to delimit the area if the distances between different part pictures are short but not if the distances are long. In this explanation it is assumed that recognition involves a search process that may be performed in a shorter time if the area of search may be delimited.

An alternative explanation of these results is that the subject has to reconstruct the relevant parts of the memory image of the original picture in order to recognize a part of the picture. This process is guided by stored information about the act of perceiving, which includes traces of successive eye movements. It is supposed that during the recognition period the subject simulates the successive fixations performed during the presentation of the original picture. More time is needed for this activity if the distances of the part pictures are longer than when they are shorter. Data supporting this hypothesis recently have been published by Noton and Stark (1971). They found that their subjects tended to fixate to same points of drawings while memorizing or recognizing a picture. In our experiment the physical distance of the part pictures were always the same during the recognition period, but it is possible that the subject had to scan the memory image of the original picture mentally in order to perform the recognition task.

The latter explanation follows closely from ideas outlined by Neisser (1967). The former is more in line with the theories adopted for retrieval of verbal material (for example, Shiffrin, 1970).

References

Collins, A. M., & Quillian, M. R. Retrieval time from semantic memory. *Journal of Verbal Learning and Verbal Behavior*, 1969, **8**, 240–247.

Haber, R. N. How we remember what we see. *Scientific American*, 1970, **223**, 104–112.

Hebb, D. Concerning imagery. *Psychological Review*, 1967, **75**, 466–477.

Kintsch, W. Models for free recall and recognition. In D. A. Norman (Ed.), *Models of memory*. New York: Academic Press, 1970. Pp. 331–373.

Mackworth, N. H., & Morandi, A. J. The gaze selects informative details within pictures. *Perception and Psychophysics*, 1967, **2**, 547–552.

Meyer, D. E. On the representation and retrieval of stored semantic information. *Cognitive Psychology*, 1970, **1**, 242–300.

Neisser, U. *Cognitive psychology*. New York: Appleton, 1967.

Norman, D. A. Comments on the information structure of memory. In A. F. Sanders (Ed.), *Attention and performance III*. Amsterdam: North-Holland Publ., 1970.

Noton, D., & Stark, L. Eye-movements and visual perception. *Scientific American*, 1971, **224**, 34–43.

Reitman, W. What does it take to remember? In D. A. Norman (Ed.), *Models of memory*. New York: Academic Press, 1970. Pp. 469–509.

Shepard, R. N., & Chipman, S. Second-order isomorphism of internal representations: Shapes of states. *Cognitive Psychology*, 1970, **1**, 1–17.

Shiffrin, R. M. Memory search. In D. A. Norman (Ed.), *Models of memory*. New York: Academic Press, 1970. Pp. 375–447.

Yarbus, A. L. *Eye movements and vision*. New York: Plenum, 1967.

Latency Mechanisms in Transcription[1]

L. H. Shaffer

Department of Psychology
University of Exeter
Exeter, England

ABSTRACT

Serial latency mechanism can be generalized by introducing buffer memories between processing stages and allowing bulk handling of codes in one or more stages. Having a buffer store enables each stage to recycle immediately and accept a new input. Such mechanisms are then well suited to describe performance in transcription skills such as copy typing. Experiments have been carried out on skilled typists in which the keyboard is an input terminal to a computer and the text is presented by the computer on a cathode-ray tube (CRT) display. The performance of one very fast typist is described in some depth. It provides extensive evidence of simultaneous activity in input, output, and control processes.

1. Introduction

The basic stochastic latency mechanism studied in human performance is one that assumes a train of processes between stimulus and response, such that completion of one process initiates the next. Such a model is appropriate for tasks in which no new stimulus can appear until a response is made to the present one. It is then sometimes possible to decompose the response

---

[1]This research was made possible by an equipment grant from the Medical Research Council.

435

latencies into the latencies of the component processes (McGill, 1963), or to associate component processes with particular aspects of the stimulus or response conditions (Sternberg, 1969). What happens, however, if new stimuli can arrive within the latency interval?

In transcription tasks there is either continual arrival of new stimuli, as in morse reception, or the stimulus sequence can be freely scanned, as in reading aloud. In performing such tasks there is typically a lag between the reception of a stimulus and its translation into response; also interresponse times are usually much shorter than would be reaction times to individual stimuli. These facts suggest two principles, one or both of which may operate in transcription skill: first, each component process can accept a new input as soon as it is free of the present one; second, stimuli are handled not singly but in batches, with consequent economies of coding. Unless all processes are synchronous, which is possible but unlikely, there must be buffer stores between them in which codes created by one process can queue for acceptance by the next.

If these principles are added to the serial latency model, they transform it into a multiple queueing model and in doing so radically alter the latency picture. In the serial model each stimulus must await the full processing of its predecessor and interresponse time (IRT) is the sum of the component latencies, but with overlapping processing of successive stimuli it is possible, in the extreme case, that IRT corresponds to the latency of the terminal process.

A task in which such a latency mechanism can be studied in great detail is copy typing. Thus far, gross measures of speed and accuracy under different conditions have been obtained from skilled typists (Hershman & Hillix, 1965; Shaffer & Hardwick, 1968), and more detailed information of IRT and errors from subjects trained on a special keyboard (Shaffer & Hardwick, 1970). These results are compatible with a transcription model that discriminates only an input process and an output process, which can overlap in time; the input process can read words and syllables but the output process takes single-letter codes from the buffer store and converts them into responses one at a time.

Facilities now have been acquired to study the performance of skilled typists in detail and what follows is a description of this work, which is still in progress.

II. Experimental Procedure

Thus far, we have been able to study the performance of four secretaries in the University, all of whom work with electric typewriters and have credited speeds of at least 60 words per minute. In the laboratory they use an electric keyboard with a standard layout of alphanumeric symbols, which is connected as an input terminal to a PDP-12 computer. It does not produce paper copy. Facing the typist is a 7 × 9 in. CRT display on which the text appears.

The computer is programmed to produce text in a single row across the center of the CRT with a vertical boundary marker at the left. When a key is struck, the text is transposed left by one symbol, the left-most symbol disappears at the boundary, and a new symbol is added at the right, so that on a given text there is a constant number of symbols on display. Transposition is virtually instantaneous. The computer stores each IRT and records which key is pressed.

The CRT provides in effect a moving window on the text whose size is variable. The position within the window of the first text letter fixes the location of the current symbol to be typed, and so it is easy to regulate how much of the display is preview of new text and how much is postview of text already typed.

The texts were all 512 symbols long, including space symbols, and were edited to contain no proper names or punctuation, so that the typist was never involved in shifts from lower- to uppercase or in carriage returns. Also she was not able to correct her errors, since any response caused the text to move on. The intention was to provide her with optimal conditions in which to produce a homogeneous transcription output. In fact a secretary may find it difficult not to introduce punctuation where she thinks it appropriate or correct an error she has detected.

The subjects came for about half an hour at a time and in the early sessions practiced typing, under these slightly novel conditions, various texts with different amounts of pre- and postview. By the end of the practice phase no differences could be detected between the performance of copying from the CRT or from a printed sheet of paper. At the end of each session their transcriptions were printed out on a teletype so that they could see their errors. This seemed to interest them more than speed measures.

In the test sessions that followed a subject was permitted to make not more than 6 errors in any one text, an error rate of just over 1%. If this was exceeded, she had to repeat the condition on a subsequent occasion. The tests were not run to any formal schedule, but altogether each subject completed a set of conditions in which preview exposure could be 1, 3, 4, 6, 8, 16, or 40 symbols coupled with a postview of 0 or 16 symbols. The texts included prose, random word sequences (obtained by reshuffling word order in a prose passage), random letter sequences (obtained by forming anagrams of words in a prose passage), and German (none of the subjects knew German or had previous occasion to type it).

III. Results for One Subject

A. Latency Statistics

The goal for a typist is to produce copy without error at the fastest rate that the keyboard will permit. It is of particular interest here to study in depth the performance of the subject SW, who came closest to this goal, having checked that there are no gross qualitative differences between her and the others.

A summary of medians and interquartile (IQ) ranges of IRT in different conditions is given in Table 1. Ordinal rather than parametric statistics are used because of the typical left skew of IRT distributions. There is no need to give separate statistics for conditions with 0 or 16 symbols of postview because they failed to produce differences in performance, and this was true for all subjects. The reason for this will become apparent later.

With an increase in the preview of prose, median latency has a negatively accelerated decrease and asymptotes at about 8 symbols. At the same time the IQ range shrinks. At the asymptote SW was typing about 9 symbols per second, with an IQ range of only 30 msec. On the convention that a word is 5 symbols, this is over 100 words per minute. Further detail is shown in the time series in Fig. 1 and the histogram in Fig. 2. Fig. 1 gives IRT as a distance from the base line, and the dots on this line represent the spaces between typed words. There is little evidence of transient or phasic fluctuation of IRT over the sequence.

Table 1. *The Median and Interquartile Range of IRT (milliseconds) for Each of the Major Experimental Conditions, from the Data of SW*

Text	Preview	Median	IQ range
Prose	40	107	92–126
	16	109	94–126
	8	110	96–127
	6	131	113–157
	4	163	134–196
	3	196	165–237
	1	443	368–536
Random word	40	104	86–122
German	40	149	129–178
Random letter	8	192	154–224
	1	545	510–590

Fig. 1. A time series of IRTs obtained from SW on a prose text with extensive preview.

The histogram has an acute peak and the general form suggests a distribution of the Laplace form. This is the form produced by a system that is paced by a periodic beat but departs from it in each cycle by an amount that is exponentially distributed (McGill, 1963). The basic Laplace distribution is a symmetrical one of two exponential curves back to back, but the histograms typically have a positive skew.

This form of histogram is preserved with preview of prose from 40 down to 8 symbols, as well as for random word text, with no shift in the peak. With German text the peak shifts to the right by 30 msec, and there is a slight increase in variance. The Laplace form appears again with a random letter text exposed 1 symbol at a time, as shown in Fig. 3, but with a five-fold increase in median latency and a considerably larger variance. The bar on the right of Fig. 3 is the frequency of latencies longer than 1 sec. On an extended scale this right tail goes up to 2 sec. The histograms in Figs. 2 and 3 contrast transcription and reaction times on a typewriter keyboard. There is virtually no overlap of the distributions.

As the preview of prose is reduced below 8 symbols, there is a progressive slowing of response and the distribution of IRT becomes increasingly diffuse. Shown in Figs. 4 and 5 are the histograms for 3- and 1-symbol preview, respectively. What is happening is that with impoverished exposure the subject tries to reconstruct the prose while she is typing, and as soon as she is confident that her prediction is correct, she accelerates and types

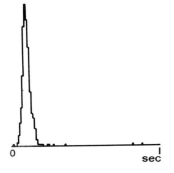

Fig. 2. A histogram of the IRTs in Fig. 1 on the interval 0–1 sec.

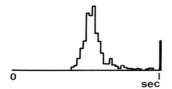

Fig. 3. A histogram of IRTs obtained from SW on a random letter text exposed 1 symbol at a time.

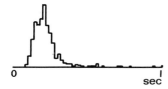

Fig. 4. A histogram of IRTs obtained from SW on prose with 3-symbol preview.

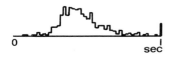

Fig. 5. As for Fig. 4, but with preview of 1 symbol at a time.

the word or phrase to completion. This opportunist tactic leads to the mixed distributions observed. The contrast between 1-symbol exposure of prose and random letter text is striking. As mentioned above, the ability to generate predictions was as good with and without postview; the material in postview could as well be kept in memory.

Note finally that German was typed at a speed intermediate between 4- and 6-symbol preview of English, whereas random letter text was typed at about the speed of English with 3-symbol preview. This indicates the amount of context that was effectively used in typing these passages.

B. Implications of the Latency Statistics

The subject SW required preview of about 8 symbols of English to type at her maximum speed (with an error rate not exceeding 1%). This figure agrees well with estimates of eye–hand span obtained by Butsch (1932), and shows that the typist adjusts this span to the amount of material she can effectively utilize.

There was a fivefold increase in latency between typing prose with free view and random letters seen one at a time. By hypothesis, if the queue in the response code buffer seldom dropped to zero then IRT in the first condition can be taken as the latency of the terminal process of reaction time measured in the second. Thus, very roughly, preterminal processing accounts for about four-fifths of reaction time, and the effect of preview is to permit a fourfold acceleration of these processes. This could come about if input processing is itself a sequence of buffered microprocesses that can overlap in time, so that a steady transfer of codes can be maintained between them. Alternatively, or in addition, there could be bulk input, such that groups of letters based upon words or syllables are read and translated in parallel into response codes.

Compelling evidence of input grouping is the effect of (familiar) grammatical structure (Shaffer & Hardwick, 1968). Hence the loss of speed on German or random letter texts. On the other hand, performance on random word text shows that grammatical factors beyond the word level are largely irrelevant. A major surprise is that skilled typists can use structure to predict ahead when preview is restricted and the continuation is reasonably determinate. Trainee subjects gave no indication of this ability (Shaffer & Hardwick, 1970). It is surprising because such prediction must occur in parallel with maintaining a response output. It is not a question of utilizing sequential redundancy to make the next response more probable; in effect the typist is projecting ahead an image of the text so that response codes for not-yet-read letters can be placed in the buffer store for future output.

All subjects shared the ability to set a typing rhythm appropriate to the text and viewing conditions even if, as with reduced preview, they made opportunist departures from this. Thus, there is preservation of the Laplace form of IRT distribution despite a shift in speed going from English to German. More dramatic examples were obtained by accident. If during typing the subject puts in an added symbol in error, then she is no longer in step with the text but will be typing the symbol to the left of the correct one (which may no longer be on display). This has the effect of giving her an extra symbol of preview. Conversely, omitting a symbol reduces preview by that amount. The result was often a spontaneous shift in performance appropriate to the new conditions. An example of this, provided by SW, is shown in Fig. 6. Starting with a 3-symbol preview of prose she added symbols at the two points indicated by arrows and the changes in both rate and variance are apparent. Thus, it appears that output rate is actively regulated in the direction of preserving a uniform speed, gauged from the resources of the input process.

We can reject completely any idea that fast typing relies only upon grouping stimuli, with no overlap of processing stages. If this were so, one should observe slow IRTs at least of the order of a full reaction time between

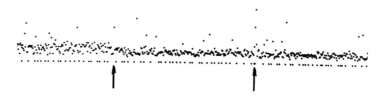

Fig. 6. A time series of IRTs obtained from SW when, starting with 3 symbol preview, she got progressively out of step with the text at the points indicated.

each group. In fact, there were none since the distributions in Figs. 2 and 3 do not overlap.

C. Errors and Error Detection

A skilled typist detects on average about half her errors (Shaffer & Hardwick, 1969a). In the present study subjects were not allowed to correct their errors, but in the case of SW typing prose with adequate preview—so that the IRT distributions are very sharp—error detections show up as marked changes in latency. When such a change is observable, it may include a speeding or slowing of the symbol that is in error, but usually shows as a speeding or slowing of the next symbol. Thus, "sentence" was typed "sentnece" with a very slow second "n"; "minor" was spelt "minmor" with a fast second "m" and a slow "o"; "since" was spelt "sinnce" with a fast second "n" and a very fast "c"; "discourse" was spelt "discovourse" with a slow "o" following the "v"; and so on. Slow responses follow both the added symbols in Fig. 6. Several subjects attributed some of their slow responses to occasions on which they felt they were about to make an error (and did not).

To detect an error, or incipient error, so quickly, a monitoring process must be able to compare two highly compatible codes, one marking the intention and the other the (incipient) execution of the response. The likeliest candidates are the response code in the output buffer and kinesthetic feedback of initiating the ballistic movement.

It is possible that monitoring may not occur on every response but may sometimes allow two or more responses to run to completion. On one occasion SW was asked to type the same prose text three times in succession. She made two errors in the first copy, each transposing a pair of letters, and in both cases the letters transposed were both typed at normal speed with a pause preceding the next symbol. It is also of interest that on the next two copies there were no errors but she paused on the first letters that had suffered inversion. Thus, in "sentry" she transposed "en" and paused on "t," then subsequently she paused on "e."

D. SERIAL LATENCY EFFECTS

Does the output process translate response codes one at a time and independently into movement? An alternative viewpoint, due to Bryan and Harter (1899), Craik (1948), and Lashley (1951) is that a typist learns response procedures for whole sequences, based upon syllables or words, that can be run off as an arpeggio of fast movements. It has even been asserted (Leonard, personal communication) that only with such procedures can high speeds be achieved. There is also the fact that striking a particular key can involve different reaching movements depending upon the previous letter typed, but this only requires that response codes embody context-sensitive rules (Shaffer & French, 1971; Wickelgren, 1969).

The data for SW were analyzed first on the assumption that only certain common words are typed as response procedures. It should be expected of such a word either that it is typed consistently faster than others or that it is typed with a characteristic latency profile over the word.

The most likely candidates for such procedures are "and" and "the" and these were inspected first, and were found to satisfy both criteria. They were typed at average speeds of 90 msec per letter, while other 3-letter words averaged 115 msec, and there was an almost invariant latency profile, despite speed changes from one occasion to another, such that the second letter was typed slower than the first and the last letter much faster. It is the terminal flourish that makes these words faster overall. This feature is absent when "and" or "the" are embedded in longer words, for example, "there."

Continuing the search through the data for SW, no other words seem to be consistently fast except, trivially, the word "a." However, looking through three successive copies of the same text, there are striking similarities of latency profiles of the same words in different copies and within a copy. The following are typical examples, with letter latencies given in 1/100ths of a second:

"though": 12 8 14 16   9 10;   9 10 14 16 10   8; 11   9 13 16   9 10;
             10   9 15 14 10   8; 11   9 14 14 10   9; 11   8 15 14 10   6,
"sun":   6 13 14;   5 12 14;   8 12 14,
"sunken":   9 12 14 17   8 12; 11 11 13 16   8 13;   9 12 13 13 16   9 13,
"ash":   9 17 12;   9 16 12; 10 16 14.

Two features go against the idea that fast typing depends upon all or most words being typed as response procedures. One is that the latency of the first letter of a word should include the time required to access a new procedure, yet first letters are typically faster than the average, not slower. The other is that the characteristic latency profile usually arises because certain letters are typed slower than average. In Fig. 2 one can detect a slight bulge on the right flank of the histogram, which represents the rump of these slow latencies and shows them to be atypical.

It does not appear that certain letters have typical latencies, or that there is a relationship between latency and frequency of usage of a letter. Witness, for example, the latencies of "s" above. The best inference seems to be that letter—and space symbol—speed is conditioned by its context. The conditioning factor is the topography of the keyboard interacting with the shape of the typist's hands and strength of her fingers. Thus, SW slows if two consecutive letters involve the same finger, or if consecutive letters on the same hand involve the medial column of the keyboard on that side (that is, the keys T, G, B on the left hand; Y, H, N on the right). Examples are the "o" in "though" and the "un" in "sun" and "sunken." Even in the common "ion" and "ing" endings the "n" is slow.

Note that "s" is typed unusually fast in "sun" but not in "sunken." Further, there is a consistent slowing on the space before "sun" which is unmotivated by anything that precedes it. The suggestion is that the typist was taking a run up to the slow "un" in the shorter word in an attempt to preserve an overall rhythm. Other examples also suggest that the speed on letters may be conditioned by their sequel, but it will require more analysis to confirm this.

A final point is that IRT typically rises slightly in the interior of long words, which amplifies an earlier finding of a relationship between word length and typing speed (Shaffer & Hardwick, 1969b). Presumably long words have to be read in fragments and this creates a problem of tracking the boundaries of these fragments during conversion into response codes.

IV. Conclusion

It should now be beyond controversy that skilled typing depends upon simultaneous input and output processing. What should now be added to earlier formulations is a control process that, in addition to starting and stopping transcription and selecting a speed–error tradeoff, has the following functions: error detection, providing a pacing rhythm selected according to the stationary conditions of the text, and modulating this rhythm to accommodate local conditions of letter transition and word length. The rapidity of output regulation suggests that it derives its information from codes in the output buffer. The nature of this information leads to the notion that the queue of codes in this buffer provides a motor image that can be scanned by the control process.

Regulation of the pacing rhythm can be based upon an estimate of the average size, or some such statistic, of the queue. It may also take into account the expectation of making errors. It was found of several subjects that if they had to repeat a condition, through exceeding the permissible number of errors, they were slower on the second occasion—even if several days had elapsed.

If there were no other sequential effects, one would explain the response privileges for "and" and "the" by postulating special response codes, each invoking a response procedure. If, however, among other context effects, it can be demonstrated that response rhythm can be modulated to anticipate particular transitions or the length of the word, then it is more economical to suppose that the control process refers to a motor image for the advance information. This preserves what is useful in the idea of a response procedure but differs from it in an important respect. Instead of having to learn a response procedure for each word the control system in effect generates a procedure based upon information in the motor image and stored information about particular transitions. The rapid detection of errors implies that response codes are copied in transfer from the buffer store to the output process, leaving the original as part of the motor image for comparison with kinesthetic feedback. Departure from the buffer occurs only when the code is displaced by subsequent material (Waugh & Norman, 1965).

References

Bryan, W. L., & Harter, N. Studies on the telegraphic language. *Psychological Review*, 1899, **6**, 345–375.

Butsch, R. L. C. Eye movements and the eye–hand span in typewriting. *Journal of Educational Psychology*, 1932, **23**, 104–121.

Craik, K. J. W. Man as an element in a control system. *British Journal of Psychology*, 1948, **38**, 142–148.

Hershman, R. L., & Hillix, W. A. Data processing in typing. *Human Factors*, 1965, **7**, 483–492.

Lashley, K. S. The problem of serial order in behavior. In L. A. Jeffress, (Ed.), *Cerebral Mechanisms in Behavior*. New York: Wiley, 1951.

McGill, W. J. Stochastic latency mechanisms. In R. D. Luce, R. R. Bush, & E. Galanter (Eds.), *Handbook of Mathematical Psychology*. Vol. I. New York: Wiley, 1963.

Shaffer, L. H., & French, A. Coding factors in transcription. *Quarterly Journal of Experimental Psychology*, 1971, **23**, 268–274.

Shaffer, L. H., & Hardwick, J. Typing performance as a function of text. *Quarterly Journal of Experimental Psychology*, 1968, **20**, 360–369.

Shaffer, L. H., & Hardwick, J. Errors and error detection in typing. *Quarterly Journal of Experimental Psychology*, 1969, **21**, 209–213. (a)

Shaffer, L. H., & Hardwick, J. Reading and typing. *Quarterly Journal of Experimental Psychology*, 1969, **21**, 381–383. (b)

Shaffer, L. H., & Hardwick, J. The basis of transcription skill. *Journal of Experimental Psychology*, 1970, **84**, 424–440.

Sternberg, S. The discovery of processing stages: Extensions of Donders' method. *Acta Psychologica*, 1969, **30**, 276–315.

Waugh, N. C., & Norman, D. A. Primary memory. *Psychological Review*, 1965, **72**, 89–104.

Wickelgren, W. A. Context-sensitive coding, associative memory, and serial order in (speech) behavior. *Psychological Review*, 1969, **76**, 1–15.

5 BINARY CLASSIFICATION TASKS

The Use of Binary-Classification Tasks in the Study of Human Information Processing: A Tutorial Survey[1]

Raymond S. Nickerson

Bolt Beranek and Newman Inc.
Cambridge, Massachusetts

ABSTRACT

A binary-classification task is one in which a decision rule partitions a set of stimuli into two exhaustive and mutually exclusive classes. This paper describes several such tasks that have been used in the past few years to study various aspects of human cognition or information processing. Attention is confined to studies in which response time has been the performance measure of primary interest. Selected results are presented. Some of the problems that have been associated with this type of research are noted. A few representative theoretical issues are discussed briefly.

I. Introduction

To put this contribution in perspective, I should indicate what I understand to be the purpose of a tutorial survey. To me, the term *tutorial* suggests a paper that covers fundamentals and assumes little or no prior knowledge of the topic. So, with apologies in advance to those who know

[1]This work was supported by the Air Force Office of Scientific Research under Contract No. F44620-69-C-0115.

449

the area well, I shall address myself primarily to those who do not. I shall try, in what follows, to do four things: (1) describe an approach to the study of certain aspects of cognition; (2) present a brief description of each of several experimental paradigms that illustrate this approach, along with a summary of some of the major findings from experiments in which such paradigms have been used; (3) note some of the problems that have been, or are, associated with this area; and (4) consider some of the types of theoretical issues that relate to this approach.

II. Binary Classification Tasks: An Approach to the Study of Human Information Processing

For our purposes a "binary-classification" task is one in which a decision rule partitions a set of stimuli into two exhaustive and mutually exclusive classes or categories. We shall be concerned in particular with binary-classification tasks in which the subject is asked to determine as quickly as possible in which of the two specified classes a stimulus belongs, and the performance measure of primary interest is response time (RT).[2] Experiments requiring "same"–"different" judgments are considered here to be examples of binary-classification experiments, inasmuch as they typically involve many possible stimuli (or stimulus pairings), whereas the number of admissible responses is two.

Few, if any, experimenters are interested in binary classification *per se*, as opposed to classification in a more general sense. Nevertheless, a fairly large number of experiments using binary-classification tasks have been performed during the last few years. So we might ask: What is the basis of the popularity of this task?

The answer, I believe, is that it allows us to manipulate the perceptual or cognitive demands of a situation while keeping the motor component simple and constant. People who do binary-classification experiments tend to be interested in decision processes as opposed to motor skills, in central as opposed to peripheral limitations to human performance. Representative of the theoretical issues that are raised are such questions as the following: How is visually presented information coded in short-term memory? How is memorized information retrieved and used in the classification process? What sorts of cognitive processes occur (or can occur) in parallel, and what sorts occur (or must occur) in series? To what extent do comparisons between

---

[2]We also will restrict our attention almost exclusively to experiments in which visual stimuli have been used, mainly because the majority of the experiments of interest have in fact used visual stimuli.

visual stimuli involve the decomposition of the stimuli into their constituent features as opposed to the holistic comparison of gestalts? To what extent do such comparisons involve the retrieval and use of "names?" What is a feature? And so on.

One of the ways to approach such questions is to attempt to measure the time required to perform tasks whose cognitive demands vary in specifiable ways. One wants, however, to be sure that the differences he obtains are indeed attributable to the cognitive, and not the motor, aspects of the task—which means keeping the latter constant. Moreover, he wants to be sure that the motor component(s) of the task represents a sufficiently small fraction of the whole to insure that the variability associated with it will not obscure the differences that he is looking for—which means keeping the motor component simple. Binary-classification tasks in which the subject is required to make a simple "yes"–"no" or "same"–"different" response, contingent upon a decision rule of arbitrary complexity, seem to satisfy these requirements.

Sufficiently many binary-classification RT experiments now have been done that it would seem appropriate to review the results and ask ourselves what we have learned from this approach to the study of human thought processes. Elsewhere (Nickerson, 1970) I have attempted a more extensive and critical review of this area. Here the review will of necessity be greatly abbreviated and somewhat superficial. A small sample of the large number of experimental paradigms that have been used and of the results that have been obtained will be considered. The paradigms that will be described, however, are not a random sample; they are what might be considered generic paradigms in that most of them represent basic themes on which many variations can be, or in fact have been, played. The results that will be described may be considered, for the most part, to be surface results, that is, results that are quite apparent from an inspection of summarized data as opposed to those that can only be detected with elaborate statistical procedures.

III. Representative Binary-Classification Tasks and Experimental Results

A. CHARACTER CLASSIFICATION[3]

Of the several tasks that we shall consider, the character-classification task that was developed and refined by Sternberg is probably the most familiar. It, or some variation of it, has been used by a fairly large number of

---

[3]With each task type, I have associated one reference that describes the method in some detail. In this case, it is Sternberg (1969).

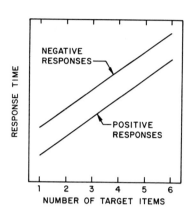

Fig. 1. Some of the main results from character classification experiments: RT increases with the number of target items at about the same rate for positive and negative responses, negative RTs being generally longer than positive RTs.

investigators during the last few years (for example, Bracey, 1969; Clifton & Birenbaum, 1970; DeRosa, 1969; Egeth & Smith, 1967; Forrin & Morin, 1969; Klatsky & Atkinson, 1970; Marcel, 1970; Nickerson, 1966; Sternberg, 1963, 1966, 1967; Wingfield & Branca, 1970).

In the simplest form of this task, the subject is given a set of n (usually from 1 to 6) letters and/or digits (*targets*) to commit to memory. He then is asked to decide as quickly as possible whether a particular character (a *probe*) is included in the target set. The question of interest is how the subject's RT and, by inference, the time required to determine whether the probe is contained in the target set, depends on the value of n. The following major findings, illustrated in Fig. 1,[4] have been obtained several times:

1. RT increases monotonically—often linearly—with n;
2. positive and negative RTs tend to increase with n at about the same rate;
3. for a given n, negative RT tends to be longer than positive RT, if positive and negative trials are equally probable.

Sternberg has inferred from the often-reported linear relationship between RT and n, and the equality of slopes of negative and positive RTs, that performance of the classification task is based on a memory-scanning process that is serial and invariably exhaustive. According to the proposed model, the probe item is compared sequentially with every target, the process terminating only after all comparisons have been made, whether or not any of the comparisons yields a match.

---

[4]This figure and Fig. 3 are idealized representations of data that have been obtained from several experiments. Examples of the results on which these fictions are based may be found in cited reports.

An obvious methodological variation on the multitarget single-probe paradigm involves the use of a single-item target set with a varying number of probes. In this case the question of interest is how RT depends on the number of probes, that is, the number of items the subject must look *at* as opposed to the number he must look *for*. The results of one such experiment (Atkinson, Holmgren, & Juola, 1969) were analogous to those obtained with a single probe and varying numbers of targets, the roles of targets and probes being reversed, of course. Specifically, RT increased linearly with probe set size, and at about the same rate for positive and negative responses, positive RTs being generally shorter than negative RTs.

In a generalized version of the character-classification task, both target and probe sets may contain more than one character, and the subject is required to decide whether *any* of the probes is included in the target set (Nickerson, 1966; Sternberg, 1967). Here, in addition to the number of targets and the number of probes, there can be an additional variable of interest, namely, the number of items the target and probe sets have in common. As shown in Fig. 2, RT tends to decrease with this variable; however, the effect of the variable may diminish greatly with practice. To my knowledge, no model has yet been developed that can account nicely for results such as those shown in this figure. The development of such a model is complicated by the fact that error rates tend to vary greatly with the independent variable and to change considerably over time. What does seem to be clear is that the comparison process must be either self-terminating

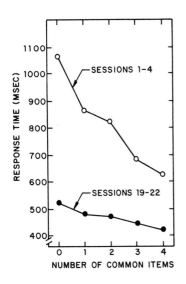

Fig. 2.   RT as a function of the number of items common to four-item target and probe sets. The two curves show performance at two levels of practice. [Data from Nickerson, R. S. Response times with a memory dependent decision task. *Journal of Experimental Psychology*, 1966, 72, 761–769. Copyright 1966 by the American Psychological Association, and reproduced by permission.]

or parallel (or both) with respect to either targets or probes, which is simply to rule out the intuitively improbable possibility that all possible target-probe comparisons are made in a serial and exhaustive fashion.

B. CLASSIFICATION VERSUS NAMING[5]

In the character-classification task, the subject must decide whether a character belongs to a specified set of characters. It is of some interest to know how the time to make such a decision compares with the time required to determine what the character is.

Apparently, the identification process is the faster of the two. Forrin, Kumler, and Morin (1966) found that subjects required less time (100–200 msec less) to name a numeral than to report whether it belonged to a specified set of four numerals. Sternberg's (1969) data also suggest that subjects can name numerals faster than they can classify them. Moreover, the result appears to hold even when the classification task involves highly familiar categories: Dick (1971) found that subjects could name characters from 100 to 200 msec faster than they could report whether they were letters or numerals. Such results leave open the question of what aspect, or aspects, of the classification task lengthens the response time. They do tend, however, to implicate relatively central factors. Input factors are ruled out inasmuch as the inputs are the same for both the naming and the classification tasks. Response organization is a possible candidate because different responses typically are required by the two tasks; however, the role of this factor is questioned by the fact that the shortest RTs are obtained in the situation (naming) for which response entropy is the greatest.

C. "SAME"–"DIFFERENT" JUDGMENTS WITH MULTIATTRIBUTE STIMULI[6]

Stimuli for this task are simple visual figures that vary with respect to such attributes (dimensions) as color, size, and shape. The subject's task is to decide whether two such stimuli are the same or different. The question of interest is how the time required to make the decision depends on the number of attributes with respect to which the stimuli differ.

The common finding, illustrated in Fig. 3, is that "different" RT varies inversely with this variable whereas "same" RT tends to be faster than would be expected from an extrapolation of the "different" RT data to the case in

---

[5]See Forrin, Kumler, and Morin (1966).
[6]See Egeth (1966).

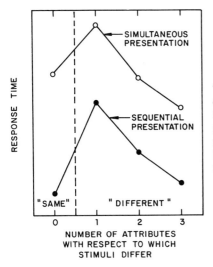

Fig. 3. Idealized results from "same"–"different" experiments with stimuli that can differ with respect to varying numbers of attributes. Negative RT tends to vary inversely with the number of attributes with respect to which stimuli differ. Positive RT is shorter than would be expected from an extrapolation of this relationship to the zero-differing-attributes case.

which zero attributes differ (Egeth, 1966; Hawkins, 1969; Nickerson, 1967b). Also, as the figure indicates, RT is generally faster if the stimuli are separated by a few seconds than if presented simultaneously. Moreover, the sequential presentation appears to shorten the "same" RTs more than the "different" RTs.

D. "Same"–"Different" Judgments with Character Sets[7]

This task is very similar to that described above, except that letters play the role here that stimulus attributes did there. On each trial, the subject judges whether two sets, of n letters each, are the same or different, "same" meaning the same letters in the same positions.

"Different" RT varies directly with the number of letters in the sets being compared, and inversely with the number of letters with respect to which any two sets differ. The latter finding (represented in Fig. 4, which is based on Bamber's data) is analogous to that obtained with Egeth's task, if one assumes that letters in fact do play the same role in this situation as do stimulus attributes in that one. Also, as in the case of the experiments with the simple visual figures, "same" RT is much shorter than would be expected from a simple extrapolation of the negative RT curves to the case of zero differing letters.

---

[7]See Bamber (1969).

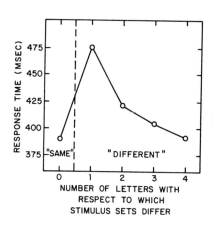

Fig. 4. "Same"–"different" RT as a function of the number of letters with respect to which two four-letter stimuli differ (data from Bamber, 1969).

The relative shortness of "same" RTs in a variety of contexts has been considered to be of some theoretical interest to several investigators. Why, one may ask, should it take less time to decide that two stimuli are the same with respect to all particulars than to decide that they differ with respect to at least one? To accommodate this apparently paradoxical result, Bamber postulated a dual-process model. The model assumes that a fast, identity-detecting process operates in parallel with a slow difference-detecting serial process. The identity-detection process treats the target and probe patterns as wholes, and elicits a response quickly *if* they match; the difference-detecting process is more analytic and plodding, treating the stimuli in terms of their features or parts. The model is nonparsimonious in the sense that it postulates two processes to accomplish a task when one is logically sufficient, but to date more parsimonious models have not been able to accommodate the result.

E. NAME- VERSUS PHYSICAL-IDENTITY MATCHING[8]

The subject is required, in this case, to decide whether two letters are the same or different. In one condition, "same" is defined as "physically identical": AA would require the response "same," whereas Aa would require the response "different." In another condition, "same" is understood to mean "same name," so in this case, both AA and Aa would be considered "same."

If the two letters of a pair are presented simultaneously, or nearly so, the following results are obtained:

---

[8] See Posner and Mitchell (1967).

1. The response "different" is made faster when the task explicitly calls for a comparison of physical features than when it must be based on a comparison of names ($RT_3 < RT_6$, Table 1).
2. Name identity can be determined faster when the stimuli are "physically identical" than when they only have the same names ($RT_4 < RT_5$, Table 1).

[For a review of the numerous experiments that have used some variant of this task, see Posner (1969).] These results have been the basis for inferences regarding the relative "depth of processing" required by different perceptual decision tasks. We shall return to this point in Section IV.

Table 1. *Results from "Same"–"Different" Judgments Based on Name versus Physical Relationships* [a,b]

	Stimulus pair		
Decision	Physically same (AA)	Physically different, same name (Aa)	Physically different, diff. name (AB)
Physically same?	1	2	3
Same name?	4	5	6

[a]After Posner and Mitchell (1967).
[b]Conditions 1, 4, and 5 call for "same" responses; conditions 2, 3, and 6 call for "different" responses.

F. WORD–PICTURE COMPARISONS[9]

Tversky (1969) and others (Fraisse, 1970; Seymour, 1970) have used tasks that, like Posner and Mitchell's (1967), involve comparisons between verbal and nonverbal stimulus representations. Tversky trained subjects to associate a different nonsense syllable with each of several simple drawings of faces. Pairs of stimuli then were presented in all possible combinations of verbal–verbal, verbal–pictorial, and so forth, the subject's task being to decide whether both items of a pair had the same name. Tversky was primarily interested in the question of how verbal and pictorial information

[9]See Tversky (1969).

is encoded in memory, and several seconds were allowed to elapse between the presentation of the two items of a pair. Moreover, the stimulus-presentation sequence was statistically structured in such a way that for any given session, the second stimulus was more than three times as likely to be of one type than of the other. Under these conditions, RT was fastest when the second stimulus was in the "expected" form, whether or not it happened to be in the same form as was the first, suggesting that the form in which such stimuli are represented in short-term memory is at least partially under the subject's control.

Fraisse (1970) has found it to take longer to determine whether a familiar word is the name of a simple visual object than to compare either two words or two objects, and Seymour (1970) found that subjects could read words and name shapes faster than they could decide whether a word was the name of a simultaneously presented shape. These results are representative of many that must be accommodated by any model that purports to account for the processing of both verbally and nonverbally represented information and the articulation of the one type of representation with the other.

G. Classification by Attribute Checking[10]

In this task the subject must decide whether a stimulus belongs to a category that is defined in terms of either a disjunction or a conjunction of some of its readily distinguished features. The independent variables of interest are the number of attributes relevant to the criterion for category membership and the number with respect to which any particular stimulus satisfies a criterion. "Red or square" is an example of a disjunctive category for which two attributes (color and shape) are relevant; "small and blue and circular" is a conjunctive category defined in terms of three attributes". A small red circle would satisfy the first criterion with respect to one attribute, and the second with respect to two. Note, however, that this stimulus would belong to the first category, but not to the second.

One of the reasons for using both disjunctively and conjunctively defined categories in the same experiment is their symmetry with respect to the relationship between number of attributes satisfying a criterion and membership versus nonmembership in the defined category. In the case of a disjunctive criterion, a stimulus is a member if it satisfies the criterion with respect to at least one attribute; it is ruled out only if it fails with respect to all relevant attributes. With a conjunctive criterion, the situation is reversed: a stimulus is a member only if it satisfies the criterion with

---

[10]See Nickerson (1967a).

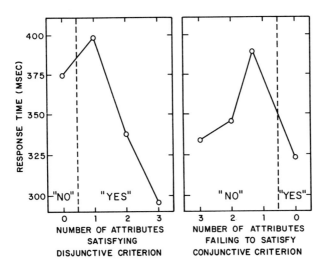

Fig. 5. RT as a function of the number of stimulus attributes satisfying (failing to satisfy) a disjunctive (conjunctive) category definition [Data from Nickerson, R. S. Categorization time with categories defined by disjunctions and conjunctions of stimulus attributes. *Journal of Experimental Psychology*, 1967, **73**, 211–219. Copyright 1967 by the American Psychological Association, and reproduced by permission.]

respect to all relevant attributes; it is a nonmember if it fails with respect to any.

The results shown in Fig. 5 also are symmetrical, to a degree. Consider first the case of a *disjunctive* criterion: for a given number of relevant attributes (three in our example), the time required to make a *positive* decision varies inversely with the number of attributes that *satisfy* the criterion; the *negative* decision is made faster, however, than would be expected from a simple extrapolation of the curve showing RT as a function of the number of attributes that *satisfy* the criterion to the zero case. With a *conjunctive* criterion, *negative* RT varies inversely with the number of attributes *failing to satisfy* the criterion (for a given number of relevant attributes), and *positive* RT is shorter than would be expected from an extrapolation of the negative RT curve to the case of zero attributes failing to satisfy the criterion.

Other results with this paradigm suggest that the disjunctive and conjunctive tasks may differ more substantially than this symmetry would suggest.[11] For example, for a given number of attributes satisfying (failing to

---

[11] Marcel (1970) who has used a similar paradigm has obtained results similar to those shown in Fig. 5 with conjunctive criteria; but with disjunctive criteria his longest RTs were associated with the case in which zero attributes satisfied the criterion. He has also shown that the curves representing positive (negative) RT in the disjunctive (conjunctive) case tend to flatten with practice.

satisfy) a criterion, RT seems to be more sensitive to the number that are relevant to the criterion in the disjunctive than in the conjunctive case. This result is not as reliable as the one mentioned above, and needs to be checked. If it holds up, it will suggest that the process of deciding that a stimulus belongs to a disjunctively defined category is different from that of deciding that it does not belong to a conjunctively defined one, in spite of the similarity of the logical requirements of the two tasks.

H. Scanning a Conceptual Category[12]

In this case, the subject must decide whether a word is the name of an item in a familiar conceptual category (as opposed to an arbitrary category defined for the purposes of an experiment). The question of interest is whether decision time will vary as a function of category size. The independent variable is manipulated by using "nested" categories; thus, the category "living thing" is considered to have more members than the category "animal."

Landauer and Freedman (1968) reported two experiments. In the first, the subject's task was to decide whether a stimulus was a member of one of the following five categories, the particular category being specified before each trial: "word," "noun," "living thing," "animal," and "dog." Every stimulus (whether positive or negative) was presented twice, once with each of two "adjacent" categories; thus, the data could be summarized in terms of the RTs associated with the larger of two categories versus those associated with the smaller, although any given category (except the largest and smallest) would be playing the role of the larger on some occasions and that of the smaller on others. For three of the two-way comparisons (noun versus living thing, living thing versus animal, and animal versus dog), the larger RT was associated with the larger category for both positive and negative responses. In the case of the fourth pairing (word versus noun), the relationship between RT and category size was reversed. (It took longer to decide whether or not a stimulus was a noun than to decide whether or not it was a word.) When the four pairings were pooled into two categories (larger versus smaller), the RT difference proved to be statistically significant in the case of negative responses but not in that of positives.

In the second experiment, Landauer and Freedman had the subjects scan lists, marking either members or nonmembers of specified categories. (Note that both positive and negative decisions are required in both cases.)

---

[12]See Landauer and Freedman (1968).

Scanning time in this experiment was greatest for largest categories with both tasks.

On balance, the results of these experiments suggest that the size of a conceptual category does determine the time required to make a decision concerning membership (or nonmembership) under certain conditions, but they also challenge the generality of the relationship and indicate the need to determine the conditions under which it does hold. (For recent pertinent experiments, see Collins & Quillian, 1970; and Meyer's contribution to this volume.)

I. SCANNING ACROSS CATEGORIES[13]

In a sense, this task is a generalization of that used by Landauer and Freedman (1968), although its use preceded that of the latter chronologically. The decision required is whether a word is the name of an item in *any* of *n* familiar categories (colors, tools, furniture, and the like), and *n* is the independent variable of interest. Category exemplars that will occur as probe stimuli may (Juola & Atkinson, 1971) or may not (Smith, 1967) be listed for the subject before he performs the task.

As might be expected, RT increases with the number of target categories, the rate of increase per category being considerably greater than the rate of increase per target obtained when the targets are enumerated explicitly, as in the more familiar character-classification paradigm. We shall consider this result again in Section V.

IV. Some Problems

In this section I shall mention what appear to me to be some problems that have been, or are, associated with binary-classification RT studies and the attendant theorizing. The problems are not all unique to this context, but they do all have implications for the interpretations that are put on the results from these sorts of experiments.

A. CONCEPTUAL PROBLEMS

There is a need for more precise definitions of many of the concepts that are used to account for experimental findings. For example, template matching is often suggested as one of the possible methods by which visual

---

[13]See Smith (1967).

stimuli might be compared. However, the term *template* has been used in a variety of ways [for a discussion of some of them, see Nickerson (1970)], and precise definitions are lacking. In the absence of details concerning how a template-matching process is assumed to work in any particular case, one may have difficulty judging how (or whether) the assumption of such a process differs *vis-à-vis* its implications regarding decision time from those of alternative processes that have been proposed.

The other side of this coin is a certain vagueness regarding what constitutes a stimulus "attribute" or "feature." (Attribute checking is often contrasted with template matching as an alternative method by which stimuli might be compared.) Garner (1970) has suggested that what experimenters have sometimes considered to be two or more attributes may be treated by the subject as a single one. Some features, he argues, are nonseparable (a stimulus that has a visual shape must also have a size) and are probably perceived in an integrated way. In this view, increasing the number of nonseparable attributes with respect to which two stimuli differ may be effectively equivalent to increasing the magnitude of the difference with respect to a single attribute. If so, whatever effects can be obtained by means of the former manipulation should be reproducible by means of the latter. Whether this proves to be the case remains to be seen. In the meantime, Garner's caveat should make us more dubious than we have been about the obviousness of what constitutes a stimulus attribute. It is interesting to note that such properties as shape, size, and color have been used as stimulus attributes in the experiments we have considered (for example, Egeth, 1966; Hawkins, 1969; Nickerson, 1967b), whereas such properties as hue, saturation, and brightness have not. One suspects that the reason for this is the tacit assumption that the latter set of properties would not be treated by the subject as individual attributes. Garner has challenged the assumption that the former set would be, and in so doing, has called attention to the problem of defining what a stimulus attribute, or feature, is.

A third conceptual problem associated with binary-classification studies has to do with the distinction between classification and recognition (or identification). Character-classification experiments commonly are referred to as experiments on character recognition. There is little evidence, however, that the processes that underlie performance in the types of classification tasks we have been considering are the same as those that mediate recognition, at least insofar as the latter term is used to connote either identification (labeling) or an awareness of having experienced a stimulus before (familiarity). The fact that it takes much less time to name a character than it takes to report whether one belongs to a class of n specified characters (Dick, 1971; Forrin *et al.*, 1966; Sternberg, 1969) strongly suggests the contrary. So, whatever else we are learning from character-classification studies, one may question whether we are learning anything about recognition *per se*.

Other conceptual difficulties stem from the somewhat uncritical way in which we have sometimes used the terms "serial" and "parallel processing." Often these terms appear to be intended to connote mutually exclusive ways in which humans might deal with information, and the possibility that many processes may be neither entirely serial nor entirely parallel is ruled out by default. Little consideration is given to the possibility that two or more processes might overlap in time, but not completely, or that one operation might be performed in parallel with another under some conditions but not under others, or that some operations might be performable in parallel but are *better* performed in series (there may be a difference in this regard between what one *does* under "normal" circumstances and what he *can do* when pressed to his limits), or that the individual's strategy may determine in part the degree of seriality with which he performs some tasks. Sometimes the terms are ambiguous with respect to the level of description intended. To say, for example, that letter recognition is a serial (parallel) process could mean either that the process of identifying a letter involves comparing it with each of a set of memorial representations of letters serially (simultaneously) or that it involves testing the input letter serially (simultaneously) for a specific constellation of features.

B. METHODOLOGICAL PROBLEMS

The binary-classification task, like any other, is subject to problems of methodology, and several have been pointed out. Hawkins (1969) noted, for example, that in "same"–"different" experiments of the type described in Section III,C, it is easy to select inadvertently stimulus pairs in such a way that the probability that the items of a pair are the same with respect to one attribute is not independent of whether they are the same with respect to another. The existence of such correlations could simplify the subject's task somewhat, and, if not appreciated by the experimenter, can lead to an erroneous interpretation of the results.

An artifact that can be obtained with the categorization-by-attribute-checking task (described in Section III,G) has been pointed out by Garner (1970). Suppose that when subjects have to decide whether a stimulus is either red or square, and it is in fact both red and square, they are faster, on the average, than when they have to base their decisions on the "faster" of these two attributes alone (for example, to determine whether the stimulus is red). Such a finding would be consistent with a model that assumed the attributes are processed in parallel in a self-terminating fashion. Garner has pointed out, however, that the result could also be an artifact of individual differences between subjects, each of whom processed the attributes in series. The reader is referred to Garner's article (1970) for a discussion of this problem.

A third problem that is at least in part methodological has to do with the physical- and name-matching paradigm of Posner and Mitchell (1967; see Section III,E). The conceptual distinction and the associated experimental paradigm that Posner and Mitchell introduced have led to numerous experiments, the results of which have provided, in my view, important clues to the nature of perceptual processes. The following comment, which is similar to one made by Kolers (1971), is intended not to challenge the general usefulness of the approach, but simply to mark a methodological point, the overlooking of which invites a misinterpretation of experimental results.

The nub of the problem is the claim that comparisons based on physical features can be made faster than those based on names, and the inference that name matches require a deeper "level" of processing than do physical matches. Consider what it means to say that two stimuli are physically the same. Clearly, it cannot mean that they are physically identical in the most literal sense, since we can be certain that no two stimuli ever are. What it must mean is that one is willing to *consider* them to be the same for some purpose—in the case of our example, for the purpose of satisfying the experimenter's presumed definition of sameness. The amount of dissimilarity one is justified in overlooking when deciding that two items are the same must depend on what he knows, or assumes, concerning the magnitudes of the differences he may encounter in the case of those stimuli that he is expected to classify as different. If he knows that (at least some of) the different stimuli differ by very little (say, about a jnd), it doubtless will be more difficult to determine that two stimuli are the same than if he can assume that different stimuli (by the experimenter's definition) *always* differ by readily discriminated amounts. It is, in fact, easy to show that one can manipulate the time required to determine sameness by varying the amount by which *different* stimuli differ (Nickerson, 1969).

In Posner and Mitchell's (1967) experiment, and in subsequent studies that have exploited the physical- versus name-identity paradigm (for example, Posner & Keele, 1967; Posner & Taylor, 1969; Posner, Boies, Eichelman, & Taylor, 1969), stimuli that were physically different (from the experimenter's viewpoint) differed by relatively large amounts. The subject did not need to look for small, difficult-to-detect differences because he knew there would be none (or, more accurately, that he could overlook them if there were any). But suppose, as Kolers (1971) has suggested, that letters were allowed to differ slightly from trial to trial (for example, the angle of a capital A were varied, or the height of the cross bar), and that the subject had the task, under one condition, of making "different" responses contingent on such physical differences, and under another condition, of comparing the stimuli with respect to their names. Would it still take less time to compare stimuli *vis-à-vis* their physical features than to compare them with respect to their names? One suspects not. If this conjecture is correct, then we are left with the conclusion that matches based on physical features can be made faster than those based on names[14] *under some conditions*, whereas the reverse relationship will hold under others. Posner (1969; see also Posner & Mitchell, 1967) has been careful to point out that while results such as those shown in Table 1 suggest different levels of processing, they do not necessarily support the idea that the hypothesized levels represent steps in a serial chain, in which a test of physical identity always precedes a comparison of names. The question that is being raised here is this: if the above conjecture regarding the contingency of the relationship between physical- and name-match RTs is correct, can *anything* of a general nature be said concerning the dependence of depth of processing on whether the task calls for a comparison of physical features or of names?

V. Some Theoretical Issues

One way to summarize the theoretical objectives of individuals working in this area is to say that the general goal has been to identify the events that occupy the interval between the presentation of the stimulus and the execution of the response, and to specify their temporal properties and relationships to each other (the order in which they occur, their durations, the extent to which they may overlap, and so on). Thus, a number of theorists have developed models that distinguish several "stages" of information processing that occupy the RT interval. These models will not be presented here; descriptions of them may be found in readily accessible sources (for example, Sternberg, 1969; Bamber, 1969; Hawkins, 1969; Posner & Mitchell, 1967). What I shall attempt to do instead is to present some conceptualizations that are at least grossly representative of the *types* of models that

---

[14]It is understood, of course, that name matches must themselves be based ultimately on the physical features of the stimuli—though not on their physical identity—inasmuch as a classification based on physical properties must underlie the retrieval from memory of stimulus names.

have been considered, and to note a few theoretical issues that are *representative* of those that have been raised. Some points concerning theoretical interpretations of specific experimental results already have been made in preceding sections.

A. CHARACTER CLASSIFICATION

Figure 6 shows several alternative conceptualizations of how the character-classification (several targets, one probe) task might be performed. There are other possibilities, of course. These are selected because they are similar to alternatives that have been suggested (Sternberg, 1967).

According to Model (a) of Fig. 6 the classification is basically a comparison of an "image" of the probe against a set of stored images of the targets. Model (b) assumes the process involves a comparison of the probe's name against target names. Model (c) assumes feature checking. In Model (d), a partially parallel process is hypothesized in which name and image matching occur simultaneously. Other combinations of image, name, and feature checking similar to Model (d) are also plausible.

To be able to select one of these conceptualizations as more tenable than the others in the light of data would be a step forward, to be sure, but only a small step. Any of these conceptualizations raises more questions than it answers—for example: What sorts of transformations are performed on the raw input during the image-forming stage? Is the input "preprocessed" and perhaps stored in some canonical form? How are names retrieved from long-term memory? Is a search process involved? If so, is it a serial search, a parallel search, a search with both serial and parallel aspects? How does the short-term memory representation of targets change as a function of time? What is the nature of the process by which the representation of a probe (whatever that representation is) is compared with the target representations? When is the comparison process terminated? (That a comparison process is involved is assumed by each conceptualization, but this assumption may itself be challenged, of course.) If feature testing is involved, what constitutes a feature? Are all the features of the probe tested against those of each target in turn, or are all of the targets compared with the probe with respect to one feature, and then with respect to another, and so on? If images and names are compared simultaneously, what triggers the response? Several of these questions have been raised and approached experimentally. The reader is referred to Sternberg (1969) for a review of several of the relevant studies.

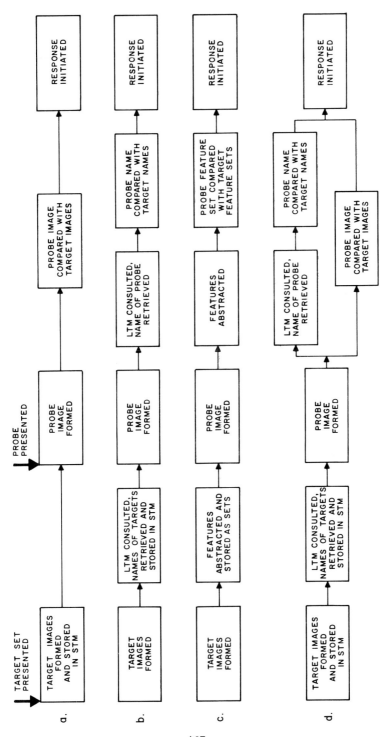

Fig. 6. Some alternative conceptualizations of the processes underlying character classification.

467

B. Attribute Checking

Consider the task of deciding whether a stimulus has *either* feature A or feature B, say, is either red or square (assuming for the moment that color and shape may be treated as separable attributes). Figure 7 shows a variety of ways in which the performance of this task might be conceptualized. In Model (a) of Fig. 7 it is assumed that the test stimulus is compared, as a whole, and serially, against representations of each of the stimuli that might occur as positive instances. (There is a tacit assumption here that the subject knows what attributes of the stimulus, if any, might be varied in addition to those that are relevant to the decision.) Model (b) represents a similar process in which the comparisons are made simultaneously. In Models (c) and (d), the process is hypothesized to be based on a comparison of stimulus features against the features that define the disjunctive category. Similar alternative representations could be developed for conjuctively defined categories.

Again, however, any one of these representations probably raises more questions than it answers. For example, the question of the exhaustiveness of the comparison process is an appropriate one to ask with respect to each: is the response made when sufficient information is acquired to warrant it, or only after all relevant comparisons have been made? In the case of the serial models (a and c), are we to assume that the order in which stimuli or attributes are checked is invariant (for a given subject, say) or random?

Unfortunately, whereas models such as those represented in Fig. 7 obviously differ in terms of hypothesized processes, they do not always make greatly divergent predictions concerning what to expect by way of experimental results. For example, although Model (c) hypothesizes a serial process, where Model (d) hypothesizes a parallel one, both predict that decision time will be inversely related to the number of stimulus attributes that satisfy the criterion, if we assume:

1. (in the case of the parallel model) the time required to compare two attributes is a random variable;

2. the comparison process is self-terminating;

3. (in the case of the serial model) attributes are checked in random order.

For the serial model, the prediction follows from the fact that the more attributes that satisfy the criterion, the fewer that will be checked, on the average, before a match is found. For the parallel model, it follows from the fact that if two tests are being carried out independently and simultaneously, the distribution of times for stimuli that satisfy both tests will be a com-

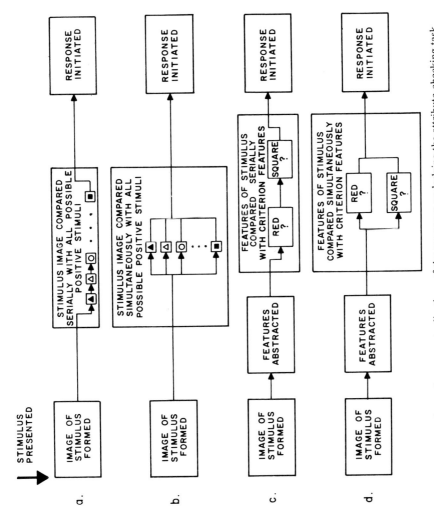

Fig. 7. Some alternative conceptualizations of the processes underlying the attribute-checking task.

469

posite distribution, the mean of which will be less than the least of the
means of the component distributions (provided the component distributions overlap; if they do not overlap, the mean of the composite distribution
will be equal to the lesser of the component means). Specifically, the composite distribution will be a distribution of minima, generated by randomly
sampling pairs of values, one from each component distribution, and
always keeping the smaller value.

When the stimulus satisfies neither of the tests (that is, it satisfies the
criterion with respect to zero attributes), the distribution of decision times
will be a distribution of maxima. In this case, if the component distributions
overlap, the mean of the composite distribution will be larger than the larger
of the component means.[15] Thus, the parallel feature-checking model predicts the same ordinal relationship between RT and the number of features
satisfying the disjunctive criterion as does the model that assumes features
are checked serially. A similar line of reasoning would show that the same
dilemma holds in the case of conjunctively defined criteria.

I do not wish to create the impression that serial and parallel models
always have the same implications for the outcomes of binary-classification
experiments, because they do not, but rather to illustrate that comparisons
that might appear at first glance to permit a crucial experiment may fail
on closer examination.

C. Scanning across Categories

Consider now the task of deciding whether a word is the name of
an item in any of n familiar categories. Several conceptualizations of the
processes that might underlie the performance of this task are shown in
Fig. 8. The first two of these are similar to those considered by Smith (1967)
and by Juola and Atkinson (1971).

The first conceptualization (Fig. 8a) assumes that the subject compares the probe word with exemplars that he generates for each target category. The second (Fig. 8b) assumes that he generates the name of the
category to which the probe belongs and compares this with the target
category names. These conceptualizations have in common the assumption
that the process involves direct comparisons between items of a kind: either
exemplars against exemplars, or category names against category names.

---

[15]It should be pointed out that the models represented in Fig. 7 imply that the longest RTs will be obtained when the stimulus satisfies (fails to satisfy) a disjunctive (conjunctive) criterion with respect to zero attributes, an implication that is at odds with the
results shown in Fig. 5.

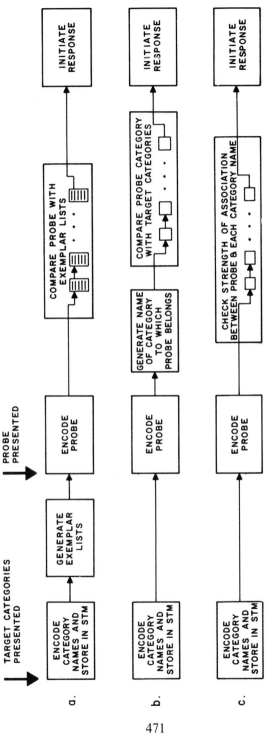

Fig. 8. Some alternative conceptualizations of the processes underlying performance of the task of scanning across categories.

471

Thus, both must postulate a generation operation. In the third conceptualization (Fig. 8c) such a direct comparison of like items is not considered to be necessary; rather, it is assumed that a probe can be checked against a category name and a direct test made of "belongingness," or "associative strength," or some such property.

Again, we see (and this is the point of this exercise) that these conceptualizations raise numerous questions. For example, what does it mean to "encode" a word stimulus? To store away in short-term memory a visual representation of a letter string? To store an "auditory" analog of that string? To store the "meaning" of the word? To activate an existing "trace" or "engram" in long-term memory?

To what extent does the encoding of the probe interfere with the retention in "active" memory of the category names or exemplar lists? [Model (a) in Fig. 8 assumes that the time between the presentation of the target categories and that of the probe is sufficient to allow the subject to generate lists of category exemplars. When the timing is such as to preclude this, the exemplar-generation process would have to occur *after* the probe is presented.] What is involved in generating a category name, given an exemplar? Does this process involve a search? If so, how is *it* organized?

Note that just a consideration of the questions of seriality and exhaustiveness as they apply to both categories and exemplars leads to a large variety of ways in which comparisons between probe and category exemplars could proceed. The probe might be compared: serially with all (some) of the exemplars of one category, then with all (some) of those of another, and so on until all (several) of the categories had been scanned; serially with one exemplar from every (several) category(ies), then with a second exemplar from every (several) category(ies), and so on, until all (some) of the exemplars from every (several) category(ies) had been checked; with all (several) exemplars of one category in parallel, then with all (several) exemplars of another category in parallel, and so forth; . . . ; with all exemplars of all categories at once.

Model (c) in Fig. 8 opens the question of a decision criterion. How does the process determine whether the association between a probe and a category name is strong enough to warrant a positive response?

VI. Concluding Remarks

We have surveyed in a cursory fashion several experimental tasks that have one feature in common: the subject must make a binary choice on the basis of a rule that partitions all stimulus possibilities into two mutually exclusive categories. The partitioning rule differs, however, from task to task, the choice of response depending on such considerations as whether the stimulus: is contained in a set of memorized stimuli; looks like another stimulus; has the same name as another stimulus; has certain specified features; is the name of a member of one or more semantic categories; and so on. Moreover, the experiments we have considered have differed greatly in many particulars other than the decision rules employed, for example, the nature of the stimuli used, the amount of training given to the subjects, the importance attached to speed versus accuracy, the specifics of the experimental sessions (stimulus intensities and durations, interstimulus intervals, the number of trials per session, the amount of presession warm-up, and the like).

Question: Is it reasonable to expect that a model might be developed that would accommodate the results from such a potpourri of tasks and experimental conditions? Clearly, no model that has been developed so far can do so. This is not a criticism of the models that exist, but simply an acknowledgment of their limitations. Model builders typically have been concerned with accounting for performance in a specific task situation such as one of those considered in Section III. Maybe the best we can expect at this point in time is a collection of models, each designed to handle some small subset of these data. On the other hand, some serious attempts to integrate such diverse results might well lead to models of considerably greater scope.

References

Atkinson, R. C., Holmgren, J. E., & Juola, J. F. Processing time as influenced by the number of elements in a visual display. *Perception and Psychophysics*, 1969, **6**, 321–326.

Bamber, D. Reaction times and error rates for "same"–"different" judgments of multidimensional stimuli. *Perception and Psychophysics*, 1969, **6**, 169–174.

Bracey, G. W. Two operations in character recognition: A partial replication. *Perception and Psychophysics*, 1969, **6**, 357–360.

Clifton, C., Jr., & Birenbaum, S. Effects of serial position and delay of probe in a memory scan task. *Journal of Experimental Psychology*, 1970, **86**, 69–76.

Collins, A. M., & Quillian, M. R. Does category size affect categorization time? *Journal of Verbal Learning and Verbal Behavior*, 1970, **9**, 432–438.

DeRosa, D. V. Transformation of sets in short-term memory: Set size reduction by deletion. *Journal of Experimental Psychology*, 1969, **82**, 415–426.

Dick, A. O. Processing time for naming and categorization of letters and numbers. *Perception and Psychophysics*, 1971, **9**, 350–352.

Egeth, H. E. Parallel versus serial processes in multidimensional stimulus discrimination. *Perception and Psychophysics*, 1966, **1**, 245–252.

Egeth, H., & Smith, E. E. On the nature of errors in a choice reaction task. *Psychonomic Science*, 1967, **8**, 345–346.

Forrin, B., & Morin, R. E. Recognition times for items in short- and long-term memory. In W. G. Koster, (Ed.), *Attention and performance II*. Amsterdam: North-Holland Publ., 1969. Pp. 126–141.

Forrin, B., Kumler, M. L., & Morin, R. E. The effects of response code and signal probability in a numeral-naming task. *Canadian Journal of Psychology*, 1966, **20**, 115–124.

Fraisse, P. Reconnaissance de l'identité physique et sémantique de dessins et de noms. Schweizerische Zeitschrift für Psychologie und Ihre Anwendungen, 1970, **29**, 76–84.

Garner, W. R. The stimulus in information processing. *American Psychologist*, 1970, **25**, 350–358.

Hawkins, H. L. Parallel processing in complex visual discrimination. *Perception and Psychophysics*, 1969, **5**, 56–64.

Juola, J. F., & Atkinson, R. C. Memory scanning for words versus categories. *Journal of Verbal Learning and Verbal Behavior*, 1971, **10**, 522–527.

Klatsky, R. A., & Atkinson, R. C. Memory scans based on alternative test stimulus representations. *Perception and Psychophysics*, 1970, **8**, 113–117.

Kolers, P. A. Some problems of classification. Paper presented at the Conference on Communicating by Language, National Institutes of Child Health and Human Development, 1971.

Landauer, T. K., & Freedman, J. L. Information retrieval from long-term memory: Category size and recognition time. *Journal of Verbal learning and Verbal Behavior*, 1968, **7**, 291–295.

Marcel, A. J. Some constraints on sequential and parallel processing, and the limits of attention. In A. F. Sanders (Ed.), *Attention and performance III*. Amsterdam: North-Holland Publ., 1970. Pp. 77–92.

Nickerson, R. S. Response times with a memory-dependent decision task. *Journal of Experimental Psychology*, 1966, **72**, 761–769.

Nickerson, R. S. Categorization time with categories defined by disjunctions and conjunctions of stimulus attributes. *Journal of Experimental Psychology*, 1967, **73**, 211–219. (a)

Nickerson, R. S. "Same"–"different" response times with multiattribute stimulus differences. *Perceptual and Motor Skills*, 1967, **24**, 543–554. (b)

Nickerson, R. S. "Same"–"different" response times: A model and a preliminary test. In W. G. Koster (Ed.), *Attention and performance II*. Amsterdam: North Holland Publ., 1969. Pp. 257–275.

Nickerson, R. S. Binary-classification reaction time: A review of some studies of human information-processing capabilities. Bolt Beranek and Newman Inc. Report no. 2004, 28 December, 1970, also to be published as *Psychonomic Monograph* No. M65, 1972.

Posner, M. I. Abstraction and the process of recognition. In K. W. Spence & G. Bower (Eds.), *Psychology of learning and motivation. Vol. III*. New York: Academic Press, 1969 Pp. 43–100.

Posner, M. I., & Keele, S. W. Decay of visual information from a single letter. *Science*, 1967, **158**, 137–139.

Posner, M. I., & Mitchell, R. F. Chronometric analysis of classification. *Psychological Review*, 1967, **74**, 392–409.

Posner, M. I., & Taylor, R. L. Subtractive method applied to separation of visual and name components of multiletter arrays. In W. G. Koster (Ed.), *Attention and Performance II*. Amsterdam: North-Holland Publ., 1969. Pp. 104–114.

Posner, M. I., Boies, S. J., Eichelman, W. H., & Taylor, R. L. Retention of visual and name codes of single letters. *Journal of Experimental Psychology Monograph*, 1969, **79** (Whole No. 1, Pt. 2).

Seymour, P. H. K. Representational processes in comprehension of printed words. *British Journal of Psychology*, 1970, **61**, 207–218.

Smith, E. E. Effects of familiarity on stimulus recognition and categorization. *Journal of Experimental Psychology*, 1967, **74**, 324–332.

Sternberg, S. Retrieval from recent memory: Some reaction-time experiments and a search theory. Paper presented at the Psychonomic Society, Bryn Mawr, Pennsylvania, August, 1963.

Sternberg, S. High-speed scanning in human memory. *Science*, 1966, **153**, 652–654.

Sternberg, S. Two operations in character recognition: Some evidence from RT measurement. *Perception and Psychophysics*, 1967, **2**, 45–53.

Sternberg, S. Memory-scanning: Mental processes revealed by reaction-time experiments. *American Scientist*, 1969, **57**, 421–457.

Tversky, B. Pictorial and verbal encoding in a short-term memory task. *Perception and Psychophysics*, 1969, **6**, 225–233.

Wingfield, A., & Branca, A. A. Strategy in high-speed memory search. *Journal of Experimental Psychology*, 1970, **83**, 63–67.

Information Retrieval Processes in "Same"–"Different" Judgments of Letter Strings

Donald Bamber   *Stanley Paine*

Psychology Service
Veterans Administration Hospital
St. Cloud, Minnesota

ABSTRACT

Various models were proposed describing how items might be retrieved from information stores which depict spatial arrays of items. An experiment involving "same"–"different" judgments of letter strings was performed to test these models. The results indicated that people are unable to retrieve a letter directly from a previously specified position in the memory trace of a letter string. Instead, items are fetched sequentially, with the order of fetching being independent of the position specified. To retrieve the desired item, it is necessary to wait for its turn in the fetching sequence.

I. Allocated Information Stores

This contribution is concerned with information retrieval from what might be called allocated information stores (AIS). The prototype of an AIS is the memory trace of a row of letters. This memory trace contains information, not only about the identity of the letters, but also their positions in the row. In general, AISs are assumed, not only to retain items, but also to associate each item with a tag which allocates that item to a particular spatial position. Suppose, for example, a person were presented with the row of letters *C V Z J*. Then, representing position tags with numerals, his

477

memory trace of the letter string would contain the pairs $(C, 1)$ $(V, 2)$, $(Z, 3)$, and $(J, 4)$.

Whenever an item is retrieved from an AIS, its position tag is retrieved with it. Retrieval of items and their position tags from an AIS may be termed either *general* or *selective retrieval*, depending on whether all items or only those items corresponding to certain spatial positions are to be retrieved. In selective retrieval, specifications of the spatial positions for which information is desired are termed retrieval cues. In the above example, if the person were asked to reproduce the entire row of letters, all four pairs of letter and position tag would be retrieved from the memory trace. That would be an instance of general retrieval. Suppose, on the other hand, the person were asked to reproduce only the first and third letters of the row. Thus, the retrieval cues would be *1* and *3*. Only the pairs $(C, 1)$ and $(Z, 3)$ corresponding to the retrieval cues *1* and *3* would be retrieved. That would be an instance of selective retrieval.

Three models of retrieval from AISs, one general and two selective, will be considered here. All of these are termed *serial models* because items are assumed to be retrieved one after another rather than simultaneously. In the general-retrieval model, pairs consisting of an item and its position tag are fetched from the AIS one after another until all items have been fetched. In the two selective-retrieval models, a set of retrieval cues are assumed to have been supplied before retrieval is begun. In the indirect selective-retrieval model, the retrieval of an item and its position tag is a two-stage process. First, an item and its position tag are fetched from the AIS; then, the position tag is checked. The order in which items and their position tags are fetched from the AIS may be predetermined or it may be random, but, in either case, the order is independent of the retrieval cues. Consequently, some inappropriate items may be fetched. After fetching an item, its position tag is checked against the retrieval cues. If the tag does not match any of the cues, the item is discarded. Only those items that have been fetched but not discarded are considered to have been retrieved. This process continues until all the desired items have been retrieved. Thus, in the example of selective retrieval given above, the pairs $(C, 1)$, $(V, 2)$, and $(Z, 3)$ all might be fetched, but $(V, 2)$ would be discarded. It can be seen that indirect selective retrieval is basically a form of general retrieval that has been modified by the addition of a tag check and the addition of the capability of stopping the fetching sequence while there are still unfetched items in the AIS. In the direct selective-retrieval model, the first and only items fetched are those items having position tags specified by the retrieval cues. Thus, there is no need for a tag check to discard inappropriately fetched items.

II. "Same"–"Different" Judgments

Bamber (1969a) performed an experiment in which the subjects were shown a row of letters and allowed to memorize it. Then, the row was removed and the subject was shown tachistoscopically a second row of letters containing the same number of letters as the first row. Let the first and second rows of letters be termed the criterion string (CS) and test string (TS), respectively. The subject's task was to indicate, by pressing one of two keys, whether the CS and TS were "same" (that is, had identical letters in identical orders) or were "different."

In discussing this experiment, it is useful to introduce the concept of the joint AIS. Now, the letters of the TS are stored in a rapidly fading visual image (Sperling, 1960; Averbach & Coriell, 1961). Neisser (1967, Chapter 2) has termed such a visual image an icon; that term will be employed here. Both the TS icon and the memory trace of the CS store information about the positions as well as the identities of the letters in the two strings. Thus, the memory trace and the icon are both AISs. In the context of the "same"–"different" judgment task, it makes sense to consider the CS memory trace and the TS icon as comprising a unified information storage and retrieval system. This system is termed the *joint AIS*.

It is convenient to conceptualize joint AIS as storing triplets consisting of a position tag and the corresponding letters from the CS and TS. Thus, if the CS was *T J K F* and the TS was *T C V F*, then joint AIS would contain the triplets $(T, T, 1)$, $(J, C, 2)$, $(K, V, 3)$, and $(F, F, 4)$. Throughout most of this paper, the joint AIS will be treated as a black box from which triplets are retrieved serially. At the end of the paper, the inner workings of joint AIS will be considered.

The above experiment was performed to test a serial, self-terminating model of "same"–"different" judgments (Egeth, 1966; Nickerson, 1970). The basic serial, self-terminating model assumes that each letter from the CS is compared with the corresponding letter from the TS, one letter pair after another. As soon as any letter pair is found not to match, the "different" response is initiated. If all the letter pairs are found to match, the "same" response is initiated. This model may be put in the form of a "verbal flow diagram" as follows.

BASIC SERIAL, SELF-TERMINATING MODEL

Step 1. Locate a previously unfetched triplet in joint AIS. If none can be found, respond "same" and terminate.

Step 2. Fetch that triplet from joint AIS.

Step 3. Does the triplet's CS letter match its TS letter? If "no," respond "different" and terminate. If "yes," return to Step 1.

The "different" response reaction times (RT) from the above experiment were consistent with the serial, self-terminating model. However, the "same" response RTs were not. The model predicts that the "same" responses should be slower than the "different" responses; however, they were faster than the "different" responses. A number of other investigators studying "same"–"different" judgments of multidimensional stimuli have found "same" responses to be faster than "different" responses (Nickerson, 1970). (When unidimensional stimuli have been employed, the opposite result has often been obtained.)

To account for the discrepancy between the results of the above experiment and the predictions of the serial, self-terminating model, a two-processor model was proposed. In this model, two stimulus-comparison processors, a fast processor and a slow processor, are assumed to operate simultaneously. The operation of the slow processor is described by the serial, self-terminating model. The fast processor can indicate only that the letter strings are "same." When the letter strings are "different," there is no output from the fast processor. When the letter strings are "same," this is indicated by both processors. However, the fast processor usually indicates this before the slow processor. Therefore, the "same" responses usually are initiated by the fast processor. When the two strings are "different," only the slow processor indicates that fact. Thus, the "different" responses are always initiated by the slow processor. This model accounts for why the "different" RTs are consistent with the serial, self-terminating model, but the "same" RTs are faster than predicted.

III. Encoding the Criterion String and Test String

Two letters are said to be physically identical if they have the same appearance; they are said to be nominally identical if they have the same name (Posner & Mitchell, 1967). Similarly, two letter strings may be said to be physically (nominally) identical if the corresponding letters from the two strings are physically (nominally) identical. In the above experiment, the CS and TS were either physically and nominally "same" or physically and nominally "different." This raises the question of whether the CS and the TS were encoded visually and then compared, or encoded verbally and then compared. Either alternative would be possible.

Conrad (1964) found that letters stored in immediate memory are encoded verbally. Posner and Keele (1967) discovered what may be the explanation of Conrad's findings. Apparently visual codes of letters decay from immediate memory within a couple of seconds. Thus, it might be expected that the CS in the above experiment would be encoded verbally. The fact that subjects can occasionally be heard mumbling the letters of the CS corroborates this view. Obviously, since the TS is stored in an icon, it must be encoded visually. How can the CS and TS be compared if the CS is encoded verbally and the TS visually? Either the TS may be recoded in a verbal form or a visual image of the CS may be generated (Posner, Boies, Eichelman, & Taylor, 1969; Tversky, 1969). Available evidence supports the latter alternative. First, RTs for judging whether two physically "different" letter strings are nominally "same" or nominally "different" are longer than RTs for judging whether two letter strings are physically and nominally "same" or physically and nominally "different" (Bamber, 1972). If the CS and TS were always encoded verbally, no such difference would be expected. Second, the subjects claim that they form a visual image of the CS before viewing the TS. Presumably, then, the subject compares a visually encoded memory trace of the CS with the TS icon.

This strategy of, first, encoding the CS verbally and subsequently generating a visual image of it may be a way of bridging the temporal gap between the presentations of the CS and TS. If the visual image of the CS were formed immediately upon viewing the CS, it might fade before the presentation of the TS.

IV. A Proposed Experiment

The experiment reported here is similar to the experiment described above (Bamber, 1969a). The primary difference between the two experiments is the following. In the present experiment, stimuli were constructed by placing a row of four white rectangles on a black background. To construct the CSs, a letter was placed in every rectangle; however, in the TSs, some of the rectangles could be left blank. The subject's task was to respond "same" if the letters actually present in the TS were physically identical to the corresponding letters in the CS, and to respond "different" otherwise. Thus, if the CS was Z F B J and the TS was *blank F blank J*, the correct response was "same." If the TS had been Z F N *blank*, the correct response would have been "different."

If a position in the TS were known to contain a blank, any comparison between the blank and the corresponding letter in the CS would be pointless. Thus, if the subject knew which positions in the TS contained letters and which contained blanks, he could selectively retrieve from joint AIS only those triplets containing no blanks. Neisser (1967, Chapter 4) has theorized that there are preattentive processes that divide the visual field into objects and attentional processes that focus various analyzing mechanisms on those objects. This theory has received some empirical support from an experiment by Shaw (1969). Conceivably, preattentive processes may locate the letters in the TS and thus provide retrieval cues for the selective retrieval from joint AIS of triplets containing no blanks. For example, if the TS were *K blank blank F*, the preattentive processes would provide the position tags *1* and *4* as retrieval cues.

Three different serial models may be proposed for the way triplets are retrieved from joint AIS in this experiment. Two models assume that preattentive processes locate the letters in the TS and provide retrieval cues specifying the positions of those letters. The triplets corresponding to those positions then are retrieved selectively from joint AIS. This gives two models because the selective retrieval may be achieved either directly or indirectly. The remaining model assumes that there are no preattentive processes. Consequently, no retrieval cues are available to the subject, and he must resort to general retrieval. Each one of these three retrieval models may be amalgamated with the basic serial, self-terminating model of "same"–"different" judgments. This yields three models of "same"–"different" judgments that differ with respect to the type of retrieval assumed. These models are outlined below. Note that the two selective models have a Step 0 and the general model does not.

GENERAL-RETRIEVAL MODEL

> *Step 1.* Locate a previously unfetched triplet in joint AIS. If none can be found, respond "same" and terminate.
> *Step 2.* Fetch that triplet from joint AIS.
> *Step 3.* Does the triplet contain a blank instead of a TS letter? If "yes," return to Step 1.
> *Step 4.* Does the CS letter of the triplet match its TS letter? If "no," respond "different" and terminate. If "yes," return to Step 1.

INDIRECT SELECTIVE-RETRIEVAL MODEL

> *Step 0.* Employ the preattentive processes to generate a set of retrieval cues specifying the positions of letters in the TS.
> *Step 1.* Locate a previously unfetched triplet in joint AIS.
> *Step 2.* Fetch that triplet from joint AIS.

Step 3. Does the position tag of the triplet match any of the retrieval cues? If "no," return to Step 1.

Step 4. Does the CS letter of the triplet match its TS letter? If "no," respond "different" and terminate.

Step 5. For every retrieval cue, has the corresponding triplet been fetched? If "no," return to Step 1. If "yes," respond "same" and terminate.

DIRECT SELECTIVE-RETRIEVAL MODEL

Step 0. Employ the preattentive processes to generate a set of retrieval cues specifying the positions of letters in the TS.

Step 1. Locate a retrieval cue for which the corresponding triplet has not yet been fetched. If none can be found, respond "same" and terminate.

Step 2. Fetch from joint AIS the triplet whose position tag matches that retrieval cue.

Step 3. Does the triplet's CS letter match its TS letter? If "no," respond "different" and terminate. If "yes," return to Step 1.

Let N denote the number of rectangles in the CS and TS. (N was fixed at four in this experiment.) Let L denote the total number of letters in the TS and let D denote the number of those letters that do not match the corresponding letter in the CS. The three main conditions in this experiment were determined by the value of D. Either the CS and TS were "same" (that is, $D = 0$), or "different" with $D = 1$, or "different" with $D = L$. Depending on whether a triplet contains a letter and a blank, or whether it contains two letters that match or mismatch, a triplet may be said to be either blank, "same," or "different." Examples of these three triplet types are: $(B, blank, 2)$, $(B, B, 2)$, and $(B, K, 2)$. Thus, joint AIS will always contain D "different" triplets, $L - D$ "same" triplets, and $N - L$ blank triplets.

The three models given above all agree on the following predictions: When the CS and TS are "same," all L "same" triplets and no "different" triplets will be fetched from joint AIS. When $D = 1$, one "different" triplet and, on the average, half of the $L - 1$ "same" triplets will be fetched. When $D = L$, one "different" triplet and no "same" triplets will be fetched.

It is with respect to the number of blank triplets fetched that the three models differ. The direct selective retrieval model predicts that no blank triplets are ever fetched. A total of $N - L$ blank triplets are stored in joint AIS. What proportion of these blank triplets do the general and indirect selective retrieval models predict will be fetched on the average? The two models agree that the proportions will be $\frac{1}{2}$ and $1/(L + 1)$ when $D = 1$ and $D = L$, respectively. When the CS and TS are "same," the indirect selective retrieval model predicts that the proportion will be $L/(L + 1)$ and the general retrieval model predicts that the proportion will be 1. The method used to derive the above predictions is presented in Bamber (1969b, Appendix 1).

Let t_s, t_d, and t_b denote the mean amount of time taken to fetch and process a "same" triplet, a "different" triplet, and a blank triplet, respectively. Let i and p denote, respectively, the mean time taken by sensory and preattentive processes in a single RT. Since the preattentive processes must always examine the same fixed number of rectangles in the TS, it is assumed that p is independent of the number of letters placed in those rectangles. For the general retrieval model, p will be zero. Depending on whether the response is "same" or "different," let m_s and m_d denote the mean time taken by motor processes in a single RT. Then, let a_s and a_d denote $i + p + m_s + t_s$ and $i + p + m_d + t_d$, respectively.

What RT predictions to these models make? These predictions can be derived by adding together the times taken by sensory, preattentive, and motor processes together with the total time spent fetching and examining triplets. By suitably combining the various terms, the following predictions of mean RT can be derived from the general retrieval model:

$$RT_{D=1} = a_d + \tfrac{1}{2}(N - 1)t_b + \tfrac{1}{2}(L - 1)(t_s - t_b), \qquad (1)$$

$$RT_{D=L} = a_d + \left(\frac{N - L}{L + 1}\right)t_b, \qquad (2)$$

$$RT_{same} = a_s + (N - 1)t_b + (L - 1)(t_s - t_b). \qquad (3)$$

The indirect selective retrieval model makes the above predictions for "different" RTs. However, for mean "same" RTs, it predicts

$$RT_{same} = a_s + (N - 1)t_b + (L - 1)(t_s - t_b) - \left(\frac{N - L}{L + 1}\right)t_b. \qquad (4)$$

According to the direct selective retrieval model, no blank triplets are ever fetched from joint AIS. Consequently, the mean RT predictions of that model can be derived by setting t_b equal to zero in Eqs. (1)–(3).

When Bamber (1969a) proposed a two-processor model, the nature of the fast processor was left unspecified. However, the fast processor was given the name *identity reporter*. Thus, it would be consistent with that name to propose that the fast processor can initiate a "same" response only when the CS and TS have the same overall appearance. Now, when the TS contains blanks, it certainly looks very different from the CS. Thus, under those circumstances, the fast processor would not respond and the "same" response should be initiated by the slow processor. Consequently, the fast processor would initiate "same" responses only when L equals N. When L is less than N, "same" responses should be consistent with a serial, self-terminating model.

Several other investigators have proposed some form or another of a two-processor model for "same"–"different" judgments. A number of these models assume that the fast processor compares stimuli on some kind of holistic basis (Nickerson, 1970). Thus, these models would agree with the conclusion that, when the TS contains blanks, "same" responses should be initiated by the slow processor.

V. Method

A. PROCEDURE

On each trial, the subject inspected the CS outside the tachistoscope. Then, he looked inside the tachistoscope, fixated his eyes, and pressed a foot-switch. Two hundred msec later, the TS appeared in the stimulus field for 100 msec. Then, the subject pressed either the "same" key or the "different" key and reported verbally whether he believed his manual response to have been correct or incorrect. He then received feedback concerning the accuracy of his response. The reaction time was measured from the onset of the TS to the manual response.

B. SUBJECTS

All four subjects were undergraduates from nearby colleges who were paid for participating. All were males except S 3. All were right-handed except S 4. "Same" responses were indicated with the dominant hand by S 1 and S 3 and with the nondominant hand by S 2 and S 4. It was desired that the error rate of each subject should be less than 3%. Consequently, all prospective subjects were given a screening test to evaluate whether, with subsequent practice, they would be able to attain that low an error rate. Four prospective subjects were screened, and it was judged that the error rates of all four would be satisfactory.

C. STIMULI

Both the CSs and the TSs were constructed by placing four white rectangles ($N = 4$) in a horizontal row on a black background. The rectangles measured 3 cm vertically by 2 cm horizontally and were separated by $\frac{1}{2}$ cm.

Letters measuring $1\frac{1}{2}$ cm in height were placed at the center of some or all of the rectangles. The CS always contained four letters. The TS contained from one to four letters ($L = 1, 2, 3, 4$) with the remainder of the rectangles left blank. The letters were drawn from the set of capital consonants: B, C, D, F, J, K, L, N, S, T, V, Z. No letter ever appeared twice within a single string. Whenever a letter appeared in both the CS and the TS, it occupied the same position in both strings.

D. Experimental Design

The experiment consisted of a practice session followed by eight experimental sessions lasting $1\frac{1}{2}$ hr each. Each session began with 20 practice trials followed by 240 experimental trials. The same 240 CSs were presented in the same order in every session. However, the TSs were varied within and between sessions in such a manner that the subject never could predict whether the TS would be "same" or "different," or how many letters it would contain, and so forth. In each session, L took on the value 4 on 96 trials and the values 1, 2, and 3 on 48 trials each. For each value of L, the CS and TS were "same" on 50% of the trials, "different" with $D = 1$ on 25%, and "different" with $D = L$ on 25%. Of course, when $L = 1$, $D = 1$ and $D = L$ are identical conditions. For each combination of L and D employed, all permutations of D "different" letters, $L - D$ "same" letters, and $N - L$ blanks occurred as TSs with equal frequency.

E. Apparatus

The stimulus field of the tachistoscope measured 6 cm vertically by 10 cm horizontally and was at an apparent distance of 100 cm. The fixation field remained on continuously and consisted of two dimly lit strips 2 cm in height bordering the upper and lower edges of the stimulus field. The subjects were instructed to fixate in the center of the dark area between the two strips. The luminances of the fixation field and of the white rectangles were roughly 3 cd m^{-2} and 60 cd m^{-2}, respectively. The force required to depress the response keys was roughly 25 gm.

F. Data Analysis

Before analyzing the RT data, a total of 2.0% of the responses were discarded: 1.3% because the subject pressed the wrong response key, 0.1% because the subject pressed both the correct and the incorrect key, and 0.6%

because the response was slower than 1300 msec. The methods used to analyze the RT data have been described elsewhere (Bamber, 1969b, Appendix 2). Z tests were employed to test statistical significance.

VI. Results and Discussion

In reporting the results of this experiment, two conventions will be followed. First, unless stated otherwise, reported results are for the mean of the four subjects. Second, when an estimate of a quantity is stated in the form $m \pm s$, m is the estimate and s is its standard error.

A. "DIFFERENT" RESPONSES

The observed mean RTs for the main experimental conditions are presented on the left side of Fig. 1. The results for individual subjects are presented in Table 1. Using a least-square method, Eqs. (1) and (2) were fit to the RT data of all the "different" conditions except the $D = 1, L = 4$ condition. The theoretical RTs derived from Eqs. (1) and (2) are presented on the right side of Fig. 1. The observed and theoretical RTs agree well for all the "different" conditions except the $D = 1, L = 4$ condition. There the discrepancy between the predicted RT and the observed RT was a highly significant 46.6 msec, the latter RT being the faster of the two. Otherwise,

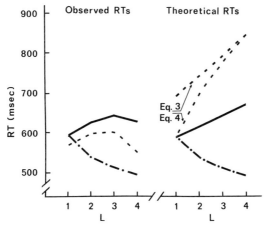

Fig. 1. Observed and theoretical mean RTs presented as a function of L: dashed line, "same"; solid line, $D = 1$; dashed–dotted line, $D = L$.

Table 1. *Mean RTs and Standard Errors (in milliseconds) of Each Subject in the Main Conditions*

Condition	S 1	S 2	S 3	S 4
D = 1				
L = 1	532.9 ± 9.3	545.9 ± 9.8	640.0 ± 6.7	662.5 ± 6.7
L = 2	540.5 ± 10.5	584.8 ± 15.9	669.2 ± 7.7	707.5 ± 10.3
L = 3	550.7 ± 15.2	609.6 ± 16.0	685.3 ± 10.6	737.5 ± 15.1
L = 4	544.7 ± 8.3	582.0 ± 12.3	687.5 ± 8.6	692.3 ± 8.0
D = *L*				
L = 2	459.1 ± 8.0	479.3 ± 5.0	610.9 ± 7.9	610.8 ± 8.6
L = 3	437.0 ± 7.5	456.4 ± 4.8	600.4 ± 5.6	565.3 ± 5.1
L = 4	418.9 + 3.1	437.9 ± 2.5	585.9 ± 3.3	542.0 ± 2.6
"same"				
L = 1	535.6 ± 6.8	509.1 ± 8.5	613.8 ± 3.7	624.3 ± 4.5
L = 2	519.3 ± 8.0	524.9 ± 8.3	661.8 ± 7.4	692.3 ± 8.2
L = 3	501.8 ± 5.8	540.1 ± 7.5	680.8 ± 7.7	702.8 ± 8.5
L = 4	430.7 ± 3.7	475.2 ± 4.8	664.4 ± 4.6	627.3 ± 4.4

combining the discrepancies between observed and theoretical RTs from all the other "different" conditions, yielded a root-mean-square discrepancy of 1.6 msec. The individual subjects showed a similar pattern of agreement between observed and theoretical RTs. A reason is suggested below why the observed RT in the $D = 1$, $L = 4$ condition was faster than predicted.

Estimates of the parameters a_d, t_s, and t_b derived from Eqs. (1) and (2) are presented in Table 2. It is apparent that the direct selective retrieval model is incorrect. Had this model been correct, the estimates of t_b would not differ significantly from zero. As it is, all the estimates of t_b are quite substantial. The estimate of t_s was significantly greater than that of t_b for each of the subjects except $S1$. As might be expected, once a triplet has been fetched from joint AIS, more time is required to process a "same" triplet than to process a blank triplet.

Table 2. *Estimates of the Parameters a_d, t_s and t_b and Their Standard Errors (in milliseconds) for Each Subject*

Subject	a_d	t_s	t_b
All *S*s	496.6 ± 1.5	117.8 ± 6.6	66.4 ± 2.9
S 1	417.0 ± 3.4	95.6 ± 13.9	76.0 ± 6.4
S 2	436.8 ± 2.6	139.2 ± 14.9	72.9 ± 6.8
S 3	587.5 ± 3.1	82.2 ± 9.8	36.0 ± 4.8
S 4	545.3 ± 2.8	154.2 ± 13.5	80.7 ± 4.8

For the $D = 1$ conditions, RT was faster when the discrepant letter was located on the left side of the TS rather than the right. For each value of L, a separate graph was made plotting RT versus the position of the discrepant letter in the TS. The best-fit slopes of these graphs were 27.7 ± 3.3, 26.4 ± 4.7, 52.6 ± 6.5 and 39.0 ± 4.5 msec for $L = 1, 2, 3$, and 4, respectively. Each of the individual subjects exhibited significant left–right position effects. Similar results have been reported by Bamber (1969b). This suggests that fetching of triplets from joint AIS often, but not always, proceeded from left to right across the CS and TS. The finding of position effects, even when $L = 1$, provides further evidence against the direct selective retrieval model.

In general, the "different" RTs are consistent with either a general retrieval model or an indirect selective retrieval model, provided that an explanation can be given as to why the mean RT in the $D = 1, L = 4$ condition was faster than predicted.

B. "SAME" RESPONSES

The observed "same" RTs are plotted as a function of L on the left side of Fig. 1. Inspection of Table 1 shows that the form of this curve varied from subject to subject. However, one point on which the results from the various subjects agree is that "same" RTs are faster when $L = 4$ than when $L = 3$. This is reminiscent of Egeth's (1966) finding that "same" RTs were faster when all dimensions were relevant than when one dimension was irrelevant.

On the right side of Fig. 1, two sets of theoretical "same" RTs are presented: one set from Eq. (3) (general-retrieval model) and one set from Eq. (4) (indirect selective-retrieval model). In deriving the theoretical "same" RTs, isochronality was assumed (Bamber, 1969a) and a_s was set equal to the previously estimated value of a_d. Choosing another value for a_s would affect only the overall height of the theoretical RT curves and would not affect their form. It is clear that the observed "same" RTs are not consistent with either a general retrieval or indirect selective retrieval model.

One way of resolving this discrepancy is to postulate a two-processor model (Bamber, 1969a; Nickerson, 1970). However, it is also clear that the particular type of two-processor model which assumes that the fast processor can initiate a "same" response only when the CS and TS have the same overall appearance is incorrect. This type of model predicts that the "same" RTs for $L = 1, 2, 3$, but not $L = 4$, should be consistent with a serial, self-terminating model. This is not the case. While some form of a two-processor model may well be correct, this particular type is not.

Not only does the number of letters contained in a TS affect "same" RTs, but so does the pattern of those letters. Table 3 shows the mean "same"

Table 3. *Mean "Same" RTs and Standard Errors (in milliseconds) for Letter Patterns in the TS*

$L = 1$		$L = 2$		$L = 3$	
sbbb	537.3 ± 4.1	ssbb	525.7 ± 5.2	sssb	572.1 ± 5.7
bsbb	553.2 ± 7.4	sbsb	611.3 ± 11.5	ssbs	616.4 ± 8.8
bbsb	586.2 ± 5.5	sbbs	615.1 ± 10.5	sbss	618.1 ± 8.1
bbbs	606.0 ± 7.2	bssb	636.3 ± 10.1	bsss	618.9 ± 7.0
		bsbs	630.4 ± 12.5		
		bbss	578.6 ± 6.4		

RT for the various letter patterns. In this table, an "s" denotes a "same" letter and a "b" denotes a blank. Although the pattern effects are large, it is difficult to find any simple way of characterizing them. However, examining the $L = 1$ pattern effects, it is clear that there is a large left–right position effect. The best-fit slope of the graph plotting RT versus the position of the solitary letter in the TS was found to be 23.9 ± 2.6 msec. This slope is not significantly different from the slope of the equivalent graph in the $L = 1$ "different" condition. The slopes for the individual subjects were all significantly greater than zero and, except for $S4$, none was significantly different from the corresponding slope in the $L = 1$ "different" condition. Posner and Taylor (1969) have performed an experiment having some features in common with the present one and have found similar position effects.

The observation of position effects in the $L = 1$ "same" condition is a critical one. This observation is consistent with an indirect selective-retrieval model but not with a general-retrieval model. In the indirect selective-retrieval model, the subject is assumed to know which positions in the TS contain letters and which contain blanks. Thus, as soon as the triplet containing the one and only letter in the TS has been fetched and found to be a "same" triplet, the subject should initiate the "same" response. So, if triplets were typically fetched in a left-to-right order, a position effect should result. However, in the general-retrieval model, the subject would have to fetch all the triplets in joint AIS before responding.

Although the position effects found in the $L = 1$ "same" condition provide strong support for an indirect selective retrieval model, how is it to be explained that the "same" RTs for $L = 2, 3,$ and 4 are incompatible with this model? One possible explanation is that, in a two-processor model of the type proposed by Bamber (1969a), the processor termed the *slow processor* may be the faster of the two processors when $L = 1$, but not when $L = 2, 3,$ and 4. The fact that the mean RT in the $L = 1$ "same" condition is faster than in the $L = 1$ "different" condition may result from a failure of the isochronality assumption (Bamber, 1969a).

C. The $D = 1$, $L = 4$ Condition

In the present experiment, the time (t_s) taken to fetch and examine a "same" triplet was estimated to be 117.8 msec. However, in a similar experiment (Bamber, 1969a) in which the TS never contained blanks, this time was estimated to be 60.2 msec. The difference between these two estimates seems rather large to ascribe entirely to differences between subjects. Presumably, at least for the "different" conditions, performance in the no-blank experiment can be described by the basic serial, self-terminating model, whereas performance in the present experiment can be described by the indirect selective-retrieval model. A comparison of the verbal flow diagrams for these two models suggests a reason for the discrepancy between the two estimates of t_s. In the basic serial, self-terminating model, t_s is an estimate of the time taken to traverse Steps 1–3 of that model. In the indirect selective-retrieval model, t_s is an estimate of the time taken to traverse Steps 1–5 of that model. Thus, the latter model has two extra steps (Steps 3 and 5) that have no counterpart in the former model. Much of the difference between the two estimates of t_s may represent the time taken to traverse those two steps.

The subjects in the present experiment eventually may have learned that, whenever the preattentive processes indicated that the TS contained no blanks ($L = 4$), they could save time by following Steps 1–3 of the basic serial, self-terminating model. Let t_3 and t_5 represent, respectively, the times taken to traverse Steps 3 and 5 of the indirect selective retrieval model. Using this strategy, the time taken to fetch and process a "same" triplet would be shortened by $t_3 + t_5$. Similarly, the time taken to fetch and process a "different" triplet would be shortened by t_3. Now, in the $D = 1$, $L = 4$ condition, an average of one and one-half "same" triplets and one "different" triplet are fetched each trial. Thus, there would be an average time saving of $2.5t_3 + 1.5t_5$ per RT. In the $D = L$, $L = 4$ condition, no "same" triplets and one "different" triplet are fetched each trial. The total time saving per RT thus would be t_3. Therefore, if t_5 were large and t_3 were small, there would be a large time saving in the $D = 1$, $L = 4$ condition and a negligible saving in the $D = L$, $L = 4$ condition. This may be why the RTs in the $D = 1$, $L = 4$ condition were faster than those predicted by the indirect selective-retrieval model.

D. Errors

The overall error rate in this experiment was 1.3%. However, this error rate was not constant across all conditions. Table 4 presents the error rate in each of the main experimental conditions. In the "same" condition, the error

Table 4. *Proportion of Responses That Were Errors in Each of the Main Conditions*

	"Same"	$D = 1$	$D = L$
$L = 1$	.013	.009	—
$L = 2$	.017	.024	.000
$L = 3$	.010	.029	.000
$L = 4$	.003	.052	.000

rate appears to be somewhat lower for $L = 4$ than that for $L = 1, 2$, and 3. This suggests that the presence of blanks in a TS that was, otherwise, identical to the CS occasionally caused a subject to respond "different." In the $D = 1$ condition, the error rate increased sharply with L. When there were redundant "different" letters in the TS ($D = L$, $L = 2, 3, 4$), there were no errors. At the end of each trial, the subject was required to report whether he believed his key-press response to have been correct or incorrect. After about 85% of the response errors, the subject reported that he had made an error. In the entire experiment, only two trials occurred where the subject responded correctly and then reported that he had made an error. Thus, the subjects were generally aware of when they made errors.

Two models of errors in the "different" conditions now will be considered. The first model, proposed by Bamber (1969a, b), assumes that these errors are caused by the rapid fading of letter images stored in the TS icon. Because RTs are faster when $L = 4$ than when $L = 3$, one would expect fewer errors when $L = 4$ than when $L = 3$. However, for $D = 1$, the opposite occurred. Evidently the model is wrong.

The second model, which may be called the premature-termination model, was proposed by Nickerson (1967). Logically, if the TS contains L letters, the subject ought to fetch and examine all of them before responding "same." However, the subject may sometimes respond "same" before examining every TS letter. Consequently, the subject may overlook a "different" letter and respond "same" incorrectly. Let K represent the mean number of TS letters actually fetched and examined before responding "same." From the $D = 1$ column in Table 4, K was estimated to be 0.99, 1.95, 2.91, and 3.79 when $L = 1, 2, 3$, and 4, respectively.

The premature termination model of errors raises the possibility of artifact in regard to some of the above conclusions. If this model is correct, it is clear that the theoretical "same" RTs calculated above are overestimates. Could this overestimation of the theoretical "same" RTs explain the discrepancy between them and the observed "same" RTs? This possibility was investigated as follows: The premature termination model and the indirect selective retrieval model were amalgamated to form a single model. Using the above estimates of K, the predictions of this model were fit to the RT data from all the "different" conditions except the $D = 1, L = 4$ condition. The new estimates of a_d (497.1 msec), t_s (120.9 msec), and t_b (66.5 msec) differed only slightly from the old estimates. The new theoretical "same" RTs were found to be only slightly faster than the old, the difference being 0.0, 4.5, 5.3, and 15.5 msec at $L = 1, 2, 3$, and 4, respectively. Clearly, the large discrepancy between the theoretical and observed "same" RTs is not an artifact due to premature termination.

VII. The Structure of Joint Allocated Information Stores

Up to this point, joint AIS has been treated as a black box from which triplets are retrieved serially. Evidence has been presented indicating that the selective retrieval of a triplet from joint AIS is achieved indirectly rather than directly. It is now time to consider the inner workings of the black box.

Joint AIS is composed of two AISs: the CS memory trace and the TS icon. Each of these AISs stores pairs consisting of a letter and a position tag. Just how might a triplet consisting of a CS letter, a TS letter, and a position tag be selectively retrieved from two such AISs? Five different models for this process are presented below. The alphabetically labeled steps in the models below are designed to replace Steps 1, 2, and 3 of the indirect selective-retrieval model.

MODEL I

> *Step a.* Fetch a previously unfetched letter and position tag from the CS memory trace.
> *Step b.* Does the position tag match any of the retrieval cues? If "no," return to Step a.
> *Step c.* Fetch from the TS icon the letter whose position tag matches the position tag just fetched from the CS memory trace.

MODEL II

> *Step a.* Fetch a previously unfetched letter and position tag from the CS memory trace.
> *Step b.* Does the position tag match any of the retrieval cues? If "no," return to Step a.
> *Step c.* Fetch a letter and position tag from the TS icon.
> *Step d.* Does the position tag from the TS match the position tag from the CS? If "no," return to Step c.

MODELS III AND IV

These models are identical to Models I and II, respectively, except that the roles of the CS memory trace and the TS icon are interchanged.

MODEL V

    Step a. Simultaneously fetch a previously unfetched letter from the CS memory trace, and the corresponding letter from the TS icon, together with their position tag.

    Step b. Does the position tag match any of the retrieval cues? If "no," return to Step a.

Thus, Model I assumes that selective retrieval occurs indirectly from the CS memory trace and directly from the TS icon. Model III assumes the reverse. Models II, IV, and V assume that selective retrieval occurs indirectly from both the CS memory trace and the TS icon.

Sperling (1960) and Averbach and Coriell (1961) presented their subjects briefly with a letter array followed by a signal which served as a retrieval cue. The subjects were instructed to report the letters in the positions specified by the retrieval cue. The accuracy of the subjects' reports declined if the retrieval cue was delayed. This indicates that the subjects modified, in accordance with the retrieval cue, the order in which they read letters out of the fading icon. Hence, it may be concluded that selective retrieval from an icon occurs directly.

Of the five models for indirect selective retrieval from joint AIS, only Model I is consistent with this conclusion. In Model I, selective retrieval from the CS memory trace occurs indirectly. As mentioned above, there is reason to believe that the CS memory trace employed in "same"–"different" judgments is visually encoded. Thus, visually encoded memory traces and icons apparently have different retrieval properties. Selective retrieval occurs indirectly in the former and directly in the latter.

VIII. Conclusions

The main conclusions drawn from this study are the following. First, as theorized by Neisser (1967, Chapter 4), before the comparison of the TS with the CS is ever begun, preattentive processes already have determined where the letters and blanks are located in the TS. Second, selective retrieval from the CS memory trace occurs indirectly. Thus, people appear to be incapable of direct selective retrieval from the visually encoded memory trace of a letter string. Third, the particular type of two-processor model that assumes that the fast processor can initiate a "same" response only when the CS and TS have the same overall appearance is incorrect.

Acknowledgments

The authors wish to thank Teresa Kucala, George Mergen, Vincent Stephens, and John Swenson for their assistance. The authors are indebted to the reviewer for his useful suggestions for improving the clarity of exposition in this paper.

References

Averbach, E., & Coriell, A. S. Short-term memory in vision. *Bell System Technical Journal*, 1961, **40**, 309–328.

Bamber, D. Reaction times and error rates for "same"-"different" judgments of multidimensional stimuli. *Perception and Psychophysics*, 1969, **6**, 169–174. (a)

Bamber, D. "Same"-"different" judgments of multidimensional stimuli: Reaction times and error rates. Doctoral dissertation, Stanford University; Ann Arbor, Michigan: University Microfilms, 1969. No. 69–17,395. (b)

Bamber, D. Reaction times and error rates for judging nominal identity of letter strings. *Perception and Psychophysics*, 1972, **12**, in press.

Conrad, R. Acoustic confusions in immediate memory. *British Journal of Psychology*, 1964, **55**, 75–84.

Egeth, H. E. Parallel versus serial processes in multidimensional stimulus discrimination. *Perception and Psychophysics*, 1966, **1**, 245–252.

Neisser, U. *Cognitive psychology*. New York: Appleton, 1967.

Nickerson, R. S. "Same"-"different" response times with multi-attribute stimulus differences. *Perceptual and Motor Skills*, 1967, **24**, 543–554.

Nickerson, R. S. Binary-classification reaction time: A review of some studies of human information-processing capabilities. Report No. 2004, December 28, 1970, Bolt Beranek and Newman, Inc., Cambridge, Massachusetts, Contract F44620-69-C-0115, Air Force Office of Scientific Research.

Posner, M. I., & Keele, S. W. Decay of visual information from a single letter. *Science*, 1967, **158**, 137–139.

Posner, M. I., & Mitchell, R. F. Chronometric analysis of classification. *Psychological Review*, 1967, **74**, 392–409.

Posner, M. I., & Taylor, R. L. Subtractive method applied to separation of visual and name components of multiletter arrays. *Acta Psychologica*, 1969, **30**, 104–114.

Posner, M. I., Boies, S. J., Eichelman, W. H., & Taylor, R. L. Retention of visual and name codes of single letters. *Journal of Experimental Psychology*, 1969, **79**(1, Pt. 2).

Shaw, P. Processing of tachistoscopic displays with controlled order of characters and spaces. *Perception and Psychophysics*, 1969, **6**, 257–268.

Sperling, G. The information available in brief visual presentations. *Psychological Monographs*, 1960, **74**(11, Whole No. 498).

Tversky, B. Pictorial and verbal encoding in a short-term memory task. *Perception and Psychophysics*, 1969, **6**, 225–233.

Effect of Stimulus Frequency on Speed of "Same"–"Different" Judgments

Lester E. Krueger

Department of Psychology
City College of the City
University of New York
New York, New York

ABSTRACT

In judging whether two stimuli are the "same" or "different," does the subject always compare or match the stimuli with each other, or does he sometimes know in some more direct fashion that the two stimuli, encoded as a single unit or gestalt, are the "same" or "different"? A single-process model was proposed in which the subject treats alike, as units, all stimulus pairs, both "same" and "different," and in which the typically longer latencies for "different" than "same" judgments are explained by the larger set of pairs, and thus the greater stimulus uncertainty, in the "different" case. To test whether stimulus pairs are encoded as units, and thus show the same effects as unitary stimuli, some letter pairs were presented more frequently than others. Further, the size of the set of "same" pairs was made equal to that of "different" pairs. The more-frequent pairs did yield shorter response times (RTs) than the less-frequent ones, but only in the "different" case, and the "same" latencies remained shorter than the "different" ones. The results support a dual-process model in which "same" judgments are handled by an image- or feature-matching process, which is at too low a level to be influenced by familiarity, and "different" judgments involve analytical, serial processes, such as naming and feature checking, which are influenced by familiarity.

I. Introduction

In judging two stimuli in the "same"–"different" choice reaction time (RT) task, subjects typically show shorter latencies for "same" than "different" stimulus pairs, which has led some investigators (for example, Bamber, 1969; Tversky, 1969) to postulate that, to a degree, different stimulus-comparison processes subserve "same" and "different" decisions. The present study tested whether a single-process model in which all stimulus pairs, both "same" and "different," are processed in the same manner might yet fit the data. The present single-process model takes as its starting point the fact that the subjects, when questioned after an experimental session, often say that they made many "matches" quite automatically, with no conscious awareness of having actually made a match. Perhaps, rather than making a perceptual match between stimulus items, the subjects made a cognitive match between the pair of stimuli, encoded as a unit, and the corresponding memory trace, which contained a response specification. When the subject sees EE, for example, he may immediately recognize the letter pair (having seen it innumerable times in words such as SEEM and FEEL) and know that the two letters are the "same," before he has had time to complete a comparison of the geometrical outlines of the two letters. Forming a representation of the stimulus pair as a unit or gestalt ought to be easier when the two stimulus items are presented simultaneously, but nonetheless is assumed also to occur when the items to be compared are presented successively.

Performing a cognitive match also ought to be easier for stimulus pairs that are more familiar or are presented more frequently, and for which the subject thus is better prepared. Rather than indicating that two different comparison processes subserve "same" and "different" judgments, the shorter latencies for "same" judgments might simply reflect the fact that typically the number of different pairs, and thus the stimulus uncertainty, is less in the "same" case. The digits 0 to 9, for example, yield ten "same" and ninety "different" pairs, so that if "same" and "different" trials were to occur with equal frequency, then a particular "same" pair of digits would occur about nine times as frequently as a particular "different" pair. If the possible "same" pairs are very numerous or infinite in number, however, as in the case of a continuous stimulus dimension, the subject would be forced to resume making direct perceptual matches. If it is assumed that these perceptual matches are made by means of a self-terminating feature-by-feature comparison process, then latencies ought to be shorter for "different" than "same" judgments because the subject need only find one differing aspect in order to know that the two stimuli are different, but must examine all features to know they are the same.

Some evidence indeed does indicate that latencies are shorter for "same" than for "different" stimuli when the stimulus set is small, but not when it is large or infinite. Bindra, Donderi, and Nishisato (1968) found shorter latencies for "same" than "different" stimuli when the stimuli differed on hue or on click versus tone, but longer latencies for "same" when the stimuli differed on line length, and they concluded that: "stimuli that are codable (i.e., which can be categorized by absolute judgment) yield a shorter latency for decision same, and noncodable stimuli (i.e., those requiring a reference stimulus for categorization) yield a longer latency for decision same [Bindra *et al.*, 1968, p. 121]." Nickerson (1969), similarly, found longer "same" than "different" latencies for tones varying in pitch, and said that: "possibly judgments requiring the comparison of stimuli with respect to such properties as pitch, loudness, length, etc., may involve image-matching processes to a greater degree or in a different sense than do judgments of stimuli for which verbal labels are readily available [p. 274]."

If the subject does encode the stimulus pair as a unit, then his latencies ought to be influenced (and in the same way) by those factors that influence choice RTs when unitary stimuli are presented. Several investigators (for example, LaBerge & Tweedy, 1964; Krueger, 1970a) have found that if frequency of occurrence is varied among a set of stimuli for which the same response is assigned, the RTs are shorter for the more frequently presented stimuli. The present experiment tested for analogous frequency effects in the "same"–"different" situation by presenting some "same" and "different" letter pairs four times as often as other "same" and "different" pairs. The more-frequent set, as well as the less-frequent set, contained only two "same" and two "different" pairs. The use of so few letter pairs (only eight in all) was designed to give the subject a maximum opportunity to come to encode each pair as a unit. Using the same number of "same" and "different" pairs was designed to eliminate the usual advantage that "same" pairs derive from coming from a smaller set of pairs. Thus, it was predicted that "same" and "different" pairs would not differ in RT, but that RT would be lower for more-frequent than less-frequent pairs.

II. Method

A. APPARATUS

Stimuli were presented on a Gerbrands Model T-3B-1 tachistoscope, which has six timers and three exposure fields (all set to maximum intensity: 4 mL), each with a semiautomatic card changer. Information on RT (measured in milliseconds by a specially built electronic timer) and on which

button the subject pressed, was recorded on punched paper tape for subsequent computer analysis. To start each trial, the subject pressed a foot
pedal connected to a remote-start switch on the tachistoscope; the switch
was rendered inoperative between trials, so that the subject could not
initiate a trial before being permitted to by the experimenter.

B. STIMULUS MATERIALS

Each stimulus pair consisted of two capital letters centered on a 4 by
6-in. white index card. The letters were typed in 12 point, IBM Courier 72,
on the same row, with 5 blank spaces between them. At 31 in. from the subject, the two letters subtended a visual angle of 1.25°.

Two sets of 400 stimulus pairs were prepared. One set, in which pairs
containing the letters B and R occurred four times as frequently as those containing H and K, was shown to half the subjects, and the other set, in which
H and K pairs were four times as frequent as B and R pairs, was shown to the
other half. Each set was composed of ten groups of 40 stimulus pairs. In one
set, the letter pairs BB, RR, BR, RB occurred eight times each, and the letter
pairs HH, KK, HK, KH occurred two times each in each group of 40. In the
other set, the frequency pattern was reversed, so that HH, KK, HK, KH
occurred eight times each, and BB, RR, BR, RB occurred two times each.
The 40 stimulus cards in a group were arranged in random order, which
remained the same throughout the experiment, but the order of the groups
of 40 was varied across the subjects. Thus each subject received ten replications or trial blocks of the basic set of conditions, which each group of
40 cards constituted.

C. PROCEDURE

The subjects were instructed to keep their eyes fixated at the location
midway between the two letters in a pair, as indicated by a prior, small black
fixation dot. On each trial, the fixation point appeared for .8 sec, then the
letter pair appeared for 1.2 sec, after which the fixation point reappeared
for 2.0 sec. The subject's response did not terminate the stimulus display,
which always remained in view for 1.2 sec. The experimenter changed the
stimulus card after the subject responded, so that 2.0–3.0 sec typically
elapsed between the end of one trial and the beginning of the next. A buzzer
briefly sounded when the subject pressed the wrong button or pressed before
the stimulus card appeared. The subject received four practice trials (letter
pairs: WW, TZ, SS, DP) before seeing the 400 stimulus cards. All RTs ex-

ceeding 3 sec or on which the subject pressed the wrong button were excluded before the RTs were averaged.

Half the subjects pressed the right button for "same" and the left button for "different," and half pressed the left button for "same" and the right button for "different." The subjects were asked to respond as quickly as possible, but not at the expense of accuracy. The subjects were paid $1.75 for the 50-min session, plus a bonus of 50¢ if their error rate was below 5% and their speed of response fell in the top quartile for all subjects.

D. SUBJECTS

Thirty City College of New York undergraduates served as subjects. All had 20/30 vision or better, as tested with a Snellen chart.

III. Results

As Eichelman (1970) has reported, the stimulus repetition effect is exhibited in both the "same"–"different" task and the choice RT task involving unitary stimuli: the RTs are lower when the same stimulus appears again in immediate succession. Eichelman found a similar, but smaller, decrease in RT for response repetitions (same response, different stimulus). In the present experiment, stimulus repetitions of less-frequent pairs were too few to analyze; on more-frequent pairs, when the same stimulus was presented twice in succession, mean RT was 42 msec lower for the second, as compared with the first presentation (sign test, $p < .001$). The stimulus repetition effect was larger for "same" (52 msec) than "different" judgments (32 msec); $F(1, 28) = 3.50$, $p < .10$. No effect of response repetition (same response, different stimulus) was found in any of the last three trial blocks, for which an examination was made: the mean RTs were 676 and 674 msec for response repetitions and nonrepetitions, respectively, in the last three blocks. The immediate stimulus repetitions, which occurred on a higher proportion of the trials for more-frequent pairs than for less-frequent ones, were removed from the data shown in Fig. 1, because the main concern of the present experiment was with a longer-lasting facilitation induced by a prior occurrence of a stimulus. Even with immediate stimulus repetitions removed, a stimulus frequency effect was found: the average RT was lower for more-frequent than less-frequent pairs; $F(1, 28) = 16.80$, $p < .001$. Also, the error rate was slightly higher for less-frequent (3.5%) than more-frequent pairs (2.5%); $F(1, 28) = 3.85$, $p < .10$.

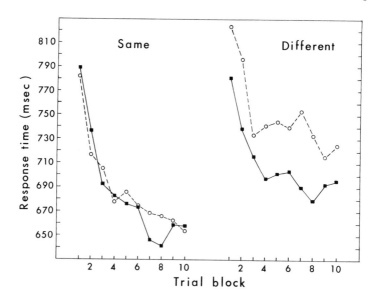

Fig. 1. Mean response time, in milliseconds, by whether stimulus pair was "same" or "different" and (■) more frequent or (○) less frequent. Each of the four more-frequent pairs occurred eight times and each of the four less-frequent pairs occurred two times within each 40-trial block. Data on immediate stimulus repetitions are excluded.

As Fig. 1 shows, the stimulus frequency effect was greater for "different" than "same" responses. The frequency × same-versus-different interaction was significant $F(1, 28) = 34.7$, $p < .001$; and, on separate analyses of variance, the 41-msec decrease in RT for more-frequent as compared with less-frequent pairs on "different" trials was significant, $F(1, 28) = 40.10, p < .001$; but the 4-msec decrease on "same" trials was not, $F < 1.0$. The frequency effect showed a slight tendency to increase over trials—the more-frequent pairs were judged 20 msec faster on the first five trial blocks and 25 msec faster on the second five trial blocks—and the trial block × frequency interaction was significant, $F(9, 252) = 2.93, p < .005$, as was also the trial block × frequency × same-versus-different interaction, $F(9, 252) = 1.86, p < .05$.

A more discernible change in Fig. 1, over the ten trial blocks, is the steady increase in the difference between "same" and "different" RTs: the trial block × same-versus-different interaction was significant; $F(9, 252) = 3.46, p < .001$. Even among the more-frequent pairs alone, RT was significantly lower for "same" than "different" judgments; $t(29) = 3.48, p < .005$. An explanation of the faster "same" RT that is based on a greater readiness to respond "same" does not seem possible, because the significantly higher error rate for "same" (3.5%) than "different" stimulus pairs (2.5%),

$F(1, 28) = 5.91$, $p < .025$, indicates, if anything, a response bias towards "different."

Most subjects, when questioned after the session, indicated that H and K were easier to discriminate than B and R, and, accordingly, the stimulus frequency effect was larger when the more-frequent set contained H and K (37 msec) rather than B and R (8 msec). The stimulus set × frequency interaction, however, was not significant; $F(1, 28) < 1.0$ Most subjects also could correctly name afterwards both letters in the more-frequent set and at least one letter in the less-frequent set. When asked how they decided whether the two letters in a pair were the same or different, five subjects could not describe what happened, one subject said the decision became automatic, four subjects said they sometimes named the letters to themselves, and 20 subjects indicated they attended only to the physical or geometrical features of the letters.

IV. Discussion

The present data do not support the cognitive-match model, which postulates that "same" and "different" stimulus pairs are processed in the same manner, namely, that the subject encodes the two stimuli to be compared as a unit and then decides whether the unit falls in the "same" or "different" category. There were an equal number of "same" and "different" pairs; yet RT remained lower for "same" than "different" judgments, and the disparity in RT even increased with practice. After this study was completed, it was discovered that Nickerson (1968), who presented letters in a pair successively rather than simultaneously, also tried, and failed, to equalize the RT for "same" and "different" by equalizing the size of the set of "same" (CC, DD) and "different" pairs (CD, DC).

If the stimulus pairs in the present study were treated as units, then stimulus frequency ought to have affected the RT, as is true for unitary stimuli; yet no effect was found for "same" judgments. Stimulus frequency, however, did affect "different" RT; the effect was nearly constant across the ten trial blocks (see Fig. 1), indicating a short-term, rather than cumulative, facilitation. Similar results of similar magnitude were found in the case of unitary stimuli by Krueger (1970a). Krueger found a 51-msec effect for a 4:1 frequency ratio, which matches well the 41-msec effect for a 4:1 frequency ratio on "different" judgments in this study. Thus, cognitive matches might yet have been made on "different" stimulus pairs.

The mean RTs were quite long, ranging between about 650 and 750 msec (see Fig. 1). Several factors might account for the long RTs. First, the letters that were paired together (for example, BR, HK) are relatively difficult to discriminate. Second, the subjects were set for accuracy as well as speed (overall error rate: 3%). Third, perhaps most important, the 12-point typed letters used in the present study are small and somewhat difficult to see at a distance of 31 in. In a further, unpublished experiment employing the same apparatus, simultaneous presentation of the letters in a pair, and 16 subjects, but using larger, 24- and 60-point Futura Demibold Quiktype dry-transfer letters, the mean RT was much lower: 542 msec for "same" and 581 msec for "different" judgments. The difference between "same" and "different" judgments was significant; $F(1, 15) = 66.13, p < .001$. The center-to-center distance was kept constant at .875 in for both the 24-point and 60-point letter pairs. During the first half of the experimental session, for half the subjects the 24-point letters were shown on 75% of the trials, and the 60-point letters on 25%, and for the other subjects the 24-point letters were shown on 25% of the trials, and the 60-point letters on 75% of the trials. The proportions were reversed for the second half of the session. The mean RT was significantly lower, though only by 11 msec, for the more-frequent letter size (556 msec) than for the less-frequent size (567 msec); $F(1, 15) = 4.54, p < .05$. The effect was slightly, but not significantly, larger for "different" (15 msec) than "same" judgments (7 msec).

V. Conclusions

The finding that stimulus frequency affects RT for "different," but not for "same" judgments, is consistent with the results of Robinson (1969), but not those of Egeth and Blecker (1971) and Hock (1971). As in the present study, these investigators all employed simultaneous rather than successive presentation of items in the stimulus pair. Robinson, using an accuracy-of-response rather than RT measure, found improved performance on "different," but not on "same" trials, for pairs of Chinese characters that had been presented repeatedly rather than only once. Egeth and Blecker manipulated familiarity by presenting trigrams rated high or low on meaningfulness and by presenting letter pairs that were oriented upright or upside down. They found that familiarity only affected the RT for "same" judgments. Similarly, Hock found on "same," but not on "different," trials that the RT was lower for dot patterns that the subjects had reproduced during preexperimental training. As to what produced these divergent findings, one clue lies in the fact that in most of Egeth and Blecker's experiments and both of Hock's experiments, latencies in the unfamiliar condition were as long as or longer for "same" as those for "different," whereas in the present experiment, the latencies in the less-frequent condition were shorter for "same." Thus, as one might expect, familiarity caused a greater decrease in RT for the type of stimulus, "same" or "different," which had a longer RT to begin with and thus was less likely to be at a minimal, irreducible RT.

The present findings (shorter RT for "same" than for "different" pairs; familiarity effect only on "different" judgments) seem more consonant with the dual-process model in which "same" judgments are based mainly on image or template matching, involving a global, holistic comparison of the two items in a pair, whereas "different" judgments are based mainly on a slower, serial process (Bamber, 1969), in which the subject may name the two letters (Krueger, 1970b) and may recheck the pair in order to determine exactly where the difference lies (Tversky, 1969). If, indeed, the template matching on "same" trials were based on a fast, relatively low-level type of form perception, then relatively little effect of familiarity would be expected (see Hochberg, 1968), as compared with the "different" judgments, where higher-level processes, such as naming, are involved.

Posner and Mitchell (1967) postulated two different processing nodes: node 1, based on physical identity (for example, A A), and node 2, based on name identity (for example, A a). The present study indicates that the simultaneous presentation of two upper-case letters does not guarantee that the subjects will remain at node 1. The subjects in this study exhibited longer latencies for "different" than "same" judgments, showed an effect of familiarity only in the "different" case, and, in the case of four subjects, reported afterwards that they sometimes named the two letters—which suggests that, whereas processing remained at node 1 for "same" pairs, it sometimes was at node 2 for "different" pairs. Egeth and Blecker, but not Posner and Mitchell, also found faster RT for "same" than "different" pairs when two upper-case letters were presented simultaneously on each trial.

Acknowledgments

This study was supported by NIH Grant HD04869-01-02. The author is grateful to Lucille Spivak, Paul Kadis, and Sheri Berenbaum for their able and conscientious assistance in collecting and tabulating the data, and for their very helpful comments. Phillip Liss and Ira Kaplan also provided very helpful comments.

References

Bamber, D. Reaction times and error rates for "same"–"different" judgments of multidimensional stimuli. *Perception and Psychophysics*, 1969, **6**, 169–174.

Bindra, D., Donderi, D. C., & Nishisato, S. Decision latencies of "same" and "different" judgments. *Perception and Psychophysics*, 1968, **3**, 121–130.

Egeth, H. E., & Blecker, D. Differential effects of familiarity on judgments of sameness and difference. *Perception and Psychophysics*, 1971, **9**, 321–326.

Eichelman, W. H. Stimulus and response repetition effects for naming letters at two response-stimulus intervals. *Perception and Psychophysics*, 1970, **7**, 94–96.

Hochberg, J. In the mind's eye. In Haber, R. N. (Ed.) *Contemporary theory and research in visual perception.* New York: Holt, 1968, Pp. 309–331.

Hock, H. S. The role of structure in the perception of familiar and unfamiliar stimuli. Unpublished doctoral dissertation, Johns Hopkins University, 1971.

Krueger, L. E. Effect of stimulus probability on two-choice reaction time. *Journal of Experimental Psychology*, 1970, **84**, 377–379. (a)

Krueger, L. E. Effect of bracketing lines on speed of "same"–"different" judgment of two adjacent letters. *Journal of Experimental Psychology*, 1970, **84**, 324–330. (b)

LaBerge, D., & Tweedy, J. R. Presentation probability and choice time. *Journal of Experimental Psychology*, 1964, **68**, 477–481.

Nickerson, R. S. Note on "same"–"different" response times. *Perceptual and Motor Skills*, 1968, **27**, 565–566.

Nickerson, R. S. "Same"–"different" response times: A model and a preliminary test. *Acta Psychologica*, 1969, **30**, 257–275.

Posner, M. I., & Mitchell, R. F. Chronometric analysis of classification. *Psychological Review*, 1967, **74**, 392–409.

Robinson, J. S. Familiar patterns are no easier to see than novel ones. *American Journal of Psychology*, 1969, **82**, 513–522.

Tversky, B. Pictorial and verbal encoding in a short-term memory task. *Perception and Psychophysics*, 1969, **6**, 225–233.

6 THEORIES OF CHOICE AND REACTION TIME

Some Observations on Theories of
Choice Reaction Time: Tutorial Review

R. J. Audley

Department of Psychology
University College London
London, England

ABSTRACT

An appraisal of theories of choice reactions is made in the light of experimental findings concerning sequential phenomena and the properties of erroneous responses, in both cases for two-choice experiments only.

A simple way of representing sequential effects is described; and it is shown that these depend on the form of the stimulus–response (S–R) code. It is concluded from an examination of the data that performance in a choice reaction is governed both by attention to a particular stimulus and by a more or less continuously varying preparation for this stimulus or its associated response. The need is indicated for confirmation of the limited experimental results on which this conclusion is based.

A sequential-decision model is shown to give the best account of the properties of errors but it is also concluded that a model of the kind suggested in the light of sequential effects would also describe the facts.

In a brief consideration of the trade off between speed and accuracy, it is concluded tentatively that this is largely achieved by the subject varying the extent to which he employs a strategy of making a response determined in advance of the arrival of the stimulus. The possible role of a preliminary stimulus sampling process is not discounted.

Finally, further evidence is cited in favor of a model of the kind inferred from an examination of sequential effects.

509

I. Introduction

There is a fortunate ambiguity in the phrase "tutorial review": for who is tutor and who tutee? Given the present audience, it was always likely that I would fill the latter role; that this will definitely be so follows from my decision to discuss theories of choice reaction time. My own interests have been mainly in the phenomena of choice when relatively difficult discriminations are required; until this year I had not carefully read the many recent papers that have greatly enlarged our knowledge of the reaction-time situation. So what I am presenting is very much like a student's first response to the mass of ideas and data with which he finds himself confronted: selective, grossly oversimplified, and in no sense a proper review of the field. At least this has the merit of keeping redundancy to a minimum, for there have been some excellent reviews of various aspects of choice reactions (for example, Kornblum, 1969; Laming, 1968, 1969; Nickerson, 1970; Smith, 1969; Welford, 1960), and who better than their authors can give a correct description of theories? [As well as the papers just cited, I am thinking particularly of Briggs and Blaha (1969), Briggs and Swanson (1970), Edwards (1965), Swensson and Edwards (1971), Falmagne and Theios (1969), Fitts (1966), Fitts, Peterson, and Wolpe (1963), Ollman (1966), Rabbitt (1968a, 1969). Yellott (1967).] This paper is therefore offered as a commentary rather than a review.

As a student one is confronted with the task of determining what observations are usually accepted as facts, what are the basic principles that form the core of various theories, and whether any of the principles can be demonstrated to be true or false. Since it seems very unlikely that any theorist expresses the whole conceptual truth and nothing but the truth, and as each author emphasizes particular phenomena, it appears desirable to select a generally acceptable corpus of facts and determine what light this throws on the validity of various principles. Facts are, of course, "facts" and have uncertainty attached to them, and the reader must be warned that I am taking a particularly simplified view of them.

Most of my commentary is devoted to two-choice reaction tasks in which the subject is presented with one of two stimuli which are easy to discriminate and to each of which he is required to make a different simple response. I will say relatively little about the influence of stimulus discriminability, or about performance in situations with more than two alternatives, or about cases where there is a many:one mapping of stimuli on to responses. The principal excuse for these restrictions of scope is that my arguments rely on more or less quantitative information about the reaction times for different responses within a given task, and there is not much of this available for situations involving either multiple choices or variations in stimulus discriminability. (In point of fact, I like to believe that the contribution by Welford to this volume indicates the way in which some of the conjectures made here could be generalized to tasks that involve more than two alternatives.) There are two subsidiary pleas. The first is easy to state: Nickerson (1970) has given a splendid account of the many: one situation, which goes into the details of stimulus discrimination. The second also concerns discriminability and requires some elaboration. I am of the opinion that tasks involving difficult discriminations exhibit considerable differences in performance characteristics from the usual choice reaction-time (CRT) task employing easily distinguishable stimuli: the main one being that, for difficult tasks, errors are made with longer average latencies than correct responses (for example, Audley, 1970; Audley & Mercer, 1968; Pike, 1968), whereas easy tasks elicit quicker errors (for example, Laming, 1968; Egeth & Smith, 1967), and in some tasks both slow and quick errors occur (Wilding, 1970). Whether the information processing strategies used for the two kinds of task are the same is the important question, and I do not believe we yet have the data to resolve this issue. Easy discriminations usually are presented in an experimental context of other easy discriminations, and difficult ones are presented in a context of similar difficulty. It seems likely that processing strategies would be selected according to the total context, and therefore we need experiments that vary this (see Shallice & Vickers, 1964; Christ, 1970; but also see Laming, 1968, p. 12). In the absence of such studies, I shall mainly ignore discriminability and, of course, its possible confounding with the number of alternatives (Crossman, 1955).

My apologia concluded, I will turn to a consideration of the "facts" and examine the success of various theories in accounting for them. But first a brief listing of the theories.

II. Some Theories of Choice Reaction Time

A. Models Based upon Statistical-Decision Theory

These regard the subject as sampling statistical information about the stimulus presented until a criterion level in favour of one of the alternatives is reached (Carterette, 1966; Edwards, 1965; Fitts et al., 1963; Laming, 1963, 1968; Stone, 1960). I will not comment on certain stochastic models that can be regarded as nonoptimal decision procedures (LaBerge, 1962; McGill, 1963; Audley, 1960: Audley & Pike, 1965; Laming, 1968, p. 22 et seq.) because hitherto they have not appeared as successful as the optimal model in predicting CRT performance when discriminability is high. However, in the light of conjectures about the characteristics of a satisfactory theory offered later in the paper, consideration should surely be given in the future to modified forms of these stochastic models (see, especially, Vickers, 1970).

B. Models Based upon Communication Theory

The applicability of the principles of optimal encoding of messages to the processing of stimuli in a choice reaction task has been strongly questioned by several authors: for example, by Kornblum (1969), Laming (1968), and Rapoport (1959). One might wonder, therefore, whether this kind of theory should still be considered. However, from the first, the concept of optimal coding has been a fruitful source of hypotheses about possible mechanisms underlying human information processing (Hick, 1952; Welford, 1960; see Smith, 1969, for a recent review). Furthermore, the quantitative expressions of the theory have continued to provide an acceptable description of the average reaction times in a variety of situations (but see Laming, 1968, Chapter 1), particularly for multiple-choice tasks, where a persisting problem is to find a plausible alternative basis for the expression $RT = a + b \log k$ (k is the number of alternatives), although there have been some more or less purely mathematical discussions of the issue (Rapoport, 1959; Laming, 1966). Finally, Briggs and his colleagues have described a remarkably detailed breakdown of the flow of information from stimulus to response, which, in part, relies on the principles of communication theory (Briggs & Blaha, 1969; Briggs & Swanson, 1970).

C. The Preparation Model of Falmagne

In the most often discussed version of this hypothesis (Falmagne, 1965), it is postulated that the subject is either prepared fully or not at all for the stimulus that is presented, and when this preparation is inappropriate, will make errors or slower correct responses. More recently, Falmagne and Theios (1969) have elaborated this model in terms of memory templates of the stimuli, which can be in different serial positions within short- and long-term memory stores. Variations in reaction time are accounted for by the duration of a serial search for the template of the stimulus presented. The similarity to the search strategies discussed by Hick (1952), Sternberg (1966), and Welford (1960) needs no elaboration; a review of these ideas is given by both Smith (1969) and Nickerson (1970).

D. FIXED-SAMPLE MODELS

These incorporate the notion that a critical factor determining the properties of choice reactions is the duration of a process by means of which the subject samples stimulus input, the duration usually being regarded as selected to achieve a given accuracy of performance.

Many authors have proposed that the total time from stimulus to response can be broken down into various stages. The minimum number suggested is three: an input time, including the collection of an adequate sample of sensory data; a decision time; and a response execution time. In the simplest version of the fixed-sample theory it is supposed that the decision time is constant within a given experiment (Stone, 1960; Laming, 1968). However, it is more plausible that the decision stage would have a variable time, dependent upon the quality of the sample information and any biases that the subject might have in processing it. Briggs and Swanson (1970) postulate a serial search through memory templates, the comparison time between input and templates being affected by the quality of the input. An alternative hypothesis is that the subject treats the sampled information in the manner postulated for detection tasks by signal-detectability theory, determining to which side it lies of some criterion. The decision time then would be a decreasing function of the distance of the sample information from the criterion (Audley & Mercer, 1968; Gescheider, Wright, & Evans, 1968; Meyers & Thomas, 1972; P. T. Smith, 1968; Thomas, 1970). There is indeed no reason why a sequential decision model of type A should not represent the second stage.

Although the fixed-sample principle obviously does not constitute a complete theory of CRT, it could be a necessary component for a successful one. This might be more especially the case for difficult discriminations, if there is an upper limit on the human capacity to integrate information over time.

E. THE FAST-GUESS MODEL

In this approach (Ollman, 1966; Yellott, 1967, 1971) it is postulated that the subject's performance reflects a mixture of two strategies: true discriminations with a high level of accuracy, and responses which are biased guesses, uninfluenced by the presented stimulus. It might be thought that this is only the basis of a useful procedure to correct for the influence of lapses in a subject's attention to his task; however, Swensson and Edwards (1971) recently have presented data strongly suggesting that subjects can only achieve a trade off between the speed and accuracy of their responses by opting for one or the other of two such distinct strategies. Yellott (1971) has incorporated Falmagne's concept of preparation for a particular stimulus in a modified version of the fast-guess model; my later comments refer to the original version.

F. MODELS EMPHASIZING THE SPECIFIC ROLE OF STIMULUS REPETITIONS AND ALTERNATIONS[1]

It is not entirely clear to me whether this involves a new principle not covered by some of the types already described. From one viewpoint, it could be regarded as a subsidiary principle to be incorporated in accounting for particular levels of expectancy and preparation in making predictions from other models, particularly types A, B and C. At one time, in the early research on this topic (Bertelson, 1963, 1965; Bertelson & Renkin, 1966), it appeared that the repetition effect was largely due to the repetition of responses and this would have necessitated its inclusion as an additional principle in all other theories. However, much later research has favored the view that the effect depends upon stimulus repetition (M. C. Smith, 1968; Hinrichs & Krainz, 1970; but see also the discussion of response processes below). It seems most appropriate to agree with Kornblum that he has shown the important role of sequential phenomena on CRT by means of the most elementary available partition of stimulus sequences—one must add, most elegantly.

G. OTHER MODELS

This is a necessary category to cover those principles which I shall not consider. Indeed OTHER might be regarded as an acronym for Other Theorists Especially Rabbitt, for I am particularly conscious of not having considered the work of this author, both on changing strategies of information processing and on the nature of errors. However, I have been asked to write about "theories"; I am prepared to believe that Rabbitt has been presenting facts.

Hardly anything has been said, thus far, about responses; as Smith (1969) has emphasized, few theories include any very explicit statements about their selection and execution. Sequential-decision theories largely dispense with a response selection stage, and template matching theorists are inclined to view the appropriate response as already attached to the templates. Briggs and Swanson (1970), however, have given a place to output

---

[1] See especially Kornblum (1967, 1969, and this volume).

processes in their partition of the events between stimulus and response.

Can we even be sure that the serial process inferred from studies of categorization is properly located when it is regarded as a comparison of the input with stimulus templates? Could it not be a search through the S–R code required by the task that follows upon an identification of the stimulus (Miller, 1970)? Once a stimulus is identified, a search through an S–R code will be increasingly important as this code becomes unusual; the time advantage gained by preparing for a given stimulus also may be facilitated by a partial retrieval of the response (Bertelson, 1963), which may interfere with the production of the correct response to another stimulus (M. C. Smith, 1968). When it comes to the execution of the response, the time for producing one response depends upon the other responses that may be called for in a task (Kornblum, 1965).

However, it appears that we have been extremely fortunate that biases induced by processes labeled variously by terms such as expectancy and preparation act principally upon stimulus analysis rather than response production. Even if there occur effects due to the partial retrieval of the response to an expected stimulus, it is the stimulus bias that exerts the controlling influence on performance, and hence, the emphasis on the stimulus in existing theories is, happily appropriate. [In the light of the paper by Sanders (1970) at the last Attention and Performance Conference and that by Kornblum here, these remarks about the dominant role of stimulus selection may merely reflect the gullibility of the present author.]

Many of these problems of understanding response processes are largely bypassed in considering two-choice tasks. Yet clearly in the case of those models in which emphasis is placed upon preparation for a particular stimulus, some additional statements are required as to the process that is initiated when this preparation is inappropriate. These might well depend upon the particular S–R code in use. Where the stimuli and responses are arranged in congruent spatial patterns, a simple readjustment of the response, as in tracking skills, may be all that is necessary, since the stimuli and responses are likely to be coded in terms of the same dimensions (Wallace, 1971). When the S–R code links symbols to spatial responses, a full retrieval of the response, via the stored code, may take place even though, in principle, the failure of the expected stimulus to appear provides sufficient information for the correct response to be made in a two-choice task.

In fact, in comparing theory and data we are faced with an almost bewildering variety of codes and responses, perhaps just because the theories say nothing about the effect of these. Such results as we do have, although valuable, are often presented in the digested form appropriate only to a particular model, usually one based on communication theory (Brainard, Irby, Fitts, & Alliusi, 1962).

III. A Comparison between Theoretical Predictions and Some "Facts"

A. SEQUENTIAL EFFECTS

It is clear from reading the recent literature that special attention should be given to sequential effects, that is, the way in which the accuracy and speed of a reaction to a stimulus is dependent upon the prior sequence of stimuli experienced by the subject and the characteristics of his responses to these. A recent experimental paper has demonstrated clearly and simply the magnitude of such effects as far as reaction times are concerned (Remington, 1969); several authors have placed them at the focus of theoretical and experimental studies that consider both time and errors (Laming, 1969; Kornblum, 1969; Falmagne, 1965). It is only fair to mention that their potential importance was made apparent relatively early (for example, Hyman, 1953), although it required the experimental studies of Bertelson (1961) to force them on our attention. Of course, because they are so dominant, their presence in the usual type of study may have obscured other important properties of the processes underlying the choice reaction. For this reason, a means of controlling them has been proposed by LaBerge, Van Gelder, and Yellott (1970).

In studies where the error rate is low, which is usually the case, we may safely use the average times of all reactions to a given stimulus as a function of prior experience and ignore the relatively minor perturbations produced by the time differences between erroneous and correct responses, which is an important issue I shall consider later.

Of course, one expects sequential effects to be complex, and it would be helpful to have some simple summary of them that would facilitate a preliminary appraisal of alternative theories. To find such a description it would seem appropriate to look for a common feature of those theories that appear to be more successful in treating sequential phenomena—those that emphasize the role of expectation or preparation for a stimulus.

Superficially, at least, any theory that gives a central role to expectancy, or a related concept, will predict that there will be a simple relation, often linear, between reaction times to the alternative stimuli, as these times are changed by the prior sequence of stimuli the subject has experienced. The reasons behind this conjecture are as follows. The typical two-choice reaction experiment ensures a perfect negative correlation between the probability of occurrence of the alternatives, and, thus, even if it is not an intrinsic property of the human subject to keep the sum of his expectancies for each possible stimulus at a constant value, exposure to the experiment is likely to force him into this strategy. It would be most interesting to observe the result of breaking this usual dependence among the occurrences of stimuli: in the two-choice case, either by sometimes presenting both stimuli and demanding both responses or by sometimes presenting neither. The responses to joint stimulation might be uninterpretable, but the single stimulus trials should throw light on the structure of expectancies. In any event, it is clear that there will usually be a linear exchange with a slope of -1 between the changing expectancies for the two stimuli; for a k-choice situation the relation between the expectancy for one alternative and the average for all others would have a slope of $-(k - 1)$. If a theory implies a linear relation between expectancy and reaction time, which is sometimes the case, then a linear exchange between the reaction times to the two stimuli is predicted. Otherwise, some other negative monotone relation would be expected. A similar treatment can be made of error rates.

Now this is obviously a very simple-minded approach that ignores many theoretical nuances, but it has the virtue of providing a convenient way of representing sequential data. Of course, theories may differ not only in the form of the time-exchange curve they predict but also in their predictions of the particular position on the curve where the data for a given prior stimulus sequence should lie. Both kinds of predictions will be examined later. Meanwhile, let us consider whether the data force any conclusions upon us.

I imagine that there is a wealth of data appropriate for the present purposes to be found in laboratories throughout the world, but there are few published reports of them. That the linear exchange occurs is implied by Laming's (1969) well-supported claim that a statistical information model provides a satisfactory account of sequential data obtained for a visual-length identification task, but the data are given in a highly digested form, and much of the analysis is focussed on the effects of particular sequences. The only published data I have located are those described by Remington (1969) and by Schvaneveldt and Chase (1969).[2] The former employed a two-choice task with an S–R code of spatially separated lights mapped onto corresponding response keys and an intertrial interval of 4 sec. Data are reported as reaction times to a given stimulus as a function of the four prior stimuli, and for two conditions in which the probabilities of the alternative stimuli are respectively in the ratios 50:50 and 70:30. The error rate was low and the published data are the average times for all responses, both correct and erroneous. In the case of the 50:50 condition, the data for the two stimuli are not given separately but are presented as average times for corresponding sequences, for example, a run of four stimuli which are the

---

[2]After this contribution was written, my attention was drawn to an analysis of sequential effects in a four-choice task by Remington (1971).

same as that to which the response is made. In the paper of Schvaneveldt and Chase, both two- and four-choice reactions were studied for a variety of S–R codes and intertrial intervals (ITIs). The codes were: two- and four-choice spatial (press an illuminated button), two- and four-choice with numerals paired in natural orders with buttons, and the same components in a four-choice task with a scrambled relation between them. The spatial code was investigated for both short (.1, .5, 1.0 sec) and long ITIs (1.0, 2.5, 8.5 sec); for the numeral–button code only the short intervals were used. The data for errors are excluded, the error-rates again being low. The results are partitioned according to the three previous stimuli only.

For the spatial code, the data of both papers approximates a linear exchange of times, although the data for Remington's 50:50 condition and those from the Schvaneveldt and Chase study where long ITIs were used suggest that there may be some systematic deviations from this. (See Figs. 1 and 2, conditions I and II.)

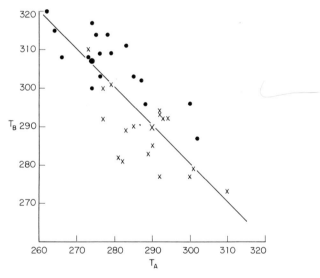

Fig. 1. The data of Remington (1969) replotted as an exchange relation between the reaction times to the two alternative stimuli, A and B. Each point is based on the average times for a particular sequence of four prior stimuli. The crosses represent data from a situation in which the two stimuli are presented with equal frequency; the closed circles come from a situation in which the stimuli occur with frequencies in the ratio 70:30. The larger symbols correspond to the overall average times for the two conditions. The straight line having a slope of − 1 was fitted by eye. As pointed out in the text, Remington does not report separate times for the two stimuli in the case of the 50:50 data. The symmetry of the above plot of these data is therefore artifactual, although it is believed that it is not likely to be a misleading representation of the complete (unknown) facts.

Fig. 2. The data of Schvaneveldt and Chase (1969) replotted in the manner described in the legend of Fig. 1. Each point now is based on the average times for a particular sequence of three prior stimuli. Conditions I and II are data for a spatial S–R code with long and short ITIs, respectively. Condition III data are for a symbolic S–R code. Again, because the reported data do not distinguish responses to different stimuli, the symmetry of the above diagram is inevitable but the slopes of its components are not determined artifactually.

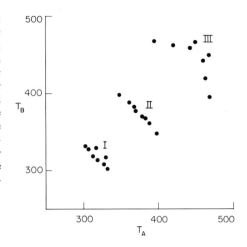

In Remington's more detailed results, these deviations exhibit an interesting pattern which, if replicable, may be important in understanding sequential effects, although the earlier-mentioned averaging procedure may have aided me in forming a simple-minded perception of the data. The most striking feature is that after a sequence where a run is terminated by an alternation (for example, AAAB, BAAB), the times for both stimuli are the same and relatively long. Further alternations lead to a decrease in the times for both stimuli, a sequence such as ABAB yielding relatively very quick responses. On the other hand, a continuing run of stimuli after the first alternation leads to the kind of variations in time that are expected on the linear exchange notion. This simple pattern suggests that an alternation ending a run of stimuli "clears the system," and performance then is determined in separate ways by a run or a continuing sequence of alternations, the latter having an overall speeding effect. However, I admit that this may be a phenomenon "the likes of which will never be seen again"; similar astrological investigations do not reveal any similar pattern in the 70:30 data, for example alternations now appear to lead to a slowing of the overall response speed. The important overall features of the data are: (a) that they would not reject the general notion of a linear exchange of times for the two stimuli; (b) the average data for the two conditions lie on the straight line that usually appears to fit the sequential data best (from different subjects for the two conditions).

The Schvaneveldt and Chase condition employing the number–button code displays a strikingly different result that would certainly, at first sight, not appear to be capable of being explained by any single principle of expectancy, that is, by postulating either a continuum of expectancy or all-or-none preparation. In both cases, a linear exchange over the whole data range would be predicted. Instead, for this code, the data suggest to me that on each trial attention is directed toward one stimulus and also, in some sense, preparation for that stimulus can also be varied in a continuous manner. The way in which this notion agrees with the facts is illustrated in Fig. 3. This possibility will be considered again when particular theories are discussed.

For the four-choice situation, the present analysis cannot be pursued very far, since the sequences of prior stimuli have been described only in terms of whether each is the same as the presented stimulus or different. Thus, one cannot tell, for example, what the effect of a run of one stimulus would have on the time for any other. It appears, however, that the slope of the exchange relation is approximately -3, as would be expected on the exchange principle. For the scrambled code, results are dominated by a strong repetition effect, the times being much faster when a stimulus is repeated, only small variations being produced by stimuli earlier in the

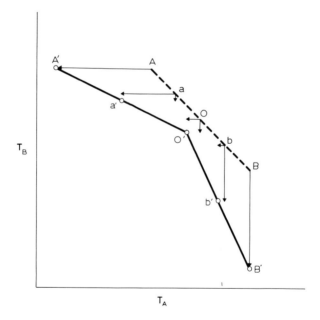

Fig. 3. Possible explanation of sequential effects for a symbolic S–R code in terms of a dual-aspect process. The dotted line AOB represents the linear exchange due to the changing probabilities of attending to each stimulus. The arrows originating from points on this exchange line represent the average degree of preparation for a stimulus when it has been selected for attention; the horizontal arrows indicate average preparation for S_A and vertical arrows that for S_B. The locus A'O'B' represents the predicted form of the data.

sequence. It is important to note that the data for both the ordered and scrambled four-choice code appear to lie on the same exchange curve.

Let us turn then to the treatment of sequential effects by the various theories.

1. Statistical-Decision Models

Laming (1969) states the sequential statistical-decision model in terms of the flow of statistical information (Kullback, 1959). The subject is viewed as receiving, in the presence of a particular stimulus, a stream of information as to which alternative is its source. To represent this stream, it is convenient to break up time t into small quanta of duration δt, so that $t = r \, \delta t$. The additional input in one of these time quanta is represented by a random variable x: the form of these sensory data is not immediately important. In a two-choice situation, the additional data comes from one of two stationary distributions with probability-density functions $f(x|S_A)$, $f(x|S_B)$, where S_A and S_B are the two stimuli. The data arriving in the rth interval constitutes information in favor of the presence of one stimulus as against the other; the increment of information in favor of S_B against S_A, δI_r, is expressed as the log likelihood ratio

$$\delta I_r = \log\{f(x_r|S_B)/f(x_r|S_A)\}.$$

The total information in favor of S_B at time t, due to the presence of a stimulus is then $\sum_{s=1}^{r} \delta I_s$. However, there may be other information available to the subject about the nature of the current stimulus: for example, that the alternatives are being presented with probabilities $\Pr\{S_A\} = 1 - p$, $\Pr\{S_B\} = p$. This constitutes a priori information, $I_0 = \log\{p/(1-p)\}$. Therefore, the total information available to the subject at time t is

$$I(t) = I(r \, \delta t) = I_0 + \sum_{s=1}^{r} \delta I_s.$$

As sensory data arrives, the information traces out a one-dimensional random walk, and it is assumed that a decision is made when the information reaches one of two boundaries I_a and I_b corresponding to each response. If the mean rate of flow of information in favor of the stimulus presented is the same for both alternatives, then $E(\delta I/S_A) + E(\delta I/S_B) = 0$, where $E(\cdot)$ indicates the expected value or average of the increments of information in favor of S_B. For this so-called symmetric decision process, the optimal decision procedure, in the sense of having a minimum average reaction time for a given overall error rate ϵ, is obtained by setting the boundaries at

$$I_a = -\log\{(1 - \epsilon)/\epsilon\}, \qquad I_b = \log\{(1 - \epsilon)/\epsilon\}.$$

[Edwards (1965) presents the model in a different way and, in addition to signal probabilities, considers the influence of costs and payoffs for various S–R outcomes and the costs of sensory data.] For a fixed error rate, the distance between the decision boundaries is always $2 \log\{(1 - \epsilon)/\epsilon\}$, and the starting point of the random walk is at I_0, determined by the *a priori* estimates of the signal probabilities.

   Laming offers a treatment of sequential effects in terms of the subject's estimates of the stimulus probabilities. These could be based on information gathered from many aspects of the subject's experience. Laming places greatest emphasis on the subject's appraisal of the relative frequency of the stimuli, and the relative frequency of alternations and repetitions: in both cases, *a priori* information based on experience prior to exposure to a stimulus sequence as well as information resulting from exposure to the sequence itself are considered. I shall not dwell on the details of his analysis which supposes a limit to the information about stimulus probabilities the subject can store. For present purposes, it suffices to state that the analysis can be interpreted as setting the starting point of the random walk at a position that is a weighted average of the stimulus probabilities estimated separately from information about the stimulus frequency and from that about the relative frequency of alternations and repetitions. There is therefore a resemblance to certain recent analyses of data from experiments in which subjects are required to predict the successive stimuli in a binary sequence (Friedman, Carterette, & Anderson, 1968).

   The effect of all aspects of prior experience is merely to change the average position of the starting point of the random walk between fixed boundaries. If we continue to assume that the mean information rate in favor of the stimulus presented is the same for both stimuli, it is clear that the sum of the average reaction times to make the two alternative responses will be constant, since a bias in favor of one response takes the starting point an equal distance from the boundary corresponding to the other—always provided that the overall error rate remains unchanged. With low error rates this will imply a linear exchange for times to the two stimuli as the prior sequence varies.

   A statistical decision model is therefore compatible with the results I have reported for spatial codes. It should also be noted that Laming's development of this treatment of sequential effects was devised to agree with his empirical finding that reaction times and errors to a stimulus could be accounted for approximately by supposing that the subjective probability of a particular stimulus being presented (and hence the starting point of the random walk) was a geometrically weighted average of the occurrences of the stimulus in the prior sequence, and of a similar average of the occurences of repetitions and alternations. (The precise form of this average is de-

scribed on page 530. If the departures from the linear exchange noticed
in Remington's 50:50 data are replicable, then the important question is
whether the speeding up of alternations is accompanied by a higher overall
error rate, which is not implausible.

The data from the symbolic codes seem to tell against the theory as it
has been elaborated thus far. Of course, it could be supposed that the subject
is not able to limit his discrimination to that between two particular single-
digit numerals, and is in a multiple-choice situation in which each has to be
discriminated from the total set. However, since the nonappearing digits are
irrelevant to the task, it would appear that informational characteristics of
the input relevant to the task stimuli should be the dominant data for the
decision process, and a linear exchange would still be predicted. It would
appear more probable that the theory needs to be modified by assuming that
the subject has selected one alternative as likely to occur and that appropriate changes are made to the corresponding response boundary, whereas
the other boundary remains at a neutral position. That is, the distance from
the starting point of the random walk to boundary corresponding to the
unattended stimulus is a constant but that to the boundary of the other
reflects the subject's expectancy concerning its presentation. It is unlikely
that a particular stimulus sequence would lead always to the choice of the
same focal alternative; if this did happen, the time-exchange relation would
take the form of an inverted L. However, a high expectancy for a given
alternative would be accompanied by a high probability of focussing upon
it and if the other alternative is attended to, the expectancy for it would be
low. The situation would then be approximately as shown in Fig. 4. In the

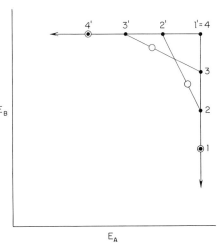

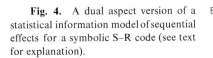

Fig. 4. A dual aspect version of a
statistical information model of sequential
effects for a symbolic S–R code (see text
for explanation).

diagram, the points labeled 1, 2, 3, and 4 represent different average expectancies for stimulus B, as a function of the prior sequence, when it is the focal alternative. The point $1'$, $2'$, $3'$, and $4'$ are the average expectancies for stimulus A for the same sequences, when it is focused upon. The overall average expectancies will lie somewhere along the lines joining corresponding points, approximately at that locus where the distances from the end points are in proportion to the expectancies. The circles in the diagram indicate likely loci from this admittedly very heuristic analysis. Whether the suggestion in the original data that the limbs of the exchange relation are linear is contrary to the present analysis is too fine a point to determine. Of course, it is also clear that whether this modification of the statistical decision model is necessary depends on the future corroboration of the Schvaneveldt and Chase data. As will be seen later, Laming's version of the sequential decision model gives a good description of other phenomena of CRT.

2. Communication Theory

From communication theory, if coding variations are possible in a two-choice situation—say, as a result of a search through various discriminating features of the stimuli—then the average message lengths for the two stimuli would be proportional to $-\log p'$ and $-\log(1 - p')$, respectively, where p' and $(1 - p')$ are subjective probabilities of the stimuli occurring after a given prior sequence. The predicted form of the exchange relation is then convex upward, and not compatible with the data available at present.

3. Falmagne's Model

A linear exchange with a slope of -1 is a direct consequence of Falmagne's (1965) approach in those cases where the subject is supposed to prepare explicitly for one of the alternatives, although the exchange now reflects the probability of this being directed toward a particular stimulus. The total possible range of variation in reaction times is the additional time required to respond to an unexpected stimulus. The interpretation and extension of the model described by Falmagne and Theios (1969) leads to certain deviations from the simple relation. If the templates of the two stimuli are shifting between any two fixed positions, the linear exchange is unaffected. If, on the other hand, the templates are sometimes both in a short-term store and, at other times, one is in the long-term store, or both are, the predicted form of the exchange relation is modified. There are at least four possible combinations of template positions, as shown in Table 1 (that is, ignoring *which* template is closer to the pole position corresponding to a state of "selective attention").

Table 1

| Combina- | Short-term store | | Long-term store | Sum of reaction times to two stimuli |
tion	Pole	Other		
A	T_1	T_2	—	Fast
B	T_1	—	T_2	Medium
C	—	T_1	T_2	Slow
D	—	—	T_1, T_2 (ordered?)	Slow

Thus, the kind of variation in the sum of reaction times to the two stimuli noticed in Remington's 50:50 data could be explained by the model. It is not entirely implausible that:

1. a first alternation might take both templates out of the buffer store;
2. continued alternations bring both templates into the buffer;
3. runs of one stimulus might lead to this template being in the pole position, the other in long-term storage;
4. it is not necessarily the case that the same effects would occur for the 70:30 condition.

As will be discussed later, Theios and Smith (1970) have preferred to describe Remington's data with the original two-state version of the model, which they claim gives a good fit.

There are at least seven possible particular states of the model, if the position of particular templates is taken into account, as shown in Fig. 5, and many possible results could be explained in an *ad hoc* way, including those for the numeral–button S–R code. But why should different codes lead to different results? It was suggested earlier that the retrieval of the response to the unexpected stimulus might involve different processes for different codes. However, it seems unlikely, from the viewpoint of the present model, that in the case of the symbolic code, the exchange relation should lie so close to an inverted L. Obviously, the modified version of the statistical decision model, suggested earlier, and the template model are different special ways of representing an information-processing structure in which there exist both attention to a given stimulus and continuous variations in expectancy for it.

4. Fixed Sample

In considering the fixed-sample model, the first question to ask is whether there is any evidence for any large variation in the time during which information is sampled under different experimental conditions. Assuming approximately optimal use of the sampled information, variations in this

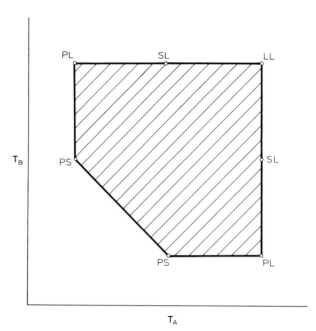

Fig. 5. Representation of the range of predictions (hatched area) of the Falmagne and Theios (1969) model concerning the time-exchange relation. The circles represent the decision times for various positions of the two stimulus templates. Each letter pair describes the positions using the following code: P = pole position in short-term memory (STM); S = other position in STM; L = template in long-term memory (LTM) (thus, LL indicates both templates in LTM). The decision times for the various positions are, of course, not necessarily spaced equally as they are in the diagram.

time would be reflected by variations in the estimates of stimulus discriminability d', when, for example, the stimulus probabilities are manipulated. Reference to Laming's (1969) Experiments I and II, shows that there, at least, overall error rates change very little, and the d's computed from the responses are extremely constant. Thus, there can be no gross changes in the distribution of input sampling times under different conditions. It is therefore necessary to consider the decision stage that follows the sampling process, and, clearly, all the other theories I am examining are prospective candidates for this. If it is proposed that a template-matching procedure constitutes the decision stage, as do Briggs and Swanson (1970), then the predictions follow those of Falmagne (1965) or Falmagne and Theios (1969). If, on the other hand, we assume that some kind of statistical-decision procedure follows, we have two alternatives: (*a*) a sequential process, already considered above; (*b*) the assumption that the subject has to determine whether the input lies to one side or the other of a criterion data value fixed by his current biases. Precise predictions of the exchange relation depend upon assumptions about the distribution of input data from the two stimuli and the method by which the subject compares the input with his criterion. The calculation of mean reaction times is difficult even then (Thomas, 1970), but median reaction times are more tractable (Audley & Mercer, 1968; Thomas, 1970). Assuming normally distributed data, and that the time to locate the input relative to the criteria is inversely proportional to the logarithm of their separation (P. T. Smith, 1968), then the exchange curve for the median reaction time is markedly convex downward. Even if other assumptions might lead to a more linear relation, it will be shown later that it is difficult to explain from this model why the reaction times of erroneous choices are faster than those of correct ones.

5. Fast-Guess Model

It is not possible to explain the linear exchange feature of Remington's data by means of the original form of the "fast-guess" hypothesis. The data include reaction times for both correct and erroneous responses to a stimulus; hence, the effect of increasing the proportion of fast guesses would be to produce changes which are orthogonal to the linear exchange. Effects of this kind observed in the data thus might be accounted for, but they clearly are not the dominant feature of the sequential phenomena.

In cases where data are presented separately for correct responses, it appears unlikely that the full range of sequential effects on reaction time could be predicted from the model unless guessing were very frequent and the error rate therefore abnormally high. For example, suppose we regard Remington's 50:50 data as entirely representing correct responses. The most extreme difference between the reaction times to stimuli A and B occurs after the sequence AAAA, when $RT_A = 273$ msec and $RT_B = 310$ msec. Assuming that the latter time is made up entirely of true discriminations and that the former is composed of a proportion $1 - q$ of true discriminations and q of guesses having a latency of, say, 100 msec, then we have

$$310(1 - q) + 100q = 273,$$

so that $q = 37/210$ for this sequence. For the 50:50 condition, however, all 16 sequences are equally likely, and the two runs of this kind would alone make a contribution to the overall error rate of $\frac{1}{8} \times \frac{1}{2} \times 37/210$, that is, more than 1%, which is close to the total rate observed in the entire experiment.

6. Models Emphasizing the Specific Role of Stimulus Repetitions and Alternations[3]

In situations where the alternative stimuli are presented in random order, without additional sequential constraints, Kornblum's analysis would lead to the same kinds of expectations concerning the time exchange relation that were obtained for models of type 1 and 3, since the relative frequencies of repetitions and alternations directly reflect the marginal stimulus probabilities. However, one might describe the results of Schvaneveldt and Chase (1969) for the number-button code in terms of a tendency to retrieve partially the response of the expected stimulus. Since the data exhibit positive recency effects, it is also possible that the departure from a linear time exchange could result from "short-circuiting" the S–R code (Bertelson, 1963) and merely repeating the previous response. It is clear that to account for the pattern of the data, the contribution to the reaction time variation of either of these processes would have to become greater as the expectancy for a stimulus increased. Such hypotheses are therefore special cases of the principle that attention to a particular stimulus and variation in the extent of preparation for its occurrence are present in CRT performance.

The examination of certain sequential phenomena therefore lends weight to a hypothesis that combines features of model types (1) and (3), which emphasize expectancy for the alternative stimuli. A further evaluation of this conclusion will be held over until certain other properties of choice reactions are considered.

There remain two other questions in connection with sequential effects which remain to be answered. These are:

1. Can the stimulus probability effect and sequential effects be accounted for in terms of the same underlying principle? By "stimulus probability effect" is meant the speeding up of the average reaction time to a more frequent stimulus, and the slowing of that to the less frequent stimulus, obtained in experiments where stimulus probabilities are varied from condition to condition.

2. Can anything be said about the properties of a stimulus sequence which determine expectancies on a given trial?

As far as available data enables us to draw a conclusion, the answer to the first question must be affirmative. To the extent that there exists a linear exchange relation of the kind already discussed, this result follows directly. Remington's data are clearly not incompatible with this, and drawing this conclusion from his results will be supported further when question 2 is

---

[3]See especially Kornblum (1969).

answered. The paper by Laming (1969) also presents a very strong case for an affirmative answer based on an independent set of data, and Kornblum's (1969) study of four-choice reactions is also in agreement, in that he shows that simple lawful relations between reaction times and first-order sequential dependencies are, by and large, all that are needed to describe his data. (The fact that the form of the exchange relation may be dependent upon the S–R code indicates the need for further studies of the signal probability effect.)

Some progress has also been made in answering the second question. Both type (1) and (3) models of expectancy theory require additional assumptions concerning the way in which current expectancies are determined, and it is obvious that discovering the proper form for these is going to be no easier than it has been for binary prediction experiments. However, there are indications that new progress is being made in studying the latter and that certain obituaries (for example, Edwards, 1969) were premature. Meanwhile, let me continue a simplified exposition.

As far as the signal-probability effect is concerned, there are certain features in common between the analyses offered by Laming (1969) and Falmagne (1965). Leaving aside the additional role that Laming and Kornblum have given to alternations and repetitions, both of the expectancy models regard the average expectancy for a signal as a geometric weighted average of its occurrences in the past. Laming's hypothesis was designed to be compatible with the results of a regression analysis that supported this conclusion, and to the extent that Falmagne relies on a stimulus sampling model for his predictions of the average probability of a subject being prepared for a particular stimulus, this leads to the same result. Of course, we are dealing in one case with continuous expectancies and in the other case with all-or-none preparation, so that predictions about the effects of particular sequences are different for the two approaches.

In many CRT studies, especially those with long intertrial intervals (Williams, 1966; Moss et al., 1967) negative recency effects are present in reaction-time data, so that we usually cannot neglect the role of alternations and repetitions. If anyone wants to pursue the question of what kind of weighting should be given even to just these two sources of expectancy, then much painstaking research will be needed. It is interesting to note that Remington's data do not exhibit negative recency and that a simple geometric weighted average of past occurrences of a stimulus describes both the stimulus probability effect and the effect of repeating a stimulus quite well.

Let us suppose that reaction time is a linear function of expectancy, E:

$$RT = a - bE.$$

The expectancy E_{in} for the ith stimulus ($i = 1, 2$) at the nth trial is assumed to be a weighted average of past occurrences of the stimulus and is therefore given by

$$E_{in} = X_{n-1} + \alpha X_{n-2} + \alpha^2 X_{n-3} + \cdots,$$

where $X_r = 1$ if the rth stimulus was S_i, and otherwise 0. The expected value of E_{in} over all sequences then is

$$\overline{E}_{in} = p_i/(1 - \alpha),$$

where $p_i = \Pr\{S_i\}$, and $\Sigma_{i=1}^2 \overline{E}_{in} \to 1/(1 - \alpha)$, the inelegance of which will not be dealt with here.

Thus, the average reaction time to S_i is a linear function of p_i; this is the case for Remington's data, which are plotted as a function of $(1 - \alpha)E$ in Fig. 6 and are fitted by the expression RT $= a - b(1 - \alpha)E$, with $a = 334$ msec and $b = 85$ msec.

For repetitions we have

$$(\overline{E}_{in}|X_{n-1} = 1) = 1 + \alpha p_i/(1 - \alpha);$$

for alternations we have

$$(\overline{E}_{in}|X_{n-1} = 0) = \alpha p_i/(1 - \alpha).$$

The difference between $(1 - \alpha)$ E for the last two expressions is $(1 - \alpha)$; hence, an estimate of $(1 - \alpha)$ is given by the difference between the reaction times for repetitions and alternations, which is predicted to be $(1 - \alpha)b$. Using the average of these reaction time differences for the three values of stimulus probability yields $\hat{\alpha} = 0.88$. The observed and predicted times for alternations and repetitions are also shown in Fig. 6, and the agreement between them is good. It is undoubtedly fortunate that Remington's data show a positive recency effect, but the present naive analysis at least has the merit of providing a simple demonstration of the compatibility of the stimulus probability effect and sequential phenomena in terms of a geometrically decaying influence of past stimulus events. I must emphasize that this analysis may be appropriate only for some S–R codes: it clearly neglects the need for a dual-aspect process claimed here to be operative for some symbolic codes.

The continuous and discontinuous models lead to different predictions about the reaction times following particular sequences. Theios and Smith (1970) claim a good fit for the discontinuous model. I have found that the continuous model, considered above, also fits tolerably well; a comparison between these descriptions would be quite gratuitous here, and is made difficult by the fact that my estimates of Remington's data points disagree with theirs. In any event, I believe it is clear that we first need to establish

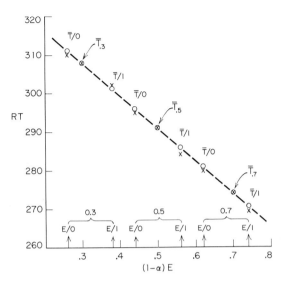

Fig. 6. Description of the effects of stimulus probability, stimulus repetition and alternation observed in the experiment of Remington (1969) in terms of an expectancy calculated as a geometrically weighted average of past occurrences of a stimulus. The times listed with numerical subscripts (.3, .5, .7) indicate the average reaction times for stimuli with those frequencies of presentation. The two points $\bar{T}/1$ and $\bar{T}/0$ on either side of each mean represent the reaction times of repetitions and alternations, respectively (see text). Open circles indicate predictions; crosses indicate observations.

whether there are any departures from a monotonic time-exchange relation, and the nature of these, before pursuing a detailed analysis of the determinants of expectancy. For this reason, I have not yet attempted to consider the predictions that would follow from a model which postulates both attention to a particular stimulus and variations in expectancy for both stimuli.

There are, of course, other ways of manipulating both the attention to a particular stimulus and the extent of the preparation for this than by varying the sequence of prior stimuli. A more exact analysis of the determinants of the time-exchange relation might then be obtained, and some of the suggestions made in the above analysis could be subjected to more stringent experimental tests.

B. THE PROPERTIES OF ERRONEOUS RESPONSES

Many reports of CRT experiments give very perfunctory accounts of data relevant to the causes and characteristics of errors. Yet these may constitute critical evidence in appraising theories. The following statements are offered as the "facts" about errors in terms of which the theories will be evaluated. They correspond closely to the issues considered by Laming (1968). Although there is unlikely to be any dispute about the first, there is little data available on the second, which obviously requires further investigation.

1a. When a response is made erroneously, the average reaction time is usually quicker than when the *same response* is made correctly.

1b. As the average reaction time of correct responses is decreased—for example, by increasing the relative frequency of the corresponding stimulus—the reaction time for that response made erroneously exhibits a closely corresponding pattern of change.

2. The ratio of the total number of errors made in the presence of each stimulus approximates to the inverse of the ratio of the corresponding stimulus probabilities:

$$R_\epsilon = \frac{\text{number of errors given } S_B}{\text{number of errors given } S_A} = \frac{\Pr\{S_A\}}{\Pr\{S_B\}}.$$

It perhaps requires emphasis that it is the total number of errors with which this expression is concerned, not the probabilities of errors conditional upon the presentation of a stimulus.

C. EVALUATION OF THEORIES

1. Statistical-Decision Models

The sequential-decision model in the form in which it has so far been considered is compatible with statement 1b but not 1a. The average time to reach a given decision boundary is independent of the stimulus presented and depends only upon the position of that boundary relative to the starting point of the decision process.

The successful prediction of statement 1b is a strong point in favor of the theory: can the theory be modified to account for faster errors? Laming proposes that since the subject has temporal uncertainty about the moment when a stimulus of either kind will arrive, he will, on some occasions at least, start sampling the experimental display in advance of the appearance of the stimulus. Consequently, he may sample data that, although not dependent upon the presence of the stimuli, will lead to random perturbations in the information as to which stimulus is responsible for the current stream of data. Thus, errors are more likely to occur when such perturbations reduce the amount of information due to the stimulus involved in a decision, and on these occasions less time than average will be taken to reach the decision boundary. Another possibility, considered by Fitts (1966), is that there are fluctuations in the boundaries of the decision process as the subject attempts to achieve a given level of performance accuracy. The latter notion will be considered later in the context of the "trade off" between speed and accuracy.

No experiment to test the adequacy of the temporal uncertainty hypothesis has been reported as yet although Laming argues in its favor on the basis of the magnitude of the time difference between correct and erroneous responses observed in different experimental conditions. When the intertrial interval is short, for example, there is little opportunity to sample "irrelevant" information, and Laming notes that the time difference tends to zero under these conditions. However, other changes obviously are taking place: the overall reaction times then are also much longer and there are higher error rates, which do not seem immediately compatible with the theory. Nonetheless, given the important agreement with statement lb, the modification needed to meet statement la certainly demands further exploration, even if it only provides a technical way of describing the influence of factors other than discrimination in a CRT task.

"Fact" 2 follows directly from the theory, the exact prediction being

$$R_\varepsilon = (1 - p - \varepsilon)/(p - \varepsilon),$$

where $\Pr\{S_A\} = 1 - p$, $\Pr\{S_B\} = p$, and ε is the overall error rate.

2. Communication Theory

For the communication-theory models, it is usually supposed that average error reaction times would be shorter than those of correct responses because an insufficiently long message has been transmitted. It would appear, however, that the predictions about the properties of errors depend upon the way in which the principles of the theory are incorporated into a particular model of CRT. If, for example, as Briggs and Swanson (1970) suppose, the critical factor in the transmission of information is the scanning of a sensory store before central processes are initiated, the latter might be might be made more difficult to perform when insufficient information is made available for them to operate upon and, hence, error RTs would be longer. However, their conclusion is that the scanning of sensory information proceeds more slowly than central processing so that I am not sure what is the final prediction. The extent to which the actual pattern of response times specified by statements la and lb can be predicted successfully depends in this case upon the hypothesized characteristics of central processing. Alternative forms of this are considered below for the fixed sample methods and for the template-comparison process postulated by Falmagne and Theios (1969).

If communication theory is accepted more literally as a model of CRT, then presumably errors occur because a particular feature of a stimulus is symbolized incorrectly or is missing from the complete message representing a stimulus. In the former case, the correct and error reaction times would be correlated on a response basis as required by statement 1b, but if transmission time is the important variable in CRT, there would not be any difference in reaction times corresponding to statement 1a. In the latter case, predictions would depend on the way in which incomplete messages are decoded, which usually is not specified. I have considered an encoding of the stimulus in terms of stimulus features only rather than in terms of templates because it is clear that the latter would imply that the reaction time to the more frequent stimulus would always be independent of its particular probability of occurrence. As far as the error ratio R_e is concerned, this fact is predicted correctly by the literal model, if the encoding of a stimulus is optimal for a given overall error rate.

In discussing these aspects of models based upon communication theory I am particularly conscious of my student status. It may also well be that, in my emphasis on the two-choice tasks, I have failed to point out possible merits of these models where more alternatives are concerned. Therefore, I would not be surprised if my analysis were challenged. However, I am inclined to regard much of this as pretty academic, and I have not striven very hard to be sure of my arguments in this section, because of the failure of the literal communication model to correctly describe the form of the time-exchange relation.

3. Falmagne's Model

To account for errors on the basis of the all-or-none preparation model, it is usually assumed that these will occur when the subject is prepared for some other stimulus than the one presented (Falmagne, 1965). Presumably this could either be an error of discrimination resulting from the inappropriate set or, alternatively, because a partially retrieved response is released prematurely. To predict faster errors in the former case, the absence of some checking stage would appear necessary (Welford, 1960). Emphasis upon response retrieval is more attractive to me, for no strong reason, except that it appears to approximate to the descriptions of error productions that sometimes are offered by subjects.

The difficulty for either version of this theory is that error reaction times are predicted to be independent of stimulus frequency since errors reflect a particular unique state. Correct responses become faster with increases in stimulus frequency because the subject is more often in an appropriately prepared state; errors, on the other hand, always occur when the subject responds as if he were in an appropriately prepared state. To account for changes in the times of errors corresponding to those of correct responses, it would again be necessary to suppose that there exists some continuous variation in the expectancy of, or preparation for, a given stimulus.

The prediction concerning the error ratio is also incorrect. For, supposing that the probability of making an error in an inappropriately prepared state is β, then

$$R_\varepsilon = \frac{\Pr\{S_B\}}{\Pr\{S_A\}} \frac{\Pr\{\text{prepared for } S_A\}}{\Pr\{\text{prepared for } S_B\}} \frac{\beta}{\beta}.$$

If the subject approximately matches his relative frequency of preparing for a stimulus with its probability of occurrence, then $\Pr\{\text{prepared for } S_A\} = \Pr\{S_A\}$, and so on, and R_ε approximates unity. The obtained result of course, might follow if the subject departed markedly from the probability matching hypothesis, but it seems implausible that he should always do so in a manner compatible with the observed error ratios. Furthermore, there is considerable evidence from studies of CRT, in which the subject is required to predict the next stimulus, that probability matching does hold for this task. Even if we make the assumption, rather inappropriate for this model, that errors also sometimes may occur when the subject is correctly prepared for a stimulus, it remains impossible to account for the observed error ratio.

A modification of this theory, which also allows for some variation in the degree of preparation for a stimulus, could lead to a correct prediction about the error ratio, although the exact form of the prediction would depend upon assumptions concerning the way in which the probability of focusing upon a particular alternative was dependent upon the expectancies for the two stimuli. Arguing very crudely, we might suppose that the subject matches both his expectancy for a stimulus and his probability of being specifically prepared for that stimulus to its probability of occurrence. If we now assume that the probability of an error is proportional to the magnitude of the expectancy operating on a given trial, then we have

$$R_\varepsilon = \frac{\Pr\{S_B\}\Pr\{\text{prepared for } S_A\}(\text{expectancy for } S_A)}{\Pr\{S_A\}\Pr\{\text{prepared for } S_B\}(\text{expectancy for } S_B)} \frac{\alpha}{\alpha},$$

where α is the constant of proportionality for the occurence of errors. Hence,

$$R = \frac{p}{1-p} \cdot \frac{1-p}{p} \cdot \frac{1-p}{p} = \frac{1-p}{p},$$

as required.

The Falmagne and Theios (1969) restatement of the model in terms of comparisons of the input with templates of the stimuli is, in essence, equivalent to allowing some degree of variation in the expectancy for a given

stimulus. Presumably, the partial retrieval of a response would occur only
for a template in the pole position, and if this were the only basis for errors,
the criticisms of the parent model would still apply. Alternatively, errors
might result from incorrectly matching the input with a template because
this is an intrinsic property of the comparison process. Errors in the comparison process could also occur because the input is of poor quality and this
possibility will be considered below in connection with fixed sample theories.

To make specific predictions about the error ratio from the Falmagne
and Theios model, we need to have assumptions additional to those so far
given by the authors. Therefore, in order to obtain some provisional results,
I will offer a rather simplified analysis. First, it seems reasonable to surmise
that errors would occur only when a stimulus is erroneously matched to a
template and that no mistakes are made when the input is being compared
with the corresponding template. Second, the proportion of errors made
when a template other than that of the presented stimulus is in the pole,
or forward, position will be greater than that for other positions. Only in
the former case is there likely to be any substantial retrieval of a response
or any strong biasing effects in the actual comparison process. It therefore
will be assumed that the error rate for a comparison with an inappropriate
template will take the value α for the pole position; and a single value $\beta < \alpha$
for all other positions.

Let T_A, and T_A' denote respectively that the template of a stimulus A is
in the pole position and some other position, on those occasions when it is
the first to be encountered, and let T_B and T_B' represent the corresponding
states for stimulus B.

The probabilities of an error for each stimulus and for each state are
then as shown in Table 2.

Table 2. *Probabilities of Error for
Each Stimulus and State*

Stimulus	T_A	T_A'	T_B	T_B'
		State		
A	0	0	α	β
B	α	β	0	0

Suppose the probability of a template being the first to be encountered
approximately matches the probability of its associated stimulus being presented:

$$\Pr\{T_A U T_A'\} = \Pr\{S_A\} = 1 - p \quad \text{and} \quad \Pr\{T_B U T_B'\} = \Pr\{S_B\} = p$$

where $p > 1 - p$. Also let x be the proportion of trials on which the state of the system is T_A, given that T_A or T_A' occur:

$$x = \Pr\{T_A \mid T_A U T_A'\}.$$

Similarly let

$$y = \Pr\{T_B \mid T_B U T_B'\}.$$

Then

$$\begin{aligned}
\Pr\{\text{error} \mid S_A\} \\
&= p\{y\alpha + (1 - y)\beta\} \\
&= p\{\alpha - (1 - y)(\alpha - \beta)\} \\
&= p\alpha\{1 - (1 - y)(\alpha - \beta)/\alpha\}.
\end{aligned}$$

Similarly

$$\Pr\{\text{error} \mid S_B\} = (1 - p)\alpha\{1 - (1 - x)(\alpha - \beta)/\alpha\}.$$

Hence, the error ratio

$$R_\varepsilon = \frac{\text{total errors} \mid S_B}{\text{total errors} \mid S_A} = \frac{p}{(1 - p)} \frac{(1 - p)\alpha\{1 - (1 - x)(\alpha - \beta)/\alpha\}}{p\ \alpha\{1 - (1 - y)(\alpha - \beta)/\alpha\}}.$$

If $\alpha = \beta$, then, as we expect from the earlier analysis of the Falmagne (1965) model

$$R_\epsilon = 1.$$

Now, R_ε depends on the values of x, y, and $(\alpha - \beta)$. The difference between the error rates for the two template positions will have the greatest effect when $\beta = 0$. In this case, we have

$$R_\epsilon = x/y.$$

Given that B is the more frequent stimulus, it seems likely (although one can produce exceptions) that its template will be relatively more often in the pole position when it is the first one encountered in the search. Thus, $y > x$, and at least it can be stated that the predicted R_ϵ is more in line with our "facts" about this ratio than the simple two-state model. To be more precise in one's predictions, more detailed assumptions would be needed, and at this stage we need more estimates of the empirical ratio, and for different S–R codes, than we need precision in the theories.

This model also does not have the difficulties of its parent hypothesis in explaining why the time to make a response erroneously should change in

concert with the time to make the same response correctly. A speeding up
of errors and correct responses is due to a particular template being pro-
portionately more often in the pole position.

4. Fixed-Sample Models

In a fixed-sample model, errors would be expected to occur when the
quality of the sensory data is relatively inadequate. For the simplest version
of this model, in which the sampling of input is followed by a decision
process of constant duration, the quality of the input would have to vary as a
result of fluctuations in sampling time if quicker errors are to be accounted
for. However, there seems to be no way by means of which we then could
explain the longer reaction times that are observed for a less frequent stimulus.

If there follows a decision as to which side of a criterion a measure of the
sampled data lies, then it appears that errors must have longer reaction
times than correct responses. For in situations with a low error rate, the data
will be close to the criterion when an error is made, and it will take longer
to decide how it should be classified. Even if the subject initiated a guess
when the data were not clear-cut, it appears likely that this must follow upon
an attempt to make a categorization, and the wrong prediction is unchanged.

If, as Briggs and Swanson (1970) propose, a template search is initiated
after sensory data have been scanned, then the prediction of differential
error rates for different stimuli would require that the search process have a
structure akin to that of my interpretation of the Falmagne and Theios
(1969) model. Of course, in a task where many templates are involved, which
more often has been the case in their research, the variation in the error rate
for a template comparison as a function of its serial position might be affected by many other factors than whether it was in the pole position.

Briggs and Swanson also suppose that the scanning of sensory data proceeds at a slower rate than the later decision process, and it would be
necessary to consider carefully the interaction between the properties of
these two stages before predictions about error rates and error reaction times
could be made. I have not yet attempted an analysis of the nature of this interaction: the important problem is whether a poor quality output of the first
stage would lead to a more ready acceptance of a template without affecting
the comparison time, or lead to an increase in the duration of this process, with
only a small effect on error rates. If Briggs and Swanson are correct in con-
cluding that it is an input scanning stage which determines the amount of information (in Shannon's sense) transmitted in performance, it is clear that
any successful theory of choice reactions must include assumptions about a
component of this kind.

5. Fast-Guess Models

For the fast-guess model, there is obviously no difficulty in explaining why errors should be quicker than correct responses. The problem here, as I have already shown, is that the extent to which correct responses are speeded up to a more frequent stimulus cannot be accounted for, if error rates are low.

The prediction of the error ratio follows a pattern similar to that for the all-or-none preparation model. If the proportion of trials on which a guess occurs is q, and p' is the probability that the response appropriate to S_B is then made, we have

$$R_\epsilon = \frac{p}{(1-p)} \frac{q\,(1-p')}{q} \frac{p'}{p'},$$

assuming that the contribution to errors from true discriminations is negligible. To account successfully for the observed values of the ratio, it again is necessary to assume a very precise deviation of guessing from a probability matching hypothesis, namely, $(1-p')/p' = (1-p)^2/p^2$, and this does not seem very plausible. I have not yet considered the implications of the modified form of the model proposed by Yellott (1971).

D. The Trade Off between Speed and Accuracy

Only the briefest of comments will be made about the way in which a subject achieves greater speed of response at the expense of accuracy. There is, as far as I know, no evidence of both being increased concomitantly at a given level of practice.

As Swensson and Edwards (1971) point out, the important distinction between models on this issue is whether they place emphasis on how much of the stimulus input is processed before a decision is made or upon how often the subject actually processes stimulus information. The former is exemplified by sequential decision models, which, taken literally, imply that a continuous trade off between speed and accuracy should be capable of being achieved by means of a single process and over a relatively wide range of the two variables. Evidence in favor of this view appeared at first to be forthcoming (Fitts, 1966), but, increasingly, it seems to be the case that the flexibility of performance, which is directly under the control of stimulus processing, is markedly limited (Howell & Kreidler, 1963; Pachella & Pew, 1968; but see Pew, 1969). On the other hand, models of the fast-guess kind, which suppose that the subject achieves the trade off by varying the extent to which he employs a strategy of making a response determined in advance of the arrival of the stimulus, have received considerable support (Yellott, 1967; and very strongly by Swensson & Edwards, 1971).

Possibly the limitations on the trade off that can be achieved by means of variations in the processing of stimulus information may be due both to a limited capacity for the temporal integration of information restricting greater accuracy of performance and to the existence of a process for scanning sensory input which can only proceed at a limited rate.

Where there is an imbalance of stimulus frequencies, it would be possible to regard fast guesses as the result of pushing the preparation for a given stimulus up to a maximum, and the results therefore might be accommodated within a model of the dual-aspect kind. When the stimuli are equally frequent, such extreme preparation would seem to be outside the range which characterizes normal accurate performance. It would, however, be most interesting to determine where the data for fast responses induced by suitable payoffs lie in relation to the time exchange curve obtained for the sequential effects of accurate performance. If they lie on the same curve, then the trade off results could be accounted for in terms of a model capable of describing accurate performance.

IV. Concluding Remarks

From many viewpoints, the sequential-decision model gives the most coherent account of the phenomena of choice reactions that I have reviewed. However, I have indicated reasons why a theory that includes the concepts of both attention to a particular stimulus and a continuously varying preparation for this stimulus could also give a good description of the same data and may be superior in other respects. One example of this kind of theory is the model of Falmagne and Theios, and, indeed, this appears to be unique in being able to comprehend, readily, distinct effects observed in the sequential data reported by Remington. However, I have not attempted to determine whether the model would explicitly predict the results observed for a symbolic S–R code, and at present I would prefer merely to conclude weakly in favor of a dual-aspect process, without specifying the mechanisms underlying the two aspects.

There is, of course, no reason to contrast the sequential and the dual-aspect theories too sharply at present. The former has the distinct advantage of providing a principle of response evocation whereas the latter only indicates, in a broad way, the kind of structure that may underlie performance. Actually, the principles of the sequential model have been given only in abstract terms, but the concept of template matching of the Falmagne and

Theios model is hardly less abstract [see Nickerson (1970) for a penetrating analysis of the concept]. Indeed, I wonder whether some uses of the term "template" do not more reflect the idea that the subject is attending to the possible occurrence of one particular stimulus, rather than referring to a particular manner of relating sensory data to a memorial representation. Thus, in a dual-aspect model, the acual choice of the stimulus to attend to would essentially define a template, and preparation for the stimulus would vary continuously either through the focusing of feature detectors, or even because of changes in the degree to which the response is retrieved.

In addition to espousing a dual-aspect notion, I would also very speculatively conclude in favor of some preliminary stimulus-sampling process with a limited range of operational durations that precedes the more central decision. I have indicated only a few points in favor of this concept, and, at the very least, further experiments along the lines of those of Briggs and his colleagues would be needed before this conclusion could be offered with any strong logical justification.

I am very conscious of having relied for my analysis on experimental results that remain to be corroborated. There are, however, some other findings relevant to my conclusions. In a number of studies in which the subject has been required to predict the next stimulus before responding to it (for example, Bernstein & Reese, 1967; Bernstein, Schuman, & Forester, 1967), a uniform finding is that reaction time to a correctly predicted stimulus is much less affected than usual by such variables as relative frequency. Such results could be regarded as some support for the notion that attention to a given stimulus is an important feature of choice reactions. The applicability of this finding to the normal CRT situation could be questioned, and sometimes leaves one with an uneasy feeling, but the data of the usual situation sometimes can be estimated quite well from those observed in a prediction task.

Evidence from similar experiments that have looked more closely at variations in reaction time for a correctly predicted stimulus also seem to indicate that there are differences in the extent to which the subject prepares for a stimulus. Although Geller and Pitz (1970) found little variation of this kind, it has been observed by Whitman and Geller (1971). Moreover, Hinrichs and Craft (1971) recently have reported differences in reaction times to the more and less frequent stimuli when these are conditional upon a correct prediction.

It also appears that some degree of dissociation can occur between the probability of attending to a particular stimulus and the level of expectancy or preparation for it. In the case of the Sternberg memory search task, it is not unreasonable to suppose that the subject would focus on a target item, even if this is not the most frequent stimulus event. Hawkins and Hosking

(1969) recently have emphasized this, and shown how the results of certain experiments using a many–one S–R code can be understood on this basis.

Finally, let me conclude, for once, more like a tutor than a tutee, by stating that my intention has been to explore the validity of various principles embodied in theories, rather than to present a convincing case for any particular theory. At least, I hope that the present analysis has suggested some ways in which these principles could be developed and tested.

Acknowledgments

This paper was written while I was on sabbatical leave in the United States. It is a pleasure to acknowledge the generous hospitality afforded me by the Institute for Advanced Study, Princeton, and by the University of California, Berkeley, during this leave. At the former, I wish especially to thank the Director and R. Duncan Luce for their kindness, and to acknowledge the support given by the Sloan Foundation. At the latter, I must first express my gratitude to the Executive Committee of the Miller Institute for Basic Research, who appointed me to a Visiting Research Professorship; and then thank Leo Postman for offering me the warm hospitality of the Institute of Human Learning.

Parts of this paper benefited greatly from a discussion with R. C. Atkinson.

References

Audley, R. J. A stochastic model for individual choice behavior. *Psychological Review*, 1960, **67**, 1–15.

Audley, R. J. Choosing. *Bulletin of the British Psychological Society*, 1970, **23**, 177–191.

Audley, R. J., & Mercer, A. The relation between decision time and relative response frequency in a blue–green discrimination. *British Journal of Mathematical and Statistical Psychology*, 1968, **21**, 183–192.

Audley, R. J., & Pike, A. R. Some alternative stochastic models of choice. *British Journal of Mathematical and Statistical Psychology*, 1965, **18**, 207–225.

Bernstein, I. H., & Reese, C. Choice reaction time and behavioral hypotheses: the effects of learning sequential redundancies. *Psychonomic Science*, 1967, **9**, 189–190.

Bernstein, I. H., Schurman, D. L., & Forester, G. Choice reaction time as a function of stimulus uncertainty and behavioral hypotheses. *Journal of Experimental Psychology*, 1967, **74**, 517–524.

Bertelson, P. Sequential redundancy and speed in serial two-choice responding task. *Quarterly Journal of Experimental Psychology*, 1961, **12**, 90–102.

Bertelson, P. S–R relationships and reaction times to new versus repeated signals in a serial task. *Journal of Experimental Psychology*, 1963, **65**, 478–484.

Bertelson, P. Serial choice reaction time as a junction of response versus signal-and-response repetition. *Nature*, 1965, **206**, 217–218.

Bertelson, P., & Renkin, A. Reaction times to new versus repeated signals in a serial task as a function of response-signal time interval. *Acta Psychologica*, 1966, **25**, 132–136.

Brainard, R. W., Irby, T. S., Fitts, P. M., & Alluisi, E. A. Some variables influencing the rate of gain of information. *Journal of Experimental Psychology*, 1962, **63**, 105–110.

Briggs, G. E., & Blaha, J. Memory retrieval and central comparison time in information processing. *Journal of Experimental Psychology*, 1969, **79**, 395–402.

Briggs, G. E., & Swanson, J. M. 1969.

Briggs, G. E., & Swanson, J. M. Encoding, decoding, and central functions in human information processing. *Journal of Experimental Psychology*, 1970, **86**, 296–308.

Broadbent, D. E., & Gregory, M. On the interaction of S–R compatibility with other variables affecting reaction time. *British Journal of Psychology*, 1965, **56**, 61–67.

Carterette, E. C. Random walk models for reaction times in signal detection and recognition. *Proceedings of the 18th International Congress of Psychology*, 1966, 84–95.

Christ, R. E. Some effects of stimulus-exposure time on choice-reaction time. *American Journal of Psychology*, 1970, **83**, 264–271.

Crossman, E. R. F. W. The measurement of discriminability. *Quarterly Journal of Experimental Psychology*, 1955, **7**, 176–195.

Edwards, W. Optimal strategies for seeking information: Models for statistics, choice reaction times and human information processing. *Journal of Mathematical Psychology*, 1965, **2**, 312–329.

Edwards, W. Decision processes research, an intemperate review. *Proceedings of the 19th International Congress of Psychology*, 1969, p. 164.

Egeth, E., & Smith, E. E. On the nature of errors in a choice reaction task. *Psychonomic Science*, 1967, **8**, 345–346.

Falmagne, J. C. Stochastic models for choice reaction time with applications to experimental results. *Journal of Mathematical Psychology*, 1965, **2**, 77, 174.

Falmagne, J. C., & Theios, J. On attention and memory in reaction time experiments. In W. G. Koster (Ed.), *Attention and Performance II, Acta Psychologica*, 1969, **30**, 316–323.

Fitts, P. M. Cognitive aspects of information processing: III Set for speed versus accuracy. *Journal of Experimental Psychology*, 1966, **71**, 849–857.

Fitts, P. M., Peterson, J. R., & Wolpe, G. Cognitive aspect of information processing: II Adjustments to stimulus redundancy. *Journal of Experimental Psychology*, 1963, **65**, 423–432.

Friedman, J. P., Carterette, E. C., & Anderson, N. H. Long-term probability learning with a random schedule of reinforcement. *Journal of Experimental Psychology*, 1968, **78**, 442–445.

Geller, E. S., & Pitz, G. F. Effects of prediction, probability, and run length on choice reaction speed. *Journal of Experimental Psychology*, 1970, **84**, 361–367.

Gescheider, G. A., Wright, J. H., & Evans, M. B. Reaction times in the detection of vibrotactile signals. *Journal of Experimental Psychology*, 1968 **77**, 501–504.

Hale, D. J. Speed-error trade-offs in the three-choice serial reaction task. *Journal of Experimental Psychology*, 1969, **81**, 428–435.

Hawkins, H. L., & Hosking, K. Stimulus probability as a determinant of discrete choice reaction time. *Journal of Experimental Psychology*, 1969, **82**, 435–440.

Hawkins, H. L., Thomas, G. B., & Drury, K. B. Perceptual versus response bias in discrete choice reaction time. *Journal of Experimental Psychology*, 1970, **84**, 514–517.

Hick, W. E. On the rate of gain of information. *Quarterly Journal of Experimental Psychology*, 1952, **4**, 11–26.

Hinrichs, J. V., and Craft, J. L. Verbal expectancy and probability in two-choice reaction time. *Journal of Experimental Psychology*, 1971, **88**, 367–371.

Hinrichs, J. V., & Krainz, P. L. Expectancy in choice reaction time: anticipation of stimulus or response? *Journal of Experimental Psychology*, 1970, **85**, 330–334.

Howell, W. R., & Kreidler, D. L. Information processing under contradictory instruction sets. *Journal of Experimental Psychology*, 1963, **65**, 39–46.

Hyman, R. Stimulus information as a determinant of reaction time. *Journal of Experimental Psychology*, 1953, **45**, 188–196.

Kornblum, S. Response competition and/or inhibition in two-choice reaction time. *Psychonomic Science*, 1965, **2**, 55–56.

Kornblum, S. Choice reaction time for repetitions and non-repetitions: A re-examination of the information hypothesis. *Acta Psychologica*, 1967, **27**, 178–187.

Kornblum, S. Sequential determinants of information processing in serial and discrete choice reaction time. *Psychological Review*, 1969, **76**, 113–131.

Kullback, S. *Information theory and statistics*. New York: Wiley, 1959.

LaBerge, D. A recruitment theory of simple behavior, *Psychometrika*, 1962, **27**, 375–396.

LaBerge, D., Van Gelder, P., & Yellott, J. I., Jr. A cueing technique in choice reaction time. *Psychonomic Science*, 1970, **7**, 57–62.

Laming, D. R. J. A statistical test of a prediction from information theory in a card-sorting situation. *Quarterly Journal of Experimental Psychology*, 1963, **14**, 38–48.

Laming, D. R. J. A new interpretation of the relation between choice-reaction time and the number of equiprobable alternatives. *British Journal of Mathematical and Statistical Psychology*, 1966, **19**, 139149.

Laming, D. R. J. *Information theory of choice-reaction times*. New York: Academic Press, 1968.

Laming, D. R. J. Subjective probability in choice-reaction experiments. *Journal of Mathematical Psychology*, 1969, **6**, 81–120.

Meyers, J. L., and Thomas, E. A. C. Implications of latency data for continuous and discrete state models of signal detection. 1972, to appear.

McGill, W. J. Stochastic latency mechanisms. In R. D. Luce, R. R. Bush, & E. Galanter (Eds.), *Handbook of mathematical psychology*. Vol. 1, New York: Wiley, 1963. Pp 309–360.

Miller, S. H. The time to recognize a visual stimulus. Unpublished doctoral thesis, London University, 1970.

Moss, S. M., Engel, S., & Faberman, D. Alternation and repetition reaction times under three schedules of event sequencing. *Psychonomic Science*, 1967, **9** (10), 557–558.

Nickerson, R. S. Binary classification reaction time: A review of some studies of human information-processing capabilities. Bolt Beranek and Newman, Inc. Report No. 2004, 1970.

Ollman, R. T. Fast guesses in choice reaction time. *Psychonomic Science*, 1966, **6**, 155–156.

Pachella, R. G., & Pew, R. W. Speed-accuracy trade-off in reaction times: Effect of discrete criterion times. *Journal of Experimental Psychology*, 1968, **76**, 19–24.

Pew, R. W. The speed-accuracy operating characteristic. In W. G. Koster (Ed.) *Attention and performance II, Acta Psychologica*, 1969, **30**, 16–26.

Pike, A. R. Latency and relative frequency of response in psychophysical discrimination. *British Journal of Mathematical and Statistical Psychology*, 1968, **21**, 161–182.

Rabbitt, P. M. A. Three kinds of error-signalling responses in a serial choice task. *Quarterly Journal of Experimental Psychology*, 1968, **20** 179–188. (a)

Rabbitt, P. M. A. Repetition effects and signal classification strategies in serial choice-response tasks. *Quarterly Journal of Experimental Psychology*, 1968, **20**, 232–240. (b)

Rabbitt, P. M. A. Errors and error-corrections in choice response tasks. *Journal of Experimental Psychology*, 1969, **71**, 264–272.

Rapoport, A. A study of disjunctive reaction times. *Behavioral Science*, 1959, **4**, 299–315.

Remington, R. J. Analysis of sequential effects in choice reaction times. *Journal of Experimental Psychology*, 1969, **82**, 250–257.

Remington, R. J. Analysis of sequential effects for a four-choice reaction time experiment. *Journal of Psychology*, 1971, **77**, 17–27.

Sanders, A. F. Some variables affecting the relation between relative stimulus frequency and choice reaction time. *Acta Psychologica*, 1970, **33**, 45–55.

Schvaneveldt, R. W., & Chase, W. G. Sequential effects in choice reaction time. *Journal of Experimental Psychology*, 1969, **80**, 1–9.

Shallice, T., & Vickers, D. Theories and experiments on discrimination times. *Ergonomics*, 1964, **7**, 37–49.

Smith, E. E. Choice reaction time: An analysis of the major theoretical positions. *Psychological Bulletin*, 1969, **69**, 77–110.

Smith, M. C. The repetition effect and short-term memory. *Journal of Experimental Psychology*, 1968, **77**, 435–439.

Smith, P. T. Cost, discriminability and response bias. *British Journal of Mathematical and Statistical Psychology*, 1968, **21**, 35–60.

Sternberg, S. High-speed scanning in human memory. *Science*, 1966, **153**, 652–654.

Stone, M. Models for choice-reaction times. *Psychometrika*, 1960, **25**, 251–260.

Swensson, R. G., & Edwards, W. Response strategies in a two-choice reaction task with continuous cost for time. *Journal of Experimental Psychology*, 1971, **88**, 67–81.

Theios, J., & Smith, P. G. Sequential dependencies in choice reaction times. *Wisconsin Mathematical Psychology Program Report*, 1970.

Thomas, E. A. C. Sufficient conditions for monotone hazard rate—An application to latency–probability curves. *Michigan Mathematical Psychology Program Report*, 1970, MMPP 70–9, 43.

Vickers, D. Evidence for an accumulator model of psychophysical discrimination. *Ergonomics* 1970, **13**, 37–58.

Wallace, R. J. S–R compatibility and the idea of a response code. *Journal of Experimental Psychology*, 1971, **88**, 354–360.

Welford, A. T. The measurement of sensory–motor performance: survey and reappraisal of twelve year's progress. *Ergonomics*, 1960, **3**, 189–230.

Whitman, C. P., & Geller, E. S. Runs of correct and incorrect predictions as determinants of choice reaction time. *Psychonomic Science*, 1971, **23**, 421–422.

Wilding, J. M. The relation between decision-time and accuracy in the identification of visual stimuli. Unpublished doctoral thesis, London University, 1970.

Williams, J. A. Sequential effects in disjunctive reaction time: Implications for decision models. *Journal of Experimental Psychology*, 1966, **71**, 665–672.

Yellott, J. I., Jr. Correction for guessing in choice reaction time. *Psychonomic Science*, 1967, **8**, 321–322.

Yellott, J. I., Jr. Correction for fast-guessing and the speed-accuracy tradeoff in choice reaction time. *Journal of Mathematical Psychology*, 1971, **8**, 159–199.

Speed-Accuracy Trade Off in Auditory Detection[1]

David M. Green

Department of Psychology
University of California, San Diego
La Jolla, California

R. Duncan Luce

The Institute for Advanced Study
Princeton, New Jersey[2]

ABSTRACT

A modified yes–no design, with response-terminated signals, a fixed dead-line, and payoffs for various stimulus–response combinations, was used to study the speed–accuracy trade off. The signal was a 1000-Hz tone presented in noise. The deadline was varied from 300 to 2000 msec, with a fixed symmetric payoff matrix, and the payoff matrix was varied with a fixed 600-msec deadline. The data are compared with four models for the speed-accuracy trade: (*a*) the fast-guess model, (*b*) a random-walk model, (*c*) a Poisson counting model, and (*d*) a Poisson timing model. When a fixed deadline is imposed on both signal and noise trials, the counting model is favored because the mean reaction time is roughly independent of both the stimulus and response and the receiver operating characteristic (ROC) plotted in normal–normal coordinates has a slope less than unity. When the deadline is imposed only on signal trials, the data favor the timing model because the mean reaction time on noise trials is a linear function of the mean reaction time on signal trials and the ROC curve has a slope greater than unity.

[1] This work was supported in part by a grant from the National Science Foundation and in part by a grant from the Alfred P. Sloan Foundation to the Institute for Advanced Study.
[2] Present address: School of Social Science, University of California at Irvine, Irvine, California.

547

I. Introduction

Two common measures of behavior are speed and accuracy. For many tasks they are inversely related, which is not surprising intuitively because accuracy arises from care and caution, and that requires time. Although the inverse relation is generally acknowledged to hold even for simple detection tasks, the precise basis for the trade off is in doubt. This hardly could be otherwise since it can only be formulated in terms of the observer's sensory–decision process, and that is still a matter of debate. Opinion ranges from, on the one hand, theories of sequential decision making, which suppose a steady accumulation of information and a response rule whose time of application is conditional on that information, to, on the other hand, simple threshold models, which suppose the sensory information is of an all-or-none character and that the trade off arises simply by varying the mix of two quite different response modes. Another school of thought bases its models on the assumption that signal energy is recoded into neural pulses, the rate of which is an increasing function of signal intensity. Since either the number of pulses in a fixed interval of time or the time for a fixed number of pulses to occur yields an estimate of the pulse rate, and hence of the signal intensity, two classes of models arise based on these statistics. Of course, as in all statistical situations, the more data accumulated, the more accurate is the estimate—the price being time. Thus, the speed–accuracy trade off is inherent in the basic idea of a pulse model, and the only question is whether detailed analyses of either model lead to a good account of the experimental results.

This contribution attempts to attack this problem experimentally. We first describe the experimental situation—basically, a response-terminated, yes–no design with a response-time deadline and payoffs for accuracy. Next, we outline the key predictions for the four models just mentioned. The data then are examined from each of these viewpoints, and one model is favored strongly. A modified deadline procedure is suggested to see if the observers can be induced to follow another model, as indeed they can. Independent of any model, this change in procedure has a very marked effect both on the reaction times and on the ROC curves.

II. Experimental Design

The beginning of each trial was marked clearly by a warning light, at which point a pure tone signal either was or was not added to the background noise. The observer was permitted one of two responses, yes or no, corresponding to the two possible types of trials. One unusual feature of the design is that the signal, when presented, remained on until the response occurred. The reason for using a response-terminated signal was to maintain statistically stationary conditions throughout the listening interval; this seems especially important when the effect of a variable deadline is studied. Following the response, information feedback was presented for .5 sec, and after another .5 sec the next trial began.

Each of three observers listened binaurally through earphones in a sound-treated room. The white Gaussian noise had a spectrum level of 40 dB. The signal, a 1000 Hz sinusoid, was either weak or intense—20 or 50 dB above the noise power density ($10 \log P/N_0$). With weak signals, performance is essentially at chance when a response must be made within 300 msec of the warning light and is nearly perfect with a 1000-msec deadline. The intense signal is roughly at the level generally used in trade-off experiments.

Each experimental session lasted about 2 hr and consisted of five runs. Each run was under one experimental condition (see below) and consisted of about 250 trials. A total of six sessions were run, so there are about 1500 trials per condition.

We recorded both the time from the onset of a trial to the response and the nature of the response. The two independent conditional response probabilities, $P(Y|s)$ and $P(Y|n)$, were estimated in the usual way. The means and variances of reaction-time distributions (MRT and VRT, respectively) also were estimated in the usual way; MRT and VRT are subscripted as needed by the presentation, s (signal) or n (noise), and/or the response, Y (yes) or N (no).

In addition to an hourly wage of $1.88, observers received points according to a payoff matrix for accuracy and a deadline for speed; these are described in the next section. The points were accumulated and converted into a bonus at the end of each run on a competitive basis among sets of three observers as follows. Let the points accumulated by the ith subject on a given run be denoted V_i, which was always positive. His share of the $0.25 bonus for that run was $V_i^2 / \Sigma_{i=1}^{3} V_i^2$.

III. Experimental Variables

Aside from the two signal levels, the two major variables were both instructional, the one intended to manipulate the speed–accuracy trade and the other, the response bias. Any response prior to the warning light was fined 25 points; as a result, such anticipations occurred with a relative frequency of less than .001. Any response following the prescribed deadline D was fined 4 points, independent of accuracy. Any response between the warning light and D was paid off according to the following matrix:

$$
\begin{array}{cc}
 & \begin{array}{cc} Y & N \end{array} \\
\begin{array}{c} s \\ \\ n \end{array} &
\left[\begin{array}{cc} X & -10 \\ & \\ -10 & Y \end{array}\right],
\end{array}
$$

where the observers were informed of the value of (X, Y) in each condition. For reasons that will become apparent, we refer to this (standard) deadline procedure as the sn deadline (signal and noise deadline).

In one experiment, (X, Y) was fixed at (10, 10), thereby producing a symmetric payoff matrix, and D was varied over the values 250, 300, 400, 500, 600, 800, 1000, 1500, and 2000 msec. The aim of this manipulation was to produce a speed–accuracy exchange. In a second experiment, D was fixed at 600 msec and the (X, Y) pair was varied over the values (20, 1)(15, 5)(10, 10)(5, 15)(1, 20) points. The aim of this manipulation was to generate an ROC curve, but without any speed–accuracy exchange. As the data will make clear, both manipulations were successful.

IV. Models

As the four models we shall test are described fully in the literature, it suffices to suggest their general nature and to state the exact predictions to be compared with data. Unfortunately, comparable predictions from the models are not available. Our policy is to accept whatever seems to be a characteristic prediction of a model, especially predictions of linear relations, and to examine the data in an absolute sense without worrying about what the other models predict. This is a sound strategy when the data unambiguously reject a model; it is much more suspect when we are inclined to accept one.

A. Fast-Guess Model

The fast-guess model (Ollman, 1966; Yellott, 1967) supposes that the observer selects on each trial one of two wholly different modes of behavior. In one, he pays attention to the signal and responds only when he has recognized it. We assume that the probability of a correct response is

a and the mean time for it to occur is μ_s. In the other mode, the observer responds as fast as he can to the onset of the signal, making no attempt to identify it; this accounts for the name of the model. He has some bias probability b for responding Y, and the mean response time is μ_g, where μ_g < μ_s. The observer uses the first mode with probability q and the second with probability $1 - q$. Any experimental manipulation that alters the probability q of paying attention generates a speed–accuracy trade off.

Let P_c and P_e denote the probabilities of correct and of error responses. Thus, if the signal is presented with probability $\frac{1}{2}$,

$$P_c = \tfrac{1}{2}P(Y|s) + \tfrac{1}{2}P(N|n)$$

and

$$P_e = 1 - P_c.$$

Let M_c and M_e denote the MRTs to correct and error responses. Then it is not difficult to show that

$$P_c M_c - P_e M_e = \mu_s(P_c - P_e).$$

We use this linear prediction to test the fast-guess model.

B. THE RANDOM-WALK MODEL

The literature includes a variety of sequential-decision models. Of these, Laming's (1968) seems to be the best worked out. The observer divides time into a sequence of equal intervals, each of which is then treated as a fixed-interval, yes–no situation. The sensory random variables (RV) observed in the several intervals are assumed to be independent and identically distributed; of course, the distribution depends upon whether or not the signal is present. Two response criteria, β_1 and β_2, are established. The decision rule has the following character. If no decision has been reached prior to the ith observation, the mean of all i observations is compared with the criteria. If it is less than β_1, respond N; if it is greater than β_2, respond Y; and if it lies between β_1 and β_2, collect the $(i + 1)$st observation and proceed as on the ith observation. The onset of the sampling is a parameter of the model; it may begin before the onset of the potential signal.

Distinctive quantitative predictions are difficult to come by in any sequential model, and so we will content ourselves with two qualitative ones. Using Laming's (1968) labeling:

B. In a two-choice experiment that signal which elicits the faster reaction, on average, has the smaller probability of error, and conversely [p. 44].

C'. In two-choice experiments errors are faster than the same response made correctly [p. 82].

C. A Counting Model

This model (McGill, 1967) assumes that the sensory trasducer converts signal energy into one or more pulse trains, which, for a constant intensity signal, are identical Poisson processes, that is, the times between successive pulses are independent, identically distributed exponential RVs. The common intensity parameter of these Poisson processes is assumed to be an increasing function of signal intensity, given that all other stimulus parameters are constant. Put another way, the expected time between pulses is a decreasing function of signal intensity.

The observer selects a time period Δ during which the number of pulses is counted. This RV is then treated just as likelihood ratio is in the theory of signal detectability (TSD), that is, if it is larger than some criterion β, he responds Y, and if it is smaller, he responds N. Two predictions follow readily. First, since the time for initiating a response does not depend on either the stimulus condition or on the response made, the observed reaction time distributions should be the same in all four cells. Second, we derive the form of the ROC curve. Let μ and v denote, respectively, the Poisson parameters corresponding to s and n, and let $z(s)$ and $z(n)$ be, respectively, the normal deviates corresponding to $P(Y|s)$ and $P(Y|n)$. Using the normal approximation to the Poisson process, the following approximate linear relation holds:

$$z(s) \cong (v/\mu)^{1/2} z(n) + \Delta^{1/2} [(\mu - v)/\mu^{1/2}]. \tag{1}$$

This agrees with the prediction of TSD but, in addition, it predicts exactly how the slope of the ROC curve decreases with increased signal intensity.

As a measure of accuracy, define d' to be the value of $z(s)$ corresponding to $z(n) = 0$, that is, to $P(Y|n) = \frac{1}{2}$. Then the speed–accuracy trade off is described in terms of the size Δ of the subject-controlled observation interval by the equations

$$\text{MRT} = \bar{r} + \Delta, \qquad d' = \Delta^{1/2}[(\mu - v)/\mu^{1/2}], \tag{2}$$

where $\bar{r}$ is the mean of the residual times not accounted for by the observation time.

D. A Timing Model

Timing models (Luce & Green, 1972) assume exactly the same pulse structure as the counting models. They differ only in the processing of the pulses. Instead of assuming that pulses are collected for a fixed time and then counted, these models assume that a fixed number of pulses are collected and the time required is measured. That time is a RV, which is treated much as in TSD except that small values—short interarrival times (IATs)—correspond to the signal rather than to the noise, because the shorter the IAT, the more likely it is that a signal is present.

We must take into account a complication that we could ignore in the counting model. We shall suppose that the stimuli activate pulse trains on J statistically identical, parallel channels (this, no doubt, is a gross over-simplification) and that the observer collects κ IATs from each channel, for a total of $J\kappa$. The response is determined by the mean of all $J\kappa$ IATs, and the time of initiation is determined by the slowest of the J channels. Thus, the response time depends on J and κ separately, not just on $J\kappa$.

Independent of the response, it can be shown (Luce & Green, 1972, Eq. 23) that the mean reaction time to the signal is of the form

$$\mathrm{MRT_s} = \bar{r} + h(J, \kappa)/\mu, \tag{3}$$

where $\bar{r}$ again denotes the mean residual time. An approximation to this function h is

$$h(J, \kappa) \simeq \kappa + 1 + (\kappa + 1)^{1/2} H(J), \tag{4}$$

where $H(J)$ is the mean of the largest of J normally distributed RVs, each with mean 0 and variance 1. A table of H is given by Tippett (1925). The equation for $\mathrm{MRT_n}$ is the same as Eq. (3), with v substituted for μ. Eliminating h from these two equations yields the testable linear relation

$$\mathrm{MRT_n} = (\mu/v)\,\mathrm{MRT_s} + \bar{r}(1 - \mu/v). \tag{5}$$

Obviously, this provides not only a test of the model, but a way to estimate μ/v and, in principle, $\bar{r}$.

A similar calculation of variances yields

$$\mathrm{VRT_n} = (\mu/v)^2\,\mathrm{VRT_s} + V(r)\,[1 - (\mu/v)^2], \tag{6}$$

where $V(r)$ is the variance of the residual distribution.

Again, using the normal approximation to the gamma, the ROC curve can be shown (Luce & Green, 1972, Eq. 31) to be approximately,

$$z(\mathrm{s}) \simeq (\mu/v)z(\mathrm{n}) + (J\,\kappa)^{1/2}\,(\mu/v - 1). \tag{7}$$

Although the linear form agrees with TSD and with the counting model, the prediction has the striking feature that the slope must be greater than 1 since $\mu > v$, which is the opposite of what is predicted by the counting model [Eq. (2)] and contrary to almost the entire body of data reported in the detection literature.

Using the same accuracy measure as in the counting model, the speed–accuracy trade off is described by Eqs. (3) and (4), together with

$$d' = (J\kappa)^{1/2}(\mu/v - 1). \tag{8}$$

In this case, κ is the subject-controlled parameter that affects both speed and accuracy. Note that this model predicts approximately the same trade off as does the counting model: MRT is approximately linear in the parameter and d' is proportional to its square root.

V. Data from the sn-Deadline Experiment

A. VARIABILITY

The deadline had the desired effect of varying the MRT from 100 to 1000 msec; it also affected the variability of the RTs. Figure 1 presents the scatter plot of standard deviation versus mean for all of the experimental data of this paper (including a deadline procedure not yet described). The open circles are data using a large signal-to-noise ratio, where the detection of the signal is no problem. The mean reaction times are short, 100–250 msec, and the variability is about 50 msec. The solid points are data using a small signal-to-noise ratio, where the detection of the signal is difficult. Although the correlation is far from 1, it is evident that the standard deviation tends to increase with MRT. A general rule of thumb is that, for these procedures and the weak signal, the standard deviation is about one-third of the mean. This fact must be kept in mind when comparing various conditions.

B. $P_c M_c - P_e M_e$ VERSUS $P_c - P_e$

The linear prediction of the fast-guess model has been tested ior easy-to-discriminate stimuli (Ollman, 1966; Yellott, 1967; Link & Tindall, 1971). In general, the fit is impressive except for conditions of extreme accuracy ($P_c \cong 1$), in which cases the data points are well above the extrapolated linear curve. Our data for both signal levels are shown in Fig. 2.

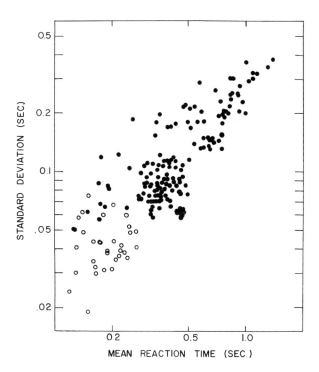

Fig. 1. Standard deviation versus mean reaction times for all conditions and observers:
($\bullet$) $10 \log P/N_0 = 20$; ($\circ$) $10 \log P/N_0 = 50$.

Those for the 50-dB signal conform to those in the literature; those for the weak 20-dB signal are much more discrepant from the theory. For the latter, a linear fit through the origin summarizes only a very narrow range of these data. Thus, we conclude that the fast-guess model does not provide an adequate description of behavior in a response-terminated, sn-deadline, Y–N detection design using weak signals.

C. MEAN REACTION TIME

Figure 3 presents the MRT_s and MRT_n data from the variable deadline experiment for each response separately. To a good first approximation, the stimulus condition does not affect the results. To the extent that this is so—recall that the data are quite variable (Fig. 1)—it disagrees with prediction C' of the random-walk model and with Eq. (5) of the timing model. It is in perfect accord with the prediction of the counting model.

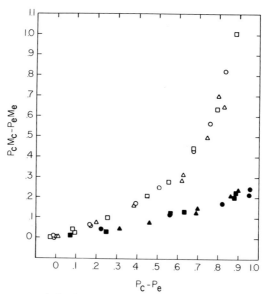

Fig. 2. Fast-guess analysis of data for sn-deadline conditions:

$10 \log P/N_0 = 20 \quad 50$

Observer 1	○	●
2	△	▲
3	□	■

Each point was generated by a different deadline value. The solid points were obtained using an easy-to-detect signal, and the open ones using a hard-to-detect signal.

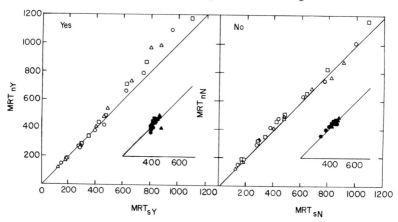

Fig. 3. The four stimulus–response mean reaction times obtained in the sn-deadline procedure: (○) Observer 1; (△) Observer 2; (□) Observer 3. The small subscript indicates the stimulus condition: s for signal, n for noise. The capital letter indicates the response: Y for yes, N for no. The open points are for conditions in which the sn deadline was varied. The solid points in the insert are the data for the condition in which the criteria was varied for a fixed, 600-msec deadline.

D. THE ROC CURVE

With a fixed deadline but a variable payoff matrix, the MRTs are approximately the same independent of either the stimulus or the response; see the insets in Fig. 3. The ROC curves for these conditions are shown in Fig. 4. The MRT data are inconsistent with prediction B of the random-walk model, and the ROC curves are grossly inconsistent with Eq. (7) of the timing model because the slopes are all less than 1. They are consistent with the counting model, and we obtain the values 1.19, 2.13, and 1.25 as estimates[2] of μ/v.

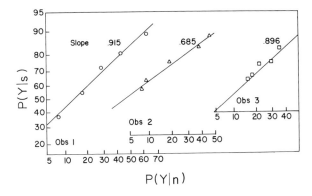

Fig. 4. ROC curves, plotted on double probability paper, for a sn-deadline of 600 msec (10 log $P/N_0 = 20$); (○) Observer 4; (△) Observer 5; (□) Observer 6. Each point is obtained from a different (X, Y) payoff condition.

VI. Intermediate Discussion

Of the four models, the data clearly favor the counting one. The question is, first, how seriously should we take this and, second, how general is the conclusion.

It is difficult to know whether an adequate repair of the fast-guess or random-walk models is possible. The data rejecting the fast-guess model

---

[2]Here and elsewhere when we examine a linear relation between two variables, both of which are random, we do both regressions and report the geometric mean of the two slopes and the arithmetic mean of the intercepts.

suggest that the observer may use more than two states and that, perhaps, he enters into some sort of sequential decision making. However, other aspects of the data did not support sequential models. It is unclear to us how seriously to take this since the predictions were simply inequalities without any indication of the magnitudes of the differences that should be found. This is, in fact, typical of sequential models; their random structure is inherently difficult to analyze, and so unless forced to it, one is inclined to search for simpler models.

Both the counting and timing models are (in this situation) very simple, and clearly the counting one is far the better of the two. That being so, one can wonder why we ever seriously entertained the timing model and, if our reasons seem adequate, what it was about this experiment that forced our observers to abandon timing behavior. Our reasons for considering timing models are both general and specific. We showed (Luce & Green, 1972) that they readily account for a wide range of psychophysical findings, including magnitude estimation as well as detection and discrimination. One new development was a theory for the detection of the onset of weak signals that are presented at random times. Unpublished simulations of that model seem, at least qualitatively, to account for some previous data (Green & Luce, 1970). Thus, we were encouraged to think it an interesting idea.

Why, then, did it fail so badly to account for the sn-deadline procedure? Although the number of IATs collected per channel, κ, is independent of the stimulus, the time to collect them is not. It takes longer to do so on n trials than it does on s trials. Therefore, either the observer chooses κ sufficiently small to avoid the deadline on n trials, in which case he does not collect as much information on s trials as he might have, or he chooses a larger κ, thereby reversing the difficulties. Clearly, in this deadline procedure, it is much more efficient to behave, if that is possible, as in the counting model: select a time, somewhat less than the deadline, and count pulses in that time. This appears to be what all three observers did.

The next question, then, is this: Can we modify the experimental design so that the timing procedure, if available, is more efficient than the counting one? Once asked, the answer is obvious: impose the deadline on only one of the stimulus conditions. It seems most natural to place it on the signal, and so we call this the s-deadline procedure. To be quite explicit: all anticipations are punished; on n trials, all responses after the warning light are paid off according to the payoff matrix; on s trials, all responses after the warning light and before the deadline D are paid off according to the payoff matrix, but responses after the deadline are fined.

VII. Data from the s-Deadline Experiment

A. $P_c M_c - P_e M_e$ versus $P_c - P_e$

The fast-guess model again is rejected, as can be seen from Fig. 5. As this plot seems little different from Fig. 2, we do not discuss it further.

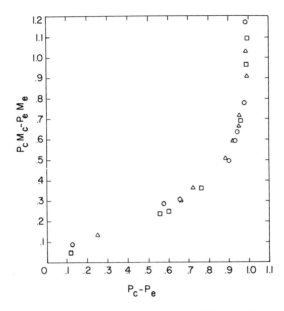

Fig. 5.   Fast-guess analysis of data obtained from different s-deadline conditions.

B. Mean Reaction Time

Figure 6 is the analog of Fig. 3. Obviously, these data are less regular, but apparently MRT is no longer independent of the stimulus. The data for the N responses agree with prediction C' of the random-walk model since errors are faster than correct responses, but those for the Y responses go in the opposite direction, at least for the longer reaction times. The basic fact revealed by this plot is that $MRT_n < MRT_s$, as is shown clearly in Fig. 7. These data disagree with the counting model and agree with the timing one. The estimates of μ/v, the slopes of the fitted line, are shown on the graph. In principle, the intercept determines $\bar{r}$; however, it appears to be too unreliable to be useful. It is easy to see why, for if $\bar{r}$ is about .2, then $\bar{r}(\mu/v - 1)$ is only about .06 sec.

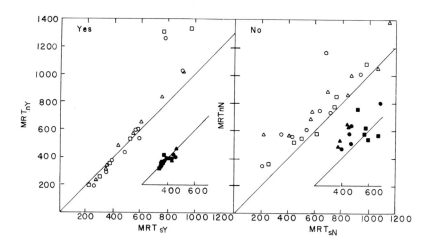

Fig. 6. The mean reaction times for various s deadlines. The figure is analogous to Fig. 3, and the same notation is used.

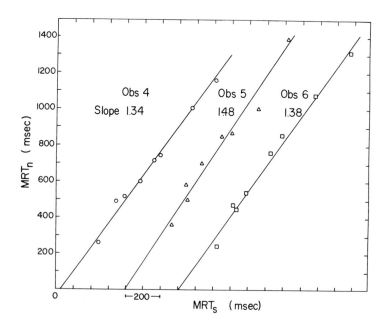

Fig. 7. The mean reaction time for noise trials versus the mean reaction time for signal trials using the s-deadline procedure. Each point was generated by a different deadline.

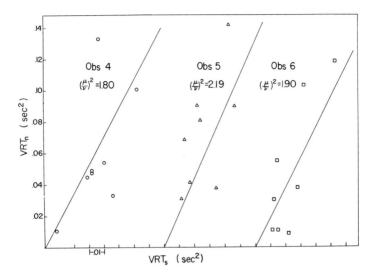

Fig. 8.   The variance of the reaction times for the two stimulus conditions using the s-deadline procedure. Each point was generated by a different deadline.

The variance data are shown in Fig. 8. The theoretical curves are those obtained from Eq. (6) using the estimates of μ/v from Fig. 7 and assuming (incorrectly, of course) that $V(r) = 0$. Given the variability of variance estimates, the fits are not bad.

C. The ROC Curve

Figure 9 presents the ROC curve for these three observers. Observe that the slopes are appreciably greater than 1, as predicted by the timing model [Eq. (7)] and in contradiction to the counting model [Eq. (1)]. In fact, the least-squares estimates of the slope of the ROC curve, which is an approximation to the ratio μ/v, are very close to the independent estimates of the same quantity obtained from the MRT (see Fig. 7). Unfortunately, this remarkable agreement between two estimates is probably fortuitous if the timing model is correct. According to that model, the time taken to accumulate $J\kappa$ pulses is a gamma distribution of order $J\kappa$. It has a mean $J\kappa/\mu$ when the signal is presented and a mean of $J\kappa/v$ when noise alone is presented. Thus, the true ROC curve is constructed by integrating the gamma distribution. Using the estimates of $\mu/v = 1.48$, obtained from the

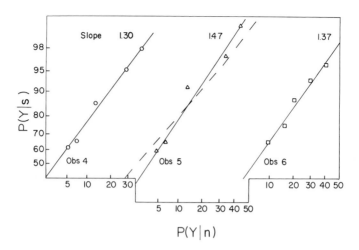

Fig. 9. ROC curves, plotted on double probability paper, for an s deadline of 600 msec. Each point was obtained from a different (X, Y) payoff condition. The dotted curve is the exact gamma curve (see text).

data for Observer 5 (Fig. 7), and estimating $J\kappa = 32$, via Eq. (7) and the data of Fig. 9, we obtain the exact prediction for the ROC curve shown as the dotted line in Fig. 9. This ROC derived from the gamma distribution is nearly linear over the major portion of the scale used in the figure, but it has a slope of about 1.20 rather than the least-squares fit to the data points of 1.47.

It is important to understand how this discrepancy arises. These two linear ROC curves actually give nearly the same fit to the data. A difference of only .01 looms very large in the standard score plots when the actual probability is less than .05 or greater than .95, and thus small differences at these extremes produce large differences in slopes. Since it is difficult to estimate such extreme probabilities accurately and since the normal approximation to the gamma has some error, the estimated slope is almost surely wrong by a sizable amount. Thus, it is not a very useful statistic except to judge crude qualitative facts such as whether the slope is greater or less than unity. It comes as an unpleasant surprise that even for gamma distribution of order 50, the normal approximation is sufficiently inaccurate to misestimate the slope by 20%. Because the gamma is not tabulated for orders beyond 50, we cannot say when this error is reduced to, say, 5%.

D. Estimation of Parameters for the Timing Model

We have estimates of μ/v from the MRT data of Fig. 7 and Eq. (5). Using the ROC curve and that estimate of μ/v, Eq. (8) yields an estimate of $J\kappa$. Using the MRT from strong signals as an estimate of $\bar{r}$, we can select $h(J, \kappa)/\mu$ so as to minimize the sum of the squared errors in Eq. 3:

$$[MRT_s - \bar{r} - h/\mu]^2 + [MRT_n - \bar{r} - (\mu/v)(h/\mu)]^2,$$

which yields the estimate

$$\frac{h}{\mu} = \frac{MRT_s - \bar{r} + (MRT_n - \bar{r})(\mu/v)}{1 + (\mu/v)^2}.$$

Another independent equation is needed to determine all of the parameters. Since we do not have one, we present in Fig. 10 for each possible value of J the corresponding values of κ and μ, where the latter follows from Eq. (3). The values of $\bar{r}$—165, 168 and 173 msec for Observers 4, 5 and 6—were the observed MRT for a very large signal-to-noise ratio $(10 \log P/N_0 = 80)$. The values of $J\kappa$ were 50 for 4, 32 for 5, and 32 for 6.

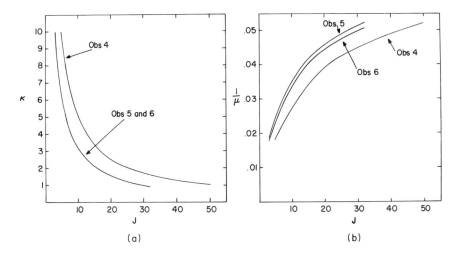

Fig. 10. Values of (a) κ and (b) $1/\mu$ for various J values. According to the timing model both κ and J are integers and the product κ times J is a constant. Its value as estimated from the data is shown in the left of the figure. Depending upon the value of J, a different $1/\mu$ estimate results, as shown in the right side of the figure. Thus, for Observer 4, if we assume κ is 3, then the number of parallel channels J is about 18, and the value $1/\mu$ is approximately .033 sec or about 30 pulses per second per channel.

VIII. The d' versus MRT Trade Off

Given the widespread use of d' to summarize sensitivity, a very natural way to represent the speed–accuracy trade off is by plotting d' versus MRT. Certainly this is an appropriate function for both the counting and timing

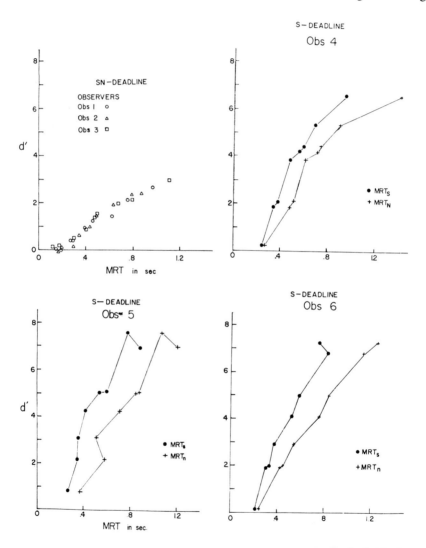

Fig. 11. Plots of d' versus MRT. The sn deadline has the three observers plotted together: (O) Observer 1; (△) Observer 2; (□) Observer 3. The s deadline shows d' plotted against both MRT_s (●) and MRT_n (+).

models. The only difficulty in constructing this function from our data is the fact that we do not have ROC curves for each deadline. However, the models say that the slope of the ROC curve is independent of either Δ in the counting model or κ in the timing model, so given our one estimate of that slope, we can estimate d' at each of the deadlines. This was done, and the resulting plots of d' versus MRT are shown in Fig. 11. Because the MRT to s and n are quite different in the s-deadline experiment, each of those three observers is described by two curves.

Qualitatively, these graphs exhibit two important features. First, the intercept corresponding to $d' = 0$ is distinctly less in the sn-deadline design than in the s-deadline one. Second, and far more spectacular, the slope of the s-deadline curves, even that corresponding to MRT_n, is considerably greater than that of the sn-deadline curves. Beyond 400 msec, the value of d' for the s-deadline is more than double that for the sn-deadline.

Is this predicted? For the counting model, Eq. (2) immediately yields

$$d' = \left(\frac{\mu - v}{\mu^{1/2}} \right) (MRT - \bar{r})^{1/2}.$$

For the timing model, matters are slightly more complicated. From Eqs. (3) and (4) we may write

$$MRT_s = \left[\bar{r} + \frac{1 + H(J)}{\mu} \right] + \left\{ \frac{\kappa + [(\kappa + 1)^{1/2} - 1] H(J)}{\mu} \right\},$$

where we have grouped the terms on the right so that the second one is 0 when κ is 0, and hence the first describes the intercept when $d' = 0$. Obviously, the intercept of the timing model, which we believe applies to the s-deadline experiment, is greater than that of the counting model, which applies to the sn experiment. The difference is $[1 + H(J)]/\mu$. Observe that if we neglect $[(\kappa + 1)^{1/2} - 1]H(J)/\mu$,

$$MRT_s \cong \bar{r} + \frac{1 + H(J)}{\mu} + \frac{\kappa}{\mu},$$

and so solving for κ and substituting in Eq. (8) we obtain

$$d' \cong \left(\frac{\mu}{v} \right) \left(\frac{\mu - v}{\mu^{1/2}} \right) \left(MRT_s - \bar{r} - \frac{1 + H(J)}{\mu} \right)^{1/2}.$$

Similarly

$$d' \cong \left(\frac{\mu}{v} \right)^{1/2} \left(\frac{\mu - v}{\mu^{1/2}} \right) \left(MRT_n - \bar{r} - \frac{1 + H(J)}{v} \right)^{1/2}.$$

We note that the rate of growth in the timing experiment for the s and n curves is μ/v and $(\mu/v)^{1/2}$, respectively, times that of the counting experiment. A direct numerical comparison is not possible, however, for two reasons. First, the observers are different. Second, the predicted growth in the timing model is only approximate. A third point is the empirical curve in the sn-deadline experiment does not really agree with the predicted, square-root form; it is more nearly linear. This discrepancy could arise for either or both of two reasons. First, the estimates of values of d' near 0 are not very stable, and so those points may be misplaced somewhat. Second, for long deadlines it is to the subject's advantage to switch to timing behavior and so raise the value of d' above that predicted by the counting model. That there may have been a little of this is suggested by the slight departure from $MRT_{sY} = MRT_{nY}$ in Fig. 3.

Our conclusion, then, is that these data are about as one would expect if the sn deadline invoked counting behavior and the s-deadline, timing behavior. Independent of any theory, however, the expirical difference in the trade-off functions is striking.

Several relevant papers have come to our attention in connection with the d' versus MRT trade off. The key one is that of Taylor, Lindsay, and Forbes (1967) in which it is shown that in a 2×2 design d'^2 is approximately linear with MRT. They replotted data of Schouten and Bekker (1967) and confirmed that $d'^2 = A(MRT - r)$. Lappin and Disch (1972), using easily discriminated visual stimuli and instructions to maintain a 25% error rate, grouped their data according to RT and then studied five different accuracy measures, including d' and d'^2 versus median RT. There was very little difference among them. Other data tending to support the d'^2 hypothesis can be found in papers by Fitts (1966), Pachella and Fisher (1972), Pachella, Fisher, and Karsh (1968), Pachella and Pew (1968), and Pew (1969).

Terminological inconsistency exists for the function relating a measure of accuracy to a measure of response time. We referred to it above as the speed–accuracy trade off, as have others; Pew suggested speed–accuracy operating characteristic (S–A OC), which seems compatible with the ROC terminology; and Lappin and Disch suggested latency-operating characteristic (LOC), which seems poor both because it has been used in at least one other way and because it emphasizes one aspect of the trade off at the expense of the other.

IX. Data from the Second sn-Deadline Experiment

After completing the above s-deadline experiment, we ran these observers in the sn-deadline procedure using a 500-msec deadline and obtained their ROC curves.

A. MEAN REACTION TIME

Table 1 shows the estimates of $MRT_n - MRT_s$ for these observers in both deadline procedures and the same thing for the first group of observers. We note that the sn deadline for these observers does not produce the negligible difference observed with the first three subjects run on this condition, as we would expect from the counting model, nor is the difference as large as that produced by the s-deadline procedure for the same observers. Rather the difference suggests some intermediate mode of behavior.

Table 1. MRT_n-MRT_s (msec) Averaged over Five Different Conditions of the ROC Curve

Observer	s-Deadline	sn-Deadline
1	—	4
2	—	3
3	—	27
4	101	35
5	185	44
6	144	42

B. THE ROC CURVE

Figure 12 presents the three ROC curves and, unlike those of Fig. 4, only one observer exhibits a slope of less than 1. The size of the slopes is noticeably smaller than those obtained with the s-deadline condition, but not nearly as small as those obtained from the first three observers using just the sn-deadline condition (Fig. 4).

One possible explanation of the change in slope of the ROC curve from the s deadline to the sn deadline is that the quality of detection is somewhat less in the sn deadline (lower d'). We therefore raised the signal level a small amount (3 dB) so that the slopes might be compared under more identical conditions. Fig. 13 shows the ROC for this condition. The slopes for two observers increase, whereas that of the third (Obs. 4) remains less than unity.

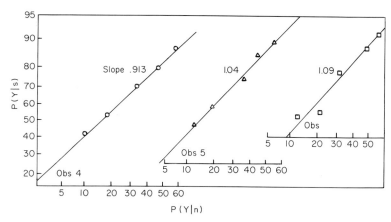

Fig. 12. ROC curves, plotted on double probability paper, for Observers 4, 5 and 6 using the sn-deadline procedure.

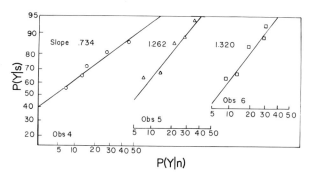

Fig. 13. ROC curves using the sn-deadline condition with signal 3 dB above those used in Figs. 9 and 12.

X. Discussion

There is little doubt that the s-deadline procedure results in unusual ROC data with slopes distinctly greater than 1. These data and the MRT data are consistent with the timing model and not with the other models. We had hoped, of course, that by changing to the sn deadline, the observers would have exhibited behavior similar to the first group of observers, which we would have interpreted as switching clearly from the timing mode to the counting mode. Both the MRT and ROC data are, roughly, half way between the two modes. It is as though the s-deadline training had created still another mode of behavior that we do not understand. One suspects that the order of experimental procedures has a strong effect and, at the least, we should run a group first on the sn deadline and follow it by an s-deadline procedure. In all likelihood, considerable instruction will be needed to shift the mode of behavior.

References

Fitts, P. M. Cognitive aspects of information processing: III. Set for speed versus accuracy. *Journal of Experimental Psychology*, 1966, **71**, 849–857.

Laming, D. R. J. *Information theory of choice-reaction times*. New York: Academic Press, 1968.

Lappin, J. S., & Disch, K. The latency operating characteristic: I. Effects of stimulus probability on choice reaction time. *Journal of Experimental Psychology*, 1972, **92**, 419–427.

Link, S. W., & Tindall, A. D. Reaction times to comparative judgments of line length. Technical Report, No. 32.

Luce, R. D., & Green, D. M. A theory of psychophysics and response times based on interarrival times of "neural" pulses. *Psychological Review*, 1972, **79**, 14–57.

McGill, W. J. Neural counting mechanisms and energy detection in audition. *Journal of Mathematical Psychology*, 1967, **4**, 351–376.

Ollman, R. T. Fast guesses in choice reaction time. *Psychonomic Science*, 1966, **6**, 155–156.

Pachella, R. G., & Fisher, D. Hick's law and the speed–accuracy trade-off in absolute judgment. *Journal of Experimental Psychology*, 1972, **92**, 378–384.

Pachella, R. G., & Pew, R. W. Speed–accuracy tradeoff in reaction time: effect of discrete criterion times. *Journal of Experimental Psychology*, 1968, **76**, 19–24.

Pachella, R. G., Fisher, D. F., & Karsh, R. Absolute judgments in speeded tasks: quantification of the trade-off between speed and accuracy. *Psychonomic Science*, 1968, **12**, 225–226.

Pew, R. W. The speed–accuracy operating characteristic. *Acta Psychologica*, 1969, **30**, 16–26.

Schouten, J. F., & Bekker, J. A. M. Reaction time and accuracy. *Acta Psychologica*, 1967, **27**, 143–153.

Taylor, M. M., Lindsay, P. H., & Forbes, S. M. Quantification of shared capacity processing in auditory and visual discrimination. *Acta Psychologica*, 1967, **27**, 223–229.

Tippett, L. H. C. On the extreme individuals and the range of samples taken from a normal population. *Biometrika*, 1925, **17**, 364–387.

Yellott, J. I., Jr. Correction for guessing in choice reaction times. *Psychonomic Science*, 1967, **8**, 321–322.

Simple Reactions with Random Countermanding of the "Go" Signal

R. T. Ollman

Bell Laboratories
Holmdel, New Jersey

ABSTRACT

On randomly selected trials of a modified simple reaction time experiment, the reaction signal was followed—after one of three possible delays—by an inhibit signal. The instructions were to respond quickly on "go" trials (no inhibit signal) while avoiding excessive errors of commission on the inhibit trials. For a model, it is proposed that when the subject detects the "go" signal, he establishes a subjective deadline. If the inhibit signal beats the deadline, the response is withheld; otherwise the response is initiated when the deadline terminates. Thus, the response time for go trials is the same, except for the additional increment of deadline delay, as the ordinary simple reaction time. By considering the distribution of go trial response times and the probability of an inhibit trial error as a function of how long the inhibit signal is delayed, and by considering also the distribution of simple reaction times, it is possible to solve for the variances of the signal detection delay, the deadline delay, and the response delay. Although there are discrepancies, some of them sizable, between the model and the data, the following provisional conclusions appear warranted: (*a*) subjects can establish deadlines to control their reaction time performance; (*b*) under some conditions the deadline distribution may be accurately described by a displaced negative exponential distribution; (*c*) the variance of the signal detection delay is substantially smaller than the variance of the response delay.

571

I. Introduction

A hypothetical process of covert time estimation figures importantly in some recently proposed reaction time models (Nickerson, 1969; Ollman & Billington, 1972). The basic notion is that the subject uses some sensory event to initiate a subjective "deadline" and then makes either a "stimulus-controlled" or else a "guess" response according to whether stimulus analysis is completed before or after the deadline terminates. The reaction time similarly is decided by whichever delay is smaller so the term "race model" also is apt.

Because they combine the "sum of" and the "minimum of" functions, these models tend to be mathematically unwieldy. For simplifying them, by treating certain random delays as constants, it is highly useful to know the relative variances for the detection, deadline, and response delays. Also, it is always desirable to know how the deadline is distributed.

A paradigm devised by Lappin and Eriksen (1966) has potential for providing this information. Their experiment randomly interleaves two trial types: (a) "go" trials on which a signal (S_1) occurs; (b) "inhibit" trials on which a second signal (S_2) occurs I sec after S_1. The instructions are to respond quickly on go trials, but to avoid responding on inhibit trials.

Suppose it takes $T_i(i = 1, 2)$ sec to detect S_i and an additional R sec to execute a response. To comply with instructions, the subject might detect S_1, institute a deadline D, and then (a) if he fails to detect S_2 within in the next D sec, initiate a response; (b) if he detects S_2 in fewer than D sec, inhibit the response. On a go trial the observable reaction time would be $T_1 + D + R$. Thus, to obtain fast performance, the subject should make D as small as possible, subject to the requirement that $T_1 + D > T_2 + I$ so that errors of commission are avoided on inhibit trials.

If T_1, T_2, D, and R are independent random variables, not directly observable, and if I_i, $i = 1, \ldots, n$ are possible values for the intersignal interval, chosen randomly by the experimenter, then some errors of commission may be expected on inhibit trials. Let p_i be the probability that a response occurs on an inhibit trial for which the intersignal interval (ISI) is I_i sec:

$$p_i = \Pr\{T_1 - T_2 + D < I_i\}, \qquad i = 1, 2, \cdots, n. \qquad (1)$$

If the distribution of $Y = T_1 - T_2 + D$ were known, for example, if it were normal, the probabilities p_i could be used to estimate the mean and the variance of Y. And if T_1 and T_2 were identically distributed, then for the inhibit trials

$$\begin{aligned} E(Y) &= E(D), \\ V(Y) &= 2V(T) + V(D), \end{aligned} \qquad (2)$$

where $E(\ )$ and $V(\ )$ indicate means and variances. Go trials observe $\mathrm{RT_g} = T + D + R$, so

$$E(\mathrm{RT_g}) = E(T) + E(D) + E(R),$$
$$V(\mathrm{RT_g}) = V(T) + V(D) + V(R). \tag{3}$$

A third pair of equations describes the ordinary simple reaction-time experiment for which the reaction time, $\mathrm{RT_s}$, is simply $T + R$. Therefore

$$E(\mathrm{RT_s}) = E(T) + E(R),$$
$$V(\mathrm{RT_s}) = V(T) + V(R). \tag{4}$$

The three variance equations are independent (those for the means are not) and have the following solution:

$$V(T) = \{V(\mathrm{RT_s}) - [V(\mathrm{RT_g}) - V(Y)]\}/2,$$

$$V(R) = \{V(\mathrm{RT_s}) + [V(\mathrm{RT_g}) - V(Y)]\}/2, \tag{5}$$

$$V(D) = V(\mathrm{RT_g}) - V(\mathrm{RT_s}).$$

For the means there is the relation

$$E(\mathrm{RT_g}) - E(Y) = E(T) + E(R) = E(\mathrm{RT_s}), \tag{6}$$

which may also be useful.

The expression $\mathrm{RT_g} = T + D + R$ recalls Snodgrass' (1969) model for time estimation responses: "a simple reaction with the additional step of delay." Because time estimation experiments require the subject precisely to produce some assigned duration, the interpolated delay will have the minimum possible variance. Similarly, in the Lappin–Eriksen paradigm it benefits the subject to set a precise deadline, to minimize $V(D)$. Thus, it is interesting that the time-estimation study of Snodgrass, Luce, and Galanter (1967) indicates that the normal distribution sometimes may provide a good description of D.

II. Method

Each trial began with a warning signal S_0 and ended 3.530 sec later. Five types of trials were interleaved randomly: (a) catch trials (10%), where only S_0 occurred; (b) go trials (21%), where only S_0 and S_1 occurred; (b) three types of inhibit trials (23% each), where S_0, S_1, and S_2 all occurred and where the ISI between S_1 and S_2 could be either I_1, I_2, or I_3 msec. The foreperiod between S_0 and S_1 lasted 700 msec, and the response key was disengaged 2600 msec after S_0.

Six ISI distributions, divided into two families of three each, were devised to create six experimental conditions. Members of the first family each cover a range (I_3-I_1) of 120 msec, and have center values (I_2) of 100, 200, and 300 msec. Members of the second family each cover a narrower range (80 msec), but have the same center values. (If the subject adapts his deadline to match I_2, then the narrow family replicates the wide family except for sampling of the deadline distribution at different—and either more or less efficient—points.) There was also a control condition consisting of 25% catch trials, 75% go trials, and conventional instructions. Each condition was conducted as a sequence of 1000 observation trials per day, with a preliminary "warm-up" series, and each subject was in the laboratory for about 90 min per day. The order of conditions was cyclic: three wide distributions in ascending order, control, three narrow distributions in ascending order, control. Five subjects were employed; no subject participated for more than two complete cycles. A total of 48 experimental sessions are reported here. In addition, there is the control condition, conducted at least twice for each subject.

The signals were small, diffused white lamps 4 ft from the subject. They were arrayed in a horizontal line, ordered from left to right at $\frac{3}{4}$-in. intervals. Lamp S_0 flashed very briefly on every trial. Once lighted, S_1 remained on until the end of the trial, and similarly with S_2. The experience of apparent movement seems not to have arisen.

The instructions, feedback, and incentives were aimed at encouraging the subject to adopt a deadline distribution that would yield $p_2 = 0.5$. If this were achieved and if the subject minimized the variance of his deadline distribution (attempted to estimate time precisely), then I_1 and I_3 would determine p_1 and p_3.

Information feedback was presented. Whenever the response switch closed, the timer revealed the time of closure; after each inhibit trial, one of three feedback lamps would identify the ISI. A particular reading of the timer was designated as the "cutoff" for encouraging the subject to set $E(D) = I_2$. If $E(T) + E(R) = 200$ msec, a reasonable value for $E(RT_s)$, then equating I_2 to $E(D)$ suggests that the cutoff should occur $I_2 + 200$ msec after S_1. Thus, with S_0 as the reference point, the cutoff was established at $I_2 + 900$ msec in each experimental condition and at 900 msec in the control condition.

To insure that this experiment will relate both to time estimation studies, which stress consistency in response times, and to reaction-time studies, which stress swiftness, it is desirable that the subject attempt simultaneously (a) to minimize the mean of $T + R$; (b) to minimize the variance of D. Accordingly, a "points" system was used for administering incentive payments. The system is more explicit but in the same spirit as the verbal instructions employed by Lappin and Eriksen (1966).

Points were lost for responding on catch trials (CTs) or failing to respond on go trials. Points were gained for a go trial response only if it occurred before the cutoff. The various inhibit trials were treated differently, depending on the ISI. For I_1 trials, points were lost for any response; for I_2 trials, points were neither won nor lost; for I_3 trials, points were earned if a response occurred, provided that it occurred before the cutoff. Points were recorded and their worth adjusted according to the skill of the subject and the apparent difficulty of the task. Earnings were in addition to a base rate of $1.25 per hr.

III. Results

A. BOUNDARY CONDITIONS

The theoretical development assumes that the signals are perfectly detectable and that subjects do not anticipate. Therefore no catch trial should receive a response and no go trial should lack a response. In fact, in 75% of the sessions the performances were perfect in both respects. Catch-trial responses tended to be concentrated in the control sessions; for all subjects but one the percentage was always less than 3 and usually less than 1. Response omissions, which sometimes occurred with three of the subjects, were concentrated in the experimental sessions and occurred on less than 1% of the trials in all sessions except three. Apparently the subjects were slightly more biased toward false responses in the control sessions than in the experimental ones.

B. CONTROL SESSIONS

The reaction times observed in the control sessions appeared to have positively skewed unimodal distributions. All estimates for $E(RT_s)$ fell between 199 and 247 msec. The estimated standard deviation of RT_s almost always lay between 20 and 40 msec for four of the subjects, and was consistently larger for the fifth.

C. EXPERIMENTAL SESSIONS

1. Go Trials

On go trials RT_g is observable. Like RT_s, it apparently followed a unimodal distribution with some degree of positive skew, although in some instances the distribution appeared strikingly linear when plotted on normal probability paper.

The instructions and feedback were effective: the product-moment correlation between $E(RT_g)$ and I_2 exceeded $+.98$ for every subject.

2. Inhibit Trials

For an inhibit trial where the intersignal is I_i, it is convenient to define the binary random variable

$$R_i = \begin{cases} 1, & \text{a response occurs} \\ \\ 0, & \text{no response occurs} \end{cases} \qquad (i = 1, 2, 3) \qquad (7)$$

without regard to the time at which the response might have occurred.

If a response occurs in the event that $Y < I_i$, then

$$\Pr\{R_i = 1\} = p_i = F(I_i), \qquad i = 1, 2, 3, \qquad (8)$$

where $F(\ )$ is the distribution function for Y. Let H be the hypothesis that specifies the form of $F(\ )$. The log-likelihood function for the inhibit trials, $\ln L(H)$, may then be written as

$$\ln L(H) = \sum_{\text{trials}} \sum_{i=1}^{3} \{R_i \ln[F(I_i)] + (1 - R_i) \ln[1 - F(I_i)]\}. \qquad (9)$$

Maximizing $\ln L(H)$ with respect to the parameters of $F(\ )$ offers a convenient way to find maximum likelihood estimates for the parameters needed for calculating $E(Y)$ and $V(Y)$. Then, for a given form $F(\ )$, the goodness of fit may be evaluated by conducting a likelihood ratio test to choose between H_0, "The R_i result from truncating an exemplar of $F(\ )$ at the points I_1, I_2, I_3"; and H_1, "The R_i result from truncating an unspecified underlying distribution with resultant unspecified probabilities p_1, p_2, p_3." The appropriate test statistic

$$-2 \ln \lambda = \ln \left\{ \max_{H_0} L(H) / \max_{H_1} L(H) \right\} \qquad (10)$$

approximately follows the χ^2 distribution for large samples. Each session observes three independent p_i, so if two parameters are estimated per session, then the statistic has one degree of freedom.

The two parameter normal and a pair of two parameter specializations of the gamma distribution were considered for Y. (The general gamma, having three parameters, is virtually assured of perfect fit.) Although the normal distribution sometimes gave excellent results, there were instances where the plot of $\hat{p}_i$ versus I_i was bowed downward on normal probability paper, possibly indicating a skewed distribution. Thus, it is surprising that

Fig. 1. Response frequencies observed on inhibit trials plotted as a function of ISI + 700 for a typical subject. The straight lines interconnect those triples observed in connection with I_1, I_2, and I_3 for each session. Data are shown in "logarithmic decumulative" form to display how they conform with the straight-line relation implied by the negative exponential distribution. (In some sessions $1 - \hat{p}_i = 0$, a result that cannot be depicted on this graph, but which is valid and is recognized as such by the numerical method for estimating parameters and measuring goodness of fit). The general-gamma and normal distributions imply that these relations will be concave downward.

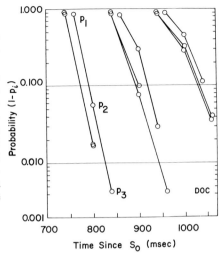

efforts to fit the nondisplaced gamma proved unavailing, even though the versatile gamma can either exhibit skewness or closely approximate the symmetrical normal distribution. Therefore, plots were made of $\log(1 - \hat{p}_i)$ versus I_i to inspect for the gamma properties that McGill and Gibbon (1965) describe. Many of the graphs (see Fig. 1) emerged as almost straight lines with various slopes and intercepts, thus indicating that Y has an exponential

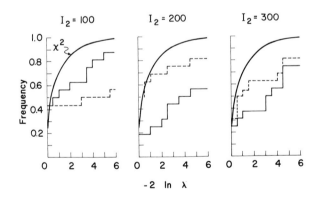

Fig. 2. Goodness-of-fit analysis for the exponential and normal distribution hypotheses concerning $F(\ )$: solid line, exponential distribution; dashed line, normal distribution. In each case the null hypothesis implies $-2 \ln \lambda$ will follow a X^2 distribution with one degree of freedom (smooth curve). For each value of I_2, 16 empirical $\hat{p}_i$-distributions were fitted. Clearly, both distribution models too often yield poor fits (large values of $-2 \ln \lambda$) and are rejected by standard significance criteria.

distribution, often displaced outward from the origin. Apparently, then, a better specialization of the gamma is that which leaves unspecified both the "time constant" and the displacement and which equates to one the remaining parameter.

Parameter estimates for the normal and the exponential distributions were found by using "hill climbing" to adjust the tentative estimates until a maximum for $\ln L(H)$ was attained. The implied value of $-2 \ln \lambda$ then was computed. The results, pooled across the five subjects but separated according to the three values of I_2, are shown as cumulative distributions for $-2 \ln \lambda$ in Fig. 2. The observed likelihoods do not conform perfectly to the predicted χ^2 distribution, and thus neither the normal nor the exponential model is entirely satisfactory. Furthermore, the pattern of their relative merit is somewhat curious: at $I_2 = 100$, the exponential is better; at $I_2 = 200$, the normal is better; at $I_2 = 300$, the normal is again better, but less markedly so.

D. Evaluation of the Model

One approach toward evaluating the deadline model notes that although both $E(RT_g)$ and $E(Y)$ will depend on I_2, the within-session difference between them is always equal to $E(RT_s)$, as indicated by Eq. (6). Two aspects of this prediction are of interest: (a) does the estimated difference $E(RT_g) - E(Y)$ have the correct magnitude in every case? (b) If there

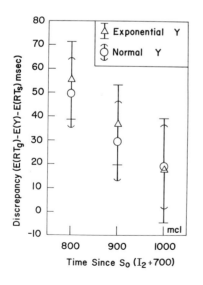

Fig. 3. Discrepancy between mean values observed in experimental sessions and control sessions shown as a function of I_2 for a typical subject: ($\triangledown$) exponential form; ($\circ$) normal form. Under the deadline model the discrepancy has an expected value of zero for each I_2. Each of the indicated 95% confidence intervals reflects, in part, the repeatability of the same control session estimates; hence they are not independent. The observed discrepancy evidently is insensitive to whether the normal or exponential form is selected for $F(\ )$.

sometimes is a discrepancy between estimates of $E(RT_g) - E(Y)$ and $E(RT_s)$, does that discrepancy depend on I_2?

The discrepancy between the average estimate for $E(RT_g) - E(Y)$ and the average estimate for $E(RT_s)$ is shown as a function of I_2 for a typical subject in Fig. 3. [The difference $E(RT_g) - E(Y)$ was estimated for each session by subtracting the estimate of $E(Y)$ from the estimate of $E(RT_g)$. The confidence intervals were computed by considering the between-sessions variance in the estimates of $E(RT_g) - E(Y)$ and in the estimates for $E(RT_s)$ and by assuming that both sets of estimates are normally distributed.] Apparently it makes little difference whether Y is assumed to follow the normal or the exponential distribution.

Clearly the deadline model is rejected by the illustrative data shown in Fig. 3: for $I_2 = 100$, the discrepancy is entirely too large; for $I_2 = 200$, the discrepancy, although somewhat smaller, is still too large. For $I_2 = 300$, the results are more acceptable. Two additional subjects exhibit almost exactly this same pattern; the remaining two subjects produce U-shaped curves with upturns at $I_2 = 300$. All five subjects show discrepancies that are significantly too large when $I_2 = 100$, regardless of which distribution is imputed to Y. A small positive discrepancy might be expected because the subjects made more errors of commission in the control conditions than in the experimental conditions. But this cannot explain why the discrepancy depends on I_2. Thus, the outcome of this analysis appears to be quite damaging to the deadline model. Moreover, it is not easily attributed to having imputed the wrong distribution to Y.

Although the deadline model could be rejected on the basis of estimates of mean values, it is nonetheless interesting also to examine the variance predictions. First, within each session, the model implies, the difference $V(RT_g) - V(Y)$ equals $V(R) - V(T)$ and thus must be independent of I_2. A reasonable way to estimate $V(RT_g) - V(Y)$ for a session is to subtract the estimate of $V(Y)$ from that of $V(RT_g)$. For combining difference estimates from various sessions, a geometric mean, rather than an arithmetic one, should be used. (Geometric averaging somewhat restrains the tendency of outliers—thought to occur on some trials—to inflate estimates for variances.)

Estimates of $V(RT_g)$ and of $V(Y)$ increase with I_2, as expected. For $V(Y)$, however, the normal and the exponential models agree that the rate of increase is relatively slow. Accordingly, estimates of $V(RT_g) - V(Y)$ are not independent of I_2; instead, the difference estimates increase vary rapidly with I_2 for four out of five subjects. This is another outcome that apparently rejects the deadline model, and which is not easily attributed simply to having imputed the wrong distribution to Y.

As a final step in the analysis of variance, the data were segregated by the I_2 values, and geometric means of estimates for $V(RT_s)$ and $V(RT_g)$ − $V(Y)$ were calculated. These values, together with geometric means of estimates for $V(RT_g)$, then were substituted into Eq. (5) to obtain estimates for $V(T)$ and $V(R)$ as functions of I_2. The deadline model predicts they will have values that are independent of I_2.

In some instances the results are nonsensical in that they indicate $V(T)$ < 0, a theoretically impossible result that arises when the estimate for $V(RT_g) − V(Y) = V(R) − V(T)$ exceeds the estimate of $V(RT_s) = V(T) + V(R)$. Because estimates of $V(RT_g) − V(Y)$ increase with I_2, indications of $V(T) < 0$ arise mainly with $I_2 = 200$ and $I_1 = 300$. Again, the pattern of this analysis is independent of which distribution is imputed to Y. The conclusion $V(T) < 0$ is indicated in 7 out of 15 cases by the normal and in 6 out of 15 cases by the exponential. Possibly, this is also an indication that $V(T)$ is relatively small compared with $V(R)$. Interestingly, there is no indication that $V(R) < 0$. Further, for those cases where $V(T) > 0$, the median estimate for $V(R)/[V(T) + V(R)]$ exceeds 0.79 for both the normal and the exponential models.

Finally, it is curious to note, if the deadline model were evaluated on the basis of estimates for mean values, then its degree of success would be an increasing function of I_2; however, if estimates of variances were the basis for judgment, then the degree of success would be a decreasing function of I_2.

IV. Discussion

There is no serious doubt that these data reject—in the narrow and technical sense—the deadline model developed above; nor is this surprising. Indeed, most investigators expect rejection when an explicit model is tested by an experiment designed specifically to be sensitive. (The spacing of the inhibit trial ISIs and the frequency of go versus inhibit trials were calculated to attain parameter estimates with the smallest feasible sampling variances.) Thus, the important question is not whether the entire model ought to be discarded on the basis of significance tests, but whether its substantive tenets have merit. Specifically, does the deadline notion have merit and, if so, what of the deadline distribution?

Recall that subjects were confronted with objective performance requirements that had been developed on the assumption that the model is exactly correct. They met these requirements well enough to earn profits and to produce a correlation between $E(RT_g)$ and the go trial cutoff that exceeds +.98 for every subject. The cutoff was linked, by means of the theory, to the ISI values used on the inhibit trials. Thus, it is doubly significant that the relation between the response probability and the ISI value is always substantially as expected from theory. The picture that emerges is one of a theory that makes predictions which are often discernibly wrong, but usually basically right. The errors, such as they are, do not warrant overturning the basic deadline concept at this time. Indeed, one might even say that the deadline conception is somewhat better founded than before and that there may be merit in considering the displaced exponential distribution for the deadline.

Finally, of course, a discrepancy from theory should be considered as a significant clue, not discounted as only a nuisance. Discrepancies involving variances can be discounted somewhat by noting that the inevitable attention lapses—they seem to have occurred at the rate of about 1%— can produce "outlier" observations that can greatly inflate variance estimates. However, difficulties involving mean values must be taken very seriously. Ultimately there remains the fact that estimates of $E(RT_g)$ – $E(Y)$ decrease, contrary to prediction, with I_2 for four out of five subjects. What makes this fact particularly telling is that it pertains entirely to the experimental condition and does not rest on a comparison with the control condition.

References

Lappin, J. S., & Eriksen, C. W. Use of a delayed signal to stop a visual reaction-time response. *Journal of Experimental Psychology*, 1966, **72**, 805–811.

McGill, W. J., & Gibbon, J. The general-gamma distribution and reaction times. *Journal of Mathematical Psychology*, 1965, **2**(1), 1–18.

Nickerson, R. S. "Same"–"Different" response times: A model and a preliminary test. A. F. Sanders (Ed.) *Attention and Performance, Acta Psychologica*, 1969, **30**, 257–275.

Ollman, R. T., & Billington, M. J. The deadline model for simple reaction times. *Cognitive Psychology*, 1972, **3** (No. 2), 311–336.

Snodgrass, J. G. Foreperiod effects in simple reaction time: Anticipation or expectancy? *Journal of Experimental Psychology Monograph*, 1969, **79**(3, Pt. 2).

Snodgrass, J. G., Luce, R. D., & Galanter, E. H. Some experiments on simple and choice reaction time. *Journal of Experimental Psychology*, 1967, **75**, 1–17.

Factors Influencing Speed and Accuracy of Word Recognition[1]

Richard C. Atkinson   *James F. Juola*

Department of Psychology   *Department of Psychology*
Stanford University   *University of Kansas*
Stanford, California   *Lawrence, Kansas*

ABSTRACT

Seven experiments, designed to investigate the effects of various factors on word recognition, are reported. For each experiment the subject memorized a list of from 16 to 54 words and then was tested with a sequence of single words; each test involved either a target word (member of the list) or distractor word (not on the memorized list). In response to each test word the subject pressed one of two keys, indicating whether the word was a target or a distractor. Response latency was shown to depend upon the number of prior tests on a given word (Experiment 1) and the length of the target list (Experiment 2). Experiments 3 and 6 demonstrated that response latency to a target word can be decreased by repeating the word in the study list or by otherwise making certain words more salient. Experiments 4, 5, and 7 showed that response latency was affected by similarities between target and distractor words and by such word characteristics as frequency, concreteness, and syllable length. The latency and error data were discussed in terms of a model for recognition which assumes that the subject either (*a*) makes an initial fast response based on the familiarity of the test word or (*b*) if the familiarity is neither high nor low, delays responding until an extended search of the memorized list is carried out. Quantitative predictions generated by the model compare favorably with the data.

[1]The preparation of this paper was supported by the National Science Foundation Grant No. NSFGJ-443 and by the National Institute of Mental Health Grant No. MH21747.

I. Introduction

   This contribution describes a series of experiments that were designed to study search and retrieval processes in long-term memory. Specifically, the problem under investigation is how a subject is able to decide whether or not a given test stimulus is a member of a predefined set of target items. For any initial set S of stimuli, a subset S_1 is defined which is of size d. Stimuli in subset S_1 will be referred to as target items; subset S_0 is the complement of S_1, and its members will be called distractor items. The experimental task involves a long series of discrete trials, where on each trial a stimulus is presented from S. To each presentation the subject must make either an A_1 or A_0 response indicating that he judges the stimulus to be either a target or distractor item, respectively. For the experiments reported in this paper, the stimuli were all visually presented words; however, the model that we shall present can be applied to a broader class of stimuli.

   In a task of the type described above it is possible to initiate a test sequence without the subject knowing the features that distinguish the target stimuli from distractors. As the discrimination is learned, the probabilities of correct responses and errors would change, eventually reaching stable performance. For our present purposes, however, it was desirable to have the target set extremely well learned prior to the experimental session. Under these conditions the subject is able to indicate with almost perfect accuracy whether the test stimulus is a target or a distractor, and the principal data are response latencies.

   There are many ways to define target and distractor sets so that varying demands are placed on the subject's memory as he makes a decision. If S_1 is distinguished from S_0 by means of a simple rule, it might be unnecessary to retrieve any information from long-term memory before making a response. For example, if S_1 is the set of all English words beginning with the letter "b" and S_0 is all the remaining English words, the subject can respond to each test word even before the name of the word is retrieved from memory. More complex rules could be constructed so that information stored in long-term memory must be accessed before a decision is made. For example, let S_1 be the set of all four-legged animal names. The subject would not only have to name the word presented on a test, but would have to retrieve some information about the semantic properties of that word before responding.

   Alternatively, no rule might suffice to distinguish target stimuli from distractors, for example, if the target set consists of a list of unrelated words previously memorized by the subject. In this case, there are at least two ways that the subject could identify target stimuli. One possibility is that the subject retrieves the contents of the long-term storage location at the address of the tested stimulus. This could include information about whether that item has been previously designated a member of S_1 (that is, the information could contain "list markers" for target words). On the other hand, if the target set is not too large, the subject could store the items in memory as a list structure and then compare the test stimulus with each item on the list. The latter process presumably takes place in experiments where the target set is limited to about six items or less that are placed in short-term memory immediately prior to the onset of a test stimulus (Sternberg, 1966). A similar scan of S_1 could occur if it is stored permanently in long-term memory and accessed at the time of test, as in the case for questions such as, "Does the number '4' occur in your home phone number?"

The task of interest for the present discussion is one in which no rule applies to the distinction between S_0 and S_1 stimuli, and the target set is too large to maintain in short-term memory. This task is comparable to that used by Sternberg (1966), but the memory sets we employ are much larger, and must be maintained in long-term memory rather than being presented shortly before the onset of every test stimulus. The questions to be answered concern the type of memory search that is necessary to make a recognition decision. Different models, incorporating the search process as one of several successive and independent stages, can be tested against latency data to determine the most probable mechanism for recognition.

II. A Prototype Experiment

Experiment 1 was designed to study the effects on response speed of repeated tests on target and distractor stimuli (Fischler & Juola, 1971). All test stimuli were selected from a common pool consisting of 48 one-syllable nouns (Thorndike & Lorge, 1944, frequency of A or AA). For each of 20 subjects a different set of 24 S_1 and 24 S_0 words were selected randomly from S. The S_1 words were given to the subject as a list to be learned in serial order, approximately 18 hr before the experimental session.

At the start of the test session the subject was allowed to study his target list for a few minutes, and then was given a written serial recall test. All subjects satisfied a preexperimental criterion by correctly recalling the lists on two successive trials (no subject made any errors).

The subject then was seated in front of a tachistoscope, in which the test words were presented one at a time. To each presentation the subject made either an A_1 or an A_0 response (indicating that the test word was a target or a distractor, respectively) by depressing one of two telegraph keys with his right forefinger. The keys were separated by a central home key on which the subject rested his finger between trials. The assignment of A_1 and A_0 responses to right or left keys was counterbalanced across the subjects.

The test sequence consisted of 120 consecutive trials that were divided into four blocks. For Block I, six target words and six distractors were randomly selected from S_1 and S_0, respectively. For Block II, the 12 Block I words were repeated, and six new targets and six new distractors were also shown. Block III included all the words presented in Block II with 12 new words (six targets and six distractors). Finally, Block IV included all the words of Block III plus the 12 remaining words in S. Thus, 12 words were presented in Block I, 24 words in Block II, 36 words in Block III, and 48 words in Block IV. The order of presentation within blocks was randomized.

The subjects were instructed to respond as rapidly as possible to each test word, while being careful to avoid making errors. No feedback was provided for correct responses, but the subjects were informed whenever an error was made. This feedback, however, was unnecessary, because the subjects were almost always immediately aware of the fact that an error had occurred. The trials were self-paced, with the test session lasting aproximately 35 min.

The mean error percentages and mean latencies for correct responses for the four trial blocks are presented in Fig. 1. Within each block, errors and latencies are plotted as functions of presentation number for targets and distractors. In each block, the mean latency of A_1 responses is greater than that of A_0 responses when target and distractor words are presented for the first time. When test words are repeated, however, positive response latency decreases whereas negative response latency increases. The strength of this interaction decreases across blocks; that is, the effects of repetitions on both positive and negative response latencies are not as great in Block IV as they are earlier.[2]

Effects similar to those observed for response latencies can be noted in the error data. The solid bars in the lower part of Fig. 1 are errors to target words, and the open bars are errors to distractors. In each block most errors to targets occurred on initial presentations, whereas most errors to distractors occurred on later presentations.

Mean positive-response latency also was plotted as a function of the serial position of the target word in the study list. There was absolutely no trend relating response latency to serial position. This was true for initial and repeated presentations of target words separately as well as for the combined data. Since this result might seem somewhat surprising, it is worth noting that in every experiment we have run using the above paradigm (this includes all

---

[2]The reduction in the strength of the interaction is apparently due to a lag effect. Juola *et al.* (1971) demonstrated that as the number of items between successive presentations of any item increases, the effect of repetition decreases. In Experiment 1, the number of trials increases by 12 from one block to the next. Thus, the lag between successive presentations of the same test word also increases.

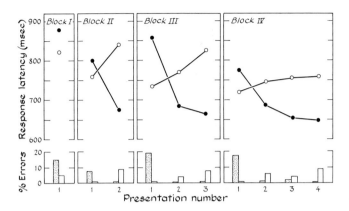

Fig. 1. Mean response latency and error percentages as functions of presentation number for targets and distractors in each of four blocks: (●) targets; (○) distractors. Incorrect responses to target words are represented by the shaded bars, and errors to distractors are represented by open bars (Experiment 1).

the studies discussed in the present paper), there has been no effect of the target word's serial position on response latency. A discussion of these results and those of the following experiment will be delayed until we have considered a model for recognition memory and developed its theoretical implications.

III. Effects of Varying the Length of the Target Set

Experiment 2 was essentially the same as the previous study except that the number of words in the target lists was varied. A population of 48 common, one-syllable nouns was used to generate lists of 16, 24, or 32 words. Subjects were assigned randomly to one of the three list-length conditions, with 24 subjects in each group. All subjects satisfied the serial recall criterion for S_1 words described for Experiment 1.

In order to replicate the design of Experiment 1 as closely as possible, only 16 target words and 16 distractors were tested for all three groups. The distractor words presented were selected randomly from the remaining items in the pool; the targets consisted of consecutive strings of 16 words from the S_1 lists (either the first, middle, or last 16 words from the 24 and 32 word sets).[3] Using this procedure, it was possible to present identical test se-

---

[3]There was no effect on response latency of the segment (beginning, middle, or end) of the target list that was tested. Therefore no further distinctions will be made between groups on this basis.

quences to all three groups of subjects. As in Experiment 1 the test trials were broken into four consecutive blocks; four target words and four distractors were presented for the first time in each block, along with all of the words presented in the previous block.

For each list length the pattern of latency and error data closely matched those presented in Fig. 1 for Experiment 1. To test for the presence of list-length effects, the data from the last two trial blocks (Blocks III and IV) were combined; mean latencies were obtained for A_1 and A_0 responses to test words that were presented for the first times, and for those that had been presented previously. These data are given in Fig. 2. Figure 2a shows mean latencies for initial presentations of target and distractor words, and Fig. 2b shows mean latencies for repeated presentations (weighted averages of those words occurring for the second, third, and fourth times). Similarities to the results of Experiment 1 can readily be pointed out: (a) positive response latency is greater than negative latency on initial presentations, but this order is reversed for repeated tests; (b) most of the errors to target words occur on initial presentations, whereas most errors to distractors occur on repeated presentations.

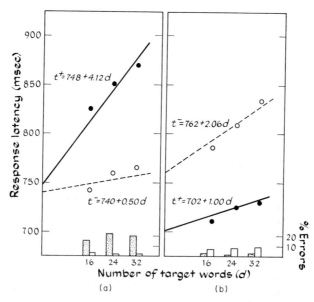

Fig. 2. Mean response latency and error percentages as functions of the length of the target list (d) (the data represent a weighted average of response latencies from Blocks III and IV), (●) targets; (○) distractors: (a) Data for initial presentations of target and distractor words; (b) Data for repeated presentations. Incorrect responses to target words are given by the shaded bars, and errors to distractors by open bars (Experiment 2). The linear functions fitted to the data are explained in a later section.

The number of target words affected response latency for all types of trials, the effect being strongest for initial presentations of target words and for repeated tests of distractors. The magnitude of the effect on response latency of adding a single word to the target set can be approximated by the slopes of straight-line fits to the data in Fig. 2. The average slope is about 2.0 msec per word for the data of Experiment 2; this value is slightly less than that obtained for a similar experiment (Juola, Fischler, Wood, & Atkinson, 1971), but is much less than the 38 msec per digit obtained for small-target sets in Sternberg's short-term memory experiment (Sternberg, 1966).

IV. A Model for Recognition

The model to be considered has been presented elsewhere (Juola, Fischler, Wood, & Atkinson, 1971) to account for latency and error data from recognition experiments like those reviewed in this paper. The model is similar to Kintsch's theory for recognition learning (Kintsch, 1967), but the processes associated with the memory states have been changed to account for response latencies as well as hit and false alarm rates.

It is assumed that each test word has associated with it a familiarity measure that can be regarded as a value on a continuous scale. The familiarity values for targets are assumed to have a mean that is higher than the mean for distractors, although the two distributions may overlap. In many recognition studies (for example, Shepard & Teghtsoonian, 1961) the target set is not well learned, but involves stimuli that have received only a single-study presentation. Under these conditions the subjective familiarity of the test stimulus leads directly to the decision to make an A_1 or A_0 response; that is, the subject has a single criterion along the familiarity continuum that serves as a decision point for making a response. Familiarity values that fall above the criterion lead to an A_1 response, whereas those below the criterion lead to an A_0 response (Parks, 1966).

The present studies differ from most previous recognition experiments in that the target stimuli are members of a well-memorized list. In this case, it is assumed that subjects can use their familiarity measure to make an A_1 or A_0 response as soon as the test stimulus is presented, or they can delay their response until a more extensive memory search has confirmed the presence or absence of the test item in the target set. This process is shown in Fig. 3. If the initial familiarity value is either above a high criterion (c_1) or below a low criterion (c_0), the subject outputs a fast A_1 or A_0 response, respectively. It the familiarity associated with the test stimulus is of an intermediate value, the subject will be less confident about which response to choose. Since instructions emphasize correct responding, the subject is likely to make a more extensive search of memory (perhaps including a scan of the target list) in seeking a match for the test stimulus.

On the nth presentation of a given item in the test sequence, there is a density function reflecting the probability that the item will generate a particular familiarity value x; the density function is $\phi_1^{(n)}(x)$ for target items and $\phi_0^{(n)}(x)$ for distractor items. The two functions have mean values $\mu_1^{(n)}$ and $\mu_0^{(n)}$, respectively. (Note that the superscript n refers to the number of times the item has been tested, and not to the trial number of the experiment.) The effect of repeating specific target or distractor items in the test sequence is assumed to increase the mean familiarity value for these stimuli. This is illustrated in Fig. 3a and b, where $\mu_1^{(n)}$ and $\mu_0^{(n)}$, shown in (b) ($n > 1$), have both shifted to the right of their initial values $\mu_1^{(1)}$ and $\mu_0^{(1)}$ shown in (a). The effect of shifting the mean familiarity values up is to increase the probability that the presentation of a repeated distractor will result in an extended memory search before a response is made, whereas this probability is decreased for repeated targets.[4]

The model can be stated mathematically by writing equations that represent the sums of times for the various memory and decision processes involved in recognition. The probability that the subject makes a correct response is assumed to be 1.0 if the familiarity value for a tested distractor word is below c_1 or if the familiarity value for a target is above c_0:

$$\Pr^{(n)}(A_1|S_1) = \int_{c_0}^{\infty} \phi_1^{(n)}(x)\, dx = 1 - \Phi_1^{(n)}(c_0), \tag{1}$$

$$\Pr^{(n)}(A_0|S_0) = \int_{-\infty}^{c_1} \phi_0^{(n)}(x)\, dx = \Phi_0^{(n)}(c_1). \tag{2}$$

Note that $\Phi(\,\cdot\,)$ designates the distribution function associated with the density function $\phi(\,\cdot\,)$.

In deriving response latencies, we shall assume that the processes involved in encoding the test stimulus, retrieving from memory information about the test stimulus, making a decision about which response to choose on

---

[4]In this paper we do not consider lag effects, that is, the number of trials intervening between one presentation of an item and its next presentation. However, such effects do exist and can be significant under some experimental conditions. To account for lag effects, we would assume that μ_i increases immediately upon the presentation of an item, but over an extended period of time gradually drifts back to its initial value. For a discussion of this problem and data see Juola *et al.* (1971).

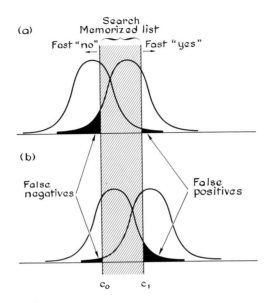

Fig. 3. Distributions of subjective familiarity values for distractor words (left) and target words (right) on the familiarity continuum: (a) the relative locations of the distributions at the start of the session; (b) the increase in the means that occurs for both distributions after the target and distractor words have been tested.

the basis of this information, and emitting a response can be represented as successive and independent stages. These stages are diagrammed in the flow chart in Fig. 4. When the test stimulus is presented, the first stages involve encoding the item and executing a rapid search of long-term memory. This initial search will yield only a limited amount of information, but it will suffice to permit the subject to arrive at an index (x) of the subjective familiarity of the test stimulus. The times required to execute these two stages are combined and represented by the quantity l in Fig. 4. The next stage is to arrive at a recognition decision on the basis of x. If $x < c_0$, a negative decision is made; if $x > c_1$, a positive decision is made. These decision times are functions of the value of x, and are given by the functions $\tau_0(x)$ and $\tau_1(x)$, respectively. If $c_0 \leq x \leq c_1$, an extended search of long-term memory is required, yielding more complete information about the test stimulus. The length of time needed for this search is assumed to be a function of d, the number of stimuli in S_1. The total time for a decision in this case is $\kappa(x) + \theta_i(d)$. In this equation $\kappa(x)$ denotes the time to make the decision to execute an extended search, and may depend upon x. The function $\theta_i(d)$ is the time to complete the search and depends upon the length of the target list d and upon whether the tested item is a target $(i = 1)$ or a distractor $(i = 0)$. The final stage of the

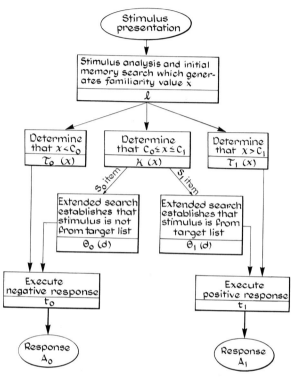

Fig. 4. Flow chart representing the memory and decision stages involved in word recognition. When a stimulus is presented, the subject arrives at a familiarity index x, and on that basis (a) decides to output a fast positive response (if $x > c_1$), or a fast negative response (if $x < c_0$), or (b) to execute a more extensive search of memory before responding (if $c_0 \ll x \ll c_1$).

process is to output a response once the decision has been made, the response time being t_0 for an A_0 response and t_1 for an A_1 response.

Equations can be derived for response latencies by weighting the times associated with each stage by the probability that the stage occurs during processing. The expected time to make an A_i response to the nth presentation of a particular stimulus drawn from set S_j (for $i, j = 0, 1$) is as follows:

$$t^{(n)}(A_1 | S_1) = \frac{\int_{c_1}^{\infty} \tau_1(x)\phi_1^{(n)}(x)\,dx + \int_{c_0}^{c_1} [\theta_1(d) + \kappa(x)]\phi_1^{(n)}(x)\,dx}{1 - \Phi_1^{(n)}(c_0)} + t_1 + l, \tag{3}$$

$$t^{(n)}(A_0 | S_1) = \frac{\int_{-\infty}^{c_0} \tau_0(x)\phi_1^{(n)}(x)\,dx}{\Phi_1^{(n)}(c_0)} + t_0 + l, \tag{4}$$

$$t^{(n)}(A_0|S_0) = \frac{\int_{-\infty}^{c_0} \tau_0(x)\phi_0^{(n)}(x)\,dx + \int_{c_0}^{c_1} [\theta_0(d) + \kappa(x)]\phi_0^{(n)}(x)\,dx}{\Phi_0^{(n)}(c_1)} + t_0 + l, \tag{5}$$

$$t^{(n)}(A_1|S_0) = \frac{\int_{c_1}^{\infty} \tau_1(x)\phi_0^{(n)}(x)\,dx}{1 - \Phi_0^{(n)}(c_1)} + t_1 + l. \tag{6}$$

In fitting the model to data from the previous experiments, several special cases will be examined. First, we shall assume that $\phi_i^{(n)}(x)$ is normally distributed with unit variance for all values of i and n. The function $\kappa(x)$ will be assumed to be a constant function of x, with value k. Finally, the function $\tau_i(x)$ will be of the following form:

$$\tau_i(x) = a_i \exp(-|c_i - x|b_i). \tag{7}$$

The function $\tau_1(x)$ is defined only for $x > c_1$, and $\tau_0(x)$ for $x < c_0$. Equation (7) can be simplified by assuming that both $\tau_1(x)$ and $\tau_0(x)$ have the same value at c_1 and c_0, respectively (that is $a_1 = a_0$), and that they decrease symmetrically as the value of $|c_i - x|$ increases (that is, $b_1 = b_0$). Two cases of this expression will be given special consideration. First, if $b_1 = b_0 = b = 0.0$, then $\tau_i(x)$ is a constant:

$$\tau_i(x) = a. \tag{8}$$

Second, if $a_1 = a_0 = k$, $\tau_i(x)$ has the same value as k when $x = c_i$:

$$\tau_i(x) = k \exp(-|c_i - x|b). \tag{9}$$

Finally, the function $\theta_i(d)$ must be specified. This function represents an extended search of long-term memory, and is assumed to be a linear function of the target set size. Two cases we wish to consider differ in the relative length of the memory search for target and distractor items. First, it could be assumed that the search times are identical for both types of items:

$$\theta_1(d) = \theta_0(d) = \alpha d. \tag{10}$$

Alternatively, it might be that the length of the memory search is shorter on positive trials than on negative trials. This situation would occur if each list item is stored in a separate memory location, and the subject retrieves the contents of each location in seeking a match for the test stimulus. When a match is obtained, the search ends; otherwise all the memory locations are checked. The time for this process is

$$\theta_1(d) = \alpha[(d + 1)/2], \tag{11a}$$

$$\theta_0(d) = \alpha d \tag{11b}$$

It should be noted that the two memory-search processes described above correspond to the exhaustive and self-terminating cases of the serial scanning model described by Sternberg (1969). Whereas Sternberg's models have proved to be extremely valuable in interpreting data from a wide variety of memory-search experiments, good fits between the models and data do not necessarily require that the underlying psychological process be serial in nature. There are alternative models, including parallel scanning models, that are mathematically equivalent to those proposed by Sternberg and yield the same predictions as Eqs. (10) and (11) (Atkinson, Holmgren, & Juola, 1969). Thus, the use of Eqs. (10) and (11) to specify the time associated with the extended memory search does not commit us to either a serial or parallel interpretation.

The model as it is now formulated predicts differences in performance as a function of the number of times an item has been tested. However, no mechanism has been incorporated to take into account improvements in performance resulting from extended practice on the task. An inspection of the data in Fig. 1 indicates that practice effects are occurring; for example, in Experiment 1 the first presentation of a distractor item in Block I produces a response latency of 819 msec, whereas the first presentation of a distractor item in Block IV has a latency of 721 msec. The theory can be amended to take into account generalized practice effects by assuming that t_0 and t_1 decrease over trials. For some experiments a meaningful analysis of the data requires an estimate of changes in t_0 and t_1 with practice. For others, the problem can be sidestepped by restricting the analysis to the later trial blocks, if it can be assumed that t_0 and t_1 have reached some asymptotic level.

V. Theoretical Predictions for the List-Length Study

The model will now be used to generate predictions for the latency and error data from Experiment 2. To avoid dealing with practice effects in this experiment, we shall confine our analysis to the data from Blocks III and IV where it seems reasonable to assume that performance is asymptotic.

Initially a value must be arbitrarily assigned to either c_0, c_1, $\mu_0^{(1)}$, or $\mu_1^{(1)}$ as a scaling parameter. Once this is done, the other parameters can be estimated from the data. We will let $c_0 = 0.0$. From the error data it is possible to estimate $\mu_1^{(n)}$, since an error to a target word occurs only if its familiarity value lies below c_0:

$$\Pr^{(n)}(A_0 \mid S_1) = \Phi_1^{(n)}(c_0). \tag{12}$$

The error proportions over the last two trial blocks for the first, second, third, and fourth presentation of a target item (averaged across the three list-length groups) were as follows: 0.171, 0.016, 0.014, and 0.007. Using the normal probability distribution it is possible to calculate that $\mu_1^{(1)} = c_0 + 0.950 = 0.950$. Similarly, $\mu_1^{(2)} = 2.14$, $\mu_1^{(3)} = 2.20$, and $\mu_1^{(4)} = 2.46$. The same procedure can be used to arrive at mean familiarity values for distractor words, since

$$\Pr^{(n)}(A_1 | S_0) = 1 - \Phi_0^{(n)}(c_1). \tag{13}$$

The error proportions for presentations one through four for distractors were 0.005, 0.039, 0.049, and 0.049, respectively. Thus, $\mu_0^{(1)} = c_1 - 2.58$, $\mu_0^{(2)} = c_1 - 1.76$, $\mu_0^{(3)} = c_1 - 1.66$, and $\mu_0^{(4)} = c_1 - 1.66$.

With c_0 set equal to zero and $\mu_i^{(n)}$ estimated from the error data, the remaining parameters can be estimated from the latency data. Four models of the theory will be used to generate fits to the data of Experiment 2. The models differ in the functions $\tau_i(x)$ and $\theta_i(d)$ as outlined below:

		$\theta_i(d)$	
	Eq. (10)		Eq. (11)
Eq. (8)	Model 1		Model 2
$\tau_i(x)$			
Eq. (9)	Model 3		Model 4

The parameters that remain to be estimated are somewhat different for Models 1 and 2 versus 3 and 4. For Models 1 and 2 there are five parameters: c_1, α, $(k + t_0 + l)$, $(k + t_1 + l)$, and $(a + t_0 + l)$. The quantities in parentheses indicate that the component parameters cannot be evaluated separately; only their sums can be estimated. For Models 3 and 4 there are five parameters: c_1, α, k, b, $(t_0 + l)$, and $(t_1 + l)$.

Our method for parameter estimation involves the data presented in Fig. 5; it is simply the weighted average of the data for the third and fourth trial blocks of Experiment 2. Parameter values are selected that minimize the sum of the squared deviations (weighted by the number of observations) between the data points in Fig. 5 and theoretical predictions. A number of problems are involved in minimizing the squared-deviation function analytically, and consequently a computer was programmed to carry out a systematic search of the parameter space until a minimum was obtained accurate to three places. The weighted sum of squared deviations for the models are as follows:

$$\text{Model 1:} \quad 3.81 \times 10^5,$$
$$\text{Model 2:} \quad 4.57 \times 10^5,$$
$$\text{Model 3:} \quad 4.35 \times 10^5,$$
$$\text{Model 4:} \quad 4.68 \times 10^5.$$

Model 1 clearly yields the best fit, and Model 3 is second; both Models 1 and 3 assume that the extended memory search is represented in Eq. (10).

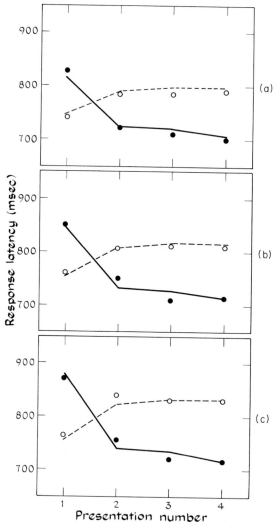

Fig. 5. Mean response latency as a function of presentation number for target and distractor words for three different list length (*d*) conditions, (●) targets; (○) distractors; (a) data for *d* = 16; (b) data for *d* = 24; (c) data for *d* = 32. The broken lines fitted to the data were generated from Model 1 (Experiment 2).

Table 1. *Parameter Values for the Two Best-Fitting Models (Experiment 2)*

Model 1	Model 3
$c_1 = 1.02$	$c_1 = .822$
$\alpha = 9.86$ msec	$\alpha = 14.1$ msec
$(k + t_0 + l) = 868$ msec	$a = k = 144$ msec
$(k + t_1 + l) = 824$ msec	$b = .320$
$(a + t_0 + l) = 731$ msec	$(t_0 + l) = 653$ msec
$(a + t_1 + l) = 687$ msec[a]	$(t_1 + l) = 609$ msec

[a]Not estimated, but computed from the above three parameters.

The parameter estimates for these two models are given in Table 1. The predicted values for Model 1 are presented in Fig. 5 as connected lines; it should be noted that the model not only fits these data but (due to the method of parameter estimation) provides a perfect fit to the error data.

The results in Fig. 5 can be replotted by considering those items receiving their first presentation ($n = 1$) and those receiving a repeated presentation ($n = 2, 3,$ or 4); in the latter case a weighted average must be taken. If this is done the data points are those presented in Fig. 2, and the straight lines in that figure are the predicted functions based on Model 1. The fits displayed in Fig. 2 could be improved upon somewhat, but it should be kept in mind that they were obtained by using parameter estimates based on a different breakdown of the data.

The latency of an error response should be fast according to the theory, since errors occur only when the secondary memory search is bypassed. The data support this prediction, and accord well with the values generated by Model 1. Specifically, the latency of an error is close to the predicted value of $l + t_0 + a = 731$ msec for an S_1 item, and to $l + t_1 + a = 687$ msec for an S_0 item. A more detailed account of error latencies is given in Juola *et al.* (1971).

A verbal interpretation of the results in terms of Model 1 would proceed as follows. When a target item is presented for the first time, the probability that an extended memory search will occur before a response is made exceeds the probability that a fast positive response will be emitted on the basis of the familiarity value of the item alone. The opposite is true for initial presentations of distractors; most trials result in fast negative responses. Thus, the mean latency is longer for initial presentations of targets than for initial presentations of distractors ($k > a$), and the list-length effect is greater for targets than for distractors. The effect of repeating tests of words is to increase the familiarity of both targets and distractors. This results in an increased mean latency for responses to distractors (since a greater proportion of trials results in an extended memory search before a response) and a decrease in response latency to targets. The magnitudes of the list-length effects are observed in change concomitantly. Although such variables as number of presentations and number of intervening items between successive presentations affect the familiarity value of an item, it is probable that all target items are about equally familiar at the start of the session. Any deviations that exist between the values most likely are due to properties of specific words or idiosyncratic responses on the part of the subject. It is apparent that the familiarity of the target item cannot be assumed to depend upon its serial position in the study list, since no serial position effects have been observed.

VI. Effects of Number of Occurrences in the Study List

Experiment 3 was designed to test the effects of repeating words in the study lists. Fifteen subjects each memorized a list of 32 words, but some of the words were repeated either once or twice in the list. Specifically, the lists contained eight single words: six words that occurred twice, and four words that occurred three times. The order of the words within the lists was randomized with the constraint that at least four words would occur between successive occurrences of a repeated word. As in the previous experiments, the subjects were instructed to learn the list in serial order, and they were tested for serial recall of all 32 items before the recognition tests began. The test session was divided into three consecutive trial blocks of 36 trials each. Within each block, the 18 target words were tested once, along with 18 distractors. Different sets of distractor words were presented in each block.

The results showed that the mean latency was significantly shorter for responses to target words that were repeated in the study lists than that for responses to those that occurred only once. This effect was obtained in all three blocks. The model that generated the best fit to the data of Experiment 2 (Model 1 of the previous section) was also used to fit the data of Experiment 3. There are at least two ways to account for the effects of repetition of words in the study list within the framework of the model. First, if the extended memory search involves the retrieval of the memorized list and a check for a match with the test stimulus, the expected length of time before a match is found is an inverse function of the number of times the target item occurs in the list. The fact that the best-fitting model assumes an exhaustive memory search, however, makes this analysis seem to be somewhat untenable; the evidence from Experiment 2 suggests that the length of the extended memory search is the same for positive and negative trials. Therefore, proposing a self-terminating scan to account for the repetition effects in Experiment 3 would seem to be theoretically inconsistent.

A second alternative would be to let the expected familiarity value for a target word be an increasing function of the number of times that the word occurred in the target set. It has been assumed previously that all target words initially have about the same familiarity value, for no experiment has shown positive response latency to be a function of the serial position of the target word. An analysis of the error data from Experiment 3 indicates, however, that repetitions in the study list increase the expected familiarities for those target words. The mean error proportions were .051, .034, and .011 for words that occurred one, two, and three times, respectively, in the target lists. Moreover, the mean error proportions for all three types of positive test trials were observed to decline across blocks (which is expected, since all target words were presented in each block). However, the mean error proportion for distractors was about .006 in all three blocks (which is also expected since distractors were not repeated from one block to the next).

The patterns observed in the data for Experiment 3, as shown in Fig. 6, can be fit by the model using the same procedure as in the previous section. The mean familiarity value for an item can be expressed as the distance from the appropriate criterion that will generate the observed error probability.

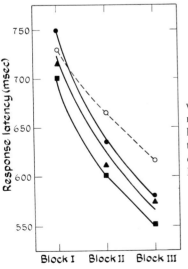

Fig. 6. Mean response latency for distractor words and for target words as a function of the number of times the word occurred in the target list for three consecutive trial blocks: (○) distractors; targets (●) 1 time, (▲) 2 times, (■) 3 times. The curved lines fitted to the data were generated from Model 1 (Experiment 3).

The fit to the data was obtained by using Model 1, and by retaining the same parameter values estimated from Experiment 2. The only difference was that in this case additional estimates of t_0 and t_1 had to be made for each trial block of the experiment. Under these conditions the predictions for Model 1 are represented by the curves in Fig. 6. As we see, the predictions of the model accord well with the observed values.

VII. Effects of Similarity of Distractors to Target Words

For Experiment 4, a list of 16 pairs of nouns was used, eight were synonym pairs and eight were homophone pairs. Fifteen subjects received different study lists made up of one target word randomly selected from each pair. The subjects were run for two consecutive daily sessions of 96 trials each. During both sessions, every target word was presented three times each. The distractor words consisted of the eight synonyms and eight homophones of the target words along with additional neutral words. [A more complete description of this experiment, along with lists of the word pairs, is presented in Juola *et al.* (1971).]

The mean latencies for the two sessions combined are given in Table 2. The results show the same pattern as in the previous studies, the response latency being much shorter for the second and third tests of target words than for the initial presentations. The mean latency of negative responses to neutral distractors was less than the latency of responses to initial presentations of target words, but was greater than that of subsequent tests.

Negative response latency to synonyms of target words was significantly greater than the latency of responses to neutral distractors. Somewhat surprisingly, the latency for homophones exceeded that of responses to synonyms. After the data had been collected, a closer examination of the homophone pairs revealed that they could be divided into two cate-

Table 2. *Mean Response Latencies (in milliseconds) for the First, Second, and Third Presentations of Target Words, and for Distractors That Vary in Similarity to Target Words (Experiment 4)*

Test word type	Latency	Test word type	Latency
Targets		Distractors	
Presentation 1	733	Homophones	793
Presentation 2	622	Synonyms	731
Presentation 3	617	Neutral words	673

gories: those that were visually quite similar to each other (only two letters were different, for example, *bored* and *board*) and those that were visually dissimilar (more than two letters were different, for example *sense* and *cents*). The mean response latency to homophone distractors that were classified as being visually similar to their respective target-word pairs was 895 msec, whereas the latency to those that were visually dissimilar was 716 msec (not significantly greater than the latency to neutral distractors).

In terms of the proposed model, it appears that the familiarity of any distractor item can be increased by including items that are similar to it in the target set. Specifically, it seems clear that semantic information is used by the subject in determining whether or not a test item is on the target list. Acoustic information apparently is not by itself an important determinant of an item's familiarity, since the relatively long latencies to homophones appear to be due to visual similarities between the words of the homophone pairs. The cause of the effect of visual similarity is not entirely clear. It may be the case that some visual information is used in judging the familiarity of the presented stimulus. It is also possible, and perhaps more likely, that visual similarity between targets and distractor words leads to confusions and errors of identification of the test stimulus before the subject can decide exactly what word is being presented. Thus, the effect of visual similarity could be due either to an increase in the expected familiarity value μ_0, of the distractor item, or it could increase the expected time for the encoding process, thereby raising the length of time for stage *1*.

VIII. Frequency, Concreteness, and Number of Syllables

The words used in Experiment 5 were selected so that they could be separated into two distinct, equally sized groups on the basis of any of three criteria: frequency in English, abstractness–concreteness, and number of syllables (one or two). Sixty-four five-letter words were used, most of these taken from the Paivio, Yuille, and Madigan (1968) noun list. The frequent words were rated either A or AA according to the Thorndike and Lorge (1944) word count, and the infrequent words were those that occurred fewer than 10 times per million. Similarly, concrete nouns were rated higher than 6.0 and abstract nouns were less than 3.0 on the Paivio–Yuille–Madigan scale. The additional words that were not present in the initial norms but were needed to complete the design were selected from the Thorndike and Lorge word lists. Three independent judges were used to pick those words that seemed to best match the originally selected words on the concreteness dimension.

The critical dimensions arranged the word pool into a $2 \times 2 \times 2$ factorial design with eight words in each cell. For each subject, four words were selected randomly from every cell to make a list of 32 target words. During the test session, all 64 words were shown in two successive random orderings to yield 128 trials.

Mean response latencies were found for each type of word for positive and negative trials separately. Means were then taken across 16 subjects, and the results are presented in Table 3. The differences between levels of the three variables were in the same direction for both positive and negative latencies, with responses to two-syllable words being faster than responses to one-syllable words, those of concrete words being faster than those of abstract words, and those of infrequent words being faster than those of frequent words. However, separate analyses of variance performed on the data for positive and negative responses showed that the only significant differences were between frequent and infrequent target words and between abstract and concrete distractors. The result for targets is similar to Shepard's (1967) finding that the probability of correct recognition of an "old" word occurring in a long sequence of words is greater if the old word is a relatively uncommon word in English. Presumably, the effect of prior study for an infrequent word is to cause a greater change in its subjective familiarity than that produced for frequent words. When an infrequently occurring word is presented as a test, and it has a relatively high familiarity value, the subject is apparently more likely to output a response on the basis of its familiarity value alone than he is for frequent target words. Two explanations for this process are that the subject may either retrieve a

Table 3. *Mean Response Latencies (in milliseconds) as Functions of Frequency, Concreteness, and Number of Syllables (Experiment 5)*

	Target words	Distractor words
High frequency	790	830
Low frequency	762	805
Abstract	785	839
Concrete	767	795
One syllable	782	824
Two syllables	770	810

higher familiarity value for infrequent target words than for frequent words, or he may adjust his criterion for a fast positive response so that c_1 is lower when a relatively rare word is tested. The latter argument is equivalent to saying that the subject compares the retrieved familiarity of a test word with its expected familiarity, which is a function of its frequency in English. If a large discrepancy occurs, the subject outputs a fast positive response before any further memory search is initiated.

Previous experiments (for example, Gorman, 1961) have shown that recognition probability for old words is higher if the words are concrete rather than abstract. A similar effect favoring responses to concrete words was noted in Experiment 5, although it was significant only for distractor items. Since abstract and concrete distractors were balanced for frequency (and, presumably, familiarity), it appears that the concreteness dimension affects l, the encoding and initial information retrieval stage of the model. The time between the stimulus onset and an estimation of the word's familiarity seems to be an increasing function of the abstractness of the distractor word, but a thorough explanation of the mechanism for this process cannot be made on the basis of the present data.

Although the number of syllables in the test word did not have a significant effect on response latency either for target or distractor words, it is interesting to note that response latencies were shorter for two-syllable words in both cases. Since all words were five letters in length it is worth noting that the two-syllable words generally contained more common spelling patterns than did the one-syllable words (for example, *tenet* versus *pique*). Presumably, words that contain more commonly occurring letter patterns should be easier to encode (decreasing the value of l) than those that have less common patterns. The total response latency to two-syllable words then should be shorter than latency for one-syllable words if all other factors are equal. This explanation is admittedly tentative, and the results presented here were not obtained to provide tests for theories of word perception. However, the arguments follow naturally from the proposed theory and account for the observed latency effects.

IX. Repression Effects on Recognition Latency

Experiment 6 was designed to determine if the procedure used in the previous studies could lend itself to the study of repression effects in recognition memory. Repression here is taken to mean forgetting which is selective to those perceptions and memories that produce anxiety. Supposedly, this type of forgetting is initiated by a mechanism that defends the subject against such anxiety. It should be possible to determine the extent of repression effects on recognition memory by using the paradigm of the previous studies. If certain target words are paired with anxiety-provoking stimuli, and then these words are presented in a recognition task, repression effects should interfere with the initial stages of processing and perhaps later search and decision processes as well. The expected result is that response latency should be greater for target words that have been associated with anxiety-provoking stimuli than for words that have been associated with neutral or positive stimuli.

Each subject memorized a target list of 16 words. The target lists then were divided into three consecutive groups of four words each (the first two and last two words were not included as they were to be tested only in a warm-up block at the start of the test session). One word from each group was assigned to one of four treatment conditions: (a) paired with a positive experience, (b) paired with a neutral experience, (c) paired with a negative experience, or (d) not paired with any experience. The positive and negative experiences were generated by the subjects. They were instructed to write down descriptions of the three most intense occasions when they had experienced feelings similar to those in, first, a list of positive emotionally-descriptive statements, and, second, a list of negative statements. Three neutral experiences were provided by the experimenter. These consisted of descriptions of routine events obtained from newspaper stories. Each of nine list words was paired randomly with one of the experiences. These pairings were achieved by having the subject write down four different associations between the given target word and the appropriate experience as assigned by the experimenter.

The test sequence was divided into a warm-up block of eight trials followed by three trial blocks of 24 trials each. All 12 experimental target words were presented once in each block along with 12 distractors, which were never repeated. The results showed that the four different treatment conditions for target words had a significant effect on positive response latency in the first trial block only. The data for Trial Block I are presented in Table 4. The latencies in the latter two blocks converged for all four conditions, with a mean response latency of 688 msec for Block II and 665 msec for Block III. The latencies for responses to distractor words were 733 msec and 711 msec for the last two blocks.

The data in Table 4 show that response latency was actually shortest for words that had been paired with negative experiences, although the mean latency was not significantly less than the time to respond to words paired with positive experiences. Both of these conditions resulted in latencies significantly below those for words paired with neutral experiences, and the mean latency for unpaired words was significantly greater than that of any other condition.

Table 4. *Mean Response Latencies (in milliseconds) to Four Types of Target Words and to Distractor Words (Experiment 6)*

Test word type	Latency
Target words	
Positive experience	755
Negative experience	733
Neutral experience	788
Unpaired	916
Distractor words	782

The results do not support the repression hypothesis of forgetting, namely, that (*a*) the pairing of negative experiences with target words will elicit anxiety when the words are presented in a recognition test, and (*b*) this anxiety will block the perception of the word or impede the retrieval of stored information about the word. Either process would result in response latency being greater for negatively paired words than for words paired with neutral or positive experiences. The data indicate that the mere pairing of a target word to any type of experience results in a shorter mean latency to that word, especially if the experience is one from the subject's own background.

The interpretation, in terms of the model, is that any effort to associate a target word with a prior experience results in a subsequent higher familiarity value for that word. This effect is evidenced by the fact that responses to target words associated with negative or positive experiences were faster than responses to distractors. This result is unusual; in all of the studies reported here, response latency for target words is greater than the response latency for distractors on their initial presentations. It appears that the familiarity value (rather than any positive or negative associations with the word) determines the speed with which the subject can make a recognition decision.

X. Recognition Latency for Words in a Semantic Hierarchy

Experiment 7 was designed to test for the effects of imposing an organizational scheme on the words of the target set. Specifically, all target words were taken from the semantic hierarchy shown in Table 5. The hierarchy of the present study is an expansion of two hierarchies used in a study by Bower, Clark, Lesgold, and Winzenz (1969). Of the 86 words in Table 5, each subject received a target set of 54. All the target sets included both words in Level

Table 5.   *Hierarchical Organization of 86 Nouns (Experiment 7)*

A.   Organism

Plant				Animal			
Vegetable	Flower	Tree	Fruit	Mammal	Insect	Bird	Fish
Carrot	Rose	Oak	Apple	Dog	Ant	Robin	Bass
Bean	Tulip	Elm	Orange	Cat	Mosquito	Eagle	Trout
Corn	Carnation	Pine	Pear	Cow	Fly	Sparrow	Shark
Pea	Daisy	Maple	Banana	Horse	Bee	Cardinal	Herring

B.   Instrument

Musical				Precision			
Brass	Woodwind	Percussion	String	Drafting	Optical	Surgical	Navigation
Tuba	Clarinet	Drum	Violin	Compass	Telescope	Scalpel	Radar
Cornet	Oboe	Cymbals	Banjo	Ruler	Microscope	Forceps	Gyroscope
Trumpet	Flute	Bells	Cello	Protractor	Monocle	Stethoscope	Sextant
Horn	Saxophone	Triangle	Guitar	Pen	Spyglass	Pincers	Altimeter

1 and the four words in Level 2. Twelve words were included from Level 3, these being either all four or only two of the exemplars of the Level 2 words. Similarly, either four or two exemplars were included under each of the Level 3 words. An example of one target set, in the form it was presented to the subject, is shown in Fig. 7. The different target sets were made such that every word within any level was used as a target equally often. Distractor words were chosen randomly from the Thorndike–Lorge list, and were matched with the words in Table 5 in length and frequency.

The subjects memorized the target set the day prior to the experiment; they were tested before the experimental session by filling in a hierarchy with blank lines drawn in where the target words appeared on the study sheet. No subjects made any errors on the recall task. During the test session all 54 target words were shown once, and 54 different distractors were also presented.

The data for the two halves of the target set were combined, and the mean latencies were found for each level. There was no effect of level within the hierarchy on positive response latency. The only significant effects were between words that were members of subsets of different sizes within Level 3 and Level 4. These subsets are denoted Level 3 (four nodes) for words that are one of the four exemplars of a Level-2 node (for example, *mammal* in Fig. 7), level 3 (two nodes) for words that are one of the two exemplars of a

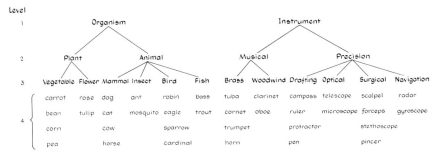

Fig. 7. An example of a semantic hierarchy containing the words presented to the subject as a target list. The level designation on the left side of the figure did not appear on the subject's copy (Experiment 7).

Level-2 node (for example, *woodwind*), Level 4 (List 4-4) for words that were one of four items listed under one of a group of four nodes in Level 3 (for example, *scalpel*), Level 4 (List 4-2) for words that were one of four items listed under one of a pair of nodes in Level 3 (for example, *carrot*), Level 4 (List 2-4) for words that were one of two items listed under one of four nodes in Level 3 (for example, *ant*), and Level 4 (List 2-2) for words that were one of two items listed under one of a pair of nodes in Level 3 (for example, *clarinet*). The mean response latencies for all types of trials are shown in Table 6.

The results do not support a memory search that follows the structure of the semantic hierarchy of Fig. 7. Even if the target words are organized hierarchically in the subject's memory, it does not appear to be the case that a search through such an organization is necessary before a recognition decision can be made. Studies that have shown effects of hierarchical organization typically have employed a task requiring the subject to recall information about more than one word (Collins & Quillian, 1969; Meyer, 1970), whereas the present task can be performed adequately if only information about the test word is retrieved.

Table 6. *Mean Response Latency (in milliseconds) for Words as Functions of Their Locations in a Semantic Hierarchy (Experiment 7)*

Test word type	Latency	Test word type	Latency
Target item			
Levels 1 and 2	728	Level 4 (List 4-4)	693
Level 3 (4 nodes)	722 733	Level 4 (List 4-2)	717 733
Level 3 (2 nodes)	755	Level 4 (List 2-4)	724
		Level 4 (List 2-2)	738
		Distractor items	708

The significant results that were obtained are more difficult to interpret than the lack of effects due to the level in a hierarchy. It seems incompatible with earlier results that the subjects can respond more quickly to an item that is a member of a large subset than to one that belongs to a smaller subset. A tentative explanation for this result can be made on the basis of the data from Experiment 4. It was demonstrated that semantic similarity between a distractor word and a target can increase the familiarity of the distractor, resulting in a slower negative response time. In the present experiment, the items that are most highly related semantically are those that share the same relative positions in the hierarchy. If the study of one word serves to increase the familiarity value of related words, then one would expect those words with the greatest number of similar words in the target set to have the highest mean familiarity. From this argument the prediction that positive response latency should be shortest to words that belong to a relatively large subset can be made if the subset contains words that are semantically related. It is clear that any words at the same level in the hierarchy are closely related semantically, and the prediction that response latencies should be shorter to a word that is one of a subset of four items at a given level than to one that is one of a subset of two is upheld by the data in Table 6. The explanation offered here is like the one proposed by Schaeffer and Wallace (1969) to account for judgments of word meanings; as in the present study, semantic similarity between test words facilitated the decision that the words belonged to the same category.

In terms of the above argument, it is important to determine whether the response speed for a given test word is increased if semantically related words have been previously tested. To do this, the means presented in Table 6 were computed for the first and second halves of the test session separately. The results clearly demonstrated that the effects of subset size within the hierarchy were only important late in the session. For the first half of the session, there were no significant differences among any of the heirarchical divisions shown in Table 6. Thus, the differential familiarities for words were not so much the result of previously studying related words, as they were due to a priming effect of the prior presentations of semantically related words.

XI. Summary and Conclusions

A simplified version of the model proposed earlier is shown in Fig. 8. It is assumed that when a stimulus word is presented for a recognition test, the subject performs an initial, rapid access of the information stored about the test item. This information provides the subject with a familiarity rating for the word. Response decisions based on the familiarity of the stimulus

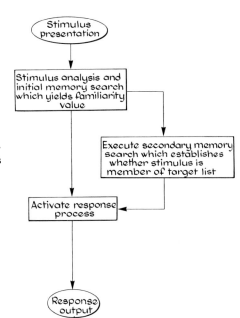

Fig. 8. Simplified flow chart representing the memory and decision stages involved in word recognition.

alone can be made very quickly, but they result in a relatively high error rate. If the results of the initial memory search do not provide the subject with enough information to respond with confidence (that is, if the familiarity value is neither very high nor very low) a secondary, extended memory search is performed before a response is emitted. The latter search virtually guarantees that the subject will arrive at the correct decision, but with a consequent increase in response latency. By adjusting the criteria for emitting responses based on familiarity alone, the subject can achieve a stable level of performance, matching the speed and accuracy of responses to the demand characteristics of the experiment.

The model provides a tentative explanation for the results of several recognition–memory experiments. The memory and decision stages are indicative of possible mechanisms involved in recognition; we do not, however, claim that they are exact descriptions of the processes involved. The comparison of data with theoretical predictions are reported mainly to show that many quantitative features of our results can be adequately described by the model. The particular parameter estimates reported are not to be interpreted too closely, since the parameter space was fairly shallow in the region where best fits were obtained; considerable play could be permitted in some of the estimates without seriously affecting the goodness of fit.

There are several encouraging points, however, which suggest that memory and decision states of the model correspond to processing stages of the subject. Introspective reports indicate that subjects may indeed output a rapid response based on initially retrieved information about the test stimulus. Subjects report that they are sometimes able to respond almost immediately after the word is presented before "knowing for sure" if the item is a target or not. The same subjects report that on other trials they recall portions of the memorized list before giving a response. The fact that subjects are always aware of their own errors also supports the general outline of the model; even if the initial familiarity of an item produces a decision to respond immediately, the extended memory search continues, and results in the subject confirming that he has or has not made the correct response. These introspective reports lend support to the general theoretical representation, and go beyond the goodness-of-fit demonstrations. No other model that we have yet considered combines these features into a workable alternative.

The data from our experiments provide clues regarding which features of the test stimuli affect the various memory and decision processes. Whereas the sources of these effects are difficult to isolate, some conclusions can be drawn. It appears that visual properties of the stimulus affect the ease with which it can be encoded and thus the speed of the initial memory search. Words that contain infrequent spelling patterns or are visually quite similar to one another can result in longer response latencies. Other factors seem to influence the familiarity of the tested word. These include the lag since the word was last activated in memory (either through exposure to certain words immediately before the test session, or through repeated tests during the session) and the presentation of items related to the test word.

Whereas we can list manipulations that affect the familiarity of words, the definition of familiarity needs to be more precise. Familiarity apparently depends on the time since the last previous exposure or retrieval of the word. A more general formulation would involve the description of a word as a stimulus and how it is represented in memory. If a word is represented as a complex of features (Anisfeld & Knapp, 1968), each feature (semantic, acoustic, visual, and so forth) might be independently time tagged when activated in memory. This activation may occur when the word itself is tested, or when words similar on one or more dimensions are presented. Familiarity then could be based upon a feature count, familiarity increasing with the number of tagged features (Kintsch, 1970).

A comparison between the data of the present experiments and those of short-term recognition studies is revealing. We have completed an experiment (Juola & Atkinson, 1971) that uses the same paradigm as Sternberg's (1966) study. The subjects were from the same pool as those who participated in the experiments reported here, and the same apparatus was used. Additionally, the stimulus words were the same as those used in Experiments 1–3. In the Juola–Atkinson experiment, each trial began with the auditory presentation of a target set of from one to four words, followed by the visual presentation of a single test word. All other features of the experiment were the same as those for the studies reported in this paper. The results showed response latency to be a linear function of the target set size, with the following best-fitting straight line: $617 + 26d$ ($d = 1$–4). In accord with Sternberg's findings, a much larger target-set effect was found in the short-term study [the slope parameter was about 38 msec in the Sternberg (1966) experiment]. Whereas the overall response speed was slower than that reported by Sternberg, it was still considerably below that of any of the long-term experiments reported in this paper.

Some conclusions can be drawn about similarities and differences between these two classes of experiments. Presumably, since new items are constantly being presented and a given stimulus may change from being a target on one trial to being a distractor on another, the subjects do not rely on the familiarity of the test stimulus in the short-term experiments. With the test set already in short-term memory, it is possible to initiate the "extended" search (in the sense of the previous discussion) without first retrieving information from long-term memory. Since this type of search is target-set dependent, the greater set-size effects observed in short-term recognition studies are expected.

The overall response latencies appear to be greater in the long-term experiments than in the short-term recognition studies. This effect is presumably due to the fact that information must be retrieved from long-term memory in the former type of experiment before a decision can be made. If an extended memory search is necessitated, additional information must be retrieved, resulting in an even longer response latency. It is interesting to note that for the models tested in the present paper, the best representation of the extended search process had the same mathematical form as the one proposed by Sternberg to account for the short-term studies (that is, linear functions with equal slope for both targets and distractors). Whereas the overall data from these two classes of experiments show marked differences, some features of the results suggest that there may be common processes involved in short-term and long-term recognition.

Acknowledgments

The authors gratefully achnowledge the assistance of Christine Wood for collecting and analyzing the data for five of the experiments reported here. Experiment 1 was run by Ira Fischler and Experiment 6 by Michael Ryan. Thanks are also due to Dexter Fletcher for assistance in writing the computer program.

References

Anisfeld, M., & Knapp, M. Association, synonymity, and directionality in false recognition. *Journal of Experimental Psychology*, 1968, **77**, 171–179.

Atkinson, R. C., Holmgren, J. E., & Juola, J. F. Processing time as influenced by the number of elements in a visual display. *Perception and Psychophysics*, 1969, **6**, 321–326.

Bower, G. H., Clark, M., Lesgold, A., & Winzenz, D. Hierarchical retrieval schemes in recall of categorized word lists. *Journal of Verbal Learning and Verbal Behavior*, 1969, **8**, 323–343.

Collins, A. M., & Quillian, M. R. Retrieval time from semantic memory. *Journal of Verbal Learning and Verbal Behavior*, 1969, **8**, 240–247.

Fischler, I., & Juola, J. F. Effects of repeated tests on recognition time for information in long-term memory. *Journal of Experimental Psychology*, 1971, **91**, 54–58.

Gorman, A. M. Recognition memory for nouns as a function of abstractness and frequency. *Journal of Experimental Psychology*, 1961, **61**, 23–29.

Juola, J. F., & Atkinson, R. C. Memory scanning for words versus categories. *Journal of Verbal Learning and Verbal Behavior*, 1971, **10**, 522–527.

Juola, J. F., Fischler, I., Wood, C. T., & Atkinson, R. C. Recognition time for information stored in long-term memory. *Perception and Psychophysics*, 1971, **10**, 8–14.

Kintsch, W. Memory and decision aspects of recognition learning. *Psychological Review*, 1967, **74**, 496–504.

Kintsch, W. Models for free recall and recognition. In D. A. Norman (Ed.), *Models of human memory*. New York: Academic Press, 1970.

Meyer, D. E. On the representation and retrieval of stored semantic information. *Cognitive Psychology*, 1970, **1**, 242–300.

Paivio A., Yuille, J. C., & Madigan, S. A. Concreteness, imagery, and meaningfulness values for 925 nouns. *Journal of Experimental Psychology Monograph Supplement*, 1968, **76**, No. 1, Part 2, 1–25.

Parks, T. E. Signal detectability theory of recognition memory performance. *Psychological Review*, 1966, **73**, 44–58.

Schaeffer, B., & Wallace, R. Semantic similarity and the comparison of word meanings. *Journal of Experimental Psychology*, 1969, **82**, 343–346.

Shepard, R. N. Recognition memory for words, sentences, and pictures, *Journal of Verbal Learning and Verbal Behavior*, 1967, **6**, 156–163.

Shepard, R. N., & Teghtsoonian, M. Retention of information under conditions approaching a steady state. *Journal of Experimental Psychology*, 1961, **62**, 302–309.

Sternberg, S. High-speed scanning in human memory. *Science*, 1966, **153**, 652–654.

Sternberg, S. Memory scanning: Mental processes revealed by reaction-time experiments. *American Scientist*, 1969, **57**, 421–457.

Thorndike, E. L., & Lorge, I. *The teacher's word book of 30,000 words*. New York: Bureau of Publications, Teachers College, Columbia University, 1944.

On Expectancy and the Speed and Accuracy of Responses

Ewart A. C. Thomas

Department of Psychology[1]
University of Michigan
Ann Arbor, Michigan

ABSTRACT

The role of expectancy in the task of detecting a weak signal is investigated by conducting an experiment in which the subject is required to detect a weak signal presented after a random delay. The view of expectancy presented here distinguishes between the effect of mean foreperiod and that of conditional probability, and it is argued that expectancy effects are qualitatively similar on detection reaction time as on simple reaction time. A theory is outlined in which the relationship between the speed and accuracy of a response depends on the quality of sensory information on which the response is based, and it is assumed that quality of information is directly related to expectancy. Although this *ad hoc* theory accounts for the present experimental results adequately, it remains to be tested rigorously through further experimentation.

I. Introduction

The notion of expectancy has been used by many authors to explain the relationship between simple reaction time (RT) and foreperiod (t) in a variable foreperiod experiment (for example, Mowrer, 1940; Näätänen, 1970; Thomas, 1970; see also the contribution of Besrest & Requin to this volume). According to Mowrer, the expectancy effect is due primarily to the mean foreperiod $E(t)$,[2] whereas the author has proposed that it is due to the

---

[1]Present address: Department of Psychology, Stanford University, Stanford, California.
[2]The symbol $E(\cdot)$ is used to denote "mathematical expectation."

conditional probability p_t that the signal would be presented at t, given that it has not yet been presented. It was argued that since $E(p_t^{-1}) = E(t) - a$, where a is the minimum foreperiod, it is possible that the mean foreperiod effect is merely a consequence of the conditional probability effect. However, the data reported in Thomas (1970) show that RT is a minimum when $t = E(t)$, which suggests that there is an additional mean foreperiod effect.

Recent studies (for example, Luce & Green, 1970) of the task of detecting weak signals that arrive at random times have prompted the question: What is the effect of expectancy on sensitivity, bias and detection RT? The present study attempts to answer this question experimentally by having subjects respond in three conditions:

Condition A. This is a simple RT task with a variable foreperiod in which the stimulus is equally likely to be a visual "noise" field alone or the noise with a small brighter patch superimposed on it (noise-plus-signal field).

Condition B. The stimulus characteristics are the same as in condition A, but here the subject is asked to discriminate between the two stimuli by pressing one or the other of two response keys.

Condition C. This is the same as condition B except that the stimuli are presented a constant time after a warning signal. This constant foreperiod is equal to the mean $E(t)$ of the foreperiod distribution used in conditions A and B.

One reason for trying to extend the notion of expectancy to account for data obtained from the detection conditions B and C is that it is conceivable that, in the free-response (vigilance) experiment, expectancy is the underlying psychological variable that mediates performance (for example, Broadbent, 1971). If this were the case, the questions that arise in the free-response task, for example, whether the performance decrement with increasing clock time is due to changes in sensitivity or in bias, could be answered by reference to other tasks in which expectancy could be manipulated. The variable foreperiod task is a good way of varying expectancy in a relatively controlled way. Hence, the results from the present experiment may be helpful in the construction of an adequate account of free-response data.

II. Method

A. Foreperiod Distributions

Two discrete foreperiod distributions J and L were used in this experiment. In both distributions the possible foreperiod values were 2, 4, 6, and 8 sec, the time being measured from a warning signal. The frequencies of

Table 1. *Frequency of Signal Presentation at 2, 4, 6, and 8-sec foreperiods*

Distribution	Time (sec) 2	4	6	8
J	12	12	18	30
L	30	18	12	12

signal presentation at the different foreperiod values in a run of 72 trials are given in Table 1, so that for J, $p_2^{-1} = 72/12 = 6$ and $E(t) = 5.8$ sec, whereas for L, $p_2^{-1} = 72/30 = 2.4$ and $E(t) = 4.2$ sec. The constant foreperiod used in condition C was 5.8 sec if distribution J was used in conditions A and B, and was 4.2 sec if distribution L was used.

B. Stimuli and Responses

The stimuli were square patches of light that were flashed onto a screen for a duration of 100 msec. The area of the noise field was 4 in.² and that of the signal was $\frac{9}{16}$ in.², the signal being superimposed on the middle of the noise field. The warning signal was four dots, which appeared on the screen near the corners of the noise field, subtending a visual angle of about 6°, for a duration of .5 sec. There were three response keys: a left, a center, and a right key. The center key only was used in condition A while the left and right keys were used in conditions B and C, the index finger of the corresponding hand being used to depress the latter two keys.

A PDP-1 computer was programmed to select either stimulus with probability $\frac{1}{2}$ and the foreperiod values in the desired frequencies in runs of 72 trials, and to record the reaction times.

The interval between a response and the next warning signal was constant within a run of trials; when distribution J was used, the interval was 4.2 sec; when L was used, it was 5.8 sec. Thus, the average intertrial interval was 10 sec in all conditions.

C. Procedure

Six subjects were tested, three under each foreperiod distribution. Each subject was tested for one practice session and six experimental sessions, each session consisting of two runs of 72 trials under one or two of the three conditions. There was a 4-min break between runs. Over the six sessions each subject had two runs of conditions A and C and eight runs of condition B.

III. Results

The data from six experimental sessions were pooled separately for each subject and for each of the conditions A, B, and C. In assessing the differential effects of the distributions J and L the data from subjects 1, 2, and 3 and from subjects 4, 5, and 6 were grouped. These grouped data were analyzed using the following:

1. *Analysis of variance on the simple RT data from condition A.* Here the three factors were the subjects (S), the presence of the signal (E), and the foreperiod (T) with 3, 2, and 4 levels, respectively, and the analysis was done on the mean RT for each combination of factor levels.

2. *Analysis of variance on the detection RT data from condition B.* Here the three factors were the subjects, the response type (R) and the foreperiod with 3, 4, and 4 levels, respectively, and the analysis was also done on the mean RT for each combination of factor levels.

3. *Analysis of variance on the detection rates from condition B.* Here the three factors were the subjects, the presence of the signal, and the foreperiod, and the analysis was done on the frequencies of the Yes response for each combination of factor levels.

The grouped data are also presented graphically.

A. SIMPLE REACTION TIME

The analysis of variance of the data from distribution J yielded significant F ratios for all three main factors, $S, E(p < .01)$, and $T(p < .01)$ and nonsignificant first-order interactions. The data, averaged over subjects 1, 2, and 3 are plotted in Fig. 1.

For distribution L the analysis of variance yielded significant F ratios for S and T $(p < .01)$ only. The data, averaged over subjects 4, 5, and 6 are plotted in Fig. 1. For both distributions, the RT-foreperiod curves decrease on the average the decrease being more marked in distribution J. The average RT for J and L are 294 and 255 msec, respectively.

B. DETECTION REACTION TIME

The analysis of variance of the data from distribution J yielded significant F ratios for $S, R(p < .001)$, and $S \times R$ $(p < .01)$ only. An inspection of the data shows that the $S \times R$ interaction is due to between-subject variability in the difference between correct "yes" and correct "no" RTs and in the difference between incorrect "yes" and incorrect "no" RTs. For all three

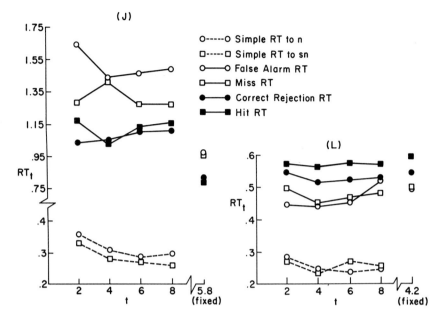

Fig. 1. Simple and Detection RT under *J* and *L* (unit of time = 1 sec).

subjects, the RTs conditional on a response are faster for correct than for incorrect responses. This last inequality will be treated as most important for the purpose of interpreting the data, so that there will be no need to consider the $S \times R$ interaction in our arguments. These data, averaged over the subjects, are presented in Fig. 1 along with the averaged data from condition C, where the foreperiod was constant at 5.8 sec. Again in condition C it will be noticed that correct RTs are faster than incorrect RTs, though the difference is smaller and the responses are faster than in condition B.

The data from distribution *L* are plotted in Fig. 1. Here the correct RTs are slower than the incorrect RTs, with the RT for each of the four response categories being approximately the same in condition C as in condition B across all foreperiod values.

C. DETECTION PROBABILITIES

The arcsine transformation was applied to the frequencies of "yes" responses in condition B and the analysis of variance was done on these transformed values. If the analysis were performed on the untransformed values, the sources of variation could be related to the concepts of *sensitivity* and *bias* as follows. Let p_{FA} and p_H denote the false alarm and hit rates at a given foreperiod value. Since noise and signal plus noise are equally likely, the probability of a "yes" response, Pr(yes), and of a correct response, Pr (correct), are given by

$$Pr(yes) = \tfrac{1}{2}(p_H + p_{FA})$$

and $$Pr(correct) = \tfrac{1}{2}p_H + \tfrac{1}{2}(1 - p_{FA})$$
$$= \tfrac{1}{2}(p_H - p_{FA}) + \tfrac{1}{2}.$$

The probability of a "yes" response is monotonically related to bias, as this concept is defined in the popular models of signal detection, for example, the theory of signal detectability and Luce's choice theory (1959), and Pr (correct) is monotonically related to sensitivity when bias is constant. Therefore, Pr (yes) is a measure of bias, and, if it is constant over a set of conditions, it would appropriate to regard Pr (correct) as a measure of sensitivity for these conditions.

The calculation of the T main effect involves summing over the two values of E, that is, computing $p_H + p_{FA}$, for each foreperiod value and then finding the variance of these sums. Therefore, a T effect can be attributed to changes in bias over the different foreperiod values. The E main effect measures the difference (squared) between p_H and p_{FA}, averaged over foreperiod values. Consequently, it measures the difference between the obtained performance level and the chance level, that is, it measures sensitivity. The $E \times T$ interaction effect measures the extent to which the difference $p_H - p_{FA}$ varies with foreperiod value, that is, the extent to which sensitivity varies with foreperiod. The other effects can be interpreted similarly, but they are not of interest here.

We shall interpret the significant effects yielded by the analysis of variance as if this analysis were performed on the untransformed values. For

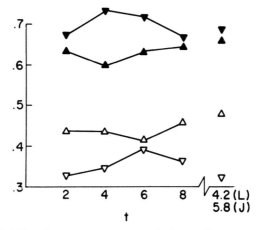

Fig. 2. Probability of a correct response and of a "yes" response under J and L; Pr (Correct), $J(\blacktriangle)$, $L(\blacktriangledown)$; Pr(Yes), $J(\triangle)$, $L(\triangledown)$.

both distributions J and L, the E effect was significant ($p < .001$), but neither the T nor the $E \times T$ effect was significant. These data, averaged over the subjects, are presented in Fig. 2, along with the data from condition C. It can be seen that, for both distributions, sensitivity is approximately constant across the foreperiod values in condition B and the fixed value in condition C; and the same is true for bias.

D. SUMMARY OF RESULTS

We will now summarize those aspects of the data that we consider relatively important:

1. There is a foreperiod effect on simple RT, the effect being larger for distribution J than for L.

2. For J only, the simple RT to the noise field is significantly slower than that to the noise plus signal field, the difference being approximately constant over the different foreperiod values.

3. There is no foreperiod effect on detection RT in condition B.

4. For distribution J, correct responses are faster than incorrect responses, whereas, for L, correct responses are slower than incorrect ones. This is true for both conditions B and C.

5. For distribution J, the RTs in condition B are slower than the RTs in condition C; the difference between the correct and incorrect RTs and that between incorrect "yes" RTs and incorrect "no" RTs are larger in condition B than the corresponding differences in condition C. For distribution L, the RTs in condition B are approximately the same as the corresponding RTs in condition C.

6. There is no foreperiod effect on sensitivity or on bias. Further, the values of the relevant parameters are approximately the same in condition B as in condition C.

IV. Theoretical Considerations in Interpreting the Data

A. EXPECTANCY EFFECTS ON REACTION TIME

It was argued in the first section that the effect of expectancy has at least two component effects: one due to the mean of the foreperiod distribution $E(t)$ (possibly degenerate) and the other due to the changes in the conditional probability of signal occurrence over the waiting period. The data used in this argument were derived from simple RT experiments. It will be convenient for us to suppose that responding to a stimulus involves at least three stages (in the sense of Sternberg, 1969): an input stage in which sensory information is encoded, a decision-making stage in which the encoded information is processed to determine whether or what responding should occur, and a response execution stage in which the appropriate motor responses are made. In the author's view, in the simple reaction task, which typically employs one suprathreshold stimulus and one response, the sensory input to be encoded is minimal and the decision-making stage is virtually eliminated. Therefore, it is felt that the expectancy effects observed in this task are effects on the response execution stage. It is now of interest to inquire whether expectancy effects remain qualitatively the same when the time taken to complete either or both of the first two stages is not negligible. Such would seem to be the case when there are two or more possible stimuli that are confusable, one with another, and when a different response is required for each stimulus.

The data yielded by the present experiment provide some answers to these questions. First, RT_t for detection appears to be independent of t, suggesting that for detection responses, unlike simple reactions, conditional probability does not affect response speed "locally," that is, differentially at the different foreperiods. Second, the fact that, for distribution J but not L, the RT in condition B is larger than that in condition C suggests that there *is* an effect of conditional probability, but that this effect is "global," probably a function of $E(p_t^{-1})$. This difference in RT cannot be attributed to the difference in mean foreperiod $E(t)$ since this is the same in conditions B and C. Third, the large difference in RT for condition C between the J and L distributions suggests that there is a mean foreperiod effect on detection responses. Fourth, the difference in simple RT to the noise and to the noise plus signal field appears to be an expectancy effect on the input stage because the difference is constant over foreperiods. It is not clear whether this effect is due to $E(t)$ or $E(p_t^{-1})$ since these two factors are confounded in distribution J. In sum, it appears that expectancy effects are qualitatively the same on detection RT as on simple RT, except that the conditional probability effect is not reflected in the RT–foreperiod curve for detection RT as it is for simple RT. These comparisons are summarized in Table 2.

In discussing the expectancy effect on detection responses no mention was made of the response process as one that determines the *accuracy* of a response. The fact that sensitivity and bias are approximately equal in conditions B and C suggests that expectancy induces a lengthening of RT in order that some predetermined error rate not be exceeded. This suggestion is the basis for a speed–accuracy model, which we now outline.

B. Speed and Accuracy as a Function of Information Quality

We will be concerned here with the input and decision-making stages of performance, and we will use two familiar concepts, the quality of sensory information and the speed-accuracy operating characteristic (OC). The

Table 2. *Components of the Expectancy Effect on Stages of Information Processing*

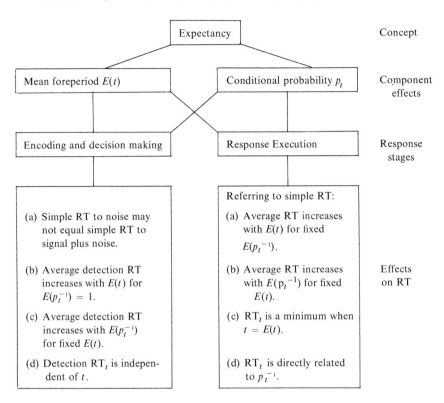

first was used by Audley and Mercer (1968) to account for the monotonic relationship between the latency and probability of response, and the second was used by Pachella and Pew (1968). The three main assumptions about these concepts are:

Assumption 1. The quality of sensory information varies randomly from trial to trial and expectancy effects on information processing time are due to changes in the quality of sensory information to be processed, greater expectancy leading to better quality.

Assumption 2. For each level of information quality there is a unique speed–accuracy OC, that is, a plot of Pr(correct) against processing time. For a given processing time, Pr(correct) increases monotonically with information quality.

Assumption 3. A speed–accuracy OC reaches its asymptote at a finite value of RT, and the asymptotic Pr(correct) is a strictly increasing function of information quality.

We also need an additional assumption about response strategy.

Assumption 4.   The subject attempts to maintain a preferred level of accuracy over changes in information quality.

From these assumptions we can make two remarks about the case where the preferred level of accuracy is intermediate, for example, 0.7.

Remark 1.   When the quality of information is high on the average, and varies little from trial to trial, the speed–accuracy relationship is determined by a speed–accuracy OC, and correct responses will be slower than incorrect responses.

Let us consider only those trials on which the (high) quality of information corresponds to the speed–accuracy OC, *AP*, shown in Fig. 3, and let $P^* = [T(P, \alpha), \alpha]$ be the point on this OC, where α is the preferred level of accuracy and $T(P, \alpha)$ is the corresponding RT. Then only on those trials where RT is less than $T(P, \alpha)$ will the Pr(correct) be less than α, from which it follows that correct responses will be slower than incorrect ones.

Remark 2.   When the quality of information is low on the average, and varies substantially from trial to trial, the speed–accuracy relationship is determined by the locus, *BPQRA*, of RTs at which the speed–accuracy OCs reach their respective asymptotes, and correct responses will be faster than incorrect responses.

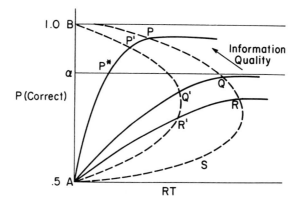

Fig. 3.   Speed–accuracy operating characteristics for different levels of quality of sensory information.

When the quality of information is low on the average, there will be trials on which the quality is such that the corresponding OCs lie uniformly below the line Pr(correct) = α, for example, AQ. Given the OC, AQ, and α, the optimal operating point is clearly Q since further processing does not improve accuracy. For these trials then the operating points will lie on $BPQRA$, and longer RTs will correspond to lower levels of accuracy.

These remarks concerning the speed-accuracy relationships in the data can be sharpened by taking account of the two sources of variability that we have introduced. The first source is the variance (v^2) of the operating point on a single OC, this variance corresponding to RT variability conditional on quality of information. The second source is the variability of information quality, and hence of OC, within a block of trials, this variability inducing a variance (w^2) of, for example, P on $BPQRA$ or P^* on the line Pr(correct) = α. Then we can restate Remarks 1 and 2 as follows:

Remark 1a. When the quality of information is high on the average and v^2 is large relative to w^2, the operating points will lie close to the OC corresponding to the modal information quality, and correct responses will be slower than incorrect ones.

Remark 2a. When the quality of information is low on the average and w^2 is large relative to v^2, the operating points lie close to $BPQRA$, and correct responses will be faster than incorrect ones.

We now can account for the results 4–6 in Section III,D by assuming that for distribution L the operating points are close to P^* in conditions B and C, whereas for distribution J, the operating points are close to Q in condition C and to R in condition B. Note that this would predict that for J the sensitivity in condition B would be less than that in condition C, a prediction not violated by the data in Fig. 2.

Alternatively, we can replace Assumption 4 by the following:

Assumption 4′. For each level of information quality, that is, for each OC, there is a preferred operating point.

If we let $B'P'Q'R'A$ denote the locus of these preferred operating points, and w'^2 denote the variance on this locus, we can argue as in Remarks 1a and 2a to reach the same conclusions.

It now remains for us to consider ways in which the strategies implied above, particularly in Assumptions 4 and 4′ and Remark 2, may be effected in practice. We can conceive of the decision-making mechanism as a non-stationary, sequential device which takes discrete samples from the memory trace of the stimulus. The decision time is determined by the number of samples taken, and the response corresponds to the stimulus which is most likely to have produced the observed sample values. Let us further suppose that each sample has two attributes, a *direction*, which is the stimulus most likely to have produced it, and a *weight*, which is the posterior probability of the most likely stimulus. The weight is assumed to depend on the quality of sensory input. For example, if the sample is a log-likelihood ratio in favor of signal plus noise over noise, the sign of the sample determines the more likely stimulus (direction) and the absolute magnitude determines the posterior probability (weight). The nonstationarity of the sampling device follows from the assumption that the sample weight decreases on the average as more samples are taken. Then we can suppose that sampling stops as soon as, or before, successive sample weights fall below a pre-determined criterion. Thus, this criterion as applied to the sample weight sets an upper limit to the decision time. When the information quality is high, the limit may not be reached, but in Remark 2 and in Assumption 4' the assumption is that it is reached when the information quality is low.

It should be noted that the above model does not presuppose that the subject has any capabilities other than those of computing the direction and weight of a sample. These are capabilities that seem necessary if stimulus-based decisions are to be made.

V. Concluding Remarks

In the simple reaction task one might say that increased expectancy corresponds to an increased bias for responding over not responding. In the choice reaction task, if one were to assume that the preparedness to make a given response would be reduced if there are other responses for which the subject should prepare equally, the response uncertainty in the task would seem to limit possible increases in the bias for responding over not responding. It would follow that the foreperiod effects evident in simple reaction time would be attenuated when one considers choice reaction time. This may account for the absence of foreperiod effects in the detection times obtained in the present experiment.

The finding that there is no foreperiod effect on bias is not surprising since, although the conditional probability of a stimulus varies with the foreperiod, the probability of signal plus noise given a stimulus is .5 for all t. However, the independence of sensitivity from foreperiod is surprising. A possible explanation, suggested by Saul Sternberg, is that because of the "long" display time (100 msec) and the efficiency of visual memory a subject does not have to attend to a stimulus at the exact moment of pre-sentation in order to identify it accurately, so that expectancy effects would be masked. Because of this possibility it might have been better to have used a task in which the subject had to attend to the stimulus when it was presented in order to be accurate; failure to do this would lead to a reduction in the quality of sensory information.

The theory presented in the previous section to account for the speed–accuracy relationships in the data is an *ad hoc* theory, and remains to be tested rigorously by data from further experimentation. The major assumption to be tested is that expectancy is related directly to quality of sensory information. At present the theory provides a framework for accounting for qualitatively different modes of responding, namely, correct responses being faster or slower than incorrect responses. The prediction is that when the preferred level of accuracy is intermediate, correct responses are slower than incorrect ones when the average quality of information is very high *or* very low (for example, when the operating points are near *S* in Fig. 3). When the average quality of information is intermediate, correct responses are faster than incorrect ones. An implicit assumption is that the preferred level of accuracy is distinct from the observed level of accuracy, but that it can be estimated from the levels of accuracy observed under conditions of little or no time uncertainty.

The notion of expectancy has had to be fortified by the notions of quality of information and speed–accuracy operating characteristic before it could account for the data. The question arises, therefore, as to whether there is much value in retaining expectancy as an explanatory concept. It is felt that the notion is still a useful one, if only because it suggests another experiment for testing the theory presented in the previous section. This experiment, in which condition C is replicated for different values of the (constant) foreperiod, is now in progress.

Acknowledgments

It is a pleasure for me to thank Miss Lillian Chappell for conducting the experiment and for her generous help in preparing the manuscript. I also wish to acknowledge the help of Mr. Alan Purdy in programming the experiment, and the helpful comments of Professor R. J. Audley. The work reported here was supported by a Faculty Research Grant from the University of Michigan.

References

Audley, R. J., & Mercer, A. The relation between decision time and relative response frequency in a blue-green discrimination. *British Journal of Mathematical and Statistical Psychology*, 1968, **21**, 183–92.

Broadbent, D. E. *Decision and stress.* New York: Academic Press, 1971.

Luce, R. D. *Individual choice behavior.* New York: Wiley, 1959.

Luce, R. D., & Green, D. M. Detection of auditory signals presented at random times II. *Perception and Psychophysics*, 1970, **7**, 1–14.

Mowrer, O. H. Preparatory set—Some methods of measurement. *Psychological Review Monograph*, 1940, No. 52.

Näätänen, R. The diminishing time-uncertainity with the lapse of time after the warning signal in reaction-time experiments with varying fore-periods. *Acta Psychologica*, 1970, **34**, 399–419.

Pachella, R. G., & Pew, R. W. Speed–accuracy trade off in reaction time: Effect of discrete criterion times. *Journal of Experimental Psychology*, 1968, **76**, 19–24.

Sternberg, S. The discovery of processing stages: Extensions of Donders' method. In W. G. Koster (Ed.), *Attention and Performance II. Acta Psychologica*, 1969, **30**, 276–315.

Thomas, E. A. C. On expectancy and average reaction time. *British Journal of Psychology*, 1970, **61**, 33–38.

7 PERCEPTION OF TEMPORAL ORDER

The Perception of Temporal Order:
Fundamental Issues and a General Model[1]

Saul Sternberg   Ronald L. Knoll

Bell Laboratories
Murray Hill, New Jersey

Dedicated to
the Memory of
Robert R. Bush

ABSTRACT

How do people judge the order of two nearly simultaneous stimuli, such as a light and a tone? We consider this question in the context of a general independent-channels model that incorporates most existing models of order perception as special cases, and which has been implicitly assumed when temporal-order judgments are used to study perceptual latency. In the model, a "decision function" converts a difference in central "arrival times" of two sensory signals into an order judgment. The psychometric function for order is regarded as a distribution function, and can be represented additively in terms of the central arrival latencies and the decision function. Various distinct decision functions correspond to various previously proposed mechanisms involving a "perceptual moment," attention switching, a threshold for arrival-time differences, and so forth (Section II).

One test of the model is to compare reaction-time measurements with order judgments (Section III). Discrepancies can be understood by an analysis of the concept of perceptual latency that recognizes the internal response to a pulse as being spread out in time (Section IV).

---

[1]A glossary of symbols and abbreviations may be found at the end of the text.

An alternative test is to determine whether experimental factors that influence two signal channels selectively have additive effects on the mean, variance, and higher cumulants of the psychometric function for order, as the general model implies. Some data confirm the model when examined in this way, but others do not. We consider extensions of the model from order judgments to other perceptual domains in which the relative arrival time of a pair of signals is thought to determine the percept. An additivity test applied to binaural lateralization favors extending the model to that phenomenon, and suggests a new method for tracing information flow in sensory channels by analyzing time-intensity trading relations at different "levels." Such an analysis reveals different effects of stimulus intensity on latency for different visual tasks, and leads to speculations about the locus of stereoscopic depth perception in relation to other processes (Section V).

The influence of attentional bias on the point of subjective simultaneity makes tests of the model difficult. However, the model suggests how to study this "prior-entry" phenomenon and determine whether attention influences the sensory channels or the decision mechanism (Section VI).

Implications of transitivity of perceived order are examined, particularly in relation to the idea of a single multisensory "simultaneity center" in the brain; some experimental tests of transitivity are reviewed (Section VIII).

The problem of perceived order of three or more stimuli bears on several important questions, including transitivity. But existing experiments with multiple stimuli shed little light on these issues (Section IX).

Several aspects of experimental method are considered (Section X).

I. Introduction

That the perceived temporal order of a pair of stimuli might not correspond to their actual order had already been recognized when experimental psychology began, and the source of errors in judgments of order and simultaneity is one of the oldest of our unsolved problems. Since the work of Bessel and other 19th century scientists, it has been known that observers differ systematically, that objectively simultaneous stimuli may consistently fail to be subjectively simultaneous, and that there are variations from one judgment to the next of the same pair of stimuli (Sanford, 1888; Dunlap, 1910).

Although the mechanisms responsible for these effects are not yet well understood, experiments involving judgments of temporal order or simultaneity have nonetheless been used to attack problems in fields that range from sensory mechanisms to psycholinguistics, including, for example, the dependence of sensory latency on stimulus intensity (Roufs, 1963), identification of speech sounds (Liberman, Harris, Kinney, & Lane, 1961), lateralization of function in the cerebral hemispheres (Kappauf & Yeatman, 1970), duration of visual images (Sperling, 1967), selective attention (Stone, 1926), comprehension of sentences (Reber & Anderson, 1970), perception of melodic lines (Bregman & Campbell, 1971), and the nature of aphasia (Efron, 1963c).

The systematic difference between objective and subjective simultaneity of a pair of stimuli can be indexed by the physical time difference necessary for the pair to appear simultaneous, or for the two possible orders to be reported with equal frequency. This *constant error* is usually attributed to differences between the times taken by signals representing the two stimuli to arrive at the place in the brain where their order is judged. These *arrival latencies* reflect detection and transmission delays that are not compensated for in perception and that may vary with attributes of the stimuli such as their intensities.

Arrival latencies must have some variability, which would limit the precision of temporal-order judgments (TOJs). (By "precision" we mean the sensitivity of judgment probabilities to changes in the interstimulus interval.) One of the reasons for an interest in the TOJ in its own right rather than only as a measure of mean latency differences, however, is the possibility that for many stimulus combinations, the precision of TOJs is controlled and limited primarily by variability of a central mechanism, rather than by variability within particular sensory channels (for example, Hirsh & Sherrick, 1961; Kristofferson, 1963).

A. EXPERIMENTAL PARADIGM

Much of this paper is concerned with experiments that use variations of the TOJ paradigm shown in Fig. 1. The stimuli are S_x, presented at time t_x, and S_y, presented at time t_y. From trial to trial the time difference $t_y - t_x = d(x,y)$ takes on various values that can be positive, zero, or negative. After each presentation the subject judges whether S_x appeared to occur before S_y (response "$t_x < t_y$") or after S_y.[2] In this way a psychometric function $F(d)$ is generated, in which the probability of the judgment that S_x preceded S_y increases monotonically with d over a range from zero to one.

It is convenient to regard $F(d)$ as the (cumulative) distribution function of a random variable, $\mathbf{D}(x, y)$, defined such that

$$F(d) \equiv \Pr\{``t_x < t_y"| d(x, y) = d\} \equiv \Pr\{\mathbf{D}(x, y) \leq d\}. \tag{1}$$

[We shall show in Section II how $\mathbf{D}(x, y)$ may be usefully represented in terms of other variables.] Two parameters of $F(d)$ are usually of interest.

---

[2] In terms of traditional psychophysics this is the "method of single stimuli," the "stimulus" on each trial being the time interval $d(x, y)$.

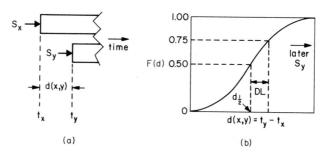

Fig. 1. Stimulus presentation and idealized data from a temporal-order experiment. (a) On each trial stimuli S_x and S_y are presented at times t_x and t_y to sensory channels x and y, respectively; the subject judges which stimulus appeared to occur first. Time proceeds from left to right. Rectangles indicate stimulus processing by channels; their left edges represent stimulus-presentation times. (b) Psychometric function relating d, the stimulation-time difference, to $F(d) \equiv \Pr\{"t_x < t_y" | d(x, y) = d\}$, the probability that S_x appears to occur before S_y.

One is the *point of subjective simultaneity* (PSS), often taken to be the 50% point: the value of $d(x, y) = d_{1/2}$ such that $F(d_{1/2}) = \frac{1}{2}$ and the two possible TOJs are equally likely.[3] [The quantity $d_{1/2}$ is the median of the **D** distribution; it will later be useful to consider the mean $d_\mu = E(\mathbf{D})$ as an alternative measure of the simultaneity point.] In general, the PSS differs from the *point of objective simultaneity* ($d = 0$). A second parameter of $F(d)$ is an index of its slope, such as the *difference threshold* [DL $\equiv \frac{1}{2}(d_{3/4} - d_{1/4})$], which can be regarded as half of the interquartile range of **D**—a measure of its dispersion. The greater the precision of judgment, or temporal resolution, the smaller is the DL. (The probability of a *correct* TOJ for a particular d-value is not a useful characterization of performance in this kind of experiment, because it depends on both the PSS and the precision of judgment; see Section X,E.)

B. EVIDENCE FOR A CENTRAL TIMING MECHANISM

One source of evidence for a central mechanism that controls the precision of TOJs is Hirsh's seminal research of a decade ago (Hirsh, 1959;

---

[3]It is worth noting that under this definition stimuli at the PSS need not necessarily give rise to a perception of simultaneity. If the required judgment was of simultaneity *versus* successiveness, rather than of one order *versus* the other, it is possible (but not necessary) that $\Pr\{"simultaneous"\}$ would be maximized for the d value that produced maximum uncertainty about order. It is also possible that for a particular stimulus pair no d value would make $\Pr\{"simultaneous"\}$ large.

Hirsh & Sherrick, 1961). These remarkable experiments showed that, with few exceptions, stimulus pairs from the same sensory modality—auditory, visual, or tactile—or from any of the three possible modality pairs give rise to TOJs of approximately the same precision. In most cases a DL $\simeq$ 18 msec was observed. An increase in d of about 80 msec produced a change from a reliable perception of S_y first [$F(d) \simeq 0$] to a reliable perception of S_x first [$F(d) \simeq 1$]. Hirsh has stressed the fact that the time separation required to resolve two identical stimuli as successive, which shows large intersensory differences as conventionally measured, is far smaller than this d-value difference.

Some aspects of Hirsh's findings now appear to depend on details of his method (see Section X), but it is fair to say that his conclusion still stands that, with few exceptions, variations in modalities and attributes of the stimuli in a pair have relatively small effects on the precision of judgments of their temporal order. This led Hirsh to conclude that the precision is limited primarily by a central mechanism serving several modalities, rather than by the sensory channels themselves.

The exceptions we know of—cases where the order of stimulus pairs with substantially smaller separations can be reliably discriminated— seem to be attributable to special modality-specific mechanisms in which stimuli interact close to the periphery, thereby generating special cues correlated with their temporal order.[4] In these cases higher centers receive signals representing the *relation* of the two stimuli, rather than only *separate* representations of the stimuli themselves. These exceptions suggest that in experiments addressed to study of the conjectured central mechanism, pairs of stimuli from different modalities should be used, to insure against contamination by peripheral sensory interactions.

---

[4]One interesting example arises when two clicks are delivered to different ears. When the time separation is small enough (≤ 2 msec, approximately) so that a fused image is perceived, the location of the image in the head depends on temporal order; under these conditions order can be reliably discriminated with time separations as small as .1 msec (Green & Henning, 1969). Because the lateralization of dichotic clicks depends on their being close in time, the lateralization phenomenon would cause the psychometric function for temporal order to be nonmonotone, rising steeply near zero and then falling before rising again when $d \simeq 15$ msec (Babkoff & Sutton, 1963). Such nonmonotone functions have also been observed for pairs of monaural clicks, with minima at about 10 msec $< d <$ 15 msec, and used as evidence for the existence of peripheral stimulus interactions which presumably influence the perceived quality of the composite stimulus (Babkoff & Sutton, 1971). Non-monotone functions raise questions about the usefulness of a concept of "temporal acuity" (White & Lichtenstein, 1963). For other examples that suggest special mechanisms, see Liberman et al. (1961), Békésy (1963), Békésy (1969), Biederman-Thorson et al. (1971), and Green (1971).

Several other kinds of evidence, in addition to Hirsh's, have been adduced for a central timing mechanism. For example, Cheatham and White have shown that regardless of sensory modality, the maximum rate at which judged numerosity increases with the duration of fast trains of identical pulsed stimuli is approximately the same (see White, 1963).[5] Eijkman and Vendrik (1965) showed that duration discrimination of filled intervals is no better when the interval is defined by two concurrent stimuli in different sensory modalities than when it is defined by a single stimulus; if a large proportion of the judgmental variability resulted from "noise" that was associated with independent sensory channels rather than with a central mechanism, one would expect averaging in the two-stimulus condition to increase discriminability. Kristofferson (1967b) has found a strong relation between the half-periods of subjects' alpha rhythms and their ability to discriminate temporal differences between bisensory stimulus pairs.

A common view is that for the time relation between two signals to be judged, their representations must be brought together somewhere in the brain. Efron (1963a, b) and Corwin and Boynton (1968) have argued from their data that there is a common "simultaneity center" for all stimulus pairs, possibly located in the dominant hemisphere. This view develops the idea of a central mechanism one step further—from a common process to one that also has a common locus.

What might limit the time resolution of a central mechanism? One possible explanation is that attention cannot be divided between sensory channels, and that during any one time period, information from only one channel can be admitted. Exact time information for signals that arrive on unattended channels would be lost. Together with assumed constraints on when attention can be switched from one channel to another, these ideas form the basis of Kristofferson's (1963, 1967a, b, 1970, this volume) account of successiveness discrimination and several other phenomena.

A second explanation of limited time resolution is that for the central processor, time is quantized into periodic samples, or perceptual "moments" (Stroud, 1955). Signals arriving at the central processor through different channels can always be admitted, but if they arrive during the same moment their order cannot be discriminated.

Although the search for a central timing mechanism has motivated some of the workers in this area, others have used the measurement of temporal-order perception as a tool in the study of individual sensory

---

[5] Recently, however, John (1971) has raised some questions about the interpretation of these studies, based partly on his demonstration of the dependence of auditory-numerosity judgments on stimulus intensity.

systems, in particular, to measure variations in sensory latency. This work has focused mainly on changes induced in the PSS by changes in one of the stimuli, which are taken to reflect corresponding changes in its arrival latency. Most of it has not been concerned with the DL and the question of temporal resolution. But Rutschmann and Baron have tested the idea that the central mechanism has perfect resolution, and that order discrimination is imperfect solely because of the variability of sensory arrival times (Baron, 1969; Gibbon & Rutschmann, 1969; Rutschmann & Link, 1964; Rutschmann, 1967, 1969).

The independent-channels model that we shall be discussing in much of this paper is a generalization of all the models of order perception we know of, and permits variability both in the channels and in the central mechanism. One of our goals in the present paper is to explore two issues in light of this general model. First, how can we use TOJs to answer questions about the channels, while making minimal commitment to a model of the central decision mechanism? Second, how can we use TOJs to answer questions about the decision mechanism, with minimal assumptions about the channels?

II. Independent-Channels Model

A. The General Model

Many of the models of TOJs that have been proposed explicitly or assumed implicitly are special cases of the general *independent-channels model* shown in Fig. 2. Stimuli S_x and S_y are presented at times t_x and t_y, where $t_y = t_x + d$. After an *arrival latency*, represented by the random variable $\mathbf{R}_x$, stimulus S_x has been detected, and a signal has been transmitted to an appropriate place in the brain, its *arrival time* being $\mathbf{U}_x = \mathbf{R}_x + t_x$. The same is true for stimulus S_y; because S_y is presented at time $t_x + d$, its arrival time is given by $\mathbf{U}_y = \mathbf{R}_y + t_y = \mathbf{R}_y + t_x + d$. The detection and transmission operations are performed by the relevant sensory channel; arrival latencies depend on stimulus attributes and possibly also on adjustable detection criteria. The TOJ depends on the *arrival-time difference* $\mathbf{U}_y - \mathbf{U}_x = \mathbf{R}_y - \mathbf{R}_x + d$, according to some *decision rule*. Stimulus attributes and the value of d do not influence the decision directly, but only indirectly by virtue of their effects on the arrival times. The decision rule induces a *decision function* G on values of $\mathbf{U}_y - \mathbf{U}_x$, associating an order-decision probability with each arrival-time difference such that for any value of d,

$$\Pr\{``t_x < t_y"\,|\,\mathbf{U}_x = U_x, \mathbf{U}_y = U_y\} \equiv G(U_y - U_x). \tag{2}$$

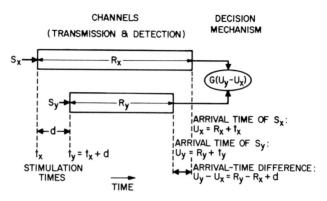

Fig. 2. Independent-channels model. Stimulus times are represented by positions of the left sides of the two boxes on a left–right time axis. Lengths of the boxes represent arrival latencies, that is, duration of the sensory transmission and detection processes on which the decision mechanism depends. The positions of the right sides represent arrival times used by the decision mechanism.

It follows that

$$F(d) \equiv \Pr\{``t_x < t_y"|d(x,y) = d\} = E\,[G(U_y - U_x)|d(x,y) = d], \quad (3)$$

where the expectation is taken over the joint distribution of U_x and U_y. We assume that G is a nondecreasing function of the arrival-time difference; this seems to exclude only those unusual cases (Section I, B) where different decision mechanisms operate at different parts of the $U_y - U_x$ range.

The sensory channels are assumed to be separate, or independent, in the sense that activity in one channel is not influenced by *what* activity occurs in the other, or by *when* it occurs. Thus, neither $\mathbf{R}_x$ nor $\mathbf{R}_y$ is influenced by the value of d, and a change in one (resulting, for example, from a change in attributes of one stimulus) has no influence on the other. One implication is that $\mathbf{R}_x$ and $\mathbf{R}_y$ are *independent in mean*: changes in one have no direct influence on the mean of the other. Given no spurious correlation of $\mathbf{R}_x$ and $\mathbf{R}_y$ (which might be caused, for example, by overall fluctuations in sensitivity or by spontaneous fluctuations in the direction of attention), it also follows that $\mathbf{R}_x$ and $\mathbf{R}_y$ are *stochastically independent*.[6] (The inferences made in all the studies we know of in which the PSS is used to measure effects of stimulus variations on sensory latency require the assumption of independence in

---

[6]Since the first kind of independence can occur without the second, it is desirable to consider them separately, just as in the case of the additive durations of processing stages (Sternberg, 1969a).

mean. They also require an *assumption of selective influence* of stimuli on channels: changes in S_x influence only $\mathbf{R}_x$ and not $\mathbf{R}_y$.)

We have deliberately avoided a precise definition of "channels," since it is not yet clear what definition would be most useful. One criterion might be the independence property of the general model: two stimuli would be associated with different channels if their arrival latencies are independent. (Channels probably would not then be identified with sensory modalities.) Such a criterion should be distinguished from one based on attentional selectivity, such as Kristofferson's (1967a), where stimuli are associated with different channels if and only if they cannot be attended to simultaneously.

B. ADDITIVE REPRESENTATION OF THE PSYCHOMETRIC FUNCTION FOR THE DETERMINISTIC DECISION RULE

According to the *deterministic decision rule*, the subject reports S_x before S_y if and only if the S_x signal arrives at the decision mechanism before the S_y signal. The decision function is the step function

$$G(U_y - U_x) \equiv \begin{cases} 0, & U_y - U_x < 0 \\ 1, & U_y - U_x \geq 0. \end{cases} \tag{4}$$

The discrimination of *arrival times* is thus perfect and unbiased; the limited precision of order judgments arises solely from variability of $\mathbf{R}_x$ and $\mathbf{R}_y$. This model has been used extensively by Rutschmann (for example, this volume) and by Baron (1969). From Eq. (3) and definition (4) it follows that

$$F(d) = \Pr\{0 \leq U_y - U_x | d(x, y) = d\}$$
$$= \Pr\{0 \leq \mathbf{R}_y - \mathbf{R}_x + d\}.$$

Using Eq. (1) we can express the psychometric function F—the distribution function of $\mathbf{D}(x, y)$—in terms of $\mathbf{R}_x$ and $\mathbf{R}_y$:

$$F(d) \equiv \Pr\{\mathbf{D}(x, y) \leq d\} = \Pr\{\mathbf{R}_x - \mathbf{R}_y \leq d\}. \tag{5}$$

This relation permits us to define the following additive representation of $\mathbf{D}(x, y)$:

$$\mathbf{D}(x, y) = \mathbf{R}_x - \mathbf{R}_y. \tag{6}$$

In short, the psychometric function is identical with the distribution function of the arrival-latency difference between channels.[7]

---

[7]This relation was used by Rutschmann and Link (1964) and Gibbon and Rutschmann (1969). The generalization to an arbitrary criterion β on the arrival-time difference is straightforward: if "$t_x < t_y$" requires $U_y - U_x \geq \beta$, then Eq. (6) becomes $\mathbf{D}(x, y) = \mathbf{R}_x - \mathbf{R}_y + \beta$.

C. Six Models of the Decision Mechanism

Model 1. The deterministic decision rule discussed above is only one of many interesting rules for converting arrival-time differences into responses. Six decision functions G, corresponding to six different decision rules, are shown in Fig. 3.

Model 2. In one variety of *perceptual-moment* theory (Stroud, 1955), time is partitioned into nonoverlapping equal intervals (moments), and two arrivals can be ordered by the decision mechanism only if they fall in different moments. The stimulus pair is assumed to occur at random relative to the phase of the moment train. The probability that a boundary between moments falls between the arrivals increases linearly with the arrival-time difference, up to the duration τ of one moment. If $|U_y - U_x| > \tau$, discrimination is guaranteed, regardless of phase. If we assume that when both arrivals occur during the same moment the two order judgments are equiprobable, the result is a linear decision function that is symmetric about zero (Fig. 3b).

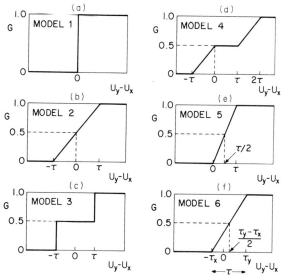

Fig. 3. Decision functions produced by six models of the decision mechanism. (a) Deterministic-decision model. (b) Perceptual-moment model with moment of duration τ. (c) Threshold model with threshold of size τ. (d) Triggered attention-switching model with three states, potential switching points separated by time τ, and attention initially biased toward channel y. (e) Triggered attention-switching model with four states, and attention initially biased toward channel y. (f) Periodic-sampling model with period $\tau = \tau_x + \tau_y$. For any model, the psychometric function depends on the arrival-latency distributions as well as the decision function.

Model 3. The function shown in Fig. 3c is produced when a *threshold* of size τ is applied to the arrival-time difference. If $|U_y - U_x| < \tau$, there is no discrimination and the two judgments are equiprobable.[8] Such a decision function has been considered by Baron(1970,1971), and also arises from a *triggered moment* process, in which a moment of duration τ is initiated by the first signal to arrive (Venables, 1960; Oatley, Robertson, & Scanlan, 1969; Mollon, 1969).

Model 4. Although it was developed for a different experimental paradigm, Kristofferson's (1963, 1970) *triggered attention-switching* theory can be applied here also. This theory applies to pairs of stimuli that cannot be simultaneously selected by attention; the decision function it generates is shown in Fig. 3d, for the case where attention is initially directed to channel y. (For initial attention to channel x, the function is displaced to the left by an amount τ.) An attentional switch is triggered by the first signal to arrive, whichever it is, but switches can be accomplished only at a series of periodic time points with period τ. Here we assume that the switch occurs at the first such time point after the arrival. A signal *registers* only when it has arrived *and* attention is switched to its channel. For order to be discriminated, attention must be switched to each channel in turn, and the signal that registers second must arrive with some delay after attention switches to its channel. If the second registration occurs without an interval between attention switching and signal arrival, then, regardless of the registration order, the same state (perceived simultaneity) is produced, and the two TOJs are equiprobable. According to this theory, then, the pattern of registrations is partitioned into three distinguishable states. Note that this is the first decision function we have considered that is not symmetric about $U_y - U_x = 0$.

Model 5. In a *four-state triggered attention-switching* theory—a variant of Kristofferson's theory not discussed elsewhere—the judgment is the same as the registration order, whether or not the second registration occurs with an interval between attention switching and signal arrival. Figure 3e shows the resulting decision function, when attention is initially directed to channel y. Although linear, like the function generated by a perceptual moment mechanism, this function is not symmetric about zero.

---

[8]This model and some of the others can be naturally elaborated by permitting variations in "response bias" or "criterion bias" parameters. In this instance, for example, the judgment probability associated with below-threshold arrival-time differences could be an adjustable response-bias parameter. (See footnote 7 for a way to introduce criterion bias in the deterministic rule.) In the present paper the specific models are presented primarily as illustrative, and will not be elaborated in this way.

Model 6. In the final model we consider (which also is not discussed elsewhere as a basis for order judgments), the sensory channels are subject to a continual *periodic sampling* process with a fixed period. Sampling may be limited to the two channels defined by the task $(\cdots, x, y, x, y, x, \cdots)$, or may include other channels as well. Arrivals at the decision mechanism are assumed to occur at random relative to the phase of the sampling process. The arrival of a signal is registered as soon as its channel is sampled; the judged order of two signals is the same as their registration order. The location of the resulting linear decision function depends on the time τ_x from the *y*- to *x*-sampling points, and the time τ_y from the *x*- to *y*-sampling points, as shown in Fig. 3f.[9] The slope of the function is governed by the period $\tau = \tau_x + \tau_y$ of the process.

D. ADDITIVE REPRESENTATION OF THE PSYCHOMETRIC FUNCTION
    FOR THE GENERAL MODEL

For the deterministic decision rule we arrived at an additive representation of the psychometric function in terms of the arrival-latency distributions [Eq. (6)]. Here we show how this result can be extended to the probabilistic decision functions exemplified by Models 2–6.

Let G represent a general decision-function—any function of arrival-time difference that is continuous, nondecreasing, and has a range from 0 to 1. All the decision functions of Fig. 3 are special cases of this one. Because of its properties, G can be regarded as a distribution function. Define $\Delta(x,y)$ to be the random variable that corresponds to G:

$$G(v) \equiv \Pr\{\Delta(x,y) \le v\}. \tag{7}$$

From Eq. (3) and definition (7) it follows that

$$F(d) = E[\Pr\{\Delta(x,y) \le \mathbf{U}_y - \mathbf{U}_x | \mathbf{U}_x, \mathbf{U}_y, d(x,y) = d\}],$$

where the expectation is taken over the joint distribution of $\mathbf{U}_x$ and $\mathbf{U}_y$, or

$$F(d) = E[\Pr\{\Delta(x,y) \le \mathbf{R}_y - \mathbf{R}_x + d | \mathbf{R}_x, \mathbf{R}_y\}], \tag{8}$$

where the expectation is taken over the joint distribution of $\mathbf{R}_x$ and $\mathbf{R}_y$. Now, $E_B[\Pr\{\mathbf{A} \le \mathbf{B} | \mathbf{B}\}] = \Pr\{\mathbf{A} \le \mathbf{B}\}$. [This can be verified by expressing the joint distribution of $\mathbf{A}$ and $\mathbf{B}$ as the product $f(A|B)g(B)$, where f and g are density functions, and expressing the expectation as an integral.] From Eq. (8) we therefore have

---

[9]An alternative interpretation of the same model involves sampling intervals rather than sampling points, and identifies τ_x and τ_y as "dwell times" on the channels of S_x and S_y, respectively, of a periodic attentional switching process limited to these channels.

$$F(d) = \Pr\{\Delta(x, y) \le \mathbf{R}_y - \mathbf{R}_x + d\}.$$

Using Eq. (1) and rearranging terms, we arrive at an expression for the psychometric function F—the distribution of $\mathbf{D}(x,y)$—in terms of $\mathbf{R}_x$, $\mathbf{R}_y$, and $\Delta(x,y)$:

$$F(d) \equiv \Pr\{\mathbf{D}(x,y) \le d\} = \Pr\{\mathbf{R}_x - \mathbf{R}_y + \Delta(x,y) \le d\}. \tag{9}$$

If we now extend definition (7) to make $\Delta(x, y)$ stochastically independent of $\mathbf{R}_x - \mathbf{R}_y$, Eq. (9) permits us to define the following additive representation of $\mathbf{D}(x, y)$:

$$\mathbf{D}(x, y) = \mathbf{R}_x - \mathbf{R}_y + \Delta(x, y). \tag{10}$$

In short, the psychometric function for the general independent-channels model, which gives the probability of a particular TOJ as a function of d, can be expressed as the convolution of the decision function with the distribution of arrival-latency differences between channels.[10] This simple but powerful implication of the general model, expressed in Eqs. (9) and (10), forms the basis of much of the remainder of this paper.

The formulation in Eq. (10) makes it clear that the shape of the psychometric function $F(d)$ depends on both Δ (the decision mechanism) and $\mathbf{R}_x - \mathbf{R}_y$ (the channels). [Thus, measuring the shape of $F(d)$ will not permit rejection of any hypothesis about the central mechanism without *some* restrictions on $\mathbf{R}_x - \mathbf{R}_y$ being assumed.] In general, the shape will reflect most strongly whichever of the two components has the greatest variance. Two extremes are represented by the theories of Rutschmann and Kristofferson. In Rutschmann's theory (for example, Rutschmann, this volume), Δ is assumed to be a constant (zero), and it is only the latency distributions that limit precision and control the shape of $F(d)$. On the other hand, in Kristofferson's theory (1963) $\mathbf{R}_x - \mathbf{R}_y$ is assumed to be a constant for any particular pair of stimuli, and only the decision function is important.

---

[10]Some readers may find the following argument helpful in understanding the basis of Eq. (10). Consider the deterministic decision function with criterion β, as discussed in footnote 7. Any (nondecreasing) decision function $G(d)$ can be represented as a probability mixture of deterministic functions with different β values, the mixing distribution being the decision function itself. For each value of β, the $\mathbf{D}(x, y)$ distribution is obtained by translation of the $\mathbf{R}_x - \mathbf{R}_y$ distribution by an amount β. Hence, the general $\mathbf{D}(x, y)$ distribution is a probability mixture of translations of the $\mathbf{R}_x - \mathbf{R}_y$ distribution, the mixing distribution being the distribution of $\Delta(x, y)$. Now a mixture of translations of a distribution is equivalent to the convolution of that distribution with the mixing distribution. Hence, to transform the $\mathbf{R}_x - \mathbf{R}_y$ distribution into the $\mathbf{D}(x, y)$ distribution one must add to $\mathbf{R}_x - \mathbf{R}_y$ the independent random variable $\Delta(x,y)$.

Existing evidence suggests that measurable variance is contributed by both the central mechanism and the channels. The similarity of DLs for TOJs within and between various modalities (Section I,B) suggests that a common mechanism limits precision and therefore contributes variance of its own. And estimates of variance from electrophysiological measurements tend to be too small to account entirely for the DL for order (for example, Chapman, 1962; Levick & Zacks, 1970; Levick, 1972; Zacks, 1972). On the other hand, given the assumption that the central mechanism is not influenced directly by stimulus variations, the finding that intensity changes not only alter the PSS (which could occur even if R_x had zero variance) but also can produce small but systematic effects on the DL (for example, Gibbon & Rutschmann, 1969) implies that arrival-time variability plays at least some role in controlling the precision of TOJs.

At the present stage of research on order perception we feel that the primary concerns should be, first, to validate the general independent-channels model and, second, assuming its validity for particular situations, to characterize the central mechanism by determining properties of the decision function. By making specific supplementary assumptions about the distributions of R_x, R_y, and Δ, one could test the general model jointly with these assumptions. But failure of such a strong model need not invalidate the general model. For this reason we consider (in Sections III and V) tests of the general model that do not require strong distributional assumptions. For similar reasons we feel it is desirable to attempt inferences from D to Δ while invoking minimal assumptions about R_x and R_y. Examples of tests requiring no assumptions about latency distributions are described in Sections VIII and IX.[11]

---

[11]One example of a general assumption that permits inferences from D to Δ is that the distribution of $R_x - R_y$ is strongly unimodal (Ibragimov, 1956). Most widely used distributions have this property, including normal, exponential, gamma, double exponential, logistic, uniform, and triangular distributions, and the beta distribution with nonnegative parameters. The convolution of a strongly unimodal distribution with a unimodal distribution must itself be unimodal. Hence, if the psychometric function is observed to have more than one inflection point (indicating multimodality of the D distribution), the decision function must also have more than one inflection point (corresponding to multimodality of the Δ distribution); such an observation would thus permit rejection of Models 1, 2, 5, and 6 of Section II,C.

A second example of a general assumption is that the $R_x - R_y$ distribution is unimodal and symmetric about its mean. (This would be true if R_x and R_y were unimodal and identically distributed.) Because the convolution of two unimodal and symmetric distributions is itself unimodal and symmetric, a unimodal Δ distribution symmetric about its mean, as in Models 1–6, then requires the D distribution to be unimodal and symmetric about its mean.

The main technical difficulty in using measured psychometric functions in conjunction with the additive representation of Eq. (10) appears to be that whereas the psychometric function easily provides estimates of *quantiles* of the **D** distribution, such as its 50 and 75% points, the additive representation most lends itself to simple statements about the mean, variance, and higher *cumulants*[12] of that distribution (see Section X, F).

In the sections that follow we describe analyses of data from a variety of studies. The analyses emphasize predicted relations among means of psychometric functions, but not higher cumulants, since these are the easiest relations to test with available data. Our conclusions depend on the assumption that although PSSs from the studies we review were not explicitly intended as estimates of means, they are approximations thereof.[13]

III. Comparison of Order Judgments and Reaction Times to Test the Independent-Channels Model

Historically, the reaction-time (RT) experiment emerged from studies of TOJs of bisensory stimulus pairs (Boring, 1950, Chapter 8). It was believed that latencies of the same internal events contributed in both tasks, so that one task would shed light on the other. It is therefore not surprising that in one modern approach to testing the independent-channels model, TOJs of stimulus pairs are compared to RTs of simple (detection) reactions to each stimulus.

(Footnote 11–*cont.*)

An inference about Δ that requires no assumptions about the latency distributions is based on the fact that the greatest mode of a convolution of two distributions can be no greater than the greatest mode of either component. A consequence is that the maximum slope of the psychometric function provides a lower bound on the slope of a linear decision function, and on the maximum slope of any decision function.

[12]Cumulants are statistics of a distribution that are closely related to its moments and that are additive for sums of independent random variables (see Kendall & Stuart, 1958).

[13]Most studies report either 50% points of psychometric functions determined by a method of constant stimuli, or estimates derived from an up-and-down staircase procedure or a method of limits. If the psychometric function is symmetric, all three methods estimate its mean; if it is asymmetric, the estimate is biased to varying degrees away from the mean and toward the median. Our assumption would be justified if, for example, the functions were sufficiently symmetric so that the bias was small.

Unfortunately, in order to permit such tests the independent-channels model must be considerably elaborated; the tests are then not of the model alone, but of its conjunction with strong supplementary assumptions. We shall see in Section V that without this elaboration the model is nevertheless susceptible to evaluation by other methods. We discuss RT tests first, however, for historical reasons, and because they raise important questions about the concept of perceptual latency (discussed in Section IV).

Extensions of the model that underlie such tests are shown in Fig. 4. The reaction time $\mathbf{T}$ is assumed to be the sum of the arrival latency $\mathbf{R}$ that controls the TOJ and the summed duration $\mathbf{M}$ of the additional processing stages that lead to the reaction. Thus, in addition to Eq. (10), we have

$$\mathbf{T}_x = \mathbf{R}_x + \mathbf{M}_x \quad \text{and} \quad \mathbf{T}_y = \mathbf{R}_y + \mathbf{M}_y. \tag{11}$$

A. COMPARISON OF $\mathbf{D}(x, y)$ AND $\mathbf{T}_x - \mathbf{T}_y$

Tests that compare $\mathbf{D}(x, y)$ to $\mathbf{T}_x - \mathbf{T}_y$ have been conducted for visual-auditory pairs by Rutschmann and Link (1964) and for pairs of flashes by Gibbon and Rutschmann (1969). Let us first consider the comparison of means. The general idea is that the mean arrival-latency difference that causes the PSS to differ from zero will also cause the mean RTs, $E(\mathbf{T}_x)$ and $E(\mathbf{T}_y)$, to differ from each other by the same amount. Two assumptions underlie this expectation. First, the "final common path" for reactions to dif-

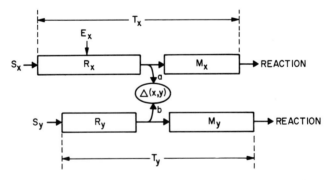

Fig. 4. Extensions of the independent-channels model that link TOJs of a stimulus pair with RTs for detection reactions to the same stimuli presented individually. The arrival time $\mathbf{R}$ is assumed to be an additive component of the reaction time $\mathbf{T}$. The summed durations of the additional stages needed for the reaction, including "motor time," are represented by $\mathbf{M}$. These additional stages are sometimes assumed to be common ($\mathbf{M}_x = \mathbf{M}_y$). Discrepancies may force relaxation of this assumption, or insertion of additional time-consuming stages at points marked a and b. An attribute of S_x, such as its intensity E_x, is shown influencing $\mathbf{R}_x$ selectively.

ferent stimuli starts at the level of the order decision; that is, the inputs to a common order-decision mechanism are the same as inputs to a common response-mechanism, and

$$E(\mathbf{M}_x) = E(\mathbf{M}_y).$$

Second, Δ is symmetric in the sense that

$$E(\Delta) = 0,$$

as in Models 1–3 of Section II,C. The result is

$$E(\mathbf{T}_x) - E(\mathbf{T}_y) = E(\mathbf{R}_x) - E(\mathbf{R}_y) = E[\mathbf{D}(x, y)] \equiv d_\mu \qquad (12)$$

In the bisensory experiment of Rutschmann and Link (1964) this test failed dramatically for both subjects: whereas the auditory $E(\mathbf{T})$ was about 45 msec shorter than the visual $E(\mathbf{T})$, the auditory stimulus had to be presented about 43 msec *earlier* than the visual to produce subjective simultaneity. Relative to Eq. (12) this represents a discrepancy of 88 msec. The discrepancy led to the conjecture that the order-decision mechanism was "further" (by 88 msec) from the auditory than from the visual channel; this corresponds to assuming an additional delay at point a or b of Fig. 4. An alternative explanation would relax the assumption that $E(\mathbf{M}_x) = E(\mathbf{M}_y)$, or the assumption that $E(\Delta) = 0$. In the flash-pair experiment of Gibbon and Rutschmann (1969), one of the two subjects showed a similar but smaller systematic discrepancy,[14] the other subject showing good agreement.

We turn now from the comparison of means to the comparison of distributions. This comparison (which also was made in both the studies cited above) tests a stronger extension of the model, involving the following further restrictions on the conditions that led to Eq. (12):

$$\Delta = 0 \qquad \text{and} \qquad \mathbf{M}_x = \mathbf{M}_y = M \text{ (a constant).} \qquad (13)$$

The first condition is equivalent to assuming the deterministic decision rule

---

[14]Let S_f be the foveal flash (left eye) and S_p be the peripheral flash (right eye). For this subject $E(\mathbf{T}_f) - E(\mathbf{T}_p) - E[\mathbf{D}(f, p)] \simeq 20$ msec, approximately independent of intensity variations in S_f. This discrepancy led Gibbon and Rutschmann (1969) to elaborate the deterministic model as in footnote 7, introducing a fixed nonzero criterion on the arrival-time difference.

The considerations that apply to such discrepancies apply also to findings like those of Halliday and Mingay (1964), who compared the difference between latency estimates of the cortical evoked potentials elicited by tactile stimulation of toe and finger to an estimate of the PSS for the same pair of stimuli, in an attempt to understand the effects of the length of conduction pathways on perceived simultaneity.

(Model 1 of Section II,C). The second asserts that all the variance in RT is due to variability in the arrival latency. The consequence is

$$\mathbf{D}(x, y) = \mathbf{T}_x - \mathbf{T}_y. \tag{14}$$

Thus, the empirical distribution function of RT differences is compared to the psychometric function. One remarkable outcome of the Gibbon and Rutschmann study is that even where these two functions differed in central tendency they agreed roughly in slope, supporting the implication from Eq. (14) that

$$\text{Var}(\mathbf{D}) = \text{Var}(\mathbf{T}_x) + \text{Var}(\mathbf{T}_y). \tag{15}$$

It should be noted, however, that Eq. (15) does not require conditions (13), but only that $\text{Var}(\Delta) = \text{Var}(\mathbf{M}_x) + \text{Var}(\mathbf{M}_y)$.

B. COMPARISON OF CHANGES IN $\mathbf{D}(x, y)$ AND $\mathbf{T}_x$: EQUALITY OF FACTOR EFFECTS

We see, then, that comparisons of $\mathbf{D}$ with $\mathbf{T}_x - \mathbf{T}_y$, even when restricted to their means, require assumptions about $\mathbf{M}_x$, $\mathbf{M}_y$, and Δ (and delays at points a and b of Fig. 4) that may be unacceptable. The failures of these comparisons suggest that either this set of supplementary assumptions, or the independent-channels model itself, is invalid. An alternative approach that links TOJs with RTs replaces the supplementary assumptions above by an *assumption of selective influence* (Sternberg, 1969b). Let E_x denote an experimentally varied attribute of S_x, such as its intensity. Assume that factor E_x influences $\mathbf{R}_x$ only—that it has no effect on $\mathbf{R}_y$ or $\Delta(x, y)$ in the TOJ, and no effect on $\mathbf{M}_x$ in the RT. The only other constraint needed is that $\mathbf{R}$ and $\mathbf{M}$ are stochastically independent.[15]

Given these assumptions, then roughly speaking any change in E_x should cause the same change in $\mathbf{T}_x$ as in $\mathbf{D}(x, y)$. That is, the effects of factor E_x on $\mathbf{T}_x$ and $\mathbf{D}(x, y)$ should be equal. Let $\mathbf{D}$, $\mathbf{D}'$ and $\mathbf{T}_x$, $\mathbf{T}_x'$ represent TOJs and RTs for E_x and E_x', respectively. Then

$$\mathbf{D} - \mathbf{D}' = \mathbf{T}_x - \mathbf{T}_x'. \tag{16}$$

Let κ_r represent the rth cumulant of a random variable (κ_1 representing the

---

[15]If this constraint is not fully satisfied, and $\mathbf{R}$ and $\mathbf{M}$ are independent in mean only, then Eqs. (16) and (17) are limited to means only.

mean, κ_2 the variance, and so forth). Equation (16) implies the equality of E_x-effects on all cumulants:

$$\kappa_r(\mathbf{D}) - \kappa_r(\mathbf{D}') = \kappa_r(\mathbf{T}_x) - \kappa_r(\mathbf{T}_x'), \qquad r = 1, 2, \dots . \qquad (17)$$

Thus, for example, a change in the PSS (measured by d_μ) induced by a change in the intensity of S_x should be the same as the change it induces in the mean RT.

There are surprisingly few studies in which both **D** and **T** have been examined for the same stimuli over a range of intensities.[16] A few tests of this kind have succeeded, the study of Roufs (1963) being perhaps the most convincing example. Roufs used onsets of 400-msec flashes, whose intensity varied over a range of two log units. He found good agreement between the effects of intensity on the PSS relative to a reference flash, and on the mean RT; both changed by about 35 msec.[17]

But there are several striking failures of such comparisons. In one study by Rutschmann (1967), where the stimuli were brief shocks to the two hands, an increase in stimulus intensity that reduced both $E(\mathbf{T})$ and $\text{Var}(\mathbf{T})$ had no systematic effect on the DL and had either no effect or an effect in the opposite direction on the PSS.[18] Sanford (1971) had subjects judge the position assumed by a rotating pointer when they detected an intensity increment of from 2 dB to 18 dB in a white noise, and also measured RTs to the same increments. Whereas the mean RT was shortened by 82 msec over this intensity range, the mean PSS changed by only 48 msec (in the appropriate direction, however).

In evaluating these apparent failures of the independent-channels model, it is important to consider the question of which RT procedure is the appropriate one, in terms of percentage of catch trials, amount of reward for speed, degree of signal uncertainty, randomized versus blocked inten-

---

[16]Numerous studies have been made of visual latency, some using TOJs and others using RT measures. Unfortunately, few studies have used both, and whereas the flashes in RT studies have usually been long, those in TOJ studies have tended to be brief. This difference may be partly responsible for the fact that the RT studies tend to reveal the larger intensity effects (see Section IV).

[17]In their comparison of the distribution functions of $\mathbf{T}_x - \mathbf{T}_y$ and $\mathbf{D}(x, y)$, Gibbon and Rutschmann (1969) used three different flash intensities, permitting comparison of interquartile ranges (related to variances) as well as 50% points or medians (approximations to means). Intensity-induced changes in medians were approximately the same, with a slight tendency for larger changes in the RT data. Changes in interquartile ranges were smaller when derived from the RT data than when observed in the psychometric function.

[18]One possible source of these puzzling findings might be stimulus interactions associated with the bilaterally symmetric cutaneous stimuli (Rutschmann, 1967). In our terms, this would mean that the two stimuli were not associated with independent channels.

sities, and the like. It has been demonstrated convincingly, at least for auditory stimuli, that the size of the intensity effect depends on such procedural variations (for example, John, 1967; Grice, 1968; Murray, 1970). Since the judgment of order requires discrimination of one stimulus from the other, the appropriateness of simple RT might be questioned. (In one promising procedure that avoids some of the difficulties in the common comparisons, an RT measurement and an order judgment are obtained on the same trial.) Finally, to assume that stimulus intensity has no effect on **M**, that is, on stages that follow the order decision, is quite possibly an error. (If **M**, as well as **R**, were reduced by increases in stimulus intensity, we would have one explanation for a larger effect of intensity on RT than on d_μ.) But it is hard to see how the most dramatic failures could be traced to issues like these. Instead one has to consider the concept of perceptual latency itself.[19]

IV. The Concept of Perceptual Latency

Much of the thinking about perception of temporal order and its relation to RT seems to incorporate two implicit assumptions: first, that the relevant internal representation of a temporally punctate stimulus event is itself punctate, and second, that the system is noiseless. Both assumptions are questionable.

Difficulties for the first assumption arise from the fact that at any level at which temporal summation occurs, that is, at which a lower-level response is integrated over time to any extent, abrupt changes in stimulus amplitude do not produce correspondingly rapid changes in response amplitude (Levinson, 1968; Sperling & Sondhi, 1968). This is also true for a system containing multiple paths that vary in transmission rate, if the internal response is provided by the sum of their outputs (Raab, 1962).

---

[19]A different kind of application of the extended independent-channels model of Fig. 4 has been made by Bertelson and Tisseyre (1969) in their attempt to determine the level of processing that mediates the effect of the frequency of a word on the mean latency, $E(\mathbf{T}_x) = \overline{\mathbf{T}}_x$, of its identification. In terms of Fig. 4, they started with the assumption that reducing word frequency causes $\overline{\mathbf{T}}_x$ to increase. They found from TOJs that it did not cause $\overline{\mathbf{R}}_x$ to increase, and inferred that it increases only $\overline{\mathbf{M}}_x$, that is, that it slows only those stages that are "above" the level at which order decisions are made. One possibility that must be considered in relation to such an application is that the stimulus feature of a flashed word that is used in judging the time of the flash may not be involved in the process that ascertains the identity of the word; if so, $\overline{\mathbf{R}}_x$ would be unrelated to $\overline{\mathbf{T}}_x$, rather than being one of its components.

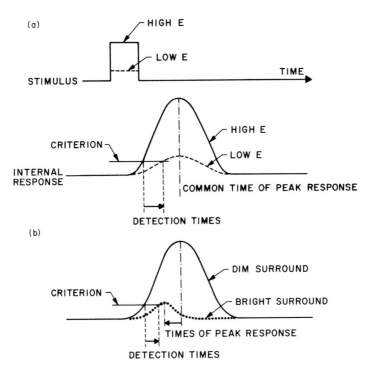

Fig. 5. Hypothetical internal responses to pulsed stimuli—here, light flashes. (a) Pulses of different intensities have different detection latencies relative to a criterion above baseline, but the same latencies to peak response. (b) Brighter annular surround reduces response amplitude, thereby prolonging detection latency, but also increases temporal resolution, thereby shortening latency of peak response.

In Fig. 5a are shown the responses that pulsed stimuli of two intensities would produce in a simple linear system with properties of a low-pass filter. The response to the more intense stimulus is simply a multiple of the response to the weaker one; thus, both responses start rising from the base line and reach their peaks at the same time. If the second implicit assumption were true—if the system were noiseless—then the initial departure from baseline could be used as a detection criterion. But in the presence of internal noise, a higher criterion (such as the one shown in the figure) is needed in order to reduce the frequency of false alarms. The particular criterion used influences not only the absolute detection latency, but also the change in latency induced by a given intensity change.

In general, unless two responses are identical in size and shape, differing by a time translation only, there *is* no uniquely defined latency difference:

the expected effect on latency of a factor such as intensity will depend on what particular feature or measure of the internal response is assumed to define its latency (see Mollon & Krauskopf, 1972). The idea of an adjustable criterion (sensitive to payoffs and instructions) applied to a temporally dispersed response has received support from a number of studies of simple RT (for example, John, 1967; Grice, 1968; Murray, 1970).

Now, it is quite possible that one feature of the internal response might be used for initiating the reaction in an RT task, and a quite different feature might serve as the time marker in a TOJ. After all, the RT task requires speed with a low false-alarm rate, whereas the TOJ requires low variance to maximize precision. Thus, TOJs might depend on the estimated time of the *peak* response, which might have less sampling variance than the delay before a response first exceeds a criterion level, because the latter, but not the former, varies with trial-to-trial fluctuations in sensitivity. In the example of Fig. 5a the peak latency is invariant, even though the detection latency changes with intensity.

A more dramatic example is shown in Fig. 5b. Suppose a brief flash is presented inside a steady annular surround. (In Section V we consider results from an experiment of this kind.) An increase in surround intensity has two effects (Alpern, 1968): it shortens the time constant of the visual system, increasing temporal resolution, and it lowers the sensitivity of the system, reducing response amplitude. It is thus possible for change in a single factor (surround intensity) to prolong the detection latency but shorten the latency of the peak.

Given such considerations, it is remarkable that RT and TOJ results ever agree. If the two measures can depend on different features of the internal response, quantitative and even qualitative disagreements do not appear critical for the independent-channels model. Relative to pulsed stimuli, onsets or offsets may provide fewer alternative features of the internal response on which order judgments might be based. This may account for the good agreement found by Roufs (1963) between effects of intensity on RTs and PSSs for light onsets in the middle range of intensities.

V. Additive-Factor Tests of the Independent-Channels Model

A. Selective Influence of Factors on Channels: Additivity of Factor Effects

It seems, then, that in order to understand the relation between TOJ and RT, one needs an explicit description of the internal response and how these two tasks depend on it. Lacking such a description, how can one test the independent-channels model? One set of consequences of the model that can be used for testing it without leaving the domain of TOJs depends on extending the assumption of selective influence mentioned in Section III,B.

Suppose there are experimental factors, A and B, that can reasonably be assumed to influence selectively the pair of channels x and y in a TOJ experiment. (For example, factor A might be the intensity of an auditory stimulus, and factor B the intensity of a visual stimulus.) The assumption means that $\mathbf{R}_x = \mathbf{R}_x(A)$ depends on the level of A but not B, $\mathbf{R}_y = \mathbf{R}_y(B)$ depends on the level of B but not A, and Δ depends on neither. Now consider $\mathbf{D}$ (representing the psychometric function) as a function of A and B:

$$\mathbf{D}(A, B) = \mathbf{R}_x(A) - \mathbf{R}_y(B) + \Delta. \tag{18}$$

Because the arrival latencies are represented additively in Eq. (18), the assumption of selective influence implies that the factor effects are additive. That is, the change produced in $\mathbf{D}$ by a change in factor A from one level to another is the same, regardless of the level of factor B. If $\mathbf{R}_x$ and $\mathbf{R}_y$ are independent in mean only, this implication applies to the PSS, $E(\mathbf{D})$, only; if they are stochastically independent, it applies to the variance and all the higher cumulants as well. In Sections V,B and V,C we consider experiments that test such implications.

It is important to note that in using TOJs to measure the effect of any factor on perceptual latency, one implicitly accepts the validity of both the selective influence assumption and the independent-channels model. Note also that the conclusions concerning additivity of factor effects hold, whatever the decision function, $\Delta(x, y)$.

B. Tests of Factor Additivity in Three Visual Experiments

Despite the importance of factor additivity for testing any independent-channels model, as well as for justifying many applications of TOJs, few studies have used factorial designs that permit the desired tests of additivity; fewer still were designed explicitly for this purpose, and those that do exist are restricted to measures of central tendency. In this section we discuss results of three such studies, all using pairs of visual stimuli.

The data shown in Fig. 6 are derived from a study by Efron (1963b) in which the stimuli were brief dichoptic flashes to different visual hemifields. For each subject, PSSs were estimated by a method of limits for each of the four conditions obtained by factorial combination of two left-flash (S_L) intensities and two right-flash (S_R) intensities. For each stimulus, the intensity

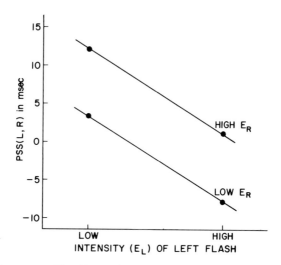

Fig. 6. Means over 20 subjects of the PSSs from four pairs of flash intensities in Efron's (1963b) experiment. On the abscissa are indicated the two intensities (E_L) of the flash to the left visual field (S_L); the parameter is the intensity (E_R) of the right flash (S_R). The PSS represents $t_R - t_L$. Also shown is the best-fitting pair of parallel lines, which represent perfect additivity of the effects of E_L and E_R on the PSS. The mean deviation of points from lines is .06 ± .21 msec; the standard error (SE) is based on the 1-*df* difference between mean deviations for right-handed and left-handed subject subgroups, regarded as sampling error.

levels were separated by one log unit. The additive model fits very well.[20]

Factor additivity can also be tested with data from a recent study by Matteson (1970). An annular surround was presented continuously to the right eye, above the fixation point. Subjects judged the order of a brief test flash (S_x) inside the annulus and a brief reference flash (S_y) presented to the other eye below the fixation point. One factor was the intensity of S_y: an increase of 2.2 log units increased the PSS $= t_y - t_x$ by 56 msec, indicating a reduction in the latency $\mathbf{R}_y$. The second factor was intensity of the test-flash surround: an increase of about 5 log units decreased the PSS by 50 msec, indicating a reduction in the test-flash latency $\mathbf{R}_x$.

Matteson's surround-intensity effect is a dramatic instance of a TOJ effect in the opposite direction from what one would expect for RTs, and is

---

[20]Some caution is called for in interpreting this result. Interaction contrasts (Sternberg, 1969a, Section 5.2) for left- and right-handed subject groups were of opposite sign, resulting in a small mean contrast with a relatively large standard error (SE). The value of the SE implies that a mean interaction contrast of as much as 2.7 msec (31% of the smaller main effect) would be needed to reach significance at the .05 level.

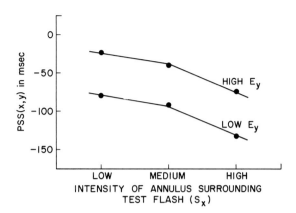

Fig. 7. Means over two subjects of the PSSs from six combinations of reference-flash (S_y) and test-flash (S_x) surround intensities in Matteson's (1970) Experiment II. On the abscissa are indicated three sets of surround intensities; the parameter is the intensity (E_y) of the reference flash. The PSS represents $t_y - t_x$. Also shown is the best-fitting pair of parallel profiles, which represent perfect additivity of the effects on the PSS of the two factors. The mean absolute deviation of points from lines is 1.3 msec. (See footnote 22.)

consistent with the analysis diagrammed in Fig. 5b.[21] Mean PSSs from two subjects, obtained by a staircase procedure, are shown in Fig. 7. Again, an additive model fits well.[22]

In our third example, however, we find clear-cut interactions when we apply what seem to be similar tests. Rutschmann (contribution to this volume, Experiment II) factorially varied the intensities of a dichoptic foveal-peripheral flash pair, using the method of constant stimuli to measure PSSs.

---

[21]In accordance with that analysis, a later study by Matteson, Lewis, and Dunlap (1971) has shown that the effect disappears or is markedly reduced when the onset of a long flash, rather than a pulse, is being judged. Presumably, the early flank of the internal response is likely to be more salient (relative to any early peak) when the stimulus is a long flash than when it is a pulse, and therefore is more likely to be the latency-defining feature for TOJs.

[22]There were actually seven levels of surround intensity; for purposes of the present analysis they were combined into three sets. Again, in this instance, the exceptional goodness of fit for the mean data should be interpreted with caution, because they represent the sum of two (nonsignificant) interactions in opposite directions for the two subjects. To express this idea quantitatively, we need an estimate of the precision of a measure of the mean interaction. To arrive at such an estimate, consider the linear component of the interaction, which can be expressed as a 1-df signed quantity for each subject simply by fitting an additive model to low- and high-intensity surrounds only. Whereas the mean data then show a mean deviation from additivity of only .6 msec, the SE of this quantity, based on the 1-df between-subject difference, is 3.8 msec.

The effects of the two factors did not add: peripheral intensity had a larger effect on the PSS when foveal intensity was high than when it was low. (See Section X,B for a possible explanation.)

C. ADDITIVE-FACTOR TEST OF AN INDEPENDENT-CHANNELS MODEL OF BINAURAL LATERALIZATION

When dichotic clicks are presented with a time separation of no more than about 2 msec, a fused auditory image is formed, located inside the head. Changes in time separation cause changes in perceived location within the head; the separation that causes the fused image to be centered can be regarded as a PSS. Furthermore, in terms of its perceived location, increasing the intensity of one of the clicks is equivalent to presenting it earlier.

Binaural lateralization is of interest in relation to temporal-order perception for several reasons. First, it seems to depend on a special peripheral mechanism that has much better resolution than that observed in most temporal-order experiments (see footnote 4). Second, and more important for our present purpose, lateralization provides an instructive testing ground for the independent-channels model, where the model is extended from order judgments to another perceptual domain in which it is thought that the relative arrival time of a pair of signals is critical in determining the percept. Finally, the relation between effects of intensity on lateralization and on TOJs outside the lateralization region exemplifies relations that may be useful in tracing information flow in sensory systems, as described in Section V, D.

An explicit independent-channels theory of lateralization was developed by both David, Guttman, and van Bergeijk (1958) and Deatherage and Hirsh (1959):

> ...the binaural lateralization mechanism, located at some point where the outputs from the two ears converge, is sensitive to time difference only. Under this hypothesis binaural intensity difference at the ears is converted to time difference according to the time–intensity trading relation [David et al., 1958].

In our terms, click intensities influence the channels selectively and have only indirect effects on the decision mechanism, mediated by the changes they induce in arrival latencies. David et al. (1959) recognized and used the implication expressed in Eq. (18) that effects of intensity on the PSS would be additive, but never tested it. A subset of the data from the Deatherage and

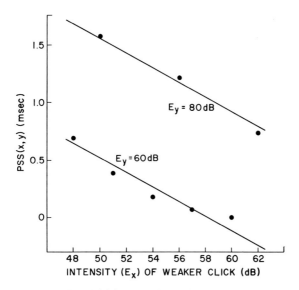

Fig. 8. Data suitable for additivity test selected from the Deatherage and Hirsh (1959) experiment on auditory localization. The points are derived from four observers' data. Each point represents an average of values from two conditions: stronger click to right ear, stronger click to left ear. The intensity (E_x) of the weaker click in peak-equivalent sound pressure level is indicated on the abscissa; the parameter is the intensity (E_y) of the stronger click. The PSS is the amount $t_y - t_x$ by which the weaker click was advanced relative to the stronger, to "center" the fused image in the head. Parallel quadratic functions fitted to this subset of the data had a negligible quadratic component; therefore, perfect additivity of the effects of E_x and E_y on the PSS is represented by parallel lines.

Hirsh (1959) study, however, provides an approximation to an appropriate factorial design; results of the test, which we regard as promising for the independent-channels model, are shown in Fig. 8.[23]

Such additivity would support not only the general model, but also the assumption of selective influence, and thus help justify using the effect of intensity on a PSS to measure an effect of intensity on latency in the sensory channel. Interpreted this way, the "time–intensity trade" in lateraliz-

---

[23]Because variability in this study was reported as being "rather large," and information about the precision of individual data points is no longer available, the deviations from the fitted functions are difficult to evaluate quantitatively.

For comments on some of the complexities of binaural lateralization that might lead one to question the applicability of the independent-channels model, see Green and Henning (1969). One complication is that experienced observers are able to report on two separate fused images produced by dichotic signals, each image having its own time–intensity trading relation (Hafter & Jeffress, 1968).

ation implies a very small effect of intensity on latency. For moderate intensities in the Deatherage and Hirsh study the effect is on the order of .05 msec/dB. We know of no studies of the effect of intensity on the PSS for exactly comparable auditory stimuli outside the fusion region, where temporal order is judged. But the studies that come closest (Hirsh, 1959, Experiment IV; Sanford, 1971) reveal an effect of intensity on auditory latency that is one or two orders of magnitude greater. This difference suggests that some of the interesting features of sensory channels might be represented by the model shown in Fig. 9.

D. Use of the Time–Intensity Trading Relation to Trace Information Flow

Figure 9 shows each channel performing a series of processing operations on the input, with the durations of more than one of the early processes influenced by stimulus intensity. Furthermore, these processes are all influenced in the same direction: the higher the intensity, the shorter their durations.[24] In the figure, for example, both R_x and R_x' are shortened by an increase in E_x. Since the arrival latency at Δ is R_x, whereas the arrival latency at Δ' is $R_x + R_x'$, the intensity effect on a PSS mediated by Δ' will be the greater. In other words, the effect of intensity on the latency of a signal is augmented as it passes through the channel. This implies that for any decision mechanisms that operate on arrival-time differences, the more processing required to produce their inputs, the greater the effect of intensity on the PSS. Given the results discussed in Section V,C—a smaller effect of intensity on PSS in binaural lateralization than in temporal order—this

---

[24]This could occur if higher intensity caused the output of a process to have both shorter latency and greater amplitude, and if greater amplitude of the input to the next process shortened its duration. Note that in a strict sense, such processes are not "stages" (Sternberg, 1969a, Sec. 3.2), because relevant features of their outputs are not independent of factors influencing their durations. The possibility of such indirect effects of intensity on later processes is supported by electrophysiological evidence (Miller & Glickstein, 1967; Miller, Moody, & Stebbins, 1969). It is also consistent with findings that intensity can have larger effects on RTs than on TOJs (Section III,B) or on latencies of visually evoked cortical responses (Vaughan, et al., 1966). For the visual system, however, the possibility of intensity effects on durations of higher processes conflicts with the common notion that there is just one locus of the effect of intensity on latency (Bernhard, 1940; Prestrude, 1971; Stevens, 1970) and that processing stages at levels above the retina contribute latency components that are independent of stimulus intensity. An error in interpreting latency–intensity functions is sometimes made when functions that are parallel on a logarithmic time scale (such as power functions with equal exponents, which may differ by a scale factor on a linear time scale) are assumed also to be parallel on a linear time scale.

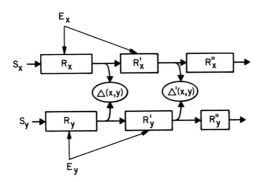

Fig. 9. Extension of the independent-channels model to judgments that depend on arrival times at different "depths" in the channel. Increasing the stimulus intensity E_x is assumed to reduce the duration $\mathbf{R}_x'$ as well as $\mathbf{R}_x$ (see footnote 24). Hence, the influence of intensity on the arrival latency $\mathbf{R}_x + \mathbf{R}_x'$ at Δ' is greater than its influence on the arrival latency $\mathbf{R}_x$ at Δ. The same applies for channel y. However, E_x and E_y must have additive effects on the PSSs associated with *both* Δ and Δ'.

argument is consistent with the view that the stimulus representation used by the binaural-lateralization mechanism is available closer to the periphery than is the representation used by the temporal-order mechanism.

An equally interesting instance of different time–intensity trading relations based on different kinds of judgment arises in vision. We consider three phenomena, all involving the perceived locations of moving objects. The Pulfrich effect is an illusion of stereoscopic depth produced when an object is moved in the frontal plane and viewed binocularly with a neutral filter over one eye (Lit, 1949). Because the filter attenuates the input to one eye, it is thought to delay the arrival of signals from that eye at the place in the brain where binocular fusion occurs. The binocular signals that arrive simultaneously therefore correspond to different locations of the moving object, the spatial disparity changing with the rate and direction of movement. As in stereograms and normal binocular vision, such changes in disparity are interpreted as changes in depth. The delay can be inferred from the size of the depth effect, and measured as a function of the amount of attenuation (Lit, 1949; Alpern, 1968). With an actual moving object, one cannot separately manipulate attenuation and delay of the stimuli to the two eyes so as to nullify the depth illusion, and thereby measure the PSS more directly. But with moving stereo displays, such direct measurement of the time–intensity trading relation at the level of binocular fusion is possible. Julesz and White (1969) have made a start in this direction, and Rogers and Anstis (1972) have reported extensive measurements.

A similar phenomenon is produced when a display of two separate objects, one above the other and moving back and forth in synchrony in the frontal plane, is viewed monocularly. When one of the objects is covered by an attenuating filter, it appears to lag behind the other (Wilson & Anstis, 1969). Here it is possible to adjust the objective lag of one movement relative to the other so as to nullify the subjective lag, thereby measuring the PSS directly, as a function of the amount of attenuation.

A third phenomenon arises when subjects attempt to align a moving dichoptic vernier display—two radial line-segments shown to different eyes while rotating at the same rate about what appears to be the same axis (Prestrude, 1971). When the display to one eye is covered by an attenuating filter the subjective alignment is disturbed; the amount of objective mis-alignment needed to restore it provides a measure of the PSS.

In studies of these three phenomena the effects of intensity on the PSS were smallest for the rotating dichoptic vernier, intermediate for stereoscopic depth, and greatest for correlated movement. Given a model of the kind diagrammed in Fig. 9, these differences in time–intensity trading relations would lead to the inference that stereoscopic depth is achieved higher in the visual system than vernier alignment, but lower than comparison of the positions of separated moving objects. But to justify this inference it would also have to be shown that for each phenomenon intensity effects in the two channels are additive, thereby demonstrating the validity of the independent-channels model in each instance.[25]

E. CHANNELS, STAGES, AND ADDITIVE FACTORS

The independent-channels model, the assumption of selective influence of factors on channels, and the additive representation of Eq. (18), together parallel closely considerations that arise when the reaction time T is regard-

---

[25]Approximate mean changes in PSSs in the three situations, in response to an increase in retinal illuminance of 1.0 to 4.0 (0 to 4.0) log trolands, are as follows:

vernier alignment (Prestrude, 1971)	23 (36) msec
stereoscopic depth (Lit, 1949)	32 (—) msec
(Rogers & Anstis, 1972)	38 (71) msec
correlated movement (Wilson & Anstis, 1969)	45 (121) msec

(Because no artificial pupil was used in the Wilson and Anstis experiment, the values above depend on corrections for pupil size that we have applied to their data. To estimate the larger value from Prestrude's data a small extrapolation was required.)

We have performed rough additivity tests on the four sets of data listed above; at this writing it appears that the independent-channels model is supported at least for the vernier and depth data.

From altogether different considerations, Julesz (1971, Ch. 3) has concluded that stereopsis is located higher in the visual system than monocular vernier acuity, but lower than movement perception.

ed as the sum of durations of two component processing stages of interest, $\mathbf{T}_a$ and $\mathbf{T}_b$, and the duration of the remaining stages $\mathbf{T}_w$. Along with this *stage theory*, an assumption of selective influence leads to an additive representation of $\mathbf{T}$ similar to Eq. (18):

$$\mathbf{T}(A, B) = \mathbf{T}_a(A) + \mathbf{T}_b(B) + \mathbf{T}_w; \tag{19}$$

the implied additivity of factor effects on $\mathbf{T}$ provides tests of the theory and assumption. In the *additive-factor method* (Sternberg, 1969a) one inverts the argument in the case of RT, seeking factors with additive effects and using them to infer the existence and nature of processing stages. In the same way, instances of additive and interacting factors in the domain of TOJs can be used to identify independent sensory channels, defined in the sense of Section II,A.

The similarities and contrasts between these approaches are instructive. In both, the basic theory involves additivity (arrival-latency difference, stage-duration sum), assumed selective influence, and implied additivity of factor effects. With RT, a subset of stages ($\mathbf{T}_a$, $\mathbf{T}_b$) can be studied that are embedded in unknown others ($\mathbf{T}_w$); with TOJs, a pair of channels ($\mathbf{R}_x$, $\mathbf{R}_y$) can be studied in the context of an unknown decision function. In both, independence in mean and stochastic independence can be separately assessed. The major difference, and one that creates greater technical difficulties for the study of channels, is that whereas the $\mathbf{T}$ distribution can be directly sampled, access to the $\mathbf{D}$ distribution is limited to points on its distribution function.

VI. Prior Entry: Effect of Attentional Bias on Temporal-Order Perception

"The stimulus for which we are predisposed requires less time than a like stimulus, for which we are unprepared, to produce its full conscious effect." This *law of prior entry* was included by Titchener (1908, p. 251) among his seven laws of attention. In our terms, the law asserts that the shifting of an attentional bias from channel x to channel y causes the $PSS(x, y) = t_y - t_x$ to increase; we call this increase the *prior-entry effect*. The effect is promising as a tool for the study of attention. But more important for our present purpose, it provides a constraint on all theories of order perception.

Shortly after Titchener published his law, Dunlap (1910) reconsidered the experiments on which it was based, and concluded that the effects claimed for attention were actually artifacts resulting from flaws in experimental method.[26] But a later study by Stone (1926), which avoided many of the early pitfalls, demonstrated the effect and provided a characterization that recent experiments (Sternberg, Knoll, & Gates, 1971) tend to confirm.

Stone's subjects judged the order of a tap (cutaneous) and a click (auditory). Stimulus times were determined by a method of constant stimuli. In different series of trials, subjects made judgments under two conditions of attentional bias induced by instruction (for example, "Attend to the click; expect the click."). The results, shown in Fig. 10, reveal a mean prior-entry effect of 46 msec, which is large relative to effects that are often of interest in temporal-order experiments. Furthermore, the findings hint at a characterization of the effect as a horizontal translation of the psychometric function, without systematic change in shape.

Perhaps the first question that should be asked in the context of the independent-channels model is whether the locus of the prior-entry effect is in the channels or in the decision mechanism. Some models of the central mechanism (Models 4, 5, and 6 of Section II,C, for example) are inherently responsive to attentional changes. Others (for example, Model 3) would require postulation of correlated changes in response bias (see footnote 8). On the other hand, some views of attention (see Moray, 1969) would locate the effect in the channels and, for example, identify an attentional bias toward a particular channel with an increase in sensitivity or a reduction in the level of a detection criterion for stimuli in that channel.[27]

The additive representation of the general model, given in Eq. (10), suggests one way of answering the question of locus. Let E_x and E_y represent intensities of stimuli S_x and S_y, respectively, and let B represent an attentional-bias factor. Suppose that B influences the decision mechanism only. Then, considering $\mathbf{D}$ as a function of E_x, E_y, and B, we have

$$\mathbf{D}(E_x, E_y, B) = \mathbf{R}_x(E_x) - \mathbf{R}_y(E_y) + \Delta(B). \tag{20}$$

The implication, as in Section V,A, is that effects of all three factors will be

---

[26]The experiments on which the law was based—"complication" experiments—were modeled after the astronomers' problem of determining when a star crossed a hairline (visual) in relation to a series of clicks (auditory). Most of them involved multiple observations of a continuously rotating pointer and a discrete acoustic stimulus, with the observer judging the position the pointer assumed when he heard the sound. Dunlap argued that the effects attributed to attention resulted from variations in the eye movements associated with the moving pointer, and found fault with the use of multiple presentations before each judgment.

[27]If this were so, the concept of perceptual latency (Section IV) would become even more troublesome, particularly since the size of an intensity effect would depend on the state of attention.

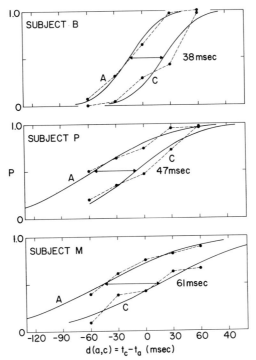

Fig. 10. Psychometric functions from Stone's (1926) experiment, with normal ogives fitted by maximum likelihood (probit analysis). Curves marked A and C represent judgments when attention was biased toward the auditory and cutaneous signals, respectively. If subjects were uncertain, they could withold their response ("$t_a = t_c$"); hence, the quantity plotted is $P = \Pr\{"t_a < t_c"\} + \frac{1}{2}\Pr\{"t_a = t_c"\}$. The DLs for conditions A and C were 19 and 20 msec, 44 and 35 msec, and 54 and 53 msec for subjects B, P, and M, respectively. Prior-entry effects, measured by differences between means of the fitted ogives, are shown.

additive. In particular, the prior-entry effect, measured as a change in the mean of the psychometric function, will be independent of stimulus intensity. But if the attention factor as well as stimulus intensity influences the channels, some interaction between effects of these factors would be expected. For example, if attentional bias is mediated by a reduced detection-criterion level (Fig. 5a), the prior-entry effect should be decreased as E_x and E_y are increased. (Figure 5a shows the higher intensity producing an internal response with a steeper slope in the criterion region. A given reduction in criterion then leads to a smaller latency reduction for a high- than for a low-intensity stimulus.)

The prior-entry effect may not be restricted to heteromodal stimulus pairs: intramodal effects have been claimed by Needham (1936), Rubin (1938), and Ladefoged and Broadbent (1960).

The existence of the effect leads to problems of method as well as to interesting questions of theory. In almost no recent studies of order perception has there been any explicit control of attentional bias. A spontaneous fluctuation of bias would induce spurious correlation among arrival latencies, destroying stochastic independence and altering the shape of the psychometric function, although it might not interfere with independence in mean. Systematic attentional shifts that were correlated with conditions could cause the independent-channels model to fail in many ways. (If a subject is free to do so, he might bias his attention to the dimmer of two flashes if intensity is not randomized, bias it differently for onsets than offsets, or bias it in a way that depends on the earlier observations on a trial with multiple observations of the same stimulus pair, or on the first observation in a forced-choice task.) On the other hand, it seems unlikely that systematic attentional shifts would produce spurious support for the independent-channels model. This observation might tempt one to argue from the successful additivity tests of Section V,B that systematic shifts of attentional bias may not occur readily.

VII. Potential Effects of Interchannel Interactions

We have seen that although attentional effects might make difficult the testing of the independent-channels model, they are not, in principle, incompatible with the model. In contrast, if there is interaction among the channels that process even heteromodal signals, as has been argued from the results of certain kinds of RT experiments, this would be fatal to the assumption of channel independence and thus to the general model. The possibility of such interaction arises from RT experiments where irrelevant signals closely precede or follow reaction signals. In general, preceding signals delay the response, as in studies of the "psychological refractory period" (Smith, 1967), and following signals facilitate it, as in studies of "intersensory facilitation" (for example, Bernstein, Rose, & Ashe, 1970). There also exists electrophysiological evidence for heteromodal interactions; for example, Thompson et al. (1963) have observed heteromodal inhibitory effects in association areas of the cat's cortex.

It is possible that these effects arise at processing stages higher up than those on which temporal-order perception depends; indeed, insofar as the independent-channels model is confirmed, such a view would gain sup-

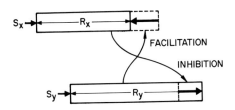

Fig. 11. Possible effects of interchannel interaction on the arrival-time difference. If interactions inferred from RT experiments were located in the channels, early activity in channel x might inhibit channel y, prolonging $\mathbf{R}_y$, and later activity in channel y might facilitate channel x, shortening $\mathbf{R}_x$. When $d(x, y) = t_y - t_x$ was positive (negative), then, $U_y - U_x$ would be increased (decreased), thereby improving discriminability.

port. But the possibility must be kept in mind that these phenomena arise at early processing stages, and reflect changes in the arrival latencies $\mathbf{R}_x$ and $\mathbf{R}_y$. This would complicate the relation between the stimulation-time difference $d(x, y)$, and the arrival-time difference $U_y - U_x$, as shown in Fig. 11. Depending on their form, these interchannel interactions could sharpen temporal discrimination: the psychometric function would represent greater discriminability than the central mechanism alone could provide. Also, depending on their form, these effects could distort the function.

VIII. Transitivity of Subjective Simultaneity and the Existence of a Common Simultaneity Center

Simultaneity in *physical* time is a *transitive relation*: if events a and b are simultaneous, and events b and c are simultaneous, then events a and c must also be simultaneous. The simultaneity point for an event pair divides possible arrangements of the pair into those that produce the two possible orders. This relation between simultaneity and order, together with the transitivity of simultaneity, implies that there can be no arrangement of events in physical time such that their order is intransitive: for all arrangements where a precedes b, and b precedes c, a must precede c. Since physically simultaneous events are not, in general, subjectively simultaneous, the transitivity relations of events in physical time need not carry over to subjective simultaneity or subjective order.

In this section we consider the concept of transitivity of subjective simultaneity and its relation to the idea that not only does a common *mechanism* mediate TOJs of most stimulus pairs, but also that this decision mechanism has a common *locus*—a "simultaneity center"—in the brain.[28] We consider some other implications of the existence of a common decision center and show that, contrary to common belief, it is neither necessary nor sufficient for transitivity. Since the issue of transitivity is nonetheless important, we review the few existing studies that are relevant to it.

A. TRANSITIVITY OF ARRIVAL LATENCIES AND DECISION FUNCTIONS

In considering the pairwise subjective simultaneity of several stimulus pairs we use $\text{PSS}(x, y) \equiv d_\mu(x, y)$ to define the simultaneity point. It is convenient to regard a stimulus S_i together with its presentation time t_i as an ordered pair (S_i, t_i). Let time values $t_x = t_x^*$, $t_y = t_y^*$, and $t_z = t_z^*$ be chosen to produce subjective simultaneity of (S_x, t_x^*) with (S_y, t_y^*) and of (S_y, t_y^*) with (S_z, t_z^*). This requires $t_y^* - t_x^* = d_\mu(x, y)$ and $t_z^* - t_y^* = d_\mu(y, z)$. The transitivity condition then implies simultaneity of (S_z, t_z^*) with (S_x, t_x^*), or $t_x^* - t_z^* = d_\mu(z, x)$. Define

$$\mathbf{I}(x, y, z) \equiv \mathbf{D}(x, y) + \mathbf{D}(y, z) + \mathbf{D}(z, x), \qquad (21)$$

and let $\bar{\mathbf{I}} \equiv E(\mathbf{I})$. The transitivity condition can then be expressed as

$$\bar{\mathbf{I}}(x, y, z) = d_\mu(x, y) + d_\mu(y, z) + d_\mu(z, x) = 0, \qquad (22)$$

and $\bar{\mathbf{I}}$ may be used as an index of intransitivity.[29,30]

Under what conditions does Eq. (22) hold? Let $\mathbf{R}_x(y)$ be the arrival latency of signal S_x when it is being ordered relative to S_y. Then, from

---

[28]It has been argued (for example, Corwin & Boynton, 1968) that a necessary condition for the judgment of order of any pair of stimuli is that internal responses to those stimuli be brought together at some locus in the brain, by way of convergent neural pathways from each sensory area.

[29]Here and elsewhere in this section it is helpful to use the complementary relation among pairs of psychometric functions (and decision functions): $\mathbf{D}(x, y)$ has the same distribution as $-\mathbf{D}(y, x)$ [and $\Delta(x, y)$ as $-\Delta(y, x)$]. Hence $d_\mu(x, y) = -d_\mu(y, x)$, and similarly for $d_{1/2}$.

[30]Note that we have defined the PSS as the mean of the psychometric function $d_\mu(x,y) = E[\mathbf{D}(x,y)]$, and not the median. This is necessary in order to develop the theory of the present section. If simultaneity is defined instead as the 50% point, then the transitivity of subjective simultaneity becomes *weak stochastic transitivity*: $\Pr\{``t_x < t_y"\} = \frac{1}{2}$ and $\Pr\{``t_y < t_z"\} = \frac{1}{2}$ implies $\Pr\{``t_x < t_z"\} = \frac{1}{2}$; the three medians, rather than the three means of Eq. (22), add to zero. Like many of the additivity properties developed earlier in this paper, the transitivity properties of the present section depend on features that the expectation does not, in general, share with the median. Hence, tests of transitivity that use the 50% points of psychometric functions are properly thought of as approximations.

Eq. (10),

$$D(x, y) = R_x(y) - R_y(x) + \Delta(x, y). \tag{23}$$

Define

$$I_R(x, y, z) \equiv [R_x(y) - R_x(z)] + [R_y(z) - R_y(x)] + [R_z(x) - R_z(y)], \tag{24}$$

and

$$I_\Delta(x, y, z) \equiv \Delta(x, y) + \Delta(y, z) + \Delta(z, x). \tag{25}$$

Then Eqs. (21) and (23) imply that

$$I = I_R + I_\Delta. \tag{26}$$

In general, for $\bar{I} = 0$ and transitivity, we must have both $\bar{I}_R = 0$ and $\bar{I}_\Delta = 0$. The quantity $\bar{I}_R$ can be regarded as an index of *arrival-latency intransitivity*. If there is a common center, as diagrammed in Fig. 12a, the arrival latency of S_x is the same, whether it is ordered relative to S_y or S_z. Hence, $R_x(y) = R_x(z) = R_x$, and similarly for the other channels, so that $\bar{I}_R = 0$ and the arrival latencies are transitive.

On the other hand, if the temporal order of different stimulus pairs is determined in different centers, and reached by pathways of different "lengths" (Fig. 12b), such that $E[R_x(y) - R_x(z)] \neq 0$, and so forth, then, in general, $\bar{I}_R \neq 0$. Furthermore, suppose that $R_x(y)$ and $R_x(z)$ are differentially influenced by stimulus intensity (E_x) as suggested in Fig. 12b. Then the amount of intransitivity $\bar{I}_R$ would depend on E_x and, conversely, the effect of E_x would depend on the stimulus, S_y or S_z, with which S_x was paired. (Note, however, that if the first process in each channel, which might represent events at the receptor level, has a long duration relative to the others, then deviations from transitivity would be small, and a precise experiment would be needed to detect them.)

That the existence of a common center is not, strictly speaking, a *necessary* condition for transitivity of arrival latencies is shown by the arrangement in Fig. 12c, in which the latency differences associated with different centers cancel each other out. To be sure, the arrangement is implausible, but the possibility should be kept in mind.

In the existing studies of transitivity (Efron, 1963a; Békésy, 1963; Corwin & Boynton, 1968), the decision rule was implicitly assumed to be deterministic and unbiased (Model 1 of Section II, C). For that model as well as Models 2 and 3, $E[\Delta(x, y)] = 0$ and, *a fortiori*, $\bar{I}_\Delta = 0$. Hence, a common center, implying $\bar{I}_R = 0$, is sufficient for transitivity of PSSs [Eq. (22)].

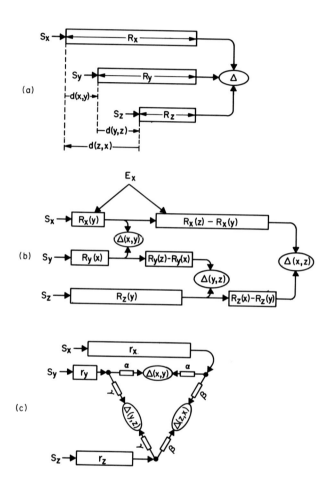

Fig. 12. Three arrangements of channels and decision centers. (a) Common decision center showing transitive arrival latencies, with stimulus times adjusted for simultaneous arrivals. (b) Different center for each pair of channels, reached by pathways of different "lengths" (that is, durations). Components of pathway durations are symbolized as in Eq. (24). Intensity (E_x) of S_x is shown influencing both parts of channel x, and therefore having a larger effect on $\mathbf{R}_x(z)$ than on $\mathbf{R}_x(y)$. In general, arrival latencies are intransitive. (c) Different centers, but with each center midway between "initial-arrival points" (large dots) of its pair of signals. The durations α, β, and γ are additional delays associated with pathways between initial-arrival points and decision centers. The arrangement produces $\mathbf{R}_x(y) = \mathbf{r}_x + \alpha$, $\mathbf{R}_x(z) = \mathbf{r}_x + \beta$, and so forth, and can be shown to give transitive arrival latencies, $\bar{\mathbf{I}}_R = 0$.

More generally, $\bar{I}_\Delta$ can be regarded as an index of *decision-function intransitivity*. Because $\bar{I}_\Delta$ may be nonzero, as in Models 4–6, the existence of a common center is not a *sufficient* condition for transitivity of PSSs.

B. FURTHER IMPLICATIONS OF A COMMON DECISION CENTER

The properties discussed in Section VIII,A can be generalized and extended in interesting ways—to relations among higher cumulants of psychometric functions, and to sets of more than three stimuli. In this section we list some of these results without proof. Note that only one of them [Eq. (30)] is used in the analyses that follow. All except Eq. (30) require us to assume that arrival latencies are stochastically independent.

Define a symmetric decision function (exemplified by Models 1–3) as one where $\Delta(x, y)$ has the same distribution as $-\Delta(x, y) = \Delta(y, x)$. All its odd cumulants are zero. For three channels with symmetric decision functions, Eq. (22), for the mean, generalizes to all odd cumulants:

$$\kappa_r[\mathbf{I}(x, y, z)] = \kappa_r[\mathbf{D}(x, y)] + \kappa_r[\mathbf{D}(y, z)] + \kappa_r[\mathbf{D}(z, x)] = 0,$$

$$r = 1, 3, \ldots . \tag{27}$$

The condition for $r = 3$, for example, implies that if one of the three psychometric functions is symmetric, then the others must be either both symmetric or both asymmetric. If both are asymmetric, the asymmetries must be of opposite sign. Some of Baron's results (1970, Fig. 2) provide a successful test of this expectation.

For the even cumulants, the most we can assert is a triangle condition on κ_2 (the variance). Assuming equal variances for the three decision functions,

$$\kappa_2[\mathbf{D}(x, y)] + \kappa_2[\mathbf{D}(y, z)] \geq \kappa_2[\mathbf{D}(z, x)]. \tag{28}$$

The triangle condition means that the sum of any two variances can be no smaller than the third.

For four (or more) channels with symmetric decision functions, paired in a simple closed chain, Eq. (27) for the odd cumulants can be generalized as follows:

$$\kappa_r[\mathbf{I}(w, x, y, z)] = \kappa_r[\mathbf{D}(w, x)] + \kappa_r[\mathbf{D}(x, y)] + \kappa_r[\mathbf{D}(y, z)]$$

$$+ \kappa_r[\mathbf{D}(z, w)] = 0, \qquad r = 1, 3, \ldots . \tag{29}$$

In particular, with or without stochastic independence,

$$\bar{I}(w, x, y, z) = d_\mu(w, x) + d_\mu(x, y) + d_\mu(y, z) + d_\mu(z, w) = 0. \tag{30}$$

With four channels the constraint on the even cumulants is stronger, however. Assuming identical decision functions or, at least, functions whose even cumulants are identical:

$$\kappa_r[\mathbf{D}(w, x)] - \kappa_r[\mathbf{D}(x, y)] + \kappa_r[\mathbf{D}(y, z)] - \kappa_r[\mathbf{D}(z, w)] = 0,$$
$$r = 2, 4, \ldots. \quad (31)$$

C. Tests of Transitivity in Three Experiments

We know of only two experiments explicitly designed to test the transitivity of subjective simultaneity; a third did so incidentally. In all three experiments, PSSs for each stimulus pair were determined in separate series of trials by a staircase procedure or a modified method of limits. (This direct approach has a potential flaw that should be kept in mind. Insofar as attentional bias is free to vary and produce prior-entry effects, bias differences among trial series where different pairs are judged could produce spurious intransitivity. See Section X,D.)

Efron (1963a, Experiment III) used four different stimuli—dichoptic flashes to left and right fields (V_L, V_R), and shocks to left and right index fingers (S_L, S_R), of a single subject. PSSs for all six possible pairs were estimated. (This is a desirable procedure since it permits four separate tests[31] of transitivity, with 3 df.) Results are summarized in Table 1. For each test, the stimuli are identified with S_x, S_y, and S_z in such a way that $d_\mu(z, x)$ differs in sign from the other two PSSs and is negative. When this is done, the deviations from transitivity (represented by the sums of three PSSs in the last column) appear to be small but systematic.[32,33]

Corwin and Boynton (1968) tested transitivity among pairs drawn from

---

[31]The appropriate test is to fit a single additive model to all six PSSs, estimating three parameters that represent mean arrival-latency differences and using the remaining 3 df for testing. Such a model accounts for 91% of the variance among the PSSs in Efron's data, and the deviations fail to reach significance at the .05 level. But for clarity, and to display the systematic nature of the deviations, we present results of separate transitivity tests based on the four subsets of three stimuli.

[32]The SE of the intransitivity index is based on the pooled variance (54 df) of the ten observations entering into each PSS.

[33]Discrepancies in the direction shown could occur if estimates from the method of limits were sensitive to starting values of d. If mean starting values were approximately the same for the six stimulus pairs, and the subject was reluctant to change his judgment either very early or very late in a series, then PSS estimates would be biased toward being close to each other in absolute value. A better method of revealing a pattern of discrepancies of this kind would be to let $d_\mu(z, x)$ in Table 1 correspond to the PSS that is largest in a fitted additive model (footnote 31), rather than letting it equal the observed PSS that differs in sign from the others, as we did. For these data the two methods give identical results.

Table 1. *Transitivity Test from Efron (1963a)*[a]

$S_x\,S_y\,S_z$	$\hat{d}_\mu(x, y)$	$\hat{d}_\mu(y, z)$	$\hat{d}_\mu(z, x)$	Intransitivity
$V_L\,V_R\,S_L$	9.75	13.25	−17.25	5.75 ± 2.03
$V_L\,V_R\,S_R$	9.77	11.25	−18.00	3.02 ± 2.03
$V_L\,S_L\,S_R$	17.25	2.50	−18.00	1.75 ± 2.03
$V_R\,S_L\,S_R$	13.25	2.50	−11.25	4.50 ± 2.03

[a]Data from one subject; values in milliseconds.

Table 2. *Transitivity Test from Corwin and Boynton (1968)*[a]

Subject	$S_x\,S_y\,S_z$	$\hat{d}_\mu(x, y)$	$\hat{d}_\mu(y, z)$	$\hat{d}_\mu(z, x)$	Intransitivity
CS	N E F	21.7	37.3	−47.0	12.0 ± 8.2
RF	N E F	−0.7	25.7	−43.0	−18.0 ± 8.7
RMB	N F E	50.0	15.0	−65.0	0.0 ± 9.3

[a]Data from three subjects; values in milliseconds.

three visual stimuli: monocularly viewed brief flashes to the fovea (F), above the fovea (N), and to the right (E). The results are summarized in Table 2, where the conventions are as in Table 1.[34] The deviations from transitivity are neither significant nor systematic in this experiment, but a more precise test is probably called for.

Interesting within-modality transitivity tests have also been reported by Békésy (1963) as "control measurements" in studies of the effects of conduction-pathway lengths on the perception of pairs of nearly simultaneous tactile stimuli. The experimenter selected three sites on the body at different distances from the brain, and applied tactile stimuli to the three possible pairs of sites. The PSS for a pair was defined as the time difference needed to localize the sensation midway between the two sites; Békésy argued that this occurred when arrival times at the brain were equal. Unfortunately, no data from these tests were reported, so it is difficult to evaluate Békésy's conclusion that the PSSs were approximately transitive.

An extensive study that provides perhaps the most convincing answer to a question of transitivity was conducted for a different purpose by Hansteen (1968, 1971). Using a staircase procedure, he measured PSSs in an attempt to

[34]The SEs are based on within-subject variation among three separate estimates of each transitivity index (2 *df*).

Table 3. *Transitivity Test from Hansteen (1968)[a]*

Subject	Test-flash intensity	$\hat{d}_\mu(c_0, t_0)$	$\hat{d}_\mu(c_1, t_0)$	V_0	$\hat{d}_\mu(c_0, t_1)$	$\hat{d}_\mu(c_1, t_1)$	V_1	Intransitivity $\bar{I} = V_0 - V_1$
TF	High	46.2	40.6	5.6	58.3	103.8	−45.5	51.1 ±9.6
	Low	−4.6	−3.0	−1.6	19.9	52.1	−32.2	30.6 ±5.8
	H–L	50.8	43.6	—	38.4	51.7	—	—
GH	High	54.3	−46.3	100.6	110.7	74.0	36.7	63.9 ±7.2
	Low	−3.6	−82.0	78.4	69.4	9.4	60.0	18.4 ±7.0
	H–L	57.9	35.7	—	41.3	64.6	—	—

[a]Data for foveal test stimuli; values in milliseconds. Differences V_0 and V_1 represent the two terms in Eq. (32).

compare the perceptual latencies of the onsets and offsets of long flashes. Since PSSs of test and comparison flashes were estimated for all four combinations of test onset (t_0) and offset (t_1) and comparison onset (c_0) and offset (c_1), the intransitivity index of Eq. (30) can be estimated. In that equation, let $w = c_0$, $x = t_0$, $y = c_1$, and $z = t_1$. By rearranging and using $d_\mu(j, k) = -d_\mu(k, j)$ we obtain

$$\bar{I} = [d_\mu(c_0, t_0) - d_\mu(c_1, t_0)] - [d_\mu(c_0, t_1) - d_\mu(c_1, t_1)]. \tag{32}$$

Thus, for transitivity to hold, the difference in PSS caused by a change from comparison onset to comparison offset should be the same whether ordering is done relative to test onset or test offset. In Table 3 we present the results for foveal test stimuli (right eye, intensities 4700 and 4.7 trolands) and peripheral comparison stimuli (left eye, intensity 470 trolands). We have averaged over variations in test-stimulus background level, since this factor had virtually no effect on PSSs for foveal tests.[35] As shown in the last column, all four tests of transitivity fail substantially, significantly, and in the same direction. The difference would imply that the amount by which test-onset latency exceeds test-offset latency is substantially less when the reference is comparison onset than when it is comparison offset.[36]

---

[35]The SEs are based on residual mean squares in within-subject analyses of variance, with 11 (16) *df* for low (high) intensity. The results for peripheral tests are not summarized here because they depended on test-background intensity and are less clear-cut.

[36]It is possible to explain this remarkable finding as an artifact based on systematic variations in attentional bias, and consequent prior-entry effects. Assume, for example, that if only one flash is turned on before the event pair to be judged, it captures the attention, whereas if both flashes are either on or off, attention is biased toward the foveal test flash. The intransitivity index then becomes an estimate of the prior-entry effect.

D. PATHWAY DIFFERENCES AND THE VARIATION OF INTRANSITIVITY WITH
   STIMULUS INTENSITY

A second notable aspect of Hansteen's results is the substantial effect of test-flash intensity on the intransitivity index $\bar{I}$. If the intransitivity were due solely to decision-function intransitivity ($\bar{I}_\Delta \neq 0$) such an effect could not occur: given a common center, the effects of E_x on $R_x(y)$ and $R_x(z)$ would be equal and $\bar{I}_R$ would be zero regardless of intensity. [See Eq. (24).] Instead, the existence of an intensity effect implies pathway differences like those shown in Fig. 12b. Assuming selective influence of E_x on channel x, the index $\bar{I}_R$ can vary with E_x if and only if the effects of E_x on $E[R_x(y)]$ and $E[R_x(z)]$ differ, and this is possible if and only if the effects of E_x on $d_\mu(x, y)$ and $d_\mu(x, z)$ differ. Such differences are illustrated by the discrepancies within each of the two pairs of intensity effects (H–L) for each subject, given in the third and sixth rows of Table 3. When either the onset (t_0) or the offset (t_1) of the test flash is judged, the effect (H–L) of its intensity on the PSS depends on whether the other event is an onset or an offset.[37]

Since either one of these two discrepancies—for t_0 or for t_1—would be sufficient to indicate pathway differences, it is not necessary to perform a full test of transitivity in order to obtain evidence bearing on the existence of a common center. In general, it is sufficient to determine whether a change in E_x has the same effect on PSS(x, y) as on PSS(x, z), where S_y and S_z are qualitatively different stimuli that would be expected to involve different decision centers if such existed. If the effects differ, as in Hansteen's study, pathway differences can be inferred. If the effects are equal, then either the arrival pathway of S_x is the same whether S_x is ordered relative to S_y or to S_z, or there are different pathways that happen to be equally influenced by intensity.

In contrast to Hansteen's results, Roufs' (1963) study contains an interesting example of equal effects of flash intensity on the PSS relative to three different reference stimuli: the onset of a flash to the same eye, the onset of a flash to the opposite eye, and the onset of a tone. For these three reference stimuli, the linear regressions of one subject's PSSs on $\log_e$ (retinal illuminance) had estimated slopes and 95% intervals of -7.6 ± 0.3 msec, -7.6 ± 1.3 msec, and -6.6 ± 1.4 msec, respectively. This result gives at least some support to the idea of a common decision center.

---

[37]Since we find an explanation in terms of different centers implausible in this instance, we are inclined to seek an alternative account. The explanation of intransitivity in this experiment in terms of attentional-bias variations (footnote 36) can be extended to cover its variation with stimulus intensity if it is assumed, for example, that where the events being judged are both offsets, the attentional bias toward the foveal flash is reduced when it is of lower intensity.

IX. Order Judgments of Multiple Stimuli

A. RELATION TO THEORETICAL ISSUES

Up to now we have considered perception of the order of stimulus pairs only. Additional light can be shed on several theoretical issues by studying the perceived order of three or more stimuli.

Suppose, for example, that there are pair-specific decision centers with intransitive arrival latencies, and that subjects judge the order of stimulus triples. Suppose further that the response on each trial is required to be an ordered triple, in which the ordering of the three pairs is inherently transitive. Then, for some temporal arrangements of the stimulus triple, the order information available at the pair-specific centers will be intransitive, and therefore not expressible in the response. Forcing intransitive perception to fit the mold of a transitive response could reduce the apparent perceptual precision. On the other hand, if intransitivity were produced solely by a common decision mechanism, such as Model 6 of Section II,C, the information available at the center on any individual trial would be transitive, in which case this difficulty would not arise.

Even if a common decision center is assumed, almost all models of the decision mechanism lead us to expect that to achieve a specified probability of "correct" order requires a greater separation between successive stimuli for triples than for pairs. This follows from the fact that a triple is correctly ordered only when all of its three component pairs are.[38] When the response is an ordered triple, the judgment of a component pair can be identified as the corresponding ordered pair embedded in the response triple. A more theoretically decisive comparison of order discrimination of pairs and triples concerns a pair in isolation versus the same pair embedded in a triple (the full response again being an ordered triple), and involves the precision of order discrimination (DL) rather than probability "correct" (which depends on both the DL and the PSS).

Insofar as the independent-channels model is applicable, embedding of a pair in a triple has no influence on arrival latencies.[39] For this reason, the

---

[38]Even if there were no variability in either arrival latencies or decision mechanism, a greater separation would be required for triples than pairs if absolute values of the three PSSs differed. For equally spaced stimulus times, the perceived order would be "correct" for each of the six possible stimulus orders only if the interstimulus interval was greater than the largest of the six PSSs (see Fig. 13).

[39]Note, however, that particularly if all three stimuli are in the same sensory modality, increasing the number of stimuli to be ordered increases the chance of peripheral stimulus interactions that would violate the independent-channels model.

comparison of isolated with embedded pairs holds promise for discriminating among models of the decision mechanism. Thus, for Model 1 (deterministic) or Model 2 (perceptual moment), embedding a pair in a triple should have no effect either on the discriminability of order or on the PSS. Baron (1970) has pointed out that for Model 3 (threshold), embedding could actually improve performance. (Suppose arrivals are in the order $U_x < U_y < U_z$, with $U_y - U_x < \tau$ and $U_z - U_y < \tau$. If, however, $U_z - U_x > \tau$, this adds enough information for the arrival times of the entire triple, including all three pairs, to be discriminated.) For Models 4 and 5 (triggered attention-switching) embedding should reduce precision. The effect for Model 6 (periodic sampling) depends on whether the period increases with the number of channels to be sampled.

When more than two stimuli are to be ordered, it is possible not only to study the perceived order of a sequence presented once, but also to study perceived order of the same sequence presented repeatedly in a recycling fashion. Such a study might be motivated by a general interest in the perceived order of elements embedded in a stream of stimuli. An interesting consequence of differences from one stimulus to another in mean arrival latency, illustrated in Fig. 13, is that arrival orders in many-cycle and single-cycle presentations could differ systematically. This could happen if not all the arrivals associated with one cycle occurred before the first arrival from the next cycle. One difficulty in interpreting results of studies with recycled stimuli is that assumptions must be made about how information from different cycles combines to determine the final judgment.

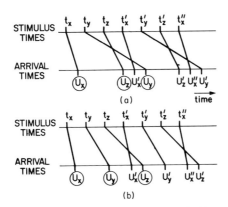

Fig. 13.   Effects on arrival sequences of recycling stimuli with equal interstimulus times. Arrivals from a single cycle are circled. (a) Single-cycle arrival order "incorrect" while recycled arrival order "correct." (b) Single-cycle arrival order "correct" while recycled arrival order "incorrect." Range of the three arrival latencies (and therefore size of largest PSS) is larger in (a) than in (b). Hence, "correct" arrival order with single cycles of all six stimulus orders requires a larger interstimulus time for (a) than for (b).

B. Characteristics of Existing Studies Using Multiple Stimuli

Relatively few published studies have been concerned with the perceived order of three or more stimuli. All involve stimuli within a single sensory modality, temporal patterns restricted to equal intervals between successive stimuli, and emphasis on "correctness" rather than separate analysis of perceptual precision (DL) and perceptual "bias" (PSS). For these reasons it is difficult to interpret the finding that even when onsets of successive stimuli are separated by 100 msec or more in recycling presentations, accuracy is far from perfect (Bregman & Campbell, 1971; Pinheiro & Ptacek, 1971; Thomas, Hill, Carroll, & Garcia, 1970; R. M. Warren, Obusek, Farmer, & R. P. Warren, 1969).

We know of only one study yielding data that permit comparison of TOJs of isolated stimulus pairs with TOJs of the same pairs embedded in triples (Hill & Bliss, 1968).[40] Results show clearly that for a stimulus pair with a given interstimulus interval, probability of "correct" report is markedly reduced when the pair is embedded in a triple, even if elements of the pair are presented first and last in the triple. Roughly speaking, for the same degree of accuracy, an embedded pair requires two or three times as much time separation as the same pair in isolation. [For example, with 60 msec between stimulus onsets, an isolated pair was correctly ordered with probability .93; with 120 msec between the onsets of S_1 and S_3 in the S_1–S_2–S_3 triple, the S_1–S_3 pair was correctly ordered in the response triple with probability .91 (from data in Hill & Bliss, 1968, Table 5).] If a finding such as this could be extended to measures of judgmental precision other than "correctness," and under conditions less subject to the limitations mentioned in Section IX,A, it would have considerable theoretical importance.

X. Comments on Experimental Method

In this section we assemble some of our impressions and preferences concerning experimental method in the study of temporal-order perception.

---

[40]This study has the virtue of using single rather than recycling presentations. A possible defect for our purposes, however, is that the stimuli presented on a trial (brief tactile stimuli on the hands, differing in location) were drawn randomly from an ensemble of 24 possible stimuli, so that identity as well as order information increased with the number of stimuli. The proportions we report here are conditional on correctness of the identity information in the response.

A. MULTIPLE-OBSERVATION METHODS

Procedures in which subjects are permitted ad lib multiple observations before each judgment have a long history in studies of temporal-order perception. For example, they were used in the "complication" experiments of the last century (Dunlap, 1910; see footnote 26), in the experiments of Hirsh (1959) and Hirsh and Sherrick (1961), and in several of the studies of order perception of multiple stimuli mentioned in Section IX,B.

If the underlying psychometric function for single observations was strictly monotonic and did not vary from trial to trial, one would expect that ad lib observations on each trial could produce indefinitely precise discrimination, limited only by the number of observations the subject chose to make (Green & Swets, 1966, Chapter 9). Such considerations make the interpretation of results from ad lib observation procedures difficult. What is remarkable, however, is the small size of the reduction actually produced in the DL when ad lib observations are permitted (Gengel & Hirsh, 1970). One possible explanation is that memory limitations prevent subjects from making full use of multiple observations (see Section XI). They might also lead to questions about the desirability of methods that require subjects to compare one presentation to their memory of one or more others, as when a standard stimulus is presented on each trial, and as in forced-choice procedures (for example, Kristofferson, 1963; Liberman et al., 1961).

B. BIASING EFFECTS OF STIMULUS RANGE

In the context of the method of single stimuli, multiple observations may have a large effect on the PSS, forcing it closer to the center of the stimulus range than does a single-observation procedure. Such a difference between procedures was demonstrated by Gengel and Hirsh (1970). This biasing effect of stimulus range may account for the consistent finding by Hirsh (1959) and Hirsh and Sherrick (1961) that in experiments where the range was centered at zero and multiple observations were used, PSSs were very close to zero.

Even with single observations on each trial, the PSSs measured with a method of constant stimuli are somewhat suspect, particularly when the range is relatively small, because of range-induced biases (Guilford, 1954, Chapter 6; Erlebacher & Sekuler, 1971). Adaptive up-and-down "staircase" methods, in which the distribution of stimuli is automatically centered approximately at the PSS, seem to us far better for measuring the PSS (Kappauf, 1969a,b; Levitt, 1971). Data from stimulus sequences controlled by such procedures may be used to estimate the entire psychometric function as well, but because the estimates of probabilities from those data may be subject to bias, an estimate of the function is perhaps better derived by the method of single stimuli with range centered on a previously measured PSS. It is instructive that of the three additive-factor tests using the PSS that were reviewed in Section V,B, the two that were relatively successful did not use the method of constant stimuli.

The stimulus range in the method of constant stimuli may also have an effect on the precision of TOJs (Hirsh & Fraisse, 1964).

Methodological developments associated with signal-detection theory (Green & Swets, 1966) have made it possible to eliminate effects of response bias (or decision criterion) when discriminability is being measured, by using the assumed dependence of bias (but not of discriminability) on explicit or implicit payoffs. But to answer many of the questions raised in this paper, the PSS ("constant error") must be measured. At present, though, there is no established method (such as using payoffs for "correctness") for disentangling changes in arrival-time means from changes in possible bias parameters. [Feedback and payoffs can easily cause transformations of the psychometric function that are approximately horizontal translations (Gengel & Hirsh, 1970).] The orderliness of some of the results reviewed in Section V,B, however, suggests that the problem of bias may not always be a serious one.

C. PURITY OF STIMULUS INFORMATION

We have already commented on the desirability of using stimuli from different sensory modalities so as to reduce the likelihood of peripheral stimulus-interactions and the special cues they might generate. For similar reasons, onsets (or offsets) are probably better than pulsed stimuli, because the internal response may be simpler, providing fewer alternative features that might be used to register time of occurrence (Section IV). (Indeed, the judged order of pulsed stimuli may depend on information combined from two observations—the order of their onsets and the order of their offsets.) If onsets or offsets are used as stimuli, however, the durations must be either long or randomized, to avoid duration cues that are correlated with temporal order.

D. CONTROL OF ATTENTIONAL BIAS

In Section VI we mentioned some of the dangers associated with uncontrolled attentional bias. One way to deal with the possibility of prior-entry effects that might vary from one condition to another is to force a particular bias. But methods that might do this have yet to be adequately tested in the context of TOJs. A second way is to randomize conditions (such as stimulus intensities) from trial to trial, so that even if the bias fluctuates it is not confounded with condition. Where condition differences are determined by stimulus features that are apparent before the events to be judged, as in Hansteen's experiment (Section VIII,C), the randomization method cannot be used. Even in the absence of this difficulty, the usefulness of the randomization method is limited if attentional bias interacts with experimental factors that influence the channels. Fluctuations in bias will, of course, add unknown variance to the psychometric function. And the randomization method may not be usable with multiple-observation or forced-choice paradigms, since one presentation might systematically influence the bias adopted for the others.

E. Dangers of Averaging

We have already cautioned against analyses based on probability of "correct" judgments in the method of single stimuli. In some studies, an average of two functions is reported: $F(d)$ for $d \geq 0$ (the part of the psychometric function to the right of zero), and $1 - F(-d)$ for $d \geq 0$ (the complement of the part of the function to the left of zero). These two measures of "correctness" estimate the same function only if D is distributed symmetrically about zero (implying a zero PSS). Even if D is symmetric, but about some value other than zero, such analyses are likely to obscure and mislead. For example, if $F(d)$ is a normal ogive with nonzero mean, the mean probability correct obtained in this way is an S-shaped function of $|d|$, rather than being the concave-downward right half of the ogive.

If there are any differences in PSS among psychometric functions, averaging will tend both to reduce the estimated judgmental precision and to lead to distortions of shape. This is true for averaging over subjects in a single-stimulus paradigm for example, and for averaging over the two presentation orders in a two-alternative forced-choice paradigm.

F. Estimation of Cumulants of the Psychometric Function

An empirical psychometric function provides us directly with a small set of quantiles of the D distribution. But the simple, distribution-free consequences of the theoretical developments presented in this paper are stated in terms of the mean, variance, and higher cumulants of the D distribution. These quantities cannot be estimated from a small set of quantiles without making assumptions about the form of the psychometric function, or the relation among the forms of a set of functions. In our view this is the most serious methodological problem associated with the ideas we have presented (see Section II,D). By fitting smooth functions from a specified family to empirical psychometric functions as, for example, in probit analysis (Finney, 1952), the problem can be completely solved, but we have little basis at present for choosing the family. The use of Spearman's (1908) method and its generalization (Epstein & Churchman, 1944; see also Finney, 1964) requires assumptions about the form of the psychometric function that are substantially weaker, and thus more acceptable. This method treats the empirical psychometric function as a cumulative grouped frequency distribution of **D** values, and leads relatively directly to estimates of its mean and higher cumulants, for which Sheppard's corrections for grouping may be appropriate (see Kendall & Stuart, 1958).

Some particular estimates using only one or two quantiles can be made on the basis of assumptions that are relatively weak and at least partially testable. For example, the assumption that the **D** distribution is symmetric about its mean permits the mean to be estimated; the assumption that a set of psychometric functions differ only in origin permits differences in mean to be estimated; the assumption that a set of functions differ only in origin and scale (have the same "shape") permits tests of additivity of variances.

XI. Real-Time Processing without Memory

As we have said earlier, all the models of temporal-order perception that we know of are special cases of the general independent-channels model, and the validity of using order judgments to measure perceptual latency depends on the validity of the model. Since the model is plausible and attractive, it seems worthwhile to emphasize some of its special features and hint at alternatives one might consider.

In the general model and its special cases, the decision mechanism is thought of as collecting all its information from the sensory channels in real time, with minimal reliance on memory. This property is particularly evident for decision mechanisms that depend on periodic sampling or attention switching.

Within each channel, none of the particular models makes use of more than one point of access to the flow of information. For example, an early stage does not feed information forward to a later stage, before the signal itself arrives, to provide a warning that attention must be switched. Instead, the level at which signals are selected by attention is the same as the level at which their arrivals control the switching of attention. Moreover, even if the detailed structure of an internal response is stored for other purposes, each channel furnishes only a single time value to the decision mechanism—a value that could be derived from the internal response by, for example, a memoryless threshold device.[41]

It is the real-time character of the processing of signals that suggests treating internal time as homogeneous at the level of the arrivals, so that the mean difference between arrival times differs at most by an additive constant from the physical difference between stimulus times. This psychophysical relation contrasts with most others, from which nonlinear internal transformations are inferred (Stevens, 1970).

For purposes of TOJs, then, we have been assuming that the internal responses to stimuli are not laid out in some display area where their structures and temporal relations can be scrutinized at leisure by the homunculus. In other words, we have assumed that the homunculus, like man, experiences the world in three dimensions rather than four. Following Efron's (1963c) lead of drawing inspiration from the antiheroes of contemporary fiction, perhaps we should consider Vonnegut's Tralfamadorians in devising an alternative model of the homunculus:

> The Tralfamadorians can look at all the different moments just the way we can look at a stretch of the Rocky Mountains, for instance. They can see how permanent all the moments are, and they can look at any moment that interests them. It is just an illusion we have here on Earth that one moment follows another one, like beads on a string, and that once a moment is gone it is gone forever.[42]

Clearly the homunculus *is* Tralfamadorian to some extent, since man can store at least crude information about the temporal structure of experience. However, if further research supports the independent-channels model, with its real-time characteristics, we would conclude that memory for temporal arrangements plays no role in TOJs of nearly-simultaneous stimuli. This could reflect a limitation on memory: stored temporal information might be incapable of yielding the fine temporal resolution of a real-time process.

---

[41]If the decision mechanism does use single time values rather than more detailed internal responses (which might differ in structure from one stimulus to another or one channel to another), this would be consistent with supposing that (*a*) equal-magnitude arrival-time differences of opposite sign are equally discriminable from simultaneous arrivals (symmetric decision function), and that (*b*) the decision function is the same, regardless of the particular events whose order is judged.

[42]From Kurt Vonnegut, Jr. *Slaughterhouse 5 or the children's crusade*, p. 23. New York: Delacorte Press, 1969. By permission of Delacorte Press and Seymour Lawrence, Inc.

Glossary

Here we provide a list of the main symbols used in order of appearance in the text, with brief definitions and numbers of the sections in which they are introduced. Note that symbols in boldface represent random variables; the same symbols in italics represent values of these random variables.

TOJ	Abbreviation of the term "temporal-order judgment." I.
S_x	Stimulus in channel x. I,A.
t_x	Time at which S_x is presented. I,A.
$d(x, y)$	$t_y - t_x$. I,A.
"$t_x < t_y$"	Subjective report that S_x appears to occur before S_y. I,A.
$F(d)$	Psychometric function: $\Pr\{"t_x < t_y"\}$ as a function of $d(x, y)$. I,A.
$\mathbf{D}(x, y)$	Random variable defined such that $\Pr\{\mathbf{D}(x, y) \leq d\} = F(d)$ is its distribution function. I,A.
$PSS(x, y)$	Point of subjective simultaneity: a value of d. I,A.
$d_{1/2}$	Median of $\mathbf{D}$ distribution: one definition of PSS. I,A.
d_μ	Mean of $\mathbf{D}$ distribution: another definition of PSS. I,A.
$E(\ )$	Expectation. I,A.
DL	Difference threshold: half the change in d required to increase $F(d)$ from .25 to .75. I,A.
$\mathbf{R}_x$	Arrival latency for S_x at locus of order-decision mechanism. I,A.
$\mathbf{U}_x$	Arrival time for S_x: $\mathbf{R}_x + t_x$. II,A.
G	Decision function giving $\Pr\{"t_x < t_y"\}$ as a function of $U_y - U_x$. II,A.
$\mathbf{\Delta}(x, y)$	Random variable defined such that $\Pr\{\mathbf{\Delta}(x, y) \leq v\} = G(v)$. II,D.
RT	Abbreviation of the term "reaction time." III.
$\mathbf{T}$	Reaction time. III.
$\mathbf{M}$	Duration, including motor time, of processing stages that "follow" order mechanism. III.
Var( )	Variance. III,A.
E_x	Attribute of stimulus S_x, such as its intensity. III,B.
κ_r	Cumulant of rth order. III,B.
$\mathbf{I}(x, y, z)$	$\mathbf{D}(x, y) + \mathbf{D}(y, z) + \mathbf{D}(z, x)$. VIII,A.
$\bar{\mathbf{I}}$	$E(\mathbf{I})$: an index of intransitivity. VIII,A.
$\bar{\mathbf{I}}_R$	Component of intransitivity associated with arrival latencies. VIII,A.
$\bar{\mathbf{I}}_\Delta$	Component of intransitivity associated with decision mechanism. VIII,A.

Acknowledgments

Discussions with several colleagues contributed to this paper; we particularly thank D. F. Andrews, F. K. Hwang, and C. L. Mallows for their advice. We also thank R. Efron, J. C. Falmagne, A. B. Kristofferson, T. K. Landauer, J. D. Mollon, R. Rutschmann, and especially L. B. Boza, C. S. Harris, and D. E. Meyer, for helpful comments on earlier drafts, and S. M. Anstis, T. R. Corwin, R. W. Hansteen, H. H. Matteson, A. M. Prestrude, and B. J. Rogers for furnishing us with unpublished details of their data.

References

Alpern, M. A note on visual latency. *Psychological Review*, 1968, **75**, 260–264.

Babkoff, H., & Sutton, S. Perception of temporal order and loudness judgments for dichotic clicks. *Journal of the Acoustical Society of America*, 1963, **35**, 574–577.

Babkoff, H., & Sutton, S. Monaural temporal interactions. *Journal of the Acoustical Society of America*, 1971, **50**, 459–465.

Baron, J. Temporal ROC curves and the psychological moment. *Psychonomic Science*, 1969, **15**, 299–300.

Baron, J. The threshold for successiveness. Unpublished doctoral dissertation, University of Michigan, 1970.

Baron, J. The threshold for successiveness. *Perception & Psychophysics*, 1971, **10**, 201–207.

von Békésy, G. Interaction of paired sensory stimuli and conduction in peripheral nerves. *Journal of Applied Physiology*, 1963, **18**, 1276–1284.

von Békésy, G. The smallest time difference the eyes can detect with sweeping stimulation. *Proceedings of the National Academy of Sciences*, 1969, **64**, 142–147.

Bernhard, C. G. Contributions to the neurophysiology of the optic pathway. *Acta physiologica Scandenavica*, **1**, Suppl. 1, 1940.

Bernstein, I. H., Rose, R., & Ashe, V. M. Energy integration in intersensory facilitation. *Journal of Experimental Psychology*, 1970, **86**, 196–203.

Bertelson, P., & Tisseyre, F. Apparent order and stimulus uncertainty. *Psychonomic Science*, 1969, **15**, 65–66.

Biederman-Thorson, M., Thorson, J., & Lange, G. D. Apparent movement due to closely spaced sequentially flashed dots in the human peripheral field of vision. *Vision Research*, 1971, **11**, 889–903.

Boring, E. G. *A history of experimental psychology.* 2nd ed. New York: Appleton, 1950.

Bregman, A. S., & Campbell, J. Primary auditory stream segregation and perception of order in rapid sequences of tones. *Journal of Experimental Psychology*, 1971, **89**, 244–249.

Chapman, R. M. Spectral sensitivities of neural impulses and slow waves in the bullfrog retina. *Vision Research*, 1962, **2**, 89–102.

Corwin, T. R., & Boynton, R. M. Transitivity of visual judgments of simultaneity. *Journal of Experimental Psychology*, 1968, **78**, 560–568.

David, E. E., Jr., Guttman, N., & van Bergeijk, W. A. On the mechanism of binaural fusion. *Journal of the Acoustical Society of America*, 1958, **30**, 801–802.

David, E. E., Jr., Guttman, N., & van Bergeijk, W. A. Binaural interaction of high-frequency complex stimuli. *Journal of the Acoustical Society of America*, 1959, **31**, 774–782.

Deatherage, B. H., & Hirsh, I. J. Auditory localization of clicks. *Journal of the Acoustical Society of America*, 1959, **31**, 486–492.

Dunlap, K. The complication experiment and related phenomena. *Psychological Review*, 1910, **17**, 157–191.

Efron, R. The effect of handedness on the perception of simultaneity and temporal order. *Brain*, 1963, **86**, 261–284.   (a)

Efron, R. The effect of stimulus intensity on the perception of simultaneity in right- and left-handed subjects. *Brain*, 1963, **86**, 285–294.   (b)

Efron, R. Temporal perception, aphasia and déjà vu. *Brain*, 1963, **86**, 403–424.   (c)

Eijkman, E., & Vendrik, A. J. H. Can a sensory system be specified by its internal noise? *Journal of the Acoustical Society of America*, 1965, **37**, 1102–1109.

Epstein, B., & Churchman, C. W. On the statistics of sensitivity data. *Annals of Mathematical Statistics*, 1944, **15**, 90–96.

Erlebacher, A., & Sekuler, R. Response frequency equalization: A bias model for psychophysics. *Perception & Psychophysics*, 1971, **9**, 315–320.

Finney, D. J. *Probit analysis: A statistical treatment of the sigmoid response curve.* (2nd ed.) London: Cambridge Univ. Press, 1952.

Finney, D. J. *Statistical method in biological assay.* (2nd ed.) London: Griffin, 1964.

Gengel, R. W., & Hirsh, I. J. Temporal order: The effect of single versus repeated presentation, practice, and verbal feedback. *Perception & Psychophysics*, 1970, **7**, 209–211.

Gibbon, J., & Rutschmann, R. Temporal order judgment and reaction time. *Science*, 1969, **165**, 413–415.

Green, D. M. Temporal auditory acuity. *Psychological Review*, 1971, **78**, 540–551.

Green, D. M., & Henning, G. B. Audition. *Annual Review of Psychology*, 1969, **20**, 105–128.

Green, D. M., & Swets, J. A. *Signal detection theory and psychophysics.* New York: Wiley, 1966.

Grice, G. R. Stimulus intensity and response evocation. *Psychological Review*, 1968, **75**, 359–373.

Guilford, J. P. *Psychometric methods.* 2nd ed. New York: McGraw-Hill, 1954.

Hafter, E. R., & Jeffress, L. A. Two-image lateralization of tones and clicks. *Journal of the Acoustical Society of America*, 1968, **44**, 563–569.

Halliday, A. M., & Mingay, R. On the resolution of small time intervals and the effect of conduction delays on the judgment of simultaneity. *Quarterly Journal of Experimental Psychology*, 1964, **16**, 35–46.

Hansteen, R. W. Visual latency as a function of stimulus onset, offset and background luminance. Unpublished doctoral dissertation, Tulane University, 1968.

Hansteen, R. W. Visual latency as a function of stimulus onset, offset, and background luminance. *Journal of the Optical Society of America*, 1971, **61**, 1190–1195.

Hill, J. W., & Bliss, J. C. Perception of sequentially presented tactile point stimuli. *Perception & Psychophysics*, 1968, **4**, 289–295.

Hirsh, I. J. Auditory perception of temporal order. *Journal of the Acoustical Society of America*, 1959, **31**, 759–767.

Hirsh, I. J., & Fraisse, P. Simultanéité et succession de stimuli hétérogènes. *L'Année Psychologique*, 1964, **64**, 1–19.

Hirsh, I. J., & Sherrick, C. E., Jr. Perceived order in different sense modalities. *Journal of Experimental Psychology*, 1961, **62**, 423–432.

Ibragimov, I. A. On the composition of unimodal distributions. *Theory of probability and its applications*, 1956, **1**, 255–260.

John, I. D. A statistical decision theory of simple reaction time. *Australian Journal of Psychology*, 1967, **19**, 27–34.

John, I. D. Some variables affecting judgments of auditory temporal numerosity. Unpublished manuscript, 1971.

Julesz, B. *Foundations of cyclopean perception.* Chicago: Univ. of Chicago Press, 1971.

Julesz, B., & White, B. Short-term visual memory and the Pulfrich phenomenon. *Nature*, 1969, **222**, 639–641.

Kappauf, W. E. An empirical sampling study of the Dixon and Mood statistics for the up-and-down method of sensitivity testing. *American Journal of Psychology*, 1969, **82**, 40–55.   (a)

Kappauf, W. E. Use of an on-line computer for psychophysical testing with the up-and-down method. *American Psychologist*, 1969, **24**, 207–211.   (b)

Kappauf, W. E., & Yeatman, F. R. Visual on- and off-latencies and handedness. *Perception & Psychophysics*, 1970, **8**, 46–50.

Kendall, M. G., & Stuart, A. *The advanced theory of statistics.* Vol. I. London: Griffin, 1958.

Kristofferson, A. B. Discrimination of successiveness: A test of a model of attention. *Science*, 1963, **139**, 112–113.

Kristofferson, A. B. Attention and psychophysical time. In A. F. Sanders (Ed.), *Attention and Performance*. *Acta Psychologica*, 1967, **27**, 93–100. (a)

Kristofferson, A. B. Successiveness discrimination as a two-state, quantal process. *Science*, 1967, **158**, 1337–1339. (b)

Kristofferson, A. B. "Attention" in R. M. Patton, T. A. Tanner, Jr., J. Markowitz, & J. A. Swets (Eds.), *Applications of research on human decisionmaking*. Washington, D.C.: NASA, 1970. Pp. 49–64.

Ladefoged, P., & Broadbent, D. E. Perception of sequence in auditory events. *Quarterly Journal of Experimental Psychology*, 1960, **12**, 162–170.

Levick, W. R. Variation in the response latency of cat retinal ganglion cells. Unpublished manuscript, 1972.

Levick, W. R., & Zacks, J. L. Responses of cat retinal ganglion cells to brief flashes of light. *Journal of Physiology*, 1970, **206**, 677–700.

Levinson, J. Z. Flicker fusion phenomena. *Science*, 1968, **160**, 21–28.

Levitt, H. Transformed up-down methods in psychoacoustics. *Journal of the Acoustical Society of America*, 1971, **49**, 467–477.

Liberman, A. M., Harris, K. S., Kinney, J. A., & Lane, H. The discrimination of relative onset-time of the components of certain speech and nonspeech patterns. *Journal of Experimental Psychology*, 1961, **61**, 379–388.

Lit, A. The magnitude of the Pulfrich stereophenomenon as a function of binocular differences of intensity at various levels of illumination. *American Journal of Psychology*, 1949, **62**, 159–181.

Matteson, H. H. Effects of surround luminance on perceptual latency. *Journal of the Optical Society of America*, 1970, **60**, 1125–1131.

Matteson, H. H., Lewis, J. H., & Dunlap, W. P. Effects of stimulus duration on temporal facilitation. Paper presented at the meeting of the Psychonomic Society, St. Louis, Missouri, November 1971.

Miller, J. M., & Glickstein, M. Neural circuits involved in visuomotor reaction time in monkeys. *Journal of Neurophysiology*, 1967, **30**, 399–414.

Miller, J. M., Moody, D. B., & Stebbins, W. C. Evoked potentials and auditory reaction time in monkeys. *Science*, 1969, **163**, 592–594.

Mollon, J. D. Temporal factors in perception. Unpublished doctoral thesis, University of Oxford, 1969.

Mollon, J. D., & Krauskopf, J. Reaction time as a measure of the temporal response properties in individual colour mechanisms. *Vision Research*, 1972, in press.

Moray, N. *Attention: Selective processes in vision and hearing*. London: Hutchinson, 1969.

Murray, H. G. Stimulus intensity and reaction-time: Evaluation of a decision-theory model. *Journal of Experimental Psychology*, 1970, **84**, 383–391.

Needham, J. G. Some conditions of prior entry. *Journal of General Psychology*, 1936, **14**, 226–240.

Oatley, K., Robertson, A., & Scanlan, P. M. Judging the order of visual stimuli. *Quarterly Journal of Experimental Psychology*, 1969, **21**, 172–179.

Pinheiro, M. L., & Ptacek, P. H. Reversals in the perception of noise and tone patterns. *Journal of the Acoustical Society of America*, 1971, **49**, 1778–1782.

Prestrude, A. M. Visual latencies at photopic levels of retinal illuminance. *Vision Research*, 1971, **11**, 351–361.

Raab, D. H. Statistical facilitation of simple reaction times. *Transactions of the New York Academy of Sciences*, 1962, **24**, 574–590.

Reber, A. S., & Anderson, J. R. The perception of clicks in linguistic and nonlinguistic messages. *Perception & Psychophysics*, 1970, **8**, 81–89.

Rogers, B. J., & Anstis, S. M. Intensity versus adaptation and the Pulfrich stereophenomenon.

Vision Research, 1972, **12**, 909–928.

Roufs, J. A. J. Perception lag as a function of stimulus luminance. *Vision Research*, 1963, **3**, 81–91.

Rubin, E. Geräuschverschiebungsversuche. *Acta Psychologica*, 1938, **4**, 203–236.

Rutschmann, J., & Link, R. Perception of temporal order of stimuli differing in sense mode and simple reaction time. *Perceptual and Motor Skills*, 1964, **18**, 345–352.

Rutschmann, R. Perception of temporal order of electrocutaneous stimuli and simple reaction time. Paper presented at the meeting of the Eastern Psychological Association, Boston, Massachusetts, April 1967.

Rutschmann, R. Perception of temporal order of auditory stimuli and simple reaction time. Paper presented at the meeting of the Eastern Psychological Association, Philadelphia, Pennsylvania, April 1969.

Sanford, A. J. Effects of changes in the intensity of white noise on simultaneity judgements and simple reaction time. *Quarterly Journal of Experimental Psychology*, 1971, **23**, 296–303.

Sanford, E. C. The personal equation. *American Journal of Psychology*, 1888, **2**, 3–38, 271–298, 403–430.

Smith, M. C. Theories of the psychological refractory period. *Psychological Bulletin*, 1967, **67**, 202–213.

Spearman, C. The method of 'right and wrong cases' ('constant stimuli') without Gauss's formulae. *British Journal of Psychology*, 1908, **2**, 227–242.

Sperling, G. Successive approximations to a model for short term memory. In A. F. Sanders (Ed.), *Attention and Performance. Acta Psychologica*, 1967, **27**, 285–292.

Sperling, G., & Sondhi, M. M. Model for visual luminance discrimination and flicker detection. *Journal of the Optical Society of America*, 1968, **58**, 1133–1145.

Sternberg, S. The discovery of processing stages: Extensions of Donders' method. In W. G. Koster (Ed.), *Attention and Performance II. Acta Psychologica*, 1969, **30**, 276–315.   (a)

Sternberg, S. Memory-scanning: Mental processes revealed by reaction-time experiments. *American Scientist*, 1969, **57**, 421–457.   (b)

Sternberg, S., Knoll, R. L., & Gates, B. A. Prior entry reexamined: Effect of attentional bias on order perception. Paper presented at the meeting of the Psychonomic Society, St. Louis, Missouri, November 1971.

Stevens, S. S. Neural events and the psychophysical law. *Science*, 1970, **170**, 1043–1050.

Stone, S. A. Prior entry in the auditory-tactual complication. *American Journal of Psychology*, 1926, **37**, 284–287.

Stroud, J. M. The fine structure of psychological time. In H. Quastler (Ed.), *Information theory in psychology*. Glencoe, Illinois: Free Press, 1955. Pp. 174–205.

Thomas, G. B., Hill, P. B., Carroll, F. S., & Garcia, B. Temporal order in the perception of vowels. *Journal of the Acoustical Society of America*, 1970, **48**, 1010–1013.

Thompson, R. F., Smith, H. E., & Bliss, D. Auditory, somatic sensory, and visual response interactions and interrelations in association and primary cortical fields of the cat. *Journal of Neurophysiology*, 1963, **26**, 365–378.

Titchener, E. B. *Lectures on the elementary psychology of feeling and attention.* New York: MacMillan, 1908.

Vaughan, H. G., Jr., Costa, L. D., & Gilden, L. The functional relation of visual evoked response and reaction time to stimulus intensity. *Vision Research*, 1966, **6**, 645–656.

Venables, P. H. Periodicity in reaction time. *British Journal of Psychology*, 1960, **51**, 37–43.

Vonnegut, K., Jr. *Slaughterhouse five*. New York: Delacorte, 1969.

Warren, R. M., Obusek, C. J., Farmer, R. M., & Warren, R. P. Auditory sequence: Confusion of patterns other than speech or music. *Science*, 1969, **164**, 586–587.

White, C. T. Temporal numerosity and the psychological unit of duration. *Psychological Monographs*, 1963, **77**, No. 12.

White, C. T., & Lichtenstein, M. Some aspects of temporal discrimination. *Perceptual and Motor Skills*, 1963, **17**, 471–482.

Wilson, J. A., & Anstis, S. M. Visual delay as a function of luminance. *American Journal of Psychology*, 1969, **82**, 350–358.

Zacks, J. L. Estimation of the variability of the latency of responses to brief flashes. *Vision Research*, 1972, in press.

Visual Perception of Temporal Order[1]

Ruth Rutschmann

Department of Psychology
Queens College,
City University of New York
and
Biometrics Research
New York State Department of Mental Hygiene
New York, New York

ABSTRACT

A systematic investigation of stimulus factors affecting the perceived temporal order (TO) of two brief visual flashes was conducted with four subjects. The experiments were based on a model that considers the interstimulus intervals (ISI) for the TO threshold as a measure of perceptual latency differences, and thus can be related to other processing speed data such as reaction time (RT). Compatible with this approach, the results indicate that ISI values vary as a function of site of stimulation and flash intensity, as well as with background conditions. Monocular, dichoptic, and binocular flash pairings produced no appreciable shift in TO judgments. The overall findings do not support the suggestion that the TO threshold is a fixed value, coincident with objective simultaneity. The effect of stimulus parameters on threshold changes was similar among subjects, while, as predictable from studies on various aspects of temporal resolution and discrimination, ISI magnitudes exhibited individual differences.

---

[1]Paper supported in part by PHS Grant MH 03616, NINDB Grant NB 05221 and NIMH Grant MH 18191.

687

I. Introduction

Empirical and theoretical generalizations on critical periods determining the speed of perceptual processing, as measured in studies of temporal resolution, have flourished in recent years (for example, Haber, 1968, 1969). In any attempt to generate laws governing temporal discriminations it is important to consider the nature of the response, that is, the task required of the subject. This investigation was primarily concerned with some psychophysical characteristics of the visual perception of temporal order (TO). If discrimination of temporal sequence is based on the time required to perceive and process brief visual inputs, judgments of TO can be used as a measure of perceptual latency (for example, Rutschmann, 1966). In contrast to simultaneity thresholds, which are based on judgments of synchrony versus asynchrony, TO thresholds are based on discrimination of relative onset and are considerably less variable, more indicative of the observer's temporal sensitivity, and also allow more easily for the use of accuracy indicators.

Based on data showing that an interstimulus interval (ISI) of 20 msec is required for 75% correct detection of the TO of two stimuli, Hirsch and Sherrick (1961) concluded that the TO threshold is a constant value, coincident with objective simultaneity and independent of stimulus conditions. It seems reasonable to expect, however, that changes in stimulus parameters will affect TO perception in a manner comparable to their effects on perceptual latency as measured by psychomotor and electrophysiological techniques. Since research on TO (Rutschmann, 1966, 1967, 1969) and on the covariation between TO and RT as a function of stimulus manipulations has already demonstrated that parallel processes are involved (Rutschmann & Link, 1964; Gibbon & Rutschmann, 1969), Hirsch and Sherrick's generalization appears untenable. Other investigators also have presented evidence on perceived simultaneity and order, in different modalities, that similarly challenge the notion of an invariant threshold (Babkoff & Sutton, 1963; Efron, 1963; Corwin & Boynton, 1968). Our approach is based on a model connecting TO and RT, as illustrated in Fig. 1. Its main feature is the notion that objective simultaneity may not result in "physiological" (Hilgard, 1933) or subjective simultaneity due to different latencies (L_1 and L_2) in processing the two stimuli (S_1 and S_2). Similarly, objective asynchrony may produce apparent simultaneity (judgment of TO at chance level). Further, the ISI for the TO threshold should correspond to the average difference in RT to S_1 and S_2, and is therefore a quantitative estimate of receptor-system latency difference to onset of stimulation. This view of a psychophysical–psychomotor relationship is based on the assumptions that: (a) latencies are independent of each other; (b) latencies do not vary with changes in the magnitude of the ISI; (c) the judgment of which stimulus is first, on TO trials, corresponds to

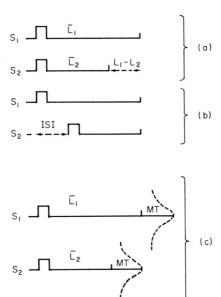

Fig. 1. Comparison of latency differences estimated from psychophysical (TO) and psychomotor (RT) measures: average perceptual latency to $S_1(\bar{L}_1, RT_1)$ is assumed longer than that to $S_2(\bar{L}_2, RT_2)$ by $L_1 - L_2$, such that at ISI $= \bar{L}_1 - \bar{L}_2 = 50\%$ response of TO. For TO measures, where $L_1 > L_2$, ISI $= \bar{L}_1 - \bar{L}_2$; (a) with simultaneous onset, response is S_2 first; (b) with asynchronous onset by ISI, response is 50% (threshold). For RT measures, where $RT_1 > RT_2$ and MT $= k$, (c) $\bar{L}_1 - \bar{L}_2 =$ ISI for 50%.

the first input processed; (d) on RT trials efferent latency (MT) to a signal is constant (k), and presumably adds little variability to total perceptual latency.

Whereas perceptual latency has been studied parametrically by psychophysical, psychomotor, and electrophysiological techniques, TO has not been systematically investigated. This report focuses on a series of experiments that attempted to fill this gap by a systematic study of the role of stimulus factors on visual TO.

II. Method

A. Apparatus

The subject was tested individually in a light-proof booth, facing a spherical background illuminated uniformly by a special projector. Test stimuli consisted of circular fields subtending $1°\ 11'$ visual angle, presented to the fovea and periphery (nasal retina) of each eye. The peripheral fields were placed at 10, 20, 30, 40, and 50° eccentricity on the horizontal meridian. Ten-msec light flashes were produced by Sylvania R1131C glow modulator tubes with ≤ 0.25-msec rise time, the luminance output of which was monitored. The subject's head and eye position was ensured by a special chin rest, and his instructions were to fixate the center of a diamond-shaped pattern formed by four miniature lamps placed at 1° from the foveal field. Surround and flash luminance was varied by means of Kodak W-96 neutral density filters. Temporal parameters of stimulation were controlled by Tektronix 162 waveform generators and calibrated by a Hewlett Packard 522B digital counter to within ±.1-msec precision. A digital recorder was used to print out trial data. Ready signals and the subject's response were given verbally via an intercom.

B. General Procedure

The subjects were familiarized with the apparatus and procedure in two preliminary unscored sessions. Each trial started with a verbal ready signal, followed by foreperiods of .8–1.0 sec and presentation of a foveal–peripheral flash pair (specific flash locations are described for each experiment separately). The subject adapted to the surround luminance for 10 min prior to the 1-hr session. The ISI between flash onsets was varied in equal interval steps according to the method of constant stimuli. The ISIs were positive (foveal flash leading), negative (foveal flash lagging), or zero (physical simultaneity). The step size and ISI ranges varied with the subject and stimulus condition: in most cases they turned out to be of the order of 10 msec and 60–80 msec, respectively. Instructions were to attend to the onset of the flashes. After each trial the subject made a forced-choice judgment of which flash appeared first, without receiving feedback.

A session consisted of four blocks of about 60 trials, with rest periods between blocks. Experiments were completed after approximately 200–400 trials per given flash pair under each stimulus condition.

C. Subjects

Four volunteer male subjects ranging in age from 16 to 27 years were tested.

D. Overall Treatment of Data

The data of each subject and stimulus condition were averaged separately for each experiment. The obtained proportions of response "foveal flash first" were plotted on a normal probability ordinate as a function of ISI, and straight lines were fitted to the data points by the method of least squares. The ISI value for 50% response and the corresponding probable error represent the subject's TO threshold (average latency difference to flash onset) and variability, respectively.

III. Site of Retinal Stimulation

EXPERIMENT 1: ECCENTRICITY OF PERIPHERAL FLASH

Given the well-known evidence on differences in structure and function across the retina (Østerberg, 1935; Poffenberger, 1912), especially as they might relate to relative latency, the location of flashes stimulating the peripheral fields of both eyes was varied. The stimulus pairs consisted of binocular foveal and monocular peripheral flashes of equal luminance, reported by the subjects as also matched in subjective brightness. In each session peripheral stimuli at two asymmetrical eccentricities in the nasal sides of the right and left eyes were presented, for example, 20 and 50°. To minimize directional eye movements and set effects, flash pairs were delivered randomly within trial blocks. A minimum of about 120 trials per flash was required to establish a reliable threshold. The subjects were questioned on phenomenal impressions (for example, brightness and movement cues) at the completion of the experiment.

Results

Highly consistent judgments were obtained with each subject within and between sessions. The TO thresholds shown in Fig. 2 indicate the average difference in latency to the foveal and peripheral flashes as a function of peripheral location, for each subject separately. The latency fluctuations with retinal position were qualitatively similar for all subjects: negative ISIs were required, indicating longer latency to peripheral flashes, increasing in value with increasing eccentricity. It is noteworthy, first, that the *absolute magnitude* of the latency difference between the fovea and peripheral sites show individual variations, a result consistent with a body of data on processing speed based on a variety of measures. Second, the individual variability of TO judgments with each flash pair was comparable across the subjects: the probable error of all TO functions was of the order of 20 msec. The graphs in Fig. 2 also show generally longer latencies to flashes stimulating the left rather than right nasal periphery.[2] In conjunction with our

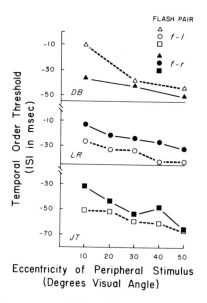

Fig. 2. ISI for 50% response of TO in light (−0.66 log mL) with binocular foveal-monocular peripheral stimuli of equal luminance (+1.24 log mL) as a function of peripheral flash location (nasal side of right and left eyes). Negative ISI = foveal flash onset delayed.

previous results (Rutschmann, 1966) an interesting generalization emerges: regardless of which eye is stimulated, flashes in the *left visual field* are perceived with a greater lag.

EXPERIMENT 2: VIEWING CONDITION

To provide further information on the contribution of peripheral versus central mechanisms in our measure of perceptual speeds, a modification of the previous experimental design was introduced intended also to determine whether a summation-like process could account for the temporal "superiority" of the fovea. Two of the subjects were tested with monocular (right or left eye), dichoptic (right or left fovea with contralateral periphery) and binocular (as in Experiment 1) flash pairs, at two eccentricities in each eye.

---

[2]It was ascertained that the deviant subject in this regard (DB) exhibited strong left-handed tendencies, an observation in line with proposals of hemispheric differences in temporal discriminations (Efron, 1963; Diamond, Rutschmann, & Bender, 1966) and in the amplitude and latency of the visual evoked response (Eason, Oden, & White, 1967; Eason & White, 1967), favoring the hemisphere dominant for speech.

The three forms of presentation were varied within blocks in a session and their order was counterbalanced between sessions. The stimulus and response conditions were otherwise identical.

Results

In Fig. 3 are shown the TO thresholds obtained for each flash pair, with type of stimulation as parameter (the data of Experiment 1 are included for comparison). The ISI values again express the same main effect, that is, the progressive lag of the peripheral system. No systematic trends attributable to type of stimulation, however, were revealed: latency differences between the fovea and periphery are *not* significantly affected by the nature of foveal stimulation. It is important that the inclusion of monocular and dichoptic viewing within the same session did not effect any appreciable shift in ISI nor in intra- and interindividual variabilities. When questioned following both experiments, the subjects reported the flashes as matched in brightness. Only one subject noticed on occasion an apparent movement between flashes, which evidently did not enter into his TO judgments in any systematic fashion.

In summary, as a function of retinal location the largest difference in latency is found between the fovea and 10°. With increasing displacement of the peripheral flash, the lag of the periphery increases on the average from about 30 to 50 msec. Beyond 10° the functions relating relative latency to eccentricity appears linear.

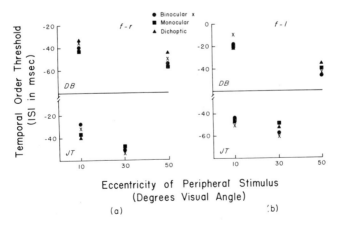

Fig. 3. ISI for 50% response of TO in light (−0.66 log mL) with equal luminance stimuli (+1.24 log mL) as a function of peripheral flash location (nasal side of right and left eyes), with type of foveal stimulation as parameter (× = corresponding points in Fig. 2).

EXPERIMENT 3: RETINAL LOCATION AND INTENSITY

Since stimulus strength is well known to be a major factor in the speed of response, it was of interest to determine the qualitative and quantitative effects of introducing an intensity difference between the various flash pairs. The precise effects of varying flash location might conceivably depend on the relative luminance of the flashes (Rains, 1963). Assuming no interaction between the two variables, and an inverse relationship between luminance and latency, the eccentricity function (Fig. 2) would shift by some constant value along the ISI axis. Empirically, our model suggests that a "constant" latency effect (change in the TO threshold) would obtain by relative increases in flash luminance or corresponding decreases in target distance. The issue of "reciprocity" here has theoretical bearing on at least two important questions that have been raised regarding visual sensitivity: the specific characteristics of temporal integration at and above threshold (Kietzman & Sutton, 1968) and the existence and measurement of processing stages (Sternberg, 1969).

In this test situation, the luminance of the foveal flash was decreased by about 2 log units relative to its original value when matched to the peripheral flashes. Two subjects were tested under conditions otherwise identical to those described for Experiment 1. Any change in the TO threshold (predictably toward less negative ISIs) with each flash pair then would reflect the increase in time of arrival of the foveal flash.

Results

The results are given in Fig. 4, wherein the original data for the equal luminance case presented in Fig. 2 are also shown to better illustrate the main finding.

It can be seen, first, that the relationship between the TO threshold and peripheral eccentricity is generally parallel to that already demonstrated. Second, the effect of dimming the foveal input is clearly expressed by an average shift of 30–40 msec toward less negative values of ISI. The single reversal in this trend occurred with subject JT at 10° in the right periphery, which was associated with an increase in probable error from 20 to about 40 msec. Otherwise, the variability of the subjects' TO judgments remained stable. With flash pairs *within* each eye the difference is relatively constant across eccentricities. Curiously, however, note that the ISIs do not change by the same amount for fovea–right and fovea–left stimuli, that is, perceived order is affected differentially depending on whether the dimmed foveal flash is presented with a right or left peripheral flash. Qualitatively this resembles the finding of monocular TO differences as a function of the visual field

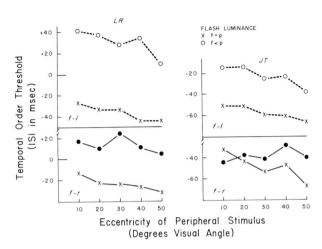

Fig. 4. ISI for 50% response of TO in light (−0.66 log mL) as a function of peripheral flash location (nasal side of right and left eyes) with equal ($f = p = +1.24$ log mL) and unequal ($f = −0.93$ log mL; $p = +1.24$ log mL) luminance flashes.

stimulated (Rutschmann, 1966) and of the laterality and location of the peripheral flash. Speculatively, possible differences in sensory magnitude between right and left peripheral signals may have produced varying degrees of subjective contrast within the range of foveal–peripheral pairs used. The precise relationships between apparent brightness of monocular and binocular inputs and their retinal location, as to how they might influence apparent sequence, require further study.

The question of an interaction between the effects of input site and intensity as suggested by Sternberg's (1969) model of RT is therefore not answered fully. Apparently the two factors are additive across, but independent within, eyes. Reciprocity between intensity and time of onset, however, appears to obtain: the overall increase in foveal latency suggests that a "trade" in physical parameters is possible, and similar in its effects to various other visual phenomena involving comparable manipulations (Lit, 1949; Kietzman, 1967; Prestrude, 1971).

IV. Effect of Luminance Differences in Light and Dark Adaptation

Reported differences in visual RT (Bartlett & McLeod, 1954) and in perceptual latencies with flash and surround luminance (Lit, 1949; Alpern, 1968; Prestrude & Baker, 1968) led to further investigation of the role of signal and surround intensity. This was accomplished by the systematic

change of both foveal and peripheral luminances over a wider range (span-
ning about 4 log units, from close to threshold to the limits of the apparatus).
One dichoptic flash pair was used, stimulating the left fovea and right
periphery at 20° on the nasal side. The data were recorded following 10
min of adaptation; light and dark surround conditions were used in separate
sessions.

The sequence of luminance values of both foveal and peripheral flashes
was counterbalanced within and between sessions. With the light background, four values of each were used. With the dark background, each
subject was tested with two levels of foveal intensity, paired with five levels
of peripheral intensity. The data obtained in about 200 trials with each
resulting flash pair again were pooled separately for each surround condition. (It was noted that no significant changes in ISI levels or variability
occurred as a function of dark adaptation within a session.)

Results

Representative thresholds of two subjects tested under light and dark
surround conditions are given in Fig. 5 as a function of peripheral flash
luminance, with foveal flash luminance as parameter. It can be seen that for
both surround conditions, thresholds vary with both peripheral and foveal
intensity.

In Fig. 5c the distance between the four functions, as compared with
ISI shifts within a given function, shows that TO thresholds in light vary
more with foveal than peripheral flash intensity: the separation between
functions, from positive to negative ISIs, is greater (about 60 msec) than

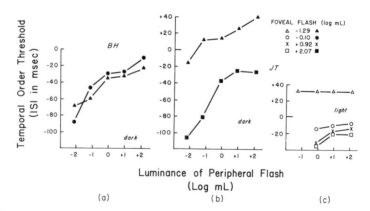

Fig. 5. ISI for 50% response of TO in light (−0.66 log mL) and darkness with one foveal
(left eye) peripheral (nasal side of right eye at 20°) flash pair as a function of peripheral flash
luminance, with foveal flash luminance as parameter.

changes within functions (about 15 msec), which asymptote at the highest intensity available.[3]

In darkness, however, larger fluctuations were produced by the intensity of the peripheral flash, yielding an overall ISI change of about 65 msec for each foveal value. The distances between functions again reveal latency changes at the fovea and, clearly, the expected inverse relationship between intensity and latency at both locations.

The main findings of this study indicate that in both light- and dark-adapted states: (a) about equal ISIs are required for threshold with equal luminance flashes, regardless of their *absolute* level; (b) relative to this "baseline," the flash the luminance of which is lowered must be delivered earlier. The perceptual latency to both foveal and peripheral flashes decreases as a negatively accelerated function of luminance.

V. Discussion

The TO method yields a reliable means of establishing quantitative and qualitative differences in perceptual latency. The major findings of the present investigation can be summarized as follows:

1. TO thresholds vary consistently as a function of the laterality and eccentricity of peripheral flashes, revealing shorter latency to a foveal flash and increasing latency with distance from the fovea.
2. There are no major differences in the functions obtained with monocular, binocular, and dichoptic flash pairs.
3. TO thresholds vary systematically with flash intensity, in both light- and dark-adapted states.
4. Individuals vary in their sensitivity to temporal intervals, but intra-individual variability remains stable throughout changes in the stimulus situation.

It is clear therefore that the TO threshold is not a fixed value, as proposed by Hirsch and Sherrick (1961), but is stimulus-bound and determined by individual differences in arrival times. This general result is in line with previous studies (Rutschmann & Link, 1964; Rutschmann, 1966, 1967) and with other reports on temporal processing phenomena that challenge the notion of a constant interval for identification of successiveness

---

[3]With the weakest foveal flash, the peripheral flash had no effect. These points were associated with a significant increase in ISI range and variability, not *systematically* related to peripheral intensity.

(Efron, 1963; Babkoff & Sutton, 1963; Corwin & Boynton, 1968). From our data it appears that the input processed first is the one at, or closest to, the center of visual fixation; the input processed second is either more distant or less intense, or both. The spatial displacements from center and stimulus strength appear to be, within limits, "tradeable."

That site of stimulation and stimulus intensity are significant factors in TO perception is compatible with a large body of literature on the effects of these variables on retinal sensitivity and perceptual speed. It is well known that spatial acuity varies across the retina (Wertheim, 1894) in relationship to differences in receptor density (Østerberg, 1935). Likewise, RT changes progressively with distance from the fovea increasing towards the periphery and being longer in the temporal than in the nasal visual field (Poffenberger, 1912; Lichtenstein & White, 1961; Rains, 1963). This agrees with the present results, as well as with a previous demonstration that TO thresholds reveal shorter latencies to nasal than to temporal flashes within one eye (Rutschmann, 1966). Significant changes in the average amplitude and latency of cortical-evoked potentials (EP) using similar flash paradigms also have been found, showing that RT covaries with changes in EP latency and varies inversely with EP amplitude (Donchin & Lindsley, 1966; Eason, Oden, & White, 1967). Although the exact conclusions to be drawn from these data are still controversial (Eason & White, 1967), perhaps due to differences in methodology, it is noteworthy that the psychophysical, psychomotor, and electrophysiological results are parallel.

As regards the behavioral measures on which we have focused, however, a reasonably direct comparison can be made. From our data, as flash eccentricity moves from 10 to 50°, the lag of the peripheral system increases by an average of .53 msec per degree of visual angle. In Poffenberger's study, the RT changes at comparable distances indicate a similar trend, though generally smaller latency differences: the largest, of the order of 6 msec, occurred between the fovea and 3°, 12 msec being the RT shift between 10 and 45°. Similar relationships between response speed and locus of stimulation have been observed in investigations of visual apparent simultaneity and movement thresholds; for example, inspection of Sweet's (1953) data indicates an increase in latency of about 5–25 msec to stimuli in the range between 5 and 40° in the periphery.

Concerning the second major stimulus factor involved, flash luminance, again the findings are consonant with a large body of RT data. An inverse relationship between intensity and latency has been found with both foveal and peripheral stimuli presented to the light- and dark-adapted eye (Bartlett & McLeod, 1954). Their report on RT as a function of flash and field luminance suggests that one of the effects of dark adaptation on response latency consists of an extension of the range, toward lower intensity values, over which latency varies minimally. This appears to be the case with TO thresholds as well (Fig. 4), which evidence a systematic and steeper change with decreases in flash luminance made possible by a darkened surround. Further, an experimental comparison of TO and RT on the same subjects, under conditions almost identical to the ones employed here, has shown that both tasks reflect about equally the effects of stimulus intensity with auditory as well as visual pairs (Rutschmann, 1969; Gibbon & Rutschmann, 1969). In support of our initial model, both tasks yield comparable descriptions of changes in latency in the expected direction. Individual differences in the absolute magnitude of latency fluctuations to a given stimulus pair, and in the amount of change across intensity conditions, were as characteristic as in all functions presented here. Analysis of the visual data suggested that intraindividual disparities in ISI levels between the TO threshold and average RT differences may reflect the operation of subjective criteria entering into the judgments of TO. It is reasonable to speculate that the individual differences typically found in discriminations of successiveness are determined at least partly by subjective decision criteria; whether and how they played a role in the present study cannot be evaluated since instructions and feedback were not manipulated. Hence, a meaningful next step is to provide information on the precise role of *response* factors in TO performance, as suggested by developments in psychophysics (see Swets, 1964) and decision-theory models of latency (Snodgrass, Luce, & Galanter, 1967; Murray, 1970).

In summary, our procedure has provided some insights into the sensory factors involved in visual temporal order, in striking conformity with predictions and information based on other measures of latency. Obviously, the paradigm bears on specific questions that have been raised regarding possible neural and attention mechanisms underlying temporal processing phenomena (Efron, 1963; Kristofferson, 1969). Accordingly, having called into question the notion of a constant TO threshold, it seems appropriate to conclude that analysis of order discriminations in terms of "correct" detection of onset differences would be fruitless. It seems more valuable to tackle specifically the psychophysical features of the relationship between objective and subjective time, between real and apparent sequence.

Acknowledgments

The author is indebted to Drs. J. Rutschmann and E. G. Heinemann, and thanks Drs. M. L. Kietzman for his helpful suggestions and critical reading of the manuscript and S. Sternberg for his stimulating comments.

References

Alpern, M. A note on visual latency. *Psychological Review*, 1968, **75**, 260–264.

Babkoff, H., & Sutton, S. Perception of temporal order and loudness judgments for dichotic clicks. *Journal of the Acoustical Society of America*, 1963, **35**, 574–577.

Bartlett, N. R., & McLeod, S. Effect of flash and field luminance upon human reaction time. *Journal of the Optical Society of America*, 1954, **44**, 306–311.

Corwin, T. R., & Boynton, R. M. Transitivity of visual judgments of simultaneity. *Journal of Experimental Psychology*, 1968, **78**, 560–568.

Diamond, S. P., Rutschmann, R., & Bender, M. B. Spatial bias and asymmetries in psychophysical judgments. *Archives of the American Neurological Association*, 1966, **91**, 145–151.

Donchin, E., & Lindsley, D. B. Averaged evoked potentials and reaction times to visual stimuli. *Electroencephalography and Clinical Neurophysiology*, 1966, **20**, 217–223.

Eason, R. G., & White, C. T. Averaged occipital responses to stimulation of sites in the nasal and temporal halves of the retina. *Psychonomic Science*, 1967, **7**, 309–310.

Eason, R. G., Oden, D., & White, C. T. Visually evoked cortical potentials and reaction time in relation to site of retinal stimulation. *Electroencephalography and Clinical Neurophysiology*, 1967, **22**, 313–324.

Efron, R. The effect of handedness on the perception of simultaneity and temporal order. *Brain*, 1963, **86** (Part II), 261–284.

Gibbon, J., & Rutschmann, R. Temporal order judgment and reaction time. *Science*, 1969, **165**, 413–415.

Haber, R. N. (Ed.), *Contemporary theory and research in visual perception*. New York: Holt, 1968.

Haber, R. N. (Ed.), *Information-processing approaches to visual perception*. New York: Holt, 1969.

Hilgard, E. R. Reinforcement and inhibition of eyelid reflexes. *Journal of General Psychology*, 1933, **8**, 85–113.

Hirsh, I. J., & Sherrick, C. E., Jr. Perceived order in different sense modalities. *Journal of Experimental Psychology*, 1961, **62**, 423–432.

Kietzman, M. L. Two-pulse measures of temporal resolution as a function of stimulus energy. *Journal of the Optical Society of America*, 1967, **57**, 809–813.

Kietzman, M. L., & Sutton, S. The interpretation of two-pulse measures of temporal resolution in vision. *Vision Research*, 1968, **8**, 287–302.

Kristofferson, A. B. Sensory attention. Technical Report No. 36, July, 1969, Department of Psychology, McMaster University, Hamilton, Ontario.

Lichtenstein, M., & White, C. T. Relative visual latency as a function of retinal locus. *Journal of the Optical Society of America*, 1961, **51**, 1033–1034.

Lit, A. The magnitude of the Pulfrich stereophenomenon as a function of binocular difference of intensity at various levels of illumination. *American Journal of Psychology*, 1949, **62**, 159–181.

Murray, H. G. Stimulus intensity and reaction time: Evaluation of a decision-theory model. *Journal of Experimental Psychology*, 1970, **84**, 383–391.

Østerberg, G. Topography of the layer of rods and cones in the human retina. *Acta Ophthalmologica Supplement*, 1935, **61**, 1–102.

Poffenberger, A. T. Reaction time to retinal stimulation, with special reference to the time lost in conduction through nerve centers. *Archives of Psychology*, 1912, **3**, 1–73.

Prestrude, A. M. Visual latencies at photopic levels of retinal illuminance. *Vision Research*, 1971, **11**, 351–361.

Prestrude, A. M., & Baker, H. New method of measuring visual–perceptual latency differences. *Perception and Psychophysics*, 1968, **4**, 152–154.

Rains, J. D. Signal luminance and position effects in human reaction time. *Vision Research*, 1963, **3**, 239–251.

Rutschmann, R. Perception of temporal order and relative visual latency. *Science*, 1966, **152**, 1099–1101. Also in R. N. Haber (Ed.), *Information-processing approaches to visual perception*. New York: Holt, 1969.

Rutschmann, R. Perception of temporal order of electrocutaneous stimuli and simple reaction time. Paper presented at the meeting of the Eastern Psychological Association, Boston, 1967.

Rutschmann, R. Perception of temporal order of auditory stimuli and simple reaction time. Paper presented at the meeting of the Eastern Psychological Association, Philadelphia, 1969.

Rutschmann, J., & Link, R. Perception of temporal order of stimuli differing in sense mode and simple reaction time. *Perceptual and Motor Skills*, 1964, **18**, 345–352.

Snodgrass, J. G., Luce, R. D., & Galanter, E. H. Some experiments on simple and choice reaction time. *Journal of Experimental Psychology*, 1967, **75**, 1–17.

Sternberg, S. The discovery of processing stages: extensions of Donders' method. *Acta Psychologica*, 1969, **30**, 276–315.

Sweet, A. L. Temporal discrimination by the human eye. *American Journal of Psychology*, 1953, **66**, 185–198.

Swets, J. A. (Ed.), *Signal detection and recognition by human observers*. New York: Wiley, 1964.

Wertheim, T. Über die indirekte Sehschärfe. *Zeitschrift für Psychologie*, 1894, **7**, 172–187.

Division of Attention in Successiveness Discrimination

Jonathan Baron

Department of Psychology
McMaster University
Hamilton, Ontario, Canada

ABSTRACT

For the general situation in which two discriminations must be made on each trial of an experiment, a "single-band" model is developed, which assumes that attention increases the probability of being correct on a task, and that at most one task is attended to on a trial. A maximum for the probability correct on both tasks, given the probability correct on each, is computed under general and specific sets of assumptions. The model is applied to data from successiveness discrimination tasks, and to the attention-switching hypothesis of successiveness discrimination.

I. Introduction

Most studies of attention involve asking a subject to do two tasks at the same time. We usually say that attention is limited when the need to perform one task impairs performance on the other. There are two different mechanisms that could account for such impairment. In the first, the subject simply cannot attend to more than one task at a time, and therefore must either give up on one task entirely, or furiously switch his attention back and forth between the two. In the second, the subject can attend to both tasks at once, although, because of a limited overall capacity (for example, Rumelhart, 1970), the presence of the second task could still impair performance on the first. These two mechanisms are exemplified by the single-band and multiple-band hypotheses, respectively, in signal-detection theory (Green & Swets, 1966), where the limitation on capacity is interpreted specifically as noise.

This paper proposes a new approach to testing whether the first, single-band, mechanism can account for impairment of one task by need to do a second, and then applies this approach to performance data on a pair of tasks in which a subject had to say whether two stimuli were simultaneous or successive. Previous attempts to test the single-band hypothesis have generally made strong assumptions about the limitation on performance of each task, for example, those made by signal detection theory (Green & Swets, 1966), which have recently been questioned by Krantz (1969), and by Baron (1971) for successiveness discrimination in particular. Other attempts, such as that of Franzen, Markowitz, and Swets (1970) have not concerned themselves with whether the subject *could* divide his attention, but whether he did so spontaneously in a situation in which it is not clear whether dividing attention between two tasks would help or hurt performance on one of them.

II. The Model

Consider two tasks in which a subject must choose between a small number of alternative responses on each trial. A task may be said to be in a state of attention or a state of nonattention. Let us define attention to task A by saying that the probability of being correct on task A with attention, P_A, is greater than the probability of being correct without attention, Q_A. The assumption of the single-band hypothesis is that at most one task can be in a state of attention. Thus, we assume that if the probability of being correct on task A is P_A, then it is Q_B on task B, the other task. We also allow the possibility that the subject attends to neither task. In this case, the probability of being correct on task A is R_A, and R_B for task B. We assume that $P_A > R_A$, $P_B > R_B$. It need not be true that $R_i = Q_i$, since special factors (such as the subject shutting his eyes and missing all the stimuli completely) may be involved in attention to neither task. In any case, P_i, Q_i, and R_i cannot be less than chance performance. We further assume that performances on the tasks are independent across all trials in which task A is in one state and task B in another. That is, if the subject attends to task A on every trial of the experiment, being correct on task A will be independent of being correct on task B. This may be considered as part of the definition of the states.

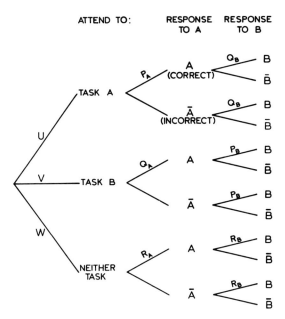

Fig. 1. Possible states of attention and correctness of responses under most general assumptions.

The entire set of possible states is illustrated in Fig. 1. The tree does not imply any ordering of decisions, but simply a way of categorizing the possibilities. Thus, U is the probability of attending to task A; V is the probability of attending to task B; and W is the probability of attending to neither. Of course, $U + V + W = 1$. We may also see that

$$p(A) = UP_A + VQ_A + WR_A, \tag{1a}$$

$$p(B) = UQ_B + VP_B + WR_B, \tag{1b}$$

$$p(AB) = UP_AQ_B + VQ_AP_B + WR_AR_B, \tag{1c}$$

where $p(A)$, $p(B)$, and $p(AB)$ represent the probability of being correct on task A, task B, and on both tasks, respectively, on a trial.

Before proceeding, it is worthy of note that no assumption is made here about *why* P_A is greater than Q_A, that is, why attention helps performance. It is, for example, possible that attention increases sensitivity, or that it changes the response bias so that percentage of correct responses will increase by movement of bias toward a more optimal point on the Response Operating Characteristic, or even that attention decreases the variability in response bias around this optimal point. The arguments for defining attention in this way, rather than in terms of a derived measure of sensitivity, are, first, that no assumptions need to be made about the nature of the threshold, and second, that the subjects, in fact, are instructed to maximize the percentage of correct responses—which gives the measure a certain face validity is nothing else.

Given the above assumptions, we may test this single-band model by holding $p(A)$ and $p(B)$ fixed, and calculating an upper bound for $p(AB)$. Since all three of these quantities can be estimated from data, it is possible to disconfirm the model by showing that $p(AB)$ exceeds the upper bound.

To find the maximum value of $p(AB)$, we fix $p(A)$ and $p(B)$, and consider $p(AB)$ to be a function of the remaining nine variables in Eqs. (1a–c). All of these nine variables are bounded by definition. Furthermore, $p(AB)$ either varies monotonically with each variable, regardless of the value of the others, or does not depend on it (for example, on W). Thus, we can find the maximum of $p(AB)$ by maximizing $p(AB)$ with respect to one variable at a time, as long as we make no premature conclusions concerning bounds on other variables.

Beginning with Q_A, let us hold all variables constant except $p(AB)$ and Q_A. From Eqs. (1a and b), it follows that

$$UP_A = p(A) - VQ_A - WR_A, \tag{2}$$

$$VP_B = p(B) - UQ_B - WR_B.$$

Substituting Eqs. (2) in the expression for $p(AB)$ in Eq. (1c), we get

$$p(AB) = Q_B [p(A) - VQ_A - WR_A] + Q_A [p(B) - UQ_B - WR_B]$$
$$+ WR_A R_R. \tag{3}$$

We can see that $p(AB)$ increases with Q_A, regardless of the values chosen for other variables, by differentiating Eq. (3) with respect to Q_A. and substituting, from Eq. (1b), for $p(B)$:

$$dp(AB)/dQ_A = V(P_B - Q_B). \tag{4}$$

Since $Q_B \leq P_B$, and since the same analysis could be done for Q_B, $p(AB)$ will be at a maximum when either $Q_A = P_A$ or $Q_B = P_B$. If both $Q_A = P_A$ and $Q_B = P_B$, then Eqs. (1a–c) become

$$p(A) \quad = (1 - W)P_A + WR_A, \tag{5a}$$

$$p(B) \quad = (1 - W)P_B + WR_B, \tag{5b}$$

$$p(AB) = (1 - W)P_A P_B + WR_A R_B. \tag{5c}$$

If, say, Q_B does not equal P_B, but $Q_A = P_A$, we can define $P_B{}^* = (UQ_B - VP_B)/(U + V)$ so that Eqs. (5b–c) hold for $P_B{}^*$ in place of P_B, so we may proceed assuming Eqs. (5a–c) in any case.

By substituting for R_A, just as we substituted for UP_A above, we find

$$dp(AB)/dP_A = (1 - W)(P_B - R_B). \tag{6}$$

This can be done for P_B as well. By substituting for P_A, we get

$$dp(AB)/dR_A = -W(P_B - R_B). \tag{7}$$

Since, by assumption, $P_B > R_B$, it is clear that $p(AB)$ increases with P_B and decreases with R_B, regardless of values of other parameters, when these other values are held constant. Likewise, $p(AB)$ increases with P_A and decreases with R_A. Furthermore, it is easily shown that for a given W and $p(A)$, P_A varies inversely with R_A, and likewise, P_B varies inversely with R_B. Thus, assuming Eqs. (5a–c), for given values of $p(A)$ and $p(B)$ we must maximize the P's and minimize the R's in order to maximize $p(AB)$.

Let us now assume that $p(A) \geq p(B)$. In this case, we can set P_A equal to its maximum possible value, 1, and R_B equal to its minimum possible value, chance performance (which we will assume henceforth to be $\frac{1}{2}$, since it is $\frac{1}{2}$ for two-choice tasks). The values of P_B and R_A will depend on our choice of W. It turns out, however, that within the constraints now imposed, our choice of W is no longer important for maximizing $p(AB)$. Specifically, we now have

$$p(A) = 1 - W + WR_A, \tag{8a}$$

$$p(B) = (1 - W)P_B + \tfrac{1}{2}W, \tag{8b}$$

$$p(AB) = (1 - W)P_B + \tfrac{1}{2}WR_A. \tag{8c}$$

By eliminating R_A and P_B, it follows that

$$p(AB) = p(B) + \tfrac{1}{2}p(A) - \tfrac{1}{2}, \tag{9}$$

which is the maximum value we have been seeking.

The assumptions made in computing this maximum are very strong. We have assumed that performance on one of the tasks with attention P_A is perfect, and that performance on the other task, when the subject attends to neither task, is at chance. Further, Q_A and Q_B will be at their maxima P_A and P_B, respectively, so that attending to one task, for this maximum, does not impair performance on the other. If $p(AB)$ is close to the maximum in Eq. (9), then Q_A or Q_B must be close to its maximum.

A special case of the model in Fig. 1 assumes that $Q_A = R_A$ and $Q_B = R_B$.

In other words, performance on a task not attended to is equally poor whether the lack of attention is due to attending to the other task or to neither. While this model is easier to reject, it is closer in conception to most of the single-band models in the literature (see Swets & Kristofferson, 1970), which assume chance performance without attention. The assumption of chance performance without attention, while even easier to reject, is not considered here because of anecdotal evidence suggesting that detection without prior attention is sometimes possible, for example, when we are bitten by a mosquito.

If we assume that

$$Q_A = R_A \qquad \text{and} \qquad Q_B = R_B,$$

Eqs. (1a–c) lead to

$$p(AB) = p(A)Q_B + p(B)Q_A - Q_A Q_B. \tag{10}$$

If either $Q_A = P_A$ or $Q_B = P_A$, the maximum value for $p(AB)$ will be

$$p(AB) = p(A)p(B), \tag{11}$$

the prediction that would result if performances on the two tasks were independent.

The following experiment on successiveness discrimination provides an example for applying the above analysis.

III. The Experiment: Method

The two tasks used each required the subject to say whether two stimuli were simultaneous or successive. Each trial began with the presentation for 1 sec of four O's in a square pattern on a cathode ray tube. The stimuli consisted of each O suddenly being replaced by an X or a Y in the same position. The letters were 8 mm high, 6 mm wide, and their centers were 25 mm apart horizontally and vertically, a visual angle of about 2.5°. The subject sat about 60 cm away in a dimly lit room. The two tasks were to say whether a pair of X's appeared successively or not, and likewise for a pair of Y's. The first X always appeared in the upper left position, and the second Y in the lower right. On half the trials, the other X appeared in the upper right and the other Y in the lower left, and on the other half, the reverse. Thus, the subject could not tell beforehand whether the two members of each stimulus pair would be oriented horizontally or vertically with respect to one another. This was done to prevent performance on one task from benefiting at the expense of performance on the other task, from a fixed order of switching attention between positions (see below).

Each pair of letters was either successive by 42 msec or simultaneous. The subject indicated his responses by pressing buttons, and could delay the onset of the next trial by holding the buttons down. On half of the trials, the first member of the Y pair preceeded the first member of the X pair by 21 msec. (The reason for this is irrelevant to the present context, and data from these trials will not be discussed here.) On the other half of the trials, the pairs began simultaneously. All conditions were presented randomly.

Four subjects were each tested for 12 sessions of 512 trials per session. Only the last 10 sessions are analyzed. Performance over these 10 sessions was relatively stable. The increase in proportion of overall correct responses between the first and the last session, for the data under consideration, were .006 for BK, .036 for KS, .066 for LW, and .054 for PM, respectively.

IV. Results and Discussion

Table 1 shows the results, and the maximum values of $p(AB)$ predicted by the strong [Eqs. (1a–c)] and weak [Eq. (10)] sets of assumptions described above. Here, $p(A)$ represents performance on the X's, and $p(B)$, the Y's. It can be seen that in no case is $p(AB)$ less than the maximum predicted by the weak set of assumptions [Eq. (11)]. [If the last five sessions alone are considered, there are two cases in which the value of $p(AB)$ falls below $p(A)p(B)$, by .002 for BK (vertical), and by .004 for LW (horizontal).] Thus, acceptance of these assumptions leads to the conclusion that the subjects in fact can attend to both tasks at once, on at least some proportion of trials.

Table 1. *Obtained Values and Predictions for p(AB) from Eqs. (9) and (11)*

Subject	Orientation within pair	Obtained values			Predicted maxima	
		$p(A)$	$p(B)$	$p(AB)$	Eq. (9)	Eq. (11)
BK	Vertical	.557	.589	.340	.372	.340
	Horizontal	.786	.674	.542	.567	.530
KS	Vertical	.737	.773	.601	.624	.570
	Horizontal	.841	.746	.654	.667	.627
LW	Vertical	.745	.722	.551	.595	.537
	Horizontal	.796	.739	.589	.639	.588
PM	Vertical	.727	.762	.565	.637	.554
	Horizontal	.787	.674	.530	.568	.530

On the other hand, the more general assumptions of Eqs. (1a–c) and (9) cannot be rejected, although one subject (KS) appears to be close. For the last five sessions, for KS (vertical), $p(A) = .714$, $p(B) = .813$ and, $p(AB) = .622$, which exceeded the maximum [Eq. (9)] of .621. This difference, of course, is not statistically significant, but is suggestive given the conservative assumptions behind Eq. (9).

One hypothesis about successiveness discrimination that can be considered in the light of the rejection of Eq. (10) is Kristofferson's attention-switching model (for example, the contribution of Kristofferson & Allan to this volume). This model holds that successiveness cannot be perceived at all unless the subject is able to switch his attention from the channel (in this case, presumably, the position) of the first stimulus, after it occurs, to that of the second stimulus in the pair, before it occurs. This model also holds that the subject can only attend to one channel at a time, and that there is a minimum time between switches.

For the data in Table 1, attending to both tasks—which clearly occurs given the assumptions of Eq. (10)—has a specific interpretation in the attention-switching model. Specifically, the subject must switch attention twice on at most half the trials, and three times on the remainder (when he uses a less-than-optimal order of switching) within the 42 msec in order to avoid having to guess on one of the tasks. (It is assumed here that the subject is able to make use of his knowledge that successiveness of the first X and the second Y implies successiveness of the Y's. If not, the subject will have to switch even more.) If the subject does not switch fast enough, he will have to guess on one of the tasks (which will be exactly as likely to be the X task as the Y task), or on both. If "not guessing" means being correct with probability P_A or P_B, and "guessing," Q_A or Q_B (assumed to be .5 in the Kristofferson–Allan model), then the assumptions of Eq. (10) are satisfied if the subject never switches more than twice in 42 msec. Since these assumptions can be rejected, the minimum time needed for switching attention must be at most 21 msec, since a considerable proportion of trials must involve attention (nonguessing) to both tasks. This is considerably lower than other estimates of the minimum switching time based on successiveness data (see the contribution of Kristofferson & Allan to this volume).

Since much of the argument for attention switching time as an explanation for errors in successiveness discrimination has been based on the constancy of the minimum switching time, it is suggested that the results presented here are additional evidence (see Baron, 1971) against this explanation. It is, however, possible that different explanations hold for different stimuli.

Acknowledgments

Ron Kinchla and Saul Sternberg provided extensive, and much appreciated, comments on an earlier version of this paper. Financial support was provided by grant A7803 from the National Research Council of Canada.

References

Baron, J. The threshold for successiveness. *Perception and Psychophysics*, **10**, 201–207, 1971.

Franzen, O., Markowitz, J., & Swets, J. A. Spatially-limited attention to vibrotactile stimulation. *Perception and Psychophysics*, **7**, 193–196, 1970.

Green, D. M., & Swets, J. A. *Signal detection theory and psychophysics*. New York: Wiley, 1966.

Krantz, D. H. Threshold theories of signal detection. *Psychological Review*, **76**, 308–324, 1969.

Rumelhart, D. E. A multicomponent theory of the perception of briefly exposed visual displays. *Journal of Mathematical Psychology*, **7**, 191–218, 1970.

Swets, J. A., & Kristofferson, A. B. Attention. *Annual Review of Psychology*, **21**, 339–366, 1970.

An Invariant Characteristic of Perceptual Systems in the Time Domain[1]

Robert Efron

Neurophysiology–Biophysics Research Laboratories
Veterans Administration Hospital
Martinez, California

ABSTRACT

Using a method of cross-modality simultaneity judgments, the perceptual onset and offset latencies for vibratory stimuli of different durations were compared. The perceptual onset latency did not alter with changes in stimulus duration. The perceptual offset latency was constant (and equal to the perceptual onset latency) only for stimuli longer than a critical value. As stimuli were made shorter than this critical value, the perceptual offset latency increased. For these brief stimuli, the sum of the perceptual offset latency and the stimulus duration was found to be a constant. Similar experiments, previously performed on the visual and auditory modalities, revealed the same invariant relationship between perceptual offset latency and stimulus duration. This relationship also was found in electrophysiological measurements of the latency of the on and off response in the visual system of the cat.

I. Introduction

The concept of "persistence of vision" refers to the idea that the conscious awareness of a visual stimulus may, under certain conditions, outlast the duration of the physical stimulus. The concept of persistence has been

---

[1]The research described in this paper has been supported in its entirety by the Veterans Administration, Department of Medicine and Surgery.

713

often invoked to "explain" at the psychological level of analysis such visual phenomena as flicker fusion (LeGrand, 1957), apparent motion and meta-contrast (Kahneman, 1967), the stereoscopic fusion of temporally disparate exposures to each eye (Efron, 1957; Engel, 1970), and the chromatic fusion of the sectors of a spinning Newton wheel (Piéron, 1952) (to name only a few).

Despite the fact that the phenomenon of persistence has been recognized in other sensory modalities such as the tactile and auditory sense (von Békésy, 1933), neither the psychophysical investigations of persistence nor the physiological studies of its neural correlates have yet provided a coherent set of data which permit the formulation of a rigorous and quantitative model of perception in the time domain that is applicable to *all* sensory modalities.

The need for such a general theory of persistence has become more critical in recent years with the introduction of three new theories that relate to temporal aspects of perceptual cognitive function. The first of these is the revival by Stroud (1955) of the perceptual-moment hypothesis—a conceptual model of information processing in the time domain that purports to account for many, if not all, of the phenomena that previously had been treated as manifestations of persistence. Although two major variants of the perceptual moment hypothesis have been proposed, neither the "discrete" moment (Bergson, 1913; Stroud, 1955) nor the traveling moment (James, 1890; Allport, 1968) hypotheses make any explicit reference to the concept of persistence. It is thus not clear if the various perceptual moment hypotheses actually incorporate the concept of persistence or ignore it entirely (see Efron & Lee, 1971).

The second area of current theory that relates to the concept of persistence is the field of attention. The various speculations concerning the shifting of attention between two sensory channels and the permissible moments in time when this switch may occur (Kristofferson, 1967a, b) similarly do not make explicit the relationship of the new theory to the phenomenon of persistence. It is not clear if these attention models are intended to subsume the phenomenon of persistence or if the effects of persistence are considered to be outside the sphere of these theories.

The third area of contemporary theory that relates to the concept of persistence are the studies of "short-term visual storage (memory)." Since the publication of Sperling's monograph in 1960, which focused on the question of short-term visual storage using the method of partial report, increasing interest has been generated concerning the phenomenon of persistence. Once again, it is not always clear if the concept of short-term visual storage is to be considered identical with "visual persistence," or if the concept of short-term storage subsumes the phenomenon of persistence as merely one particular manifestation of the wider phenomenon of storage (see Haber & Standing, 1969).

The experimental program described here was initiated for the purpose of studying the precise relationship between the duration of a stimulus applied to a receptor system and the duration of the perceptual experience of that stimulus. The details of the method and some of the findings for the visual and auditory modalities already have been published (Efron, 1970a, b, c, d). The broad goals of these investigations were:

1. to develop and validate a method which could be applied to any perceptual modality [methods such as that reported by Haber and Standing (1969), Kahneman (1967) and Allport (1968) are suitable for vision but not for auditory and tactile senses];

2. to compare, in the various sensory modalities, the time course of perception as a function of stimulus duration (as well as other stimulus parameters);

3. to relate these findings to the various hypotheses concerning the perceptual moment, attention switching, and short-term (iconic) storage;

4. to correlate these findings with the electrophysiological properties of the various perceptual pathways.

The specific purpose of the present report is to add to the previously reported findings in the visual and auditory modalities some recently obtained data in the vibratory modality which point strongly to the existence of an invariant characteristic of *all* perceptual systems in the time domain. Also to be presented are electrophysiological studies of the on and off responses in the visual system which are closely correlated with the psychophysical findings.

II. The Experimental Paradigm

The psychophysical method used in the present experiments is a modification of one used by Sperling (1967). The subjects were required to make judgments of simultaneity between stimuli presented in two modalities. In the first experiment (Efron 1970c), brief auditory stimuli (0.1-msec clicks) were used as "indexing" stimuli to estimate the durations of the perceptions of longer visual stimuli. In the second experiment (Efron 1970c), brief (5-msec) visual stimuli were used as "indexing" stimuli to estimate the durations of the perceptions of longer auditory stimuli. In the third experiment, reported in detail here, brief auditory stimuli (0.1-msec clicks) or brief visual stimuli (5-msec light flashes) were used to estimate the durations of the perceptions of longer vibratory stimuli. In each experiment the subject judged the simultaneity of the index stimulus delivered in one modality to the onset and then to the offset of a longer stimulus delivered to a different modality. Since the three experiments are methodologically identical, only the vibratory experiment will be used to illustrate the means by which the duration of the perception was measured.

A vibratory stimulus was delivered to the tip of a finger and a brief "index" stimulus was presented to another modality. The two stimuli initially were presented asynchronously so that the subject had no difficulty observing that the onset of the index stimulus preceded the onset of the vibratory stimulus. This asynchrony was reduced by 10-msec steps until the subject first reported that the *onsets* of the vibratory stimulus and the index stimulus were simultaneous. The temporal location of the index stimulus in relation to the onset of the vibratory stimulus at the point of subjective simultaneity was recorded in milliseconds. The stimuli then were presented sufficiently asynchronously so that the subject had no difficulty observing that the onset of the index stimulus was much later than the onset of the vibratory stimulus. The asynchrony again was reduced in 10-msec steps until he reported that the *onsets* of the two stimuli were simultaneous. The temporal location of the index stimulus in relation to the onset of the vibratory stimulus at the point of subjective simultaneity was recorded once again. The mean value of these two determinations was used as a measure of the cross-modal timing error of the *onsets* of the two stimuli.

Immediately upon completion of the above two determinations, the subject was asked to report when the onset of the index stimulus was simultaneous with the *offset* of the vibratory stimulus. The same method of descending limits from alternate (temporal) directions was used.

The two procedures just described are illustrated diagrammatically in Fig. 1a and b. The large, horizontal open rectangle denotes the vibratory stimulus which commenced (arbitrarily) at the 500th msec after the start of an electronic clock. The black bar just above the vibratory stimulus denotes the perception of the vibratory stimulus. It will be noted that the onset of the perception of the vibration is delayed with reference to the physical onset of the stimulus by the interval of time denoted by A. This interval includes all time utilized in activating the neural receptors in the skin, the time expended in transmission of the neural volley from the fingertip to the brain, and all other delays that might occur before this neural volley gives rise to the conscious awareness that a vibratory stimulus has commenced. Interval A will be referred to as the perceptual onset delay of the vibratory stimulus. It will also be noted in Fig. 1a and b that the perceptual experience of the vibratory stimulus outlasts the physical stimulus. This results from the same types of transmission and other delays which

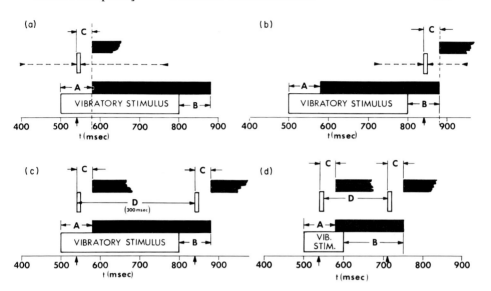

Fig. 1. Experimental paradigm (see text).

affected the perceptual onset. The perceptual offset delay of the vibratory stimulus is indicated by interval B.

A similar set of considerations affects the perception of the index stimulus, which is illustrated as a small open rectangle. In the experiments to be reported the index stimulus was either a click or a brief light flash. Interval C denotes the perceptual onset latency of the index stimulus. Since the intensity and other parameters of the index stimulus do not change throughout the experiment, interval C is assumed to be constant. The perceptual offset delay of the index stimulus has not been illustrated since it is not relevant to the experimental paradigm.

Figure 1a represents the temporal position of the index stimulus in relation to the onset of a 300-msec vibratory stimulus when the subject reports that the onsets of the two stimuli are simultaneous. This is represented by the synchrony of the onsets of the two perceptions (indicated by the dotted vertical line). It will be noted in Fig. 1a that when the onset of two perceptions are simultaneous, the onsets of the two physical stimuli are asynchronous. (This follows from the fact that the perceptual onset delay for the index stimulus and the vibratory stimulus will depend on their respective pathway lengths and intensities and will only rarely be identical.) The temporal location of the onset of the index stimulus (which results in simultaneous perceptions) is indicated by a small vertical arrow along the time base. This value (referred to in Tables 1, page 722, and 2, page 723, as "Index at on") is obtained, as already mentioned, from the mean of the two descending trials in opposite temporal directions which are indicated by the dotted horizontal arrows adjacent to the index stimulus.

Figure 1b represents the temporal position of the index stimulus in relation to the offset of the vibratory stimulus when the subject reported that the onset of the index stimulus was simultaneous with the *offset* of the vibration. Note that the offset of the perception of vibration is simultaneous with the onset of the perception of the index stimulus and that the onset of the index stimulus is not synchronous with the offset of the vibratory stimulus. The temporal location of the onset of the index stimulus (which results in simultaneous perceptions) is indicated by the small vertical arrow along the time base. This value (referred to in Tables 1 and 2 as "Index at off") also is obtained from the mean of the two descending trials in opposite temporal directions which are indicated by the dotted horizontal arrows adjacent to the index stimulus.

Figure 1c illustrates how D, the perceptual duration, was derived from the two procedures illustrated in Fig. 1a and b. D thus represents the temporal interval between the two small vertical arrows drawn on the time base. In the example illustrated, the amount of asynchrony between the two stimuli in Fig. 1a is equal to and in the same direction as that found in Fig. 1b. From this fact, coupled with the assumption that interval C remains constant, it follows that the perceptual onset delay (A) was equal to the perceptual offset delay (B), and that the duration of the vibratory perception was precisely equal to the duration of the vibratory stimulus. It should be stressed that while this experimental method does not provide any information concerning the absolute magnitude of A, B, or C, it nevertheless permits a determination of the absolute magnitude of D. In the experiments to be described, the magnitude of D was determined as a function of the duration of the vibratory stimulus.

The conventional definition of persistence, that is, that the perception of a stimulus continues for some period after the end of the stimulus, does not take full cognizance of the fact that the perceptual offset delay may be equal to the perceptual onset delay. In such a case it is somewhat misleading to use the term "persistence" because the psychological event (the perception) does not, in fact, persist for any longer than the physical event. The psychological event, that is, the perception, is merely displaced temporally. For this reason, the term persistence will be used in a more restricted sense in this paper as occurring only when the perceptual offset delay (B) is *longer* than the perceptual onset delay (A). Only under these circumstances does the perception persist for a longer period of time than the duration of the stimulus. This is illustrated in Fig. 1d for a 100-msec stimulus.

III. Method

A. SUBJECTS

The experimental subjects were college or high school students, paid for their services, who had no knowledge of the purpose of the experiments. Initially, all subjects reported appreciable difficulty in making the cross-modal simultaneity judgments, even for the longest (800-msec) vibratory stimulus. The standard deviation of 20 observations (where one observation was the difference between one value of the onset judgment and one value of the offset judgment) was often as much as ±50–60 msec. After several hours experience, they learned to maintain their judgmental criteria as indicated by a decreasing standard deviation. Only two subjects who could perform consistently with a standard deviation below ±20 msec then were used for the formal experiment. Four other subjects were rejected due to excessive variation. Although RD (a 22-year-old male) was able to perform the cross-modality experiment using a click as the index stimulus and maintain low standard deviations, the four other (rejected) subjects could not achieve this level of performance. For reasons that remain obscure, the major complaint of these four subjects was that the click seemed to interfere with the perception of the "off" of the vibration. They reported that it was difficult to attend to both stimuli at the same time. For this reason, a brief (5-msec) light flash was substituted for the click. SL (a 17-year-old female), one of the four previously rejected subjects, completed the experiment using the light flash as the index stimulus; the other three rejected subjects were not retested. Since the results using two different index stimuli are comparable, both sets of data will be reported.

B. EQUIPMENT

1. Experiment I: Vibration.

The vibratory stimulus consisted of a small probe (1.8-mm diameter) that just barely protruded from a hole in a metal plate. The finger rested on the plate, the probe stimulating the pulp of the fingertip. The probe was attached to a vibrator (Ling Model 102), which was driven by a power amplifier (Ling Model 25). The input to the power amplifier was a 100 ± 2-Hz sinusoidal output from an oscillator. The output was shaped by an electronic switch (Grason-Stadler 829 E) to provide a pulse with controllable rise and decay times. The degree of skin deformation (peak to peak) was estimated to be 0.04 in. by a linear transducer (Hewlett-Packard Model 7DCTD) through which the probe passed.

The auditory index stimulus (used for subject RD) consisted of an unfiltered and unshaped dichotic click produced by a pulse of .1 msec delivered to Koss Pro/4 headphones. The intensity of the click was 80 dB SPL when measured at a frequency of 2000 pulses/sec.

The visual index stimulus (used for subject SL) consisted of a 5-msec flash from a glow modulator lamp (Sylvania R1131C). The subject looked directly at this 11.0 ft-L source, which subtended a visual angle of 10′.

The stimuli were controlled by a digital timing system (Iconix Model 6257-6010-6083) which provided (a) gating pulses to the Grason-Stadler switch to turn on and off the vibratory stimuli, and (b) a trigger to a pulse generator (Tektronix Type 161), the output of which was either fed into the earphones to produce the click or which was utilized to gate the glow modulator tube. The accuracy of these digital timing circuits was ±0.01 msec.

2. Experiment II: Vision.

The visual stimulus consisted of a circular homogenous disc of light subtending a visual angle of 1°40′. It was viewed monocularly in the dark through an artificial pupil. The field was illuminated by a glow-modulator tube covered by a red filter. The luminance was 3.14 ft-L. The index stimulus was a click. (For details, see Efron, 1970c.)

3. Experiment III: Audition.

The auditory stimulus consisted of a gated coherent sinusoidal tone burst of 2000 Hz presented dichotically to both ears at 50 dB (re .0002 microbars) via earphones. The index stimulus was a 5-msec flash from a glow modulator tube of 3.4 ft-L. (For details, see Efron 1970c.)

C. Experimental Procedure

The method of descending limits using 10-msec steps already has been described. The judgment of simultaneity of the *onset* of the vibratory stimulus with the onset of the index stimulus was made twice, once from each direction (see Fig. 1a). The two limiting values were recorded and averaged. This mean represented one "on" observation. This was followed immediately by a judgment of simultaneity of the *offset* of the vibratory stimulus with the onset of the index stimulus (see Fig. 1b). The two limiting values were recorded and averaged. This mean represented one "off" observation. The duration of the perception (D) was obtained by subtracting the value (in milliseconds) of the "off" observation from the value of the "on" observation. This procedure provided one value of D. The entire procedure was repeated 20 times, providing a mean and standard deviation for D. The data also permitted an analysis of the mean and standard deviation of all 20 "on" and "off" observations.

The subjects were allowed to develop their own criteria for judging simultaneity. The starting points of each run were varied randomly to avoid any tendency to count the number of stimuli presented. The subjects were not informed of the magnitude of their errors, nor were they ever informed which pair of stimuli were physically simultaneous.

Subject RD received vibratory stimuli with a rise and decay time of approximately 3 msec. Nineteen vibratory stimuli durations were used. The durations selected were 10, 20, 30, 40, 50, 60, 70, 80, 100, 120, 130, 140, 160, 200, 250, 300, 400, 500, and 800 msec.

Since the short rise and decay time of the vibratory stimuli used in subject RD might have produced unique onset and offset transients that conceivably could have been utilized by the subject in performing the cross-modal simultaneity judgments, the second subject (SL) received vibratory stimuli having 10-msec rise and decay times. With these longer rise and decay times, it was not possible to use vibratory stimuli that were shorter than 30 msec. The vibratory stimuli which were used with subject SL were 30, 40, 60, 70, 90, 100, 110, 120, 130, 140, 150, 200, 400, and 800 msec in duration.

With both subjects, the different stimulus durations were presented in random order. All data required to calculate 20 values of D for each stimulus duration was obtained in a single experimental session lasting approximately $1\frac{1}{2}$ hr.

Subject SL was also tested with a stimulus shorter than the critical duration which varied in amplitude. This was done to ascertain if the perceptual duration varied inversely with intensity as had been the case in the visual modality (Efron, 1970c; Efron & Lee, 1971). Since the dynamic range of the tactile modality is appreciably more restricted than the visual, it was not possible to use stimuli of widely different amplitudes. For this experiment, one 60-msec stimulus was used that was just above the vibratory threshold. This was compared, at a subsequent session, with a 60-msec stimulus of approximately 10 times the amplitude.

IV. Results

The effect of variation of the duration of the vibratory stimulus on D, the perceptual duration, can be seen in Table 1 and Fig. 2 (subject RD), where a click was used as the index stimulus. Table 2 and Fig. 3 (subject SL) give the results when a flash was used as the index stimulus.

Table 1. *Data for Subject RD*

Stim. on	Index (click) at on: mean	Stim. off	Index (click) at off: mean	Stimulus duration	Perceptual duration: mean[a]
500	511.25 ± 7.76	510	622.50 ± 10.70	10	111.25 ± 13.46
500	505.75 ± 7.48	520	621.00 ± 13.14	20	115.25 ± 13.81
500	501.50 ± 6.71	530	629.75 ± 12.92	30	128.25 ± 16.08
500	513.25 ± 8.16	540	636.25 ± 7.05	40	123.00 ± 10.56
500	504.75 ± 9.66	550	620.75 ± 13.31	50	116.00 ± 13.04
500	516.00 ± 7.36	560	654.25 ± 10.55	60	138.25 ± 11.62
500	496.50 ± 7.27	570	621.25 ± 8.41	70	124.75 ± 10.19
500	504.50 ± 10.37	580	626.25 ± 12.02	80	121.75 ± 15.67
500	504.25 ± 6.13	600	631.50 ± 9.05	100	127.25 ± 10.70
500	505.50 ± 6.05	620	671.25 ± 8.72	120	165.75 ± 8.63
500	498.00 ± 6.77	630	652.50 ± 7.16	130	154.50 ± 10.87
500	517.00 ± 8.49	640	651.25 ± 9.72	140	134.25 ± 13.70
500	555.00 ± 9.87	660	709.00 ± 7.71	160	154.00 ± 14.01
500	500.25 ± 4.44	700	704.50 ± 10.50	200	204.25 ± 9.50
500	543.00 ± 6.37	750	786.25 ± 7.59	250	243.25 ± 11.62
500	515.75 ± 6.13	800	792.00 ± 9.23	300	276.25 ± 10.99
500	504.50 ± 7.24	900	912.00 ± 8.80	400	407.50 ± 10.20
500	509.50 ± 8.57	1000	1008.75 ± 9.01	500	499.25 ± 14.17
500	521.25 ± 5.59	1300	1315.00 ± 6.88	800	793.75 ± 8.09
	511.97 ± 16.20 = Mean of *all* "Index at on mean."				

[a]For the first nine entries the slope is +.13, $r = +.26$, $y = (+.13)x + 115.72$. For the last nine entries the slope is +.98, $r = +.99$, $y = (+.98)x + 2.53$. CD = 133.16.

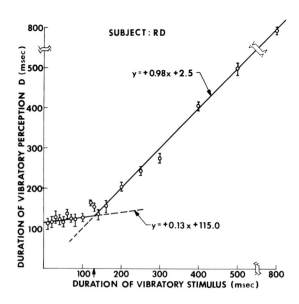

Fig. 2. Perceptual duration as function of vibratory stimulus duration using click as index stimulus.

722

Table 2. *Data for Subject SL*

Stim. on	Index (flash) at on: mean	Stim. off	Index (flash) at off: mean	Stimulus duration	Perceptual duration: mean[a]
500	502.00 ± 10.44	530	606.75 ± 13.50	30	104.75 ± 19.77
500	517.75 ± 11.86	540	624.75 ± 16.74	40	107.00 ± 17.58
500	509.25 ± 9.90	560	621.50 ± 10.01	60	112.25 ± 14.55
500	502.50 ± 14.00	570	617.75 ± 12.62	70	115.25 ± 23.70
500	514.25 ± 17.94	590	634.75 ± 18.17	90	120.50 ± 23.39
500	530.75 ± 11.73	600	654.25 ± 12.38	100	123.50 ± 17.93
500	507.50 ± 11.30	610	628.75 ± 14.13	110	121.25 ± 20.77
500	512.50 ± 9.25	620	634.75 ± 12.92	120	122.25 ± 15.60
500	510.75 ± 10.17	630	636.50 ± 12.58	130	125.75 ± 13.11
500	508.25 ± 11.27	640	651.75 ± 11.95	140	143.50 ± 17.48
500	509.50 ± 13.17	650	656.25 ± 9.72	150	146.75 ± 16.88
500	513.00 ± 10.81	750	749.50 ± 12.56	250	236.50 ± 16.47
500	510.00 ± 8.89	900	920.75 ± 10.29	400	410.75 ± 15.58
500	510.00 ± 12.35	1300	1305.50 ± 9.30	800	795.50 ± 14.86
	511.28 ± 6.97 = Mean of *all* "Index at on mean."				

[a]For the first 9 entries the slope is $+.20$, $r = +.35$, $y = (+.20)x + 99.72$. For the last 5 entries the slope is $+.99$, $r = +.99$, $y = (+.99)x - 1.12$. CD $= 127.65$.

The vibratory stimulus was always started on the 500th msec of each trial (see the first column of Tables 1 and 2). The mean and standard deviation of the 20 observations of onset simultaneity for each stimulus duration are found in the second column. The third column contains the time when the vibratory stimulus ended and the fourth column contains the mean and standard deviation of the 20 observations of offset simultaneity. The fifth column lists the duration of the vibratory stimulus and the sixth column lists the mean difference and standard deviation of this difference between the onset and offset observation on 20 repetitions. The slope, correlation coefficient, and empirical equation for each segment of the line are given as a footnote to each table. The last number (CD), included in the footnote, represents the value of the intercept of the two empirical equations and is the estimate of the critical stimulus duration.

In Figures 2 and 3, only the perceptual duration (sixth column) is plotted against stimulus duration. The brackets denote the standard deviation (from the sixth column) of each value of D.

From these two tables and graphs, it can be seen that the perceptual duration was equal to the stimulus duration for stimuli longer than the critical duration: the slope for the diagonal portion of both figures lies close to a slope of $+1.00$, and for both subjects the experimentally derived slope was $+.99$. The difference is statistically insignificant.

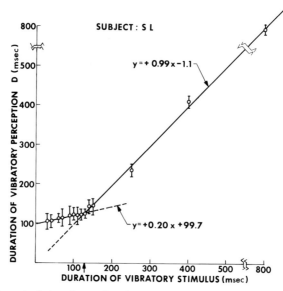

Fig. 3. Perceptual duration as function of vibratory stimulus duration using flash as index stimulus.

For stimuli shorter than the critical duration, the experimentally derived slope was +.13 ($t = 3.35$, $df = 178$) for subject RD and was + .20 ($t = 4.84$, $df = 178$) for subject SL. These empirical slopes are significantly different ($p < .01$) from a hypothetical slope of zero. Although this is a quantitatively small discrepancy, it does indicate that for the vibratory modality the perceptual duration is not precisely constant.

The fact that virtually identical functions were obtained in the two subjects with the utilization of different index stimuli indicates the general applicability of the method of cross-modality simultaneity judgments.

In the experiment on the effect of a tenfold alteration of intensity on subject SL (not illustrated), a difference of 14.17 msec was obtained in perceptual duration; the longer perceptual duration being obtained for the less intense stimulus. This difference was statistically significant at the .01 level (one-tailed test). Because of the restricted dynamic range of the vibratory modality, it was not possible to test this effect with more intense vibratory stimuli. Further increase in amplitude of vibration resulted (for a 60-msec stimulus) in the experience of a tap on the finger and a loss of the vibratory quality.

The similarity of these results in the vibratory modality to those obtained in the visual and auditory senses can be seen in Fig. 4 (vision) and Fig. 5 (audition). These graphs contain the data previously reported (Efron, 1970c) on different subjects from those who participated in the vibratory experi-

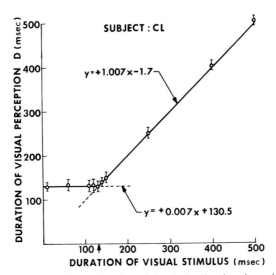

Fig. 4. Perceptual duration as function of visual stimulus duration using click as index stimulus.

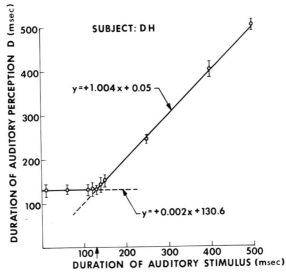

Fig. 5. Perceptual duration as function of auditory stimulus duration using flash as index stimulus.

ment. Whereas the standard deviation obtained in the vibratory experiment was larger than those obtained for the visual and auditory experiments, and the slope of the curve for the shorter stimulus durations was not quite zero, the overall similarity of the three functions is not in doubt. Also worth noting is the similarity in critical duration between the three modalities when stimuli of midrange intensity were employed.

The results of the experiments in all three modalities can be summarized:

1. The perceptual onset delay (see interval A in Fig. 1 and the second column, Tables 1 and 2) is independent of stimulus duration. The shape of the function relating stimulus duration to perceptual duration thus is determined exclusively by changes that occur in the perceptual offset delay (see interval B in Fig. 1 and the fourth column, Tables 1 and 2).

2. For all stimuli *longer* than a critical duration, the perceptual offset and perceptual onset delays are virtually identical (B = A). As a consequence, the duration of the perception is precisely equal to the duration of the stimulus, and the slope of the diagonal portion of Figs. 2, 3, 4, and 5 is thus +1.00. Whereas the entire perception is temporally displaced and lags the stimulus, there is no persistence (as defined earlier) since the perception does not persist for a longer duration than the stimulus.

3. For stimuli *shorter* than the critical duration, the perceptual offset delay (B) was longer than the perceptual onset delay (A). For these brief stimuli the relationship between perceptual offset delay and stimulus duration can be expressed in the form $B + X = k$, where B is the perceptual offset delay, X is the stimulus duration, and k is a constant that depends on stimulus parameters. It logically follows from this relationship that the perceptual offset delay is time-locked to the *stimulus onset*. The net effect of this feature of the perceptual offset delay as stimuli are made more brief is to maintain a perceptual duration which is of constant value.

4. The critical stimulus duration (CD), defined as the value of X where the two segments of the graph intersect, is approximately 110–150 msec for all modalities.

5. The CD varies inversely with stimulus intensity and is possibly affected by other stimulus properties as well [see Allport (1970) for effects of surround level in the visual system].

V. Electrophysiological Correlations

The discovery in three different modalities of the invariant relationship $B + X = k$, and the implication that the perceptual offset delay is time-locked to the stimulus *onset* for stimuli for which this relationship holds, suggests the existence of a fundamental physiological mechanism common to all perceptual systems. One feature of all sensory systems is the occurrence of "on" and "off" responses, that is, potentials time-locked to the on and off of a stimulus. A study thus was undertaken to determine if the latency of the on and off responses in the visual system have the necessary characteristics to account for the psychophysical properties of the perceptual onset and offset delay. (Similar experiments are currently in progress for other modalities.) The experiments utilize electrodes of sufficiently large tip size to record only the summed potential derived from many individual units discharging synchronously.

Using conventional stereotaxic and electrophysiological techniques (to be described in detail subsequently; Efron, 1973), recordings were obtained from the optic nerve, optic tract, lateral geniculate, striate and peristriate cortex of cats lightly anesthesized with Fluothane®. One pupil was dilated with atropine and the cornea was covered with a clear contact lens. The other eye was occluded with an opaque contact lens. Eye movements were abolished with gallamine. A white light flash of 975 ft-L, derived from a glow modulator tube, was delivered to the eye via a fiber optic bundle of 6-mm diameter, which was placed in direct contact with the corneal contact lens. Although the on responses were usually large and easily recorded, the off responses were frequently small and difficult to identify unequivocally in the background of electrode and brain-wave "noise." Conventional averaging techniques subsequently were applied to the evoked potentials, which had been recorded on an FM tape recorder to increase the detectability of the off response. The peak of the on and off response (hereafter referred to as peak latency) usually could be identified within an error of ±.5 msec by averaging the responses to 175 identical stimuli. The peak latency of the on and off response thus was ascertained for a number of different flash durations ranging between 5 and 160 msec. (On several occasions, a high-intensity strobe flash of approximately 3μsec was utilized for studying still shorter flash durations.)

Since the electrophysiological findings will be reported in detail elsewhere (Efron, 1973), only the general conclusions that held true for all anatomical sites from the optic nerve to the peristriate cortex will be given. These will be illustrated from a representative recording from the optic nerve.

A. At all anatomical sites the off response tended to be appreciably smaller in amplitude than the on response, and was reduced still further in amplitude by reducing stimulus luminance, deepening the level of anesthesia, or altering of the acid–base balance. The off response also characteristically decreased in amplitude as the stimulus duration was shortened. In a number of experiments, particularly with lower stimulus luminance, the off response attenuated so markedly with decreasing stimulus duration that useful data could not be obtained. In contrast, the on response was much less affected by changes in these variables.

In addition to these changes in the amplitude of the off response for stimuli shorter than the critical duration, the peak latency of the off response was also more variable. This "time jitter" (which is effectively eliminated in the computer averages) was not observed for the on responses that were tightly time-locked at all stimulus durations.

B. The peak-latency of the on response was constant and was independent of stimulus duration (luminance being held constant). This feature can be seen in Fig. 6 and Fig. 7a.

C. For stimuli longer than a critical duration, the peak latency of the off response was equal (± 4 msec) to the peak latency of the on response. This feature can be seen in the data of Fig. 6 and Fig. 7b for stimulus durations in excess of 60 msec. The *interval* between the on and off response for stimuli longer than 60 msec was thus equal to the stimulus duration (see Fig. 7c).

D. For stimuli shorter than 50 msec, the peak latency of the off response increased dramatically. This increase in the peak latency of the off response closely approximated the relationship $B' + X = k'$, where B' is the peak latency of the off response, X is the stimulus duration, and k' is a constant that appeared to depend on flash luminance, level of light adaptation, and depth of anesthesia. Under the conditions used in the particular experiment on the optic nerve, which is illustrated here, the critical duration was estimated to be 48.0 msec. This estimate is derived from the intersection of the two linear regression lines of Fig. 7c. As in the psychophysical experiments, the off response for all stimuli shorter than the critical duration was time-locked to the *onset* of the stimulus.

This last finding raises the obvious question: "Why is this response, which is time-locked to the onset of the stimulus, called an "off" response?" Inspection of Fig. 6 will make this point clear. Each tracing, an average of 175 responses, is arranged in order of descending stimulus duration (although experimentally obtained in random order). For the longest stimulus durations, the on and off responses are unequivocally identifiable and have equal latencies. As the stimulus is made progressively shorter, the off response is seen to shift to the left; its latency remains essentially unchanged for all stimulus durations greater than 50 msec. However, as the stimulus is made shorter than 50 msec, the off response no longer shifts to the left but remains at the *same* location on the tracings. That is, its increase in latency follows the relationship $B' + X = k'$: The off response thus becomes time-locked to the stimulus onset. If the recordings obtained with the shortest stimuli (under 50 msec) were examined in isolation, it would be natural to assume that this wave (which is referred to here as an off response) is merely a late component of a complex on response. It is only by observing the entire sequence of tracings, beginning with the longest stimuli where the off response is unequivocal, that the off response can be identified

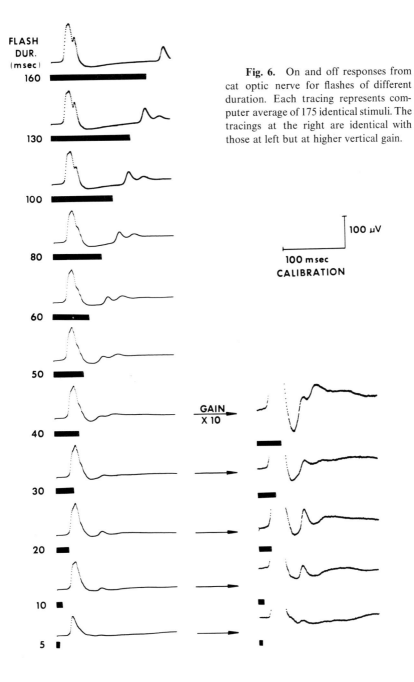

Fig. 6. On and off responses from cat optic nerve for flashes of different duration. Each tracing represents computer average of 175 identical stimuli. The tracings at the right are identical with those at left but at higher vertical gain.

FLASH
DUR.
(msec)
160

130

100

80

60

50

40

30

20

10

5

GAIN
X 10

100 μV

100 msec
CALIBRATION

729

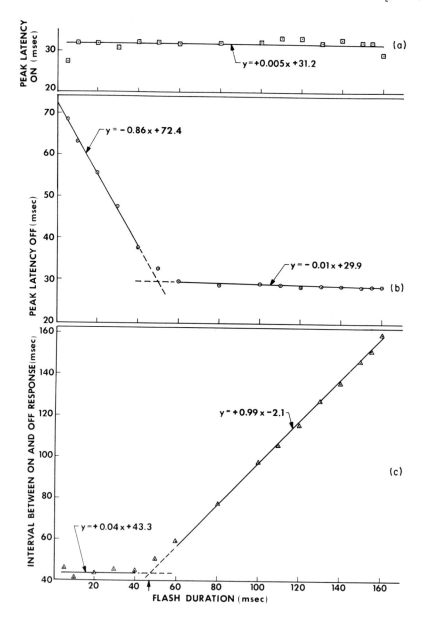

Fig. 7. (A) Peak latency of optic nerve on response as function of flash duration. (B) Peak latency of optic nerve off response as function of flash duration. (C) Interval between peak-on and peak-off response as function of flash duration. The data are derived from tracings of Fig. 6.

unambiguously for the shorter stimuli. It is also to be noted that the off response for the short stimuli is in a location where *no* such component exists from the longer stimuli.

In Fig. 7b, the peak latency of the off response (derived from a larger number of recordings than could be reproduced in Fig. 6) is plotted as a function of stimulus duration. Two linear components are seen: The horizontal component, for stimuli of 60 msec and longer, has a slope of $-.013$. The diagonal component, for stimuli shorter than 50 msec, has a slope of $-.86$. In other experiments (not illustrated) the slope varied between $-.80$ and -1.08. These variations are due, in part, to the time jitter of the off response, and to small changes in the physiological state of the animal. These electrophysiological findings in the visual system are virtually identical to those found in the psychophysical function on the two subjects previously reported (Efron, 1970c).

In Fig. 7c, the temporal *interval* between the peak of the on and off response is plotted as a function of stimulus duration. As would be expected, the shape of this curve is identical (save for the difference in critical duration) as was found in Figs. 2, 3, 4, and 5. The slope of the horizontal component is $+.044$ and the slope of the diagonal component is $+.99$—values that are in remarkably close agreement with those obtained in the psychophysical experiments.

The striking correlation between the psychophysical results obtained in man and the electrophysiological findings in the cat suggest that the unique temporal characteristics of the perceptual offset delay may be a direct consequence of the latency properties of the off response. The further finding, that the relationship of $B' + X = k'$ is obtained in as peripheral a location as the optic nerve, suggests that this temporal characteristic is impressed on the sensory system after only a relatively small number of synaptic connections. The fact that an identical function was obtained at all higher levels in the neuraxis is thus merely a consequence of the latency characteristics of the off response of the ganglion cells of the retina. (The striate cortex, for example, could not respond with an off response until it had received the off discharge from the ganglion cells.)

The correlation between the psychophysical and electrophysiological findings, impressive as they may be, nevertheless require a cautious interpretation. First, the psychophysical data is derived from man (with a duplex retina) whereas the electrophysiological data comes from the cat, which has a predominantly rod retina. Second, the visual data on man was obtained with a small ($1°40'$) stimulus of relatively low luminance (3.14 ft-L), whereas the data on the cat was derived from a large, diffuse stimulus of 975 ft-L. (The use of larger and more intense stimuli in the latter experiments was necessary because of the small amplitude of the off response with less intense and small stimuli. The use of less intense stimuli in man was found to be necessary because intense stimuli provoked so much glare and after images that the cross-modality simultaneity method could not be used.) Third, the use of an anesthetized animal inevitably raises questions as to the effect of the anesthesia itself. Finally, the critical duration in the human experiments was approximately 130 msec, whereas the CD in the electrophysiological experiment illustrated was 48.0 msec and ranged in various experiments between 35 and 50 msec. Whereas this difference could be due merely to the difference in stimulus luminance (since it is in the appropriate direction), it might be due also to the differences in the retina, anesthesia, level of light adaptation, and perhaps other, as yet unidentified, factors. Despite this cautious approach, the electrophysiological data appear to correlate strongly with the psychophysical findings that have been reported.

VI. Discussion

The psychophysical experiments described in this paper have been presented in terms of "perceptual duration." The concept of "perceptual duration," illustrated diagrammatically by the solid black bar in Fig. 1, refers to the real-time duration of a perception (that is, the process of awareness itself). Ideally, it would be desirable to invent a special instrument that started a clock when a perception of a stimulus commenced and stopped the clock when the perception ended. The difference between the two clock readings would correspond exactly to this concept of perceptual duration. The method of cross-modality simultaneity judgments of perceptual onset and perceptual offset, while falling short of this ideal, may provide a reasonable approximation to this hypothetical device. The correlations between the psychophysical results using this method and the electrophysiological findings suggest that the method does indeed provide a close approximation and this will be assumed for the remaining discussion.

What is the relationship, if any, between perceptual duration (as defined above) and the "subjective" or "perceived" duration of a stimulus? More specifically: Is the "subjective" or "perceived" duration of a stimulus determined by the real-time duration of the perception of that stimulus? In the experiments that have been described, the real-time perceptual duration was found to be essentially constant for all stimuli shorter than the critical duration. Stimuli shorter than the critical duration could thus never be discriminated *on the basis of "perceived" duration* if the "perceived" duration was exclusively determined by perceptual duration. Although a large body of literature (for example, Creelman, 1962; Zacks, 1970; Allan, Kristoffer-

son, & Wiens, 1971) attests to the fact that subjects *can* discriminate between
two brief stimuli of different duration (even when the two stimuli are equal-
ized for total energy or matched for equal loudness or brightness), the fact
that such stimuli can be discriminated does not necessarily mean that they
are discriminated on the basis of the "perceived" duration (Zacks, 1970).
Other subjective cues may still remain which enable the subjects to make the
discrimination. Since this critical issue has not been resolved yet, it is impossible to decide, *on the basis of the duration discrimination experiments cited
above*, if the "perceived" duration of a stimulus is determined exclusively
by the perceptual duration.

   However, there is other evidence indicating that the "perceived" duration is *not* determined by perceptual duration. The results of all experiments
on the "perceived" duration of brief stimuli have shown that subjects
generally report that the more intense of two equally brief stimuli appears
to be of longer duration. That is, "perceived" duration varies *directly* with
stimulus intensity. In contrast, the results of the present experiments on the
vibratory sense reveal that perceptual duration varies *inversely* with stimulus
intensity. A similar inverse relationship has been found also in the visual
modality (Efron, 1970c; Efron & Lee, 1971). In addition, all studies on flicker
fusion threshold have shown that critical flicker fusion increases (and persistence presumably decreases in duration) with increasing luminance. If
the duration of persistence varies inversely with intensity, then it would
follow that perceptual duration (which is determined by persistence for the
brief stimuli used in flicker fusion experiments) would also vary inversely
with intensity. Finally, this inverse relationship has been found in experiments on the duration of "short-term visual storage" reported by Sperling
(1960) and by Haber and Standing (1969), and in experiments on the "perceptual moment" reported by Allport (1968, 1970). Since perceptual duration
and "perceived" duration fail to show any parallelism with respect to the
effect of intensity, it is possible to reject the hypothesis that the subjective
or "perceived" duration of brief stimuli is determined by perceptual duration.

   The most striking finding in this series of experiments is the invariant
relationship between perceptual offset delay and stimulus duration ($B + X
= k$). The discovery of this heretofore unsuspected property of perceptual
systems, coupled with its presence in three different sensory modalities, and
supported by electrophysiological studies in the visual system, prompts some
speculation as to the biological role which might be served by this ubiquitous
relationship. It would seem reasonable to suspect that the physiological
mechanism which underlies this invariant property serves to ensure the
conscious registration of brief suprathreshold stimuli for a sufficient period
of time to allow the extraction of biologically important information that

otherwise would be lost. The mechanism seems to operate by maintaining the conscious experience of the stimulus for a minimum period. For example, if the value of CD is 130 msec, and the stimulus is 10 msec in duration, this process ensures that the perception is maintained for an additional 120 msec—achieving a total of 130 msec. On the other hand, if the stimulus is 100 msec in duration, the perception is maintained only for an additional 30 msec. If the stimulus is longer than 130 msec, there may be no need (from an information retrieval standpoint) for the perception to have a longer duration than the stimulus. It may be for this reason that no persistence is found for stimuli longer than the critical duration. The physiological evidence suggests that it is the off response which may terminate the perception. Without such an off signal reaching some higher neural center, the perception might be maintained for appreciably longer periods. Expressed in terms of models of short-term (visual) storage, the off response may serve to "erase" or "reset" the iconic store (wherever this might be located anatomically).

It should be emphasized that the conclusions presented in this paper are derived from studies of single stimuli presented on a dark or silent background—conditions that almost never occur outside a laboratory setting. A significant effect on perceptual duration of preceding, concurrent, and subsequent stimulation of the same (or adjacent) receptors would be expected. In audition, Gol'dburt (1961) has reported that partially masked "target" tones always were perceived as shorter in duration than unmasked tone bursts of the same duration. In vision, Liss (1968) reported that partially masked visual displays were perceived as shorter in duration compared to unmasked visual stimuli of the same duration. Whereas both these studies pertain to "perceived" duration and may not reflect a change in real-time perceptual duration, a recent paper by Haber and Standing (1970), using a method of cross-modality simultaneity judgments, provides data which indicates that the perceptual duration of brief visual stimuli can be cut short or arrested by presentation of a poststimulus burst of visual noise. It would be of interest to explore the effects of auditory and tactile "noise" bursts on perceptual duration in these latter two modalities to see if they are identical to the effect in vision described by Haber and Standing. If this should be the case, it would provide still further evidence in support of the existence of identical information processing mechanisms in all perceptual systems.

Note Added in Proof

Recent single-unit recordings from the lateral geniculate nucleus of the unanesthetized cat have revealed the existence of "off-center" neurons whose latency of discharge (as a function of flash duration) is closely described by the equation $B + X = k$. This finding suggests that the "gross" off-responses described in this article may accurately reflect the discharge characteristics of a relatively large population of off-center neurons.

Acknowledgments

I would like to thank M. Corder and M. Strachan for patiently performing all the experiments on the vibratory sense that are reported here and for their assistance in the electrophysiological studies.

References

Allan, L. G., Kristofferson, A. B., & Wiens, E. W. Duration discrimination of brief light flashes. *Perception and Psychophysics*, 1971, **9**, 327–334.

Allport, D. A. Phenomenal simultaneity and the perceptual moment hypothesis. *British Journal of Psychology*, 1968, **59**, 395–406.

Allport, D. A. Temporal summation and phenomenal simultaneity: Experiments with the radius display. *Quarterly Journal of Experimental Psychology*, 1970, **22**, 686–701.

Bergson, H. *Creative evolution*. New York: Holt, 1913.

Creelman, C. D. Human discrimination of auditory duration. *Journal of the Acoustic Society of America*, 1962, **34**, 582–593.

Efron, R. Stereoscopic vision: Effect of binocular temporal summation, *British Journal of Ophthalmology*, 1957, **41**, 709–730.

Efron, R. The relationship between the duration of a stimulus and the duration of a perception. *Neuropsychologia*, 1970, **8**, 37–55.   (a)

Efron, R. The minimum duration of a perception. *Neuropsychologia*, 1970, **8**, 57–63.   (b)

Efron, R. Effect of stimulus duration on perceptual onset and offset latencies. *Perception and Psychophysics*, 1970, **8**, 251–254.   (c)

Efron, R. The measurement of perceptual durations. *Studium Generale*, 1970, **23**, 550–561.   (d)

Efron, R. The latency of the off response in the visual system as a function of flash duration. 1973 (in preparation).

Efron, R., & Lee, D. The visual persistence of a moving stroboscopically illuminated object. *American Journal of Psychology*, 1971, **84**, 365–376.

Engel, G. R. An investigation of visual responses to brief stereoscopic stimuli. *Quarterly Journal of Experimental Psychology*, 1970, **22**, 148–166.

Gol'dburt, S. N. Persistence of auditory processes within microintervals of time. *Biophysics*, 1961, **6**, 76–81.

Haber, R. N., & Standing, L. G. Direct measures of short-term visual storage. *Quarterly Journal of Experimental Psychology*, 1969, **21**, 43–54.

Haber, R. N. and Standing, L. G. Direct estimates of the apparent duration of a flash. *Canadian Journal of Psychology*, 1970, **24**, 216–229.

James, W. *The principles of psychology*. New York: Holt, 1890.

Kahneman, D. An onset-onset law for one case of apparent motion and metacontrast. *Perception and Psychophysics*, 1967, **2**, 577–584.

Kristofferson, A. B. Successiveness discrimination as a two-state, quantal process. *Science*, 1967, **158**, 1337–1339.   (a)

Kristofferson, A. B. Attention and psychophysical time. *Acta Psychologica*, 1967, **27**, 93.   (b)

LeGrand, Y. *Light, colour and vision*. London: Chapman & Hall, 1957.

Liss, P. Does backward masking by visual noise stop stimulus processing? *Perception and Psychophysics*, 1968, **4**, 326–330.

Piéron, H. *The sensations, their functions, processes and mechanisms*. London: Frederick Muller, 1952.

Sperling, G. The information available in brief visual presentation. *Psychological Monographs*, 1960, (Whole No. 498).

Sperling, G. Successive approximations to a model for short-term memory. *Acta Psychologica*, 1967, **27**, 285–292.

Stroud, J. M. The fine structure of psychological time. In H. Quastler (Ed.), *Information theory in psychology*. Glencoe, Illinois: Free Press, 1955. Pp. 174–205.

von Békésy, G. Über die Horsamkeit der Ein-und Ausschwing-vorgange mit Berucksichtigung der Raumakustik. *Annalen der Physik*, **16**, 844, 1933.

Zacks, J. L. Temporal summation phenomena at threshold: Their relation to visual mechanisms. *Science*, 1970, **170**, 197–199.

Successiveness and Duration Discrimination[1]

Alfred B. Kristofferson   *Lorraine G. Allan*

Department of Psychology
McMaster University
Hamilton, Ontario, Canada

ABSTRACT

An "attention-switching" theory of successiveness discrimination and a "quantal onset–offset" theory of duration discrimination are reviewed. A successiveness experiment is reported which confirms a prediction of the former theory. Taking that data into account, the duration theory is developed to include forced choice successiveness discrimination. The two theories are compared on their ability to summarize the data of two experiments. Finally, the quantal onset–offset theory is used to describe some new results in duration discrimination.

The quantal onset–offset theory shows some promise in explaining duration discrimination under certain conditions. However, successiveness discrimination data are more consistent with the attention-switching theory. Both theories make use of the concept of a quantum of psychophysical time.

Successiveness discrimination would seem to be a special case of duration discrimination. In what follows, we examine the problem of accounting for both within a single theory.

---

[1]This research was supported by the National Research Council of Canada (Grant No. APA-112) and by the U.S. National Aeronautics and Space Administration (Grant No. NGR-52-059-001).

737

I. Successiveness Discrimination

Some of you will recall an *attention-switching theory* of successiveness discrimination which was discussed at the first of these meetings (Kristofferson, 1967a). According to that theory, discriminating two events that are in separate channels as successive is limited by the time required to switch attention between the channels. If the events are the offsets of a light and a tone, then in order to tell that the light goes off before the tone rather than simultaneously with the tone, it is necessary to be attending to the light, to note its offset, and then to switch to the channel of the tone and note that the tone terminates after the switch is complete. On a two-alternative forced-choice trial, with simultaneous offsets for the standard pair and offsets separated by time t for the variable pair, if t is sufficient for switching to occur, then a correct response will result.

The theory also said that the switching of attention is under the control of a periodic process, so that switching can occur only at time points separated by one time quantum. For that reason, the time that must elapse following the offset of the light until switching is complete is uniformly distributed over a range from zero to one quantum and the resulting successiveness discrimination function should be linear, going from chance to 100% over a range of one quantum.

In a later paper (Kristofferson, 1967b), it was shown that the conditions necessary for the ideal one-quantum function described above can be approximated but probably not completely achieved. The function shown in

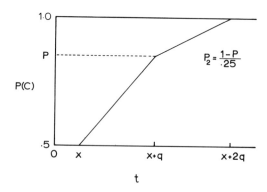

Fig. 1. Forced-choice successiveness discrimination. The graph shows the form of the function predicted by the two-state, attention-switching theory. $P(C)$ is the proportion of correct responses and t is the size of the interval between the offsets of the signals in the variable pair. P_2 is the probability of being in a two-quantum state; hence, P can assume values only between .75 and 1.0. The intercept x is interpreted as the difference in afferent latency between the two signals.

Fig. 1 is predicted by the *two-state successiveness model*, which is identical to the original theory except that the observer is said to be in a two-quantum state on P_2 of the trials. In a two-quantum state his distribution of switching times is uniformly distributed over a range from zero to two quanta. It should be noted that the predicted psychometric function shown in Fig. 1 is based on the assumption that the observer is attending to the light channel when a stimulus pair is presented. The successiveness discrimination data presented in that paper (Kristofferson, 1967b) were consistent with this assumption. Those data will be considered again later.

As a psychophysical model, the attention-switching theory is a simple two-state model with no response biases. It provides a mechanism for generating either of two states: "successive" or "simultaneous." And, it says that these are, in fact, the only states. There are no "degrees of simultaneity." That is, when attention switches to the tone channel and the tone has already gone off, it does not matter how long ago that offset occurred. The trace of the offset of the tone conveys no useful temporal information.

In Fig. 1, positive values of t mean that the light preceded the tone by t; negative values mean the reverse. Zero is simultaneity in the stimulus, x is simultaneity in the display areas, and q is the quantum size. If "coding as successive" depends only on attention switching and not at all on the temporal information, which may be contained in a decaying trace, the successiveness discrimination function should be identical for all intervals between the two offsets of the standard pair between $(x - q)$ and x. If the observer always attends to the light channel when a stimulus pair is presented, the performance should be the same when the light offset follows the tone offset by $(x - q)$ msec in the standard as when it precedes it by x msec because

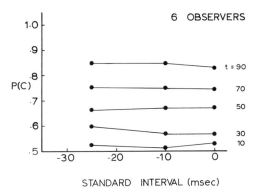

Fig. 2. The effect of change in the interval between offsets of the standard stimulus pair upon forced-choice successiveness discrimination for five values of the interval of the variable pair. Negative values mean that the sound terminates before the light. Average $P(C)$ for six observers.

all standards between $(x - q)$ and x msec have either zero or one time point between them. Since the first internal signal for intervals in this range is the tone offset, two time points are required for the two offsets to be judged as successive if the observer is in a one-quantum state and four if he is in a two-quantum state. Thus, all standard intervals between $(x - q)$ and x msec will be coded as simultaneous.

Figure 2 shows that that is the case. In this experiment we used the same kinds of signals and the same procedure as before (see Kristofferson, 1967b). Five values of t were included, as indicated in the figure, and three different intervals between the offsets of the standard pair, 0, -10, and -25 msec, respectively. The 30 combinations were intermixed randomly. There are several hundred responses for each of six observers in each data point. Varying the interval of the standard over a fairly wide range causes no effect.

II. Duration Discrimination

In a recent paper (Allan, Kristofferson, & Wiens, 1971), we presented data on the discrimination of differences in duration between brief light flashes. On the basis of those data, which cover only the restricted range of durations between 50 and 150 msec, we proposed a theory of duration discrimination. A brief sketch of this "*quantal on–off*" theory is shown in Fig. 3.

The coding of a stimulus as "short" or "long" is based upon an internal quantity I in the manner shown in the figure. The dimension I is the difference between the internal beginning and end of the signal. Repeated presentations of the same stimulus give rise to a distribution of values of I triangular in form because all variance in I is due to variance in the latencies of the "on" and "off" signals, and they are each assumed to be distributed uniformly and independently over a range of one quantum.

The triangular distributions of I are the convolutions of the two identical uniforms, and they span one quantum above and one quantum below their expected values. Since q in time quantum theory is independent of stimulus duration, that theory would expect the variance of I to be independent of stimulus duration also. Our finding (Allan et al., 1971) that variance is the same for durations of 50 and 100 msec led to the development of this theory.

The light flash experiments used a single-stimulus recognition method. In any session there were only two possible stimuli, S_0 (the base duration) and S_1 (base duration plus Δt). One stimulus was presented on a trial and the observer had to say either "short" or "long." We assume that the observer sets a criterion C on the I axis, and responds "long" when I exceeds C. One can calculate d_q, the distance between the means of the two distributions in quantal units, from the probabilities of a long response conditionalized on

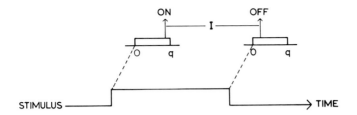

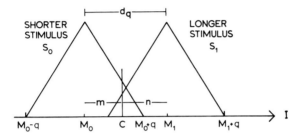

Fig. 3. The quantal onset–offset theory for single stimulus duration discrimination: $d_q = m + n$, where $m = 1 - [2P(L/S_0)]^{1/2}$ and $n = 1 - \{[2 - 2P(L/S_1)]\}^{1/2}$. When $I > C$, response $= L$. Repeated presentations of a stimulus of fixed duration give rise to a triangular distribution of internal intervals. For a longer stimulus, the distribution is shifted upward, but its variance is unchanged. The equations permit the calculation of d_q when the criterion is situated in the area of overlap between the two means.

the two stimulus events, as long as neither conditional probability equals zero or one.

Some of the data are displayed in Fig. 4 as average d_q values for six observers. As the difference in duration of the long and short flashes increases, d_q increases as a zero-intercept straight line. This means that 1 msec of stimulus duration has the same value in terms of quantal units of I anywhere within the range studied here. There is no distortion in the mapping of stimulus time into mean psychophysical time. Also, it would seem that mean psychophysical time changes in perfect correspondence to stimulus time, at least above 50 msec: there is no indication of a minimum internal duration of the kind discussed by Efron in this volume at this level.

III. Application of Duration Theory to Successiveness

We turn next to question whether the quantal onset–offset theory can account for successiveness discrimination and whether it compares favourably to the attention-switching theory in that regard. Whereas it may seem

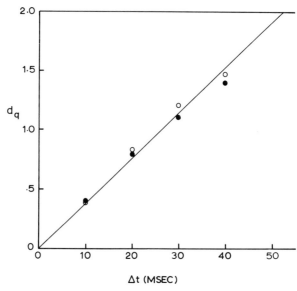

Fig. 4. Duration discrimination in terms of the distance d_q for light flashes of two brief base durations and four values of the difference between the "longer" and "shorter" flash: ($\circ$) $t = 50$; ($\bullet$) $t = 100$. Average d_q for six observers. (Data from Experiment 2 of Allan, Kristofferson, & Wiens, 1971.)

that the results shown in Fig. 2 above rule out the onset–offset theory, such is not the case, as we shall show.

All of the successiveness data we will be considering were obtained using a two-alternative forced-choice method. One application of the quantal on–off theory to the forced-choice paradigm is pictured in Figure 5. In conceptualizing the forced-choice procedure, in which the observer receives a sample from each distribution on a trial, it is customary to assume that quantity is preserved in the samples and that the observer operates on a difference between the two quantities (Green & Swets, 1966). However, our results in Fig. 2 above strongly suggest that such an assumption would not be satisfactory here.

Instead, we assume that on each trial each of the two stimulus pairs is coded as either successive or simultaneous. When the variable is coded as successive and the standard as simultaneous a correct response occurs. When both are coded either successive or simultaneous, the probability of being correct is one-half; when the variable is coded as simultaneous and the standard as successive, a wrong response occurs. Thus, this is a two-state model in which the distributions of I and the criterion generate the state probabilities.

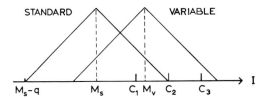

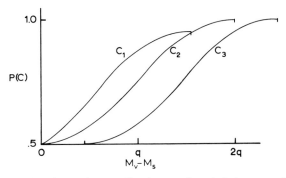

Fig. 5. Adaptation of quantal onset-offset theory to forced-choice successiveness discrimination: $P(C) = \frac{1}{2}\{P[(I > C)/\text{var}] - P[(I > C/\text{std}] + 1\}$. When $I > C$, Response = successive. When the criterion is located at C, a sigmoid successiveness discrimination function like that labeled C is predicted by the theory.

The form of the successiveness function will depend upon the position of the criterion and upon the mapping of stimulus time into I. When the criterion is set at the upper bound of the standard distribution, as C_2 in Figure 5, the successiveness function is the one labeled C_2 in the lower diagram. It is a fully-bounded sigmoid function, rising from chance to perfect performance over a range of two quanta. The effects of having the criterion within (C_1) and outside (C_3) of the standard distribution also are shown. Note that these functions assume that C remains fixed with respect to the standard distribution as $(M_v - M_s)$ is varied. One would use randomly intermixed values of the variable interval in any experiment to which the model would be applied.

We have reanalyzed the two-state successiveness data (Kristofferson, 1967b) for each of the 13 observers individually according to this model. Predicted functions were calculated for each cell of a large matrix of q and C

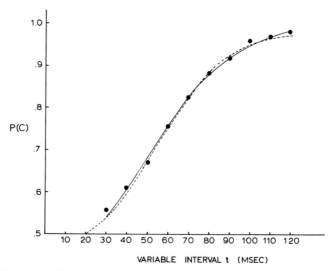

Fig. 6. Average best-fitting functions for each of the two theories to the successiveness discrimination data for 13 observers reported by Kristofferson (1967b). The solid line is the attention-switching theory and the dotted line is the quantal on–off theory. Data points are mean $P(C)$ values.

values, to the nearest millisecond, and the pair of values that yielded the smallest squared-difference between obtained and predicted was determined. This analysis was carried out for each individual subject. Thus, for each subject, a predicted $P(C)$ was derived for each value of the variable interval. The average of these predicted values was calculated over subjects for each variable interval, and the result is shown as the dotted line in Fig. 6. The same calculations for the attention-switching theory are represented by the solid line. Do not be misled by the shape of the obtained function because it is an average of observers with quite different parameters.

Both theories provide very good best fits. The average difference between obtained and predicted is −.0002 for the attention-switching theory and .0031 for the onset–offset theory; the mean absolute differences are .0054 and .0057, respectively. The attention-switching theory is somewhat better but there is insufficient ground to choose between them here.

It turns out that a basis for choice exists in the data described above on the effect of the standard interval. We estimated the parameters q and C for each observer using those trials for which the standard interval was zero and used those parameters to predict each observer's performance with the other standard intervals. The result can be seen in Fig. 7. The quantal onset–offset theory, represented by the dotted line, fails in this instance. It does so because the criterion is located below the upper bound of the zero standard

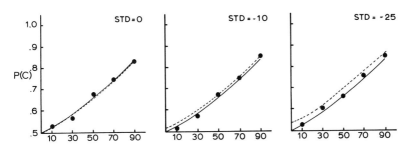

Fig. 7. Average successiveness discrimination functions for six observers for each of three values of the standard interval. The data are the same as in Fig. 2. The curves are the average functions predicted by the two theories using the parameters determined from the data for standard = 0, the solid line for the attention-switching theory, and the dotted line for the quantal on–off theory.

distribution, for some subjects, and the theory predicts an increase in performance that does not exist, at least for the −25-msec standard.

In a similar way the parameters of the attention-switching model were estimated from the zero standard data and predicted functions were calculated. Since x was equal to or greater than zero for every subject, the predicted functions are identical for the three standards. The solid lines show the result. The attention-switching theory describes this set of data very well indeed.

IV. Some Other Results Concerning Duration Discrimination

It may seem odd to propose a theory of duration discrimination that flies in the face of the "first fact" of duration discrimination. That fact, of course, is that threshold Δt is some function of base duration [for a summary of several studies, see Creelman (1962)]. Had we not found a situation, as in the light flash experiment, in which duration discrimination occurs and is not a function of base duration, we could not make this start toward a theory. Actually, our theory proposes one mechanism for the discrimination and certainly there are other mechanisms as well. The theory keeps us within the context of time quantum theory but it is obviously incomplete as a theory of duration discrimination.

It will be necessary to try and add to the theory, from experimental results, that which will account for the dependence of the discrimination upon base duration.

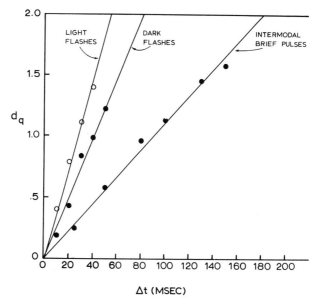

Fig. 8. Duration discrimination in terms of d_q for a base duration of 100 msec. The markers used to define the durations differ for the three cases as described in the text.

Complexities emerge immediately, especially when you begin with brief durations as we have. Some of the complications have interestingly simple features, however, as Fig. 8 demonstrates. This shows d_q as a function of Δt for a base duration of 100 msec. Each set of data is the average of the parameters of several subjects. The three sets differ in the kinds of "markers", which define the duration for the subject. The light flash data are the same data discussed above (Fig. 4). For the "dark flashes," the interval was defined by turning off a light for the prescribed time. In the intermodal case, the beginning of every interval was defined by a ten msec light flash and the end by a 10-msec tone burst. The method of single stimulus [as described above and in Allan *et al.* (1971)] was used in all cases and different subjects were involved in the three experiments. These experiments were done in our laboratory by Marnie McKee, for dark flashes and Robert Rousseau, for the intermodal case. A report is available which details the dark flash experiments (McKee, Allan, & Kristofferson, 1970).

A zero-intercept straight line is obtained in all three cases, implying the interpretation given above for light flashes. The average quantum size is very different, however, being in the range reported for successiveness discrimination only for the dark flashes, whereas the light flashes are roughly half that value and the intermodal case is about double. The quantum size is the value of Δt for which d_q is 1.0. For the three lines in Fig. 8 the values are approximately 27, 41, and 91 msec, respectively.

Thus, the kind of marker used is very significant for durations near 100 msec. However, the results of several other experiments require us to add that variations in the values of certain stimulus parameters of the markers, such as intensity and duration, are probably inconsequential. Our best guess at present is that the differences between markers seen in Fig. 8 are probably not due to "sensory cues" or "excitation interaction." That is, the insensitivity of the discrimination to changes in the physical energy in the markers makes it seem unlikely that the discriminations are based upon internal quantities which are functions of stimulus energy.

For durations less than 100 msec, other cues, such as loudness or pitch, undoubtedly become important in some cases, although apparently not for light flashes at 50 msec. Dark flashes at 50 msec are clearly another matter. Performance is at a higher level, and the d_q function is nonlinear for every subject (see McKee, Allan, & Kristofferson, 1970).

If the time intervals are presented entirely to the auditory modality, one sees a rather different pattern of results. We are using "empty auditory intervals" defined by two 10-msec tone bursts in this investigation and the results to date are summarized in Fig. 9.

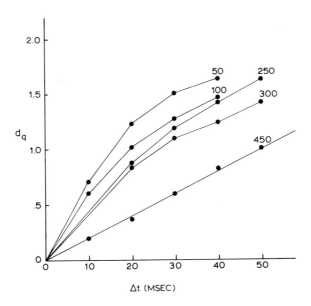

Fig. 9. Duration discrimination in terms of d_q for five base durations (shown in milliseconds) when the markers are two brief tone bursts.

Five observers were studied with base durations of 50 and 100 msec using the same design and single-stimulus method as in the light-flash experiments. The curves are concave downward, a feature seen for every individual subject, and performance is slightly higher for 50 than for 100, although the difference in Δt for a $P(C)$ of 0.75 is only 2 or 3 msec.

Three additional observers provided the data at base durations of 250 and 300 msec. The results are similar to those of the first group. Because of the small number of individuals it is not possible to conclude that performance is lower for the second group even though there is no overlap between the groups.

A third group, of three new observers, was tested at 450 msec, and here there is a marked lowering of performance. Also, the d_q function becomes linear with an average quantum of 50 msec. For every individual observer there is a linear d_q function at 450.

These results indicate, but only tentatively at this time, that the range of brief durations over which the quantal onset-offset model does not hold is much wider when the interval is wholly auditory than it is when the interval is defined by the other kinds of markers described above. Perhaps some additional mechanism, or some entirely different mechanism, is available for duration discrimination in the auditory modality up to about 400 msec.[2] We do not know yet the extent to which the onset–offset model will hold in the range above 400 msec for auditory intervals. Those experiments are being done now.

We have been unable to find any quantitative theory which describes adequately our results for brief auditory intervals. Creelman's (1962) counter theory is not satisfactory. His parameter λ, which reflects the rate of firing of the source of pulses which are counted, varies as a function of both base duration and of Δt, decreasing with increasing Δt at each base duration and increasing with increases in base duration for the data shown in Fig. 9. Our attempts to apply this formulation in other experiments on brief auditory durations have not been successful either (Carbotte & Kristofferson, 1971). This was also the case with light flashes (Allan et al., 1971), and with dark flashes (McKee et al., & 1970).

We have not used the term "psychological duration" in this paper, although we have done so before (Allan et al., 1971). What is the dimension I? If it is psychological duration, then we conclude from within temporal

---

[2]Again, we doubt that it is a matter of excitation–interaction because Carbotte has shown that changing the amplitude of the auditory markers over a wide range has no effect upon the discrimination. Carbotte's results from our laboratory are not yet available. It is possible that very short-term memory is involved at brief durations in audition and we have formulated a theory to that effect (Carbotte & Kristofferson, 1971), but with only limited success thus far.

quantum theory that psychological duration is continuous rather than quantized; that is, that psychological time *is* the hypothetical variable I as defined in Fig. 2. But it is quite possible that the decision between "long" and "short" is based upon the relative times of occurrence of instantaneous events, a stimulus event and an internally timed criterion event triggered by the stimulus onset, and not upon a measure of a time interval. That would be compatible with the way we have described successiveness discrimination and in a sense reduces both successiveness and duration discrimination to the problem of temporal order. The dimension I may be no more than real time within the central nervous system, describing the temporal relations among events which in their turn are directly responsible for psychological duration.

References

Allan, L. G., Kristofferson, A. B., & Wiens, E. W. Duration discrimination of brief light flashes. *Perception and Psychophysics*, 1971, **9**(3B), 327–334.

Carbotte, R., & Kristofferson, A. B. Discrimination of brief empty time intervals. Technical Report No. 21, Department of Psychology, McMaster University, Hamilton, Canada, March, 1971.

Creelman, C. D. Human discrimination of auditory duration. *Journal of the Acoustical Society of America*, 1962, **34**, 582–593.

Green, D. M., & Swets, J. A. *Signal detection theory and psychophysics*. New York: Wiley, 1966.

Kristofferson, A. B. Attention and psychophysical time. *Acta Psychologica*, 1967, 27, 93–100. (a).

Kristofferson, A. B. Successiveness discrimination as a two-state quantal process. *Science*, 1967, 158, 1337–1339. (b)

McKee, M. E., Allan, L. G., & Kristofferson, A. B. Duration discrimination of brief visual off-flashes. Technical Report No. 42, Department of Psychology, McMaster University, Hamilton, Canada, June, 1970.

Author Index

Number in italics refer to the pages on which the complete references are listed.

Subject Index

CONTENTS OF PREVIOUS SYMPOSIA

Reprinted from *Acta Psychologica*, Vol. 27, 1967. Copyright © North-Holland Publishing Company Amsterdam.

Attention and Performance

A. F. Sanders, Editor
Institute for Perception RVO-TNO
Soesterberg, The Netherlands

Topic 1 SINGLE-CHANNEL THEORY AND INFORMATION PROCESSING

Topic 2 REACTION PROCESSES

A. F. SANDERS, Some aspects of reaction processes

P. RABBITT, Time to detect errors as a function of factors affecting choice response time

J. F. SCHOUTEN and J. A. M. BEKKER, Reaction time and accuracy

G. L. WOLFENDALE, Decision times in signal detection

R. M. PICKETT, Response latency in a pattern perception situation

A. F. SANDERS and W. TER LINDEN, Decision making during paced arrival of probabilistic information

S. KORNBLUM, Choice reaction time for repetitions and non-repetitions—a re-examination of the information hypothesis

B. FORRIN and R. E. MORIN, Effects of context on reaction time to optimally coded signals

E. T. KLEMMER, Sequencies of responses to signals encoded in time only

J. A. MICHON and N. J. L. VAN DER VALK, A dynamic model of timing behaviour

N. S. KIRK and J. FEINSTEIN, An investigation of the relation between inspection and repairing performance of burlers and menders in the worsted woollen industry

M. M. TAYLOR, P. H. LINDSAY and S. M. FORBES, Quantification of shared capacity processing in auditory and visual discrimination

Topic 3 PHYSIOLOGICAL CORRELATES OF ATTENTION AND REACTION TIME

Introductory remarks

R. T. WILKINSON, Evoked response and reaction time

M. HAIDER, Vigilance, attention, expectation and cortical evoked potentials

J. W. H. KALSBEEK and R. N. SYKES, Objective measurements of mental load

E. H. VAN OLST, J. F. ORLEBEKE and S. D. FOKKEMA, Skin conductance as a measure of tonic and phasic arousal (Abstract)

Topic 4 SHORT TERM MEMORY AND INFORMATION PROCESSING

Introductory remarks

M. I. POSNER, Short term memory systems in human information processing

G. SPERLING, Successive approximations to a model for short term memory

Reprinted from *Acta Psychologica*, Vol. 30, 1969. Copyright © 1969 by North-Holland Publishing Company   Amsterdam.

Attention and Performance II

W. G. Koster, Editor
Institute for Perception RVO-TNO
Soesterberg, The Netherlands

Chapter 1.   INFORMATION PROCESSING AND REACTION TIME

A. T. WELFORD, A. H. NORRIS and N. W. SHOCK, Speed and accuracy of movement and their changes with age . . . .
R. W. PEW, The speed-accuracy operating characteristic . . . .
E. P. KRINCHIK, The probability of a signal as a determinant of RT . . .
R. HYMAN and C. UMILTÀ, The information hypothesis and non-repititions
S. KORNBLUM, Sequential dependencies as a determinant of choice reaction time: a summary. . . . .
I. D. JOHN, Mediating processes in choice reaction tasks . . . .
J. ANNETT, Payoff and the refractory period . . . .
D. KOVAČ, From reaction time to the measuring of promptness . . . . .
G. H. MOWBRAY and J. F. BIRD, The simple reaction time as an aid in determining the sign of a visual transient response . . . .
P. FRAISSE, Why is naming longer than reading? . . . .
M. I. POSNER and R. L. TAYLOR, Subtractive method applied to separation of visual and name components of multiletter arrays . . . .
N. C. WAUGH, The effects of recency and repetition on recall latencies . . .
B. FORRIN and R. E. MORIN, Recognition times for items in short- and long-term memory . . . .

Chapter 2.   PSYCHOLOGICAL REFRACTORY PERIOD AND SINGLE CHANNEL THEORY

P. BERTELSON and F. TISSEYRE, The time-course of preparation: confirmatory results with visual and auditory warning signals . . . .
R. DAVIS and F. A. GREEN, Intersensory differences in the effect of warning signals on reaction time . . . .
R. GOTTSDANKER, Interacting responses to crowded signals . . . .

Reprinted from *Acta Psychologica*, Vol. 33, 1970. Copyright © 1970 by North-Holland
Publishing Company Amsterdam.

Attention and Performance III

A. F. Sanders, Editor
Institute for Perception RVO-TNO
Soesterberg, The Netherlands